PASCAL BY EXAMPLE

"... reading programs might not be such a bad idea from the point of view of learning about programming."

Gerald Weinberg
The Psychology of Computer Programming

Pascal by Example

From Practice to Principle in Computer Science

Barry A. Burd
Drew University

Saunders College Publishing
Harcourt Brace Jovanovich College Publishers

Fort Worth Philadelphia San Diego New York Orlando Austin
San Antonio Toronto Montreal London Sydney Tokyo

Requests for permission to make copies of any part of the work
should be mailed to: Permissions Department, Harcourt Brace
Jovanovich, Inc., 8th Floor, Orlando, FL 32887

ISBN: 0-15-568162-1

Library of Congress Catalog Card Number: 91-73219

Printed in the United States of America

Copyrights and acknowledgements appear on page 971 which
constitutes a continuation of the copyright page.

To
Ruth and Sam,
Sam and Jennie,
Jennie and Harriet

Preface

Pascal by Example is a unique, innovative textbook for a course that has come to be known as CS1. The name CS1 comes from various reports of the Association for Computing Machinery (ACM) and the Institute of Electrical and Electronic Engineers (IEEE). CS1 is the first college-level course for students who intend to major in computer science.

The most recent report of the ACM/IEEE Joint Task Force defines *programming* as ". . . the entire collection of activities that surround the description, development, and effective implementation of algorithmic solutions to well-specified problems. While this definition is not to be construed to mean simply 'coding in a particular language or for a particular machine architecture,' it does necessarily include the mastery of highly stylized skills in a particular programming language or languages." What we see here is the need for a carefully balanced blend of skills and ideas. A good CS1 textbook needs to teach the hard and fast rules of a programming language, but it must also transcend these rules and reveal the broader nature of the software life cycle.

To achieve the desired blend this book breaks new ground in presenting Pascal programming by an example-driven approach. In using this approach, the student examines examples of algorithm design and computer programming and, in the process, discovers some of the fundamental concepts underlying the discipline of computer science.

The earliest college-level textbooks in computer science introduced programming in what might be called a feature-driven fashion. Each chapter covered an aspect of a programming language—IF statements, loops, arrays, procedures, and so on. The books described each language feature using a pleasant compromise between the rigor of a manual and the simplicity of a tutorial. Each feature was illustrated with a brief fragment of code, and longer examples (complete programs) were saved for the ends of chapters.

It eventually became apparent that modularity and top-down thinking was an important key to good programming. It also became clear that students developed habits—good or bad—toward modularity early in a computer science course. So, in order to establish good habits, procedures migrated from the latter halves of books toward the front. But then there was a problem. Procedures are "global" features of a language, and their usefulness is apparent only in the context of a complete program. Illustrating a procedure with only a program fragment would simply not do.

Therefore, complete programs started taking a more prominent place in introductory computer science books. Each chapter provided several complete programs, perhaps at the ends of several sections. And yet the primary emphasis was still the feature-driven approach. Computer programming was still seen as a sequence of language features which, when accumulated in sufficient amounts, could be used to do some useful work.

Pascal by Example represents a departure from the feature-driven approach. *Pascal by Example* is, as the title suggests, example-driven. Each section is organized in a way that moves the student from practice in programming to the fundamental principles of computer science. Each section is divided into subsections, with the pivotal subsection entitled **Program Example**. Each program example is a complete program, which can be compiled and run on any implementation of ANSI Standard Pascal. We use complete programs rather than fragments of code because the former present the entire syntactic and stylistic context in which particular Pascal language features can be used. A complete program is also executable, modifiable, and testable.

An introduction to computer science needs, of course, to be much more than just Pascal syntax. It should include problem solving, abstraction, algorithm development, programming style, documentation, program verification, and many other important concepts. We need to introduce the student to the discipline of programming—to allow the student to internalize the concepts of the software life cycle instead of just writing a program. To this end, the subsections in each section of the text have been ordered to capture the essence of the software life cycle. The ordering of subsections is as follows:

- Specifications
- Designing a Program
- Program Example
- Sample Runs
- Observations
- Further Discussion
- Traces
- Programming Style
- Structure
- Testing and Debugging

Subsections

After a brief discussion of the new ideas of a section, the specific problem to be solved (e.g., "Compute the yearly interest on a savings account") is revealed in the **Specifications** subsection. In many cases the specifications are given in a rigorous input/process/output format. The rigorous format serves two purposes: it clarifies any lurking ambiguities in the statement of the problem and it shows how a potentially ill-defined problem can be defined precisely.

In **Designing a Program** the author "thinks out loud" about how the specifications should be turned into working Pascal code. We don't emphasize any single method in these subsections. Instead we try to present a wide variety of approaches including pseudocode, Nassi–Shneiderman charts, and hierarchy diagrams. In some sections we emphasize top-down design; in others we discuss the microscopic details (i.e., Should this assignment statement go before, inside, or after the loop?). Very often this thinking out loud conjures up a new feature of Pascal. The usefulness of each new feature becomes apparent as we design our program.

The **Program Example** is a complete program that has been compiled and tested. The student can run, test, and enhance each program example. Each such example is followed by a section in which several **Sample Runs** of the program are shown. These runs have been cut and pasted from actual sessions on various implementations of ANSI Standard Pascal. Every effort has been made to make these programs portable. Most of this book's program examples can run under Turbo Pascal with little or no modification.

In the subsections entitled **Observations** and **Further Discussion**, we explain new Pascal features in detail and discuss the concepts that were used in writing the program example. The **Observations** subsection tends to point specifically to the program example. Instead of discussing each Pascal feature as an isolated entity we discuss the way in which the feature helped us solve a problem and write a program. The **Further Discussion** subsection deals with the same concepts in a broader sense; it examines all aspects of a particular Pascal feature, not just the aspects that are illustrated in the most recent program example.

In the **Traces** subsection we stimulate intuitions and encourage students to picture what's going on inside the program. We use a wide variety of techniques to help the student visualize the workings of the algorithm (e.g., desk-checking tables, tree diagrams, or drawings of cells in linked lists).

In a **Programming Style** subsection we talk about some of the choices we made in writing the program and why we made them. This is a very important part of each chapter where we try to instill in the student an understanding of two (partially conflicting) notions: that there is often more than one good way to design an algorithm or write a program and that some ways are better than others. In this subsection we emphasize readability, elegance, efficiency, documentation, and self-documentation. While language features are useful, we want the student to learn that there are other, more fundamental lessons to be learned from each program example.

In **Structure** subsections we discuss control flow and program complexity. Among other things, this subsection provides a preview of the subsequent Data Structures course. Early introduction of this material in the computer science curriculum is of definite benefit.

In the **Testing and Debugging** subsections we emphasize the "follow-through" portion of the software life cycle. This is a serious difficulty for many students—a weakness that can be remedied by repeated demonstration of various testing strategies. Each strategy is particularly suited to the program example at hand.

All this is done without compromising the important technical concepts of an introductory computer science course such as searching, sorting, recursion, stacks, queues, and trees. Because of its growing importance, we have devoted three sections to object-oriented design with Turbo Pascal. In addition to all this, the book includes over one thousand exercises.

A new kind of textbook requires new ways of teaching and learning. *Pascal by Example* isn't meant to be read from cover to cover, nor is it meant to be taught from cover to cover. As you use this book, you'll find your emphasis changing from the feature-driven to the example-driven approach. You'll want to examine each program example, carefully considering whatever Pascal features are new in the example. *Pascal by Example* is more "spiral" than any other introductory computer science book. Pascal features aren't introduced in the "logical" order found in a manual. Instead they're introduced on a need-to-know basis; features are introduced in order to help solve the problem at hand.

Pascal by Example is enriched with outstanding pedagogy. A collection of exercises follows the narrative portion of each section. The exercises are divided into several groups.

- Keywords to Review
- Questions to Answer
- Things to Check in a Manual
- Experiments to Try
- Changes to Make
- Programs and Subprograms to Write
- Things to Think About

Keywords to Review is a list of the new terms that were introduced in the section. The student should go back and review any terms that seem unfamiliar. Then there's a selection of **Questions to Answer**. Many of these should be fairly straightforward for the student, but we've included a few questions that require more than a "surface-level" understanding of the material. In all cases these are "hands-off" exercises. They can be tackled quickly, without the aid of the computer.

In a subsection entitled **Things to Check in a Manual** the student is asked to consult an authoritative source in order to discover certain implementation-dependent details about Pascal. The most important goal of the subsection is to give the student practice in reading and understanding a formal description of a language, as given in a manual.

In an **Experiments to Try** subsection, the student is asked to make some very *specific* changes to the **Program Example** and then rerun it. For instance, what happens if you put a semicolon before an ELSE or if you move the initialization inside the loop or if you regroup the subprograms? This subsection should be extremely helpful in anticipating pitfalls before they occur, in a very concrete way, and in fostering a sense of independence, showing students how to answer "what if" questions.

All the changes suggested in an **Experiments to Try** subsection are easy to perform. However, in the **Changes to Make** subsection students are asked to modify the program example, often to add more features or to make the program more robust. In **Changes to Make** exercises, the student still has the original program example as a template, but now the student is asked to think carefully about *how* to make various modifications. This helps ease the way into the next subsection, **Programs and Subprograms to Write**, where the student is asked to "start from scratch," designing and testing a program that uses the ideas discussed in the section.

Finally, in the subsection entitled **Things to Think About**, the student is given some meaty ideas to consider. The questions in this section should stimulate open-ended thinking, further reading, class discussion, and spirited debate.

Several other ideas have guided the writing of this book. One of these is the notion that students should see the most versatile and most powerful features first. For that reason, we introduce WHILE loops long before FOR loops, procedures before functions, and VAR parameters before value parameters. We do this as early as possible because we want to give instructors the opportunity to create meaningful, challenging assignments. Even in the earliest chapters, students can write useful programs and consider interesting applications. Following this notion, we introduce, in Chapter 2, as many simple, useful syntactic features of Pascal as we can. The next eight chapters are ordered according to the same principle: introduce the versatile features as early as possible; begin by illustrating these features in short programs; and expand to longer programs as the chapters progress.

One of the most intractable difficulties facing students in CS1 is not being able to construct the simple-but-subtle algorithms—finding the smallest of one hundred integers or comparing the average of the sums with the sum of the averages. By introducing the versatile features first, an instructor can get students to think about problems like these as soon as possible.

Another principle that guided the writing of this book was the early introduction of subprograms. The book's first subprogram appears in Chapter 2, and subprograms are the central focus of Chapter 3. We have carefully chosen examples that make meaningful use of subprograms. Students are turned off when they see a simple problem complicated by decomposition; by the time my readers see a procedure, in Section 2.5, they're using it to switch the values of two variables. This shows students that decomposition is a useful tool that helps reduce a real problem to simple components.

The last guiding principle is an attempt to strike a comfortable balance between teaching Pascal and teaching language-independent problem solving. The example-driven approach, with its emphasis on complete programs, suggests that this is first and foremost a Pascal textbook. But the student needs to understand that Pascal is only a piece of a larger endeavor—creating algorithms and solving problems. How do we blend the two approaches?

We begin by agreeing to a need for concreteness, accepting that the only way to teach swimming is to put people in the water and the only way to teach programming is to have students write programs. We further agree that certain practical issues about Pascal (What's the syntax? How do WHILE statements work? What does "pass by reference" mean?) must be addressed in the book. These issues should be discussed plainly and directly, in language that doesn't confuse the practical issues with the underlying problem-solving principles.

We also agree that the book must be rich in material that deals with problem decomposition, abstraction, algorithm development, programming style, and program testing. This material needs to be integrated with the Pascal-language material, so the student sees the discipline of programming as one consistent subject and not two partially-related topics. The book should introduce as many ideas from software engineering as possible and should get the student to begin thinking about data structures.

The ideal solution is to structure the text so that each section has two different kinds of subsections. The **Program Example, Sample Runs, Observations,** and **Further Discussion** subsections are reserved mainly for Pascal-language issues, while the subsections entitled **Specifications, Designing a Program, Traces, Programming Style, Structure,** and **Testing and Debugging** are devoted to software engineering and data structures issues.

Pascal by Example comes with a full complement of supplements. A student disk, which contains each of the book's program examples, is available in either of two forms: one with programs in ANSI Standard Pascal, the other with programs that run under Turbo Pascal. A carefully written *Instructor's Manual* contains notes on Turbo Pascal, hints on teaching various topics, and rationales for the approaches taken at many points in the book. It also contains solutions to most of the exercises in the textbook. An instructor's disk, containing solutions to exercises, is also available. Finally, *Laboratory Manual for Computer Science* by Steven N. Kass takes the student through the course in 15 hands-on laboratory experiences.

Although *Pascal by Example* is a highly individualistic work, it could not have been written without the help of others. My editor, Richard Bonacci, deserves an enormous amount of thanks and praise. His undying faith in this project has guided it from being a few ideas on paper into a complete book. His firm belief in the integrity of the work has kept me on track, even when I may otherwise have faltered.

Then there's my family. In the five years it's taken to write this book my wife has done more to support a frantic author than any person can be expected to do. She's kept the family afloat from the beginning of the project to the end, and for this I can never thank her enough. The kids have brought an unmeasurable amount of joy to our home and have waited with patience over repeated promises that "Daddy will be done soon." They're still too young to know that not all dads write books.

And of all the people who provided technical assistance, special thanks go to Steven Kass. His judgment on technical matters is flawless. And the amazing thing is, he always makes time to give it. The advice and support that he's provided over the past few years have been the grease that keeps this wheel turning. I would also like to thank my colleagues Norma Gilbert and Alan Candiotti for reading the manuscript and Chris Van Wyk and Bruce Klein for testing all the programs in the book.

Mary Douglas guided the project in its production stages and worked carefully with me on all the last minute (actually, last year) details. Without her help, I would have taken a lot longer to finish the book, and it wouldn't have been as good a book. Special thanks go to Joan Pendleton who edited the manuscript, to Nancy Benedict, who designed the book, and to Chris Ritter who provided the cover photograph.

Finally, I would like to express my gratitude to all the colleagues who were kind enough to review some or all of the manuscript. Their suggestions were critical to the development of this project: Michael Berman, Glassboro State College; Marcus Brown, University of Alabama at Tuscaloosa; Chuck Burchard, Pennsylvania State University at Erie; Richard Carney, Camden State Community College; Louis Gioia, Nassau Community College; Steven Kass, Drew University; Mike Michaelson, Palomar College; Louise Moser, University of California at Santa Barbara; Michael Rothstein, Kent State University; Jesse H. Ruder, Jr., Austin Community College; Dale Shaffer, Lander College, Greenwood, South Carolina; Chris Van Wyk, Drew University; Carolyn Wheless, University of Alabama at Tuscaloosa; and Ray Zarling, California State University at Stanislaus.

Barry A. Burd

Contents

Chapter 4

Elementary File Handling   198

Chapter 5

Nested Control Flow   215

Chapter 6

Repetition   263

Chapter 7

Simple Types 315

Chapter 8

Decision Making 353

Chapter 9

More Algorithms 411

Chapter 10

Array Types

467

Chapter 11

More on Arrays

555

Chapter 12

Records and Sets

605

Chapter 13

More on Subprograms

685

Chapter 14

Pointers

757

Chapter 15

More on Files

871

Appendixes

Index   972

1
Preliminaries

Computers and Programs

What is a computer?

A **computer** is a machine that processes information. It shares this information (with people, other machines, etc.) by receiving input and producing output. **Input** is information that's "put in" to a computer, and **output** is information that the computer "puts out." The computer **processes** its input in order to produce its output. Taken together, the computer's input, its output, and the values that it processes are called **data**.

Today the overwhelming majority of computers use electronic components (chips, transistors, etc.) to process data. But this may change someday. Already experiments with optical computers use light rays instead of voltages to represent data. And some researchers are thinking about biological computers that use live neurons, cells from living brains, to process data.

Example 1

some simple problems

(a) Input: Two numbers
   Output: The sum

A computer uses its input to produce its output. In this case the computer does some simple arithmetic.

(b) Input: Two numbers
   Output: The larger of the two

To produce this output, the computer makes a simple decision; it chooses between two alternatives. It "decides" which of two numbers should be its output. Of course, the computer doesn't make any conscious effort when it

1

"decides," and it doesn't make a value judgment. In this case, the computer performs a simple comparison.

(c) Input: Five pairs of numbers

Output: Five sums, one for each pair of numbers

To produce this output, the computer repeats a simple arithmetic operation (addition) five times, each time with a different pair of numbers.

(d) Input: A list of names and addresses and the name "Barry Burd"

Output: Barry Burd's address.

To produce this output, the computer looks through the list of names until it finds the name "Barry Burd." It looks for the address listed beside that name. This address is produced as output. You'll see later that this can all be done by having the computer make some decisions, as in (b) above, and repeat things, as in (c) above. In fact, every example in this book can be done with decisions and repetitions.

Looking for an item, such as the name "Barry Burd," in a list is called **searching**.

searching

(e) Input: A list of names and addresses

Output: The same list, rearranged so that the last names are in alphabetical order

sorting

Rearranging a list so that its items are in order is called **sorting**.

(f) Input: The name, hourly pay rate, and the number of hours worked this week for each employee in the company

Output: A printed paycheck for each employee in the company

This is a very practical input/output example. Many of the examples in this book aren't as immediately practical as this one. See items (a), (b), and (c) above, for instance. So keep the following in mind: An example that doesn't seem very practical often contains ideas that are building blocks. These building blocks can be used to construct more complex, practical examples.

---

programs

The computer processes its input to produce its output. To do this, it follows a set of instructions called a **program**. The purpose of this book is to teach you how to write good programs. A person who writes programs is called a **programmer**, and the act of writing programs is called **programming**.

Normally a program is written for a particular person or group of people. Such a person is called a **user**. When you're learning to write programs, you write simple practice programs for your own benefit. So in this situation you're the programmer and the user. In this text, we'll refer to you by either name, whichever is most appropriate in the given context.

The instructions in a program can't be written in ordinary English, because ordinary English can be ambiguous.

Example 2

Question: "What do you get when you add two and two?"

programming in English? The question is in ordinary English. An answer represents a unique way of interpreting the question. Some possible answers are:

Child: "A pat on the head from my father."

Engineering student: "I get my calculator."

Logician: "Twenty-two."

Mathematician: "A composite number."

Philosopher: "You get the answer to the question 'What do you get when you add two and two?'"

The child thinks that "get" means "receive." The engineering student thinks that "get" means "fetch." The logician thinks that "add" means "symbolically combine." The mathematician thinks that a general answer, rather than a specific answer, should be given. The philosopher thinks that "What do you get . . ." is a linguistic question. There are many ways to interpret this simple question because the question has many possible meanings. Ordinary English can be ambiguous.

Of course there's an obvious way to interpret the question "What do you get when you add two and two?" and most fluent speakers of English would interpret it "correctly." But that's only because it's such a simple question. When questions and instructions are complex, they can have many correct interpretations.

Example 3

Reread the descriptions of input and output given in item (e) of Example 1. The descriptions are written in ordinary English. Will addresses, as well as names, be rearranged? Will first names, as well as last names, be rearranged? You probably assume that they will, but the description of the output doesn't make this clear. It says that the list will be rearranged, but it doesn't say precisely what kind of rearranging will be done. It doesn't make sense to rearrange last names without rearranging the rest of the information, so it's safe to assume that all information should be rearranged and that the description of the output is incomplete.

By limiting the grammar and vocabulary of English, the language can be made unambiguous. But then you no longer have ordinary English. You

programming
languages

have a new language that can't really be called English. It's a programming language. A **programming language** is a language in which people can give unambiguous instructions to computers. There are hundreds of different programming languages in use. Some of them are very much like English; others are not.

Example 4

(a)
```
IF SALES-AMOUNT IS LESS THAN GOAL
    MOVE 100.00 TO COMMISSION
ELSE
    MOVE 500.00 TO COMMISSION.
```

COBOL

This is part of a program written in a language called **COBOL**. COBOL is very much like English. These instructions tell the computer to give the salesperson a $100 or $500 commission, depending on his or her sales amount.

(b)
```
IF salesAmount < goal THEN
    commission := 100.00
ELSE
    commission := 500.00
```

Pascal

This is part of a program written in a language called **Pascal**. Like the COBOL program, it tells the computer to give the salesperson a $100 or $500 commission. Some people say that the COBOL program is easier to understand because the COBOL instructions look more like English. Others claim that the Pascal program is easier to understand because it's more concise.

(c)
```
commission = (sales_amount < goal) ? 100.00 : 500.00;
```

C

This is part of a program written in a language called **C**. Like the COBOL and Pascal programs, it tells the computer to give the salesperson a $100 or $500 commission. Programs written in C are very concise and usually don't look like ordinary English.

---

about Pascal

The programming language used in this textbook is Pascal. Pascal was created in the late 1960s and early 1970s by Niklaus Wirth. His intent was to devise a language in which instructions could be expressed simply and naturally. Since its creation, Pascal has become a universal language for computer science.

Programs written in Pascal tend to be very readable. When we use the word **readable** we mean "readable by people." It's possible to write a program so cryptic that only computers can make sense of it, but it's difficult for people to correct errors in and make needed changes to such a program.

Programs written in Pascal also tend to be very elegant. **Elegance** is a difficult word to define but it generally means "aesthetically pleasing." It takes some programming experience to understand the difference between a program that's aesthetically pleasing and one that's not.

1.1 Exercises

Key Words to Review

computer	searching	user
input	sorting	programming language
output	program	Pascal
data	programmer	readable
process	programming	elegance

Questions to Answer

QUE 1.1.1 Reread the definition of a computer at the beginning of this chapter, and explain why a copper pipe, with its liquid input and output, doesn't fit the definition.

QUE 1.1.2 Explain the difference between a user and a programmer. Are you a user, a programmer, or neither, when you
a. use a word processor to prepare legal documents?
b. permanently change the way a word processor reacts to having someone press an arrow key (←, ↑, →, ↓)?
c. have someone enter your desired airline reservation into the computer system?
d. enter a customer's desired airline reservation into the computer system?
e. take apart a computer and replace one of its circuit boards?

QUE 1.1.3 State two important features of the Pascal programming language.

QUE 1.1.4 Reread item (e) of Example 1, and then reread Example 3. Change the wording of item (e) in Example 1 to answer the criticisms in Example 3.

QUE 1.1.5 Change the wording of item (e) in Example 1 to answer the following criticism:

The wording of item (e) doesn't preclude the possibility that the input looks like this:

```
Barry Burd
Harriet Ritter
Sam Burd
18 Myrtle Avenue
21 Winding Way
36 Madison Avenue
```

After all, if it's a list of names and addresses, maybe all the names come before any of the addresses.

QUE 1.1.6 Each of the following sentences is ambiguous; that is, each sentence has more than one possible meaning. Find at least two meanings for each sentence:
a. Put Mommy in the car behind us.
b. I want David Copperfield to read.

c. Lather-rinse-repeat.
d. I'll put the bandage on myself.
e. Everything shouldn't be blue.
f. Chew one tablet three times a day until finished.
g. I saved everyone five dollars.
h. Everybody loves somebody sometime.
i. Cars towed at owner's expense.
j. Add five pairs of numbers together.
k. I forgot to be nice for a year.
l. Our cream is so gentle that it never stings most people, even after shaving.
m. I hope that someday you love me as much as Amy.
n. John wrote a love letter to his wife, and he was very angry.
o. If he were to learn that wild bears are related to dogs, and never hurt people, then he'd be happier.

Things to Think About

THI 1.1.1   Reread the definition of a computer at the beginning of this chapter, and discuss whether a human being, with input via the five senses and output with words and actions, fits or doesn't fit the definition.

1.2

Computer Software

statements   Each instruction in a program is called a **statement**. When the computer follows the instruction, we say that it's **executing** the statement and that it's **running** the program. As each statement is executed, the computer is said to perform an **action**. To describe the action that's performed, we often refer to the **effect** of having the computer execute the statement.

Some statements are very simple; others are fairly complex.

Example 5

(a) "Let x be the number 10" is an English translation of the Pascal statement

```
x := 10
```

(b) "Add 1 to the value of x" is an English translation of the Pascal statement

```
x := x + 1
```

(c) "If y is a positive number then
        let x be the number 10
    otherwise
        add 1 to the value of x."

This is an English translation of the Pascal statement

```
IF y > 0 THEN
   x := 10
ELSE
   x := x + 1
```

In item (c) we have what's called a **structured statement**. It's a statement because it's an instruction to the computer. (It tells the computer first to check to see if y is positive, and then to do something to x.) It's structured because it contains other statements, the statements from items (a) and (b) of this example. A statement that contains other statements is called a structured statement. A statement that doesn't contain other statements is called a **simple statement**. The statements in items (a) and (b) of this example are simple statements.

---

code

software

translation

If we put several statements together but still don't have a complete program, we call this set of statements a program fragment or just a **fragment**. Another way of referring to a set of statements is to call it **code**.

Each statement in Pascal is composed of many **characters**. For instance, the third Pascal statement in Example 5 is composed of the characters I, F, blank space, y, blank space, >, and so on. Some of the characters combine to form **words**. For instance, I and F combine to form the word IF.

We use the word **software** to describe all the instructions that we give to a computer in the form of programs, statements, words, characters, etc. Normally a computer can't execute the statements we give it until these statements are translated into electronic signals consisting of low voltages and high voltages. When we talk about these voltages, we commonly use the number 0 to represent the low voltage and 1 to represent the high voltage. So even though we say the computer "executes" the statement

```
x := 10
```

it really executes the translation of that statement into electronic signals. The statements written with these signals are much more detailed than the ones in a Pascal program. They tell the computer exactly where inside its circuitry to move each piece of information. One Pascal statement can get translated into several statements in this **machine language**.

Computers have two different ways of doing the translation. To understand the difference, let's think about the two kinds of people who translate information from French into English.

First there's the person who sits down with a document written in French and creates a second document written in English. This kind of translator gets an entire French-language document before starting any work and then translates it to create a new document—the English translation. So when this person is done, we have an entirely new

compilers and
interpreters

document—one that English-speaking people can understand. To make a connection with computer terminology, let's call this person a **compiler**.

Then there's the person we call an **interpreter**. An interpreter listens while a French-speaking person talks and translates out loud, sentence by sentence even phrase by phrase. Our interpreter starts as soon as the French-speaking person utters the first sentence, without waiting for an entire French-language document to be created. And the interpreter "speaks" the translated version, never creating a new English-language document.

So computers translate programs either by compiling or by interpreting. When a computer *compiles* a program, it takes the entire program and translates it to create a new "program," whose symbols are all 0's and 1's. After compilation we have two programs, one written in Pascal and another written in machine language. When a computer *interprets* a program, it takes each Pascal statement, translates it, executes it, and then goes on to the next Pascal statement. The computer doesn't wait to examine the entire Pascal program before beginning its translation, and it doesn't create a new translated copy of the program.

linkers

Now there's one more step in translating a program that we haven't mentioned yet. Most programs can't be run without calling on other programs to do certain specialized tasks. These other programs are stored in the computer, can be used by anyone's program, and need to be **linked** with each person's program before they can be used. After your program is compiled it has to be linked with the other programs it needs in order to run.

In sum, the computer doesn't really run your original program. Instead it runs something that was obtained from your program by compilation and linkage. In spite of this, it's common to say that the "computer runs your program." In fact, it's common to say that *you* compile, link, and run your program, even though the computer does these things.[1]

algorithms

Now recall that a program is a set of statements—a set of instructions to be (translated and) executed. The idea behind a particular program is called an **algorithm**. Example 4 contains three program fragments, written in three different languages, but the idea behind each of these fragments is the same: give the salesperson a $100 or $500 commission, depending on his or her sales amount. Even though these three fragments look very different they all represent the same algorithm.

We can represent an algorithm by writing it in English. For instance, the following statement is a representation of the algorithm of Example 4:

If the salesperson's sales-amount is less than the desired goal then
    pay the salesperson a $100.00 commission
otherwise
    pay the salesperson a $500.00 commission.

---

[1]Throughout this text we'll always speak of your implementation's Pascal *compiler*, rather than a Pascal interpreter. But most of the ideas we discuss will be applicable to interpreters as well as compilers.

But an algorithm is an idea and we shouldn't confuse the idea with a representation of the idea. We can write the statement in English in a different way:

Pay the following commission to the salesperson:
$100.00 for total sales less than the goal;
$500.00 for total sales greater than or equal to the goal.

And we can write it in French instead of English:

Si le montant de la vente du vendeur est moins que le montant voulu alors
payez au vendeur une commission de $100.00
autrement
payez au vendeur une commission de $500.00.

We can also write it in any of the languages in Example 4, and it's still the same idea. It's still the same algorithm.

When we write an algorithm in English (or in any other spoken language), it's helpful to indent some of the phrases. In the examples given, each line describing one of the various payment alternatives is indented. When we use **indentation**, we can see at a glance which parts of the algorithm depend on other parts. Indented English is so useful, and so important, that it's been given a name. It's called **pseudocode**. Once we've solved a problem completely and correctly using pseudocode, it's usually very easy to translate the pseudocode into Pascal code. When we do this, we say that the Pascal code **implements the algorithm** that's described in the pseudocode.

pseudocode

1.2 Exercises

Key Words to Review

statement	fragment	interpreter
execute	code	link
run	character	algorithm
action	word	pseudocode
effect	software	indentation
simple statement	machine language	implement an algorithm
structured statement	compiler	

Questions to Answer

QUE 1.2.1 Explain the difference between a program and an algorithm.

QUE 1.2.2 Explain the difference between a compiler and an interpreter.

QUE 1.2.3   What are some of the differences between a language like Pascal and a machine language?

QUE 1.2.4   Here are three descriptions of algorithms, given in ordinary English prose. All three represent instructions for searching for a name in a telephone book. Two of them describe the same algorithm, and the other describes a different algorithm. Which two describe the same algorithm?

a. Examine each name in the book, starting with the first and working your way forward, until you find the name you're looking for.

b. Open to the middle of the telephone book. If the name you find there is alphabetically earlier than the name you're looking for, throw away the first half of the book. If the name you find there is alphabetically later than the name you're looking for, throw away the latter half of the book. If the name you find there is the name you're looking for, stop.

Repeat the instructions above with smaller and smaller sections of the book until you've found the name you're looking for.

c. Open to the beginning where the names start. Look at the entry that's at the upper-leftmost part of that page. Does it contain the name you're looking for? If so, then stop. If not, then dispose of that entry and move

- downward one entry, if you're not at the end of a column

- to the top of the next column on that page, if you're at the end of a column but not at the end of a page, and

- to the upper-leftmost part of the next page, if you're already on the last entry on a page.

Repeat the instructions above until you find the name you're looking for.

QUE 1.2.5   We want an algorithm with input and output as follows:

Input: A list with one hundred numbers in it; some numbers appear more than once in the list

Output: The number that appears most often in the list

Write an algorithm, in clear, unambiguous English, to transform the given input into the required output. Have a friend critique your algorithm. Are any of the instructions subject to possible misinterpretation? Rewrite the algorithm so that none of its instructions are open to misinterpretation.

QUE 1.2.6   Consider the following list of numbers:

5 3 5 9 2 5 1 3 9 9

The numbers 5 and 9 both appear three times in the list. Now reread the algorithm you wrote for Exercise Que.1.2.5. When your algorithm is given this list of numbers as its input, which number, 5 or 9, will it produce as its output? Rewrite the algorithm so that when it receives this input, its output contains both numbers, 5 and 9.

QUE 1.2.7   Here's another algorithm for you to write:

Input: Twenty numbers

Output: The sum of the twenty numbers

When you write the algorithm, assume that the person following your instructions will have only enough room to write one number at a time on the page, and can remember only two or three numbers at a time (while doing mental arithmetic).

QUE 1.2.8   Write an algorithm with the following input and output:

> Input: Four numbers; exactly one of them is negative
>
> Output: Only one of the four numbers—the one that's negative

Assume that the person following your instructions has only enough room to keep one number on a piece of paper.

QUE 1.2.9   Write an algorithm (a set of instructions) for a driver to follow at an intersection. Does your algorithm cover all possible situations?

QUE 1.2.10   Write a complete, unambiguous set of instructions for buying soda from a vending machine.

QUE 1.2.11   Write a complete, unambiguous set of instructions for using the cash machine at a particular bank.

1.3

Computer Hardware

devices and media

The term **hardware** is used to describe any piece of equipment that's a tangible part of a computer. A **device** is any piece of hardware that's used to supply input to the computer or obtain output from the computer. In contrast, a **medium** is a place where data are stored. Very often, a medium is associated with a particular device. The device reads data from the medium and gives it to the computer as input; or the device takes output from the computer and stores it on the medium.

disks

For example, a **floppy disk** is a square-looking object, usually either 5 1/4 inches or 3 1/2 inches wide. The material inside the disk is like the material on a cassette tape. It can be used to store data magnetically, just as a cassette tape stores music or video images. A floppy disk is an example of a medium. Of course a disk is useless without a device that can put data onto it and take data off of it. A device that moves data from a computer to a disk and from a disk to a computer is called a **disk drive**.

Actually there are two kinds of disks in common use—floppy disks (otherwise known as **diskettes**) and **hard disks**. Hard disks are rigid; floppy disks are "floppy" (except possibly for the rigid plastic that covers the disk). More information can be stored on a hard disk than on a floppy disk, but hard disks are more expensive than floppy disks. Also, floppy disks are **removable**—they can easily be removed from the disk drive by a user. The user can put the disk in another computer's drive or maybe place a different floppy disk in the original drive. In contrast, many hard disks aren't removable—they're **fixed**. They're installed in the computer at the factory

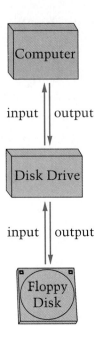

and can be removed only by taking the computer's cabinet apart. Floppy disks are usually found only on small computers; hard disks are normally found on larger computers as well as small computers.

keyboard

Here's an example of a device that's not associated with any particular medium—a **keyboard**. A computer keyboard looks very much like a typewriter keyboard. Whatever you type on the keys is sent electronically to the computer.

A keyboard is a device since it's used to supply input to the computer. Of course you could say that a keyboard "reads data from the user's brain or fingertips (the medium) and gives it to the computer as input," but that's stretching the terminology quite a bit.

screen

In this book, we need to be concerned with only a few kinds of devices and media. We've already discussed the keyboard and the disk. Another device that's found on most computer systems is a **screen** (also known as a monitor, cathode ray tube, CRT, video display unit, or VDU). A computer screen works very much like a television screen. The computer's output (words, pictures, etc.) is **displayed** visually on the screen. Looking at the whole cycle, the computer receives input from the keyboard, uses it to produce output, and sends the output to the screen.

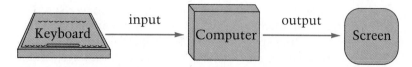

But there's one "wrinkle" in this simple picture: Computer screens are usually set up to display more than just the computer's output. Whenever you press a key on the keyboard, the letter or number that you've typed shows up immediately on the screen. The computer screen is being used to display the input that you're entering on the keyboard, so you can see what you're typing as you type it. This is called **echoing**.

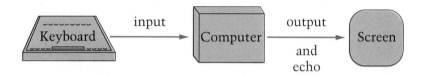

On a large computer a keyboard combined with a screen is called a **terminal**.

Terminal

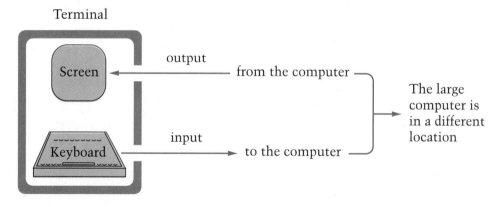

computers of various sizes

By a "large computer" we mean a **minicomputer** or a **mainframe**—a computer that can be used by many users, all at the same time.

If you're not using a large computer, you're probably using a **microcomputer** (also called a personal computer or a PC). A microcomputer is a keyboard, a computer, a screen, and some disks all in one place. It's usually small enough to fit on your desk. It's designed to be used by only one person at a time.

Some terminals put the computer's output on paper instead of on a screen. This paper/keyboard combination is the same as the screen/keyboard combination, but it creates a paper copy of the output and the echoed input instead of a screen image. The print mechanism used to put characters on paper is usually slower than a screen would be, but it creates a permanent, removable copy of the output and the echoed input.

hard copy

The paper copy that's produced is called **hard copy**. (No, screen output is never called "soft copy.") The disadvantages of hard copy are that it takes up space and the computer takes more time creating hard copy than it does creating a screen image. Printing on paper involves mechanical parts that move very slowly. Displaying images on a screen is a purely electronic process that's very fast.

The advantage of hard copy over screen output is that it creates a more permanent record of the output. If people want to see a screen's output, they have to come to the screen. With hard copy, a permanent image of the output is printed on paper. It doesn't go away when the screen is turned off, and it (the paper) can be taken anywhere, shown to other people, saved for future reference, etc.

One way to speed up the creation of hard copy is to use a **printer**. A printer is a device that accepts relatively large amounts of output from the computer and puts it on paper rather quickly. A printer might be attached to a microcomputer, or several users might share a common printer on a large computer. In either case, the user has a keyboard and a screen, and all the echoing is done on the screen, not the printer. We don't want the printer to be slowed down by having to display each character that's being typed on the keyboard. Instead the printer is being used for substantial amounts of output, which can be printed at least a full line at a time. This speeds up the creation of hard copy.

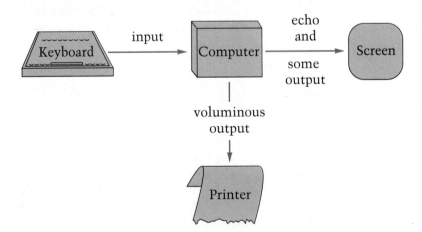

magnetic tape

One important medium we haven't mentioned yet is **magnetic tape**. Information can be recorded on magnetic tape just as sound is recorded on an audiocassette tape, and pictures are recorded on a videotape. The device that's used to record data onto tape and read the data off of the tape is called a **tape drive**. A tape is mounted on the drive just as an audiocassette is inserted into a tape deck (or a videotape is inserted into a VCR).

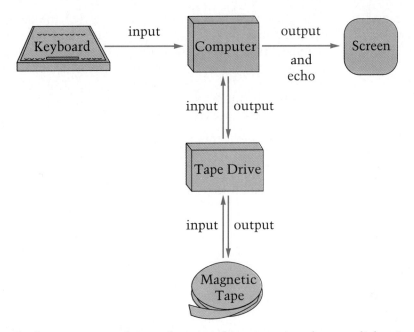

The best way to understand tapes is by comparing them to disks. A tape can store much more information than a floppy disk, and all tapes are removable. This makes tape the perfect medium for long-term storage of data. A tape can be taken off its tape drive and put away until it's needed. Days, months, or years later, the tape can be mounted on the tape drive and the data on the tape can be sent back to the computer.

Next, a tape is shaped like a long ribbon, while a disk is shaped like a platter. This shape makes a big difference. Think about the difference between an audiotape and a record on a stereo turntable. It takes a long time to find a song in the middle of an audiotape. You have to fast-forward the tape until you get to the right spot. It takes much less time to find a song on a record. You move the needle arm so that it's right above the song, lower the needle arm, hear a loud scratch, and then the song begins playing.

In the same way, it takes a long time to find information that's recorded in the middle of a magnetic tape, and not nearly as long to find information that's recorded in the middle of a disk. Using the proper terminology we say that magnetic tape permits only **serial access** to the data, while disks permit **direct access**. In other words, if you have to add, remove, or examine a small piece of information that's in the middle of a huge collection of data, you're much better off storing the huge collection of data on a disk. If, on the other hand, you just want to store a huge collection of data for use later on, you're better off storing it on a tape.

In this section we've listed just a few of the devices and media that can be used to communicate with a computer. Many computers have other hardware, including optical disks, "mice," speakers, optical scanners, etc. Consult your instructor for more details.

serial access
and direct
access

other
hardware

Input and Output in This Book

your own system's hardware

In this book we almost always assume that the device used for input is a keyboard or a disk drive and the device used for output is a screen. The computer that you use to do the exercises might be different from this. For instance, you may be using punched cards for input and a printer for output. If that's the case, there's no need to throw away this book! Almost everything in the book applies to cards as well as keyboard and printer as well as screen. Just remember that

- one of your cards corresponds to one line typed on the keyboard and echoed on the screen, and
- one of your hard copy lines printed on paper corresponds to one line displayed on the screen

1.3 Exercises

Key Words to Review

hardware	fixed disk	microcomputer
device	keyboard	hard copy
medium	screen	printer
floppy disk	display	magnetic tape
disk drive	echo	tape drive
diskette	terminal	serial access
hard disk	minicomputer	direct access
removable disk	mainframe	

Questions to Answer

QUE 1.3.1   Find out what "brand name" of computer you'll be using to do the programming exercises in this book. What kind of computer is it—a microcomputer, a minicomputer, a mainframe, or some other kind of computer?

QUE 1.3.2   Find out what kind of disk your computer has—a hard disk or a floppy disk? A fixed disk or a removable disk? How many disk drives are available to you?

QUE 1.3.3   For each of the following items, tell whether it's part of the computer's software, part of the computer's hardware, or neither:
a. a floppy disk   b. a fragment of a Pascal program   c. an algorithm
d. a statement

QUE 1.3.4   Explain the difference between a device and a medium. Which of the following are devices, and which are media?
a. paper   b. disk drive   c. screen   d. floppy disk

QUE 1.3.5   What are some of the differences between hard disks and floppy disks?

QUE 1.3.6   Explain the difference between output and echo.

QUE 1.3.7   What are some of the differences between a microcomputer and a minicomputer (or a mainframe)?

QUE 1.3.8   What are the advantages of magnetic tape over disks? What are some of the disadvantages?

QUE 1.3.9   What is it about the "shape" of a magnetic tape that makes a tape "serial"? What is it about the "shape" of a disk that makes it not be serial?

QUE 1.3.10   For each of the following situations, tell whether you'd store your information on a disk or on a magnetic tape:
a. billing information on each of the current customers, to be used by telephone operators when customers call about their accounts
b. billing information on each person who was a customer from 1940 to 1959, to be used only if a class action lawsuit is brought against the company by a group of these customers

1.4

Using a Computer

When a computer follows a set of instructions, we say that it's running a program. So how do we get a computer to run a program? To answer the question, it's helpful to begin with a simple analogy. We'll compare using a computer with controlling a robot. (The same technology that makes computers work helps to build robots.)

Let's say you have a robot that does household chores. You tell it to clean the kitchen floor. The robot doesn't already know how to clean a floor, so you give it the following set of instuctions:

How to clean the kitchen floor:

> Get a mop, a bucket, and some soap.
> Fill the bucket with soap and water.
> Repeat the following until the entire floor has been
> covered with soap and water:
> > Squeeze any water that's on the mop into the bucket;
> > Dip the mop in the bucket;
> > Put the mop on the floor and move it around over a few square feet.
> Empty the bucket.
> Put away the mop, bucket, and soap.

Notice that this set of instructions involves decision making and repetition. The robot has to repeat three steps (Squeeze/Dip/Put) several times and has to decide when to stop repeating those steps. For future reference notice that, in the text of the instructions, these three steps are *separated* from one another by semicolons. There are three steps and only two semicolons.

Each of the instructions given to the robot is like a statement in a program. The whole program is a collection of statements that the robot must follow. You give the program (this set of statements) to the robot, and then the robot goes into the kitchen and starts cleaning the floor.

While the robot was listening to your instructions, it was following another set of instructions. It was following instructions such as

Operating system:

> If the human isn't talking, sit quietly.
> Listen while the human talks.
> The human just said "Get a mop." Here's what it means when it's translated into the electronic signals that you understand: "0010011100 . . ."
> When the human's done talking, run the program that's being given to you.
> Don't say "Yes, master"; it makes you sound like a dumb machine. Instead say "Yo!" or "No sweat."

operating system

The robot follows instructions like these whenever it's not running any of your programs. These instructions govern the operation of the robot. An **operating system** is a large set of instructions that governs the operation of a computer.

Let's say the robot is sitting quietly. It's executing the first of its operating system instructions. You can get the robot's attention by saying

Command:

"Robot, come here and listen to me tell you how to clean a kitchen floor."

commands

This is an instruction to the robot, but we won't liken it to a statement in a program. It tells the robot that it's *about to be given a program*. This kind of instruction is called a **command**. A command is an instruction that the computer receives while it's following its operating system instructions. Most commands tell the computer something *about* programs. The command shown tells the robot that the next several sentences it hears form a complete program whose name is "How to clean the kitchen floor."

After you've recited the "How to clean the kitchen floor" program to the robot, it's likely that you'll say something like this:

Another command:

"That's how you clean the kitchen floor. Now go do it."

When you say this, you're giving the robot a command that tells it to run the "How to clean the kitchen floor" program.

Now back to computers. While a computer executes operating system instructions, it can accept many different commands. Some of them are given in the next example.

Example 6

typical
commands

(a) Allow me to use the computer. My name is. . . . To prove that I'm not lying about my name, here's my password. . . .

(b) What follows is the text of a program whose name is. . . . Echo it on the screen as I type it in.

(c) Translate (compile, link, etc.) the Pascal program whose name is. . . .

(d) Run the program (or, more correctly, run the translated version of the program).

(e) Make the following changes to the program whose name is. . . .

(f) Run the program again.

(g) Give me a list of programs that I've created.

(h) Delete the program whose name is . . . from the list.

(i) Good bye, for now. The next time anyone tries to use this terminal, be sure to ask for a password.

command
languages

We've translated these commands into English because each computer has its own language for accepting commands. No computer accepts commands in English, although many **command languages** are very much like English. Computers generally don't accept commands in programming languages like Pascal, because these programming languages aren't designed for expressing instructions like the ones in Example 6. Since command languages vary from computer to computer, this book can't tell you how to get any particular computer to run a program, but it can tell you what kinds of commands you'll be using and what steps you'll follow. Here are the steps:

1. If you're using a microcomputer, the computer has to be turned on, and perhaps a floppy disk has to be inserted into one of the computer's disk drives.

creating and
running a
program

2. If you're using a minicomputer or a mainframe, the computer doesn't have to be turned on because it stays on most of the time (so that various people can use it). Instead of turning the computer on, you have to identify yourself to the computer by typing certain information on the keyboard. This is called **logging on.** Most of these computers expect you to identify yourself and type in a **password** when you log on. Typing in the correct password assures the computer that you're identifying yourself correctly (and not trying to gain access to the computer by pretending to be someone else).

3. You type in the text of a program. You do this using an **editor.** Here's how an editor works:
   a. You type in a command to indicate that you want to use the editor.

b. You type in an instruction that, when translated into English, says "I'm about to type in a program. Store the characters that I type in and give them (the program) the following name: _____." The program has to be given a name so that you can refer to it later (when you want to run it, for instance). Storing a program, along with a name for the program, is called **saving the program**.

c. You type in the program. As you do this the text of the program is recorded on a disk. The program is saved.

d. You type in a special character (or characters) indicating that you've finished typing in your program. The character used differs from one computer to another. When you type in this character, it means "Don't interpret the next thing I type in as part of my program, because I'm finished typing in my program."

e. You type in an instruction that, when translated into English, says "I want to stop editing."

Some of the steps listed above may seem redundant. If you've typed in a command saying that you want to use the editor, why do you have to indicate that you're about to type in a program? When you use the editor, you can do many things. Typing in a program is only one of them. Making changes to a program is another. You have to tell the editor which of these things you want to do.

Now here's a subtle point: an editor is really a program. It's a program that helps you type in your own programs. When you're using the editor, the computer is running the editor program!

4. After you use the editor, you type in a series of commands to get the computer to run your program. Some computers require that you type in three commands; others require only one command. If you type in three commands, it's because the work of running a program is broken down into three separate steps—compile the Pascal program, link it with other code that it needs in order to run, and finally run the translated code.

5. When the computer tries to compile, link, and run your program for the first time, it's very likely that there will be some trouble. Perhaps you used an equal sign (=) instead of a colon and an equal sign (:=) (see item a in Example 5). Maybe you typed a 10 after the := when you meant to type the number 100. If the computer has trouble compiling, linking, or running your program, it produces **error diagnostics**. An error diagnostic is a message, usually displayed on the screen, that tells you that there's trouble and tells you what kind of trouble it might be. There are two things you should remember about error diagnostics:

error diagnostics

a. They can be misleading. This is because it's very difficult for the computer to correctly decide what kind of trouble it encountered. When you're writing in ordinary English, if you misspell a word and write "hom," how can someone else tell if you meant to write "home" or "him"? Sometimes it's easy to tell from the context; sometimes it's not.

"When I play a role I immerse myself totally in the character's personality. I went back to Milwaukee this summer and played Hamlet. It was fun being hom. Anyway, Method Acting is. . . ."

Be skeptical about the information given in error diagnostics. Be patient with misleading error diagnostics.

b. You should always read the error diagnostics very carefully. Think about what they say. Are they as cryptic and misleading as they seem to be, or are they giving you valuable information that it might take you hours to discover on your own? It may take a lot of time to decipher an error diagnostic, but doing this will save time in the long run.

6. After reading the error diagnostics and figuring out what's wrong with your program, the next step is to make corrections to the text of the program. You do this using the editor. Here's how it works:

a. You type in a command to indicate that you want to use the editor.

b. You type in an instruction that, when translated into English, says "I'm about to make changes to the text of the program whose name is _____. Get a copy of the program, and display it on the screen."

c. You type in instructions that indicate what changes should be made to the text of the program.

d. You type in an instruction that, when translated into English, says "I'm finished making changes. Save the new version of the program."

e. You type in an instruction that, when translated into English, says "I want to stop editing."

7. You try to run the program again, as in item 4.

8. You repeat items 5, 6, and 7 over and over again, editing and running, until you're satisfied with the results. (Notice! Even this list of things to do involves repetition.)

9. Finally, you inform the computer that you no longer want to use it. If it's a microcomputer, you just turn off the machine. If it's a minicomputer or a mainframe, you **log off**. To do this you type in a command that, when translated into English, says "I'm leaving now. Be sure to ask for log on information before letting anyone use this keyboard again."

implementations

Taken all together, a particular kind of computer along with an operating system and an interpreter or a compiler, is called an **implementation**. Let's say you know exactly what implementation you're using; for example, you know that you're using a VAX 6310 computer with the operating system VMS 5.2 and the Pascal 4.0 compiler. Then in theory you know exactly how to get the computer to run a Pascal program, and you know exactly what the computer will do when it runs the program.

Turbo Pascal

But implementations differ from one another quite a bit. For instance, if you're using an implementation called **Turbo Pascal**, you'll skip over several of the steps we've just described in getting a computer to run a program. Turbo Pascal's **programming environment** divides your screen into several **windows** and reduces the need to type in long wordy commands. Typically, any single "command" we described earlier can be issued in Turbo Pascal with just one **keystroke** (that is, just by pressing a single key.)

Pascal standards

There are even Pascal programs that run correctly on one implementation and incorrectly on another. Two manuals describe the Pascal language. They're called ANSI/IEEE 770 X3.97-1983 and ISO 7185[2]. Each manual describes, in as much detail as possible, the actions that an implementation should take when it translates and runs a Pascal program. In spite of all the detail that's spelled out in these manuals, implementations vary in the way they handle Pascal programs.

differences among implementations

In this text, we describe a simplified form of the rules in the ANSI/IEEE manual. Most of these rules are obeyed by all implementations. A rule that isn't obeyed by all implementations is called an **implementation-dependent** rule. When you write a program that uses such a rule, the actions taken by your implementation may differ slightly from the actions described in this book. To find out exactly how your implementation behaves you can ask your instructor, look in your particular implementation's manual, or experiment by writing a few small programs and seeing what your implementation does. It's always best to look in manuals or to write a few small programs. No instructor, good or bad, knowledgeable or ignorant, knows all there is to know about a particular implementation.

1.4 Exercises

Key Words to Review

operating system	editor	programming environment
command	saving a program	window
command language	error diagnostics	keystroke
log on	log off	implementation-dependent
password	implementation	

Questions to Answer

QUE 1.4.1   Find out how to edit and run a Pascal program on your computer. Try it with the following program:

---

[2]ANSI stands for American National Standards Institute, IEEE stands for Institute of Electrical and Electronic Engineers, and ISO stands for International Standards Organization.

```
PROGRAM WriteName (output);
{Writes the name of this book on the screen.}

BEGIN {WriteName}
  WriteLn ('Pascal by Example')
END.  {WriteName}
```

Keep a log describing any mistakes you made while trying to edit and run the program. Next to each "mistake," describe how the computer responded to the mistake. Also describe what you did to correct the mistake.

QUE 1.4.2 Find out whether your implementation has a Pascal compiler, a Pascal interpreter, or both. If it has both, find out which you'll normally be using to do the programming exercises in this book.

QUE 1.4.3 Explain the difference between a statement and a command. For each of the items that follows, tell whether it's the English-language translation of a statement, a command, or neither:
a. Do what's asked of you in part (c) of this exercise.
b. Which way to the computer?
c. Find the first ten digits of *pi*.
d. Explain the meaning of life.
e. Don't do what's asked of you in part (d) of this exercise. It's impossible to do.

QUE 1.4.4 Make a list of some of your implementation's operating system commands—the commands that you'll be using most often in this course.

QUE 1.4.5 Find out how you can get help when you're stuck trying to do something on the computer. Is there a "help station" at your school? Does your implementation have a command that you can type in to get more information when you're stuck?

Things to Check in a Manual

In subsections entitled Things to Check in a Manual, you'll be asked to discover facts about Pascal by consulting an authoritative source—for example, the ANSI Standard Pascal manual or the manual that comes with your particular implementation. Most of the "Pascal facts" we ask you to look up would be difficult to check just by experimenting on the computer. The goal of these subsections is not to have you learn esoteric facts about Pascal, but rather to give you some practice in reading and understanding a formal description of a language, as is given in a manual.

MAN 1.4.1 Look in your implementation's manual to see if it claims to obey the rules of ANSI Standard Pascal or the rules of ISO Standard Pascal. If not, is there a "disclaimer" section describing the ways in which your implementation differs from either of these standards?

Things to Think About

THI 1.4.1 Throughout this chapter we've emphasized that every set of instructions can be written using decision making and/or repetition. Try to think of a set of instructions that involves some mechanism other than decision making and repetition. Write down the instructions so that you can reevaluate your opinion about this as you read through the book. What problem does your set of instructions solve? Can the instructions be rewritten so that the problem is solved using only decision making and/or repetition?

Chapter Summary

A *computer* is a machine that processes *input* in order to produce *output*. To do this, it follows a set of instructions called a *program*. Each instruction in a program is called a *statement*. These statements are written in a specialized language called a *programming language*. By reading this book, you'll learn how to write good programs using the programming language *Pascal*.

Each statement in a program is composed of several *characters*, some of which combine to form *words*. Any portion of a program is called a *program fragment* or is sometimes referred to as *code*. The word *software* is used to describe all the programs we give to a computer to run.

Before a program can run, it needs to be translated from Pascal into *machine language*. Instead of using ordinary characters, a machine-language program is "written" in low voltages and high voltages, which we often represent as 0's and 1's. A machine-language program gives the computer many more details about what it should do than it gets in a Pascal program.

There are two ways a computer can translate a Pascal program. A *compiler* takes a complete Pascal program, translates it into machine language and saves the translated copy. An *interpreter* takes statements of the Pascal program, one at a time, and executes them. It doesn't save any copies of the translated statements. Once a program is compiled, it needs to be *linked* with the other programs it needs in order to run.

The idea behind a program is called an *algorithm*. We say that the program *implements* the algorithm. An algorithm can be implemented many different ways, by many different programs, but it's still the same algorithm. If we want to describe an algorithm without committing ourselves to a particular language or program, we often describe it using *pseudocode*.

The term *hardware* is used to describe any piece of equipment that's a tangible part of a computer. A *device* is any piece of hardware that's used to supply input to the computer, or obtain output from the computer. A *medium* is a place where data are stored. The following table summarizes various media and the devices with which they are associated:

	Medium	**Device**
Input	— punched cards	keyboard —
Output	— paper	screen printer
Input and output (storage)	disk tape	disk drive tape drive

An *operating system* is a large set of instructions that governs the operation of a computer. An instruction to a computer's operating system is called a *command*. Taken all together, a particular kind of computer along with an operating system and an interpreter or a compiler is called an *implementation*. Each implementation has its own language for commands and its own *implementation-dependent* rules for translating and running Pascal programs. For that reason, there's no single set of steps for writing and running a Pascal program that will work for every implementation. As you read this book, you should look in your implementation's manuals and experiment with various programs to learn the rules that your implementation follows.

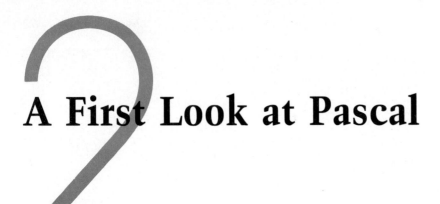

A First Look at Pascal

2.1

A Simple Program Illustrating REAL Arithmetic

An item sold in a department store normally costs $15.49, but this week it's on sale at half price. If sales tax is 5 percent and the customer gives us a $20.00 bill, how much change should we give the customer?

REAL

Our goal is to write a Pascal program to solve this simple problem. The first thing we need to do is to see how Pascal handles REAL numbers. A REAL number is a number with a decimal point, like 3.14 or -0.333. Even the numbers 1.0 and 0.00, when they're written with decimal points, are REAL numbers.

The following program demonstrates some of the concepts we need.

Program Example

```
PROGRAM RealArithmetic (output);
{Performs simple arithmetic on REAL numbers.}
   VAR
      a, b,
      sum, difference,
      product, quotient,
      parens, noParens  : REAL;
BEGIN {RealArithmetic}
   a := 1.5;
   b := 2.7;

   sum        := a + b;
   difference := a - b;
   product    := a * b;
   quotient   := a / b;
```

```
      parens     := (a + b) * b;
      noParens   :=  a + b * b;

      WriteLn ('sum              ', sum       :5:2);
      WriteLn ('difference       ', difference:5:2);
      WriteLn ('product          ', product   :5:2);
      WriteLn ('quotient         ', quotient  :5:2);
      WriteLn ('with parentheses ', parens    :5:2);
      WriteLn ('without parens   ', noParens  :5:2)
END.   {RealArithmetic}
```

Sample Runs

This program has no input. (The user doesn't type anything on the keyboard while the program runs.) Every time the program runs, the same output shows up on the screen:

```
sum                4.20
difference        -1.20
product            4.05
quotient           0.56
with parentheses  11.34
without parens     8.79
```

Observations about the Program Example

The following pseudocode can help you understand what this program does. Each line of pseudocode corresponds to one or more lines in the program:

Assign the value 1.5 to a.
Assign 2.7 to b.
Add a and b to get the value of sum.
Subtract b from a to get difference.
Multiply a and b to get product.
Divide a by b to get quotient.
Evaluate (a + b) * b, and put the result into parens.
Evaluate a + b * b, and put the result into noParens.
Display the values of sum, difference, product, quotient, parens, and noParens on the screen.

Now we'll take a more detailed look at what each line in the program is doing.

PROGRAM

• PROGRAM RealArithmetic (output);

This is the first line of a PROGRAM. The name of the program is RealArithmetic. The program produces some output, which appears on the screen.

output

Recall, from Section 1.4, that when you save a program using the editor, you give the program a name. *That name doesn't have to be the same as the name you give it on this first line of the program.* A program can have two different names—one that you write on its first line and another one that you give it when you save it using the editor.

program name

parameter list

The word (output) in parentheses is called a **parameter list**. As the compiler translates Program RealArithmetic, this parameter list tells the compiler how the program will interact with the outside world. In this case, the outside world is called output. When the word output appears in a program's parameter list, it always stands for the screen.

- {Performs simple arithmetic on REAL numbers.}

This tells us what the program does. Since this information is enclosed in curly braces { }, the computer doesn't act on it. It's just something we can read when we examine the text of the program. Any informative **comment** text that's enclosed in curly braces { } is called a **comment**.

- VAR
```
    a, b,
    sum, difference,
    product, quotient,
    parens, noParens  : REAL;
```

In an algebraic equation, like

$$x + y = 4$$

the letters x and y are the names of variables. Each variable can store a value. For instance, in the equation given, the variable x might store the value 1, and y might store the value 3.

variables and values

The same is somewhat true in a computer program: a **variable** is a place to store a **value**. More accurately, it's a location in the computer's memory where a value can be stored—a storage location.

VAR declaration part

The lines of code given above form what's called the VAR **declaration part** of the program.[1] When the compiler translates Program RealArithmetic, this VAR declaration part tells it that the variable names used in the program are a, b, sum, difference, product, quotient, parens, and noParens. It also says that each of these variables can contain a REAL number value.

---

[1]Note: In this text we'll usually refer to something like

```
VAR
    a, b,
    sum, difference,
    product, quotient,
    parens, noParens  : REAL;
```

as the VAR declaration part (of the program), or more simply as the VAR declarations (plural). To refer to a portion of the VAR declaration part in which one or more variables are declared, such as

```
    parens, noParens  : REAL;
```

we'll use the phrase VAR declaration (singular).

```
• a := 1.5;
  b := 2.7;

  sum        := a + b;
  difference := a - b;
  product    := a * b;
  quotient   := a / b;

  parens     := (a + b) * b;
  noParens   :=  a + b * b
```

assignment statement

Each of these statements makes the computer assign a value to a variable. They are called **assignment statements**. Notice that an asterisk * is used for multiplication and a slash / is used for division. Note also that parentheses are used to force addition to be done before multiplication. Without the parentheses, a + b * b means "multiply b by b and *then* add a." We'll say more on this in the next subsection.

WriteLn

```
• WriteLn ('sum              ', sum        :5:2)
```

This statement tells the computer to display several things on the screen: the word sum, followed by several blank spaces, followed by the value stored in the sum variable.

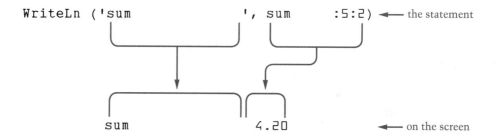

Let's look at each part of this WriteLn separately.

Whatever we put inside single quote marks in the WriteLn gets displayed on the screen exactly as we see it in the WriteLn—blank spaces and all:

```
WriteLn ('sum              ', sum        :5:2)
```

Then the word sum inside the WriteLn without quote marks

```
WriteLn ('sum              ', sum        :5:2)
```

tells the computer to display the value stored in the variable sum. The numbers :5:2 in the WriteLn

```
WriteLn ('sum              ', sum        :5:2)
```

tell the computer to use five places to write the value of sum, and tell it that two of the five places should be to the right of the decimal point.

When the value of `sum` appears on the screen, it looks like this:

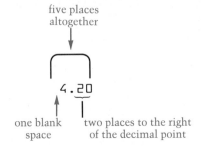

The letters `Ln` in `WriteLn` stand for the word *Line*. When a `WriteLn` is executed, the last thing it does is to go to the start of a new line on the screen. The program's next `WriteLn`

```
WriteLn ('difference            ', difference:5:2);
```

will display things starting at the beginning of this new line.

parts of a Pascal program

This program, like every Pascal program, is divided into several parts. The program contains:

```
PROGRAM RealArithmetic (output);
```
← a program heading

```
{Performs simple arithmetic on REAL numbers.}
```
← a comment

```
VAR
   a, b,
   sum, difference,
   product, quotient,
   parens, noParens  : REAL;
```
← a VAR declaration part

```
BEGIN {RealArithmetic}
   a := 1.5;
   b := 2.7;

   sum        := a + b;
   difference := a - b;
   product    := a * b;
   quotient   := a / b;

   parens     := (a + b) * b;
   noParens   :=  a + b * b;

   WriteLn ('sum             ', sum       :5:2);
   WriteLn ('difference      ', difference:5:2);
   WriteLn ('product         ', product   :5:2);
   WriteLn ('quotient        ', quotient  :5:2);
   WriteLn ('with parentheses ', parens   :5:2);
   WriteLn ('without parens   ', noParens :5:2)
END.   {RealArithmetic}
```
← a program body

Every program's body starts with the word BEGIN and finishes with the word END, and a period. Comments can go anywhere in the program.

comments

Every program should have a comment immediately after the program heading to explain and summarize the purpose of the program. A comment that comes immediately after the heading is called a **prologue comment**.

In addition to having a prologue comment, we've decided to surround the program body with comments that remind us what program we're reading ({RealArithmetic}). In longer and more complicated programs, this will help us keep track of the various pieces of our code.

Further Discussion

REAL numbers

A number with a decimal point, like 1.5, 2.7, or −3.33, is a REAL number in Pascal. Even the numbers 0.00 and 5.0 are REAL numbers when they're written with decimal points. Whenever we put a REAL number in the text of Pascal program, we must put digits before and after the decimal point. This means we can put statements like

```
a := 1.0
```

and

```
b := 0.5
```

in our Pascal programs, but we can't use statements like

```
a := 1.
```

and

```
b := .5
```

There are two kinds of "words" in Program RealArithmetic: words we made up for this example, and words that have specific meanings in the Pascal language. For instance, the word PROGRAM is the first word of every Pascal program. It's called a **reserved word** because it can be used only as the first word in a program. We can't make up a variable name called program, and we certainly wouldn't want to—it would be so confusing! For a complete list of Pascal's reserved words, see Appendix A in the back of this book.

reserved words

The words we made up for this example are all *names* of things; for example, variable names (a, b, sum, etc.) and the program name (RealArithmetic). Actually, instead of saying that RealArithmetic, a, b, and sum are "names" for things, we should be calling these words **identifiers**. An identifier is a name for something because it identifies that thing. In Pascal, you can create an identifier by using any combination of letters and digits, as long as you begin with a letter. For instance,

identifiers

```
sum
sum2
x5y29z9
thisIsAnIdentifier
karlAteABanana
```

are all valid identifiers in the Pascal language, but for various reasons none of the following are valid identifiers:

```
5GoldenRings
another#
this has blank spaces
a$
```

We've just given a few sentences, in English, to tell you how to make a Pascal identifier. English sentences are all right, but there's a nicer way to describe rules for forming identifiers and other parts of Pascal programs. You **syntax diagrams**   can describe rules with pictures called **syntax diagrams**. The word **syntax** is used in computer science in place of the word *grammar*. A syntax diagram describes things that are "grammatically correct" in the Pascal language.[2]

The syntax diagram for identifiers looks like this:

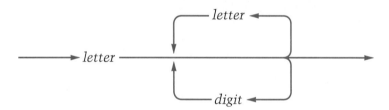

Follow the arrows any way you like. Whenever you get to the word *letter*, pick a letter. Whenever you get to the word *digit*, pick a digit.

Forming the identifier sum2:

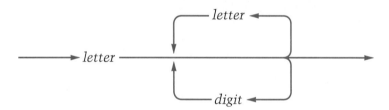

---

[2]Many times in this text we say that certain code is "correct," "valid," "permissible," "legal," "has no errors," etc. These terms are synonymous and their meaning is quite clear. But to be absolutely precise, we define them here: An example (or part of an example) is "correct," "valid," "permissible," "legal," "has no errors," etc. when it obeys the rules set out in the ANSI and/or ISO standard or it obeys rules that are followed by many of the current Pascal implementations.

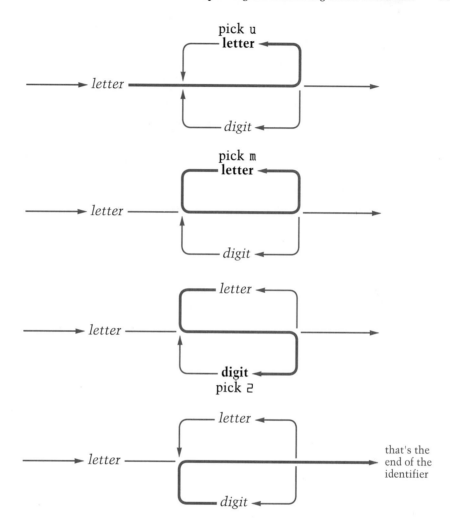

In the syntax diagram, we put the words *letter* and *digit* in italics, because these words refer to other diagrams. For instance, there's another diagram— the diagram for *digit*—on the next page. The symbols in the diagram are not in italics, because these symbols actually get written in our Pascal programs. We'll refer to syntax diagrams from time to time in this text. To see a complete set of syntax diagrams for Pascal, look at Appendix C.

The statements in a program's body are preceded by the word BEGIN and followed by the word END and a period. To show the compiler where one statement ends and the next begins, statements need to be separated **semicolons** from one another by **semicolons**. That's why the assignment statements in Program RealArithmetic end with semicolons. There's no semicolon after the very last WriteLn's closing parentheses because the word END

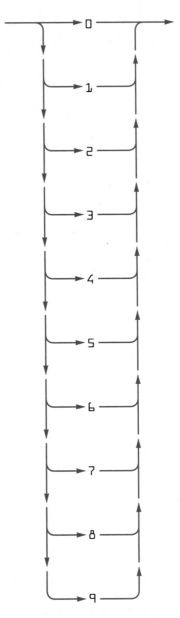

isn't considered to be a statement. (It doesn't really tell the computer to perform an action.) Since semicolons only separate statements from one another, the WriteLn doesn't need to be separated from the END.

The placement of semicolons in a Pascal program is often confusing to the beginning programmer. It helps to think of the program body as if it were written on one line, like this:

```
BEGIN   a:=1.5  ;   b:=2.7  ;   sum:= ...   ;   WriteLn(...)  END.
```

Writing it this way makes it clear that semicolons aren't used to terminate statements, they're used to separate statements from one another.

Evaluating expressions, like the ones used to assign values to parens and noParens, involves **precedence rules**. In the Observations subsection we hinted at one of the precedence rules:

precedence
rules

When there are no parentheses, * is performed before +.

This is actually part of a larger rule:

Precedence Rule 1: When there are no parentheses, * and / are performed before + and −.

So in the expression

the * and / are done first:

and then the − and + operations are performed: −28.0

But in doing this example, we glossed over one important point: In the very last step, which do we do first, the + or the −? More generally, when there are no parentheses, and Precedence Rule 1 still doesn't tell us anything about the order in which operations are performed, how do you know which operations are performed first? The question is answered by Precedence Rule 2.

Precedence Rule 2: When there are no parentheses, and Rule 1 still doesn't tell us anything about the order in which operations are performed, the operations are performed *from left to right*.

So in the expression

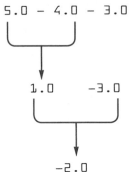

the leftmost subtraction is performed first:

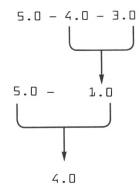

and then the rightmost subtraction is performed:

It makes a difference which subtraction is performed first. If we'd performed the rightmost subtraction first, we would have obtained a different answer:

Precedence Rule 2 often goes by the name **left-to-right associativity**.

When we began this section we promised we'd be solving a real-life problem about an item on half-price sale. Throughout the section we've been solving that problem all along. Perhaps this isn't apparent because we've been using words like `product` instead of `tax`, and `difference` instead of `change`. Now that we've got the Pascal tools, it's easy to turn them into a useful program. Here it is:

An item sold in a department store normally costs $15.49, but this week it's on sale at half price. If sales tax is 5 percent and the customer gives us a $20.00 bill, how much change should we give the customer? And, by the way, what would be the tax on the item if the customer had a coupon for $1.00 off?

```
PROGRAM HalfPriceSale (output);
{Computes sale price, tax, total, change.
 When the customer brings a coupon, computes only the tax.}
   VAR
     price, amtTendered, salePrice,
     tax, total, change, couponTax : REAL;
```

```
BEGIN {HalfPriceSale}
   price        := 15.49;
   amtTendered := 20.00;
   salePrice   := price / 2.0;
   tax         := salePrice * 0.05;
   total       := salePrice + tax;
   change      := amtTendered - total;

   couponTax   := (salePrice - 1.00) * 0.05;

   WriteLn ('price       ', price      :6:2);
   WriteLn ('tendered    ', amtTendered:6:2);
   WriteLn ('sale price  ', salePrice  :6:2);
   WriteLn ('tax         ', tax        :6:2);
   WriteLn ('total       ', total      :6:2);
   WriteLn ('change      ', change     :6:2);
   WriteLn ('with coupon ', couponTax  :6:2)
END.   {HalfPriceSale}
```

2.1   Exercises

Key Words to Review

REAL	assignment statement	identifier
PROGRAM	WriteLn	syntax diagram
output	BEGIN	syntax
parameter list	END	letter
comment	program heading	digit
variable	prologue comment	semicolon
value	program body	precedence rules
VAR declaration	reserved word	parentheses

Questions to Answer

QUE 2.1.1 For each "word" given below, tell whether the word can be used as a Pascal identifier. If not, tell why not.
a. AssignmentStatement
b. B$
c. PROGRAM
d. ImNotAnIdentifier
e. bARRY

QUE 2.1.2 Rewrite the following algebraic expressions as Pascal expressions:
a. $\dfrac{a + b}{2.0}$
b. $3.142r^2$ (Hint: r^2 is the same as "r times r.")
c. $x^2 + 3x + 5$

QUE 2.1.3 Rewrite the following Pascal expressions as algebraic expressions:
a. a - b
b. (a / b) * c
c. a / (b * c)

          d. x - y - z
          e. a * a * a

QUE 2.1.4 In each of the program fragments given below, find the final value of the variable x:

          a. a := 7.0;
             b := 1.0;
             x := a - b - b
          b. a := 14.1;
             b := -2.3;
             c := 3.0;
             x := a + b * c
          c. a := 2.4;
             b := 6.1;
             x := a/b/b

QUE 2.1.5 Modify the syntax diagram for an identifier so that only names with three or fewer characters are syntactically correct.

QUE 2.1.6 Here's a syntax diagram for a program heading:

Program heading:

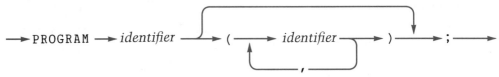

          Based on what you see in this syntax diagram, which of the following lines are legal program headings?
          a. PROGRAM ProgramName (output);
          b. PROGRAM;
          c. PROGRAM Prog;
          d. PROGRAM FirstProg (input, output);
          e. PROGRAM GoodProg (input)(output);
          f. PROGRAM 6thProgram (output);
          g. PROGRAM Family (Barry, Harriet, Sam, Jennie);

QUE 2.1.7 Here's a part of the syntax diagram that shows how you can represent a REAL number in a Pascal program:

          Translate this diagram into an English-language sentence that explains exactly how REAL numbers *can* and *cannot* be represented.

Things to Check in a Manual

MAN 2.1.1   Many implementations have more reserved words than the ones listed in Appendix A. Look in your manual and find a list of your implementation's reserved words. It's important to have a list like this, because these are the words that you may not use as identifiers.

MAN 2.1.2   Some implementations will behave as if `planetsInOtherSolarSystems` and `planetsInOtherGalaxies` are the same identifier, because the first fourteen characters of **planetsInOther**SolarSystems are the same as the first fourteen characters of **planetsInOther**Galaxies. Look in your manuals to find out if your implementation does this. (Note: Your implementation may use a different number—not necessarily fourteen.)

Experiments to Try

In this subsection we'll ask you to

- make changes to Program `RealArithmetic`, and
- try to compile and run the program with the changes

With each change the new program will fall into one of several categories:

- The compiler may not be able to compile the new program. That means the new program has a *syntax error*. A syntax error in Pascal is like a grammar error in English. A program with a syntax error can't be compiled because the grammar error makes the program meaningless. (The program may look meaningful to you; but with one tiny syntax error, like a missing semicolon, the whole program will be meaningless to the compiler.)

- The compiler may be able to compile the new program, but the computer may encounter a difficulty while trying to run the new program. This is called a *run-time error*. For instance, if your instructions are meaningful, but they tell the computer to divide a number by zero, you'll have a run-time error. At this point the computer will stop running your program. This is called *aborting* the run of your program.

    A run-time error is usually caused by another sort of "error," called a *logic error* (or a *bug*). In a logic error, the programmer has written code that doesn't correctly solve the given problem. Note the difference: a run-time error is something that happens while the computer is running your program; a logic error is a mistake made by the programmer while writing a program. The two kinds of errors often go hand in hand.

In either of the two situations given, the computer will display *error diagnostics* on the screen. An error diagnostic is a message telling the user or programmer that something went wrong while the program was being compiled or run. When you do these experiments, you should look carefully at any error diagnostics the computer gives you. With each error diagnostic, ask yourself how this diagnostic pinpoints the cause of the error.

There are two other possible outcomes of making changes to Program `RealArithmetic`:

- The computer may be able to compile and run the new program. In this case, you should look carefully at the program's new output to understand the effects of the change that you made.

- The change may not make any difference at all. In this case, you should ask yourself why the change makes no difference. Sometimes you won't be able to answer the question, so you can just hold the experiment in your mind for later reference.

In any case, it will help you to keep a log of these experiments. Here's a sample portion of a log:

Date	Exercise	Effect	Remarks
10/2	Exp.2.1.1	Syntax error (or ; expected	Program name must be one word
10/3	Exp.2.1.2	No effect	Uppercase vs. lowercase doesn't matter
10/3	Exp.2.1.13	Run-time error divide by zero	?? b was assigned the value 2.7 in an earlier statement. Have to think about this later.

Here are some experiments for you to try with Program `RealArithmetic`:

EXP 2.1.1   Change the name `RealArithmetic` to `Real Arithmetic`, with a blank space.

EXP 2.1.2   Change `PROGRAM` to `program` (that is, write it with lowercase letters).

EXP 2.1.3   Remove the word `VAR`.

EXP 2.1.4   Remove the variable name `noParens` from the program's `VAR` declaration (but don't change the line where `noParens` is assigned a value).

EXP 2.1.5   Remove the semicolon after the word `REAL`.

EXP 2.1.6   Remove one of the semicolons in the program's body.

EXP 2.1.7   Add a semicolon after the last `WriteLn`'s closing parenthesis.

EXP 2.1.8   Change `:=` to just plain `=` in one of the assignment statements.

EXP 2.1.9   Change the first assignment statement to `a := 1.0`

EXP 2.1.10   Change the first assignment statement to `a := .5`

EXP 2.1.11   Change the first assignment statement to `1.5 := a`

EXP 2.1.12   Change the second assignment statement to `a + b := 4.2`

EXP 2.1.13   Put a new statement `b := 0.0` after the statement that says `b := 2.7`

EXP 2.1.14   Change `noParens` to `noparens` (with a lowercase p) in the `VAR` declaration only.

EXP 2.1.15   Change `noParens` to `no_parens` everywhere in the program. If your implementation likes this (that is, if it allows the *underscore* _ character to appear in identifiers), try `_no_parens` and then try `no____parens`.

EXP 2.1.16   In a `WriteLn`, leave off the `:5:2`.

EXP 2.1.17   In a `WriteLn`, leave off the `:2`.

Changes to Make

In the Changes to Make exercises we'll be asking you to make modifications to each section's program example. We'll also ask you to test your modified program to see if it runs correctly. In this first set of Changes to Make exercises, we ask you to modify Programs RealArithmetic and HalfPriceSale.

CHA 2.1.1   Modify Program RealArithmetic so that the values of sum and difference are written on one line, the values of product and quotient are written on another line, and the values of parens and noParens are written on a third line.

CHA 2.1.2   Modify Program HalfPriceSale so that it computes the total price and the change when the customer brings a dollar-off coupon.

CHA 2.1.3   Modify the Program you wrote for Exercise Cha.2.1.2 so that the dollar gets taken off after the tax has been added.

Programs and Subprograms to Write

WRI 2.1.1   Write a Pascal program that computes the area of a circle with a radius of 7 inches.

WRI 2.1.2   Write a Pascal program that computes and writes the Celsius equivalents of the Fahrenheit temperatures 32°, 70°, and 212°. The formula to convert Fahrenheit to Celsius is

$$C = \frac{5}{9}(F - 32)$$

WRI 2.1.3   Modify the program you wrote for Exercise Wri.2.1.2 so that it prints the Kelvin equivalents of 32°, 70°, and 212°. To get the Kelvin temperature, add 273.15° to the Celsius temperature.

WRI 2.1.4   Write a Pascal program that computes and writes the surface area and volume of a box whose dimensions are 5 feet by 6 feet by 7.5 feet.

WRI 2.1.5   The price of a tire is $97.50, with an additional excise tax of $10.25. The labor cost of lifting the car to install any number of tires is just $15.00. Write a program that writes the total cost of buying and installing four new tires.

WRI 2.1.6   Write a program that computes 5 percent interest on a principal amount of $253.21. Then it computes the new principal (the old principal, plus the interest).

WRI 2.1.7   Write a program that computes the percentage increase or decrease in sales if this week's sales are $21,584.00 and last week's sales were $19,550.00.

2.2

A Simple Program Illustrating INTEGER Arithmetic

How many quarters can you get for 273 cents? Once you've made the change, how much do you have in quarters, and how many cents do you have left over?

INTEGER

We'll end this section with a program to solve this simple problem. But first we need to see how Pascal handles INTEGERs. An INTEGER is a "whole number"—a number without a decimal point. Numbers like 3, –35, and 0 are examples of INTEGERs.

Here's a program that shows how simple arithmetic with INTEGERs is done in Pascal.

Program Example

```
PROGRAM IntegerArithmetic (input, output);
{Performs simple arithmetic on INTEGERs.}

   VAR
      a, b, result : INTEGER;
      realNum      : REAL;

   BEGIN {IntegerArithmetic}
      Write  ('Enter two numbers (integer space integer): ');
      ReadLn (a, b);

      result  := a + b;
      WriteLn ('sum          ', result:5);

      result  := a - b;
      WriteLn ('difference ', result:5);

      result  := a * b;
      WriteLn ('product      ', result:5);

      realNum := a / b;
      WriteLn ('quotient      ', realNum:5:2);

      result  := a DIV b;
      WriteLn ('quotient      ', result:5);

      result  := a MOD b;
      WriteLn ('remainder  ', result:5)
   END.   {IntegerArithmetic}
```

Sample Runs[3]

As you can see by the program heading, this program has input. The statement ReadLn (a, b) makes the computer suspend execution of the program and wait for the user to type in values (on the keyboard) for the variables a and b. The way ReadLn (a, b) works, the user is expected to type two integers, separated by at least one blank space. As the user types, the screen has a *cursor* that shows where the next character will appear. On most screens, the cursor looks like a line _, a box ▮, or a hook ⌐. On many screens the cursor blinks on and off constantly.

After typing in the second integer, the user is expected to press the "return" key.[4] The computer will not resume execution of the program until the user presses this key.

---

[3]A few implementations behave in a "surprising" way when we have a Write followed by a ReadLn as we do in Program IntegerArithmetic and in many other examples in this text. Run Program IntegerArithmetic on your own computer. If your computer wants you to type in two numbers *before* it prints the message Enter two numbers (integer space integer): then you might need to change the Writes to WriteLns in all of these examples. Consult your instructor for more details.

[4]Some keyboards have a key marked "newline" rather than "return"; others use a key marked "enter." Throughout this text, we'll refer to this key as the "return key."

Here's what a run of Program `IntegerArithmetic` might look like:

```
Enter two numbers (integer space integer): 121 10<return>
sum             131
difference      111
product         1210
quotient        12.10
quotient        12
remainder       1
```

The user types the

```
121 10
```

and presses the return key, and the computer types all the rest.

If you're new to computers, you might be confused at first when the computer "suspends execution of the program." After displaying the words

```
Enter two numbers (integer space integer):
```

the computer won't do anything. It will just sit there, waiting for you to type in two numbers and press the return key. Once you've done this, the computer will display its six values on the screen.

When Program `IntegerArithmetic` runs, the user can type in any two integer values for a and b. In the discussion that follows, we'll usually fix our sights on this particular run, in which the user gives a and b the values 121 and 10.

Observations

- ```
  VAR
      a, b, result : INTEGER;
      realNum      : REAL;
  ```
  The variable `realNum` is a `REAL` variable (just like those in Program `RealArithmetic`). But a, b, and `result` are variables that store `INTEGER` values.

- `ReadLn (a, b)`

`ReadLn`

`ReadLn` stands for "Read a Line." When the computer executes this statement, the user types in two numbers, presses the return key, and the computer assigns values (those two numbers) to the variables a and b. The significance of reading "a line" is this: when a `ReadLn` is executed, the last thing the computer does is *prepare for reading at the start of a new line.* For instance, if the computer is executing

```
ReadLn (a, b)
```

and the user types in

```
121 10 26 <return>
```

then the computer assigns 121 to a, 10 to b, and then "prepares for reading at the start of a new line" by skipping over the 26. (*Nothing* gets assigned the value 26. Even if the program had another `ReadLn`, this
```

second `ReadLn` would start reading at the beginning of the next line of input.)

Notice how a `ReadLn` is different from a `WriteLn`: there are normally no colons in a `ReadLn`. When we ask the computer to read a value from the keyboard, we don't tell it how many places (digits, spaces, decimal point) we'll be using. We expect the computer to examine what we've typed in and determine this on its own.

- `realNum := a / b`

INTEGER
operations

In ordinary mathematics, when you divide 121 by 10, you get 12.10. So dividing one `INTEGER` by another `INTEGER` gives you a `REAL` number. This is what happens in Pascal when you use a slash `/` to represent division. With this assignment statement the `REAL` value 12.10 is assigned to the `REAL` variable `realNum`.

- `result  := a DIV b`

Sometimes you want to divide an `INTEGER` by another `INTEGER` and get an `INTEGER` result. This is what happens in Pascal when you use the word `DIV` to represent division. You can think of a `DIV` b as "the number of times b goes into a." Ten goes into one hundred twenty-one 12 times, so the value of 121 DIV 10 is 12, not 12.10.

It's easy to forget the difference between `/` and `DIV`, so try to keep it in mind when you're writing your programs or reading other people's programs.

- `result  := a MOD b`

When 10 goes into 121, you get a remainder of 1. You can think of a MOD b as "the remainder when a is divided by b." So in this statement, the value 1 is assigned to the `INTEGER` variable `result`.

- `result  := a + b;`
  - .
  - .

  `result  := a - b`
  - .
  - .

Now we see why a name like `result` is called a *variable name.* Its value can vary. In one statement, the value of `result` becomes 131, and in a later statement its value becomes 111. In fact, the variable `result` is given a new value five times during the run of Program `IntegerArithmetic`.

- `Write ('Enter two numbers (integer space integer): ');`
  `ReadLn(a, b)`

Write

When the computer finishes doing a `Write` (rather than a `WriteLn`) it doesn't go to the start of a new line on the screen. The computer uses enough places to display whatever material it needs to Write, and then it leaves the cursor at the end of that material, still on the same line.[5]

So after the computer has executed this Write, the screen looks like this

```
Enter two numbers (integer space integer): ▊ ◀── cursor
```

not like this

```
Enter two numbers (integer space integer):
▊ ◀── cursor
```

And then when the ReadLn is executed and the user types values for a and b, the screen looks like this

```
Enter two numbers (integer space integer): 121 10
```

not like this

```
Enter two numbers (integer space integer):
121 10
```

A message that asks the user to type something in, like the message

```
Enter two numbers (integer space integer):
```

prompt

is called a **prompt**. Always remember that inside the WriteLn you need to enclose the prompt in single quotes.

- WriteLn ('sum   ', result:5)

The number 5, after the colon, tells the computer to use five positions on the screen to display the value of result. So when the value of result appears on the screen, it looks like this

```
  131
↑↑
```

two blank spaces

Further Discussion

The precedence rules given in Section 2.1 said nothing about the operators DIV and MOD. It's easy to enlarge Precedence Rule 1 so that it includes DIV and MOD:

precedence rule

Precedence Rule 1: When there are no parentheses, *, /, DIV, and MOD are performed before + and −.

So in the expression

the DIV is done first, giving

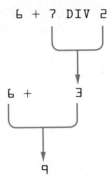

and finally

When we began this section we promised we'd be solving a real-life problem about changing cents into quarters. Now it's time for us to make good on the promise:

How many quarters can you get for some certain number of cents? Once you've made the change, how much do you have in quarters, and how many cents do you have left over?

Program Example

```
PROGRAM MakeChange (input, output);
{Converts number of cents to number of quarters.
 Also tells how many cents are left over.}
   VAR
     cents, quarters, leftOver : INTEGER;
     amount                    : REAL;
BEGIN {MakeChange}
   Write  ('How many cents? ');
   ReadLn (cents);
   quarters := cents DIV 25;
   amount   := cents / 100;
   WriteLn ('You get '          , quarters:2,
            ' quarters with $ ', amount:5:2);
   leftOver := cents MOD 25;
   amount   := quarters * 25 / 100;
   WriteLn (amount:5:2, ' in quarters with ',
            leftOver:2, ' cents left over  ')
END.   {MakeChange}
```

Sample Runs

```
How many cents? 273
You get 10 quarters with $  2.73
 2.50 in quarters with 23 cents left over
```

Observations In Program MakeChange we see the same principles in action as those we illustrated in Program IntegerArithmetic:

- We use cents DIV 25 to find out how many quarters we can get for cents-many pennies (how many times 25 goes into cents).

- We use `cents MOD 25` to find out how many cents we have left over (the remainder when `cents` is divided by 25).

- We use a slash `/` to divide two `INTEGER`s and get a `REAL` number. (Taking `25 / 100` gives us the `REAL` value 0.25—the value of a quarter.)

As you can see, we've been discussing the fundamental tools we need for solving the change-making problem all along in this section.

Programming Style

What is programming style?

Let's say we have a problem that we want solved, and we describe the problem to two different people. Each person writes a program to solve the problem. The two programs aren't exactly alike. Even though they solve the same problem, there are differences in the way they do it. In this case, we say that the two people have different **programming styles**.[6]

Here's another way to state the same issue: When you're writing a program to solve a particular problem, you have lots of choices to make. Some of these choices are made for you, by either your instructor, your supervisor, or obvious common sense. But often you have choices that aren't so straightforward, where the benefit of one alternative isn't so clear, or where the number of alternatives may make the choice difficult. In any case, the set of choices you make defines your own programming style.

In art or in fashion, there's such a thing as good style and such a thing as bad style. The same is true in programming, but in programming the dividing line between good and bad is often more clear-cut. For instance, you might tolerate and even admire a short story for its curious sense of ambiguity, but you'd be appalled by an ambiguous program that's meant to send a rocket ship to Venus.

In these sections on Programming Style, we'll try to indicate what constitutes good style and the ways in which good style is superior to bad style.

documentation

Our first observation is about documentation. The word **documentation** refers to the material that helps people understand what the program is meant to do, how well it does what it's meant to do, what ideas were used in writing the program, how to use the program, etc. Some documentation is separate from the code itself—a user's manual, a programmer's guide, etc. But some documentation is actually built into the code. When documentation is built into the code it's called **internal documentation**.

A comment is a form of internal documentation. Comments like

```
{Performs simple arithmetic on INTEGERs.}
```

---

[6]In this text we use a very broad definition of the word *style*, as in Kernighan and Plauger's book *The Elements of Programming Style*.

help us understand what a program is doing. A program can run correctly without comments; but if the program doesn't have enough comments, then it isn't readable. An unreadable program is a bad program, even if it "runs correctly."

2.2   Exercises

Key Words to Review

INTEGER	MOD	programming style
ReadLn	Write	documentation
return key	prompt	internal documentation
DIV		

Questions to Answer

QUE 2.2.1   Explain the difference between / and DIV.

QUE 2.2.2   Explain the difference between DIV and MOD.

QUE 2.2.3   Tell exactly what the user is expected to do while Program IntegerArithmetic is running (that is, tell exactly what keys should be pressed and when). If, at certain points during the run of the program, the user has to decide what to do, explain exactly what options the user has.

QUE 2.2.4   What's the difference between WriteLn and Write?

QUE 2.2.5   Give an example to show that if you ignore what Precedence Rule 1 says about DIV and MOD, you could get a wrong answer when you're trying to evaluate an expression.

QUE 2.2.6   Evaluate each of the following expressions:
a. 10 DIV 5
b. 10 DIV 4
c. (15 DIV 2) * 2
d. (16 DIV 2) * 2
e. (17 DIV 2) * 2
f. 16 MOD 4
g. 17 MOD 4

QUE 2.2.7   Make up a syntax diagram for assignment statements such as

```
result := -291
```

in which a variable is given a certain integer value. Design the diagram so that the integer value can be with or without a sign.

Experiments to Try

EXP 2.2.1   In Program IntegerArithmetic change result := a DIV b to realNum := a DIV b.

EXP 2.2.2   In Program IntegerArithmetic change realNum := a / b to result := a / b.

EXP 2.2.3   In Program IntegerArithmetic add the statement result := realNum DIV b.

EXP 2.2.4   When Program IntegerArithmetic prompts you for two numbers, type in two letters instead.

EXP 2.2.5   When Program IntegerArithmetic prompts you for two numbers, hit the space bar several times before you type in the first number.

EXP 2.2.6   When Program IntegerArithmetic prompts you for two numbers, hit the return key several times before you type in the first number.

EXP 2.2.7   Leave off the :5 when you WriteLn the value of result.

Changes to Make

CHA 2.2.1   Modify Program IntegerArithmetic so that it has just one WriteLn at the bottom that displays all six numbers on one line, like this:

```
sum 131   diff 111   prod 1210   quot 12.10   quot 12   rema 1
```

To do this, you might want to create some new variable names.

CHA 2.2.2   Redo Exercise Cha.2.2.1 so that it uses the original variable names result and realNum, but has several Writes (not WriteLns) scattered throughout the program.

Programs and Subprograms to Write

In many exercises throughout the book we ask you to "modify," "redo," or "rewrite" a program you wrote for an exercise in an earlier section. In addition to making the required changes, you should always ask yourself three questions:

- If you'd known that we'd eventually be asking for these modifications, would you have done the original exercise differently?
- Considering what you knew about Pascal when you wrote the original program, are there any ways your program could have been better?
- Considering what you've learned about Pascal in the intervening sections, what improvements can you make to the original program?

WRI 2.2.1   Write a Pascal program that reads in the number of bottles of Barry Cola you have and computes how many complete six-packs you can make. The program should also tell you how many bottles will be left over.

WRI 2.2.2   Write a Pascal program that tells you how many full-hour comp-sci lectures you can attend in 743 minutes (or any number of minutes) and how many minutes you'll have left over for lunch.

WRI 2.2.3   Modify the program you wrote for Exercise Wri.2.1.6 so that the user can type in a principal amount and an interest rate during the run of the program.

WRI 2.2.4   Modify the program you wrote for Exercise Wri.2.1.7 so that the user can type in amounts for this week's sales and last week's sales during the run of the program.

2.3

Decision Making

In Section 1.1 we noted that the basic building blocks of algorithms and programs are **decision making** and **repetition**, and so in this section we study a Pascal program that uses decision making.

Specifications

problem
specifications

When we solve a problem, we follow several steps. The first step, of course, is to define the problem. In attempting to define a problem it's very helpful to write a precise statement of the problem. A precise statement of a problem is called a set of **specifications** (or specs, for short). As you write specifications for a problem, you might see that you're having trouble stating the exact nature of the problem; that is, you may have difficulty describing exactly what your new algorithm should do. This means you haven't defined your problem in complete detail. Writing specs for a problem forces you to think about it in complete detail.

The specs for this section's program example are quite simple:

Input: The scores of two teams

Output: The same two scores, written on two separate lines—one right above the other. The winner's score is on the top line; the loser's score is on the bottom line.

Designing a Program

Here's a paragraph to describe how the problem will be solved:

Read the two scores; call them `home` and `visitor`. Then compare the scores. If `home` is bigger, write `home` on the screen, and then write `visitor`. Otherwise, write `visitor` on the screen, and then write `home`.

To turn this paragraph into pseudocode, we do some indenting and trim some of the fat:

Read `home` and `visitor` from the keyboard.
If `home` > `visitor`
   write `home` on the screen
   write `visitor` on the screen
otherwise
   write `visitor` on the screen
   write `home` on the screen

To write a program, we turn the pseudocode into Pascal code:

```
ReadLn (home, visitor);

IF home > visitor THEN
   BEGIN
      WriteLn ('home    ', home   );
      WriteLn ('visitor ', visitor)
   END
ELSE
   BEGIN
      WriteLn ('visitor ', visitor);
      WriteLn ('home    ', home   )
   END
```

Then, to create a complete program, we need a program heading and a VAR declaration.

Program Example

```
PROGRAM Scores (input, output);
{Reads two scores; writes the winner's score on top.}

   VAR
      home, visitor : INTEGER;

BEGIN {Scores}
   Write  ('Enter two scores (home space visitor): ');
   ReadLn (home, visitor);

   IF home > visitor THEN
      BEGIN
         WriteLn ('home    ', home   );
         WriteLn ('visitor ', visitor)
      END
   ELSE
      BEGIN
         WriteLn ('visitor ', visitor);
         WriteLn ('home    ', home   )
      END
END.  {Scores}
```

Sample Runs

Here's what a run of Program Scores might look like:

```
Enter two scores (home space visitor): 75 31
home            75
visitor         31
```

The user may type in two other numbers:

```
Enter two scores (home space visitor): 16 54
visitor         54
home            16
```

The user may even type in the same number twice:

```
Enter two scores (home space visitor): 80 80
visitor         80
home            80
```

Observations

- WriteLn ('home   ', home   )

  If we omit the colon in this WriteLn, the computer takes a predetermined number of places to display the value of home. Notice that the computer we used in doing our sample runs takes ten places for each integer. It puts eight blank spaces in front of a two-digit number, four blank spaces in front of a six-digit number, etc.

- IF home > visitor THEN
  ```
    BEGIN
      WriteLn ('home    ', home    );
      WriteLn ('visitor ', visitor)
    END
  ELSE
    BEGIN
      WriteLn ('visitor ', visitor);
      WriteLn ('home    ', home    )
    END
  ```

IF statement

The simplest mechanism in Pascal for making decisions is the IF statement. Taken together, the lines given above form an IF statement. An IF statement is a **structured statement** (see Section 1.2) because it contains other statements. The IF statement given contains four WriteLns. The first two WriteLns make up the IF statement's THEN-part. The last two WriteLns form the ELSE-part of the IF statement. The THEN-part is what gets executed when the value stored in home is greater than the value stored in visitor; the ELSE-part is what gets executed when the value stored in home isn't greater than the value stored in visitor (for instance, if home happens to be equal to visitor!).

So the action taken when the IF statement is executed depends on whether home > visitor is TRUE or FALSE. This expression

```
home > visitor
```

is called a **condition**.

Further Discussion

Now we have to be just a bit more precise. There are rules in Pascal that say:

- a THEN-part can contain only one statement, and
- an ELSE-part can contain only one statement

BEGIN and END

How can this be true when the THEN- and ELSE-parts in Program Scores each have two WriteLns? The answer is: We can combine several statements into a single statement with the words BEGIN and END. This makes

```
BEGIN
  WriteLn ('home    ', home    );
  WriteLn ('visitor ', visitor)
END
```

into a single statement, and also makes

```
BEGIN
  WriteLn ('visitor ', visitor);
  WriteLn ('home    ', home   )
END
```

into a single statement. These newly-formed combinations are called **compound statements**. A compound statement is a special kind of structured statement; it's a structured statement that's formed just by adding the words BEGIN and END. In this example, the IF statement, which is a structured statement, contains two compound statements. Each of these compound statements contains two simple statements (two WriteLns).

```
IF home > visitor THEN
  BEGIN
    WriteLn (.. , home   );◄── simple statement ⎫ structured
    WriteLn (.. , visitor) ◄── simple statement ⎬ compound
  END                                            ⎭ statement          structured
ELSE                                                                ── IF
  BEGIN                                                                statement
    WriteLn (.. , visitor);◄── simple statement ⎫ structured
    WriteLn (.. , home   ) ◄── simple statement ⎬ compound
  END                                            ⎭ statement
```

use of
semicolons

Notice, once again, that the semicolon is used to separate statements from one another. The THEN-part could have been written all on one line

```
BEGIN   WriteLn (.. , home  ) ; WriteLn (.. , visitor)   END
```

to illustrate this point.

You can think of the words BEGIN and END as a way of grouping together all the statements in the THEN-part and all the statements in the ELSE-part. Without the BEGIN and END, the compiler wouldn't know how many statements were in the ELSE-part when translating the program.

```
ELSE
  WriteLn ('visitor ', visitor);
  WriteLn ('home    ', home   )◄── Is this WriteLn inside the ELSE-part?
```

In this last bit of code, a glance at the indentation makes it look as if WriteLn ('home   ', home   ) is in the ELSE-part, but Pascal compilers don't "glance" at indentation. If we forget to use BEGIN and END, then WriteLn ('home   ', home   ) is *not* in the ELSE-part, so the program won't run correctly. It won't satisfy our specifications.

One more note: The > sign in

comparison
operators

```
IF home > visitor THEN
```

is the mathematical symbol for "greater than." You can use other symbols to do comparisons:

Symbol	Meaning
>	greater than
<	less than
=	equal
>=	greater than or equal
<=	less than or equal
<>	not equal

Notice that we use = rather than : = to compare two numbers. We may have an `IF` statement that begins like this

```
IF amountPaid = amountOwed THEN
```

If you mix up the :=, which is used for assignments, and the =, which is used for comparisons, the compiler will give you an error diagnostic.

use of parentheses

Another thing you can do to form comparisons is to use the words `AND`, `OR`, and `NOT`. For instance, you can write

```
IF (paid = owed) AND NOT (customerKind = special) THEN
```

But notice! These compound conditions can be a bit tricky. You have to remember to use parentheses, because

```
IF paid = owed AND NOT customerKind = special THEN
```

won't work. You also can't get away with something like

```
IF -5 < x < +5 THEN
```

Instead you have to write

```
IF (-5 < x) AND (x < +5) THEN
```

We'll say more on all this in Section 8.1.

Structure

Notice how we indent lines inside an `IF` statement:

```
IF home > visitor THEN
  BEGIN
    WriteLn ('home    ', home    );
    WriteLn ('visitor ', visitor)
  END
ELSE
  BEGIN
    WriteLn ('visitor ', visitor);
    WriteLn ('home    ', home    )
  END
```

indentation

This indentation is important for several reasons. For one thing, it adds to the readability of the program. For another, it helps us understand the program's *structure*. You see, a program is very much like an outline. It has main headings, subheadings, sub-subheadings, etc. Like an outline, the lines of a good program are indented to show the reader what parts are subordinate to what other parts.

Actually, when you think about what an IF statement does, you can almost picture yourself standing at a fork in a road. The important word here is "picture." An IF statement puts a certain picture in your mind, and this picture can be very useful. In a complicated program, with lots of IFs, the picture can help you understand what the program does and why it works the way it does.

Nassi-Shneiderman chart

One kind of picture that computer scientists find very helpful for understanding programs is called a **Nassi-Shneiderman chart** (an **NS chart**, for short). Using an NS chart the programmer can get a nice pictorial sense of how a program works without the undisciplined flow patterns that some of the older charting methods permit.

Here's an NS chart for Program Scores:

PROGRAM Scores:

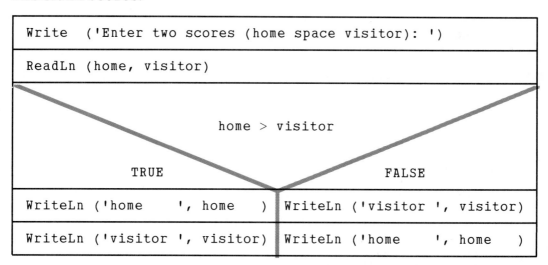

In an NS chart, an IF statement is represented by a big Y-shape with the THEN-part on the TRUE side and the ELSE-part on the FALSE side.

2.3 Exercises

Key Words to Review

decision making	THEN-part	>=
repetition	ELSE	<=
specifications (specs)	ELSE-part	<>
Write	condition	AND
IF	compound statement	OR
IF statement	>	NOT
structured statement	<	Nassi-Shneiderman (NS)
THEN	=	chart

Questions to Answer

QUE 2.3.1   For each line in Program Scores, explain why the line ends with a semicolon or why it doesn't end with a semicolon.

QUE 2.3.2   Explain why we need BEGINs and ENDs inside the IF statement in Program Scores.

QUE 2.3.3   Here's the syntax diagram for a compound statement:

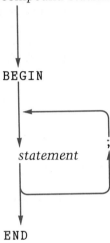

compound statement:

Use the diagram to explain why you normally don't put a semicolon before the word END.

Experiments to Try

Here are some experiments you can try with Program Scores:

EXP 2.3.1   Put a semicolon after the THEN-part's END—that is, put the semicolon between the words END and ELSE.

EXP 2.3.2   Remove the ELSE-part's BEGIN and END.

EXP 2.3.3   Run the whole program to see how many blank spaces your implementation uses to write the values of home and visitor.

Changes to Make

CHA 2.3.1   Modify Program Scores so that it reads two numbers and writes only the smaller of the two.

CHA 2.3.2   Modify Program Scores so that, when the two scores are equal, the value of home gets written on top.

CHA 2.3.3   Modify Program Scores so that the value of home almost always gets written on top; that is, the value of home is written on top unless visitor is bigger than home by at least 100.

Scales to Practice

When you learn to play a musical instrument, you always have to practice your scales. Scales are little exercises that are meant to limber up your fingers. They aren't meant to sound good, and you wouldn't want to hear someone play scales at a recital or a concert. But when you practice your scales, you gain skills that you can use when you play "real" music.

The same is true in learning to write computer programs. There are lots of practice programs you can write that don't do anything particularly useful, but that contain the basic building blocks to help you learn how to write useful programs. We've decided to call these practice programs "scales."

PRA 2.3.1 Write a program that reads two REAL numbers and then reads a third number, which is an INTEGER. The program writes the sum of the REAL numbers if the INTEGER is 0; otherwise, it writes the product of the REAL numbers.

PRA 2.3.2 Write a program that reads two integers and writes

```
first number divides evenly into second number
```

or

```
first number does not divide evenly into second number
```

whichever is appropriate.

PRA 2.3.3 Write a program that reads two numbers and writes their *absolute difference*. The absolute difference of two numbers is what you get when you subtract the two numbers and then ignore any minus sign. For example, the absolute difference of 6 and 4 is 2; the absolute difference of 3 and 5 is also 2.

PRA 2.3.4 Write a program that writes the largest of three numbers using the following algorithm:

Find the larger of the first two numbers; call it big.
Write the third number or big, whichever is larger.

Programs and Subprograms to Write

WRI 2.3.1 Write a program that reads a salesperson's total sales and prints the salesperson's commission: 5 percent of total sales if total sales are below $10,000; 7 percent of total sales otherwise.

WRI 2.3.2 Modify the program you wrote for Exercise Wri.2.3.1 so that it prints the phrase Big winner! for salespeople whose commission is more than $10,000 and prints Nice job! for all the others.

WRI 2.3.3 Write a program that reads a dollar amount for an item and another amount called the spending limit. The program prints a message telling whether or not we can afford to buy the item. Assume a 7 percent sales tax added to the price of the item.

WRI 2.3.4 Write a program that reads two numbers and writes the quotient of the two numbers after rounding. For example, if the input is 10 and 3, the output is 3; if the input is 11 and 3, the output is 4.

2.4

Another Algorithm to Solve the Same Problem

There's always a tendency, once you've found a solution to a problem, to push the problem aside and go on to something else. The thinking is something like "Whew! I solved that one—now I can forget about it. What's next?"

But in this book we'll stress over and over again that when you've found a solution to a problem, you should *step back and examine that solution*. When you look over your work, you can discover many things about it. Perhaps

you can improve upon it;

there's another way you could have done it;

it doesn't really work; or

it was really a stroke of genius.

In this section we illustrate the point by showing that the Scores problem of Section 2.3 could have been solved in quite a different way.

Specifications

Input: The scores of two teams.

Output: The same two scores, written on two separate lines—one right above the other. The winner's score is on the top line; the loser's score is on the bottom line.

These are the same specifications as in Section 2.3.

Designing a Program

Here's how we'll solve the problem:

This time we call the two scores score1 and score2. We read the scores. If score2 is bigger than score1, then before we write the scores we *switch* the values stored in score1 and score2 so that score1 contains the larger score. So by the time we get to writing the scores, we're sure that score1 contains the larger score. We always write score1 on the top line and then write score2 on the bottom line.

Pseudocode for this algorithm follows:

The *Switcher* algorithm:

If score1 < score2 then
    switch the values of score1 and score2.
Whether the values have been switched or not,
    write score1, followed by score2.

**Program
Example**

```
PROGRAM Switcher (input, output);
{Reads two scores and switches them if neces-
 sary to write the winner's score on top.}
   VAR
     score1, score2, temp : INTEGER;
BEGIN {Switcher}
   Write  ('Enter two scores (integer space integer): ');
   ReadLn (score1, score2);

   IF score1 < score2 THEN
     BEGIN
       temp   := score1;
       score1 := score2;
       score2 := temp
     END;
   WriteLn ('winner ', score1);
   WriteLn ('loser  ', score2)
END.  {Switcher}
```

**Sample
Runs**

```
Enter two scores (integer space integer): 16 54
winner        54
loser         16
```

Observations   We start with values for score1 and score2:

score1   score2

| 16 | 54 |

switching two
values

Since score1 is less than score2, we decide to switch the two values.
The "switch" is done in three steps:

1. temp := score1

   Put the value of score1 aside,
   in a temporary storage location,
   called temp.

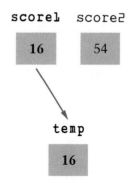

score1   score2

temp

2. `score1 := score2`

   Put the value of `score2` into `score1`.

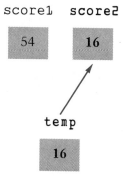

3. `score2 := temp`

   Put the value of `temp` into `score2`.

Now the values of `score1` and `score2` have been switched.

   Beginning programmers sometimes try to do the switch with just two statements

```
score1 := score2;
score2 := score1
```

but then `score1` and `score2` don't really get switched. Here's what happens instead:

1. We start with values for `score1` and `score2`:

score1	score2
16	54

2. `score1 := score2`

   Put the value of `score2` into `score1`.

   score1   score2

   54 ← 54

3. `score2 := score1`

Put the value of `score1` into
`score2`. (Since `score1` and
`score2` already have the same
value, this statement doesn't
really do anything.)

score1   score2

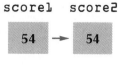

Instead of switching the values of `score1` and `score2`, we've managed
to put the original value of `score2` into both `score1` and `score2`.

Needing an extra `temp` variable isn't an isolated phenomenon. Suppose
we have a glass of coffee and a cup of milk. If we wanted to turn this into a
glass of milk and a cup of coffee we'd need to use an extra `temp` container.
This phenomenon—needing an extra "container" to do a switch—is one of
the many real-life principles that spill over into computer science.

```
• IF score1 < score2 THEN
     BEGIN
        temp   := score1;
        score1 := score2;
        score2 := temp
     END;
  WriteLn ('winner ', score1)
```

ELSE-less IF

Notice that the `IF` statement in Program `Switcher` has no `ELSE`-part.
This is permissible in Pascal. The `ELSE`-part of an `IF` statement can be
omitted if it's not needed, but the `THEN`-part can never be omitted.

Traces

If we look at a program's input and output in a sample run, we tend to think
of the program as a black box. A **black box** is a program that transforms its
input into its output without our having any knowledge of how the program
works. We see input going into the box and output coming out of the box,
but we don't see what happens inside the box. When we want to avoid
getting bogged down in details, it's useful to think of a program as a black
box.

But often we're interested in knowing how a program works. When this
is the case, seeing the program's input and corresponding output isn't
enough. We need to think of the program as a **glass box**—a box whose walls
are transparent so that we can see what's inside. In particular, we need to see
the steps that the program uses to get from its input to its output. A **trace**
is a chart that shows these steps. When you make a trace, you play the role
of the computer, writing down the effect of each statement that the
computer executes.

**writing a
program trace**

To write a trace of a program, first write down each of the program's
variable names and the word `output`.

```
 ┌──── Switcher ────────────────────────┐
 │                                       │
 │  score1   score2   temp   output      │
 │                                       │
 │                                       │
 │                                       │
 └───────────────────────────────────────┘
```

Next, read each statement in the body of the program. For each statement, ask yourself what the computer does when it executes that statement.

- If the computer changes the value of a variable (or gives that variable a value for the first time), put that new value in the trace. Put it under the variable name.
- If the computer writes to the screen, put the information that the computer writes in the trace. Put it under the word output.

Now let's make a trace for Program Switcher. When the ReadLn is executed, the variables score1 and score2 are given values. We don't know what values they'll be given, because we don't know what the user will type in. So we make up some values. Let's say the user types in 16 followed by 54:

```
 ┌──── Switcher ────────────────────────┐
 │                                       │
 │  score1   score2   temp   output      │
 │    16       54                        │
 │                                       │
 │                                       │
 └───────────────────────────────────────┘
```

Then score1 is less than score2, so the computer does a switch. Here's what happens:

First the computer executes temp := score1

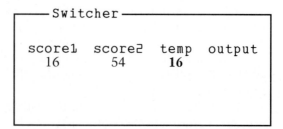

```
 ┌──── Switcher ────────────────────────┐
 │                                       │
 │  score1   score2   temp   output      │
 │    16       54      16                │
 │                                       │
 │                                       │
 └───────────────────────────────────────┘
```

then it executes `score1 := score2`

```
┌──────Switcher────────────────────────┐
│                                       │
│  score1   score2   temp    output     │
│    16       54       16               │
│  **54**                               │
│                                       │
│                                       │
└───────────────────────────────────────┘
```

and then `score2 := temp`

```
┌────────Switcher──────────────────────┐
│                                       │
│  score1   score2   temp    output     │
│    16       54       16               │
│    54      **16**                     │
│                                       │
│                                       │
│                                       │
└───────────────────────────────────────┘
```

Finally, the computer executes the two `WriteLns`

```
┌──────Switcher────────────────────────┐
│                                       │
│  score1   score2   temp    output     │
│    16       54       16               │
│    54       16              54         │
│                             16         │
│                                       │
└───────────────────────────────────────┘
```

This gives us a trace in which we show the effect of each statement that "changes" the value of a variable (or changes what's in the output):

```
ReadLn (score1, score2);
```

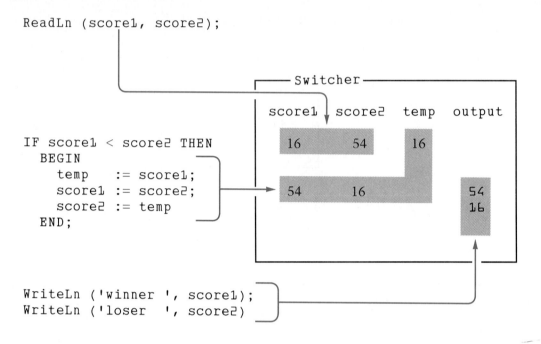

```
IF score1 < score2 THEN
   BEGIN
      temp   := score1;
      score1 := score2;
      score2 := temp
   END;
```

```
WriteLn ('winner ', score1);
WriteLn ('loser  ', score2)
```

Notice how we added new values to the trace. We moved this way:

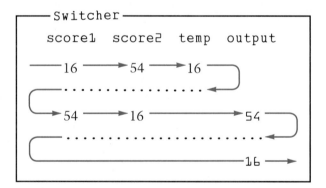

We move the way a typewriter moves: left to right, then return to start a new line, then left to right again. We never move upward, and we never move leftward along a line. This would make the trace very confusing to read. If we moved upward to an earlier line to illustrate the action of the first WriteLn:

```
┌─── Switcher ───────────────────────────────────┐
│                                                  │
│   score1     score2    temp     output          │
│    16          54        16       54            │
│    54          16                                │
│                                                  │
│                                                  │
└──────────────────────────────────────────────────┘
```

then it would look as if the `WriteLn` had been executed before `score1 := score2` and `score2 := temp`.

Programming Style

Which program is better?

Now we've seen two ways to solve the "bigger score first" problem—one way with Program `Scores` and another way with Program `Switcher`. So how do we choose between them? There are no pat answers to this question, but here are some thoughts on the subject:

1. In favor of `Scores`: `Switcher` is a bit more complicated. The three statements that do the switch need to be written very carefully, or the switch won't work.

2. In favor of `Switcher`: `Scores` has more `WriteLn`s in it, and the `WriteLn`s spread into both of the `IF` alternatives. This is a concern since we always like to contain a program's input and output to as small a region of the code as we can. Reading and writing are often the two trickiest things a program can do, so it's handy to have just a "narrow tunnel" of `ReadLn`s and `WriteLn`s where the program can communicate with the outside world.

3. In favor of `Scores`: `Switcher` involves an extra variable `temp`. This could mean that `Switcher` takes up more places in the computer's memory area. Using up one more memory location is no great loss; but if we choose Program `Switcher`, it's helpful to keep in mind that we're making this sacrifice. The sacrifice becomes magnified when we're dealing with ten thousand sets of opponents, instead of just two teams.

4. In favor of `Switcher`: There are situations where we may need to do a switch. After we've displayed the winner on top, we may have code to send different prizes to the winner and the loser. In this case it's useful to have only one variable `score1` which we *know* contains the higher of the two scores.

5. In favor of `Scores`: `Switcher` may take longer to execute than `Scores` because `Switcher` can take four steps:

   Read two numbers
   Decide whether to switch
   Switch (maybe)
   Write two numbers

whereas `Scores` always takes only three steps:

Read two numbers
Decide which alternative (`THEN` or `ELSE`) to execute
Write two numbers

It would be nice if we could count these reasons and say that `Scores` wins because it's got three reasons and `Switcher` has only two. But things usually aren't that simple. We'll have several Programming Style subsections throughout this text to help you make the subtle judgments needed to choose between good algorithms and bad algorithms, readable programs and unreadable programs, elegant code and inelegant code.

2.4   Exercises

Key Words to Review

black box   glass box   trace

Questions to Answer

QUE 2.4.1   Write two more traces for Program `Switcher`: one in which `score1` is larger than `score2` and one in which `score1` and `score2` are equal.

QUE 2.4.2   Explain why we need three variables to switch the values contained in two variables.

QUE 2.4.3   Is there any way to rearrange the assignment statements in Program `Switcher` (that is, change the order in which these three statements are executed) so that the switch still gets done correctly?

QUE 2.4.4   Explain why it's important, when writing a trace, to "move the way a typewriter moves."

QUE 2.4.5   Make an NS chart for Program `Switcher`.

Changes to Make

CHA 2.4.1   Modify Program `Switcher` so that it uses two temporary variables, `temp1` and `temp2`, and `score2` never gets directly assigned to `score1`.

CHA 2.4.2   Modify Program `Switcher` so that it works with three scores `score1`, `score2`, and `score3`. Make sure that your new program does enough switching so that only one `WriteLn` is needed in the code. Once you've done this exercise, hold on to your work so you can compare it with Exercise Cha.2.5.3.

Scales to Practice

PRA 2.4.1   Write a program that reads in four numbers, a, b, c, and d, and *rotates* their values; that is, a ends up with b's old value, b ends up with c's old value, c ends up with d's old value, d ends up with a's old value. Use as few variables as possible.

PRA 2.4.2   Redo Exercise Pra.2.4.1, but this time do a *shift* rather than a rotation. That is, make a end up with b's old value, b end up with c's old value, c end up with d's old value, but don't change the value of d.

PRA 2.4.3   In Exercise Pra.2.4.1 we do a *left rotation* on the values of a, b, c, and d. Rewrite the program so that it does a *right rotation:* that is, a ends up with d's old value, b ends up with a's old value, etc.

Programs and Subprograms to Write

WRI 2.4.1   Write a program that reads two dollar amounts (for two items) and another amount called the spending limit. In three separate messages the program tells whether we can afford the first item, whether we can afford the second item, and whether we can afford to buy both items.

Things to Think About

THI 2.4.1   Notice the orderly pattern in the code used to switch the values of two variables:

```
temp   := score1;

score1 := score2;

score2 := temp
```

Is this orderliness just a coincidence, or does it have something to do with the way we do the switching?

2.5

Procedures

Let's look once again at the pseudocode for Program Switcher:

The *Switcher* algorithm:

```
If score1 < score2 then
    switch the values of score1 and score2.
```

Whether the values have been switched or not,
write score1, followed by score2.

The pseudocode says we should switch the two values, but it doesn't say *how* we'll switch the values. That's because the pseudocode deals only with the topmost layer of the problem. It doesn't deal with the details.

Now wouldn't it be nice to translate the pseudocode into Pascal code that deals only with the problem's topmost layer? First we'd trim some extra words from the pseudocode:

The *Switcher* algorithm:

```
If score1 < score2 then
   switch score1 and score2.
Write score1 and score2.
```

then we'd change the punctuation a bit:

```
IF score1 < score2 THEN
   Switch (score1, score2);
WriteLn (score1);
WriteLn (score2)
```

This code is almost written in English, and the nice thing about it is, it's really part of a Pascal program! The program looks something like this:

```
PROGRAM IntroToProcedures (input, output);
{Reads two scores and switches them if necessary (with
 a procedure) to write the winner's score on top.}
  VAR
    score1, score2 : INTEGER;

  {----------}

  PROCEDURE Switch (VAR a, z : INTEGER);
  {Switches the values of two numbers, a and z.}
    VAR
      temp : INTEGER;
  BEGIN {Switch}
    {The details of switching belong here.}
  END;  {Switch}

  {----------}

BEGIN {IntroToProcedures}
  Write  ('Enter two scores (integer space integer): ');
  ReadLn (score1, score2);

  IF score1 < score2 THEN
    Switch (score1, score2);

  WriteLn ('winner ', score1);
  WriteLn ('loser  ', score2)
END.   {IntroToProcedures}
```

In this code we still haven't given any details about how the switching will be done. That's good. We're working on the program *from the top, downward.* First we solve the topmost layer of the problem, and then we work our way down to the details.

When we've finished writing Program `IntroToProcedures`, the detailed code for switching will look very much like the code in Section 2.4, but with a few differences. We'll explore these differences in the next several pages.

Program Example

```
PROGRAM IntroToProcedures (input, output);
{Reads two scores and switches them if necessary (with
  a procedure) to write the winner's score on top.}
  VAR
    score1, score2 : INTEGER;

  {----------}

  PROCEDURE Switch (VAR a, z : INTEGER);
  {Switches the values of two numbers, a and z.}
    VAR
      temp : INTEGER;
  BEGIN {Switch}
    temp := a;
    a    := z;
    z    := temp
  END;  {Switch}

  {----------}

BEGIN {IntroToProcedures}
  Write  ('Enter two scores (integer space integer): ');
  ReadLn (score1, score2);

  IF score1 < score2 THEN
    Switch (score1, score2);

  WriteLn ('winner ', score1);
  WriteLn ('loser  ', score2)
END.  {IntroToProcedures}
```

Sample Runs

A run of Program `IntroToProcedures` looks the same as a run of Program `Switcher`.

Observations

procedure heading

• `PROCEDURE Switch (VAR a, z : INTEGER);`

This is the first line of a PROCEDURE whose name is `Switch`. A procedure is a **subprogram**—a "program within a program." Procedure `Switch` is a subprogram of Program `IntroToProcedures`. (Go back to the whole Program Example and notice that Procedure `Switch` is written inside Program `IntroToProcedures`.) Since Program `IntroToProcedures` isn't a "sub" of anything, it's called a **main program**.

Procedure `Switch` has a parameter list. The parameter list tells the compiler how the procedure will interact with the outside world. In this case the so-called "outside world" is the main program—Program

`IntroToProcedures`. This interaction with the main program takes place using two values. The interesting thing about these values is that the main program knows these values by the names `score1` and `score2`, and the procedure knows these values by two different names, `a` and `z`. Here's how it works: The line

```
PROCEDURE Switch (VAR a, z : INTEGER);
```

is called a **procedure heading** and the statement

```
Switch (score1, score2)
```

procedure call   is referred to as a **procedure call**. The main program runs first, starting with the statement

```
Write  ('Enter two scores (integer space integer): ')
```

When the procedure call `Switch (score1, score2)` is reached, the computer "matches" the variables `score1` and `score2` with the variables `a` and `z`:

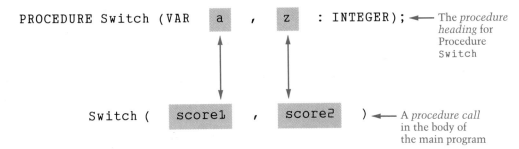

PROCEDURE Switch (VAR   a   ,   z   : INTEGER); ◄── The *procedure heading* for Procedure `Switch`

Switch (score1   ,   score2   ) ◄── A *procedure call* in the body of the main program

and then starts running the code that's inside Procedure `Switch`.

```
PROCEDURE Switch (VAR a, z : INTEGER);
{Switches the values of two numbers, a and z.}
   VAR
      temp : INTEGER;
BEGIN {Switch}
   temp := a;
   a    := z;
   z    := temp
END;   {Switch}

{----------}

BEGIN {IntroToProcedures}
   Write  ('Enter two scores (integer space integer): ');
   ReadLn (score1, score2);

   IF score1 < score2 THEN
      Switch (score1, score2) ;

   WriteLn ('winner ', score1);
   WriteLn ('loser  ', score2)
END.  {IntroToProcedures}
```

Anything that happens to a and z inside Procedure Switch actually gets done to the variables score1 and score2. So the values stored in the variables score1 and score2 get switched.

Notice that a and score1 are in the same positions (the first) in their respective parameter lists, and z and score2 are in the same positions (the second) in their respective parameter lists:

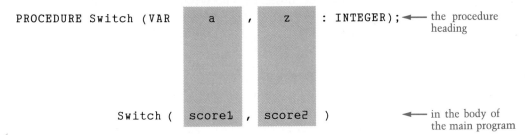

```
PROCEDURE Switch (VAR     a      ,     z     : INTEGER);  ←— the procedure
                                                            heading



         Switch (  score1  ,  score2  )    ←— in the body of
                                              the main program
```

That's why a gets matched up with score1 and z gets matched up with score2.

Now we have to be careful about what it means to "match" variables. We'll be very specific about this in Section 3.2. In the meantime, here's the proper terminology:

procedure calling and parameter passing

1. We say that Procedure Switch is **called** from the main program and then the code in Procedure Switch begins executing. After the code in Procedure Switch is finished being executed, we **return** to the main program.

2. The variables a and z (the variables that appear in the procedure heading) are called **formal parameters**. The variables score1 and score2 (the variables that appear in the procedure call statement) are called **actual parameters**.

3. What we've been calling the "matching" of variables is more properly called **parameter passing**. We say that score1 and score2 are *passed* to a and z.

● PROCEDURE Switch (**VAR** a, z : INTEGER);

Notice the word VAR in the heading of Procedure Switch. We'll talk more about this (what it does, when it's needed, when it's not needed) in Section 3.9. For now, just remember to put it in. It tells the computer to use a certain method, called **pass by reference**, to pass score1 and score2 to a and z.

pass by reference

● VAR
      temp : INTEGER;

In this problem, we never need to use the variable temp in the main program. We only use temp inside Procedure Switch. By putting temp's declaration inside Procedure Switch we prevent ourselves from accidentally referring to temp in the main program. Then if we accidentally put a statement like `temp := 3` in the main program's body, the compiler will give us an error diagnostic.

local variables

A variable like `temp`, which is declared inside a procedure, is called a **local variable**. In this program, the variable `temp` is local to Procedure `Switcher`. A local variable can't be used outside the procedure in which it's declared.

Notice the difference between the local variable `temp` and the formal parameters `a` and `z`. The formal parameters are used to communicate with the main program; the local variable is used strictly inside the subprogram.

Further Discussion

naming of formal parameters

In Program `IntroToProcedures`, the variables `score1` and `score2` got passed to `a` and `z`. So we actually had four variable names to hold two values. Sometimes it's good to have extra variable names, and sometimes it's not.[7] In Program `IntroToProcedures`, we could have avoided a bit of confusion by giving the same names to the formal and actual parameters, like so:

```
PROGRAM SameNames (input, output);
{Reads two scores and switches them if necessary (with
 a procedure) to write the winner's score on top.}
   VAR
      score1, score2 : INTEGER;

   {----------}

   PROCEDURE Switch (VAR score1, score2 : INTEGER);
   {Switches the values of two numbers, score1 and score2.}
      VAR
         temp : INTEGER;
   BEGIN {Switch}
      temp   := score1;
      score1 := score2;
      score2 := temp
   END;   {Switch}

   {----------}

BEGIN {SameNames}
   Write  ('Enter two scores (integer space integer): ');
   ReadLn (score1, score2);

   IF score1 < score2 THEN
      Switch (score1, score2);

   WriteLn ('winner ', score1);
   WriteLn ('loser  ', score2)
END.   {SameNames}
```

---

[7]For examples in which it's definitely better to have extra variable names, see Exercise Cha.2.5.3 and Program `Crossover` in Section 3.3.

In Program SameNames, the actual parameters score1 and score2 match up with formal parameters that are also named score1 and score2

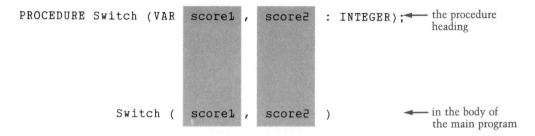

PROCEDURE Switch (VAR score1 , score2 : INTEGER); ◄—— the procedure heading

Switch (score1 , score2) ◄—— in the body of the main program

so that we can avoid some of the confusion that comes from changing variable names. But beware: Program SameNames still has four score variables! It has two variables named score1 and two variables named score2. There's a score1 in the main program and a score1 inside Procedure Switch. The only thing that connects the two score1 variables is the procedure call Switch (score1, score2), with its formal parameter list. To see this phenomenon in action, try Exercise Exp.2.5.4.

Traces

tracing a procedure

In Section 2.4 we traced Program Switcher by writing the values of its variables inside a box. Since Program IntroToProcedures contains a subprogram within a main program, we'll trace it by making a box within a box.

First we write down each of the main program's variable names and the word output. When ReadLn is executed, the variables score1 and score2 are given values.

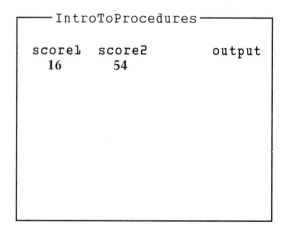

```
┌──── IntroToProcedures ────────────┐
│                                   │
│   score1    score2      output    │
│     16        54                  │
│                                   │
│                                   │
│                                   │
│                                   │
│                                   │
│                                   │
└───────────────────────────────────┘
```

Since score1 is less than score2, Procedure Switch is called. This opens a new box. In the new box, we write down the names of Switch's formal parameters (a and z) and Switch's local variable (temp). We give a and z the values that we've already given to score1 and score2.

```
┌──────── IntroToProcedures ────────────────┐
│                                            │
│   score1   score2          output          │
│     16       54                            │
│          ┌──── Switch ────────┐            │
│          │  a        z    temp │           │
│          │  16      54         │           │
│          │                     │           │
│          └─────────────────────┘           │
│                                            │
│                                            │
└────────────────────────────────────────────┘
```

Notice that we write a directly under score1, and we write z directly under score2. We do this to remind ourselves that

anything that happens to a inside Procedure Switch actually gets done to score1

anything that happens to z inside Procedure Switch actually gets done to score2.

So anything that happens to a and z inside Procedure Switch actually gets done to the variables score1 and score2. Since temp is local to Procedure Switch and doesn't match with any variable in the main program, it's written in a column of its own.

Inside Procedure Switch, the values of a and z are exchanged:

```
┌──────── IntroToProcedures ────────────────┐
│                                            │
│   score1   score2          output          │
│     16       54                            │
│          ┌──── Switch ────────┐            │
│          │  a        z    temp │           │
│          │  16      54     16  │           │
│          │  54      16         │           │
│          └─────────────────────┘           │
│                                            │
│                                            │
└────────────────────────────────────────────┘
```

When we return from Procedure Switch to the main program, score1 and score2 have new values

```
┌──── IntroToProcedures ─────────────────────┐
│                                            │
│   score1    score2           output        │
│     16        54                           │
│                                            │
│     ┌──── Switch ──────────────┐           │
│     │   a        z      temp   │           │
│     │   16       54      16    │           │
│     │   54       16            │           │
│     └──────────────────────────┘           │
│                                            │
│     54        16                           │
│                                            │
└────────────────────────────────────────────┘
```

and these values are written as output:

```
┌──── IntroToProcedures ─────────────────────┐
│                                            │
│   score1    score2           output        │
│     16        54                           │
│                                            │
│     ┌──── Switch ──────────────┐           │
│     │   a        z      temp   │           │
│     │   16       54      16    │           │
│     │   54       16            │           │
│     └──────────────────────────┘           │
│                                            │
│     54        16              54           │
│                               16           │
│                                            │
└────────────────────────────────────────────┘
```

2.5 Exercises

Key Words to Review

PROCEDURE	called	actual parameter
subprogram	return	parameter passing
main program	passed	pass by reference
procedure heading	formal parameter	local variable
procedure call		

Questions to Answer

QUE 2.5.1   Explain why it's good to deal with the topmost layer of a problem before dealing with the problem's details.

QUE 2.5.2   Put numbers beside the statements in Program `IntroToProcedures` to show the order in which the statements are actually executed.

QUE 2.5.3   Explain the differences between an actual parameter and a formal parameter.

QUE 2.5.4   Explain the differences between a local variable and a variable that's declared in the main body of the program.

QUE 2.5.5   Explain the differences between a local variable and a procedure's formal parameter.

QUE 2.5.6   In describing Program `SameNames` why do we insist that the program "has *two* variables named `score1`"?

Experiments to Try

EXP 2.5.1   Put a new statement `temp := 3` in the main program's body.

EXP 2.5.2   Remove the word `VAR` from `Switcher`'s procedure heading. Put `WriteLn`s in various places in the program, to see how the values of the formal and actual parameters change as the program is executed.

EXP 2.5.3   Repeat Exercise Exp 2.5.2 with Program `SameNames`.

EXP 2.5.4   In this section's Further Discussion subsection, we emphasized that the only connection between a formal parameter and an actual parameter is a procedure call, with its formal parameter list. Try running Program `ConnectParams`.

```
PROGRAM ConnectParams (output);
{Illustrates how the main program's 'x' might have
 nothing to do with a formal parameter named 'x'.}
  VAR
    x, y : INTEGER;
  {----------}
  PROCEDURE AddOne (VAR x : INTEGER);
  {Adds 1 to **whatever** variable is passed to it.}
  BEGIN {AddOne}
    x := x + 1
  END;  {AddOne}
  {----------}
BEGIN {ConnectParams}
  x := 5;
  y := 100;
  AddOne (y);
  WriteLn (x:4, y:4)
END.  {ConnectParams}
```

EXP 2.5.5   Change the heading of Procedure `Switch` to

```
PROCEDURE Switch (VAR z, a : INTEGER);
```

To help you see what's going on inside Procedure Switch it might help to add the statement WriteLn (a,z) several times inside the body of the procedure.

EXP 2.5.6   In the heading of Procedure Switch change the word INTEGER to the word REAL.

Changes to Make

CHA 2.5.1   Write a procedure called Obtain that prompts the user to Enter two numbers: and then ReadLns the numbers. Modify Program IntroToProcedures so that it uses Procedure Obtain.

CHA 2.5.2   Modify Program MakeChange of Section 2.2 so that the calculations are done in two separate procedures—one before the first WriteLn and another before the second WriteLn. Writing the answers is done in the main program.

CHA 2.5.3   Modify Program IntroToProcedures so that it works with three scores: score1, score2, and score3. Make sure that your new program makes enough calls to Procedure Switch.

Scales to Practice

PRA 2.5.1   Modify Exercise Pra.2.3.1 so that all the prompting and reading is done in a procedure.

PRA 2.5.2   Modify Exercise Pra.2.4.1 so that the rotation of the four values is done by a procedure, which is called from the main program.

Programs and Subprograms to Write

In each of these exercises you're asked to decompose a problem into one or more parts using procedures. Each exercise suggests how the problem should be decomposed. You should do each exercise as it's stated; but with each exercise, you should try decomposing the problem into different pieces from those that we've suggested. In each case you should ask yourself, "Which is the best way to decompose the problem?" (By the "best" way we mean the most natural way, the most elegant way, the most useful way, etc.)

WRI 2.5.1   Modify Exercise Wri.2.2.1 so that computing the number of six-packs and the number of bottles left over is done by a procedure. The reading and writing should be done in the main program. In writing the procedure and the main program be sure to pass the number of bottles, the number of six-packs, and the number of bottles left over as parameters.

WRI 2.5.2   Combine the programs you wrote for Exercises Wri.2.1.2 and Wri.2.1.3 by creating a procedure that takes the Fahrenheit temperature and computes the Celsius and Kelvin temperatures.

WRI 2.5.3   Write a program that reads a number of cents and calls a procedure to get the number of quarters, dimes, nickels, and pennies you can get for that number of cents. It displays the answers with one or more WriteLns in the main program.

WRI 2.5.4   Write a program that reads the ages of five children, in order of increasing age. Then it calls a procedure that calculates the average age of the five children and the median age of the five children (the median is the age of the middle child).

WRI 2.5.5 Redo Exercise Wri.2.5.4, but this time have the procedure calculate either the average or the median age of the children, depending on whether the user answers with a 1 or a 2 when asked which piece of information is needed.

Things to Think About

THI 2.5.1 Think of some real-life day-to-day situations in which it helps to think about a problem "from the top, downward."

2.6

Repetition

Once again, the basic building blocks of algorithms and programs are decision making and repetition. In this section we look at a Pascal program that uses repetition.

Specifications As a part of a bar graph a statistician may want to write six asterisks (*) in a line, or twenty plus signs (+) in a line.

Input: A number (called symbolsNeeded) and a character (called symbol)

Output: The symbol character is to be written on the screen symbolsNeeded–many times

Designing a Program

Here's how we write down what we want to do using ordinary English prose:

First we read symbolsNeeded, then we read symbol and write it symbolsNeeded-many times.

To turn this into pseudocode we add some indentation:

Read symbolsNeeded.
Read symbol.
Do the following symbolsNeeded-many times:
    Write symbol.

To implement this pseudocode, we need a way to do the writing "symbolsNeeded-many times." So let's expand on the pseudocode a bit:

Read symbolsNeeded.
Read symbol.
No symbols have been written so far.
As long as the number of symbols that have been written is less than symbolsNeeded, do
    Write symbol,
        add 1 to the count of symbols written so far.

And here's how we translate this pseudocode into Pascal code:

```
ReadLn (symbolsNeeded);
ReadLn (symbol       );

symbolsWritten := 0;
WHILE symbolsWritten < symbolsNeeded DO
  BEGIN
    Write (symbol:1);
    symbolsWritten := symbolsWritten + 1
  END
```

Now we'll look at the whole program.

Program Example

```
PROGRAM OneBar (input, output);
{Prints one of the bars in a bar graph.}

  VAR
    symbolsNeeded  : INTEGER;
    symbol         : CHAR;
    symbolsWritten : INTEGER;

BEGIN {OneBar}
  WriteLn ('How many?    ');
  ReadLn  (symbolsNeeded );
  WriteLn ('What symbol? ');
  ReadLn  (symbol        );
  WriteLn;

  symbolsWritten := 0;
  WHILE symbolsWritten < symbolsNeeded DO
    BEGIN
      Write (symbol:1);
      symbolsWritten := symbolsWritten + 1
    END;
  WriteLn
END.  {OneBar}
```

Sample Runs

```
How many?
9
What symbol?
*

********
```

Observations

- VAR
    ..
    symbol : CHAR;

CHAR

We've already seen REAL variables and INTEGER variables. Here's a CHAR variable. We've given it the name symbol.

The word CHAR stands for CHARacter. Any single character can be stored in a CHAR variable. For instance, we could store the asterisk (*) character in the variable symbol. Alternatively we could store a plus sign (+), a percent sign (%), etc. Any single letter (such as A or a) is a character. Even a single digit (such as 6) can be a character.

types

Now let's make our terminology a bit more precise. Words like REAL, INTEGER, and CHAR are the names of **types.** When the compiler translates Program OneBar, the VAR declaration given tells it that the variable named symbol is of type CHAR. By knowing a variable's type, the computer knows what values that variable may (and may not) assume. For instance, variables of type CHAR can assume the values A, B, C, $, &, 1, 2, etc. Variables of type INTEGER can assume values like −3, −2, −1, 0, 1, 2, 3, . . . , 10, 11, . . . , 245, 255, etc.

incrementing a counter

• symbolsWritten := symbolsWritten + 1

An assignment statement isn't the same as an algebraic equation. The algebraic equation

$$s = s + 1$$

has no solution, because it says something like "nine equals ten," which isn't true. But a statement like

```
symbolsWritten := symbolsWritten + 1
```

is legal in Pascal. It tells the computer to change the value of symbolsWritten. Here's how:

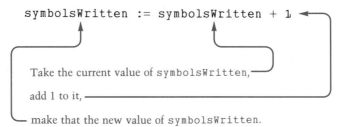

```
symbolsWritten := symbolsWritten + 1
```

Take the current value of symbolsWritten,

add 1 to it,

make that the new value of symbolsWritten.

The statement adds 1 to the value of symbolsWritten. There's a special name for a variable that gets 1 added to it. It's called a **counter** When we add 1 we say that we're **incrementing** the counter.

```
• WHILE symbolsWritten < symbolsNeeded DO
    BEGIN
      Write (symbol:1);
      symbolsWritten := symbolsWritten + 1
    END
```

This is called a WHILE statement. It makes the computer execute

```
BEGIN
  Write (symbol:1);
  symbolsWritten := symbolsWritten + 1
```

looping

```
END
```

many times. Here's what the computer does:

Check to see if `symbolsWritten < symbolsNeeded`, and if it is,
  Write a `symbol`,
  Add 1 to the count of the `symbolsWritten` so far,

Check again,
  Write again,
  Add 1 again,

Check again, etc.

The thing that's being checked over and over again

`symbolsWritten < symbolsNeeded`

is called a **condition** and each repetition of the three steps (Check/Write/Add) is called an **iteration**. The whole purpose of a `WHILE` statement is to force an action like

Write a `symbol`,
Add 1 to the count of the `symbolsWritten` so far,

to be iterated several times. That's why a `WHILE` statement is often referred to as a `WHILE` **loop**.

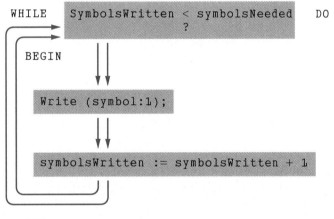

```
WHILE    SymbolsWritten < symbolsNeeded    DO
                          ?

    BEGIN


        Write (symbol:1);


        symbolsWritten := symbolsWritten + 1



    END
```

Just as in an `IF` statement, the lines inside a `WHILE` statement are surrounded by `BEGIN` and `END`. The words `BEGIN` and `END` are used to group together the statements that need to be iterated.

So how does the loop ever stop "looping"? Each time we do an iteration of our `WHILE` loop, the value stored in `symbolsWritten` gets 1 added to it:

`symbolsWritten := symbolsWritten + 1`

And eventually the condition

`symbolsWritten < symbolsNeeded`

no longer holds true. When this happens the computer stops iterating the `WHILE` loop. Instead it goes on and executes whatever statement comes right after the `WHILE` loop:

```
symbolsWritten := 0;
WHILE symbolsWritten < symbolsNeeded DO
  BEGIN
    Write (symbol:1);
    symbolsWritten := symbolsWritten + 1
  END;
WriteLn ◄── When symbolsWritten < symbolsNeeded
            is no longer true the computer goes on to
            execute this WriteLn
```

- `symbolsWritten := 0`

initialization

This statement is called an **initialization**. It gives `symbolsWritten` the **initial value** of zero. If we hadn't first given `symbolsWritten` a value, it wouldn't have made sense to compare `symbolsWritten` to `symbolsNeeded` in the `WHILE` statement's condition:

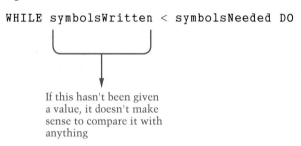

```
WHILE symbolsWritten < symbolsNeeded DO
```

If this hasn't been given
a value, it doesn't make
sense to compare it with
anything

The initialization is also needed for the assignment statement that's inside the loop. Recall that

```
symbolsWritten := symbolsWritten + 1
```

means "add 1 to the current value of `symbolsWritten`." This makes sense only if `symbolsWritten` currently has a value; otherwise, we're just trying to add 1 to "garbage." (Instead of calling it "garbage," it usually sounds better to say that the value of `symbolsWritten` is **undefined**. Nevertheless, it's still garbage!)

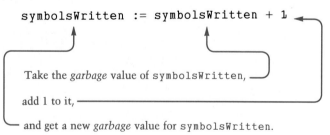

```
symbolsWritten := symbolsWritten + 1
```

Take the *garbage* value of `symbolsWritten`,

add 1 to it,

and get a new *garbage* value for `symbolsWritten`.

So before we start any iterations of the WHILE statement, we want to give symbolsWritten an initial value.

Now symbolsWritten keeps a count of the number of symbols that have already been written. Before the WHILE statement begins, no symbols have been written; and so it makes sense that we've chosen 0 for the initial value of symbolsWritten. In the first iteration of the WHILE statement, we'll get 1 added to symbolsWritten, which will give us

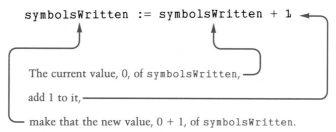

This first time around, symbolsWritten gets the value 0 + 1, which is 1. In the second iteration, symbolsWritten starts with the value 1, so we get

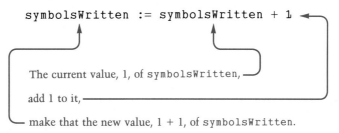

So then symbolsWritten gets to be 2. And so on. That's exactly what we want to happen.

The Writes and WriteLns in Program OneBar are worth careful examination. Let's look at a few of them.

- WriteLn ('What symbol? ');
  ReadLn (symbol   );
  WriteLn;

parameterless
WriteLns

When you tell the computer to WriteLn but don't tell it what to write, it just goes to the start of a new line on the screen. Usually this looks the same as having the computer write a single blank line on the screen.

For instance, in Program OneBar the statement

```
WriteLn ('What symbol? ')
```

puts a prompt on the screen and then goes to the start of a new line

```
What symbol?
```

So the next `WriteLn;` just goes to the start of *another* new line.

```
What symbol?
```

That is, it makes a blank line on the screen. This blank line separates the prompts and echoed input from the program's output.

```
How many?
9
What symbol?
*
```
                         ←——— A blank line
```
*********
```

- ```
  WHILE symbolsWritten < symbolsNeeded DO
     BEGIN
        Write (symbol:1);
        symbolsWritten := symbolsWritten + 1
     END
  ```

  Inside the loop we've decided to `Write (symbol:1)` instead of `WriteLn (symbol:1)`. Executing `Write` doesn't bring us to the start of a new line. So all the `symbols` are written on the same line.

- ```
  WHILE symbolsWritten < symbolsNeeded DO
     BEGIN
        Write (symbol:1);
        symbolsWritten := symbolsWritten + 1
     END;
  WriteLn
  ```

  Even after doing the last `Write (symbol:1)`, the computer hasn't yet gone to the start of a new line. This last `WriteLn` makes sure that, after writing all the `symbols`, the computer goes to the start of a new line on the screen. Anything else the computer might display (such as a message from the operating system) gets written on this new line.

```
NEXT COMMAND PLEASE> run OneBar
How many?
9
What symbol?
*

*********
NEXT COMMAND PLEASE> logoff    ←——— The operating system's prompt
                                    appears on the next line,
                                    after the line of asterisks.
```

Further Discussion

Now look once more at the pseudocode for one of the loop's iterations:

Check to see if `symbolsWritten < symbolsNeeded`, and if it is,
    Write a `symbol`,
    Add 1 to the count of the `symbolsWritten` so far.

Notice that the checking of the WHILE statement's condition

```
symbolsWritten < symbolsNeeded
```

is always done at the "top" of the loop, at the beginning of each iteration, before the execution of the compound statement. This is important. In Sections 6.1 and 6.6 we'll see why.

Traces

tracing a loop

Sometimes it's useful to write a trace as a series of rows instead of a series of columns. In this case you start by writing the program's variable names down the page, instead of across the page. The trace for Program OneBar looks best if you write names in the following order:

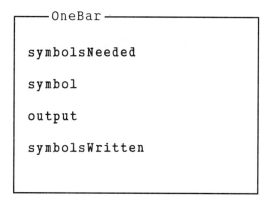

Next, read each statement in the body of the program. When you read a statement, ask yourself what the computer does when it executes that statement. (If you don't know what the computer does when it executes a statement, don't give up or guess; find out!) Here's what you'll get if you trace the program with 9 for symbolsNeeded and * for symbol:

Reading values for symbolsNeeded and symbol:

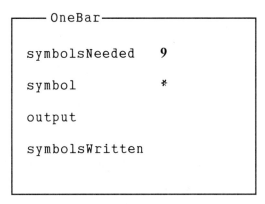

Initializing `symbolsWritten`:

```
┌──── OneBar ─────────────────────────┐
│                                     │
│  symbolsNeeded    9                 │
│                                     │
│  symbol           *                 │
│                                     │
│  output                             │
│                                     │
│  symbolsWritten   0                 │
│                                     │
│                                     │
└─────────────────────────────────────┘
```

After the first `WHILE` loop iteration:

```
┌──── OneBar ─────────────────────────┐
│                                     │
│  symbolsNeeded    9                 │
│                                     │
│  symbol           *                 │
│                                     │
│  output             *               │
│                                     │
│  symbolsWritten 01                  │
│                                     │
│                                     │
└─────────────────────────────────────┘
```

After the second `WHILE` loop iteration:

```
┌──── OneBar ─────────────────────────┐
│                                     │
│  symbolsNeeded    9                 │
│                                     │
│  symbol           *                 │
│                                     │
│  output             **              │
│                                     │
│  symbolsWritten 012                 │
│                                     │
│                                     │
└─────────────────────────────────────┘
```

And, finally, after the ninth `WHILE` loop iteration:

```
┌──────── OneBar ────────────────────────┐
│                                         │
│   symbolsNeeded      9                  │
│                                         │
│   symbol             *                  │
│                                         │
│   output             *********          │
│                                         │
│   symbolsWritten     0123456789         │
│                                         │
│                                         │
└─────────────────────────────────────────┘
```

Programming Style
choosing identifiers

Making up good identifiers is an art, not a science; but it's a very important part of programming style. Here are some general rules of thumb for creating useful identifiers:

1. An identifier should be informative. It should remind us of its purpose. It should tell us, easily and unambiguously, what thing is being "identified." By this criterion, `symbolsNeeded` is a better identifier than just `needed` because it gives us more information about the purpose of the variable being named.

2. It should be possible to use the identifier in the pseudocode and still have the pseudocode flow naturally, like ordinary English. Look again at the pseudocode we used in designing Program `OneBar`:

Read `symbolsNeeded`.
Read `symbol`.
No `symbols` have been `Written` so far.
As long as the number of `symbols` that have been `Written` is less than `symbolsNeeded`, do
  Write `symbol`,
  add 1 to the count of `symbols Written` so far.

From this pseudocode, we easily wrote Pascal code with the variables `symbolsNeeded`, `symbol`, and `symbolsWritten`.

3. An identifier shouldn't be too short. Some programmers like to use single-letter identifiers. They write programs that look like this:

```
PROGRAM OneBar (input, output);

VAR
    n : INTEGER;
    s : CHAR;
    w : INTEGER;
```

```
    BEGIN {OneBar}
      WriteLn ('How many?      ');
      ReadLn  (n);
      WriteLn ('What symbol? ');
      ReadLn  (s);
      WriteLn;

      w := 0;
      WHILE w < n DO
        BEGIN
          Write (s:1);
          w := w + 1
        END
    END.  {OneBar}
```

This version of OneBar is admirably concise, but it's harder to read than the original version, especially if the reader isn't familiar with the bar-graph problem.

4. An identifier shouldn't be too long. Long names tend to clutter up a program. They keep you from seeing the whole program at a glance. Compare our original Program OneBar with

```
PROGRAM OneBar (input, output);
{Prints one of the bars in a bar graph.}

  VAR
    symbolsNeededOnTheLine        : INTEGER;
    symbolOfTheBarGraph           : CHAR;
    symbolsAlreadyWrittenOnTheLine : INTEGER;
BEGIN {OneBar}
  WriteLn ('How many?          ');
  ReadLn  (symbolsNeededOnTheLine);
  WriteLn ('What symbol?       ');
  ReadLn  (symbolOfTheBarGraph   );
  WriteLn;

  symbolsAlreadyWrittenOnTheLine := 0;
  WHILE symbolsAlreadyWrittenOnTheLine < symbolsNeededOnTheLine DO
    BEGIN
      Write (symbolOfTheBarGraph:1);
      symbolsAlreadyWrittenOnTheLine := symbolsAlreadyWrittenOnTheLine + 1
    END
END.  {OneBar}
```

Which version is easier to read?

This rule often conflicts with the first three rules. Generally the most "informative" names are the long, cumbersome ones. Making up identifier names always means striking a good balance among the various rules of thumb.

5. It's often tempting to make up cute identifiers. A statement like

```
tasty := pizza + (2 * cheese)
```

may be "informative" in one sense or another, but it's very frustrating to see when you're trying to read someone else's program and get it to work. Sad to say, this temptation should be avoided.

self-documenting code

Using informative identifiers is an easy way to help a program be **self-documenting**. The phrase self-documenting refers to ways in which the code, exclusive of any comments, makes itself more understandable. An informative identifier does this. It "reminds" you of its purpose whenever it's used. If informative identifiers are used, you can look at a very narrow fragment of code

```
IF home > visitor THEN
```

and get some idea of what it does. Good identifiers even help keep your thinking clear while you write the program. Whenever you write a program, take time to decide on the best possible identifiers.

Structure

NS chart for a WHILE statement

In Section 2.3 we saw how to make an NS chart for an IF statement. An NS chart for a WHILE loop has a sideways "L" in it. Here's the NS chart for Program OneBar:

PROGRAM OneBar:

ReadLn (symbolsNeeded);
ReadLn (symbol);
WriteLn;
symbolsWritten := 0;

WHILE symbolsWritten < symbolsNeeded DO	
	Write (symbol:1);
	symbolsWritten := symbolsWritten + 1

2.6   Exercises

Key Words to Review

CHAR	DO	initialization
type	loop	initial value
counter	iteration	undefined
increment	condition	self-documenting
WHILE		

Questions to Answer

QUE 2.6.1   Critique the following names for variables in Program Switcher (Section 2.4):
a. num1 and num2
b. i and j
c. winner and loser
d. home and visitor
e. hi and lo
f. rocky and bullwinkle

QUE 2.6.2   Write a trace of the following program:

```
PROGRAM RepeatSomething (input, output);
{Write a prologue comment to describe what I do.}

   VAR
      i, x, y, sum : INTEGER;
   BEGIN {RepeatSomething}
      i := 1;
      WHILE i <= 5 DO
         BEGIN
            Write  ('Enter two integers: ');
            ReadLn (x, y);
            sum := x + y;
            WriteLn (i);
            WriteLn (sum);
            i := i + 1
         END
   END.  {RepeatSomething}
```

QUE 2.6.3   Explain why symbolsWritten needs to be given an initial value in Program OneBar.

QUE 2.6.4   Write an NS chart for the program in Exercise Que.2.6.2.

Things to Check in a Manual

MAN 2.6.1   Does your implementation have a limit on the number of letters that can appear in an identifier?

MAN 2.6.2   Find out what to do to stop a program while it's running if you have a program that, for some reason, won't stop running on its own. You'll need to know this to do Exercises Exp.2.6.2 and Exp.2.6.4.

Experiments to Try

EXP 2.6.1   Remove the reserved word DO from the WHILE statement in Program OneBar.

EXP 2.6.2   Put a semicolon immediately after the word DO in the program's WHILE statement. (See Exercise Man.2.6.2.)

EXP 2.6.3   Take the statement symbolsWritten := 0 out of Program OneBar. What does your implementation do when the value of a variable hasn't been defined?

EXP 2.6.4   Move the statement symbolsWritten := 0 so that it's inside the WHILE loop in Program OneBar. (Note: If the new program won't stop running, see Exercise Man.2.6.2.)

EXP 2.6.5   Run Program OneBar with symbolsNeeded equal to zero.

EXP 2.6.6   Run Program OneBar with symbolsNeeded equal to 1000.

EXP 2.6.7   When Program OneBar prompts you for a symbol, give it the number 8. (Compare this with Exercise Exp.2.2.4.)

EXP 2.6.8   When Program OneBar prompts you for a symbol, just hit the return key. (Compare this with Exercise Exp.2.2.6.)

Changes to Make

CHA 2.6.1   A single line of asterisks makes such a scrawny looking bar graph. Modify Program OneBar so that it writes a bar that's two symbols deep.

CHA 2.6.2   Repeat Exercise Cha.2.6.1, but this time make a bar whose upper and lower lines can use two different symbols.

            ****
            +++++++++

CHA 2.6.3   Modify Program OneBar so that it writes a bar with two symbols that alternate:

            ++*+*+*+

            Don't worry if your program writes one extra symbol (ten instead of nine). We'll fix that later. (See Exercise Cha.5.4.3.)

CHA 2.6.4   Repeat Exercise Cha.2.6.1, but this time make a bar that's three lines deep and can use two different symbols, with one set of symbols enclosing the other, like this:

            ****
            +++++++
            ****

CHA 2.6.5   Modify Program OneBar so that it writes a half-length bar (approximately). For example, if symbolsNeeded is 9 and symbol is – then it writes only

            –––––

CHA 2.6.6   Modify Program OneBar so that it writes a double-length bar. For example, if symbolsNeeded is 4 and symbol is + then it writes

            ++++++++

Scales to Practice

PRA 2.6.1   Modify Exercise Pra.2.3.1 so that the user enters the letter s to see the sum and the letter p to see the product (instead of 0 for sum and anything else for product).

PRA 2.6.2   Write a program that writes the squares of all the even integers that range from 1 to 20 (4, 16, 36, . . ., 400).

PRA 2.6.3   Redo the program you wrote for Exercise Pra.2.6.2, but this time have the program write the square of each number the user types in until the user enters a negative number. (Note: The square of that final negative number should be printed too.)

Programs and Subprograms to Write

WRI 2.6.1   Write a program that uses a WHILE loop to write the numbers of the dates in this year's January that fall on a Tuesday (for example, 2, 9, 16, 23, 30).

WRI 2.6.2   *(An example from physics)* Write a program that writes the values of $(1/2)gt^2 + v_0t + d_0$ for t equal to 0.0, 0.5, 1.0, etc. (up to 4.0). This formula gives the height of an object at time t if it starts off at height d_0 with an initial velocity of v_0. Let g remain constant at -32.0 feet per second[2]; let v_0 be 5.5 feet per second; and let d_0 be 6 feet.

WRI 2.6.3   Write a program that reads the costs of several meals. For each meal it calculates a 7 percent tax and a 15 percent tip and writes the resulting total. The program stops when the user enters a zero cost.

WRI 2.6.4   Write a program that reads the record high and and record low temperatures for the month. Then it keeps reading more temperatures until it reads one that's not between the record high and low. Finally it writes a message indicating that the record has been broken.

Things to Think About

THI 2.6.1   In Chapter 1 we emphasized that every set of instructions can be written using decision making and/or repetition. In this chapter we saw how to instruct the computer to do decision making and repetition. Decision making can be done with an IF statement, and repetition can be done with a WHILE statement. This should give you a more concrete idea of what we mean by "decision making" and "repetition." With this enhanced understanding, reconsider your answer to Exercise Thi.1.4.1.

Chapter Summary

A REAL number is a number with a decimal point, and an INTEGER is a "whole number"—a number without a decimal point. In Pascal you can combine two REAL numbers with any of the operators +, −, *, or /. You can combine two INTEGERs with any of the operators +, −, *, /, DIV, and MOD. When an expression has more than one operator in it, the compiler uses *precedence rules* to decide the order in which the operations are performed.

There are two kinds of "words" in a Pascal program: *reserved words* and *identifiers*. Each reserved word has a certain predetermined meaning in Pascal. In contrast, an identifier is a word that's chosen as the name of something (a variable, a subprogram, a program) by an individual programmer. When you're writing a program, it's always important to choose informative identifiers.

A Pascal program is composed of several parts, including

a program *heading*

a VAR *declaration part*

a program *body*

In addition, several *comments* help us understand what a program is doing. A program can run correctly without comments, but if the program doesn't have enough comments then it isn't readable. An unreadable program is a bad program, even if it "runs correctly."

In each Pascal program, a program heading gives the name of the program and tells whether the program receives input from the keyboard, whether it sends output to the screen, etc.

The variables used in a program are declared in the program's VAR declaration part. In the VAR declaration part, each variable is declared to be of a particular *type*. The types we used in this chapter are REAL, INTEGER, and CHAR. Other types will be discussed in the chapters to come.

The body of a program contains statements that are separated from one another by semicolons. The statements we discussed in the chapter are

assignment statements,

IF statements,

WHILE statements,

ReadLns and WriteLns

ReadLns and WriteLns actually belong to a category of statements named *procedure calls*, which will be discussed in detail in Chapter 3.

An assignment statement is used to assign a value to a variable. An IF statement is used to make a decision (that is, to decide which of the statements within it should be executed). A WHILE statement is used for repetition (that is, to cause repeated execution of the statements within it). Both IF statements and WHILE statements contain *conditions*. A condition can contain operators such as >, <, =, >=, <=, and <>. You can also use AND, OR, and NOT in a condition; but when you use these words, you must be careful to put in the proper parentheses.

By creating a *procedure* we can translate pseudocode into Pascal code that deals first with a program's "topmost layer." This allows us to solve a program from the top, downward. We start by solving the topmost layer of the problem, and then we work our way down to the details. This is a very important ingredient in the design of good programs.

A procedure, just like a program, has a heading, a V A R declaration part, and a body. The heading has a parameter list that includes the procedure's *formal parameters*. The V A R declaration part is where the procedure's *local* variables are declared. The body of the procedure contains one or more statements.

When a statement called a *procedure call* is reached, the *actual parameters* in the call are *passed* to the *formal parameters* in the procedure.

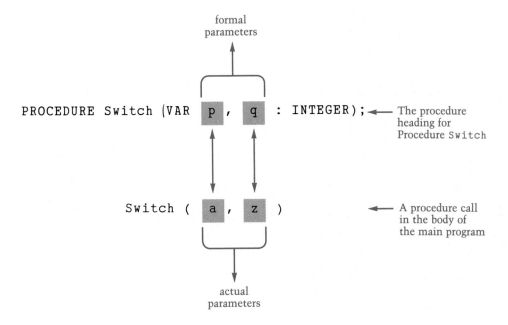

Then the statements in the body of the procedure are executed. After this, control is *returned* to the point in the code where the procedure was called.

3 Problem Decomposition Using Subprograms

When you have something important to do, and you don't want to be concerned with the details of how it gets done, you hand the task over to a specialist. You may drive a car every day, but when it needs fixing, you take it to a mechanic—a specialist in car repair. You don't ask the mechanic what size alternator it needs; you just say "Fix it." When the repairs are done, the mechanic returns the car to you.

The same kind of thing happens when you write a program. There are certain details that you want to push into the background. To take care of these details you can call on a specialist, a program that's already been written or one that you'll write later when you're not busy concentrating on the broader outline of the problem. Eventually this "specialist program" becomes part of your broader program, so the specialist is called a **subprogram**.

subprograms

In fact, it's not unusual for several programmers to work on one project. One programmer may write the main program, while other programmers write subprograms. So we can think of the programmers who write the subprograms as the specialists, writing the details of the tasks given to them by the main programmer.

Whether you're working with other programmers or working alone, subprograms help you focus your attention on one part of the problem at a time. Of course, before you focus attention on any details, you have to decide where the lines will be drawn between various parts of the problem; that is, you have to decide how you're going to decompose the problem. You have to ask yourself "What's the best way to break this problem into parts?" This is a very important step in the problem-solving process. In fact, it's no exaggeration to say that **decomposition** of the problem is the most important step in the problem-solving process. When a problem has been properly decomposed, its parts are all very clear and simple, and they can each be solved with very little effort.

problem decomposition

In this chapter, we'll decompose problems with the two kinds of subprograms that are available in Pascal: *procedures* and *functions*.

95

3.1

Pass By Value

Specifications Since Program OneBar is still fresh in your mind from Section 2.6, let's expand on that same problem. We want a bar graph that shows the total salaries of women and men in the United States, in hundreds of millions of dollars, over a three-year period. To make the graph easy to read, different characters will be used to make the bars for women's and men's salaries. The bars for women's salaries will be made of Ws; the bars for men's salaries will be made of Ms.

Designing a Program First we'll turn the specs into some imperative sentences, written in English prose:

> For each of the three years, make two bars on the graph. The first bar, for women's salaries, is made of Ws; the second bar, for men's salaries, is made of Ms.

Then we turn the prose into pseudocode:

> For each of the three years,
>   get the total women's Salaries and men's Salaries for the year
>   make a women's bar (with womensSal-many Ws),
>   make a men's bar (with mensSal-many Ms).

We can see immediately how this pseudocode will translate into Pascal:

```
year := 1990;
WHILE year < 1993 DO
  BEGIN
    ReadLn (womensSal, mensSal);
    MakeBar {with womensSal-many W's};
    MakeBar {with mensSal-many M's};
    year := year + 1
  END
```

Of course we haven't done much to translate "make a women's bar" and "make a men's bar" from pseudocode into Pascal. All we've done is make up a new identifier MakeBar and write it twice inside a loop, as if the computer would know how to MakeBar on its own. At this point, we don't worry about how the computer will actually MakeBar. We want to keep our minds focused on the broad outline of the problem, and the broad outline of the problem is to get the computer to do something several times. Making a bar is a smaller subproblem.

In the terminology of program design, we're working on the topmost part of the problem: instructing the computer to do something for each of three years. At this point we aren't giving too many details about what that

top-down design

"something" is that the computer has to do for each of three years. Those details aren't at the top of the problem. They're farther down. Another way of describing what we're doing is this: we're decomposing the problem into simpler parts. The top part is the three-year loop, and the bottom part is making a single bar.

Actually, to write the code for a procedure named `MakeBar`, we can borrow from our old Program `OneBar`:

```
symbolsWritten := 0;
WHILE symbolsWritten < symbolsNeeded DO
  BEGIN
    Write (symbol:1);
    symbolsWritten := symbolsWritten + 1
  END;
WriteLn
```

But now the values of `symbolsNeeded` and `symbol` will come from the main program. They'll be parameters that are passed to Procedure `MakeBar` from the main program.

```
PROCEDURE MakeBar (symbolsNeeded : INTEGER; symbol : CHAR);
```

The heading of Procedure `MakeBar`

```
MakeBar (womensSal, 'W');
MakeBar (mensSal  , 'M')
```

Calls to Procedure `MakeBar` from the body of the main program

So notice what we've done: we've taken what might have been a complicated program and decomposed it into two simple parts. We worked on these parts in two separate steps. In the first step we created the broad outline: a three-year loop in which there are several calls to a "specialist" named `MakeBar`. At this point, `MakeBar` was just a black box. It was the name of something that had to get done, with no details about how `MakeBar` would do it.

Then, in the next step, we took this nebulous thing called `MakeBar`, and we *refined* our notion of what it is; that is, we filled in its details. In fact, one of the names for what we've done is **stepwise refinement**.

stepwise refinement

So here's the problem-solving process that comes from the notions of **top-down design**, problem decomposition, and stepwise refinement:

Decompose the problem into parts.
Write pseudocode for the broad outline of the problem,
  listing the parts, but giving no detail for each part.
Then, taking each part as a problem in and of itself,
  Decompose the part into smaller parts.
  Write pseudocode for the part . . . etc.

The code for Program `BarGraph` follows.

Program Example

```
PROGRAM BarGraph (input, output);
{Prints a bar graph of women's and
 men's salaries spanning three years.}

  VAR
    year                : 1990..1993;
    womensSal, mensSal : INTEGER;

  {----------}

  PROCEDURE MakeBar (symbolsNeeded : INTEGER; symbol : CHAR);
  {Prints one of the bars in a bar graph.}

    VAR
      symbolsWritten : INTEGER;

  BEGIN {MakeBar}
    symbolsWritten := 0;
    WHILE symbolsWritten < symbolsNeeded DO
      BEGIN
        Write (symbol:1);
        symbolsWritten := symbolsWritten + 1
      END;
    WriteLn
  END;   {MakeBar}

  {----------}

BEGIN {BarGraph}
  WriteLn ('      WOMEN''S AND MEN''S SALARIES'   );
  WriteLn ('(in hundreds of millions of dollars)');
  WriteLn;

  year := 1990;
  WHILE year < 1993 DO
    BEGIN
      Write   (year:4, ' - Women''s and men''s salaries: ');
      ReadLn  (womensSal, mensSal);

      MakeBar (womensSal, 'W');
      MakeBar (mensSal  , 'M');
      WriteLn;

      year := year + 1
    END
END.   {BarGraph}
```

Sample Runs

```
      WOMEN'S AND MEN'S SALARIES
(in hundreds of millions of dollars)

1990 - Women's and men's salaries: 12 24
WWWWWWWWWWWW
MMMMMMMMMMMMMMMMMMMMMMMM

1991 - Women's and men's salaries: 15 26
WWWWWWWWWWWWWWW
MMMMMMMMMMMMMMMMMMMMMMMMMM

1992 - Women's and men's salaries: 19 28
WWWWWWWWWWWWWWWWWWW
MMMMMMMMMMMMMMMMMMMMMMMMMMMM
```

Observations

- `MakeBar (womensSal, 'W');`
  `MakeBar (mensSal  , 'M')`

single quotes

Look at the actual parameters in the two calls to `MakeBar`. In the first call, one of the actual parameters is `'W'`. When we put single quotes around any number of characters, we're referring to the characters themselves. Thus `'W'` represents the letter "double-u," while just plain old `W`, without the quotes, would refer to a variable named `W`.

The first time `MakeBar` is called, it's passed the letter `'W'`, so it writes a row of `W`s on the screen. The second time it's called it's passed the letter `'M'`, so it writes a row of `M`s on the screen.

- `PROCEDURE MakeBar (symbolsNeeded : INTEGER; symbol : CHAR);`

The heading of Procedure `MakeBar`

.
.

`MakeBar (womensSal, 'W');`
`MakeBar (mensSal  , 'M')`

Calls to Procedure `MakeBar` in the body of the main program

The heading of Procedure `MakeBar` has no `VAR` in its parameter list. This means that

1. Nothing that happens to `symbolsNeeded` in the subprogram is done to `womensSal` or to `mensSal` in the main program.

2. Nothing that happens to `symbols` in the subprogram is done to `'W'` or to `'M'` in the main program.

More precisely,

1. Any change made to the value of `symbolsNeeded` in the subprogram has no effect on the values of `womensSal` or `mensSal` in the main program.

parameter without a VAR

2. Any change made to the value of `symbol` in the subprogram has no effect on the values of `'W'` or `'M'` in the main program.

Indeed, in this example, it wouldn't make sense to change the values of `mensSalaries` or `womensSalaries`, since the program gets these values from the user and doesn't calculate these values itself. And it certainly wouldn't make sense to change the values of `'W'` or `'M'` in the main program. `'W'` isn't a variable; it's a character; and it can't be changed from being the letter `'W'` to being anything else.

- `VAR`
  `year : 1990..1993;`

subrange

Instead of just saying that `year` is an `INTEGER`, we can be more specific. In this `VAR` declaration we create a **subrange** `1990..1993` of the INTEGERs. With year declared to be in this subrange, the only values year can have are 1990, 1991, 1992, and 1993. That's exactly what we want! If, when we write the body of Program BarGraph, we make a mistake and let year get to be 1994, the run of the program will be aborted and the computer will give us an error diagnostic.[1]

Notice that in the VAR declaration we're allowing year to get all the way up to 1993, even though we'll be making bars only for the years 1990 to 1992. We do this because we want year to get to be 1993. When year gets to be 1993, the test

```
WHILE year < 1993 DO
```

fails, and the computer exits from the WHILE loop.

- WriteLn ('   WOMEN''S AND MEN''S SALARIES'   )
                      ↑↑   ↑↑

single quotes side by side

If we want to display a single quote mark we need to put *two* quote marks side by side in our Write or WriteLn. With just a single quote mark:

```
WriteLn ('      WOMEN'S AND MEN'S SALARIES'   )
```

the compiler would see two messages '   WOMEN' and 'S SALARIES' and some miscellaneous characters S AND MEN in between them:

```
WriteLn ( |'      WOMEN'|S AND MEN|'S SALARIES'|   )
```

Further Discussion

abstraction

One way to understand the role of subprograms is to think of them as a form of **abstraction**. The word *abstract* means "disassociated from any specific instance."[2] We usually apply it to an entity that's somehow lacking in detail. In the case of a Pascal subprogram, a call to the subprogram tells us (the human readers) that something will be done, but it doesn't tell us any of the details of what will be done. To learn about the details, we'd have to look at the subprogram's body.

Now in many areas of study, it's bad to be "lacking in detail." It could mean that you don't know something you should know. But in program-

---

[1]With many implementations, you have to do something extra when you compile Program BarGraph in order for this "range checking" to be done. For instance, on a VAX with VMS, you compile bargraph.pas by typing $pascal/check=subrange bargraph as opposed to

$pascal/check=nosubrange bargraph

With Turbo Pascal you turn range checking on or off by toggling Range checking in the Options/Compiler menu.

[2]This definition is taken from *Webster's New Collegiate Dictionary*, and is reprinted with permission.

ming, it's useful to hide details. Here are some of the advantages of hiding details:

- A program should be easy to read and to understand. Just like any other piece of technical writing, a program is easier to read if it has a *summary*—a place where the main points are given and the details are omitted. The main body of Program BarGraph can be taken as a summary of the action of the whole program. Similarly, the single line

```
MakeBar (womensSal, 'W')
```

can be taken as a summary of the action of Procedure MakeBar. All the details are given in the body of Procedure MakeBar.

- A program should be well organized, because a well-organized program represents well-organized thinking. A well-organized program resembles an outline, with main headings, subheadings, sub-subheadings, etc. In Pascal, the "main headings" are in the main program, and the "subheadings" are in the subprograms.

procedural abstraction

So creating a subprogram is a way of making the program more *abstract*—that is, making it lack detail. For that reason, subprograms are considered to be part of a grander notion called **procedural abstraction** Procedural abstraction is a good thing, because when we're thinking about the broad outline of an algorithm, details tend to get in the way. If we think about the big problem and the details all at once, we tend not to solve the problem from the top down, in outline form. Instead, we end up seeing the problem as long series of steps, with each step having equal importance and with no sense of how the steps are organized into a whole.

pass by reference

In Program IntroToProcedures (Section 2.5) the formal parameters a and z were preceded by the word VAR. Because of this, any changes we made to a and z inside Procedure Switch caused changes in the values of score1 and score2. To use the proper terminology, we say that a and z (and the corresponding actual parameters, score1 and score2) were being **passed by reference.** Pass by reference is sometimes called **pass by variable** because, when this parameter passing mechanism is used, the actual parameter *must* be a variable. Another way to say the same thing is to refer to a and z as VAR **parameters**. This reminds us that the word VAR appears in the formal parameter list.

pass by value

In Program BarGraph, the formal parameters symbolsNeeded and symbol aren't preceded by the word VAR. Because of this, we say that symbolsNeeded and symbol (and the corresponding actual parameters, womensSal, 'W', mensSal, and 'M') are **passed by value**. Sometimes we say the same thing by referring to symbolsNeeded and symbol as **value parameters**. Even if Procedure MakeBar made changes to the values of symbolsNeeded or symbol inside Procedure MakeBar, this would not cause a change in the values of womensSal, 'W', mensSal, or 'M'.

When we have many formal parameters in a subprogram heading, the word VAR applies to all parameters up to the next colon. For instance, in

```
PROCEDURE Draw (VAR thickness, breadth : REAL;
                length, width, height  : REAL;
                VAR dotsDrawn          : INTEGER);
```

the variables thickness, breadth, and dotsDrawn are passed by reference, and the variables length, width, and height are passed by value.

Traces

Recall the trace we made in Section 2.5. In that section we used pass by reference; and so when we made a trace, we wrote our formal parameter names directly under the corresponding actual parameter names. This reminded us that, with pass by reference, any change made to the value of the formal parameter has an effect on the value of the actual parameter.

tracing pass by value

When we use pass by value, we *don't* write the formal parameter name under the actual parameter name. This is to remind us that, with pass by value, any change made to the value of a formal parameter has *no* effect on the value of the actual parameter.

Here's a trace of Program BarGraph to illustrate the point:

```
┌──────────────────────── BarGraph ─────────────────────────────┐
│                                                                │
│ year womensSal mensSal                              output     │
│ 1990     12      24                                   1990     │
│              ┌─────────────────────────────────────────┐      │
│              │ symbolsNeeded symbol symbolsWritten      │      │
│              │      12          W          0        W   │      │
│              │                             1        W   │      │
│              │                             2        W   │      │
│              │                             3        W   │      │
│              │                             4        W   │      │
│              │                             5        W   │      │
│              │                             6        W   │      │
│              │                             7        W   │      │
│              │                             8        W   │      │
│              │                             9        W   │      │
│              │                            10        W   │      │
│              │                            11        W   │      │
│              │                            12            │      │
│              └─────────────────────────────────────────┘      │
│                                                                │
│              ┌─────────────────────────────────────────┐      │
│              │ symbolsNeeded symbol symbolsWritten      │      │
│              │      24          M          0        M   │      │
│              │                             1        M   │      │
│              │                             2        M   │      │
│              │                             3        M   │      │
   Etc.                                      .        .
                                             .        .
```

In this trace, notice that `symbolsNeeded` isn't written under `womensSal` or `mensSal` even though `womensSal` is passed to `symbolsNeeded` the first time the procedure is called, and `mensSal` is passed to `symbolsNeeded` the second time the procedure is called.

Structure

To represent a subprogram call in an NS chart, we create a box that's a bit smaller than the box we already have:

NS chart with a subprogram

PROGRAM BarGraph

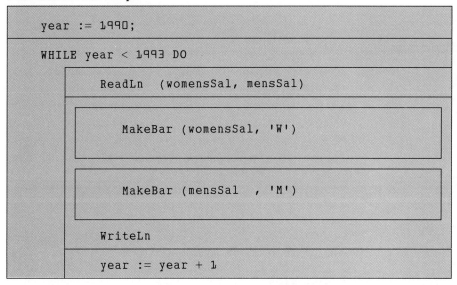

Then we make a separate NS chart to represent the action of the subprogram:

PROCEDURE MakeBar (symbolsNeeded : INTEGER; symbol : CHAR);

```
symbolsWritten := 0

WHILE symbolsWritten < symbolsNeeded DO
        Write (symbol:1)
        symbolsWritten := symbolsWritten + 1

WriteLn
```

3.1 Exercises

Key Words to Review

subprogram	subrange	pass by variable
decomposition	abstraction	VAR parameters
stepwise refinement	procedural abstraction	pass by value
top-down design	pass by reference	value parameters

Questions to Answer

QUE 3.1.1 Explain the difference between pass by reference and pass by value.

QUE 3.1.2 Explain the relationship among the following three notions: top-down design, problem decomposition, and stepwise refinement.

QUE 3.1.3 What are the advantages of decomposing a problem into parts?

QUE 3.1.4 Look again at the Scales and the Programs and Subprograms exercises in Section 2.5. Are there any places in these programs where we could have used pass by value instead of pass by reference? Explain.

QUE 3.1.5 Write a *heading* for a procedure that accepts two numbers and calculates the quotient of the two numbers as well as the remainder you get when you do the division.

QUE 3.1.6 Explain how you would *decompose* each of the following problems. At this point, don't worry about how you'd actually write code to solve the problems:
a. Draw a picture of a house using dashes (–) and exclamation points (!).
b. Draw a picture of a person, using whatever characters on the keyboard are best suited to the task.
c. Write the alphabet several times in a diagonal striped shape:

```
abcdefghijklmnopqrstuvwxyz   abcdefghijklmnopqrstuvwxyz
 abcdefghijklmnopqrstuvwxyz   abcdefghijklmnopqrstuvwxyz
  abcdefghijklmnopqrstuvwxyz   abcdefghijklmnopqrstuvwxyz
   abcdefghijklmnopqrstuvwxyz   abcdefghijklmnopqrstuvwxyz
    abcdefghijklmnopqrstuvwxyz   abcdefghijklmnopqrstuvwxyz
```

d. Search through a document for every occurrence of the word *the*.

Things to Check in a Manual

MAN 3.1.1 Find out if, with your implementation, there's a way to turn range checking on and off.

MAN 3.1.2 Find out if your implementation has a Halt feature. When your program reaches a Halt, it ends its execution immediately, even if the Halt isn't at the end of the program's main body. (Note: Some implementations may have other names for what we call Halt.)

Experiments to Try

EXP 3.1.1 In the VAR declaration of Program BarGraph, change 1993 to 1992. Don't change anything else in the program. This is a test to see if your implementation is doing range checking. If the program runs without an error diagnostic, see Exercise Man.3.1.1.

EXP 3.1.2 Remove the single quote marks surrounding the letters W and M in the calls to Procedure MakeBar.

Changes to Make

CHA 3.1.1 Make all changes needed to have Program BarGraph report salaries for the years 2010 to 2015.

CHA 3.1.2 Change Program BarGraph so that the first and last years it covers (for example, 1990 and 1992) are stored in variables whose values are read in while the program runs.

CHA 3.1.3 Rewrite Program Scores, Section 2.3, so that the values of home and visitor are read in the main program but are written by a subprogram. The decision about which value is to be printed first is made in the same subprogram.

Programs and Subprograms to Write

WRI 3.1.1 Write a procedure that receives a number via its parameter list and writes that number on the screen. If the number is positive, it gets written near the left edge of the screen. If it's negative, it gets indented by several blank spaces. For example:

```
984.22
            -55.56
2567.32
            -10.00
```

WRI 3.1.2 Write a procedure whose parameters contain the price per gallon for two blends of gasoline (regular and super) and the number of gallons desired. The procedure calculates the price of that number of gallons for both the regular and super blends.

WRI 3.1.3 The streets in my city are numbered "1st street," "2nd street," etc. (up to "19th street"), and each street has forty houses on it. The houses on "12th street" are numbered 1200, 1201, etc., up to 1239, with the even-numbered houses on the left side of the street and the odd-numbered houses on the right side.

- How many houses are there in my city?
- Exactly where (what street, what side, what house number) is the 476th house located?
- Write a program that reads a number n and calls a procedure that figures out exactly where the nth house is located (what street, what side, what house number).

WRI 3.1.4 In financial analysis we can find a company's *acid test ratio* by subtracting the company's inventory from its assets and then dividing by its liabilities.

Write a program that reads the inventory, assets, and liabilities of a company and then writes the value of the company's acid test ratio.

Your program will be aborted if it tries to divide a number by zero. So put in an `IF` statement to check and make sure that this isn't about to happen. If it is, call a subprogram that writes a warning message on the screen saying that an `Illegal-divide-by-zero` is about to take place.

WRI 3.1.5   Modify the program you wrote for Exercise Wri.3.1.4 so that the subprogram writes one of two possible warning messages—`Inventory greater than current assets` or `Zero liabilities`—depending on which warning applies. One of the subprogram's parameters is an `INTEGER` with the value 1 or 2; 1 for `Inventory greater than current assets`, and 2 for `Zero liabilities`.

WRI 3.1.6   First do Exercise Man.3.1.2 to see if your implementation has a `Halt` feature. If it does, redo Exercise Wri.3.1.4 so that your program calls itself to a halt after writing the warning message.

WRI 3.1.7   *(This exercise uses some concepts from elementary physics.)* Assume that a particle starts at position (x_1,y_1). It has constant velocity v_x in the x direction and constant velocity v_y in the y direction. With these velocities its new position (x_2,y_2) after time t will be given by the equations

$$x_2 = x_1 + v_x t$$
$$y_2 = y_1 + v_y t$$

These equations are a modified form of the *Galilean transformations.* Write a procedure that takes x_1, y_1, v_x, v_y, and t, and calculates x_2 and y_2.

3.2

Parameter Passing—How It's Done

In Section 2.5 we promised to discuss the means by which parameters are "passed" from a subprogram call to the subprogram itself. We'll do that in this section. Since there are two ways to pass information to subprograms, we need to discuss two passing mechanisms. With the first passing mechanism, we put the word `VAR` before the parameters in the subprogram's heading. We call this *pass by reference.* Here's how this method of passing parameters works:

how pass by reference is done

Look once again at Program `IntroToProcedures` in Section 2.5. In that program we have a *procedure call* and a *procedure heading.* The procedure call has two **actual parameters**, `score1` and `score2`. The procedure heading has two **formal parameters**, a and z. When the procedure is called, the actual parameter `score1` is passed to the formal parameter a. Likewise, the actual parameter `score2` is passed to the formal parameter z.

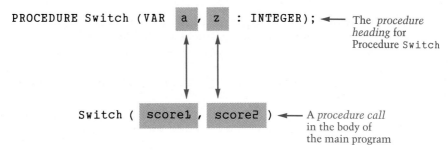

Because of the word VAR in the procedure heading, score1 and score2 are passed by reference to a and z. The effect of pass by reference is that anything that happens to a inside Procedure Switch actually gets done to score1. Likewise, anything that happens to z inside Procedure Switch actually gets done to score2.

Now here's what *really* happens when we do pass by reference: Let's say the user originally typed in 32 for score1 and 54 for score2. Then the variable names score1 and score2 refer to memory locations where the values 32 and 54 are stored.

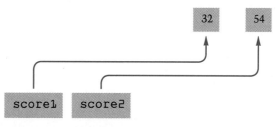

When the procedure call Switch (score1, score2) is encountered, the computer makes a refer to the memory location where 32 is stored and makes z refer to the memory location where 54 is stored. Another way to say this is that the computer makes a refer to the same memory location as score1 and makes z refer to the same memory location as score2.

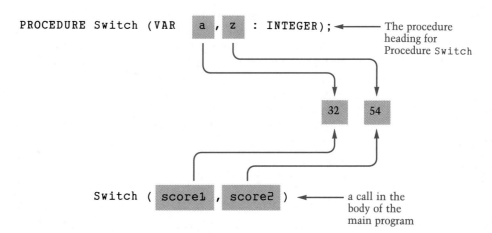

After this "matching" is done, the code inside Procedure Switch is executed. This code switches the values of a and z, so a gets to be 54 and z gets to be 32.

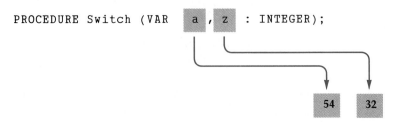

But remember that a refers to the same memory location as score1, and z refers to the same memory location as score2.

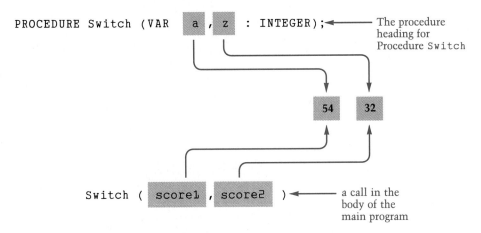

So really score1 has just received the value 54, and score2 has just received the value 32. The values of score1 and score2 have been switched!

That's how a pass by reference is actually done. Now what about the other passing mechanism, *pass by value*? Let's look at Program BarGraph from Section 3.1. We'll examine one of the two procedure calls and MakeBar's procedure heading.

how pass by value is done

The first procedure call has actual parameters, womensSal and 'W'. The procedure heading has formal parameters symbolsNeeded and symbol. When the procedure is called, the actual parameters womensSal and 'W' are passed to the formal parameters symbolsNeeded and symbol.

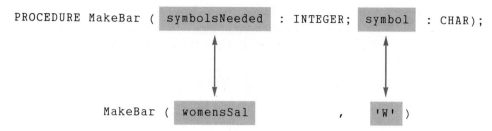

Because the word VAR isn't used in the procedure heading, womensSal is passed by value to symbolsNeeded, and 'W' is passed by value to symbol. The effect of pass by value is that nothing that happens inside Procedure MakeBar to the values of symbolsNeeded and symbol can change the values of womenSal or 'W'.

Now here's what *really* happens when we do pass by value: Let's say the user typed in 12 24 when prompted for women's and men's salaries. Then the variable name womensSal refers to a memory location where the value 12 is stored. It also happens that the actual parameter 'W' refers to a memory location where the letter "double-u" is stored.

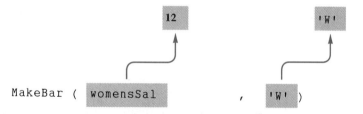

When pass by value is used, the formal parameters refer to their own memory locations—extra locations beyond those referred to by the actual parameters.

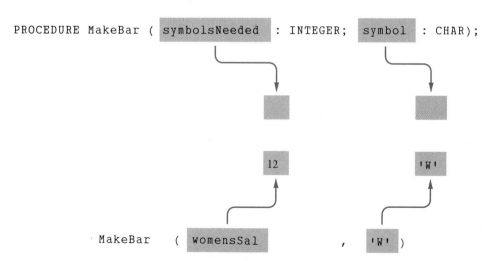

When the procedure call MakeBar (womensSal, 'W') is encountered, the computer takes *copies* of the values in the womensSal and 'W' locations and puts them into the symbolsNeeded and symbol locations.

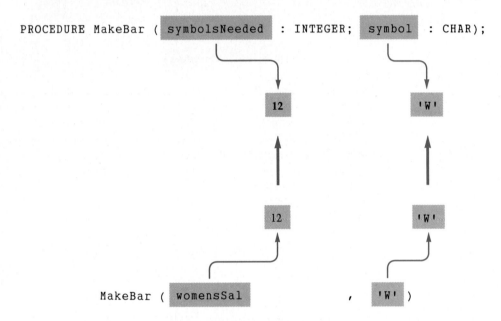

Notice that the computer does not make symbolsNeeded refer to any location that was referred to in the main program. And it doesn't make symbol refer to any memory location that was referred to in the main program. If we accidentally put statements like

```
symbolsNeeded := 13;
symbol       := 'N'
```

in the body of Procedure MakeBar, these will not refer to the memory locations of womensSal and 'W':

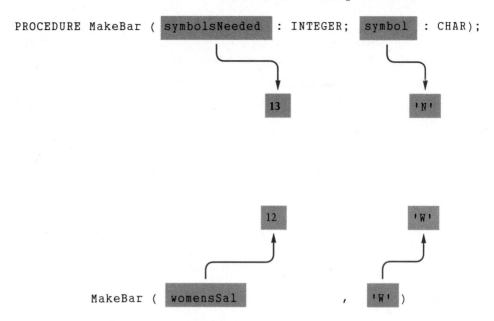

so it will have no effect on the values of womensSal and 'W' in the main program. When the code inside Procedure MakeBar is finished being executed and we return to the main program, womensSal will still have the value 12, and of course 'W' will still refer to the letter "double-u." That's how pass by value is done.

3.2   Exercises

Key Words to Review

pass by reference   formal parameter   pass by value
actual parameter

Questions to Answer

QUE 3.2.1   In any subprogram call we must have the same number of variables as in the subprogram's heading. Why?

QUE 3.2.2   Let's change our call to Procedure MakeBar:

        MakeBar (amount, ch)

without changing the procedure's heading:

    PROCEDURE MakeBar (symbolsNeeded : INTEGER; symbol : CHAR);

Why is it important that amount be of type INTEGER and ch be of type CHAR?

QUE 3.2.3   Would Procedure Switch have worked if we had used pass by value? Why, or why not?

QUE 3.2.4   Would Procedure MakeBar have worked if we had used pass by reference? Why, or why not?

QUE 3.2.5   Each of the following problems can be solved using subprograms. For each problem, write a procedure heading and a prologue comment. For each of the formal parameters in the procedure heading, tell whether pass by reference or pass by value should be used (and why). At this point you shouldn't worry about how you'd write the subprogram bodies:

a. A subprogram that increases a variable's value by 1.

b. A subprogram that prompts the user for the total number of inches of rainfall for each of three months and then reads each of these three totals.

c. A subprogram that receives, via its formal parameter list, the total number of inches of rainfall for each of three months and makes a chart on the screen showing the variation in rainfall over these three months.

d. A subprogram that takes a number of inches and converts it into yards, feet, and inches (for example, 105 inches is 2 yards, 2 feet, 9 inches). This subprogram doesn't read anything from the keyboard or write anything to the screen. It communicates entirely through its formal parameter list.

Experiments to Try

EXP 3.2.1   Remove the word VAR from the heading of Procedure Switch.

EXP 3.2.2   Change the heading of Procedure Switch to

```
PROCEDURE Switch (VAR a : INTEGER; z : INTEGER);
```

EXP 3.2.3   Change the heading of Procedure MakeBar to

```
PROCEDURE MakeBar (VAR symbolsNeeded : INTEGER;
                   VAR symbol        : CHAR)  ;
```

EXP 3.2.4   Change the heading of Procedure MakeBar to

```
PROCEDURE MakeBar (symbol : CHAR; symbolsNeeded : INTEGER);
```

and change the calls to

```
MakeBar ('W', womensSal);
MakeBar ('M', mensSal  )
```

EXP 3.2.5   Change the heading of Procedure MakeBar to

```
PROCEDURE MakeBar (symbol : CHAR; symbolsNeeded : INTEGER);
```

and try to run the program without making any other changes.

Changes to Make

CHA 3.2.1   Modify Program IntroToProcedures (Section 2.5) so that Procedure Switch has four formal parameters. Two of them receive the original values of score1 and score2 and the other two are used to send back two new values that are in the correct order. Move the program's IF statement so that it's inside Procedure Switch.

3.3

Parameter Passing—More Examples

When you leave off the VAR and do pass by value, you lose something and you gain something. You lose the ability to have the subprogram change the actual parameters' values. But you gain the safety of knowing that the subprogram won't accidentally change the actual parameters' values.

In this section we'll do several experiments to demonstrate some of the subtler points concerning pass by reference and pass by value. In each experiment we'll be considering a different scenario illustrating the way in which actual parameters can be passed to formal parameters. We'll examine each program carefully to see exactly what effect the parameter-passing mechanism has on the values of all the variables.

Specifications

Input: A principal amount and an interest rate

Output: A new principal amount, after one year's interest has been added

Program Example

```
PROGRAM Interest (input, output);
{Computes interest on a loan.}

   VAR
      principal, intRate : REAL;

   {----------}

   PROCEDURE AddInterest (VAR principal : REAL ;
                              intRate        : REAL);
   {Adds one year's interest.}
   BEGIN {AddInterest}
      principal := principal + (intRate/100.0 * principal)
   END;  {AddInterest}

   {----------}

BEGIN {Interest}
   Write      ('Enter principal and interest rate: ');
   ReadLn     (principal, intRate);

   AddInterest (principal, intRate);

   WriteLn    ('New principal: ', principal:6:2)
END.  {Interest}
```

Sample Runs

```
Enter principal and interest rate: 200.00 5.0
New principal: 210.00
```

Observations
* `principal := principal + (intRate/100.0 * principal)`
  The variable `principal` is called an **accumulator**. An accumulator is like a counter (see Section 2.6) except some value other than 1 gets

added to it. In this case the value being added to `principal` is (`intRate/100.0 * principal`). Here's what happens when the interest rate is 5.0 (5 percent):

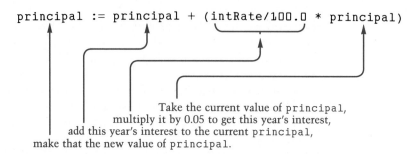

```
principal := principal + (intRate/100.0 * principal)
```

Take the current value of `principal`,
multiply it by 0.05 to get this year's interest,
add this year's interest to the current `principal`,
make that the new value of `principal`.

Notice how the `intRate` gets divided by 100.00. This brings a percentage (like 5.0 percent) down to a decimal value (like 0.05).

Remember, in the discussion of counters, how we emphasized that a counter needs to be initialized. The same is true of accumulators. In this program the variable `principal` gets its initial value when the statement

initializing an accumulator

```
ReadLn (principal, intRate)
```

is executed. Without first having this **initialization**, we'd get

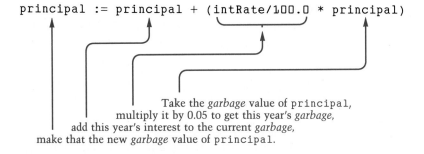

```
principal := principal + (intRate/100.0 * principal)
```

Take the *garbage* value of `principal`,
multiply it by 0.05 to get this year's *garbage*,
add this year's interest to the current *garbage*,
make that the new *garbage* value of `principal`.

Further Discussion

The word `VAR` in the heading of Procedure `AddInterest` enables the procedure to change the value of the main program's `principal` variable. To prove this, we can momentarily remove the `VAR`:

with VAR vs. without VAR

```
PROGRAM Interest (input, output);
  {Tries to compute interest on a loan -
  accidentally uses only pass by value.}
    VAR
      principal, intRate : REAL;
    {----------}
```

```
PROCEDURE AddInterest (principal : REAL ;
                       intRate   : REAL);
{Tries to add one year's interest –
 accidentally uses only pass by value.}
BEGIN {AddInterest}
  principal := principal + (intRate/100.0 * principal)
END;  {AddInterest}

{----------}
BEGIN {Interest}
  Write       ('Enter principal and interest rate: ');
  ReadLn      (principal, intRate);

  AddInterest (principal, intRate);

  WriteLn     ('New principal: ', principal:6:2)
END.  {Interest}
```

and then notice what happens:

```
Enter principal and interest rate: 200.00 5.0
New principal: 200.00
```

When the statement

```
WriteLn     ('New principal: ', principal:6:2)
```

is executed in the main program's body, the value of `principal` is still 200.00, not 210.00! Even though the actual and formal parameters both have the name `principal`, they're not the same variable. The value of `principal` in the main program doesn't get changed. To see what's going on, we can put a few `WriteLns` in Procedure `AddInterest`.

```
PROCEDURE AddInterest (principal : REAL ;
                       intRate   : REAL);
{Tries to add one year's interest –
 accidentally uses only pass by value.}

BEGIN {AddInterest}
  WriteLn ('Before adding interest: ', principal:6:2);
  principal := principal + (intRate/100.0 * principal);
  WriteLn ('After  adding interest: ', principal:6:2)
END;  {AddInterest}
```

Here's a run with our new version of `AddInterest`:

```
Enter principal and interest rate: 200.00 5.0
Before adding interest: 200.00
After  adding interest: 210.00
New principal: 200.00
```

Inside the procedure, the value of `principal` gets increased from 200.00 to 210.00. But the `principal` variable that's part of the main program retains its original value of 200.00.

global variables

The variables `principal` and `intRate`, declared in Procedure `AddInterest`, are formal parameters; and the other variables `principal` and `intRate`, declared in the main program, are called **global** variables. But what do we mean by the word *global?* After all, *global* means "everywhere." We use the word *global* because the main program's variables aren't restricted to being used only in the main body. They can *accidentally* be used inside a subprogram. We emphasize the word *accidentally*, because using a main program's variable inside a subprogram is considered bad programming practice. Here's an experiment to show you the kind of thing you should avoid doing:

```
PROGRAM UsingGlobals (input, output);
  VAR
    principal, intRate : REAL;
  {----------}
  PROCEDURE AddInterest;
  {Adds one year's interest.}
  BEGIN {AddInterest}
    principal := principal + (intRate/100.0 * principal)
  END;  {AddInterest}
  {----------}
BEGIN {UsingGlobals}
  Write      ('Enter principal and interest rate: ');
  ReadLn     (principal, intRate);

  AddInterest;

  WriteLn    ('New principal: ', principal:6:2)
END.   {UsingGlobals}
```

In this program, there's only one variable named `principal` and only one variable named `intRate`. They're declared in the main program and used both in the main program and in the subprogram. The subprogram has no formal parameters of its own; and when the subprogram is called, it's called without any actual parameters (and without any parentheses). Since there's only one `principal` variable in this program, the assignment statement inside Procedure `AddInterest` actually changes the value of the main program's `principal` variable. A run of Program `UseGlobal` looks just the way it would if we'd used pass by reference:

```
Enter principal and interest rate: 200.00 5.0
New principal: 210.00
```

But it's always better to use pass by reference to achieve this effect.

When a subprogram refers to a global variable, it's as if the subprogram is "borrowing" the global variable without the main program's permission. The main program isn't listing the variable as an actual parameter, and so it isn't giving the subprogram permission to use the variable. If the subprogram uses the variable anyway, as a global variable, the subprogram is breaking a sacred trust. The danger here is that the subprogram may actually change the value of the global variable, without having the possibility of a change announced in any of the parameter lists.

You see, the most important purpose of a parameter list is self-documentation. The parameter list tells the human reader what variables are being exchanged between the main program and the subprogram and what variables are in danger of being changed by the subprogram. Without a parameter list, we lose the ability to read that information at a glance.

undesirable side effects

If a subprogram does manage to change the value of a global variable, this change is called a **side effect**. The name is meant to be derogatory, like the unwanted side effects of certain prescription drugs.

Now here are some examples to demonstrate some of the trickier aspects of parameter passing. First we'll rewrite the program example of Section 2.3 so that it makes use of a procedure:

```
PROGRAM MoreScores (input, output);
{Reads two scores; writes the winner's score on top.}

   VAR
     home, visitor : INTEGER;

   {----------}

   PROCEDURE WriteLnTwo (hi, lo : INTEGER);
   {Writes two values on two separate lines.}

   BEGIN {WriteLnTwo}
     WriteLn (hi);
     WriteLn (lo)
   END;   {WriteLnTwo}

   {----------}

BEGIN {MoreScores}
   Write  ('Enter two scores (home space visitor): ');
   ReadLn (home, visitor);

   IF home > visitor THEN
     WriteLnTwo (home, visitor)
   ELSE
     WriteLnTwo (visitor, home)
END.   {MoreScores}
```

By creating Procedure `WriteLnTwo` we avoid having to repeat code like

```
BEGIN
   WriteLn (...);
   WriteLn (...)
END
```

more than once in the program. This is a nice example to show how we can avoid repetitious code by creating a subprogram. Anything that has to be done more than once (like writing two numbers on two separate lines) is a good candidate for being considered as a separate "part" of the problem when we're doing problem decomposition.

**doing without
BEGIN and
END**

Notice the IF statement in the program's main body. This is our first example of a structured statement without any BEGINs or ENDs. When a THEN-part has only one statement in it, the words BEGIN and END can be omitted. The same holds true for an ELSE-part with only one statement and for a loop with only one statement.

**actual and
formal
parameter
names**

The main thing this program illustrates is why we'd want to make up new names for our formal parameters. In this program we made up the new names hi and lo. We could have used the old names home and visitor, and the program would have worked correctly; but we would have had some very confusing code:

```
PROGRAM Crossover (input, output);
{Shows how having identical actual and
 formal parameter names can be confusing.}

   VAR
      home, visitor : INTEGER;

   {----------}

   PROCEDURE WriteLnTwo (home, visitor : INTEGER);
   {Writes two values on two separate lines.}

   BEGIN {WriteLnTwo}
      WriteLn (home);
      WriteLn (visitor)
   END;   {WriteLnTwo}

   {----------}

BEGIN {Crossover}
   Write ('Enter two scores (home space visitor): ');
   ReadLn (home, visitor);

   IF home > visitor THEN
      WriteLnTwo (home, visitor)
   ELSE
      WriteLnTwo (visitor, home)
END.   {Crossover}
```

Whenever the THEN-part was executed the actual parameters and the formal parameters would match up exactly the way we'd expect:

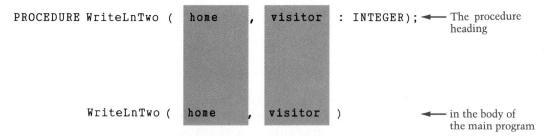

```
PROCEDURE WriteLnTwo ( home    , visitor  : INTEGER);  ◄── The procedure
                                                           heading



     WriteLnTwo ( home    , visitor  )                 ◄── in the body of
                                                           the main program
```

But when the ELSE-part was executed, this program would give us a confusing name switch:

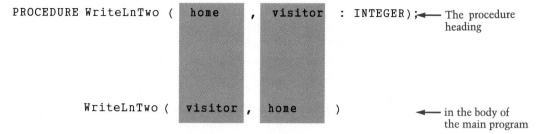

Whenever there's a chance of this happening, it's best to make up new names for the subprogram's formal parameters.

lifetime of a local variable

In this chapter we've been comparing the main program's global variables with the subprogram's local variables. One thing to keep in mind about a local variable is that it ceases to exist when the computer returns from the subprogram call. Here's an example:

```
PROGRAM Automatic (output);
{Shows how the local variable 'x' ceases to
 exist after each call to 'CallMeTwice'.}

  {----------}

  PROCEDURE CallMeTwice;
  {Local 'x' is undefined each time
   this procedure starts running.}

    VAR
      x : INTEGER;
  BEGIN {CallMeTwice}
    WriteLn ('Before assignment: ', x);
    x := 5;
    WriteLn ('After  assignment: ', x);
    WriteLn
  END;  {CallMeTwice}

  {----------}

BEGIN {Automatic}
  CallMeTwice;
  CallMeTwice
END.  {Automatic}
```

The first time Procedure `CallMeTwice` is called, its local variable x hasn't been given a value. This is a nasty situation, and your computer may give you an error diagnostic. But the question we want answered is: What will be the value of x the *second* time `CallMeTwice` is called? You may think x would retain the value 5 that was assigned to it at the end of the first call, but this isn't the case. Different implementations give you different results. Here's what we got when we ran Program `Automatic` under Turbo Pascal:

```
Before assignment: -29911
After  assignment: 5

Before assignment: -29911
After  assignment: 5
```

The local variable x ceased to exist when the computer returned from the first call to Procedure `CallMeTwice`. At the beginning of the second call, x was created afresh with the garbage value -29911. The technical way to talk about x's "ceasing to exist" is to say that the **extent** of a local variable such as x is limited to one execution of the procedure in which x is declared.

lifetime of a
VAR parameter
So here's one important use of pass by reference: to force a variable to retain its value from one subprogram call to another. For an example, we return to Program `Interest`, which we examined in the beginning of this section:

```
PROGRAM Interest (input, output);
{Computes two years' interest on a loan.}
   VAR
     principal, intRate : REAL;
   {----------}
   PROCEDURE AddInterest (VAR principal : REAL ;
                              intRate      : REAL);
   {Adds one year's interest.}
   BEGIN {AddInterest}
     principal := principal + (intRate/100.0 * principal)
   END;  {AddInterest}
   {----------}
BEGIN {Interest}
   Write       ('Enter principal and interest rate: ');
   ReadLn      (principal, intRate);

   AddInterest (principal, intRate);
   WriteLn     ('New principal: ', principal:6:2);

   AddInterest (principal, intRate);
   WriteLn     ('New principal: ', principal:6:2)
END.  {Interest}
```

This new version of Program `Interest` calls `AddInterest` twice and computes the new principal for two consecutive years:

```
Enter principal and interest rate: 200.00 5.0
New principal: 210.00
New principal: 220.50
```

Notice that the `principal` keeps increasing from one call of Procedure `AddInterest` to the next. This is because the most recent `principal` value is getting communicated back and forth between the main program and the subprogram. Pass by reference is responsible for this. If we hadn't used pass by reference, the `principal` wouldn't have been updated correctly.

We started this section by saying that you lose something and gain something with pass by value. We've seen some examples to show what you lose—you lose the ability to have the subprogram change the actual parameters' values. But you gain the safety of knowing that the subprogram won't accidentally change the actual parameters' values.

When I send parts of this textbook to my manuscript editor, I never send the originals—I send copies. I wouldn't let anyone make changes to my precious originals. That's the essence of pass by value. The main program sends a *copy* of the value of a variable to the subprogram. That way, the "precious" value of the original variable can't be destroyed.[3]

Value parameters are safer.

Here's an example to show the safety that we gain. Recall that in our original Procedure `AddInterest` we divide `intRate` by 100.00. This brings a percentage (like 5.0 percent) down to a decimal value (like 0.05).

```
principal := principal + (intRate/100.0 * principal)
```

Let's see what happens if we take the unnecessary risk of actually changing the value of `intRate` with an assignment statement.

```
intRate    := intRate/100.00;
principal := principal + (intRate * principal)
```

This is indeed an unnecessary risk. If `intRate` goes from 5.0 down to 0.05 the first time `AddInterest` is called, will it go from 0.05 all the way down to 0.0005 the second time `AddInterest` is called?

Here's the complete program:

```
PROGRAM Interest (input, output);
{Computes two years' interest on a loan.}
  VAR
    principal, intRate : REAL;

  {----------}

  PROCEDURE AddInterest (VAR principal : REAL ;
                             intRate        : REAL);
  {Adds one year's interest.
   Notice the way 'intRate' is used.}
  BEGIN {AddInterest}
    intRate    : intRate/100.00;
    principal := principal + (intRate * principal)
  END;  {AddInterest}

  {----------}

BEGIN {Interest}
  Write       ('Enter principal and interest rate: ');
  ReadLn      (principal, intRate);

  AddInterest (principal, intRate);
  WriteLn     ('New principal: ', principal:6:2);

  AddInterest (principal, intRate);
  WriteLn     ('New principal: ', principal:6:2)
END.  {Interest}
```

[3]Here again we have the analogy we used to start off this chapter. The manuscript editor is compared to a subprogram—a *specialist* at editing textbooks.

What saves us here is pass by value. The change we make to `intRate` inside Procedure `AddInterest` has no effect on the main program's `intRate`. So when Procedure `AddInterest` is called for the second time, the main program's `intRate` is still 5.0:

```
                                  5.0
    AddInterest (principal,   intRate   );

    WriteLn      ('New principal: ', principal:6:2);

                                  5.0
    AddInterest (principal,   intRate   );

    WriteLn      ('New principal: ', principal:6:2)
```

Once again it can be divided by 100.00 to get the correct decimal value 0.05, and the program runs correctly. Thus pass by value is a safety mechanism. Even if we take some foolish risks in our subprogram, pass by value protects us by not allowing the damages to spread to the main program.

restrictions with VAR parameters
Of course, we should admit that there's also some safety built into pass by reference. Take, for instance, the heading

```
    PROCEDURE AddInterest (VAR principal : REAL ;
                                intRate       : REAL);
```

and the call

If you try this, the compiler will give you an error diagnostic. When you use pass by reference, the actual parameter must be a variable. It doesn't make sense to pass the number 200.00 by reference, because passing it by reference would mean that the subprogram can change the value of 200.00. But 200.00 isn't a *variable*. Its value can't be changed.

The same sort of reasoning holds for things like:

```
    PROCEDURE AddInterest (VAR principal : REAL ;
                                intRate       : REAL);
        .
        .
        .
    AddInterest (principal1 + principal2, intRate1 + intRate2);
```

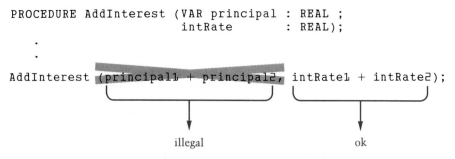

If you try this, the compiler will give you an error diagnostic, because it doesn't make sense to have Procedure `AddInterest` change the value of `principal1 + principal2`. How much of that change would affect `principal1`, and how much would affect `principal2`?

3.3 Exercises

Key Words to Review

accumulator	global	extent
initialization	side effect	

Questions to Answer

QUE 3.3.1 What are the advantages and disadvantages of pass by reference? Of pass by value?

QUE 3.3.2 In your own words, explain the difference between pass by reference and pass by value.

QUE 3.3.3 In a subprogram heading, what can go wrong if you accidentally leave off a VAR where it should be?

QUE 3.3.4 Explain what we mean when we say that "a local variable ceases to exist when the computer returns from the subprogram call." What can we do to "fix" this?

QUE 3.3.5 Can a number, like `100.00`, be the actual parameter when pass by reference is used? If so, why does it work? If not, why not?

Things to Check in a Manual

MAN 3.3.1 With normal subprogram calling, a compiler creates only one copy of the subprogram's code. Then during a run of the program, when the computer reaches a subprogram call, it starts executing that single copy. Thus, in a program containing many calls to the same subprogram, this copy of the subprogram can be executed many times.

This differs from inline execution. With inline execution, the compiler makes several copies of the subprogram's code. One copy is actually substituted at each point where you've placed a call to the subprogram. Does your implementation provide a way to execute subprograms inline? If so, does your manual give advantages and disadvantages of inline calling?

Experiments to Try

EXP 3.3.1 Remove the VAR from the parameter list of Procedure `AddInterest`. See what happens when the main program
a. calls `AddInterest` once
b. calls `AddInterest` a second time

EXP 3.3.2   Consider the version of Procedure `AddInterest` that contains the statement

```
intRate   := intRate/100.0
```

Change `intRate` to a `VAR` parameter in this procedure, and see if the program still gives you the correct answer.

EXP 3.3.3   In Program `Crossover` change one of the calls to Procedure `WriteLnTwo` to

```
WriteLnTwo (home, home)
```

EXP 3.3.4   Make a trace of the following program:

```
PROGRAM TestReference (output);
{Tests your understanding of pass by reference.}
  VAR
    x : INTEGER;

  {----------}

  PROCEDURE AssignToFirst (VAR a, b : INTEGER);
  {What does this procedure do to the variable b?}
  BEGIN {AssignToFirst}
    a := 2;
    WriteLn ('b = ', b:2)
  END;  {AssignToFirst}

  {----------}

BEGIN {TestReference}
  x := 1;
  AssignToFirst (x, x);
  WriteLn ('x = ', x:2)
END.  {TestReference}
```

Then run the program to see if your trace is correct.

EXP 3.3.5   Put the words `BEGIN` and `END` around each of the calls to `WriteLnTwo` in Program `Crossover`.

Changes to Make

CHA 3.3.1   Modify Program `Interest` so that it computes compound interest after some number of years (not just one year). The number of years is entered by the user.

CHA 3.3.2   Modify Program `BarGraph` (Section 3.1) so that it reads values like 1200000000.00 instead of just 12, for "twelve-hundred million dollars."

Scales to Practice

PRA 3.3.1   Write a procedure that uses its parameter(s) to count the number of times it's been called. Every third time it's called it displays the message `That makes three more!`

PRA 3.3.2   Modify the procedure you wrote for Exercise Pra.3.3.1 so that it has an additional `CHAR`-type parameter. The new procedure displays the message `That makes three more As!` every *third* time it receives an `A`. It can receive other characters in between receiving three As. So, for instance, if it's called thirteen times and receives the letters

    B A A C D A A E A E C A C

then it will display the message exactly two times:

    B A A C D A A E A E C A C

PRA 3.3.3   Modify the procedure you wrote for Exercise Pra.3.3.2 so that it displays the message only after it's received three As *in a row*.

PRA 3.3.4   Take your age, subtract 5 from it, multiply the number you get by 3, add 4 to the result, double the number you've obtained, add the result to 22, and finally divide what you've got by 6. This should give you your age again! Write a program that puts this trick to the test by passing a number from one procedure to another. Each of the procedures (called Subtract5, MultBy3, Add4, etc.) has only one parameter.

Programs and Subprograms to Write

WRI 3.3.1   When you buy a particular bond at a discount, you pay $975.61. Ninety days later, when the bond matures, you can redeem it at $1000.00—its face value. Write a program that makes a table showing the value of the bond for each day between the day of purchase and the ninetieth day. Use a subprogram like this section's AddInterest to find the value of the bond from one day to the next.

WRI 3.3.2   The shift lever on a car with an automatic transmission has six positions

        Low1 Low2 Drive Neutral Reverse Park

Inside the car there's some electronic circuitry that keeps track of this, using the following numeric codes:

Low1	Low2	Drive	Neutral	Reverse	Park
1	2	3	0	-1	-10

Write a procedure that keeps track of which position the shift lever is in. It takes a numeric code value (1,2,3,0,−1, or −10) and a movement (2 = move the stick rightward two positions; −1 = move the stick leftward one position; 0 = don't move the stick; etc.) and finds the resulting numeric code value. For example, Start in Neutral (0) and move leftward one position (−1) means go into Drive (3).

Write a main program that calls this procedure several times. The main program starts the car off in Park and repeatedly reads shift lever movements from the keyboard until the car goes back into Park.

3.4

Functions

In Pascal there are two kinds of subprograms: procedures and functions. You've already seen how to create a procedure. In this section you'll see how to create a **function**.

In truth, procedures and functions are very much alike. They differ in a very subtle way: The purpose of a function is to calculate a single value, like the area of a rectangle or the E in $E = mc^2$. On the other hand, the purpose of a procedure is usually to perform an action; for example, to write one of the bars of a bar graph or switch the values of score1 and score2.

Don't become too concerned about the difference between procedures and functions. Everything that you can do with a function can also be done with a procedure, and vice versa. Making the choice between a procedure and a function is a matter of programming style.

Specifications

If you start reading this book at 10:30, and read for 3 hours and 40 minutes, you'll be finished at 2:10.

In this sort of a problem, you're really adding together two "amounts of time" to get a third "amount of time":

	hours	minutes
When you start:	10	30
plus		
How long you work:	3	40
equals		
When you finish:	2	10

Notice that "time amounts" don't get added the way ordinary numbers do. They use DIV and MOD and a few other tricks.

Input: Two "time amounts" (hour1, minute1 and hour2, minute2)

Output: The "sum" (hourNew, minuteNew) of the two time amounts

In general, we'll expect our time amounts to work exactly as they do on a twelve-hour clock. After 12 o'clock comes 1 o'clock; after 59 minutes comes 0 minutes; etc. For simplicity, we'll ignore A.M. and P.M.

Designing a Program

In this section we'll concentrate on just one part of the problem—adding hours together. The MOD operation will help us do it. When we start at 10 o'clock and do three hours' work, we should finish at 1 o'clock:

```
(hr1 + hr2) MOD 12
( 10 +  3 ) MOD 12
     13     MOD 12
         1
```

But if we work only two hours we have to use MOD and then adjust our answer a bit:

```
(hr1 + hr2) MOD 12
( 10 +  2 ) MOD 12
     12      MOD 12
           0
```

which somehow changes into

```
12 o'clock
```

We can fix this by making a few changes in the original MOD formula, but it seems more intuitive to just make a special case for "0 hours":

```
IF hrNew = 0 THEN
   SumOfHours := 12
ELSE
   SumOfHours := hrNew
```

A complete program follows.

Program Example

```
PROGRAM SumOfHoursDriver (input, output);
{Test driver for a function that
 adds together two hour-amounts.}
   VAR
      hour1, hour2, hourNew : INTEGER;
   {----------}
   FUNCTION SumOfHours (hr1, hr2 : INTEGER) : INTEGER;
   {Adds together two hour-amounts.}

      VAR
         hrNew : INTEGER;

   BEGIN {SumOfHours}
      hrNew := (hr1 + hr2) MOD 12;
      IF hrNew = 0 THEN
         SumOfHours := 12
      ELSE
         SumOfHours := hrNew
   END;   {SumOfHours}
   {----------}

BEGIN {SumOfHoursDriver}
   Write  ('Enter (hours space hours): ');
   ReadLn (hour1, hour2);

   hourNew := SumOfHours (hour1, hour2);

   WriteLn  ('Combined time is ', hourNew:2, ' o''clock')
END.   {SumOfHoursDriver}
```

Sample Runs

```
Enter (hours space hours): 10 3
Combined time is  1 o'clock
```
―――――――――
```
Enter (hours space hours): 10 2
Combined time is 12 o'clock
```
―――――――――
```
Enter (hours space hours): 0 0
Combined time is 12 o'clock
```

Observations   At the beginning of this chapter, we drew a comparison between subprograms and specialists. Each subprogram has a certain specialty—like switching the values of two variables or drawing part of a bar graph.

Of course, in real life there are two kinds of specialists. Some specialists perform services, and others answer questions. For instance, a car mechanic is a service specialist. You give the mechanic your car; and when you get your car back, it's been changed somehow (for the better, we hope). But how about an expert witness at a murder trial? The witness is really there to answer a question—Was the suspect insane or not?

In Pascal, a specialist that performs a service is called a procedure, and a specialist that supplies an answer is called a function.

function subprogram heading

- `FUNCTION SumOfHours (hr1, hr2 : INTEGER) : INTEGER;`

  This is the heading for a subprogram whose name is `SumOfHours`. This subprogram accepts two values, the values of `hr1` and `hr2` (its formal parameters), and gives us an answer, the time that's `hr2`-many hours after `hr1`.

  Go back and notice the word *answer* in the preceding paragraph. Since `SumOfHours` gives us an answer, it's called a *function subprogram*. That's why we use the word `FUNCTION`, rather than `PROCEDURE`, in the heading. The answer that's given to us by Function `SumOfHours` is called the function's **result value**.

  Since a number of hours can't have a decimal point, the result value of Function `SumOfHours` is going to be an `INTEGER`. We say that the **result type** of Function `SumOfHours` is `INTEGER`, and in the heading we put : `INTEGER`; after the function's formal parameter list.

  `FUNCTION SumOfHours (hr1, hr2 : INTEGER) : `**`INTEGER;`**

  Remember: Procedures don't supply answers, and they don't have result values, so a procedure heading just ends with a semicolon.

- ```
  IF hrNew = 0 THEN
     SumOfHours := 12
  ELSE
     SumOfHours := hrNew
  ```

establishing a result value

  Inside the function subprogram's body, we give the function a result value by assigning a value to the name of the function. One of these two assignments to the name `SumOfHours` will be executed, and that's how the computer will decide what value the function returns.
  ```

Let's say, for instance, that `hr1` is 10 and `hr2` is 2. Then `hrNew` will be 0, so the `THEN`-part

```
SumOfHours := 12
```

gets executed. So the answer returned by this call to Function `SumOfHours` (that is, the function's result value) will be the number 12.

calling a function

• `hourNew := SumOfHours (hour1, hour2)`

This is how we call a function subprogram from the body of the main program. We don't just write the function's name and a parameter list; we do something with the name. In particular, *we make use of the fact that the function's name has a value.* In this example, we assign that value (the number 12, perhaps) to a variable named `hourNew`. In another program we may have done something like:

```
WriteLn( SumOfHours (hour1, hour2) )
```

That is, we'd use the result value by writing it on the screen.

Now here's a picture to illustrate how values move back and forth when Function `SumOfHours` is called:

```
PROGRAM SumOfHoursDriver (input, output);
      .
      .

   FUNCTION SumOfHours ( hr1, hr2  : INTEGER) : INTEGER;
                      .
                      .
   BEGIN {SumOfHours}
               .
               .

        SumOfHours  :=  12
                      .
                      .

   END;  {SumOfHours}
         .
         .
   BEGIN {SumOfHoursDriver}
         .
         .


   hourNew  :=  SumOfHours  ( hour1, hour2 )
         .
         .

   END.  {SumOfHoursDriver}
```

When the function is called

When returning from the function

Further Discussion

comparing functions with procedures

The text of a function is different from the text of a procedure in two very important ways:

- Inside the function's body, the function's name is given a value.

```
SumOfHours := 12
```

or

```
SumOfHours := hrNew
```

This is because the purpose of a function is to calculate a single value (the function's result value).

In contrast, a procedure's name is never given a value.

- The heading of a function ends with a colon followed by a type name.

```
FUNCTION SumOfHours (hr1, hr2 : INTEGER) : INTEGER;
```

This is called the function's result type. It tells the compiler what type of result value the function will return. If the result value is INTEGER, the function's result type is INTEGER; if the result value is REAL, the function's result type is REAL, etc.

In contrast, the heading of a procedure never ends with a result value.

```
PROCEDURE MakeBar (symbol : CHAR);
```

The call to a function is different from a call to a procedure in one very important way:

- When we call a function, we use its result value.

```
hourNew := SumOfHours (hour1, hour2)
```

In contrast, when we call a procedure, we just give its name.

```
MakeBar (womensSal, 'W')
```

restrictions on the use of a function's name

A call to a function has a value so it can be used as part of an expression. For instance, we can do something like

```
oneHourMore := SumOfHours (hour1, hour2) + 1
```

or even

```
If SumOfHours (hour1, hour2) > 12 THEN
   WriteLn ('Error')
```

But there's one thing we *cannot* do:

Inside the body of a function subprogram, we can assign a value to the function name as many times as we want, but we can never use the function name to refer to the value that we've assigned to it.

Take, for instance, the following illegal code:

```
FUNCTION SumOfHours (hr1, hr2 : INTEGER) : INTEGER;
{Adds together two hour-amounts.}
   VAR
      hrNew : INTEGER;
BEGIN {SumOfHours}
   SumOfHours := (hr1 + hr2) MOD 12;      {← OK}
   IF SumOfHours = 0 THEN                  {← no good}
      SumOfHours := SumOfHours + 12;       {← no good}
   WriteLn (SumOfHours:2)                  {← no good}
END;  {SumOfHours}
```

First we assign a value to SumOfHours. Let's say SumOfHours gets the value 1. That's OK. But then we mistakenly try to use the name SumOfHours to refer to this number 1. That's not legal.

In Chapter 13 we'll talk more about this issue and see that "using" a function's name inside the function's body has a very different meaning from what you might expect. For now, just don't do it. Inside the body of a function, don't use the function's name in a WriteLn, on the right side of an assignment statement, as part of the condition in an IF statement, etc.

Traces

When we make a trace for a function subprogram, we put the function's result value under the function's name

tracing a
function
subprogram

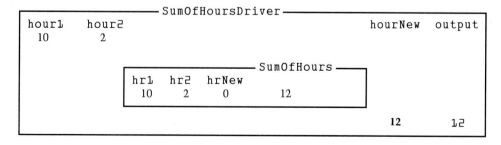

and then when we return from the function, we show how the function's result value is used. In this example, the function's result value is assigned to the variable hourNew.

Programming Style

comparing procedures and functions

There isn't anything mysterious about a function subprogram. It's just like a procedure; but it returns a result value, and its heading looks a bit different. (The statement that calls a function looks a bit different too.) It's just that certain tasks lend themselves nicely to procedures, and others work better when they're written as functions.

To show how procedures and functions are so similar, let's rewrite the program example so that it calls a procedure rather than a function:

```
PROGRAM AddHoursDriver (input, output);
{Test driver for a procedure that
 adds together two hour-amounts.}

  VAR
    hour1, hour2, hourNew : INTEGER;

  {----------}

  PROCEDURE AddHours (hr1, hr2        : INTEGER ;    {Changed!!!}
                           VAR SumOfHours : INTEGER);    {Changed!!!}
  {Adds together two hour-amounts.}

    VAR
      hrNew : INTEGER;

  BEGIN {AddHours}
    hrNew := (hr1 + hr2) MOD 12;
    IF hrNew = 0 THEN
      SumOfHours := 12
    ELSE
      SumOfHours := hrNew
  END;  {AddHours}

  {----------}

BEGIN {AddHoursDriver}
  Write ('Enter (hours space hours): ');
  ReadLn (hour1, hour2);

  AddHours (hour1, hour2, hourNew);                  {Changed!!!}

  WriteLn  ('Combined time is ', hourNew:2, ' o''clock')
END.  {AddHoursDriver}
```

Notice: only a few lines of the program need to be changed (the lines with the comment Changed!!!). In the subprogram heading, the result type is replaced by a VAR parameter, and the subprogram is given a new name.[4]

```
FUNCTION   SumOfHours (hr1, hr2 : INTEGER) : INTEGER;


PROCEDURE  AddHours (hr1, hr2          : INTEGER ;    {Changed!!!}

                          VAR SumOfHours : INTEGER);    {Changed!!!}
```

---

[4]In this discussion, it's handy to use the nickname VAR parameter to refer to "a parameter that's passed by reference."

In the main program, hourNew is no longer the object of an assignment. Instead, it's an actual parameter.

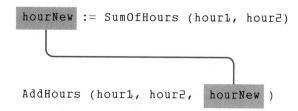

choosing
subprogram
names

That's it! No other changes are necessary.

When we give a procedure or a function a name, we should always remember the following guideline:[5]

A procedure's name should be a verb or a verb phrase. A function's name should be a noun or a noun phrase.

We do this because a procedure *does something* and a function's name *has a value* (that is, a function's name is something). If we follow this guideline, then it's easy to fit our subprogram names into the pseudocode:

Add the Hours, hour1 and hour2, to get the New hour:
    AddHours (hour1, hour2, hourNew)

The New hour is the Sum Of the Hours, hour1 and hour2:
    hourNew := SumOfHours (hour1, hour2)

So how do you know when to create a function rather than a procedure or a procedure instead of a function? There are no hard and fast rules, but there are a few rules of thumb:

Which to use?

1. If you've written a procedure that has exactly one VAR parameter (like Procedure AddHours), then it should probably be changed into a function. After all, the purpose of such a procedure is to compute one value (the value of the VAR variable), and that's exactly what functions are meant to do.

2. If you've written a function that has VAR parameters, then it should probably be changed into a procedure. This function would compute values for its VAR parameters in addition to computing its result value. But a function isn't meant to compute more than one value. Only a procedure should compute more than one value. When a function has a VAR parameter, we say that the function has *side effects*. Side effects are

---

[5]For more on this guideline, see Section 8.3.

undesirable because they violate the compute-one-value philosophy of functions.

3. If you've written a function that has a `ReadLn` in it, then it should probably be changed into a procedure. This is because a function's formal parameter list is supposed to name all the values the function uses to arrive at its result. If we put a `ReadLn` in the middle of the function, it's as if the function is sneaking off to the side (to your keyboard) and getting another value to use. It violates the spirit of the *function* notion.

In several examples to come, we'll see that these rules are by no means absolute.

Testing and Debugging

In the Experiments exercises of Section 2.1 we described syntax errors, run-time errors, and logic errors. Of course we'd like our programs to be error-free, so one might imagine that finding and correcting errors (that is, *debugging*) is an important part of the programming endeavor. In subsections entitled Testing and Debugging, we'll give you hints on detecting and correcting errors in your programs.

Our first hint is about detecting errors in procedures and function subprograms. Take another look at Program `SumOfHoursDriver`. How is the work divided between the function and the main program? Clearly the function does almost all the work. The main program does some input and output, but its principal purpose is to call Function `SumOfHours`.

When we went about solving the problem of adding hour-amounts together, we solved it with a function subprogram. That's fine, but we can't issue a command to tell the operating system to run a subprogram. A subprogram can only run when it's called as part of a complete program. Now eventually we'll put Function `SumOfHours` into a larger program—one that adds minutes as well as hours, has nice looking output, etc. But for now, we just want to see if our Function `SumOfHours` works. So we write a simple program around the function; that is, we write a main program whose sole purpose is to call Function `SumOfHours` so that the function can be run and tested. A main program of this kind is called a **test driver**. We'll be using test drivers over and over again in our program examples and in the exercises.

test driver

3.4   Exercises

Key Words to Review

function	result type	test driver
result value	side effect	

Questions to Answer

QUE 3.4.1   Explain the situations in which we'd use a procedure rather than a function or a function rather than a procedure.

QUE 3.4.2   Explain the differences in syntax between the heading of a procedure and the heading of a function. Why do these syntactic differences make sense, given the different ways in which procedures and functions are used?

QUE 3.4.3   Explain the differences in syntax between a call to a procedure and a call to a function. Why do these syntactic differences make sense, given the different ways in which procedures and functions are used?

QUE 3.4.4   Why do we say that "everything that you can do with a function can also be done with a procedure, and vice versa"?

QUE 3.4.5   Why is it stylistically improper for a function to have a `VAR` parameter?

Experiments to Try

EXP 3.4.1   Remove the entire `IF` statement from Function `SumOfHours`. This means that the name `SumOfHours` never gets anything assigned to it inside the body of the function. Does your implementation tolerate this? If so, what value does the call `SumOfHours (hour1, hour2)` receive?

EXP 3.4.2   Add the statement

```
MakeBar := 9
```

at the end of Procedure `MakeBar` in Section 3.1.

EXP 3.4.3   Remove the final `:INTEGER` from the heading of Function `SumOfHours`.

EXP 3.4.4   In the main body of Program `SumOfHoursDriver`, change

```
hourNew := SumOfHours (hour1, hour2)
```

to

```
SumOfHours (hour1, hour2)
```

Changes to Make

CHA 3.4.1   Modify Program `SumOfHoursDriver` so that it distinguishes between A.M. and P.M.

CHA 3.4.2   Modify Function `SumOfHours` so that it uses a twenty-four-hour clock. Twenty-four-hour clocks (used in many parts of the world) have hours numbered 0 through 23, instead of 1 to 12. With a twenty-four-hour clock, midnight is called 0:00, one minute after midnight is called 0:01, etc.

Programs and Subprograms to Write

WRI 3.4.1   Modify Exercise Wri.2.2.1 so that computing the number of six-packs is done by a function subprogram and counting the number of bottles left over is done by another function subprogram. The reading and writing should be done in the main program.

WRI 3.4.2   Redo Exercise Wri.2.1.5, this time having a function subprogram that accepts the number of tires purchased and returns the price of that many tires.

WRI 3.4.3   Redo Exercise Wri.2.3.1, this time using a function subprogram to compute the commission.

WRI 3.4.4   The price of heating oil is $0.99 per gallon during the summer months (June to August) and $1.15 per gallon during the rest of the year. Write a function that takes an amount of heating oil (in gallons) and a month number (1 to 12) and returns the cost of the oil. Write a main program that reads the amount of heating oil used in each of twelve months and writes the total cost of heating oil for the year.

WRI 3.4.5   In an introductory computer science course there are three programming projects, two exams, and a final. The projects collectively count 30 percent toward the student's grade, the two exams count another 30 percent, and the final counts 40 percent. Each instrument (project, exam, final) is graded on a scale of 1 to 100.

Write a function that takes the six scores for a student's projects, exams, and final and returns an overall course grade in the range of 1 to 100.

Write another function that takes an overall grade, and returns a letter grade (a CHAR-type value) based on the following scale:

A = 90–100
B = 80–89
C = 70–79
D = 60–69
F = below 60

Use these two functions in a main program that reads six scores for a student and writes the student's letter grade.

3.5

Subprograms Calling Other Subprograms

Let's continue with our discussion of the time-amounts problem. In Section 3.4 we added only hours together. In this section we'll add hours and minutes.

Designing a Program   Adding minutes is just a bit more complicated than adding hours. Of course we can use MOD 60 the way we used MOD 12 for hours

```
(min1 + min2) MOD 60
```

But then when we go over 60 minutes, the number of hours gets changed. For instance, if we add 30 minutes and 40 minutes we get 1 hour and 10 minutes. Here's how it's actually calculated:

Calculating hours:		Calculating minutes:	
(min1 + min2) DIV 60		(min1 + min2) MOD 60	
(30 + 40) DIV 60		(30 + 40) MOD 60	
70	DIV 60	70	MOD 60
	1		10

Now let's say we start working at 2:30 and work for 3 hours and 40 minutes. Here's what we get from all the formulas we have so far:

	hours	minutes
When you start:	2	30
plus		
How long you work:	3	40
equals		
When you finish:	5 hours	1 hour + 10 minutes

As a final step, we've got to add 5 hours and 1 hour to get 6 hours (giving a final finishing time of 6:10). Fortunately we already have Function SumOfHours from Section 3.4 to add hour amounts for us.

```
hrNew := SumOfHours (hrNew, hrsFromMinutes)
hrNew := SumOfHours (  5  ,        1     )
hrNew := 6
```

So here's what we have when we put it all together:

```
PROCEDURE AddMinutes  (min1, min2          : INTEGER ;
                       VAR hrNew, minNew : INTEGER);
{Adds together two minute-amounts.}
  VAR
    hrsFromMinutes : INTEGER;
BEGIN {AddMinutes}
  hrsFromMinutes := (min1 + min2) DIV 60;
  hrNew          := SumOfHours (hrNew, hrsFromMinutes);
  minNew         := (min1 + min2) MOD 60
END;  {AddMinutes}
```

But now notice that Procedure AddMinutes contains a call to Function SumOfHours; that is, one subprogram is calling another subprogram. This is certainly a legitimate thing to do. We'll look at it a little more deeply later in this section. For now, let's just look at the code. Our program AddTimes just combines what we did in Section 3.4 with this new procedure AddMinutes. We've also thrown in a couple of procedures to help us do input and output:

- Procedure ReadLnTime prompts for values of hr and min and reads them from the keyboard.
- Procedure WriteLnTime makes the hr and min look like a time of day when it writes them. It writes

  10:02

  instead of

  10 2

The complete code follows.

Program Example

```
PROGRAM AddTimes (input, output);
{Adds together two time-amounts.}

  VAR
    hour1,   minute1,
    hour2,   minute2,
    hourNew, minuteNew : INTEGER;

  {----------}

  PROCEDURE ReadLnTime (VAR hr, min : INTEGER);
  BEGIN {ReadLnTime}
    Write  ('Enter the time (hours space minutes): ');
    ReadLn (hr, min)
  END;   {ReadLnTime}

  {----------}

  FUNCTION SumOfHours (hr1, hr2 : INTEGER) : INTEGER;
  {Adds together two hour-amounts.}

    VAR
      hrNew : INTEGER;

  BEGIN {SumOfHours}
    hrNew := (hr1 + hr2) MOD 12;
    IF hrNew = 0 THEN
      SumOfHours := 12
    ELSE
      SumOfHours := hrNew
  END;   {SumOfHours}

  {----------}

  PROCEDURE AddMinutes  (min1, min2        : INTEGER ;
                         VAR hrNew, minNew : INTEGER);
  {Adds together two minute-amounts.}

    VAR
      hrsFromMinutes : INTEGER;

  BEGIN {AddMinutes}
    hrsFromMinutes := (min1 + min2) DIV 60;
    hrNew          := SumOfHours (hrNew, hrsFromMinutes);
    minNew         := (min1 + min2) MOD 60
  END;   {AddMinutes}

  {----------}

  PROCEDURE WriteLnTime (hr, min : INTEGER);
  BEGIN {WriteLnTime}
    Write  (hr:2);
    Write  (':');
    IF min < 10 THEN
      BEGIN
        Write ('0');
        Write (min:1)
      END
```

```
         ELSE
           Write (min:2);
         WriteLn
      END;  {WriteLnTime}

      {----------}

   BEGIN {AddTimes}
      ReadLnTime (hour1, minute1);
      ReadLnTime (hour2, minute2);

      hourNew := SumOfHours (hour1, hour2);
      AddMinutes (minute1, minute2, hourNew, minuteNew);

      WriteLn;
      Write          ('The combined time is ');
      WriteLnTime (hourNew, minuteNew)
   END.  {AddTimes}
```

**Sample
Runs**

```
Enter the time (hours space minutes): 2 30
Enter the time (hours space minutes): 3 40

The combined time is  6:10
```
————————————
```
Enter the time (hours space minutes): 10 30
Enter the time (hours space minutes):  3 40

The combined time is  2:10
```

Observations

**Who can call
whom?**

If you look at Program AddTimes you'll find two calls to Function
SumOfHours—one call from the main program and another from Procedure AddMinutes.

```
PROGRAM AddTimes (input, output);
       .
       .

{----------}
```

```
FUNCTION SumOfHours (hr1, hr2 : INTEGER) : INTEGER;
       .
       .

BEGIN {SumOfHours}
       .
       .

END;   {SumOfHours}
```

```
{----------}
```

```
PROCEDURE AddMinutes    (min1, min2      : INTEGER ;
                         VAR hrNew, minNew : INTEGER);
       .
       .

BEGIN {AddMinutes}
       .
   hrNew := SumOfHours (hrNew, hrsFromMinutes);
       .
       .

END;   {AddMinutes}
```

```
{----------}
       .
       .

BEGIN {AddTimes}
       .
   hourNew := SumOfHours (hour1, hour2);
       .
       .

END.   {AddTimes}
```

There are several ways to explain why the compiler allows us to do this. The simplest (though not quite accurate) way to explain it is to say that the heading of Function SumOfHours

```
FUNCTION SumOfHours (hr1, hr2 : INTEGER) : INTEGER;
```

comes before each of these calls in the text of the program. So by the time the compiler reaches these calls, it already knows what SumOfHours means and can call the function appropriately. If we moved Function

SumOfHours so that it appeared below Procedure AddMinutes, then Procedure AddMinutes would no longer be allowed to call Function SumOfHours:

```
PROGRAM AddTimes (input, output);
     .
     .
     .
  {----------}
```

```
PROCEDURE AddMinutes    (min1, min2        : INTEGER ;
                         VAR hrNew, minNew : INTEGER);
     .
     .
BEGIN {AddMinutes}
     .
   hrNew := SumOfHours (hrNew, hrsFromMinutes);    ◄──── Now this call is illegal!
     .
END;   {AddMinutes}
```

```
  {----------}
```

```
FUNCTION SumOfHours (hr1, hr2 : INTEGER) : INTEGER;
     .
     .
BEGIN {SumOfHours}
     .
END;   {SumOfHours}
```

```
  {----------}
     .
     .
BEGIN {AddTimes}
     .
   hourNew := SumOfHours (hour1, hour2);
     .
END.   {AddTimes}
```

The compiler would give us an error diagnostic, because when it reached this first call to Function SumOfHours, it wouldn't yet know what SumOfHours means.

Now let's see if we can be a bit more precise about which subprograms can call which other subprograms. There's a rule in Pascal that goes something like this:

Scope Rule: An identifier can be used anywhere after the place where it's declared, as long as it's being used inside the program or subprogram in which it's declared.

In the case of a subprogram name, "using" the name means calling the subprogram. And the name is declared in the subprogram heading. So for subprograms, this rule says

Scope Rule: A subprogram can be called anywhere after the place where its heading appears, as long as it's being called inside the program or subprogram in which its heading appears.

scope   We use the word **scope** to describe the portion of a program in which a particular identifier can be used. So these are called scope rules. The scope rules have lots of subtleties, so we won't analyze them very much here. We'll just shade in the part of Program `AddTimes` where Function `SumOfHours` can be called and notice that both calls to Function `SumOfHours` are legal, because they both appear in the shaded region. More on this in Section 3.8.

```
PROGRAM AddTimes (input, output);
{Adds together two time-amounts.}
   VAR
      hour1,   minute1,
      hour2,   minute2,
      hourNew, minuteNew : INTEGER;
   {----------}
   PROCEDURE ReadLnTime (VAR hr, min : INTEGER);
   BEGIN {ReadLnTime}
      Write ('Enter the time (hours space minutes): ');
      ReadLn (hr, min)
   END; {ReadLnTime}
   {----------}
```

```
FUNCTION SumOfHours (hr1, hr2 : INTEGER) : INTEGER;
{Adds together two hour-amounts.}

    VAR
      hrNew : INTEGER;

  BEGIN {SumOfHours}
    hrNew := (hr1 + hr2) MOD 12;
    IF hrNew = 0 THEN
      SumOfHours := 12
    ELSE
      SumOfHours := hrNew
  END;  {SumOfHours}

  {----------}

  PROCEDURE AddMinutes  (min1, min2         : INTEGER ;
                         VAR hrNew, minNew : INTEGER);
  {Adds together two minute-amounts.}

    VAR
      hrsFromMinutes : INTEGER;

  BEGIN {AddMinutes}
    hrsFromMinutes := (min1 + min2) DIV 60;
    hrNew          := SumOfHours (hrNew, hrsFromMinutes);
    minNew         := (min1 + min2) MOD 60
  END;  {AddMinutes}

  {----------}

  PROCEDURE WriteLnTime (hr, min : INTEGER);
  BEGIN {WriteLnTime}
    Write  (hr:2);
    Write  (':');
    IF min < 10 THEN
      BEGIN
        Write ('0');
        Write (min:1)
      END
    ELSE
      Write (min:2);
    WriteLn
  END;  {WriteLnTime}

  {----------}

BEGIN {AddTimes}
  ReadLnTime (hour1, minute1);
  ReadLnTime (hour2, minute2);

  hourNew := SumOfHours (hour1, hour2);
  AddMinutes (minute1, minute2, hourNew, minuteNew);

  WriteLn;
  Write        ('The combined time is ');
  WriteLnTime (hourNew, minuteNew)
END.  {AddTimes}
```

143

Structure

hierarchy charts

When the subprograms start piling up, the way they do in Program `AddTimes`, it helps to make a diagram. One kind of diagram that's particularly helpful is called a **hierarchy diagram**. A hierarchy diagram is very much like a company's organizational chart.

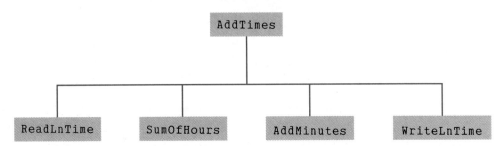

The main program, `AddTimes`, is the "boss" and the subprograms are its "underlings." Another way to think about a hierarchy diagram is to think of it as a family tree. `AddTimes` is the parent, and its children are `ReadLnTime`, `SumOfHours`, and `AddMinutes`, `WriteLnTime`. In fact, looking at the children from left to right, it helps to think of `ReadLnTime` as the oldest child, `SumOfHours` as the next oldest, etc.

Traces

tracing nested
subprogram
calls

When a subprogram calls another subprogram, we get a trace that has a box within a box within the main box.

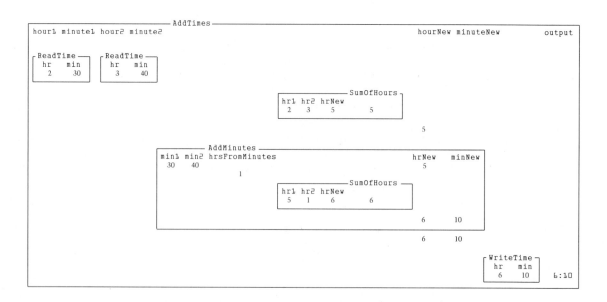

3.5   Exercises

Key Words to Review

scope   hierarchy diagram

Questions to Answer

QUE 3.5.1   Explain, in your own words, the rule that permits Function SumOfHours to be called from Procedure AddMinutes.

QUE 3.5.2   In Program AddTimes can Function SumOfHours be called by a statement that's in the body of Procedure WriteLnTime? Why, or why not?

QUE 3.5.3   Is there a subprogram of Program AddTimes that cannot be called from the main body of Program AddTimes? Why, or why not?

Experiments to Try

EXP 3.5.1   Move Function SumOfHours so that it comes after Procedure AddMinutes.

EXP 3.5.2   Move WriteLnTime so that it's where ReadLnTime currently is, and move ReadLnTime so that it's where WriteLnTime currently is.

Changes to Make

CHA 3.5.1   Rearrange the decomposition of Program AddTimes so that the IF statement that's presently inside Function SumOfHours is a subprogram in and of itself (called Procedure AdjustHours). Rewrite Function SumOfHours so that it calls AdjustHours. Then rewrite Procedure AddMinutes so that it calls AdjustHours (instead of SumOfHours).

Programs and Subprograms to Write

WRI 3.5.1   Write a program that subtracts times. It reads a finishing time and the amount of time it took to do a particular task and writes the starting time of the task.

WRI 3.5.2   Write a program that reads an airplane's departure and arrival times and writes the length of the flight (in hours and minutes).

WRI 3.5.3   Write a program that divides a time amount by an integer value. Your program reads the amount of time allotted for work, and the number of tasks that need to get done in that time. If each of the tasks is to take the same amount of time, how long should each task take?

3.6

Pascal's Pre-Declared Subprograms

In this section we discuss subprograms that have no headings and no bodies. We just call them! We don't need to supply headings or bodies, because these subprograms are built into the Pascal language. They're **pre-declared** subprograms. Any Pascal program can call any of these subprograms.

pre-declared subprograms

We've already used a few of these subprograms:

ReadLn   Reads zero or more values, and then prepares for reading at the start of a new line

WriteLn   Writes zero or more values, and then prepares for writing at the start of a new line

ReadLn and WriteLn

You may be surprised to hear ReadLn and WriteLn referred to as procedures. When you call ReadLn it looks a lot like any other procedure call:

```
ReadLn (base, height)
Switch (score1, score2)
```

but the pre-declared ReadLn procedure is a bit different from a procedure that the programmer could create. Unlike the procedures we've been creating in this chapter, ReadLn can take any number of actual parameters, and the parameters don't need to be of a particular type:

```
VAR
   symbolsNeeded : INTEGER;
   base, height  : REAL;
   a, b, c       : CHAR;
ReadLn (symbolsNeeded);

ReadLn (base, height);

ReadLn (a, b, c)
```

A call to WriteLn can also have any number of actual parameters, and the parameters don't have to be of a particular type. In addition to this, a WriteLn call can have colons in it:

```
PROGRAM WriteLnDemo (output);
{Demonstrates the use of WriteLn.}
   VAR
     i, j : INTEGER;
     r    : REAL;
```

```
BEGIN {WriteLnDemo}
   i := 6;
   j := 2;
   r := 3.14;
   WriteLn (i:3, j:3, r:8:2);
   WriteLn (6:i, 10:j, r:i+j:j)
END.  {WriteLnDemo}
```

The output of Program `WriteLnDemo` takes up two lines. The first line looks like this:

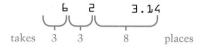

and the second line looks like this:

On the second line of output the two numbers are squished together. It's hard to tell where one number begins and the other ends, because we left only two places to write the 10.

Note that some subprogram calls don't have an actual-parameter list. In Section 2.6 we first called Procedure `WriteLn` without supplying an actual-parameter list.

```
WriteLn;
```

When we call a subprogram without any actual parameters, we just leave off the parentheses. In the case of `WriteLn`, the computer just goes to the start of a new line, without having displayed any values.

Read and Write

We've already used the pre-declared procedure `Write`—an alternative to `WriteLn`. There's also an alternative to `ReadLn`.

`Read`   Reads one or more values; doesn't necessarily prepare for reading at the start of a new line.

`Write` Writes one or more values and doesn't prepare for writing at the start of a new line.

Program Example

```
PROGRAM ReadDemo (input, output);
{Shows how 'Read' works, as opposed to 'ReadLn'.}
   VAR
      x, y : INTEGER;
BEGIN {ReadDemo}
   Write   ('Enter two integers: ');
   Read    (x);
   Read    (y);
   ReadLn;
```

```
Write    ('The integers are:   ');
WriteLn (x:2, y:2);

WriteLn ('--------------------');

Write    ('Enter two integers: ');
ReadLn  (x, y);

Write    ('The integers are:   ');
WriteLn (x:2, y:2)
END.   {ReadDemo}
```

Sample Runs

```
Enter two integers: 1 5
The integers are:   1 5
--------------------
Enter two integers: 3 9
The integers are:   3 9
```

Observations

- ```
  Read    (x);
  Read    (y);
  ReadLn
  ```

  These three statements can take the place of the single statement

  ```
  ReadLn  (x, y)
  ```

  because Read doesn't gobble up everything up to the start of the next line.

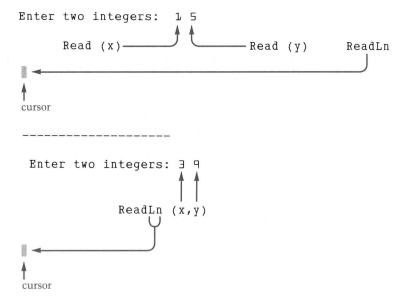
  ```

ReadLn, Read, WriteLn, and Write are pre-declared procedures. The following are a few of Pascal's pre-declared functions, along with programs that demonstrate the way they're used.

Sqrt

Sqrt A function that returns the square root of a number. Accepts either an INTEGER or a REAL number as its actual parameter, but always returns a REAL number.

Program Example

```
PROGRAM UseSqrt (input, output);
{Demonstrates Pascal's pre-declared 'Sqrt' function.}
  VAR
    number  : INTEGER;
    sqrRoot : REAL;
BEGIN {UseSqrt}
  Write  ('Enter an integer: ');
  ReadLn (number);

  sqrRoot := Sqrt (number);
  WriteLn ('Square root is ', sqrRoot:3:1)
END.  {UseSqrt}
```

Sample Runs

```
Enter an integer: 16
Square root is 4.0
```
_____

```
Enter an integer: 10
Square root is 3.2
```
_____

```
Enter an integer: -16
```
Error diagnostic – can't take the square root of a negative number

Sqr

Sqr A function that returns the square of a number. Accepts either an INTEGER or a REAL number as its actual parameter. If you give it an INTEGER it returns an INTEGER. If you give it a REAL it returns a REAL.

Program Example

```
PROGRAM UseSqr (input, output);
{Demonstrates Pascal's pre-declared 'Sqr' function.}
  VAR
    number, square : INTEGER;
BEGIN {UseSqr}
  Write  ('Enter an integer: ');
  ReadLn (number);

  square := Sqr (number);
  WriteLn ('Square is ', square:2)
END.  {UseSqr}
```

Sample Runs

```
Enter an integer: 4
Square is 16
```

```
Enter an integer: 0
Square is  0
```

```
Enter an integer: -4
Square is 16
```

Observations For a variable called x, the value of $Sqr(x)$ is the same as x * x. So why have a pre-declared function Sqr? Well if we want to find the square of

```
(5*x - 3*y/145) + (28 - z)/6 + 31145 MOD q
```

then

```
Sqr ((5*x - 3*y/145) + (28 - z)/6 + 31145 MOD q)
```

is more readable and less error-prone than

```
((5*x - 3*y/145) + (28 - z)/6 + 31145 MOD q) *
          ((5*x - 3*y/145) + (28 - z)/6 + 31145 MOD q)
```

The Sqr version may also run faster because, in that version, the computer will most likely be calculating the value of

```
(5*x - 3*y/145) + (28 - z)/6 + 31145 MOD q
```

only once.

Program Example

Sqr—another example

```
PROGRAM HowSqrWorks (output);
{'Sqr' returns an integer or real,
   depending on what's been passed to it.}

BEGIN {HowSqrWorks}
   WriteLn ('Square of 5   is ', Sqr(5)   :2);
   WriteLn ('Square of 5.0 is ', Sqr(5.0):4:1)
END.  {HowSqrWorks}
```

Sample Runs

```
Square of 5   is 25
Square of 5.0 is 25.0
```

Observations There are really two pre-declared functions, both with the same name Sqr. One of them takes an INTEGER for an actual parameter and returns an INTEGER result. The other takes a REAL number for an actual parameter and returns a REAL result. The Pascal compiler decides which of the pre-declared functions you're trying to call by examining the actual parameter that you supply. This is called **overloading**. The name Sqr is said to be overloaded because it has more than one meaning.

Trunc   Trunc A function that "turns a REAL number into an INTEGER." To be more precise, it accepts a REAL number and cuts off any digits to the right of the decimal point to obtain an INTEGER.

So this function accepts a REAL number as its actual parameter and returns an INTEGER.

**Program
Example**

```
PROGRAM UseTrunc (input, output);
{Demonstrates Pascal's pre-declared 'Trunc' function.}
  VAR
    number: REAL;
    truncation : INTEGER;
BEGIN {UseTrunc}
  Write  ('Enter a real number: ');
  ReadLn (number);

  truncation := Trunc (number);
  WriteLn ('Truncation is ', truncation:3)
END.  {UseTrunc}
```

**Sample
Runs**

```
Enter a real number: 10.6
Truncation is  10
```
_____

```
Enter a real number: -10.6
Truncation is -10
```
_____

```
Enter a real number: 8.0
Truncation is   8
```

Odd

Odd A function that accepts an INTEGER and tells you whether the INTEGER value is odd or not.

**Program
Example**

```
PROGRAM UseOdd (input, output);
{Demonstrates Pascal's pre-declared 'Odd' function.}
  VAR
    number : INTEGER;
BEGIN {UseOdd}
  Write  ('Enter an integer value: ');
  ReadLn (number);

  IF Odd (number) THEN
    WriteLn (number:3, ' is odd.')
  ELSE
    WriteLn (number:3, ' is even.')
END.  {UseOdd}
```

**Sample
Runs**

```
Enter an integer value: 13
 13 is odd.
```
_____

```
Enter an integer value: 42
 42 is even.
```
_____

```
Enter an integer value: 0
  0 is even.
```

Observations Checking `IF Odd (number)` is the same as checking

```
IF number MOD 2 = 1
```

but when you use Function `Odd` the computer can make optimal use of the way `number` is represented in its memory and thus do the checking more quickly. Besides, `Odd (number)` is more self-documenting than `number MOD 2 = 1`.

We've said that Function `Odd` accepts an `INTEGER` but we haven't mentioned what type of value is returned by Function `Odd`. We'll discuss this in Section 8.3.

In the next section we'll see a program that uses these functions to solve a real-life problem.

3.6   Exercises

Key Words to Review

pre-declared subprogram	`Trunc`
`Sqrt`	`Odd`
`Sqr`	
overloading	

Questions to Answer

QUE 3.6.1   What's the difference between `ReadLn` and `Read`? Between `WriteLn` and `Write`?

QUE 3.6.2   Consider each of the pre-declared subprograms discussed in this section. In what way(s) is each different from a subprogram that can be created by the programmer?

Experiments to Try

EXP 3.6.1   Run Program `UseSqrt` and give it a negative value for `number`.

EXP 3.6.2   Run Program `UseSqrt` and give it 0 for the value of `number`.

EXP 3.6.3   Modify Program `UseSqrt` so that `number` is a `REAL` variable. Then run the new program.

EXP 3.6.4   Repeat Exercises Exp.3.6.1 to Exp.3.6.3 with Program `UseSqr` instead of `UseSqrt`.

EXP 3.6.5   Change `:2` to `:4:1` in Program `HowSqrWorks`.

Changes to Make

CHA 3.6.1   Modify Program `UseSqrt` so that it writes the largest `INTEGER` value that's less than or equal to the square root of `number`.

CHA 3.6.2   Modify Program `UseSqr` so that it writes the value of `number` taken to the eighth power.

CHA 3.6.3   Modify Program `UseTrunc` so that, with negative numbers, it "truncates downward." That is, it writes −11 when the user enters −10.6.

3.7

Using Pascal's Pre-Declared Subprograms

Specifications   A builder needs to make diagonal braces for walls of various heights. The lumber used to make the braces come in lengths 2 feet, 4 feet, 6 feet, etc. When it's finally installed, the brace will form the hypotenuse of a triangle, like this:

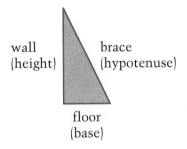

wall
(height)

brace
(hypotenuse)

floor
(base)

Input: The floor and wall measurements (that is, the base and height of the triangle)

Output: The length of lumber that the builder should buy

Designing a Program   First, we have to determine the size of the hypotenuse. To do this we use a formula from trigonometry:

$$\text{hypotenuse} = \sqrt{\text{base}^2 + \text{height}^2}$$

To translate this into Pascal, we use the `Sqr` and `Sqrt` functions.

```
hypotenuse  := Sqrt ( Sqr(base)+Sqr(height) )
```

After we find the hypotenuse there's still more work to do. This hypotenuse could be a number like 10.6 feet. We need to turn this into 12 feet, an even integer that's bigger than 10.6. (Remember—lumber doesn't come in 10.6-foot or 11-foot sizes.) The translation from 10.6 to 12 takes two steps. First we turn 10.6 into 11; then we turn 11 into 12. Here's how:

First step (turning 10.6 into 11)   We find an integer that's at least as large as 10.6. To do this, we truncate the number 10.6 and add 1. Here's an NS chart to show what we do:

Algorithm `NextInteger`:

Truncate the hypotenuse   (that is, shave the .6 off of 10.6, giving 10)
Add 1 (giving 11).

Second step (turning 11 into 12)   We want an algorithm that adds 1 to odd numbers like 11, but leaves even numbers alone.

Algorithm `NextEven`:

The number is odd?	
TRUE	FALSE
Add 1 to the number	Don't add 1

So our program will have two subprograms: `NextInteger` and `NextEven`.
    Now once in a while we'll want to skip the "add 1" step in Algorithm `NextInteger`. For instance, if we start out with a hypotenuse of 8.0, we don't want to force the builder to buy 9 or 10 feet of lumber.

Algorithm `NextInteger`:

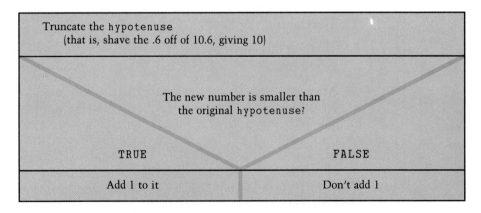

Truncate the hypotenuse (that is, shave the .6 off of 10.6, giving 10)	
The new number is smaller than the original hypotenuse?	
TRUE	FALSE
Add 1 to it	Don't add 1

When we write the code, each of these charts will be turned into a separate subprogram. Meanwhile, the main program has a chart of its own:

PROGRAM Braces:

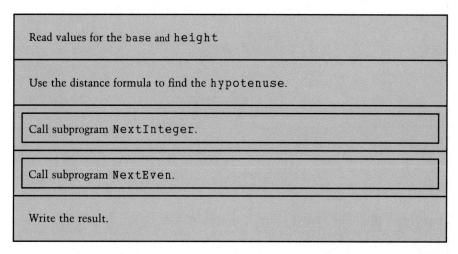

Notice! We make a separate chart for each subprogram and one for the main program.

The code follows.

Program Example

```
PROGRAM Braces (input, output);
{Computes the length of lumber a builder needs to buy
 in order to brace a wall with a certain 'height'
 from a certain 'base'.  Lumber only comes in even
 lengths: 2', 4', 6', etc.}
   VAR
      base, height, hypotenuse : REAL;
      lengthToBuy              : INTEGER;

   {----------}

   FUNCTION NextInteger (hypotenuse : REAL) : INTEGER;
   {Find an integer that's at least as large as the hypotenuse.}
      VAR
         m : INTEGER;
   BEGIN {NextInteger}
      m := Trunc (hypotenuse);
      IF m < hypotenuse THEN
         m := m + 1;
      NextInteger := m
   END;   {NextInteger}

   {----------}
```

```
          FUNCTION NextEven (lengthToBuy : INTEGER) : INTEGER;
          {If necessary, add 1 to 'lengthToBuy', to make it even.}
          BEGIN {NextEven}
            IF Odd (lengthToBuy) THEN
              NextEven := lengthToBuy + 1
            ELSE
              NextEven := lengthToBuy
          END;   {NextEven}

          {----------}

     BEGIN {Braces}
        Write  ('Enter base and height (real space real): ');
        ReadLn (base, height);

        hypotenuse  := Sqrt ( Sqr(base)+Sqr(height) );
        lengthToBuy := NextInteger (hypotenuse);
        lengthToBuy := NextEven (lengthToBuy);

        WriteLn ('Buy ', lengthToBuy:2, ' feet.')
     END.   {Braces}
```

Sample Runs

Here are four sample runs:

```
Enter base and height (real space real): 6.0  8.0
Buy 10 feet.
_____

Enter base and height (real space real): 2.9  4.0
Buy  6 feet.
_____

Enter base and height (real space real): 4.0  4.0
Buy  6 feet.
_____

Enter base and height (real space real): 3.0  4.0
Buy  6 feet.
```

You should write a trace for each of these runs, to make sure you understand how Program Braces works.

Observations

changing a variable's value with a function

- lengthToBuy := NextEven (lengthToBuy)

In this statement, a call to Function NextEven is used to modify the value of the variable lengthToBuy. Looking at the statement, we notice that lengthToBuy is the function's actual parameter, but it's also the variable to which we assign the function's result value. It's quite common for function subprograms to be used this way. It's like a statement that increments a counter:

```
x := x + 1
```

Here the variable x appears on both sides of the :=, just as the variable lengthToBuy appears on both sides of the := when we call Function NextEven.

Further Discussion

In Program `Braces` we used seven of Pascal's pre-declared subprograms—`Write`, `ReadLn`, `Sqr`, `Sqrt`, `Trunc`, `Odd`, and `WriteLn`. Pascal has several other pre-declared subprograms. Here's a list of some of the pre-declared functions:[6]

more
pre-declared
functions

`Round` Takes a `REAL` number and returns an `INTEGER` that's close to the `REAL` number by rounding upward or downward. Here are some examples:

hypotenuse	`Round` (hypotenuse)
31.78	32
31.25	31
31.50	32
−31.78	−32
−31.25	−31
−31.50	−32

Compare `Round` with the pre-declared function `Trunc` from Section 3.6.

`Abs` Takes an `INTEGER` or a `REAL` number and returns the absolute value of the number. If you give it an `INTEGER` it returns an `INTEGER`; if you give it a `REAL` it returns a `REAL`. So, `Abs (−3)` is 3, `Abs (−3.14)` is 3.14, `Abs (3.14)` is 3.14, and `Abs (0)` is 0.

Each of the following functions takes either an `INTEGER` or a `REAL` number for its actual parameter. Either way, these functions always return `REAL` results.

`Sin` Returns the trigonometric sine of the number you give it. (The number is taken as an angle expressed in radians.)

`Cos` Returns the trigonometric cosine of the number you give it. (The number is taken as an angle expressed in radians.)

`ArcTan` Returns the inverse tangent (the arctangent) of the number you give it. (The value that's returned is to be taken as an angle expressed in radians.)

`Ln` Returns the natural logarithm of the number you give it (the logarithm with base e).[7]

`Exp` Takes a number, say x, and returns the value e^x.

---

[6]For a more complete list, see Appendix B.

[7]Note: e is a number, very near 2.71828, that's important in many scientific and mathematical applications.

Ln and Exp can be used to take a number to any power. For instance, you can find the value of $3^{2.5}$ with the statement

```
WriteLn ( Exp(2.5 * Ln (3)) : 8:3 )
```

This comes from the mathematical formula

$$x^y = e^{y \ln x}$$

You can also use Ln to find the logarithm of a number to any base. For instance, you can find the value of $\log_{10}5$ with the statement

```
WriteLn ( Ln(5)/Ln(10) : 8:3 )
```

This comes from the mathematical formula

$$\log_b x = \ln x / \ln b$$

If you need to know why these formulas work, consult any calculus text.

Testing and Debugging

Now let's think about what we might do *after* we've written a program. We'll probably want to make sure the program runs correctly. But what do we mean by "runs correctly"? There are two possibilities:

What does "runs correctly" mean?

- *We've written the specs well.* They provide a precise statement of the problem in complete detail; that is, they tell us exactly how the program should behave—what output it should give for every possible input. Then the program "runs correctly" as long as it satisfies the specifications; that is, for every possible input, the program gives the output that's predicted in the specifications.

- *We've written imprecise or incomplete specs.* Then it's harder to say what "runs correctly" really means. Probably it means something like "for every possible input the program does what we think it should do." If the specs are somewhat complete it means "for some inputs the program does what the specs say, and when the specs don't say anything, the program does what we think it should do." Most likely it means we should rewrite the specs.

In any case, running correctly has something to do with "for every possible input," the program gives the appropriate output.

Now how can we test the program to make sure it's running correctly? If we go by our definition of "running correctly," we might be tempted to run the program millions of times—once for every possible input. The input to Program Braces is two REAL numbers, so we'd have to run Program

Braces with every possible pair of REAL numbers. It's hard to imagine how we'd go about making a list of all possible pairs of REAL numbers:

```
0.0    0.0        ◄──── a base and a height
0.0    0.000001   ◄──── another base and height
0.0    0.000002   ◄──── another base and height
  .                       .
  .                       .
  .                       .
0.000001   0.0              etc.
0.000002   0.0
  .
  .
  .
0.000001   0.000001
  .
  .
  .
6.0    8.0
6.0    8.000001
  .
  .
  .
```

exhaustive
testing

This approach, called **exhaustive testing**, is clearly not the right way to go.

Instead of testing the program with all possible inputs we've got to test it with some sensible collection of inputs called **test cases**. This collection of test cases has to be large enough to convince us that the program runs correctly for all possible inputs, and small enough so that we can complete the testing in a reasonable amount of time.

paths of
execution

Now how do we go about choosing a "sensible" collection of test cases? One approach is to choose an input from each of the program's paths of execution. If we look at the NS chart for Program Braces we can easily see what we mean by a **path of execution**:

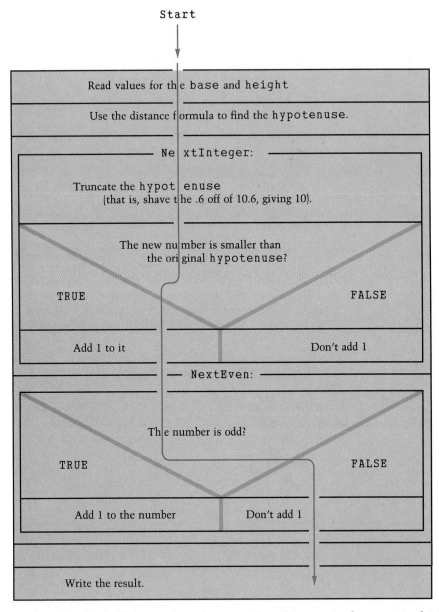

The path that's illustrated in the preceding diagram is the one in which the computer decides to go "left" at the "smaller than original hypotenuse" question and then "right" at the "number is odd" question. There are four possible paths that the computer can take during a run. Each possible path is called a path of execution. Each path is actually a set of choices, deciding which THEN-parts are executed and which are skipped. The four possible paths are:

Path 1 (skip both THEN-parts):

```
IF m < hypotenuse THEN
   m := m + 1



         .
         .

IF Odd (lengthToBuy) THEN
   NextEven := lengthToBuy + 1
ELSE
   NextEven := lengthToBuy
         .
         .
```

Input that makes Program Braces take Path 1:

6.0   8.0

Path 2 (execute both THEN-parts):

```
IF m < hypotenuse THEN
   m := m + 1
         .
         .
         .
IF Odd (lengthToBuy) THEN
   NextEven := lengthToBuy + 1
ELSE
   NextEven := lengthToBuy
         .
```

Input that makes Program Braces take Path 2:

2.9   4.0

Path 3 (skip one THEN-part):

```
IF m < hypotenuse THEN
   m := m + 1
         .
         .
         .
IF Odd (lengthToBuy) THEN
   NextEven := lengthToBuy + 1
ELSE
   NextEven := lengthToBuy
         .
         .
```

Input that makes Program Braces take Path 3:

4.0   4.0

Path 4 (skip the other THEN-part):

```
IF m < hypotenuse THEN
   m := m + 1
         .
         .
         .
IF Odd (lengthToBuy) THEN
   NextEven := lengthToBuy + 1
ELSE
   NextEven := lengthToBuy
         .
         .
         .
```

Input that makes Program
Braces take Path 4:

3.0   4.0

Notice that in the Sample Runs for Program Braces we did four runs. Each run represents one of the four possible paths of execution. (Check this! See Exercise Que.3.7.5.)

In any case, we've managed to use the program's paths of execution to guide us in choosing test cases. Instead of testing Program Braces with a large and random set of inputs, we've chosen one input from each path of execution. We can think of it in the following way:

The set of all possible inputs to Program Braces is a huge collection of REAL-number pairs. This collection is naturally divided into four groups:

The paths of execution of Program Braces:

Path 1	Path 2
Path 3	Path 4

From each path we've chosen a representative input—an input that will represent all the inputs in that path when we're testing the program.

The paths of execution of Program Braces:

Path 1	2.9 4.0
6.0 8.0 Path 1	Path 2
4.0 4.0 Path 3	Path 4
	3.0 4.0

Now we can't be absolutely sure that the program runs correctly after we've tested it by running it four times. But we can't possibly do exhaustive testing; and by choosing a representative from each path of execution, at least we know that we've tried every "road" on the "map" at least once.

glass box testing

Using paths of execution is one example of something we call **glass box testing**. If we have some understanding of the way a program or subprogram works, we call it a glass box. Recall from Section 2.4 that a glass box is a box that we can "see into." We have to see the internal workings of Program Braces in order to figure out what its paths of execution are. (We have to look at its IF statement and decide which THEN-parts are skipped and which are not skipped.)

Using paths of execution is a good way to test a program, but it's not the only way. In a very large program, the number of paths of execution can be enormous. We'll explore other ways to choose test cases in the chapters to come.

3.7 Exercises

Key Words to Review

Round	ArcTan	test cases
Abs	Ln	path of execution
Sin	Exp	glass box testing
Cos	exhaustive testing	

Questions to Answer

QUE 3.7.1 What's the difference between Trunc and Round?

QUE 3.7.2 Why isn't it always practical to use exhaustive testing to find out if a program works correctly?

QUE 3.7.3 Find all paths of execution of Program Scores in Section 2.3.

QUE 3.7.4 Find all paths of execution of Program Switcher in Section 2.4.

QUE 3.7.5 You should make sure that each of this section's Sample Runs is in the path of execution that we claim it's in. Write a trace for each of these runs. For each trace, check to make sure that we've labeled the run with the correct path number.

Things to Check in a Manual

MAN 3.7.1 Find a list of the pre-declared subprograms that are provided by your implementation.

Experiments to Try

EXP 3.7.1   Change the main body of Program `Braces` so that it looks like this:

```
BEGIN {Braces}
   Write  ('Enter base and height (real space real): ');
   ReadLn (base, height);

   Write  ('Buy ');
   Write  (NextEven(NextInteger(Sqrt(Sqr(base)+Sqr(height)))):2);
   WriteLn (' feet.')
END.  {Braces}
```

EXP 3.7.2   What happens when you apply `Round` to a number that's got zeros to the right of the decimal point, like `3.000`?

Changes to Make

CHA 3.7.1   Rewrite `NextInteger` so that it's a procedure.

CHA 3.7.2   Modify Program `Braces` so that the value of the `hypotenuse` is found by calling a function subprogram.

CHA 3.7.3   Add statements to various parts of Program `Braces` so that when it's done running, it writes the number of the path of execution that was taken (1,2,3, or 4).

Scales to Practice

PRA 3.7.1   Write and test a function that rounds an `INTEGER` value to the nearest hundred. For example, it accepts 5293 and returns 5300.

PRA 3.7.2   *(This exercise requires knowledge about trigonometry.)* Use Pascal's pre-declared subprograms to write functions that find
a. the tangent of an angle
b. the secant of an angle
c. the inverse sine of a number (given in radians).

Programs and Subprograms to Write

WRI 3.7.1   The savings plan at your bank pays 6 percent interest each year, and at the end of each year you take the interest and deposit it back into the plan. To find out how much money you have after n-many years, you can use the formula

Amount after *n* years = original principal $\star$ $(1 + 0.06/n)^n$

Write a function subprogram that takes the original principal, the interest rate, and the number of years, and returns the amount of money you have after that many years. In testing this function subprogram, compare its result with the answers you get when you use Program `Interest` from Section 3.3.

WRI 3.7.2   Do you know the square root of 9? How accurately can you guess the square root of 12? Write a procedure that accepts an integer and a real number (like 12 and 3.47) and writes a message such as

```
3.47 is within 0.01 of the square root of 12
```

The digits of the "within" number should be mostly 0s along with a single 1 (like 10, 0.1, 0.0001, etc.). To test your procedure, write a main program that reads an integer n and then repeatedly asks the user for guesses about the square root of n.

WRI 3.7.3 *(An example from biology)* Measurements of the bones of many mammals show that the diameter, *d*, of a species' femur (its thighbone) is related to the mass, *m*, of a typical member of the species by the following formula:

$$d = 5.2m^{0.36}$$

In this equation, *d* is given in millimeters and *m* is given in kilograms. Write a function subprogram that takes a mammal species' mass and returns the diameter of the species' femur.

WRI 3.7.4 *(A continuation of Exercise Wri.3.7.3)* Now you might be interested in knowing the approximate size of your *own* femur. Write some functions to convert back and forth between English and metric system units. Here are the conversion formulas:

1 pound = 0.454 kilograms (when measured on Earth)
1 inch = 25.4 millimeters

Then write a main program that reads your weight, in pounds, and writes the approximate diameter, in inches, of your femur.

WRI 3.7.5 *(To do this problem, it helps to know something about quadratic equations.)* Write a program to use the quadratic formula

$$x = \frac{-b + \sqrt{b^2 - 4ac}}{2a} \quad \text{or} \quad \frac{-b - \sqrt{b^2 - 4ac}}{2a}$$

to solve equations of the form

$$ax^2 + bx + c = 0$$

Your program will be aborted if you try to use Sqrt to find the square root of a negative number. So put in some code to check the value of $b^2 - 4ac$ and print a warning message if it's negative (or, if possible, have your program print a message and then halt. See Exercise Man.3.1.2.)

WRI 3.7.6 *(To do this problem, you need to know about* x-y *coordinates—from geometry.)* Let's say we have two points (x_1, y_1) and (x_2, y_2) on a plane. The distance between these two points is given by the formula

$$\text{dist} = \sqrt{(x_2 - x_1)^2 + (y_2 - y_1)^2}$$

Write a function subprogram that accepts the coordinates of two points and computes the distance between them.

WRI 3.7.7 *(Continuation of Exercise Wri.3.7.6)* A triangle is *equilateral* if all three of its sides have the same length. It's called *isosceles* if only two of its sides have the same length. It's called *scalene* if its sides all have different lengths. Write a program that reads coordinates for three points in the x-y plane, and writes a message telling what kind of triangle is formed by the points.

WRI 3.7.8 *(This exercise uses some concepts from physics.)* An "amount of sound" is often measured in units called *decibels*. The formula is

$$\text{sound level in decibels} = 10 \star \log_{10} \frac{\text{sound intensity}}{\text{intensity of the quietest audible sound}}$$

The intensity of quietest audible sound is around 10^{-12} watts per square meter; a human voice is normally about 3.1×10^{-6} watts per square meter; and the painful sound of a subway train screeching to a halt is around 1 watt per square meter. Write a function subprogram that accepts a value for sound intensity and computes the sound level in decibels. Find the values of your function for the following sounds:

Sound	Sound intensity (in watts per square meter)
whispering	1.6×10^{-6}
the sound inside a car at 60 mph	3.1×10^{-5}
car without a muffler	1.0×10^{-2}

WRI 3.7.9   *(This exercise uses some concepts from physics.)* To compute the location of an "event" in Einstein's theory of relativity, we use the *Lorentz transformation.* Assume that one observer observes an event at location x_1 and time t_1. A different observer is moving past the first observer with speed v. This second observer will measure the location of the event to be

$$x_2 = \frac{x_1 - vt_1}{\sqrt{1 - (v/c)^2}}$$

where c is the speed of light (186,000 miles per second). Write and test a function subprogram that accepts values for x_1, t_1, and v, and returns the value of x_2.

WRI 3.7.10   *(Continuation of Exercise Wri.3.7.9)* Einstein's theory of relativity does strange and unexpected things to time. In the situation described in the preceding exercise, the two observers will disagree on the time at which the event occurred. The second observer will measure the time of the event to be

$$t_2 = \frac{t_1 - (vx_1/c^2)}{\sqrt{1 - (v/c)^2}}$$

Write a function subprogram that accepts values for x_1, t_1, and v, and returns the value of t_2.

3.8

Nested Decomposition

When my child isn't feeling well, I take the child to a pediatrician—a specialist in dealing with children's health. If the pediatrician suspects that it's a behavioral problem, then we get referred to a child psychologist—a subspecialist in dealing with a particular aspect of children's health. The moral to this story is that a specialist can refer a problem to another specialist.

Here's what we have if we translate all this into the language of computing: If a main program can have a subprogram, what about the subprogram having a "sub-subprogram"? It's not only possible—in some cases it's also desirable. In this section we'll see why.

Specifications   The income of the Harriet Ritter Trucking company is based on the total mileage driven by its trucks. It's $1.60 per mile. The firm's regular operating costs (for gas, drivers' salaries, etc.) are $1.10 per mile. But in addition to its regular operating costs, the firm pays yearly road taxes based on the following formula:

Road tax = $2,500.00 +
$0.17 for each mile driven in excess of 5,000 miles.

The first $2,500.00 is called the base tax amount and the extra $0.17 per mile is called the secondary tax rate. Neither tax is levied for companies that are "inactive"; that is, companies whose trucks travel 0 miles in a given year.

The firm's profit is equal to its income minus its regular operating costs and road taxes. We want a program that makes a table showing the firm's profits for mileages ranging from 0 miles to 30,000 miles, in increments of 2,000 miles.

Designing a Program   The specs say "a table showing the firm's profits for mileages ranging from 0 miles to 30,000 miles," so we'll need a loop:

Main program:

For the mileages 0, 2000, 4000, etc., up to 30000,
    write the mileage, and the corresponding Profit.

So how do we compute the Profit? Let's create a function to do it:

Main program:

    Function Profit:
        The code to compute the Profit goes here.
For the mileages 0, 2000, 4000, etc., up to 30000,
    write the mileage, and write Profit(mileage).

Function Profit is a "specialist"—an expert at doing the Profit computation. By putting Function Profit in the pseudocode, we're delaying details about the way in which the profit is computed. At this point, we're concentrating on the main loop—the topmost part of the problem.

Now the specs say that "the firm's profit is equal to its income minus its operating costs and road use taxes," so we'll have

Main program:

    Function Profit:
        Profit := Income − operating Cost − Tax

For the mileages 0, 2000, 4000, etc., up to 30000,
    write the mileage, and write Profit(mileage).

So in order to compute the Profit, we need to compute the Income, the operating Cost, and the Tax. Why not have the Profit function call on three other functions—"experts" at doing the Income, Cost, and Tax computations?

Main program:

    Function Profit:

        Function Income:
            The code to compute the Income goes here.

        Function Cost:
            The code to compute the Cost goes here.

        Function Tax:
            The code to compute the Tax goes here.

        Profit := Income − operating Cost − Tax

For the mileages 0, 2000, 4000, etc., up to 30000,
    write the mileage, and write Profit(mileage).

We're thinking about how the profit is to be computed, but still we're delaying details. We're delaying details about the way in which the income, operating cost, and road tax are computed.

Now look once again at this pseudocode and notice where we're putting Functions Income, Cost, and Tax: we're putting them inside Function Profit. They'll be functions within a function—subprograms of the Profit subprogram. Why? Because computing the income, operating cost, and road tax are *subproblems* of the Profit problem. Computing the road tax is something we have to do in order to compute the profit, just as computing the profit is something we have to do in order to solve the main problem. When we think about writing the main loop, we want to put aside the details of computing the profit. Similarly, when we get around to writing a formula to compute the profit, we want to defer the details of computing the road tax. This is top-down thinking. It leads us naturally to writing a subprogram within a subprogram.

When we finally write the code, we'll say that Functions Income, Cost, and Tax are local to Function Profit. That's because these functions will be declared within Function Profit and can be called only by Function Profit. It's very much like a subprogram having its own local **nested** variables. When we declare one subprogram to be local to another **subprograms** subprogram, we say that subprograms are being **nested**

Of course, the nesting can go on for many levels. For instance, when it comes to computing Tax we have to consider the BaseTax and the SecondaryTax. This gives us two subprograms within the Tax subprogram.

Main program:
   Function Profit:
      Function Income:
         The code to compute the Income goes here.
      Function Cost:
         The code to compute the Cost goes here.
      Function Tax:
         Function BaseTax:
            The code to compute the BaseTax goes here.
         Function SecondaryTax:
            The code to compute the SecondaryTax goes here.
         The code to compute the Tax goes here.
      Profit := Income − operating Cost − Tax
   For the mileages 0, 2000, 4000, etc., up to 30000,
      write the mileage, and write Profit(mileage).

Now, at last, here's the code:

Program Example

```
PROGRAM Trucking (output);
{Makes a table of trucking-company profits for
 mileages ranging from 0 to 30000 miles.}
   CONST
      startMiles      =      0   ;
      stopMiles       = 32000    ;
      milesIncrement  =  2000    ;
      incomePerMile   =      1.60;
      costPerMile     =      1.10;
      baseTaxAmount   =  2500.00;
      cutoff          =  5000    ;
      secTaxRate      =      0.17;
   VAR
      mileage : startMiles..stopMiles;
   {----------}
   FUNCTION Profit (mileage : INTEGER) : REAL;
   {Given a particular mileage, computes the profit.}
      {----------}
      FUNCTION Income (mileage : INTEGER) : REAL;
      {Given a particular mileage, computes the income.}
      BEGIN {Income}
         Income := mileage * incomePerMile
      END;   {Income}
```

```
{----------}
FUNCTION Cost (mileage : INTEGER) : REAL;
{Given a particular mileage, computes the operating cost.}
BEGIN {Cost}
  Cost := mileage * costPerMile
END;  {Cost}

{----------}
FUNCTION Tax (mileage : INTEGER) : REAL;
{Given a particular mileage, computes the road tax.}

  FUNCTION BaseTax (mileage : INTEGER) : REAL;
  {Computes the base tax.}
  BEGIN {BaseTax}
    IF mileage = 0 THEN
      BaseTax := 0.00
    ELSE
      BaseTax := baseTaxAmount
  END;  {BaseTax}

  {----------}
  FUNCTION SecondaryTax (mileage : INTEGER) : REAL;
  {Computes the secondary tax.}
  BEGIN {SecondaryTax}
    IF mileage <= cutoff THEN
      SecondaryTax := 0.00
    ELSE
      SecondaryTax := secTaxRate * (mileage - cutoff)
  END;  {SecondaryTax}

  {----------}

BEGIN {Tax}
  Tax := BaseTax (mileage) + SecondaryTax (mileage)
END;  {Tax}

{----------}
BEGIN {Profit}
  Profit := Income(mileage) - Cost(mileage) - Tax(mileage)
END;  {Profit}

{----------}
BEGIN {Trucking}
  WriteLn ('Miles    Profit');

  mileage := startMiles;
  WHILE mileage < stopMiles DO
    BEGIN
      WriteLn (mileage:5, Profit(mileage):10:2);
      mileage := mileage + milesIncrement
    END
END.  {Trucking}
```

Sample Runs

```
Miles      Profit
    0        0.00
 2000    -1500.00
 4000     -500.00
 6000      330.00
 8000      990.00
10000     1650.00
12000     2310.00
14000     2970.00
16000     3630.00
18000     4290.00
20000     4950.00
22000     5610.00
24000     6270.00
26000     6930.00
28000     7590.00
30000     8250.00
```

Observations

- CONST
  ```
  startMiles      =        0   ;
  stopMiles       =    32000   ;
  milesIncrement  =     2000   ;
  incomePerMile   =        1.60;
  costPerMile     =        1.10;
  baseTaxAmount   =     2500.00;
  cutoff          =     5000   ;
  secTaxRate      =        0.17;
  ```

constant
definitions

This is called the **constant definition** part of a program. A **constant** is an identifier whose value cannot be changed during the run of the program. In Program Trucking the names startMiles, stopMiles, miles-Increment, etc. are constants. We use these constants at several points in the program. We use them in the VAR declaration to define a subrange for the variable mileage

```
VAR
   mileage : startMiles..stopMiles;
```

and we use them many times in the body of the program

```
SecondaryTax := secTaxRate * (mileage - cutoff)
```

A constant definition part must come before any VAR declaration parts, as in Program Trucking. Notice that constant definitions look a bit different from VAR declarations. They don't have colons in them. Instead, they have equal signs (=).

Now here are some things we *cannot* do with constants: We can't have a statement that changes the value of a constant.

```
ReadLn (startMiles)
stopMiles :=stopMiles + 500
```

We can't even have code that *threatens* to change the value of a constant, like the VAR in

```
PROCEDURE Adjust (VAR m : INTEGER);
        .
        .
        .
Adjust (milesIncrement)
```

• PROGRAM Trucking (output);
```
        .  .
          .
VAR
   mileage : startMiles..stopMiles;
{----------}
FUNCTION Profit (mileage : INTEGER) : REAL;
```

type names in formal parameter lists

Compare the declarations of mileage in the main program and in the functions' formal parameter lists. In the functions, we dispense with subranges and declare mileage to be an ordinary INTEGER. Why? Because parameter lists like

```
FUNCTION Profit (mileage : 0..32000) : REAL;
```

or

```
FUNCTION Profit (mileage : startMiles..stopMiles) : REAL;
```

aren't allowed in Pascal. You might think this is an arbitrary rule and that you'd never know about the rule unless you read this page. But that's not the case at all. Look at the syntax diagram for a formal parameter list:

formal parameter list:

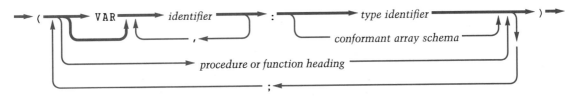

There's no mention of a subrange along the top line of the diagram. All we can put after the colon is a type identifier—a single identifier that's the name of some type.

So what do we do if we want to protect the `mileages` in our subprograms with subranges? We'll see what we can do when we get to Section 4.2.

In Section 3.5 we talked about the conditions under which one subprogram can call another subprogram. Now we need to elaborate on that discussion. Recall the Scope rule in Pascal, which said

> Scope Rule: An identifier can be used anywhere after the place where it's declared, as long as it's being used inside the program or subprogram in which it's declared.

In the case of a subprogram name, "using" the name meant calling the subprogram. And the name was declared in the subprogram heading. So for subprograms, this rule said

> A subprogram can be called anywhere after the place where its heading appears, as long as it's being called inside the program or subprogram in which its heading appears.

In this section we look carefully at that last phrase "as long as it's being called inside the program or subprogram in which its heading appears." In particular, the part of Program `Trucking` where Function `Income` can be called is shaded on the next two pages:

```
PROGRAM Trucking (output);
{Makes a table of trucking-company profits for
 mileages ranging from 0 to 30000 miles.}
   CONST
     startMiles      =       0   ;
     stopMiles       = 32000     ;
     milesIncrement  =  2000     ;
     incomePerMile   =       1.60;
     costPerMile     =       1.10;
     baseTaxAmount   =  2500.00;
     cutoff          =  5000     ;
     secTaxRate      =       0.17;
   VAR
     mileage : startMiles..stopMiles;

   {----------}

   FUNCTION Profit (mileage : INTEGER) : REAL;
   {Given a particular mileage, computes the profit.}

     {----------}

     FUNCTION Income (mileage : INTEGER) : REAL;
     {Given a particular mileage, computes the income.}
     BEGIN {Income}
       Income := mileage * incomePerMile
     END;   {Income}

     {----------}

     FUNCTION Cost (mileage : INTEGER) : REAL;

     {Given a particular mileage, computes the operating cost.}
     BEGIN {Cost}
       Cost := mileage * costPerMile
     END;   {Cost}

     {----------}

     FUNCTION Tax (mileage : INTEGER) : REAL;
     {Given a particular mileage, computes the road tax.}

       FUNCTION BaseTax (mileage : INTEGER) : REAL;
       {Computes the base tax.}
       BEGIN {BaseTax}
         IF mileage = 0 THEN
           BaseTax := 0.00
         ELSE
           BaseTax := baseTaxAmount
       END;   {BaseTax}

       {----------}
```

```
      FUNCTION SecondaryTax (mileage : INTEGER) : REAL;
      {Computes the secondary tax.}
      BEGIN {SecondaryTax}
        IF mileage <= cutoff THEN
          SecondaryTax := 0.00
        ELSE
          SecondaryTax := secTaxRate * (mileage - cutoff)
      END;  {SecondaryTax}


      {----------}

    BEGIN {Tax}
      Tax := BaseTax(mileage) + SecondaryTax(mileage)
    END;  {Tax}


    {----------}

  BEGIN {Profit}
    Profit := Income(mileage) - Cost(mileage) - Tax(mileage)
  END;  {Profit}

  {----------}
BEGIN {Trucking}
  WriteLn ('Miles    Profit');

  mileage := startMiles;
  WHILE mileage < stopMiles DO
    BEGIN
      WriteLn (mileage:5, Profit(mileage):10:2);
      mileage := mileage + milesIncrement
    END
END.  {Trucking}
```

It includes code from the heading of Function Income on downward, but it only includes the code that's inside Function Profit—the subprogram in which Function Income appears. This is why we say that Function Income is local to Function Profit. Function Income can't be called from anywhere outside Function Profit. For instance, the following call would be illegal and would cause the compiler to give you an error diagnostic:

```
PROGRAM Trucking (output);

   {----------}
```

```
FUNCTION Profit (mileage : INTEGER) : REAL;

   {----------}

   FUNCTION Income (mileage : INTEGER) : REAL;
   BEGIN {Income}
      .
   END;   {Income}


   {----------}

   FUNCTION Cost (mileage : INTEGER) : REAL;
   BEGIN {Cost}
      .
   END;   {Cost}


   {----------}

   FUNCTION Tax (mileage : INTEGER) : REAL;

   BEGIN {Tax}
      .
      .
   END;   {Tax}

   {----------}

BEGIN {Profit}
      .
END;   {Profit}
```

```
   {----------}
BEGIN {Trucking}
      .
   WriteLn ( Income(mileage):8:2 )  ◀── This call is illegal!
      .
END.   {Trucking}
```

This is illegal because

- Function Income is declared inside Function Profit, but
- the call to Function Income is in the main body, not anywhere inside Function Profit.

At first this may seem to be an unfair restriction, but it's actually a good safeguard. By making Income be local to Function Profit, we're saying that we expect Income to be called only from Function Profit and that the compiler should interpret any other call to Income as an error—an accident about which we want to be notified.

Structure

nesting vs. no
nesting

In Section 3.5 we made a hierarchy diagram of Program AddTimes. The relationship among the various parts of the program was simple—we had a main program and four subprograms. So in the hierarchy diagram we had a parent and four children.

Since Program Trucking has nested subprograms, the hierarchy diagram for Program Trucking has grandchildren in it.

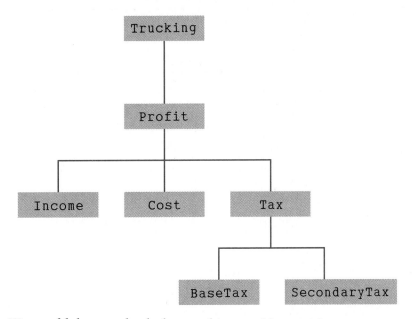

We could have solved the trucking problem without using nested subprograms:

```
PROGRAM Trucking2 (output);
{Makes a table of trucking-company profits for
 mileages ranging from 0 to 30000 miles.}

  CONST
    startMiles      =       0   ;
    stopMiles       = 32000     ;
    milesIncrement  =  2000     ;
    incomePerMile   =     1.60;
    costPerMile     =     1.10;
    baseTaxAmount   =  2500.00;
    cutoff          =  5000     ;
    secTaxRate      =     0.17;
  VAR
    mileage : startMiles..stopMiles;

  {----------}
```

```
FUNCTION Income (mileage : INTEGER) : REAL;
{Given a particular mileage, computes the income.}
BEGIN {Income}
  Income := mileage * incomePerMile
END;  {Income}

{----------}

FUNCTION Cost (mileage : INTEGER) : REAL;
{Given a particular mileage, computes the operating cost.}
BEGIN {Cost}
  Cost := mileage * costPerMile
END;  {Cost}

{----------}

FUNCTION BaseTax (mileage : INTEGER) : REAL;
{Computes the base tax.}
BEGIN {BaseTax}
  IF mileage = 0 THEN
    BaseTax := 0.00
  ELSE
    BaseTax := baseTaxAmount
END;  {BaseTax}

{----------}

FUNCTION SecondaryTax (mileage : INTEGER) : REAL;
{Computes the secondary tax.}
BEGIN {SecondaryTax}
  IF mileage <= cutoff THEN
    SecondaryTax := 0.00
  ELSE
    SecondaryTax := secTaxRate * (mileage - cutoff)
END;  {SecondaryTax}

{----------}

FUNCTION Tax (mileage : INTEGER) : REAL;
{Given a particular mileage, computes the road tax.}
BEGIN {Tax}
  Tax := BaseTax (mileage) + SecondaryTax (mileage)
END;  {Tax}

{----------}

FUNCTION Profit (mileage : INTEGER) : REAL;
{Given a particular mileage, computes the profit.}
BEGIN {Profit}
  Profit := Income(mileage) - Cost(mileage) - Tax(mileage)
END;  {Profit}

{----------}
```

```
BEGIN {Trucking2}
  WriteLn ('Miles      Profit');

  mileage := startMiles;
  WHILE mileage < stopMiles DO
    BEGIN
      WriteLn (mileage:5, Profit(mileage):10:2);
      mileage := mileage + milesIncrement
    END
END.  {Trucking2}
```

In this new program `Trucking2`, all functions are just subprograms of the main program. None of them are local to any of the others. Here's the new hierarchy diagram:

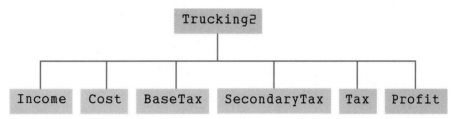

All the functions in this diagram are **siblings**. If we wanted to call Function `Income` from the main program, we could certainly do it.

```
PROGRAM Trucking2 (output);
    .
    .
    {----------}

    FUNCTION Income (mileage : INTEGER) : REAL;
    BEGIN {Income}
        .
    END;  {Income}

    {----------}

    FUNCTION Cost (mileage : INTEGER) : REAL;
    BEGIN {Cost}
        .
    END;  {Cost}

    {----------}
```

```
FUNCTION BaseTax (mileage : INTEGER) : REAL;
BEGIN {BaseTax}
   .
END;      {BaseTax}
```

{----------}

```
FUNCTION SecondaryTax (mileage : INTEGER) : REAL;
BEGIN {SecondaryTax}
   .
END; {SecondaryTax}
```

{----------}

```
FUNCTION Tax (mileage : INTEGER) : REAL;

   .
BEGIN {Tax}

   .
END;   {Tax}
```

{----------}

```
FUNCTION Profit (mileage : INTEGER) : REAL;
BEGIN {Profit}
   .
END;   {Profit}
```

{----------}

```
BEGIN {Trucking2}
   .
   .
   WriteLn ( Income(mileage):8:2 )   ←── Now this call is legal!
   .
END.   {Trucking2}
```

Sometimes it's best to use subprogram nesting and other times it's not. If you never want to compute Income on its own, only Income as a term in the formula for Profit, then you want to make Income be a subprogram of Function Profit and thus protect yourself from accidentally calling Income in any other context. On the other hand, if at times you may want to compute Income for its own sake, then Function Income

safety in nesting

shouldn't be nested within any other subprograms. It's all a question of what you need. You must always weigh the anticipated need for a subprogram against the safety of knowing that a subprogram won't accidentally be called from the wrong part of the code.

Programming Style

how to decompose

Dividing a program into subprograms is a little bit like cutting it into pieces. How do you know where to make the cuts?

Often the pseudocode gives you some good clues. First, think of a subprogram as a unit that "does" something. Any "doing" should be represented in the pseudocode as a verb. So to find the subprograms hidden in the pseudocode, look for the important verbs. For instance, in the pseudocode for the bar-graphs problem, each occurrence of the verb "make" in

    For each of the three years,
        make a women's bar,
        make a men's bar.

becomes a subprogram.

When you use this method to create subprograms, it's very likely that each subprogram you create will "do" one and only one thing, corresponding to the action of one and only one verb. This is good, because a subprogram shouldn't do many different unrelated things. A subprogram that does too many things doesn't hold itself together very well in the programmer's mind. When a subprogram does one and only one thing, we **cohesion** say that the subprogram has a property called **cohesion**.

In this chapter we've examined several ways to decompose a problem—using procedures and functions, perhaps nesting them within one another, etc. These are all instances of a more general notion called modularity. The **modularity** word **modularity** stands for the various ways in which we can break a problem into parts, using subprograms, or perhaps some other features that aren't part of ANSI Standard Pascal. Whatever we use, and whichever language we choose for implementing the solutions to our problems, we'll always find that modularity—dividing the problem into smaller, more manageable pieces—is the key to finding the best, most elegant, most workable solution to our problem.

3.8 Exercises

Key Words to Review

nested subprogram	constant definition	cohesion
CONST	siblings	modularity
constant		

Questions to Answer

QUE 3.8.1   In what situations is it desirable to have one subprogram nested inside another?

QUE 3.8.2   Look again at Exercise Cha.3.5.1. Explain why the new procedure AdjustHours can't be nested inside Function SumOfHours.

QUE 3.8.3   What are the advantages of using a CONST definition?

QUE 3.8.4   Looking at the syntax diagram for a formal parameter list, explain why the word VAR applies only to the parameter large in the heading

```
PROCEDURE Move (VAR large       : INTEGER;
                    small       : INTEGER;
                    countLg, countSm : INTEGER);
```

QUE 3.8.5   When must you use BEGIN and END in an IF statement or a WHILE statement?

QUE 3.8.6   In Program Trucking, why can't Functions Income, Cost, or Tax be called from the program's main body?

QUE 3.8.7   What's the similarity between a local variable and a local subprogram?

Experiments to Try

EXP 3.8.1   Put a call to Function Cost in the main body of Program Trucking.

EXP 3.8.2   Put a call to Function Cost in the body of Function Income.

EXP 3.8.3   Try to compile the following program:

```
PROGRAM TwoMyReads (input, output);
  VAR
    i : INTEGER;
    r : REAL;

  {----------}
  PROCEDURE MyRead (VAR i: INTEGER);
  BEGIN {MyRead}
    Read (i)
  END;   {MyRead}

  {----------}
  PROCEDURE P (VAR i : INTEGER; VAR r : REAL);

    {----------}
    PROCEDURE MyRead (VAR r : REAL);
    BEGIN {MyRead}
      Read (r)
    END;   {MyRead}

    {----------}
  BEGIN {P}
    MyRead (i);
    MyRead (r)
  END;   {P}

  {----------}
```

```
BEGIN {TwoMyReads}
  P (i,r);
  WriteLn (i,r)
END.  {TwoMyReads}
```

Can you explain the results you get?

Changes to Make

CHA 3.8.1 Take each of the constants defined in Program Trucking and discuss whether it's rightly been made a constant or instead should be changed to a variable whose value is read in during the run of the program. Modify Program Trucking so that each of these constants (or perhaps the ones you think should be changed) are turned into variables.

CHA 3.8.2 Modify Program IntroToProcedures, Section 2.5 so that the decision about whether or not to Switch is made in a subprogram. The old procedure Switch should be called by this new subprogram.

CHA 3.8.3 Modify Program BarGraph (Section 3.1) so that Procedure MakeBar is nested inside another procedure. This other procedure reads a salary figure and then calls MakeBar to make the appropriate bar.

CHA 3.8.4 Modify AddTimes in Section 3.5 so that it's a procedure instead of a program. When you do this, you'll want to take all the reading and writing out of AddTimes and instead have AddTimes communicate information using parameters. Once you've done this, write a main program (a test driver) that calls your new Procedure AddTimes.

Programs and Subprograms to Write

WRI 3.8.1 A customer's monthly telephone bill is computed using the formula

base rate + cost for individual calls + tax

The base rate is a certain fixed amount—depending on the kind of service the customer gets (pulse dialing or touch tone). The cost for each call depends on three things—the number of minutes for the call, the region to which the call was made ("local" or "long distance"), and the time of day the call began (day, evening, or night). Finally the tax is a certain percentage of the base rate plus the cost for individual calls.

Here's a table giving actual amounts for the quantities just described:

Item	Amount
Base rate—pulse dialing	$15.00
Base rate—touch tone	18.00
Cost per minute for a call:	
Local	
daytime	0.05
evening	0.03
nighttime	0.02
Long distance	
daytime	0.20
evening	0.15
nighttime	0.12
Tax	7%

Write a program that writes the total amount of a customer's telephone bill after reading in all the needed information (type of service, and for each call the number of minutes, the region to which the call was made, etc.). Use constants to represent the amounts given in the table.

WRI 3.8.2   First do Exercise Wri.3.8.1. Then modify your program so that customer's phone bill includes an additional 3 percent tax on long distance calls only. When you were doing Exercise Wri.3.8.1 would you have done anything differently if you'd been able to anticipate this change?

WRI 3.8.3   Twenty years ago I bought a house for $14,500.00. Now it's worth $56,000.00. I don't live in the house anymore, so I have to decide whether to sell it, or keep it and try to find someone to rent it. If I sell it for $56,000.00 then I have to pay the realtor a 6 percent commission. I also have to pay taxes—28 percent federal and 7 percent state taxes. (Note: taxes are paid on the difference between the sale price of $56,000 and the base price of $14,500.) I can take what's left, invest it, and get an 8 percent return. If I rent it then I can probably get $500 a month from the tenant; but I still have to pay property tax, which is about $1000 per year, and repairs, which cost about $1500 per year.

Write a program that helps me decide whether I should sell the house or keep it. Have your program read in all the dollar amounts and percentages given in the statement of the problem. Run the program more than once, each time with different dollar amounts and percentages.

WRI 3.8.4   *(Continuation of Exercises Wri.3.7.9 and Wri.3.7.10)* Write and test a procedure that accepts values for x_1, t_1, and v and finds the values of x_2 and t_2. To do most of its work this new procedure should call the subprograms you wrote for Exercises Wri.3.7.9 and Wri.3.7.10.

3.9

A Look at Object-Oriented Programming (Supplementary)

In this chapter we've been decomposing problems into smaller subproblems—with procedures, functions, nested subprograms, etc. In each section on Designing a Program we went through the reasoning that leads to one particular decomposition of a problem into smaller parts. Now the question arises: If we're given a problem to solve, is there a recipe we can follow for decomposing it?

Unfortunately, there isn't. Decomposing problems takes practice, patience, and experience. In general, there's no algorithm we can give that tells us how to decompose every program into smaller subprograms. But several authors have suggested useful ways of thinking about decomposition. And one particular approach called **object-oriented programming** (or **OOP**, for short) has become very popular in the last few years.

In this section we present a very simple view of the way OOP prescribes that we decompose problems. Our discussion will focus on only one small aspect of OOP, and to do this we'll need to use a feature that's not available in ANSI Standard Pascal. We'll borrow a feature from Turbo Pascal called the **unit**. If you're using ANSI Standard Pascal, the program example in this section won't compile on your computer. But that's OK. You can learn a lot about OOP just by reading through the example. And our example isn't very far from being legal in the ANSI standard. A little rearranging here and there will make it legal. Perhaps your implementation has some feature of its own that works very much like Turbo Pascal's units.

Specifications   In this section we rework our solution to the "time-amounts" problem of Section 3.4.

> Input: Two "time amounts" (hour1, minute1 and hour2, minute2)
>
> Output: The "sum" (hourNew, minuteNew) of the two time amounts

We'll decompose the problem a new way, using Turbo Pascal units to represent pieces of the problem.

Designing a Program

classes of data

The time-amounts problem is made up of three natural **classes** of data: hours, minutes, and times. What we call a time, such as 12:15, is actually a combination of the two other data classes—hours and minutes. So when we decompose our problem, we decompose it into three parts:

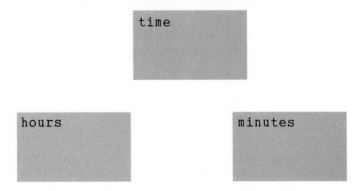

For each of the three parts, we ask ourselves, "What are the operations that we want to perform with this class of data?" or more simply, "What do we want to do with `hours`? . . . with `minutes`? . . . with `time`s?" Of course we want to add two `time`s together, but we also want to read a time-amount from the keyboard and write a time-amount to the screen.

```
time
   ReadLnTime
   AddTimes
   WriteLnTime
```

So now we've described a certain class of data that we call `time`. It consists of the numbers we normally think of as times (12:00, 1:15, 2:30, etc.) together with the collection of operations that we perform on times. Each of these operations will be implemented with a Pascal subprogram. When we put all this together into a conceptual box, we say that we're **encapsulating** everything we need to know about `time`s.

Turbo Pascal's units

Our goal is to write a Turbo Pascal unit that contains exactly what we've described in the `time` box—subprograms to `ReadLnTime`, `AddTimes`, and `WriteLnTime`. But first we have to think about how we're going to perform each of these operations. Let's think first about `ReadLnTime`. Here's how we did it in Section 3.5:

```
Write ('Enter the time (hours space minutes): ');
ReadLn (hr, min)
```

Notice the reference to `hr` and `min`, and remember that we're planning to make `hours` and `minutes` be parts of the decomposition in their own right.

```
time
   ReadLnTime
   AddTimes
   WriteLnTime
```

```
hours
```

```
minutes
```

This means we'll need two more Turbo Pascal units—one to encapsulate hours and another to encapsulate minutes. In order to do something like ReadLn (hr, min), we'll have to say how to Read an Hour in our hours unit and how to Read a Minute in our minutes unit.

```
time
   ReadLnTime
   AddTimes
   WriteLnTime
```

```
hours
   ReadHour
```

```
minutes
   ReadMinute
```

In fact, what we call a time is always a combination of a number of hours and a number of minutes, no matter what operation we're performing on it. So just as we can break down ReadLnTime into ReadHour and ReadMinute, we can also break down AddTimes into AddHours and AddMinutes and break down WriteLnTime into WriteHour and WriteMinute.

```
time
   ReadLnTime
   AddTimes
   WriteLnTime
```

```
hours
   ReadHour
   AddHours
   WriteHour
```

```
minutes
   ReadMinute
   AddMinutes
   WriteMinute
```

Now notice the way this is organized in the diagram. It's not organized according to who calls whom, the way it would be in a hierarchy diagram. Instead it's organized as three different classes of data. We'll implement each class of data with a Turbo Pascal unit. A unit is simply a collection of definitions and declarations. It contains declarations of subprograms to implement the operations associated with a particular class of data.

For instance, the unit that implements hours follows.

Program Example

```
UNIT HoursU;
{Provides operations on 'hour-type' values.}


INTERFACE
  CONST
    oneHour = 1;

  PROCEDURE ReadHour   (VAR hr   : INTEGER);
  FUNCTION  SumOfHours (hr1, hr2 : INTEGER) : INTEGER;
  PROCEDURE WriteHour  (hr       : INTEGER);


IMPLEMENTATION
  PROCEDURE ReadHour (VAR hr : INTEGER);
  BEGIN {ReadHour}
    Read (hr)
  END;  {ReadHour}

  {----------}
  FUNCTION SumOfHours (hr1, hr2 : INTEGER) : INTEGER;
  {Adds together two hour-amounts.}

    VAR
      temp : INTEGER;

  BEGIN {SumOfHours}
    temp := (hr1 + hr2) MOD 12;
    IF temp = 0 THEN
      SumOfHours := 12
    ELSE
      SumOfHours := temp
  END;   {SumOfHours}

  {----------}
  PROCEDURE WriteHour (hr : INTEGER);
  BEGIN {WriteHour}
    Write (hr:2)
  END;   {WriteHour}

END. {HoursU}
```

Sample Runs???

Look! A unit has no body of its own. We can't run it on its own. The procedures that we've put into the HoursUnit have to be called from somewhere else. Since we can't run HoursU on its own, we don't have any sample runs yet.

Observations

- ```
  UNIT HoursU;
      .
      .
  INTERFACE
      .
      .
  IMPLEMENTATION
      .
      .
  END. {HoursU}
  ```

  Here's the structure of a unit. Sandwiched in between the header `UNIT HoursU;` and the unit's `END` there are two sections: an `INTERFACE` section and an `IMPLEMENTATION` section. Let's look at each section individually.

- ```
  INTERFACE
     CONST
        oneHour = 1;
  PROCEDURE ReadHour   (VAR hr    : INTEGER);
  FUNCTION  SumOfHours (hr1, hr2  : INTEGER) : INTEGER;
  PROCEDURE WriteHour  (hr        : INTEGER);
  ```

`INTERFACE`

The `INTERFACE` section tells exactly what we need to know in order to make use of the facilities that are provided by the unit. For instance, one "facility" provided in the `HoursUnit` is Procedure `WriteHour`. In order to "make use of" Procedure `WriteHour`, we need to know how to call it. In particular, to write the procedure call

```
WriteHour (hr)
```

we need to know

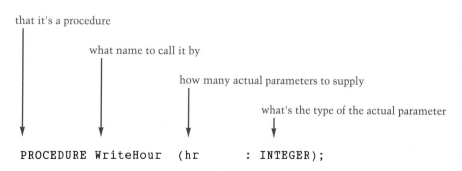

So now we know exactly what a subprogram heading is for: it gives the "outside world" precise instructions for calling the subprogram.

The constant definition in this `INTERFACE` section is an interesting aspect of OOP. We'll examine it in a moment.

```
• IMPLEMENTATION
    PROCEDURE ReadHour (VAR hr : INTEGER);
    BEGIN {ReadHour}
      Read (hr)
    END;   {ReadHour}
    {----------}
        .
        .
        .
    Etc.
```

IMPLEMENTATION The IMPLEMENTATION section gives details about the way in which the facilities in the unit are implemented. These are details that we do not need to know if we're just making use of the facilities. For instance, if we just want to *call* Procedure WriteHour, we don't need to know what's inside the *body* of Procedure WriteHour. Nothing inside the procedure's body would help us write a call like

```
WriteHour (hr)
```

(Of course before we call Procedure WriteHour we should have some idea of what the procedure will do for us. But that's another story. We don't need to look at the body to find that out. Instead we should look at whatever documentation has been provided.)

Now let's look at the unit that implements minutes.

Program Example

```
UNIT MinutesU;
{Provides operations on 'minute-type' values.}


INTERFACE
  USES HoursU;
  PROCEDURE ReadMinute  (VAR min         : INTEGER);
  PROCEDURE AddMinutes   (min1, min2      : INTEGER ;
                          VAR hrNew, minNew : INTEGER);
  PROCEDURE WriteMinute (min              : INTEGER);


IMPLEMENTATION
  PROCEDURE ReadMinute (VAR min : INTEGER);
  BEGIN {ReadMinute}
    Read (min)
  END;   {ReadMinute}
  {----------}
```

```
PROCEDURE AddMinutes  (min1, min2         : INTEGER ;
                       VAR hrNew, minNew : INTEGER);
{Adds together two minute-amounts.}
BEGIN {AddMinutes}
  minNew := min1 + min2;
  WHILE minNew >= 60 DO
    BEGIN
      hrNew  := SumOfHours (hrNew, oneHour);
      minNew := minNew - 60
    END
END;  {AddMinutes}

{----------}

PROCEDURE WriteMinute (min : INTEGER);
BEGIN {WriteMinute}
  IF min < 10 THEN
    BEGIN
      Write ('0');
      Write (min:1)
    END
  ELSE
    Write (min:2)
END;  {WriteMinute}
END. {MinutesU}
```

Observations

•
```
minNew := min1 + min2;
WHILE minNew >= 60 DO
  BEGIN
    hrNew  := SumOfHours (hrNew, oneHour);
    minNew := minNew - 60
  END
```

Compare this with the way we added minutes together in Section 3.5.

```
hrsFromMinutes := (min1 + min2) DIV 60;
hrNew          := SumOfHours (hrNew, hrsFromMinutes);
minNew         := (min1 + min2) MOD 60
```

information hiding

We do it a bit differently in this section because of an important notion called **information hiding**. When we practice information hiding, we make sure that the only unit containing details about hours is the HoursUnit; that is, we hide details about hours from all the other units. But this means we can't use our old statement

```
hrsFromMinutes := (min1 + min2) DIV 60
```

in the new version of Procedure AddMinutes. Doing so would mean we had a formula to calculate hrsFromMinutes right inside the MinutesUnit. That wouldn't be any good, because information hiding tells us to put hours calculations only in the HoursUnit.

Of course, when we add two minute-amounts together, we can gain an extra hour. So Procedure AddMinutes has to have *some* way of increasing the number of hours. If we do information hiding, the proper way to do it is to have AddMinutes *call a procedure whose details are hidden inside the* HoursUnit.

```
hrNew := SumOfHours (hrNew, oneHour)
```

So now we have to rearrange our algorithm a bit. In the OOP code, we have a WHILE loop that keeps adding oneHour and subtracting 60 minutes until it runs out of minutes. To add oneHour it makes this call to Function SumOfHours. The details of Function SumOfHours are hidden inside the HoursUnit.

Now what about this constant oneHour that we use in the call to Function SumOfHours? As it stands currently, the program would run correctly if we used the number 1

```
hrNew := SumOfHours (hrNew, 1)
```

but once again we would be violating the spirit of information hiding. After all, this number 1 would represent the notion of "a single hour," and this statement in the MinutesUnit has no business knowing anything about hours or "single hour"s. All it should know how to do is to call subprograms from the HoursU unit. Only the HoursUnit gets to deal with such details as the meaning of "a single hour."

That's why the HoursUnit has this CONST definition

```
CONST
   oneHour = 1;
```

This is where the HoursUnit stores its knowledge of what "a single hour" really means. Since this CONST definition is in the INTERFACE section of HoursU, the nickname oneHour is made available for use by other units. Units like MinutesU can make reference to the name oneHour, but only HoursU has control over the *value* of the constant oneHour. That's exactly the way it should be. All information about hours should be encapsulated inside a single unit—the HoursUnit.

• USES HoursU;

USES

This line, at the top of the MinutesU unit, simply warns the compiler that MinutesU will be using things from the HoursU unit—like the constant oneHour, the function SumOfHours, etc.

Earlier in this section we said that "a time is always a combination of a number of hours and a number of minutes." This means that when we write our TimeU unit, we should borrow heavily from the HoursU and MinutesU units. That's exactly what we do.

Program Example

```
UNIT TimeU;
{Provides operations on 'time-type' values.}


INTERFACE
  USES HoursU, MinutesU;
  PROCEDURE ReadLnTime  (VAR hr, min      : INTEGER);
  PROCEDURE AddTimes     (hr1, min1        : INTEGER ;
                          hr2, min2        : INTEGER ;
                          VAR hrNew, minNew : INTEGER);
  PROCEDURE WriteLnTime (hr, min          : INTEGER);


IMPLEMENTATION
  PROCEDURE ReadLnTime (VAR hr, min : INTEGER);
  BEGIN {ReadLnTime}
    Write      ('Enter the time (hours space minutes): ');
    ReadHour   (hr);
    ReadMinute (min);
    ReadLn
  END;  {ReadLnTime}
  {----------}
  PROCEDURE AddTimes (hr1, min1         : INTEGER ;
                      hr2, min2         : INTEGER ;
                      VAR hrNew, minNew : INTEGER);
  {Adds together two time-amounts.}

  BEGIN {AddTimes}
    hrNew := SumOfHours (hr1, hr2);
    AddMinutes (min1, min2, hrNew, minNew)
  END;  {AddTimes}
  {----------}
  PROCEDURE WriteLnTime (hr, min : INTEGER);
  BEGIN {WriteLnTime}
    WriteHour   (hr);
    Write        (':');
    WriteMinute (min);
    WriteLn
  END;  {WriteLnTime}
END. {TimeU}
```

Observations In its INTERFACE section, the TimeUnit provides three subprograms to perform operations on time-amounts—ReadLnTime, AddTimes, and WriteLnTime. But notice that in the bodies of these subprograms we never do any direct handling of any hour values or minute values. Instead, we do subprogram calls. In fact, every single line in the bodies of these three subprograms contains a call to another subprogram. This is because time is really a combination of hours and minutes—and all the operations on time can be broken down into operations on hours and operations on minutes.

Now where do we start executing all this? All we have in our units are subprograms. None of these units has a body of its own. We need a "main" program that starts calling all these subprograms. Our main program will look a lot like program `AddTimes` from Section 3.5. The biggest difference is that our new main program will call subprograms that aren't declared within it. It will call subprograms that are declared in the units that it `USES`.

```
PROGRAM TimeProgram (input, output);
{Driver for a set of time units.}

  USES TimeU;

  VAR
    hour1,   minute1,
    hour2,   minute2,
    hourNew, minuteNew : INTEGER;
BEGIN {TimeProgram}
  ReadLnTime (hour1, minute1);
  ReadLnTime (hour2, minute2);

  AddTimes (hour1,   minute1,
            hour2,   minute2,
            hourNew, minuteNew);

  WriteLn;
  Write         ('The combined time is ');
  WriteLnTime (hourNew, minuteNew)
END.  {TimeProgram}
```

Sample Runs

```
Enter the time (hours space minutes): 2 30
Enter the time (hours space minutes): 3 40

The combined time is  6:10
```

So that's the way problems are decomposed when we do object-oriented programming. OOP provides a new way of thinking about decomposition. It tells us that we should start by asking ourselves what classes of data we have in the problem. In an OOP decomposition, each "piece" of the problem is the encapsulation of a particular class of data.

Of course this is barely even the tip of the OOP iceberg. There's a lot more to OOP than what we've discussed in this section. We'll have more to say about OOP in some supplementary sections at the ends of other chapters.

3.9   Exercises

Key Words to Review

object-oriented programming (OOP)	unit	encapsulation
	INTERFACE	information hiding
class	IMPLEMENTATION	USES

Questions to Answer

QUE 3.9.1   In the beginning of this section we said "there's no algorithm we can give that tells us how to decompose every program into smaller subprograms." Describe the extent to which object-oriented programming provides just such an algorithm.

QUE 3.9.2   Explain one of the purposes of a unit in Turbo Pascal.

QUE 3.9.3   Why does a Turbo Pascal unit normally not have a body?

QUE 3.9.4   Describe the relationship between the INTERFACE and IMPLEMENTATION sections of a Turbo Pascal unit. In particular, why do we need each section?

QUE 3.9.5   In this section we complained that

```
hrsFromMinutes := (min1 + min2) DIV 60
```

shouldn't be in the MinutesU unit, because it would have the MinutesU unit doing too much with hour amounts. But then we said it's all right to have

```
hrNew := SumOfHours (hrNew, oneHour)
```

in the MinutesU unit. What's the difference?

QUE 3.9.6   In this section we complained that

```
hrNew := SumOfHours (hrNew, 1)
```

shouldn't be in the MinutesU unit, because it would have the MinutesU unit doing too much with hour amounts. But then we said it's all right to have

```
hrNew := SumOfHours (hrNew, oneHour)
```

in the MinutesU unit. What's the difference?

QUE 3.9.7   Translate the body of the TimeProgram into pseudocode and see how much the pseudocode and the Pascal code are alike.

QUE 3.9.8   Rethink each of the decompositions you gave for Exercise Que.3.1.6 in light of what you now know about object-oriented programming.

QUE 3.9.9   Explain how you would use OOP to decompose each of the following problems. At this point, don't worry about how you'd actually write code to solve the problems:
a. Find the average of a list of test scores.
b. In a list of test scores, find the score that occurs most often.
c. Alphabetize a list of employee names.
d. Search a list of employees to find all the employees whose zip code is 07940.

Things to Check in a Manual

MAN 3.9.1   Find out if your implementation has some feature of its own that does the work of Turbo Pascal's units.

Changes to Make

CHA 3.9.1   Create a new function IncrementHour that adds 1 to the number of hours. This new function is called by Procedure AddMinutes and calls Function SumOfHours. In which unit does Function IncrementHour belong?

Things to Think About

THI 3.9.1   In the beginning of this section we said "there's no algorithm we can give that tells us how to decompose every program into smaller subprograms." Can you give general rules to describe the way in which you normally go about decomposing problems?

Chapter Summary

Problem decomposition is the single most important step in the problem-solving process. When a problem has been properly decomposed, its parts are all very clear and simple, and they can each be solved with very little effort. When you're deciding how to decompose a problem it's essential to design your solution from the top, downward.

> Decompose the problem into parts.
> Write pseudocode for the broad outline of the problem,
>   listing the parts, but giving no detail for each part.
> Then, taking each part as a problem in and of itself,
>   Decompose the part into smaller parts.
>   Write pseudocode for the part . . . etc.

First you work on the "big picture," putting the smaller details on the back burner. Then, in successive steps, you make refinements that help you get a handle on some of the smaller details. Layer by layer you work your way downward until you've designed a solution for the problem in its smallest details.

By creating subprograms we achieve a measure of *procedural abstraction*. This means that the work of solving a particular part of a problem has been abstracted—that is, details about the algorithm we used have been removed from our immediate view. Procedural abstraction is a good thing, because when we're thinking about the broad outline of an algorithm, details shouldn't get in the way.

In Pascal there are two ways to pass parameters—*pass by reference* and *pass by value*. With pass by reference, anything that happens to the *formal parameter* during the execution of the subprogram also gets done to the *actual parameter*. Using pass by reference we can change the value of an actual parameter. With pass by value, nothing that happens to the formal parameter during the execution of the subprogram has any effect on the actual parameter. Using pass by value does not change the value of the actual parameter.

In this chapter, we decomposed problems with the two kinds of subprograms that are available in Pascal: *procedures* and *functions*. In general, the purpose of a procedure is to perform an action, and the purpose of a function is to calculate a single value. Since procedures and functions have different purposes, the syntax for writing and calling them is a bit different. At the end of a function heading we put a colon and a type name to indicate what *result type* is returned by the function. Inside the body of a function, the function's name is given a value. This is the *result value* that's returned by the function. And when the function is called, we must use its result value.

In a Pascal program we can have subprograms calling other subprograms as long as we observe the *Scope Rule*:

Scope Rule: An identifier can be used anywhere after the place where it's declared, as long as it's being used inside the program or subprogram in which it's declared.

In addition to having subprograms that are written by the programmer, Pascal provides certain *pre-declared* subprograms. Some of these pre-declared subprograms do things for us that we wouldn't otherwise be able to do (for example, ReadLn, WriteLn, and other subprograms for input and output). Many of the pre-declared subprograms do things that we can already do, but do them more efficiently (for example, Sqr and Odd). A few of them have special features that can't be used in subprograms that are written by the programmer (such as, WriteLn's colons). See Appendix B for a complete list of Pascal's pre-declared subprograms.

ANSI Standard Pascal doesn't have units, but if we add units to our language we can begin to do *object-oriented programming (OOP)*. In OOP we decompose a problem by looking for the different classes of data in the problem. We encapsulate a particular class of data by putting everything we need to know about it into one part of the code. In this section a "part" of the code was a Turbo Pascal unit. An OOP decomposition works best when we remember to do *information hiding*. With information hiding, each unit contains details about only one particular class of data.

Elementary File Handling

4.1

Reading and Writing

This chapter is something of a "detour." We're going to veer away from the development of algorithms and show you a few examples concerning input and output using files.

What is a file?   A **file** is a collection of information. If you start up your editor, type in a few words, and save them with the name words.txt, then you've created a file that the computer knows by the name words.txt. On most computers, a file that's created this way is stored on a disk. The file can contain words or numbers or even the text of a Pascal program.

Specifications   The first program in this chapter copies characters from one disk file to another. We'll use the names inFile and outFile for the two files. So our program copies characters *from* the inFile *to* the outFile. While the program does this, it also echoes the characters to the screen.

Note: The program in this section will work only if the inFile has just one line in it. For files with more than one line, see Section 5.1.

Designing a Program

The pseudocode for a file-copy program is fairly simple:

> As long as you haven't reached the end of the input file,
> keep doing the following:
>> Read the next character from the input file,
>> Write that character to the output file,
>> Write that character to the screen
>> (that is, echo the character.)

Program Example

```
PROGRAM Copy (inFile, outFile, output);
{******************************************************************************
 *                                                                           *
 * Author      : Barry Burd, Math/CS Department, Drew University             *
 * Date        : February 13, 1991                                           *
 * Reviewed by : Chris Van Wyk                                               *
 *                                                                           *
 * Purpose:                                                                  *
 *   Copies 'inFile' to 'outFile', and displays the results on the screen.   *
 *                                                                           *
 * Algorithm used:                                                           *
 *   As long as we're not at the end of the inFile,                          *
 *     Read a character (into the variable 'ch') from the inFile,            *
 *     Write the character to the outFile,                                   *
 *     Write the character again, this time to the screen.                   *
 *                                                                           *
 * Variables:                                                                *
 *   ch : CHAR -- stores each character as it's read from the inFile (and    *
 *                also as it's written to the outFile and to the screen).    *
 *                                                                           *
 * Known bugs and limitations:                                              *
 *   Doesn't work if the inFile is more than one line long.                  *
 *                                                                           *
 * Interfaces:                                                               *
 *   Called by issuing the operating system's 'run' command.                 *
 *                                                                           *
 *   Files:                                                                  *
 *     inFile  : Created by the user with an editor.  (See known bugs!)      *
 *     outFile : Created by this program - a copy of the inFile.             *
 *     output  : The screen                                                  *
 *                                                                           *
 *   Subprograms called:                                                     *
 *     Newly created subprograms : None.                                     *
 *     Pre-declared subprograms  : Reset, Rewrite, Read, Write.              *
 *                                                                           *
 ******************************************************************************}
```

```
VAR
   ch               : CHAR;
   inFile, outFile : TEXT;
BEGIN {Copy}
  Reset   (inFile);
  Rewrite (outFile);
  WHILE NOT Eof(inFile) DO
    BEGIN
      Read  (inFile,  ch);
      Write (outFile, ch);
      Write (output,  ch)
    END
END.  {Copy}
```

Sample Runs

Several things happen before, during, and after a run of Program Copy:

- Before the program runs, you edit a file and save it, perhaps with the name infile.dat.[1] Maybe the file contains a line with Noam Chomsky's sentence

  ```
  Colorless green ideas sleep furiously.
  ```

- When you run Program Copy, the line Colorless green ideas sleep furiously shows up on your screen.

- After the program is finished running, you can edit a file, perhaps named outfile.dat, that contains the same line Colorless green ideas . . .

Observations

program parameters

- PROGRAM Copy (**inFile**, outFile, output);

  Instead of reading from the keyboard, whose name is input, we're reading from a disk file that will be known to our Pascal program by the name inFile. We could have given the file any name we wanted. We chose inFile because we wanted to suggest the idea of an input File.

- PROGRAM Copy (inFile, **outFile, output**);

  Instead of writing just to the screen, whose name is output, we're copying to a file that will be known to our Pascal program by the name outFile. Since we'll be echoing characters to the screen as well, we still include the word output in the program heading.

naming files

  Now here's something that might be a bit confusing: when we refer to our disk files in operating system commands or with our editor, we might not call them inFile and outFile. If we're using a VAX with VMS, we probably call them infile.dat and outfile.dat when we're editing them. On other systems we may use different names.

---

[1]To see why we say "perhaps," read the first of the Observations.

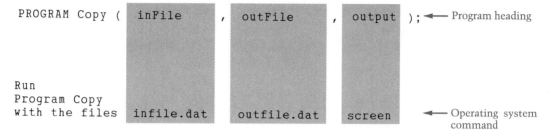

<pre>
PROGRAM Copy (│ inFile   , │ outFile   , │ output │); ◄── Program heading

Run
Program Copy
with the files │ infile.dat   │ outfile.dat   │ screen │ ◄── Operating system
                                                               command
</pre>

So how do you make the connection between the file's name *inside* the Pascal program and the name you give the file when you use the editor? It depends on your implementation. Each system has its own way of working this problem out. To find out how your implementation does it, you'll need to look at your computer's manuals or talk to your instructor.

- VAR
   inFile, outFile : TEXT;

TEXT files

We can't just make up a new name without telling our program what the name stands for. The word TEXT is built into the Pascal language. It stands for a certain kind of file. For now, all the files we create will be declared to be of type TEXT. Roughly speaking, a TEXT file is the kind of file that you can create with your editor.

- Reset (inFile)

Reset

We've created a disk file with our editor. This Reset tells the computer to get that file ready so that the Pascal program can read from it. Reset is a pre-declared procedure. Notice that Reset is called only once in Program Copy. That's the way it should be. Once the file is made ready, the program can read all the characters in the file.

- Rewrite (outFile)

Rewrite

Rewrite is a pre-declared procedure. This call to Rewrite tells the computer to get outFile ready so that the Pascal program can write to it. Notice that Rewrite is called only once in Program Copy.

- Read (inFile, ch)

reading from a file

When we tell the computer to Read, we have to tell it that the reading should be done from the inFile, rather than from the keyboard. We do it by putting the word inFile in the beginning of Read's parameter list. It's as simple as that.

- Write (outFile, ch)

writing to a file

On this line we're telling the computer to write the value of ch to the outFile rather than to the screen.

• `Write (output,  ch)`

We want the computer to echo its characters to the screen. We could do this with just

`Write (ch)`

but in this program we included the word `output` just to emphasize that `output` is the name of a file. It's the *screen* file.

• `WHILE NOT Eof(inFile) DO`

`Eof`

`Eof` is a pre-declared function. It stands for *End of file*. This loop keeps iterating as long as the reading hasn't reached the end of the `inFile`.[2]

Programming Style

Notice the prologue comment in Program `Copy`. It's more detailed and elaborate than the prologue comments in our earlier programs. Is it "better"?

prologue comments

We'll answer this question with a few other questions: Who will eventually be reading the program? What will they need to know about it? What information will be most helpful? Here are some typical scenarios:

1. The program is part of a computer science text called *Pascal by Example*. Everyone knows who wrote the text because his name appears in it several dozen times, in different contexts. Also, the program is surrounded by Specifications, Designing a Program, and Observations subsections that give us most of the information appearing in this prologue comment.

   In this context, a huge prologue comment is helpful as a one-time teaching tool but would hardly be useful in each program example.

2. The program is one of several hundred programs to be used in a business environment. Several thousand people will use the program; and when the program's author leaves the company, someone will be asked to examine the code and make some changes.

   In this context it's *essential* that the documentation be complete, precise, accurate, detailed, etc. If you look at each piece of information in the expanded prologue comment, you'll be able to think of some way in which it would be helpful to a person who's examining the code. Notice in particular the part entitled `Known bugs and limitations`. In computer programming, we should never try to hide or even gloss over a program's bugs and limitations. On the contrary, we should make very prominent notices to draw attention to these things. Otherwise, people will have to deal with them when they come up by surprise. Ugly surprises like this aren't helpful to anyone—certainly not to the user or the author of the program.

3. The program is one of several assignments that you're handing in as part of the work in an introductory computer science course. The instructor will grade about thirty Program `Copy`s—one for each student.

---

[2] To find out what type of value Function `Eof` returns, see Section 8.3.

Certainly the instructor needs to know who wrote the program. Perhaps the statement of purpose isn't so important if all thirty copies of the assignment are handed in at the same time. But what if you hand yours in late and the instructor doesn't get around to grading it with the others? Then it helps to have a statement of the program's purpose at the top. Or what if you did something wrong and the instructor wants to check and make sure you understood the assignment?

A description of the algorithm helps the instructor understand what you intended to do while you were writing the code. It also shows how your thinking was organized. And what about a paragraph telling exactly what sort of input the program expects to receive—numbers, characters, upper or lower case, in which columns, how many blank spaces, how many lines, etc.? This is extremely helpful because it permits the instructor to run the program and test it with some other input data. Of course each instructor has different expectations on what kind of documentation should accompany each assignment. Ask your own instructor for details.

Now remember that all three scenarios assume that people will actually read the program itself. We're not talking about users—the people who just run the program without ever seeing the code. Prologue comments aren't very useful to users because prologue comments are buried in the code, which the users never see.

external documentation   The users have a whole different set of needs. They need **external documentation**—documentation that's separate from the program itself. They also need a different kind of information. They shouldn't know about variables, algorithms, or subprograms.

The users need documents that describe the software from various perspectives. A **user's guide** should introduce the software in a way that's fairly easy to read and comprehend. A **reference manual** should give a very complete and rigorous description of the software. It should be readable, but not necessarily "easy" to read. For the novices there may even be a **tutorial**—a step-by-step tour of the software—a set of very carefully guided experiments to try. Even with external documentation we must remember to ask the questions: Who will eventually be using the program? What will they need to know about it? What information will be most helpful to them?

4.1 Exercises

Key Words to Review

file	Reset	user's guide
input	Rewrite	reference manual
output	Eof	tutorial
TEXT	external documentation	

Questions to Answer

QUE 4.1.1   List any way(s) in which reading from a disk file is different from reading from the keyboard.

QUE 4.1.2   In Program Copy why do we make sure that Reset is executed only once?

QUE 4.1.3   Look at the prologue comment in Program Copy. For each piece of information in the comment, give a scenario in which that piece of information would be helpful to someone who's examining the code.

QUE 4.1.4   Look at the prologue comment in Program Copy. What other pieces of information, not given in this prologue comment, might be helpful to someone who's examining the code?

Things to Check in a Manual

MAN 4.1.1   Find out how to make a connection between the name used for a file inside a Pascal program and the name used for the file outside the program (for example, by the editor).

Experiments to Try

EXP 4.1.1   Run Program Copy; but before you do, make sure that there's no inFile anywhere on your system.

EXP 4.1.2   Run Program Copy; but before you do, make sure that there's nothing in your inFile. In other words, edit the inFile and save it, but don't put any characters in it.

EXP 4.1.3   Remove the statement Reset (inFile) from Program Copy.

EXP 4.1.4   Remove the statement Rewrite (outFile) from Program Copy.

EXP 4.1.5   Move the statement Reset (inFile) so that it's the first statement inside the WHILE loop.

EXP 4.1.6   Move the statement Rewrite (outFile) so that it's the first statement inside the WHILE loop.

Changes to Make

CHA 4.1.1   Modify Program Scores from Section 2.3 so that it gets its input from a disk file and sends its output to a disk file.

CHA 4.1.2   Modify Program Copy so that it stops copying the single-line inFile when it reads a period character. Make sure your program puts a period at the end of the outFile and writes a period at the end of the line on the screen.

CHA 4.1.3   Modify Program Copy so that it alternates, copying odd-numbered characters to the outFile and even-numbered characters to another file called outFile2. For instance, if the inFile contains

        Ceaand   ytohui sr?

then the outFile will contain

        Can you r

and `outFile2` will contain

    ead this?

Before running the new Program `Copy` make sure your `inFile` has an even number of characters in it.

Scales to Practice

PRA 4.1.1   Write a program that simply writes three numbers to a file. Then write another program that reads the three numbers back from the file.

PRA 4.1.2   Write a program that reads thirty single-digit numbers, stored all on one line on a disk file, and writes the sum. After you have the program working, edit the disk file and a few of the numbers. Then test the program again.

Programs and Subprograms to Write

WRI 4.1.1   Modify the program you wrote for Exercise Wri.2.5.4 so that it reads the ages of the children from a disk file.

WRI 4.1.2   Modify the program you wrote for Exercise Wri.3.1.4 so that it writes the acid test ratio into a disk file, but writes the warning message (if any) on the screen.

WRI 4.1.3   Modify the program you wrote for Exercise Wri.3.3.2 so that it writes a *history file* as it runs. A history file contains a list of everything that happened during the run of a particular program. In this case, the history file contains a record of all the positions the shift lever stops in. For instance, a history file that looks like this:

$$-10 \quad -1 \quad \quad 3 \quad -1 \quad -10$$

might have the following interpretation:

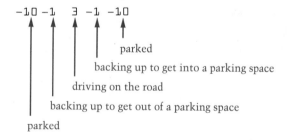

4.2

Using Files

Let's consider again the bar-graph problem from Section 3.1. Look at the sample run given in that section. When the user types in a number, it gets echoed on the screen and shows up as if it were part of the output.

```
1990 - Women's and men's salaries: 12 24
WWWWWWWWWWWW
MMMMMMMMMMMMMMMMMMMMMMMM
```

Now what if you don't want the prompt and the user's input to get mixed up with the program's output? Perhaps the input for each bar is a sequence of nine salary numbers, one for each of nine regions of the country. You may not want the nine numbers to clutter up the appearance of the bar graph.

```
1990 - Women's and men's salaries for each of nine regions:
1 1 1 2 1 1 2 1 2
2 3 1 4 2 1 5 2 4
WWWWWWWWWW
MMMMMMMMMMMMMMMMMMMMMMMM

1991 - Women's and men's salaries for each of nine regions:
2 1 1 3 1 1 3 1 2
3 3 1 5 2 1 5 2 4
WWWWWWWWWWWWWW
MMMMMMMMMMMMMMMMMMMMMMMMMM

1992 - Women's and men's salaries for each of nine regions:
3 2 1 3 1 1 4 2 2
4 3 1 5 2 1 6 2 4
WWWWWWWWWWWWWWWWW
MMMMMMMMMMMMMMMMMMMMMMMMMM
```

Here's what you can do: You can store the input numbers in a disk file. When the program reads its input from a disk file, the numbers won't be echoed on the screen, and so they won't get mixed in with the program's output. You can create an input disk file by going into the editor, just as if you're about to type in a program. But instead of typing in a program, you type in the program's input. You type it with return keys and all, as if the program were running and executing ReadLns—only the program isn't running when you do this. For instance, our Program OnlyBars will have a line that looks like this:

```
Read (salaries, nextSal)
```

It tells the computer to read the value of nextSal from the salaries file. This line will be executed nine times (once for each region of the country) and then the computer will execute

```
ReadLn (salaries)
```

So when you create the input file with the editor, you might begin by typing in

```
1 1 1 2 1 1 2 1 2<return key>
```

You're simply typing on the editor as if the computer were executing nine Reads followed by a ReadLn.

In fact, in Program OnlyBars this sequence of nine Reads followed by a ReadLn is done six times in a loop; and so when you get into the editor, you may type in something like this:

```
1 1 1 2 1 1 2 1 2<return key>
2 3 1 4 2 1 5 2 4<return key>
2 1 1 3 1 1 3 1 2<return key>
3 3 1 5 2 1 5 2 4<return key>
3 2 1 3 1 1 4 2 2<return key>
4 3 1 5 2 1 6 2 4
```

Program Example

```
PROGRAM OnlyBars (salaries, output);
{Prints a bar graph of women's and men's salaries
 spanning three years.  Each year's salary figures
 represent totals from nine regions.}
  CONST
    startYear = 1990;
    stopYear  = 1993;
  TYPE
    yearType = startYear..stopYear;
  VAR
    year                : yearType;
    womensSal, mensSal  : INTEGER;
    salaries            : TEXT;

  {----------}


  PROCEDURE ObtainTotalSal (VAR salaries      : TEXT    ;
                            VAR symbolsNeeded : INTEGER);
  {Obtains total salary for nine regions.
   Reads each of nine regions and forms a total.}
    CONST
      startRegion = 1;
      stopRegion  = 10;
    TYPE
      regionType = startRegion..stopRegion;
    VAR
      region  : regionType;
      nextSal : INTEGER;
  BEGIN {ObtainTotalSal}
    symbolsNeeded := 0;
    region := startRegion;
    WHILE region < stopRegion DO
      BEGIN
        Read (salaries, nextSal);
        symbolsNeeded := symbolsNeeded + nextSal;
        region := region + 1
      END;
    ReadLn (salaries)
  END;   {ObtainTotalSal}

  {----------}
```

```
PROCEDURE MakeBar (symbolsNeeded : INTEGER; symbol : CHAR);
{Prints one of the bars in a bar graph.}
  VAR
    symbolsWritten : INTEGER;
BEGIN {MakeBar}
  symbolsWritten := 0;
  WHILE symbolsWritten < symbolsNeeded DO
    BEGIN
      Write (symbol:1);
      symbolsWritten := symbolsWritten + 1
    END;
  WriteLn
END;   {MakeBar}

{----------}

BEGIN {OnlyBars}
  WriteLn ('      WOMEN''S AND MEN''S SALARIES'   );
  WriteLn ('(in hundreds of millions of dollars)');
  WriteLn;

  Reset (salaries);
  year := startYear;
  WHILE year < stopYear DO
    BEGIN
      ObtainTotalSal (salaries, womensSal);
      ObtainTotalSal (salaries, mensSal  );

      WriteLn (year:4);
      MakeBar (womensSal, 'W');
      MakeBar (mensSal  , 'M');
      WriteLn;

      year := year + 1
    END
END.   {OnlyBars}
```

Sample Runs

If, when you edit the input data, you type in

```
1 1 1 2 1 1 2 1 2
2 3 1 4 2 1 5 2 4
2 1 1 3 1 1 3 1 2
3 3 1 5 2 1 5 2 4
3 2 1 3 1 1 4 2 2
4 3 1 5 2 1 6 2 4
```

then the output on the screen will look like this:

```
        WOMEN'S AND MEN'S SALARIES
(in hundreds of millions of dollars}
1990
WWWWWWWWWW
MMMMMMMMMMMMMMMMMMMM
1991
WWWWWWWWWWWWW
MMMMMMMMMMMMMMMMMMMMM
1992
WWWWWWWWWWWWWWWWW
MMMMMMMMMMMMMMMMMMMMMMMM
```

Observations   Just as in Program Copy, we put a new file name, salaries, in the program's heading. Then in the VAR declarations we declare salaries to be a TEXT file. In the beginning of the main program's body, we Reset the salaries file; and then when we Read, we make sure to Read from salaries:

```
Read (salaries, nextSal)
```

passing a file to a subprogram   Since this Read takes place in a subprogram, we have to send the file name salaries to the subprogram. It appears in the subprogram's parameter list:

```
PROCEDURE ObtainTotalSal (VAR salaries       : TEXT     ;
                          VAR symbolsNeeded : INTEGER);
```

so when we call the subprogram, we supply the name salaries as an actual parameter:

```
ObtainTotalSal (salaries, womensSal);
ObtainTotalSal (salaries, mensSal   )
```

Notice that in the subprogram's heading, salaries has the word VAR in front of it. If we omit the word VAR the compiler will give us an error diagnostic. Now does this mean that Procedure ObtainTotalSal makes changes to the salaries file? Why would it make changes to the salaries file if it just Reads data from the file?

Well, Reading is more than just "getting information." Among other things Reading means "moving to the next piece of information" in the file. And from the point of view of Procedure ObtainTotalSal, this movement is really a change. More on this in Section 15.2.

```
• CONST
    startYear = 1990;
    stopYear  = 1993;
  TYPE
    yearType = startYear..stopYear;
  VAR
    year : yearType;
```

We could have declared

```
VAR
  year : startYear..stopYear;
```

or even

```
VAR
  year : 1990..1993;
```

type definitions

but instead we decided to give the subrange a name. We call it yearType. The new name is defined in a part of the program that we call the **type definition part.** With this new definition, the word yearType becomes the name of a type, just the way INTEGER, REAL, and CHAR are the names of types (see Section 2.6). The only difference is that the names INTEGER, REAL, and CHAR are **predefined** in the Pascal language and the name yearType isn't.

A type definition part must come after any CONST definitions and before any VAR declarations, as in our main program OnlyBars, and in its subprogram ObtainTotalSal.

Further Discussion

When we define a new type name, we can use that name in other parts of the program. For instance, in Section 3.8 we had difficulties protecting all our mileage variables with subranges, because things like

advantages of using type definitions

```
FUNCTION Profit (mileage : 500..20500) : REAL;
```

or

```
FUNCTION Profit (mileage : startMiles..stopMiles) : REAL;
```

aren't allowed in Pascal. But if we create a new type name

```
PROGRAM Trucking (output);
      .
      .
CONST
  startMiles =   500;
  stopMiles  = 20500;
TYPE
  mileageType = startMiles..stopMiles;
VAR
  mileage : mileageType;
```

then all our mileage variables, even the ones that are formal parameters, can be restricted to subranges:

```
FUNCTION Profit (mileage : mileageType) : REAL;
```

Another advantage of creating a new type name is *self-documentation.* Wherever we use words like yearType or mileageType they tell us something about what they stand for. A subprogram heading like

```
FUNCTION Profit (m : mileageType) : REAL;
```

is much more informative than

```
FUNCTION Profit (m : INTEGER) : REAL;
```

And then there's one more way to understand new type names. In Section 3.1 we talked about subprograms being a form of *procedural abstraction.* At this point we can describe another kind of abstraction called *data abstraction.* Once again, the word *abstract* means "lacking in detail." In this case, it means that the details about the data (the variables and their types) are moved out of conspicuous view. This is good, because it pushes the details to a place where they belong, where they won't get in the way of our thinking about the "big picture."

In Program OnlyBars we have a variable named year. The "details" about year are that values of year must lie within the range 1990 to 1993. These details are moved out of conspicuous view (that is, abstracted) when we create a new type, named yearType, and declare year to be of type yearType. When we look at the declaration

```
VAR
   year : yearType;
```

we understand that we're talking about a collection of years, but we don't necessarily clutter our minds with details about which years. That is, this detail about the data has been abstracted. It's been moved out of the way (into a type definition).

In many areas of study, it's bad to be "lacking in detail." It could mean that you don't know something you should know. But in programming, it's useful to hide details. It means you're thinking about the problem in layers. First you concentrate on the topmost layer, where yearType could stand for any range of years—not just 1990 to 1993. Once you fully understand this topmost layer, you can move into the next layer, where specific years have been chosen. First you look at the abstract, then the concrete, then the even-more-concrete, etc. That's how it should be done.

Testing and Debugging

We obtained the data for this section's Sample Run by examining a copy of the *Statistical Abstract of the United States.*[3] When you're testing a program to see if it runs correctly, it's always good to use some "real-life" data. There are two ways to get real-life data.

alpha and beta testing

One way is to have the programmer look it up in books or try to recall it from experience or common sense. This is called **alpha testing**. The essence of alpha testing is that it's done by the programmer or at least that it's done within the company where the program was written.

Of course we could also get real-life data by giving the program to the real-life users and letting them test it. We might give Program OnlyBars to a team of demographers. Along with the program, we'd give them a careful warning that they're helping to test the program and that, until the testing

---

[3]Published yearly by the Department of Census of the U.S. Department of Commerce.

is done, they should not rely on the program's results. This kind of testing is done all the time. It's called **beta testing**.

glass box
testing and
black box
testing

Now recall from Section 3.7 that when we do *glass box testing*, we find test data by examining the code. The program is a "glass box"—a box whose contents are visible. In contrast, beta testing is a form of **black box testing**. In black box testing, we make use of no knowledge about the way the program works. Instead, we get our test data by thinking about the problem that the program should solve. More precisely, when we do beta testing we give the program to its eventual users and let them think about the problem that the program should solve.

4.2   Exercises

Key Words to Review

predefined	beta testing	type definition part
black box testing	TYPE	data abstraction
alpha testing		

Questions to Answer

QUE 4.2.1   Let's say you're using the editor to create a disk file—a file that's going to be read by a Pascal program. How can you tell when to start a new line in the file that you're editing?

QUE 4.2.2   Explain why we use only pass by reference when we send the name of a file to a subprogram.

QUE 4.2.3   What is *data abstraction?* How is it different from *procedural abstraction?* In what ways is it similar?

Changes to Make

CHA 4.2.1   Modify Program OnlyBars so that it writes a salary total (in hundreds of millions of dollars) beside each bar. For example,

```
1990
WWWWWWWWWWW 12
MMMMMMMMMMMMMMMMMMMMMMMM 24
```

CHA 4.2.2   Modify Procedure MakeBar so that it makes the four-digit year be a part of its bar:

```
WW 1990 WWWW
MM 1990 MMMMMMMMMMMMMMM
```

Of course you'll want to assume that each bar is long enough to have the year in it, plus two spaces and some symbols.

CHA 4.2.3   Create a separate subprogram to write the following title at the top of the bar graph:

```
        WOMEN'S AND MEN'S SALARIES
    (in hundreds of millions of dollars)
           from 1990 to 1992)
```

Programs and Subprograms to Write

WRI 4.2.1   A disk file contains a starting balance and a set of transactions that might occur in a checking account

```
 984.22   starting balance
 -55.56   check written
2567.32   paycheck deposited
 -10.00   service charge on checking account
```

Use this information to print a bank statement containing two columns. The left column contains all the amounts credited to the account (deposits, etc.), and the right column contains all the amounts debited from the account (checks written, service charge, etc.) To do this problem, just write a main program that calls the procedure you wrote for Exercise Wri.3.1.1.

WRI 4.2.2   Modify the program you wrote for Exercise Wri.3.4.5 so that it makes optimal use of subranges. In particular, create a subrange called letterGradeType and make use of it in the main program and in the function that returns letter grades.

WRI 4.2.3   In this section we talked about creating the salaries file with your implementation's editor. Now it's time to write a program that

- prompts the user for women's and men's salaries in nine regions over a three-year period
- reads these values from the keyboard
- creates the salaries file by writing these values to the disk

Things to Think About

THI 4.2.1   Discuss the advantages of reading from a disk file, as opposed to reading from the keyboard. What about writing to a disk file, as opposed to writing to the screen? Given several examples of problems in which one or the other technique would be better.

Chapter Summary

A *file* is a collection of information. In this chapter we discussed *disk files*—collections of information stored on disk. We can create a disk file using an editor and then have our Pascal program Read the file. (We did this in Program Copy with the inFile and in Program OnlyBars with the salaries file.) Another thing we can do is have our Pascal program Write a file and then, if we like, examine the file using an editor. (We did this in Program `Copy` with the `outFile`.)

Before a Pascal program `Reads` from a disk file, it has to `Reset` the file. Before it `Writes` to a disk file, it has to `Rewrite` the file. Pascal's pre-declared procedures `Reset` and `Rewrite` prepare a file for reading and writing.

In Pascal, you can create a new type name in the *type definition part* of the program. There are several reasons why this is a useful thing to do. When you create a new type, you can refer to it in other parts of the program (for example, in a subprogram parameter list). When someone sees the type name in the program, they can understand the overall purpose of the type without having to deal with the details about the type. This is an example of *data abstraction.*

Thorough documentation is an important part of any program. When you're writing documentation, the key questions to ask are, Who will eventually be reading the program? What will they need to know about it? What information will be most helpful to them?

5
Nested Control Flow

In Section 3.7 we introduced the notion of a path of execution. A path of execution is one of the ways the computer can "travel" through the program—one of several possible routes. It's a way that **control** of the computer can **flow** from one statement to another.

In the same section, we saw how an IF statement can help determine the flow of control in a program. But a WHILE statement affects the control flow too. For instance, in the fragment

```
ReadLn (x);
WHILE x < 10 DO
  BEGIN
    WriteLn ('Hello world');
    x := x + 1
  END
```

the WHILE statement makes the program "travel" through the WriteLn several times. How many times? It depends on the initial value of x.

structured statements

IF statements and WHILE statements are examples of **structured statements**, statements that can contain other statements. Some of these "other" statements can themselves be structured statements, as we'll see in this chapter's examples. When one structured statement includes another, we say that the statements are **nested**. The first example in this chapter has a WHILE statement inside another WHILE statement.

5.1
File Copying Revisited

Recall Program Copy in Section 4.1 in which we copied a file, with only one line, to another file. Most files have more than one line, so we'd like to extend Program Copy to make it more useful.

Designing a Program

There's an old nursery rhyme that goes

> Each wife had seven sacks,
> Each sack had seven cats,
> Each cat had seven kits;

It reminds us of the task that's before us:

> Each file had several lines,
> Each line had several characters;

Let's begin with a slight modification of the pseudocode for our old version of Program Copy:

> As long as you haven't reached the end of the input line,
> keep doing the following:
>   Read the next character from the input file,
>   Write that character to the output file,
>   Write that character to the screen
>   (that is, echo the character.)

This is what we want to do for each line of our new file. In other words, we want to perform the actions described by this pseudocode many times. So we want all this to be *repeated* inside a loop:

> As long as you haven't reached the end of the input file,
> keep doing the following:
>   As long as you haven't reached the end of the input line,
>   keep doing the following:
>   Read the next character from the input file,
>   Write that character to the output file,
>   Write that character to the screen
>   (that is, echo the character.)

Notice how we're combining two loops, with one of them inside the other. The first loop tells us to process several lines. Then, each time we process a particular line, the second loop tells us to process several characters. This pseudocode will lead us to Pascal code that has two WHILE statements, with one of them inside the other. When we talk about them we'll refer to them as the **inner loop** and the **outer loop**. So here's our first draft of the Pascal code:

```
{This code won't quite work!}
WHILE NOT Eof(inFile) DO
   WHILE NOT Eoln(inFile) DO
      BEGIN
         Read (inFile,  ch);
         Write(outFile, ch);
         Write(output,  ch)
      END
```

Eoln is a pre-declared function. It stands for *End of line*.

Now this code is almost correct, but not quite. The corrected version is given in the Program Example that follows. Let's look at it first, and then we'll discuss why it's correct.

Program Example

```
PROGRAM Copy (inFile, outFile, output);
{Copies inFile to outFile, and
 displays the results on the screen.}
   VAR
      ch                : CHAR;
      inFile, outFile : TEXT;
BEGIN {Copy}
   Reset   (inFile);
   Rewrite (outFile);
   WHILE NOT Eof(inFile) DO
      BEGIN

         WHILE NOT Eoln(inFile) DO
            BEGIN
               Read  (inFile,  ch);
               Write (outFile, ch);
               Write (output,  ch)
            END;

         ReadLn  (inFile);
         WriteLn (outFile);
         WriteLn
      END
END.  {Copy}
```

Sample Runs

A run of this program is the same as a run of Program Copy from Section 4.1, except this program works even with files containing more than one line. For example,

```
Colorless green ideas
sleep furiously.
This is the third line.
Here are five numbers:
  1 2 3
 4
 5
```

Observations   Here's what a file of type TEXT looks like:[1]

TEXT files

```
<character> <character> .. <character> <end-of-line indicator>
<character> <character> .. <character> <end-of-line indicator>
   .
   .
<character> <character> .. <character> <end-of-line indicator>
<end-of-file indicator>
```

---

[1]Note: In this section we describe the way files are handled in many implementations of ANSI Standard Pascal. Your own implementation may differ from this. Consult your instructor or your implementation's manual for more details.

end-of-line indicator

It's a sequence of lines, where each line contains several characters. Interspersed among the ordinary characters are several occurrences of a "special character" that we'll call the *end-of-line indicator*. On many implementations the end-of-line indicator isn't a character at all. It's just a place that the computer keeps track of. But it will be useful for us to think of this "place" as "special character" of some sort. That is, when we see

```
The first line.
The second line.
```

displayed on the screen, we'll picture a file whose content is

```
The first line.end-of-line indicatorThe second line.end-of-line indicator
```

end-of-file indicator

At the end of every file there's another "special character" called the *end-of-file indicator*. It keeps track of the place where one file ends and another begins.[2]

In Program Copy we use Pascal's pre-declared Eoln function to find out if the computer is about to read the end-of-line indicator.[3] When using Eoln, it's important to remember that this function finds out if we're at the end of the line, but it doesn't prepare the computer for reading at the start of the next line. Here's an experiment to show you what we mean:

Program Example

```
PROGRAM EolnDemo (inFile, output);
{*****************************************************************
 * Shows how the pre-declared 'Eoln' function works.  Comments *
 * tell what the program does with the following 'inFile':     *
 *                                                             *
 *      ab                                                     *
 *      c                                                      *
 *****************************************************************}
  VAR
    ch      : CHAR;
    inFile : TEXT;
BEGIN {EolnDemo}
  Reset (inFile);
  Read (inFile, ch);                              {reads 'a'}
  Read (inFile, ch);                              {reads 'b'}
  IF Eoln (inFile) THEN
    WriteLn ('I''m at the end of the line.');

  IF Eoln (inFile) THEN
    WriteLn ('I''m still at the end of the line.');
```

---

[2]In the examples that follow, we'll frequently use *end-line* for the end-of-line indicator and *end-file* for the end-of-file indicator.

[3]To find out what type of value Function Eoln returns, see Section 8.3.

```
IF Eoln (inFile) THEN
   WriteLn ('Even now I''m at the end of the line.');
ReadLn (inFile);                              {Prepares for reading}
                                              {at the start of a new}
                                              {line.  That is, moves}
                                              {us past the end-line}
                                              {indicator.}

IF Eoln (inFile) THEN
   WriteLn ('Am I still at the end of the line?');
Read (inFile, ch)                             {reads 'c'}
END.  {EolnDemo}
```

Sample Runs

With the following inFile:

```
ab
c
```

How Eoln works

the output of Program EolnDemo will be

```
I'm at the end of the line.
I'm still at the end of the line.
Even now I'm at the end of the line.
```

This illustrates that you can call Eoln more than once, without doing any Reads or ReadLns between the calls, and Eoln will be TRUE each time.

Now let's get back to Program Copy. Our original translation of the pseudocode was missing one thing. It never called Read or ReadLn after testing for Eoln:

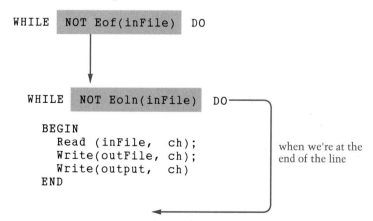

```
{This code won't quite work!}
     WHILE   NOT Eof(inFile)   DO


         WHILE   NOT Eoln(inFile)   DO
             BEGIN
                Read (inFile,  ch);
                Write(outFile, ch);
                Write(output,  ch)
             END
```

when we're at the end of the line

So this code would never prepare for the reading of a new line; that is, it would never push the computer past the end-of-line indicator. In order to push the computer past the end-of-line indicator, we need a ReadLn:

```
WHILE NOT Eof(inFile) DO
   BEGIN
```

```
WHILE  NOT Eoln(inFile)  DO ──────┐
                                  │
   BEGIN                          │
      Read (inFile,   ch);        │
      Write(outFile,  ch);        │  when we're at the
      Write(output,   ch)         │  end of the line
   END;                           │
                                  │
   ReadLn  (inFile);  ◄───────────┘
   WriteLn (outFile);
   WriteLn
END
```

And since we're going to the beginning of a new line in the inFile, we need to do the same thing in the outFile and on the screen. That's why our code has two extra WriteLns.

5.1 Exercises

Key Words to Review

| control flow | nested statements | outer loop |
| structured statements | inner loop | |

Questions to Answer

QUE 5.1.1   What's the relationship between the terms *structured statements* and *nested statements?*

QUE 5.1.2   Why does the file-copying problem lend itself naturally to the use of nested loops?

QUE 5.1.3   Explain the use of the terms *outer loop* and *inner loop.*

QUE 5.1.4   Make an NS Chart for the new version of Program Copy that appears in this section.

Experiments to Try

EXP 5.1.1   Run Program EolnDemo on your own computer to make sure it behaves the way we claim it does.

EXP 5.1.2   Remove ReadLn (inFile) from Program Copy (but first look at Exercise Man.2.6.2).

EXP 5.1.3   Run Program Copy with an empty inFile; that is, the inFile has been created, but it has nothing in it.

EXP 5.1.4   Run Program Copy with no inFile; that is, the inFile has not been created at all.

Changes to Make

CHA 5.1.1 Modify Program `Copy` so that it copies only the `inFile` to the screen, but it copies one page (that is, one "screenful") at a time. The new program, which we'll call Program `More`, repeatedly displays 22 lines from the `inFile`, displays the message

```
--More--
```

on the twenty-third line, and waits for the user to hit the space bar followed by the return key

```
--More-- <return>
```

before displaying another 22 lines.

CHA 5.1.2 There are many improvements you can make on your `More` program from Exercise Cha.5.1.1.

a. Allow the user to type an equal sign, followed by the return key.

```
--More--=<return>
```

When the program receives this input, it takes the last line that it displayed and writes a message telling how many lines this is from the first line of the file.

b. Allow the user to type the letter q, followed by the return key.

```
--More--q<return>
```

This ends a run of Program `More`.

We'll make some other improvements on Program `More` in the chapters to follow.

Programs and Subprograms to Write

WRI 5.1.1 Write a program that reads a six-letter password from the keyboard and compares it with the six-letter word that it reads from a stored file. If the two words are the same, the program sends the message

```
You are now logged on.
```

to the screen; otherwise, it sends the message

```
Incorrect password.
```

to the screen.

WRI 5.1.2 Write a program that compares the contents of two stored files to see if the two files contain exactly the same characters. If they do, the program prints the message

```
The files are identical.
```

If not, then the program prints the remainders of the lines in the two files, starting from the points where the two files are different.

WRI 5.1.3 There are two ways to represent the changing of lines in poetry. One way is simply to start writing on a new line:

Into the old pond
A frog suddenly plunges.
The sound of water.

and another way is to represent the change of lines with a slash:

The peasant hoes on./The person who asked the way/Is now out of sight.

Write a program that reads a file containing one of the Japanese Haiku given above. In the file, the poem is written on several lines. The program writes the same poem on a new file using slashes.

Here's another Haiku you can use to test your program:

The morning-glory
Has captured my well-bucket.
I will beg water.

WRI 5.1.4   (*Linear search of a file*) Use your editor to create a file that's several lines long. Then write a program that searches for the letter B in the file. At the end of its run, the program reports either the line number where a B first appears or a message saying that there are no Bs in the file.

5.2

Loops with Sentinels

In this chapter we're looking at structured statements that contain other structured statements. This section contains another example of a loop within a loop.

Specifications You're an instructor and you need to tally up the points on each of forty student exams. It's easy to make mistakes when you do this arithmetic in your head, so you use a calculator. But with a calculator, you can hit the wrong button and not see much evidence that you've made a mistake. So you write a "no frills" program that helps you subtract numbers (the number of points off on each question) from 100. The numbers that you enter stay on the screen for a long while, so you can catch any mistakes you make.

With this program, all you have to do is type in numbers and hit the return key. The total starts at 100 and goes down as you type more numbers. When you're done with a student's exam, you just type in a zero. This tells the computer to print the student's exam score and start at 100 again. When you're done with all the exams, you type a -1.

Input: Several student "exams," followed by the number -1

exam
exam
    .
    .
exam
-1

Each student's "exam" consists of several "points-off" scores, followed by the number 0 (which indicates the end of that exam). Each number that's typed in is immediately followed by the return key.

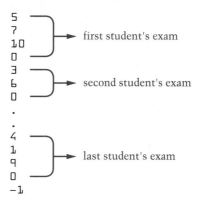

Output: After each student's exam, the program writes the total score for that exam (which is what you get when you subtract all the points-off scores from 100).

Notice that 0 and −1 are read in as if they're ordinary data, but once they're read in they don't get treated like ordinary data. Instead of being subtracted from a student's exam score, they're used to tell us something about the data—namely, that we're at the end of some part of the data. **sentinel values** Values like 0 and −1 are called **sentinel** values.

Designing a Program

One of the most important skills in computer programming is knowing how to simplify a problem in order to make it more manageable. In this instance we'll simplify our problem by temporarily choosing to handle only one student's exam. In the next section we'll consider the whole problem once again. So here's a restatement of the specs:

Input: A student's "exam," which consists of several "points-off" scores, followed by the number 0 (which indicates the end of that exam). Each number that's typed in is immediately followed by the return key.

Output: After reading the points-off scores, the program writes the total score for that exam (which is what you get when you subtract all the points-off scores from 100).

So we'll need a loop of some kind:

As long as we haven't reached the end of the exam data, keep doing the following:
   Read the number of points off for an incorrect answer,
   Subtract that many points off from the total exam score.

We use this pseudocode to get the first draft of the code:

```
CONST
  endExamSentinel = 0;
     .
     .
WHILE nextInput <> endExamSentinel DO
   BEGIN
     ReadLn (nextInput);
     total := total - nextInput
   END
```

But this won't work, because the first time we do the test

```
nextInput <> endExamSentinel
```

nextInput won't have a value. We'd better try putting the first
ReadLn (nextInput) before that comparison:

```
CONST
  endExamSentinel = 0;
     .
     .
ReadLn (nextInput);
WHILE nextInput <> endExamSentinel DO
   BEGIN
     ?
     ?
   END
```

But now when we enter the WHILE loop, we have a nextInput value that
needs to be subtracted from the exam total. So what do we want to do
each time inside the loop? First we want to subtract that nextInput from
the exam total, and then we want to read another nextInput value.

```
CONST
  endExamSentinel = 0;
     .
     .
ReadLn (nextInput);
WHILE nextInput <> endExamSentinel DO
   BEGIN
     total := total - nextInput;
     ReadLn (nextInput)
   END
```

This is a very common way to set up a WHILE loop. The general format is

Read some data.
While the data satisfies some condition, do the following:
    process the data;
    read more data.

We'll certainly need to use this format whenever we deal with sentinels.

Once we've figured out how to write the program's main WHILE loop, writing the rest of the program is easy.

Program Example

```
PROGRAM PointsOnOneExam (input, output);
{Tallies the scores for one exam.}
  CONST
    topPossible     = 100;
    endExamSentinel = 0;
  VAR
    nextInput, total : INTEGER;

  {----------}

  PROCEDURE PromptAndReadLn (VAR nextInput : INTEGER;
                                 sentinel   : INTEGER);
  BEGIN {PromptAndReadLn}
    Write  ('Points off (or ', sentinel:2, '): ');
    ReadLn (nextInput)
  END;   {PromptAndReadLn}

  {----------}

BEGIN {PointsOnOneExam}
  PromptAndReadLn (nextInput, endExamSentinel);
  total := topPossible;

  WHILE nextInput <> endExamSentinel DO
    BEGIN
      total := total - nextInput;
      PromptAndReadLn (nextInput, endExamSentinel)
    END;

  WriteLn ('Total on this exam: ', total:3)
END.   {PointsOnOneExam}
```

Sample Runs

```
Points off (or  0): 4
Points off (or  0): 1
Points off (or  0): 9
Points off (or  0): 0
Total on this exam:  86
```

Observations

- `total := total - nextInput`

accumulating with subtraction

  `total` is an accumulator that counts downward from 100. That's why `nextInput` always gets subtracted from `total`.

5.2   Exercises

Key Words to Review

sentinel

Questions to Answer

QUE 5.2.1   Give the reasoning behind the placement of calls to Procedure `PromptAndReadLn` in Program `PointsOnOneExam`.

QUE 5.2.2   Give the reasoning behind the placement of the `total := topPossible` statement in Program `PointsOnOneExam`.

QUE 5.2.3   When writing Program `PointsOnOneExam` why did we create Procedure `PromptAndReadLn`?

QUE 5.2.4   Write a trace for Program `PointsOnOneExam`.

Changes to Make

CHA 5.2.1   Modify Program `PointsOnOneExam` so that a sample run of the program looks like this:

```
Points off: 4
   More(y or n)? y
Points off: 1
   More(y or n)? y
Points off: 9
   More(y or n)? n
Total on this exam:   86
```

In this section you can use a `WHILE` loop to write this program. In Section 6.6 you'll learn a more natural way to write the same program.

Programs and Subprograms to Write

WRI 5.2.1   The data from a survey of television viewing habits look like this:

```
1  3  0  5  -1
```

These data tell us that we surveyed four households. The first household had one television set, the second had three sets, the third had none, and the fourth had five sets. All the data are contained on a single line. The sentinel -1 tells us that we're at the end of the data.

Write a program that reads these data and writes the number of households in the survey, the total number of television sets in the survey, and the average number of television sets per household.

WRI 5.2.2   Modify the program you wrote for Exercise Wri.2.6.2 so that it stops looping when it finds that the object begins to go downward. In this way our program can find an approximate value for the maximum height that the object will attain.

5.3

Nested Loops with Sentinels

Designing a Program

In Section 5.2 we simplified the points-off problem to deal with only one student's exam. In this section we'll go back to the original problem.

You have several students' exams, and on each exam there are a number of answers with points taken off. Once again it's like the old nursery rhyme

constructing nested `WHILE` *loops*

Each run had several exams,
Each exam had several incorrect answers;

The pseudocode is bound to look something like this:

As long as we haven't reached the end of all the data,
keep doing the following:
    As long as we haven't reached the end of this exam's data,
    keep doing the following:
        Read the number of points off for an incorrect answer,
        Subtract that many points off from this exam's total score.

So we'll surely have a program that has a loop within a loop.

But once again the hard part is figuring out where to put all the other statements: the `ReadLn`s, the initializing statements, etc. Here's the first draft of the code:

```
WHILE nextInput <> stopRunSentinel DO
  BEGIN

    WHILE nextInput <> endExamSentinel DO
      BEGIN
        total := total - nextInput
      END

  END
```

for each incorrect answer

for each exam

Now where do we have to `ReadLn (nextInput)`? Certainly we need to do it before we do the test

```
nextInput <> stopRunSentinel
```

So we want a `ReadLn` at the top of the code:

```
ReadLn (nextInput);
WHILE nextInput <> stopRunSentinel DO
  BEGIN

    WHILE nextInput <> endExamSentinel DO
      BEGIN
        total := total - nextInput
      END

  END
```

Then we notice that the statement

```
total := total - nextInput
```

will use up this value of nextInput; so, after subtracting nextInput from total, we have to read a new value for nextInput:

```
ReadLn (nextInput);
WHILE nextInput <> stopRunSentinel DO
  BEGIN
    WHILE nextInput <> endExamSentinel DO
      BEGIN
        total := total - nextInput;
        ReadLn (nextInput)
      END

  END
```

So far so good. Now when this ReadLn (nextInput) reads a zero (the endExamSentinel), that means it's time to leave the inner loop and write the total for this exam:

```
ReadLn (nextInput);
WHILE nextInput <> stopRunSentinel DO
  BEGIN
    WHILE nextInput <> endExamSentinel DO
      BEGIN
        total := total - nextInput;
        ReadLn (nextInput)
      END;

    WriteLn (total:3)
  END
```

But then the computer will get right to the line where it tests for the endExamSentinel:

```
ReadLn (nextInput);

WHILE  nextInput <> stopRunSentinel  DO

  BEGIN

    WHILE  nextInput <> endExamSentinel  DO

      BEGIN
        total := total - nextInput;
        ReadLn (nextInput)
      END;


    WriteLn (total:3)

END
```

So right after we `WriteLn (total:3)` we'd better read in another value for `nextInput`:

```
ReadLn (nextInput);
WHILE nextInput <> stopRunSentinel DO
  BEGIN
    WHILE nextInput <> endExamSentinel DO
      BEGIN
        total := total - nextInput;
        ReadLn (nextInput)
      END;
    WriteLn (total:3);
    ReadLn (nextInput)
  END
```

This is the thinking we use to decide where to put the `ReadLn`s in Program `Points`.

Program Example

```
PROGRAM Points (input, output);
{Tallies the scores for several exams.}
  CONST
    topPossible      = 100;
    endExamSentinel = 0;
    stopRunSentinel = -1;
  VAR
    nextInput, total : INTEGER;
  {----------}

  PROCEDURE PromptAndReadLn (VAR nextInput : INTEGER;
                                 sentinel      : INTEGER);
  BEGIN {PromptAndReadLn}
    Write  ('Points off (or ', sentinel:2, '): ');
    ReadLn (nextInput)
  END;   {PromptAndReadLn}
  {----------}
BEGIN {Points}
  PromptAndReadLn (nextInput, stopRunSentinel);
  WHILE nextInput <> stopRunSentinel DO
    BEGIN
      total := topPossible;
      WHILE nextInput <> endExamSentinel DO
        BEGIN
          total := total - nextInput;
          PromptAndReadLn (nextInput, endExamSentinel)
        END;
      WriteLn ('Total on this exam: ', total:3);
      WriteLn;
      PromptAndReadLn (nextInput, stopRunSentinel)
    END
END.   {Points}
```

Sample
Runs

```
Points off (or  -1): 5
Points off (or   0): 7
Points off (or   0): 10
Points off (or   0): 0
Total on this exam:   78

Points off (or  -1): 3
Points off (or   0): 6
Points off (or   0): 0
Total on this exam:   91

Points off (or  -1): 4
Points off (or   0): 1
Points off (or   0): 9
Points off (or   0): 0
Total on this exam:   86

Points off (or  -1): -1
```

5.3 Exercises

Questions to Answer

QUE 5.3.1 Give the reasoning behind the placement of calls to Procedure `PromptAndReadLn` in Program `Points`.

QUE 5.3.2 Give the reasoning behind the placement of the `total := topPossible` in statement Program `Points`.

QUE 5.3.3 Write a trace for Program `Points`.

QUE 5.3.4 Write an NS Chart for Program `Points`.

Experiments to Try

EXP 5.3.1 Run Program `Points` and type in negative values (other than −1) when prompted for numbers of points off.

EXP 5.3.2 Run Program `Points` and type in −1 (attempting to end the entire run of the program) when you see the prompt

```
Points off (or   0):
```

EXP 5.3.3 Run Program `Points` and type in 0 when you see the prompt

```
Points off (or  -1):
```

Changes to Make

CHA 5.3.1 Modify Program `Points` so that the `topPossible` isn't always 100—it's a value that the user supplies at the beginning of each run.

CHA 5.3.2 Modify Program `Points` so that the `topPossible` isn't always 100—it can vary from one student's exam to another. The user is prompted for a new `topPossible` value whenever the sentinel −1 is typed in. The program ends its run when the value of `topPossible` becomes zero.

CHA 5.3.3   Redo Exercise Cha.5.3.2 so that the program ends when the sentinel value −2 is typed in.

CHA 5.3.4   Modify Program `Points` so that a sample run of the program looks like this:

```
Points off: 3
  More(y or n)? y
Points off: 6
  More(y or n)? n
Total on this exam:   91

More exams(y or n)? y

Points off: 4
  More(y or n)? y
Points off: 1
  More(y or n)? y
Points off: 9
  More(y or n)? n
Total on this exam:   86

More exams(y or n)? n
```

Compare this exercise with Exercise Cha.5.2.1.

Programs and Subprograms to Write

WRI 5.3.1   Modify the program you wrote for Exercise Wri.4.2.1 so that the disk file can contain several transactions on each line

```
984.22   starting balance

-55.56   2567.32   -10.00
-21.54   -606.00   50.00   -32.99
```

At the end of each line, the program writes a *subtotal*—the amount in the account with the transactions that it's read so far.

WRI 5.3.2   Modify the program you wrote for Exercise Wri.5.2.1 so that it works for several cities. The data for the last of the cities end with −2 rather than −1.

WRI 5.3.3   It costs $2.50 just to get into a taxicab in New York City, and once you're in the cab it costs an extra $1.75 for each mile of travel. Write a program that makes a table of costs for various numbers of one-mile trips, two-mile trips, three-mile trips, etc.

```
Number     Mileage per trip
of trips   1  2  3  4  5  6  7  8  9  10
1
2
3
4
```

Each row of the table should stop when the cost exceeds $15.00.

Things to Think About

THI 5.3.1   Can you give a general set of guidelines to describe the kind of problem whose solution requires nested loops?

5.4

More Statement Nesting

Specifications   Input: Several numbers (each of type INTEGER)

Output: The smallest of these numbers

Designing a Program   The problem seems so simple. A human might just glance at ten numbers and "pick" the smallest, but computers can't "glance." And what does it mean to "pick" a number?

To be truthful, a human can "glance" at only one number at a time. This glancing happens so fast that we get the impression that we're glancing at several numbers at once. To find the smallest of several numbers, a computer has to do several simple comparisons. That is, several times it has to answer a question like

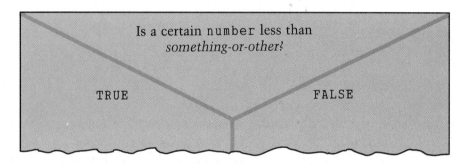

But what's the "something-or-other" that the computer needs to compare its numbers to? The answer is simple and ingenious: throughout the entire algorithm, the computer should keep track of the smallest value that it's read so far and compare all new numbers it reads to that smallest. Several times the computer should do

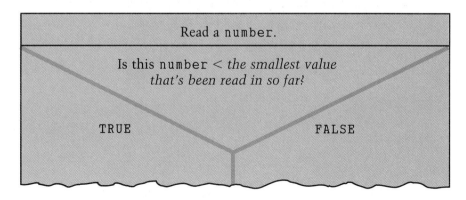

If the answer to the < question is "yes," the computer should change its mind about what it thinks is the smallest value it's read so far:

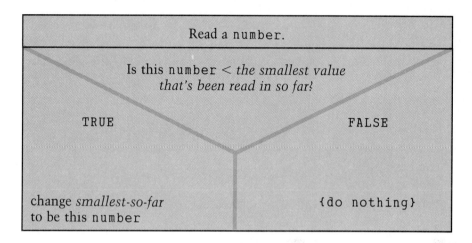

So we'll have a simple IF statement that compares number to the smallest-so-far. But remember that this IF statement will have to be executed several times—once for each number that the computer can read in. The IF statement will have to be inside a WHILE statement:

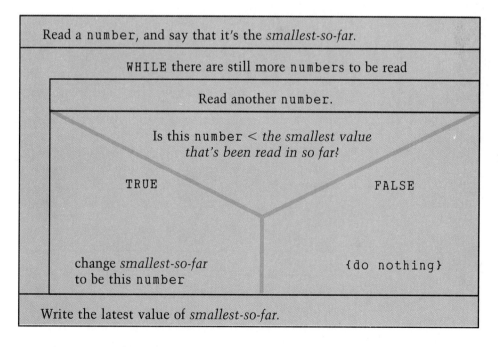

The code follows.

**Program
Example**

```
PROGRAM Minimum (input, output);
{Writes the smallest of the
 numbers given to it as input.}
   VAR
     min, number : INTEGER;
BEGIN {Minimum}
  WriteLn ('Enter one or more integer values.');
  WriteLn ('(Terminate by indicating end-of-file): ');
  ReadLn (min);
  WHILE NOT Eof(input) DO
    BEGIN
      ReadLn (number);
      IF number < min THEN
        min := number
    END;
  WriteLn;
  WriteLn ('The smallest is ', min:5)
END.   {Minimum}
```

**Sample
Runs**

```
Enter one or more integer values.
(Terminate by indicating end-of-file):
10
-1
5
<end-of-file indicator>
The smallest is    -1
```

Normally, the phrase *<end-of-file indicator>* won't appear on the screen. We've put it in our sample run to show where the user indicates "end-of-file." More on this in the Observations.

Observations

initialization

• ReadLn (min)

Here's another example of an *initialization*. This program needs an initialization because we need to have given values to number and min before the condition number < min is tested. For number there's never any problem, because number always gets a value right before the condition is tested:

```
ReadLn (number);
IF number < min THEN

   .

   .
```

But min normally gets its values from the assignment statement that comes after the test is done:

```
IF number < min THEN
  min := number
```

The difficulty occurs when number < min is tested for the very first time. At that point, the assignment statement min := number has never been executed, so `min` has to have been given an initial value. This is done in the initialization.

Eof(input)

- WHILE NOT Eof(input) DO

Since Section 4.1 we've been using Pascal's pre-declared `Eof` function to tell if the computer has reached the end of a file. But is `input` a file? The answer is "yes." The word `input` refers to the file that consists of all the information the user types in at the keyboard during the run of the program. Even though `input` isn't a disk file, it's still considered to be a file. Likewise, all the information that gets written to the screen (the `output`) is a file.

But how does the computer know when it's reached the end of this input file? Almost every implementation has a way for the user to tell the computer "I'm not going to type any more in." On many implementations, the user does this by holding down a key marked "control" (or "ctrl") while hitting one of the letter keys.

By the way, a call to `Eof` without a parameter list

```
WHILE NOT Eof Do
```

is the same as calling it with `input` in its parameter list

```
WHILE NOT Eof(input) DO
```

This holds true of calls to `Eoln` as well.

Traces

detailed tracing

When we trace Program `Minimum` we'd like to show a bit more detail than we've shown in our earlier traces. Instead of just showing the values of variables, let's also show exactly what the user types in (the `input`) and what happens to the two conditions `Eof(input)` and `number < min`:

```
┌──────────────────────── Minimum ──────────────────────────┐
│                                                            │
│  input         Eof(input)   number   number < min   min   output │
│   10                                                  10         │
│   -1           FALSE          -1        TRUE         -1          │
│    5           FALSE           5        FALSE                    │
│ <end-of-file>  TRUE                                       -1     │
│                                                            │
└────────────────────────────────────────────────────────────┘
```

Testing and Debugging

robustness

We have quite a bit to say about testing Program `Minimum`. First we have to talk about robustness. A program that can deal sensibly with a wide variety of input situations, including the unexpected situations, is described as being **robust**. One situation that always needs to be considered is the situation where the program receives no input.

Advice: It's always useful to think about how a program will behave if it receives no input.

For instance, what if an uncooperative user ignores the hint given in Program Minimum's prompt?

```
Enter one or more integer values.
(Terminate by indicating end-of-file):
<end-of-file indicator>
```

Then the computer will try to execute the first ReadLn (min), but instead of getting a value for min, it will see the end-of-file indicator. So the program will be aborted and a nasty-looking error diagnostic will appear.

This is bad. Program Minimum could be just one program in a sequence of programs that get executed automatically, one after another. If a run of Program Minimum gets aborted, it could spoil the whole sequence.

dealing with no data

So what do we do? We enclose most of the program's body in an IF statement that deals with the no-input possibility.

```
PROGRAM Minimum (input, output);
{Writes the smallest of the
 numbers given to it as input.}
  VAR
    min, number : INTEGER;
BEGIN {Minimum}
  WriteLn ('Enter one or more integer values.');
  WriteLn ('(Terminate by indicating end-of-file): ');
  IF Eof(input) THEN
    BEGIN
      WriteLn ('No input values have been read, but');
      WriteLn ('  end-of-file has been encountered ');
      WriteLn ('Minimum value being set arbitrarily to zero.');
      min := 0
    END
  ELSE
    BEGIN
      ReadLn (min);
      WHILE NOT Eof(input) DO
        BEGIN
          ReadLn (number);
          IF number < min THEN
            min := number
        END;
      WriteLn;
      WriteLn ('The smallest is ', min:5)
    END
END.   {Minimum}
```

If the program runs with no input, it doesn't just get aborted. It does the best it can at guessing a smallest value. In all likelihood, this guess (zero) isn't going to be a meaningful answer to the problem the user is trying to solve, but at least the program's added `WriteLn`s send a message to the screen warning the user that something may have gone wrong.

Now that we've made Program `Minimum` sufficiently robust, it's time to talk about testing the program. In earlier chapters we talked about testing our programs by doing several trial runs. Now let's approach the testing issue from a different point of view. Let's "test" Program `Minimum` by reading the program carefully and convincing ourselves that the program will work.

Actually this approach isn't quite "testing." It's one step in a much broader endeavor, called program verification. The term **program verification** refers to activities that we do to convince ourselves that a program works correctly. The act of testing, where we actually run the program with sample data, is just one form of program verification.

program verification

So we want to convince ourselves that Program `Minimum` works just by "reading" the program. Of course by "reading" we don't mean a brief glance at the code and a "Yes, it looks like that'll work." We'll do a very detailed reading of the program, and we'll actually prove that Program `Minimum` works correctly.

a proof of correctness

Now here's what we really intend to prove about Program `Minimum`:

> At the end of each `WHILE` loop iteration, the variable `min` holds the smallest value that's been read in so far.

As long as the user provides any input at all, this assertion about `min` is certainly true before the first `WHILE` loop iteration. That's when the computer executes its first `ReadLn`

```
ReadLn (min)
```

At that point in time, the value in `min` isn't just the smallest value that's been read in so far, it's the only value that's been read in so far.

Now what happens during the first iteration? The computer reads a `number`. If this `number` is smaller than `min`, then the value in `min` gets replaced by this smaller `number`.

```
IF number < min THEN
    min := number
```

But if `number` is larger than `min`, the value in `min` doesn't get replaced. In either case, `min` ends up with the smaller of the two values that have been read in. So at the end of the first iteration, `min` holds the smallest value that's been read in so far.

In the second iteration, a new `number` gets compared with `min`, which holds the smaller of the first two values. Perhaps this new `number` is so small that it replaces the smaller of the first two values. Or maybe it's large enough so that it doesn't replace the smaller of the first two values. In either case, `min` ends up with the smallest of the first three values that are read in.

And so on. After each iteration `min` holds the smallest value that's been read in so far.[4]

So what? As long as the user has provided any input at all we know that `min` always holds the smallest value that's been read in so far. But at the end of the program the words "so far" have special meaning, because no other values will be read in. So then we can say

> At the end of the program, the variable `min` holds the smallest value that has been, *or will be*, read in.

In other words, Program `Minimum` works correctly. It does what the specs say it should do.

What we've just done is to actually prove that Program `Minimum` works correctly. We've done what's called a **proof of correctness**. To do this proof, we took an assertion

> The variable `min` holds the smallest value that's been read in so far.

and showed that this assertion is true at the end of every iteration of the program's WHILE loop. In other words, we showed that the truth of this assertion doesn't vary from one iteration to another. An assertion like this is called a **loop invariant**, because its truth doesn't vary. Loop invariants are used frequently in proving that programs run correctly.

testing vs.
proofs of
correctness

Now let's compare this proof that we just did with our old testing methods—running the program several times, each time with different input data. When we run the program several times, what we're really showing is that the program runs correctly with a representative collection of input data. We're hoping that our collection is large enough to represent any input the program can possibly be given, but we can't be sure of this. All we can say is "It works for all the data that we actually used in doing the test."

In contrast, a proof of correctness is an attempt to show that the program works correctly for *every* possible input. Reread the proof of correctness for Program `Minimum` and notice that it doesn't mention any particular values for `number`, nor does it say anything about how many `numbers` will be typed in before end-of-file is indicated. A proof of correctness is intended to be very general indeed.

---

[4]A reader who's familiar with mathematical induction will recognize that we're using it implicitly in this proof.

5.4   Exercises

Key Words to Review

robust   proof of correctness   loop invariant
program verification

Questions to Answer

QUE 5.4.1   True or false? When you initialize a variable, you always set it equal to zero. Explain.

QUE 5.4.2   Explain the strategy used in Program Minimum for finding the smallest of several values.

QUE 5.4.3   Expand the trace of Program OneBar (Section 2.6) so that it keeps track of whether or not symbolsWritten < symbolsNeeded.

QUE 5.4.4   In a certain sense a proof of correctness gives us more information than doing several test runs. Why?

QUE 5.4.5   Show that, as long as x is greater than or equal to zero, the assertion

The current value of x plus the current value of y equals twice the *original* value of x.

is an invariant for the loop in Program Proof1:

```
PROGRAM Proof1 (input, output);
{Prints double the value that's input.}
   VAR
      x, y : INTEGER;
BEGIN {Proof1}
   ReadLn (x);
   y := x;
   WHILE x > 0 DO
      BEGIN
         y := y + 1;
         x := x - 1
      END;
   WriteLn (y:3)
END.   {Proof1}
```

Use this invariant to prove that Program Proof1 prints double the value that's given to it as input.

QUE 5.4.6   Show that, as long as x is greater than or equal to zero, the assertion

y is equal to z * (z - x)

is an invariant for the loop in Program Proof2:

```
PROGRAM Proof2 (input, output);
{Prints the square of the value that's input.}
   VAR
      x, y, z : INTEGER;
BEGIN {Proof2}
   ReadLn (x);
   y := 0;
   z := x;
   WHILE x > 0 DO
      BEGIN
         y := y + z;
         x := x - 1
      END;
   WriteLn (y:3)
END.  {Proof2}
```

Use this invariant to prove that Program Proof2 prints the square of the value that's given to it as input.

Things to Check in a Manual

MAN 5.4.1   Is there a way, with your implementation, to indicate the end of the keyboard input file? If so, what is it?

Experiments to Try

EXP 5.4.1   Run the first version of Program Minimum (without the added lines to insure robustness) and indicate end-of-file immediately after the program starts running.

EXP 5.4.2   Add the following statement immediately after the IF statement in Program Minimum:

```
WriteLn ('        Smallest so far: ', min:5)
```

EXP 5.4.3   In addition to the statement you added for Exercise Exp.5.4.2, add the following statement immediately before the IF statement in Program Minimum:

```
Write ('number < min: ', number < min)
```

EXP 5.4.4   Let's try to change Program Minimum so that the user is prompted for each number that's entered. Add a WriteLn inside the WHILE loop. (Put it immediately before the ReadLn). Does the program do what you'd expect it to do? This behavior will be explored thoroughly in Section 15.2.

Changes to Make

CHA 5.4.1   Modify Program Minimum as follows:

Input: A number, stored in the variable size; and several other numbers, each stored in the variable available

Output: The smallest available value that's at least as big as size

This output of this new program is called the *best fit*.

CHA 5.4.2 Modify Program `Minimum` so that, instead of `Reading` a value for `min` before the `WHILE` loop, it assigns a very large number to `min`—a number larger than any that will be read from the keyboard. (For instance, assume that none of the numbers read from the keyboard will be larger than 999.)

CHA 5.4.3 Reconsider your solutions to Exercises Cha.2.6.3 and Cha.2.6.4 in the light of what you now know about combining `IF` statements and `WHILE` statements.

CHA 5.4.4 Modify Procedure `MakeBar` so that it writes only two asterisks, in two positions specified by the main program:

```
*           *
```

(In all the other positions that come before the second asterisk, it writes blank spaces.) Have the main program call the new procedure in such a way that an X made of asterisks gets written on the screen.

CHA 5.4.5 Modify Program `Copy` (Section 5.1) so that it takes its input from the keyboard and deposits this data into a disk file. It keeps reading characters from the keyboard until the user indicates end-of-file. (Note: Don't have your program attempt to send any prompts to the screen.) This is an editor in its most primitive form. The program can be used to create a file, but not to modify the file as it's being created.

CHA 5.4.6 Modify Program `Copy` (Section 5.1) so that it omits any blank spaces when copying to the `outFile`, but doesn't omit them when copying to the screen.

CHA 5.4.7 Modify Program `Copy` (Section 5.1) so that it has an `IF` statement inside a `WHILE` loop, instead of nested loops. For example,

```
If Eoln(inFile) THEN
    .
    .
```

Many programs involving nested loops can be modified to have an `IF` statement inside a loop. What other programs that we've done can be modified this way? Which programs can't be modified this way?

CHA 5.4.8

Modify Program Copy so that it assumes that each line of the
  inFile is exactly sixty characters long. When it creates t
he outFile, it creates lines that are only fifty characters
long. For instance, if the inFile contains this paragraph,
then the outFile contains ::::::::::::::::::::::::::::::::::::

Modify Program Copy so that it assumes that each l
ine of the inFile is exactly sixty characters long
. When it creates the outFile, it creates lines t
hat are only fifty characters long. For instance,
 if the inFile contains this paragraph, then the o
utFile contains ::::::::::::::::::::::::::::::::::::

Scales to Practice

PRA 5.4.1 Write a program that satisfies the following specifications:

Input: A number, stored in the variable `size`; and several other numbers, each stored in the variable `available`

Output: The first `available` value that's at least as big as `size`

This output of this new program is called the *first fit*.

PRA 5.4.2 Write a program that keeps reading numbers until five of the numbers that it has read are between 50 and 100. Then it writes the sum of these five numbers.

PRA 5.4.3 Modify the program you wrote for Exercise Pra.5.4.2 so that the program stops when it finds five numbers in a row between 50 and 100.

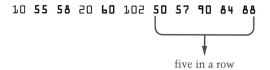

10 55 58 20 60 102 50 57 90 84 88

five in a row

PRA 5.4.4 A disk file has several lines, with one number on each line. Write a program that reads the file and looks for places where the number on a line is different from the number on the previous line.

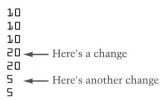

10
10
10
20 ◄─── Here's a change
20
5 ◄─── Here's another change
5

To report a place where this occurs, the program tells how many lines it is from the top of the file.

PRA 5.4.5 Modify the program you wrote for Exercise Pra.5.4.4 so that the disk file contains REAL numbers and the program reports any place where the numbers on two consecutive lines differ by a certain amount epsilon. The value of epsilon is read from the keyboard when the program begins its run.

PRA 5.4.6 Modify Program Minimum so that it makes use of a Function PickOne, which returns the smaller of the two numbers given to it. This gives you a program that we'll call FindValue. Then, without changing the main body of Program FindValue, modify the new Function PickOne so that the program writes the sum of the numbers that it reads.

PRA 5.4.7 Modify Function PickOne (from Exercise Pra.5.4.6) once again, this time making the program subtract "points off" amounts on students' exams, as in Program PointsOnOneExam (Section 5.2).

Programs and Subprograms to Write

WRI 5.4.1 Write a program that reads a state's rainfall (in inches) for twelve successive months (January to December). Then it writes

the highest month's rainfall and the number of the month in which it occurred, the lowest month's rainfall and the number of the month in which it occurred, and the average monthly rainfall.

Have your program do this for several states.

WRI 5.4.2 In a supermarket you have a choice of buying several different packages of hamburger meat.

```
A 2.15  6.77
B 7.50 14.90
C 5.25 15.75
```

The letter identifies a particular package. The number after the letter tells how many pounds of meat are in the package. The last number on a line gives the price of the package. Write a program that reads this information and tells you which package has the cheapest meat in it.

WRI 5.4.3 *(The dice game "craps.")* Here are the rules for playing craps: The first time you roll the dice:

If you get a 7 or 11, you win.

If you get a 2, 3, or 12, you lose.

If you get any other number (called a point), then you keep rolling.

You keep rolling until:

You get the point number again, in which case you win.

You get a 7, in which case you lose.

Write a program that repeatedly reads numbers between 2 and 12 until the player wins or loses. Before it stops running it writes one of the two messages Win! or Lose!

WRI 5.4.4   Your company has two kinds of employees—hourly and salaried. The hourly employees receive paychecks every week and the salaried employees receive paychecks every month. Write a program that prints the numbers (from 1 to 365) of the days in the year when paychecks of one kind or another need to be issued. For example,

```
 7    Issue hourly paychecks
14    Issue hourly paychecks
21    Issue hourly paychecks
28    Issue hourly paychecks
31    Issue salaried paychecks
35    Issue hourly paychecks
 .
 .
 .
Etc.
```

WRI 5.4.5   A bit is like a digit, except that a bit can only be 0 or 1. Write a program that does the following:
a. Reads seven bits and keeps track of whether an even or an odd number of them are 1's. These first seven bits are called *data bits.*
b. Then reads an eighth bit, called a *parity bit.* A parity bit of 0 tells us that an even number of data bits should have been 1's. A parity bit of 1 tells us that an odd number of data bits should have been 1's.
c. Writes OK if the parity bit gave us the correct information and not OK otherwise.

5.5

Nested IFs

In this section we examine nested IF statements—IF statements that contain other IF statements.

Specifications   Input: Three numbers

Output: The largest of the three

Designing a Program   You'd think that if you have such a simple problem, there would be only one or two ways to solve it. But there are many different ways to solve this problem. Here's one way:

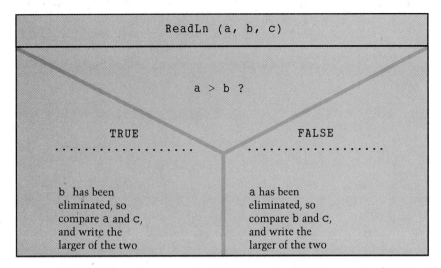

First we compare a with b and eliminate the smaller value.[5] Then we compare the remaining value with c. Now here's the same algorithm, with a little more detail added:

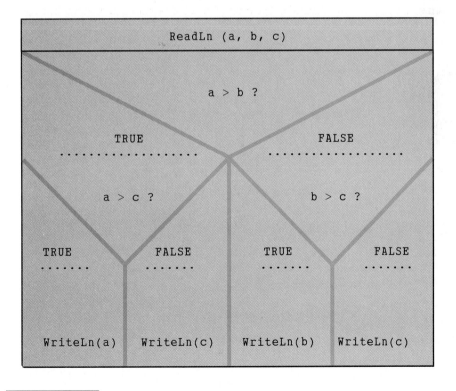

---

[5]Unless, of course, a and b happen to be equal.

When we translate the NS chart into a program, we get an "outer" IF statement, with two "inner" IF statements inside it:

Program Example

```
PROGRAM ThreeWay (input, output);
{Finds the largest of three numbers.}
  VAR
    a, b, c : REAL;
BEGIN {Threeway}
  Write  ('Enter three real numbers: ');
  ReadLn (a, b, c);
  Write  ('The largest is ');
  IF a > b THEN
    {b has been eliminated}
    IF a > c THEN
      WriteLn (a:5:1)          {1}
    ELSE
      WriteLn (c:5:1)          {2}
  ELSE
    {a has been eliminated}
    IF b > c THEN
      WriteLn (b:5:1)          {3}
    ELSE
      WriteLn (c:5:1)          {4}
END.  {ThreeWay}
```

Sample Runs

Program ThreeWay has four paths of execution. In each path, a different WriteLn gets executed. To make things easy to follow, we've added numbers, in comments, to the WriteLns in Program ThreeWay.

Here's a sample run that follows WriteLn path {1}:

```
Enter three real numbers: 16.0  8.0  5.0
The largest is  16.0
```

and here's a sample run that follows WriteLn path {3}:

```
Enter three real numbers: 8.0  16.0  5.0
The largest is  16.0
```

and WriteLn path {2}:

```
Enter three real numbers: 8.0  5.0  16.0
The largest is  16.0
```

and finally WriteLn path {4}:

```
Enter three real numbers: 5.0  8.0  16.0
The largest is  16.0
```

Programming Style

Nested IFs are certainly useful, but sometimes they make a program difficult to read. Here's a new program, NoNesting, that does *almost* the same work as Program ThreeWay but avoids nested IFs:[6]

alternatives to the use of nested IFs

```
PROGRAM NoNesting (input, output);
{Finds the largest of three numbers.}
   VAR
      a, b, c : REAL;
BEGIN {NoNesting}
   Write  ('Enter three real numbers: ');
   ReadLn (a, b, c);
   Write  ('The largest is ');
   IF (a >= b) AND (a >= c) THEN
      WriteLn (a:5:1);
   IF (b >= a) AND (b >= c) THEN
      WriteLn (b:5:1);
   IF (c >= a) AND (c >= b) THEN
      WriteLn (c:5:1)
END.   {NoNesting}
```

Of course, Program NoNesting has trouble of its own. The compact collection of conditions is hard to read and easy to write incorrectly.

One nice way to avoid nesting is to create a subprogram for the inner IF statement.

```
PROGRAM AvoidNesting (input, output);
{Finds the largest of three numbers.}
   VAR
      a, b, c : REAL;
   {----------}
   FUNCTION MaximumOf (x, y : REAL) : REAL;
   {Finds the larger of two numbers.}
   BEGIN {MaximumOf}
      IF x > y THEN
         MaximumOf := x
      ELSE
         MaximumOf := y
   END;   {MaximumOf}
   {----------}
```

---

[6]To find out why we say *almost*, do Exercise Exp.5.5.1. To find out how to change *almost* into *always*, see Section 8.4.

```
BEGIN {AvoidNesting}
   Write  ('Enter three real numbers: ');
   ReadLn (a, b, c);
   Write  ('The largest is ');
   IF a > b THEN
      {b has been eliminated}
      WriteLn (MaximumOf(a,c) : 5:1)
   ELSE
      {a has been eliminated}
      WriteLn (MaximumOf(b,c) : 5:1)
END.  {AvoidNesting}
```

In Program `AvoidNesting`, the outer and the inner `IF` statements have been separated. The main program is much simpler (and easier to read) than the nested `IF`s in Program `ThreeWay`. Notice the use of formal-parameter names x and y instead of a, b, or c. The names a and c might have been useful for the first call to `MaximumOf`:

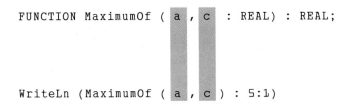

```
FUNCTION MaximumOf ( a , c  : REAL) : REAL;



WriteLn (MaximumOf ( a , c ) : 5:1)
```

but they'd have been very confusing when we tried to understand the second call to `MaximumOf`:

```
FUNCTION MaximumOf ( a , c  : REAL) : REAL;



WriteLn (MaximumOf ( b , c ) : 5:1)
```

Now since we have this nice Function `MaximumOf`, let's use it as much as we can. In Program `AvoidNesting`, the outer `IF`, in the program's main body, finds the maximum of a and b. Instead of doing this with an `IF` statement, we can just call Function `MaximumOf`

```
MaximumOf(a,b)
```

and then take whatever result we get and use `MaximumOf` to compare it with c:

```
MaximumOf( MaximumOf(a,b), c)
```

The complete program is astoundingly simple:

```
PROGRAM UseMaxFunction (input, output);
{Finds the largest of three numbers.}
  VAR
    a, b, c : REAL;

  {----------}
  FUNCTION MaximumOf (x, y : REAL) : REAL;
  {Finds the larger of two numbers.}
  BEGIN {MaximumOf}
    IF x > y THEN
      MaximumOf := x
    ELSE
      MaximumOf := y
  END;  {MaximumOf}

  {----------}
BEGIN {UseMaxFunction}
  Write  ('Enter three real numbers: ');
  ReadLn (a, b, c);
  Write  ('The largest is ');

  WriteLn (MaximumOf( MaximumOf(a,b), c) : 5:1)
END.  {UseMaxFunction}
```

If you absolutely must have nested IFs, remember to add comments to make your program more readable. In the original Program ThreeWay, each comment explains four lines of the program.

5.5 Exercises

Questions to Answer

QUE 5.5.1 Explain why Program ThreeWay has four paths of execution.

QUE 5.5.2 How many paths of execution does Program NoNesting have? What about Program AvoidNesting? Program UseMaxFunction?

QUE 5.5.3 Give four sets of input for Program ThreeWay—one representative for each of the four input classes. In each set, make all three numbers be negative.

QUE 5.5.4 Repeat Exercise Que.5.5.3, this time making two out of three numbers be negative in each set.

Experiments to Try

EXP 5.5.1 Run Program ThreeWay with the input

```
5.0  5.0  5.0
```

Then run Program NoNesting with the same input.

EXP 5.5.2 Change all the > signs to < signs in Program ThreeWay. What does the program do now? After you've made this change, can you change the WriteLns so that the program still finds the largest of the three numbers?

Changes to Make

CHA 5.5.1 Rewrite Program ThreeWay so that it writes all three of the numbers given to it. The largest is written on the first line, then the next largest on the second line, and finally the smallest on the third line.

CHA 5.5.2 Modify Program ThreeWay so that it writes nothing when the largest number is a negative number.

CHA 5.5.3 Modify Program ThreeWay so that it writes nothing when the largest number is an odd number.

CHA 5.5.4 Modify Program ThreeWay so that it writes the largest of four values (even though a program like Program Minimum from Section 5.4 might be better suited to this task).

Programs and Subprograms to Write

WRI 5.5.1 We want a program that reads two sales amounts (one for today and another for several days ago) and computes the average daily increase or decrease in sales. In order to do this, the program also has to read the number of days between the two sales amounts. If sales amounts have increased, the program should report it this way:

```
Average daily increase is $   138.61
```

And if the sales amounts have decreased, the program should report it this way:

```
Average daily decrease is $    96.22
```

Your program should be on the lookout for the user's accidentally entering a zero for the number of days between the two sales amounts. If this happens, the program should print an error message and not report any increase or decrease.

5.6

A Careful Look at the IF Statement

Program ThreeWay in Section 5.5 made very heavy use of IF **statements**. So it's time we took a careful look at the IF statement and the way it works.

IF statement
syntax

Here's the syntax diagram for the IF statement:

IF *statement:*

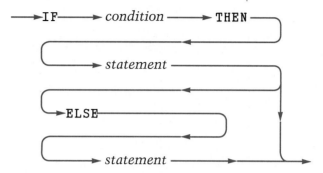

And here's another set of syntax diagrams that give us the same information in a slightly different way:

IF *statement:*

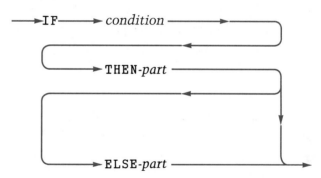

THEN-*part:*

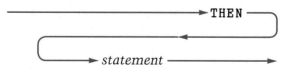

ELSE-*part*

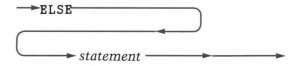

Now notice that a THEN-part has only one statement in it. The same is true of an ELSE-part. But we know from earlier examples that if we use BEGIN and END, we can put as many statements as we like in the THEN-part or the ELSE-part. So what's going on? To help figure it out, we have to look at the (simplified) syntax diagram for a statement:

statement syntax

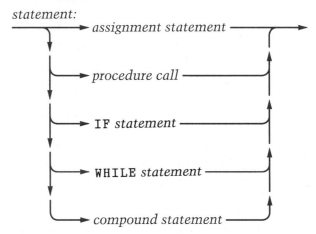

statement:

assignment statement

procedure call

IF statement

WHILE statement

compound statement

There are several different kinds of statements, and one of them is a **compound statement**. Here's what a compound statement looks like:

compound statement syntax

compound statement:

BEGIN

statement

;

END

At this point, we seem to have created a circular definition. A statement, if we choose, can be a compound statement. If it is, then it has statements in it. Does it make any sense to define a statement in terms of itself? Maybe we could use this definition to create a bottomless statement pit: We write a compound statement that contains a statement, which happens to be a compound statement, which in turn contains a compound statement etc.

```
BEGIN
  BEGIN
    BEGIN
          .
          .
      {infinitely many BEGIN's}
      {infinitely many END's  }
          .
          .
    END
  END
END
```

This can't be right!

But we can fix it. The definition of a statement is fine as long as we agree not to make bottomless pits like the one we made above. A definition of this kind is called a **recursive definition**. Among other things, recursive definitions allow us to put IF statements inside other IF statements.

recursive definitions

```
IF condition THEN
    statement ◄—This statement can be an IF statement
ELSE
    statement
```

This is exactly what we do in Program ThreeWay.

Now notice how few semicolons Program ThreeWay has. Starting from the first IF there are about ten lines of code without a single semicolon! Why?

semicolons in IF statements

It's because Pascal uses semicolons to separate the statements in a compound statement from one another. The only compound statement in Program ThreeWay is the whole body of the program.

```
BEGIN {Threeway}
  Write  ('Enter three real numbers: ');
  ReadLn (a, b, c);
  Write  ('The largest is ');
  IF a > b THEN
    {b has been eliminated}
    IF a > c THEN
      WriteLn (a:5:1)              {1}
    ELSE
      WriteLn (c:5:1)              {2}
  ELSE
    {a has been eliminated}
    IF b > c THEN
      WriteLn (b:5:1)             {3}
    ELSE
      WriteLn (c:5:1)             {4}
END.   {ThreeWay}
```

One large compound statement

This compound statement contains four other statements. It contains:

```
Write   ('Enter ...
ReadLn (a, b, c)
Write   ('The largest ...
a huge IF statement.
```

These four statements are separated from one another with semicolons. The IF statement happens to contain other statements, but this doesn't change the fact that the compound statement contains only four statements.

Pascal's use of semicolons is made a bit more complicated by something called the **null statement**. Here's the syntax diagram for a null statement:

null statement

null statement:

This is no misprint. The null statement has no characters in it. It's nothing. It instructs the computer to do nothing. Now, how can so much nothing make any difference? Let's see what happens when we add a harmless semicolon to Program ThreeWay:

```
IF  a > b  THEN;
   {b has been eliminated}
   IF  a > c  THEN
      WriteLn (a:5:1)      {1}
   ELSE
      WriteLn (c:5:1)      {2}

   .
   .
```

When the compiler looks at this, it actually sees

```
IF  a > b  THEN
   null statement; {i.e., do nothing}    ⎤→ a complete
                                          ⎦  IF statement
IF  a > c  THEN
   WriteLn (a:5:1)              {1}       ⎤
ELSE                                       ⎥→ another (separate)
   WriteLn (c:5:1)              {2}       ⎦  IF statement
```

After doing nothing about a > b, the computer goes on to test IF a > c. It does this test whether a > b is true or not.

Actually, there's even more trouble here than what we just described. There's another ELSE in Program ThreeWay that comes right after this code. The problem is that this second ELSE no longer belongs to an IF statement! Here's what the compiler sees:

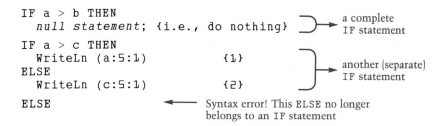

```
IF a > b THEN
   null statement; {i.e., do nothing}              a complete
                                                   IF statement
IF a > c THEN
   WriteLn (a:5:1)           {1}
ELSE                                               another (separate)
   WriteLn (c:5:1)           {2}                   IF statement

ELSE                            Syntax error! This ELSE no longer
                                belongs to an IF statement
```

The same sort of thing happens if you put a semicolon right before an ELSE. When you do

```
IF a > c THEN
   WriteLn (a:5:1);          {1}
ELSE
   WriteLn (c:5:1)           {2}
```

the compiler actually sees

```
IF a > c THEN
   WriteLn (a:5:1);          {1}          a complete
                                          IF statement
ELSE                                      Syntax error!
   WriteLn (c:5:1)           {2}
```

Reminder!

In fact, for a beginning Pascal programmer, putting a semicolon before an ELSE is a very common cause of syntax errors. *So you should remember never to put a semicolon before an* ELSE.

the dangling ELSE problem

Now if we make a slight change to the specs for Program ThreeWay, we discover an interesting feature of nested IF statements:

Input: Three numbers

Output: The largest of the three, as long as it's the first or the second number; no output at all if the largest is the third

Maybe we can satisfy the new specifications by just removing the WriteLn (c:5:1) statements from Program ThreeWay.

```
PROGRAM DanglingElse (input, output);
{This program doesn't do what we'd expect it to do.}
  VAR
    a, b, c : REAL;
BEGIN {DanglingElse}
  Write  ('Enter three real numbers: ');
  ReadLn (a, b, c);
  Write  ('The largest? ');
  IF a > b THEN
    IF a > c THEN
      WriteLn (a:5:1)              {1}
  ELSE
    IF b > c THEN
      WriteLn (b:5:1)             {3}
END.  {DanglingElse}
```

It looks as if we've just removed the ELSE-parts from the two inner IF statements. It's certainly legal to have an IF statement without an ELSE-part. But there's a difficulty here. Let's look at a sample run:

```
Enter three real numbers: 8.0  16.0  5.0
The largest?
```

That's strange. We removed WriteLn (c:5:1) from the program but now the value of b, which is 16.0, is refusing to be written! Why?

It's because the first IF statement has no ELSE-part. That is, when the test a > b fails, there's no alternative action for the program to take, so the program does nothing.

This may be a little confusing because the program's indentation makes it look as if the first IF statement has an ELSE-part. But a Pascal compiler never uses a program's indentation to translate a program. Instead it checks to see if the program follows the syntax diagrams correctly. When it translates a set of nested IFs, it uses the following additional rule:

Nested IF Rule: No matter how the program is indented, an ELSE always belongs to the nearest IF to which it can possibly belong.

So in the code

```
IF a > b THEN
  IF a > c THEN
    WriteLn (a:5:1)              {1}
ELSE
```

the ELSE must belong to the second IF, not the first.
So here's what we've really got in Program DanglingElse:

```
BEGIN {DanglingElse}
   Write  ('Enter three real numbers: ');
   ReadLn (a, b, c);
   Write  ('The largest? ');
```

```
   IF a > b THEN  ◄──────── an IF without an else

     IF a > c THEN

       WriteLn (a:5:1)                    {1} ────────► THEN-part


   ELSE


       IF b > c THEN
         WriteLn (b:5:1)                  {3} ────────► ELSE-part
END.   {DanglingElse}
```

In order not to be misleading, the program should have been indented this
way:

```
PROGRAM DanglingElse (input, output);
{This program doesn't do anything sensible,
 but at least its indentation isn't misleading.}
   VAR
     a, b, c : REAL;
BEGIN {DanglingElse}
   Write  ('Enter three real numbers: ');
   ReadLn (a, b, c);
   Write  ('The largest? ');
   IF a > b THEN
     IF a > c THEN
       WriteLn (a:5:1)                {1}
     ELSE
       IF b > c THEN
         WriteLn (b:5:1)              {3}
END.   {DanglingElse}
```

Now at last it's clear that if a isn't greater than b, nothing will be written.
   Deciding which IF statement has an ELSE-part is called the **dangling
ELSE** problem. We can protect ourselves against dangling ELSEs by putting
BEGINs and ENDs in the right places. Here are two ways to do it:

```
PROGRAM DontWriteC (input, output);
{Finds the largest of three numbers, but only
 if it's the first or the second of the numbers
 that were given as input.}
    VAR
       a, b, c : REAL;
BEGIN {DontWriteC}
   Write  ('Enter three real numbers: ');
   ReadLn (a, b, c);
   Write  ('The largest? ');

   IF a > b THEN

      {b has been eliminated}
      IF a > c THEN
         WriteLn (a:5:1)              {1}
      ELSE
         BEGIN
         END

   ELSE

      {a has been eliminated}
      IF b > c THEN
         WriteLn (b:5:1)             {3}
      ELSE
         BEGIN
         END

END.   {DontWriteC}
```

In Program DontWriteC, we have two compound statements that contain only the null statement. When the computer executes either of these statements, it does nothing. (That's good. We want it to do nothing rather than having it write c.) Notice that these "do nothing" compound statements help us avoid the dangling else problem.

Now here's another alternative:

```
PROGRAM AnotherDontWriteC (input, output);
{Finds the largest of three numbers, but only
 if it's the first or the second of the numbers
 that were given as input.}
    VAR
       a, b, c : REAL;
BEGIN {AnotherDontWriteC}
   Write  ('Enter three real numbers: ');
   ReadLn (a, b, c);
   Write  ('The largest? ');

   IF a > b THEN

      {b has been eliminated}
      BEGIN
        IF a > c THEN
           WriteLn (a:5:1)                {1}
      END
```

```
          ELSE
            {a has been eliminated}
            BEGIN
              IF b > c THEN
                WriteLn (b:5:1)              {3}
            END
    END.   {AnotherDontWriteC}
```

Notice how we've avoided the dangling else problem in this program. The program's only ELSE is forced to belong to the desired IF because

```
        IF a > c THEN
            WriteLn (a:5:1)          {1}
        END
      ELSE
        {a has been eliminated}
          .
          .
```

just can't be an IF statement. The word END gets in the way.

Now we've done something very unusual in Program AnotherDont-WriteC. We've created compound statements that don't "group together" several smaller statements. For instance

```
      BEGIN
        IF b > c THEN
            WriteLn (b:5:1)
      END
```

is a compound statement with only one statement in it: an IF statement. This is a rare occurrence in Pascal.

5.6 Exercises

Key Words to Review

statement	recursive definition	dangling ELSE
compound statement	null statement	

Questions to Answer

QUE 5.6.1 Would we be able to create structured statements if we couldn't use recursive definitions to describe our language? Explain.

QUE 5.6.2 Describe the dangling ELSE problem.

QUE 5.6.3   In Pascal, every IF statement must have a THEN-part.

```
IF condition THEN
    do something that's important
```

But there are situations in which we'd want a THEN-part to do nothing

```
IF condition THEN
    don't do anything
ELSE
    do something that's important
```

Can you think of a way to do this in Pascal? Can you think of a situation in which we'd want to do this?

QUE 5.6.4   Look once again at Program DanglingElse in this section. Will the WriteLn commented with the number {3} ever be executed? Why, or why not?

QUE 5.6.5   Add semicolons as needed to the following program:

```
PROGRAM ThreeVariables (input, output)
{Add semicolons to this program.}

  VAR
    a, b, c : REAL

BEGIN {ThreeVariables}
    Write  ('Enter three real numbers: ')
    ReadLn (a, b, c)

    WHILE a > c DO
      IF a > b THEN
        BEGIN
          a := a - 1
          WriteLn ('a ', a:5:1)
        END
      ELSE
        BEGIN
          WriteLn ('b ', b:5:1)
          a := a - 2
        END

    END.   {ThreeVariables}
```

Experiments to Try

EXP 5.6.1   In Program ThreeWay (Section 5.5) add a semicolon after the program's last WriteLn (the one that's commented with the number {4}).

EXP 5.6.2   In Program ThreeWay (Section 5.5) add a semicolon after the program's next-to-last WriteLn (the one that's commented with the number {3}).

EXP 5.6.3   In Program ThreeWay (Section 5.5) add a semicolon after the program's first THEN:

```
IF a > b THEN;
```

EXP 5.6.4   Take any program that compiles with no error diagnostics. In the main body of the program, change a semicolon into a triple semicolon.

```
x := 10;;;
```

EXP 5.6.5 Take any program that compiles with no error diagnostics. In the VAR declaration part of the program, change a semicolon into a triple semicolon.

```
VAR
   x : INTEGER;;;
```

EXP 5.6.6 Compile and run the following program:

```
PROGRAM DoNothing;
{Contains one null statement.}
BEGIN
END.
```

Changes to Make

CHA 5.6.1 Turn Program DontWriteC (Section 5.6) into Program DontWriteA.

CHA 5.6.2 Turn Program AnotherDontWriteC (Section 5.6) into AnotherDontWriteB.

Chapter Summary

A structured statement is a statement that can contain other statements. Some of these "other" statements can themselves be structured statements. When we do this, we say that the statements are *nested*.

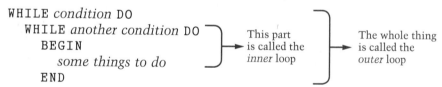

```
WHILE condition DO
   WHILE another condition DO
      BEGIN
         some things to do
      END
```

This part is called the *inner* loop

The whole thing is called the *outer* loop

A TEXT file is a sequence of lines, where each line contains several characters. Interspersed among the ordinary characters are several occurrences of a "special character" that we'll call the *end-of-line indicator*. At the end of every file there's another special character called the *end-of-file indicator*. Pascal's pre-declared Eoln function tells us if the computer is about to read the end-of-line indicator. The pre-declared Eof function tells us if the computer is about to read the end-of-file indicator.

When reading values in a WHILE loop, it's often necessary to put the first Read or ReadLn before the loop. This insures that the WHILE statement's condition can be tested when the WHILE statement is encountered for the first time. Then inside the loop, the reading will typically be the last thing to be done.

Read some data.
While the data satisfies some condition, do the following:
   process the data;
   read more data.

Any combination of structured statements can be nested—loops within loops, IFs within loops, IFs within IFs, loops within IFs, etc. In particular, nested IFs can become tricky if we forget the Nested IF Rule:

Nested IF Rule: No matter how the program is indented, an ELSE always belongs to the nearest IF to which it can possibly belong.

In a Pascal program the placement of semicolons requires some care. For instance the code

```
IF a > b THEN;
```

contains a *null statement,* which may not be obvious at first glance. Pascal's null statement has no characters in it, and when it's executed it doesn't perform any action. However, the null statement can have a significant impact on the way in which the compiler views the program.

A semicolon is most troublesome if it's accidentally placed immediately before the word ELSE. This creates a syntax error and so should never be done.

If we want to show that a program works correctly for all possible inputs, not just certain sample inputs, we can do a *proof of correctness.* In a proof of correctness, we often deal with an assertion called a *loop invariant.* The goal of the proof is to show that the loop invariant is true at the end of each loop iteration.

Repetition

The WHILE Statement in Depth

We've used the WHILE statement in many programs, and in this section we'll take a very simple WHILE loop, dissect it, and examine some of its subtleties.

Specifications

Input: Several grades on an exam, read from a file (called gradeFil)

Output: The average of the grades

Program Example

```
PROGRAM FindAverage (gradeFil, output);
{Finds the average of several grades.}
  CONST
    sentinel = -1;
  TYPE
    gradeType = -1..100;
    natural   =  0..MAXINT;
  VAR
    grade       : gradeType;
    sum, count  : natural;
    average     : REAL;
    gradeFil    : TEXT;
BEGIN {FindAverage}
  Reset (gradeFil);
  count := 0;
  sum   := 0;
  ReadLn (gradeFil, grade);
```

```
    WHILE grade <> sentinel DO
      BEGIN
        count := count + 1;
        sum   := sum + grade;
        ReadLn (gradeFil, grade)
      END;

    average := sum / count;
    WriteLn ('The average of the grades is ', average:6:2)
  END.  {FindAverage}
```

Sample Runs   With the following gradeFile:

```
87
100
75
93
-1
```

the output of Program FindAverage looks like this:

```
The average of the grades is  88.75
```

Observations

• TYPE
    natural   =   0..MAXINT;

MAXINT

The name MAXINT is **predefined** in the Pascal language. MAXINT is the largest value that a variable of type INTEGER can have. The value of MAXINT varies among implementations, but typical values are 32767 and 2147483647 (which happen to be the same as $2^{15} - 1$ and $2^{31} - 1$).

Further Discussion

Here's the syntax diagram for the WHILE statement:

WHILE statement syntax

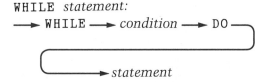

WHILE *statement:*

condition testing in the WHILE statement

We'll say that each WHILE statement contains another statement, called the *repeated statement.* Of course the repeated statement can be a simple statement or a structured statement. Often it's a compound statement.

It's nice to have a general understanding of the connection between WHILE statements and repetition, but it's also important to make this general understanding more precise. Here are some things to remember:

1. The testing of the condition is done at the "top" of the loop, at the beginning of each iteration, before the execution of the repeated statement.

2. The testing of the condition is done only at the "top" of the loop, at the beginning of each iteration. It's never done during the execution of the repeated statement.

3. Execution of the WHILE statement doesn't end until, upon testing, the condition is found to be FALSE.

We'll deal with each item in turn:

First, condition testing is done at the "top" of the loop. Because of this, it's possible to have a WHILE statement whose repeated statement is never executed. This happens in Program FindAverage if the first thing in the gradeFil is the sentinel value −1. If your program has a WHILE statement whose repeated statement never seems to get executed, check to see if the WHILE statement's condition is FALSE when it's first tested.

Second, condition testing is done only at the "top" of the loop. To illustrate this point, let's try changing Program FindAverage so that it has only one ReadLn:

```
PROGRAM FindAverage2 (gradeFil, output);
{Finds the average of several grades.}
  CONST
    sentinel = -1;
  TYPE
    gradeType = -1..100;
    natural   =  0..MAXINT;
  VAR
    grade       : gradeType;
    sum, count  : natural;
    average     : REAL;
    gradeFil    : TEXT;
BEGIN {FindAverage2}
  Reset (gradeFil);
  count := 0;
  sum   := 0;
  grade := 0;
  WHILE grade <> sentinel DO
    BEGIN
      ReadLn (gradeFil, grade);
      count := count + 1;
      sum   := sum + grade
    END;
  average := sum / count;
  WriteLn ('The average of the grades is ', average:6:2)
END.  {FindAverage2}
```

At first glance this program makes some sense. The statements inside the loop seem to occur in a fairly sensible order. The variable grade is initialized to 0 before the loop to make the condition

```
WHILE grade <> sentinel DO
```

be TRUE. But Program FindAverage2 doesn't work correctly. Here's what happens during the last iteration:

```
WHILE grade <> sentinel DO
  BEGIN
    ReadLn (gradeFil, grade);    ←——grade becomes −1,
                                     which is equal to the
                                     sentinel, but

    count := count + 1;          ←—— The iteration isn't
    sum   := sum + grade         ←—— stopped. These two
                                     statements still get
                                     executed.
  END
```

The sentinel value −1 gets added into the sum as if it were a regular grade!

Third, execution doesn't end until, upon testing, the condition is found to be FALSE. The difficulty is, there's nothing in the syntax of the WHILE statement to insure that the condition will ever become FALSE. It's easy to make up a WHILE statement whose condition never becomes FALSE.

```
{This code has an infinite loop!}
WHILE grade <> sentinel DO;
  BEGIN
    count := count + 1;
    sum   := sum + grade;
    ReadLn (gradeFil, grade)
  END
```

Because of the semicolon after the DO, the computer takes this code to be the same as

```
{This code has an infinite loop!}
WHILE grade <> sentinel DO
  {null statement};
BEGIN
  count := count + 1;
  sum   := sum + grade;
  ReadLn (gradeFil, grade)
END
```

So the computer just executes the null statement over and over again, testing the value of grade each time. Of course the null statement does nothing to change the value of grade, so grade never becomes −1, and the execution of the WHILE loop never ends. A loop like this is called an **infinite loop** because its execution never ends (unless the program is aborted).

infinite loops

Notice that the mere presence of the words BEGIN and END doesn't make any sort of a loop. In this bad example, the words BEGIN and END just group together three statements, for no particular reason.

From this last example it may seem as if all infinite loops are easy to detect. This isn't true. See Exercises Que.6.1.1 and Que.6.1.2 for harder examples.

Programming Style

Program FindAverage2 doesn't quite work correctly because the computer doesn't jump out of the middle of a WHILE loop. There's actually a way to try to rescue Program FindAverage2, but it's frowned upon by most good programmers. Here it is:

```
PROGRAM DontUseGoto (gradeFil, output);
{Finds the average of several grades.}
  LABEL
    99;
  CONST
    sentinel = -1;
  TYPE
    gradeType = -1..100;
    natural   =  0..MAXINT;
  VAR
    grade       : gradeType;
    sum, count : natural;
    average     : REAL;
    gradeFil    : TEXT;
BEGIN {DontUseGoto}
  Reset (gradeFil);
  count := 0;
  sum   := 0;

  WHILE 1 + 1 = 2 DO
    BEGIN
      ReadLn (gradeFil, grade);
      IF grade = sentinel THEN
        GOTO 99;
      count := count + 1;
      sum   := sum + grade
    END;
  99:
  average := sum / count;
  WriteLn ('The average of the grades is ', average:6:2)
END.  {DontUseGoto}
```

GOTO
Programming with GOTOs is like traveling around Paris by swimming through its sewer system. There are lots of nice short cuts, but none of them are worth taking. Don't use GOTOs in your programs.

Structure

resources

In economics, a **resource** is an entity whose supply is potentially limited. For any particular resource, the demand might possibly exceed the supply. When this happens the resource has to be divided carefully among those who need it.

The same is true in computer science. A resource is any aspect of computer usage that can possibly be in short supply. For instance, let's assume that your computer center has 100 microcomputers and that, on one particular afternoon, 150 people show up needing to use microcomputers. Then the collection of microcomputers at your computer center is a resource. The use of these microcomputers must be monitored carefully, and policies must be created to insure that use of these machines is allocated fairly.

Perhaps your computer center has no microcomputers, but instead it has a large minicomputer, or mainframe, that can accommodate many users at once. In this case the privilege of logging on and using the various parts of the computer (disks, central processing unit, etc) is a resource. Only a certain number of users can be logged on at once, and those users must use the computer's parts according to an orderly schedule.

time and space   There are two resources that figure prominently in the theory of computer science. They're called **time** and **space**. Time is a measure of how long a program takes to run, and space is a measure of how much memory the program uses while it's running. These resources are of special interest for two reasons:

- They apply to all computers—microcomputers, minicomputers, mainframes, etc.—and to all programs.
- They're very basic resources. A more complicated resource (like the number of floppy disks in a box or the number of users who can log on to a minicomputer at one time) can usually be analyzed as a combination of the basic resources time and space.

With the gradeFile we gave in this section's Sample Runs, Program FindAverage takes 5 seconds to run on our microcomputer and 3 seconds to run on our minicomputer. These numbers tell us a little bit about Program FindAverage, but mostly they tell us about the relative speeds of our micro- and minicomputers. We want a way of measuring time consumption that helps us compare programs, not computers.

So let's divide the body of Program FindAverage into three parts:

```
BEGIN {FindAverage}
   Reset (gradeFil);
   count := 0;                              ⎫
   sum   := 0;                              ⎬⟶ Part I.
   ReadLn (gradeFil, grade);                ⎭

   WHILE grade <> sentinel DO               ⎫
      BEGIN                                 ⎪
         count := count + 1;                ⎬⟶ Part II
         sum   := sum + grade;              ⎪
         ReadLn (gradeFil, grade)           ⎪
      END;                                  ⎭

   average := sum / count;                  ⎫⟶ Part III
   WriteLn ('The average ... )              ⎭
END.   {FindAverage}
```

Let's say that on a particular computer Part I takes 1/10th of a second to run and Part III takes 1/10th of a second to run. Then let's assume that each iteration of the WHILE loop takes 1/100th of a second to run. If there are *n*-many grades to be averaged, then the WHILE loop will be iterated *n* times. So the total amount of time for Program FindAverage to run will be

$$\text{Running time of Program } \texttt{FindAverage} = \begin{aligned} &= 1/10 && + (n * 1/100) + && 1/10 \text{ seconds} \\ &= 10/100 + && n/100 && + 10/100 \text{ seconds} \end{aligned}$$

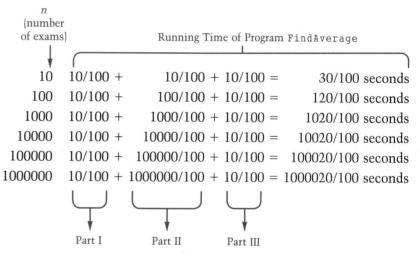

Part I   Part II   Part III

Now let's imagine that Program FindAverage is being used for the SATs—an exam that's given nationally. In this case, the number of exams in the gradeFil can be astronomical:

n
(number
of exams)   Running Time of Program FindAverage

10	10/100 +	10/100 + 10/100 =	30/100 seconds
100	10/100 +	100/100 + 10/100 =	120/100 seconds
1000	10/100 +	1000/100 + 10/100 =	1020/100 seconds
10000	10/100 +	10000/100 + 10/100 =	10020/100 seconds
100000	10/100 +	100000/100 + 10/100 =	100020/100 seconds
1000000	10/100 +	1000000/100 + 10/100 =	1000020/100 seconds

Part I   Part II   Part III

If we simplify the fractions, we get:

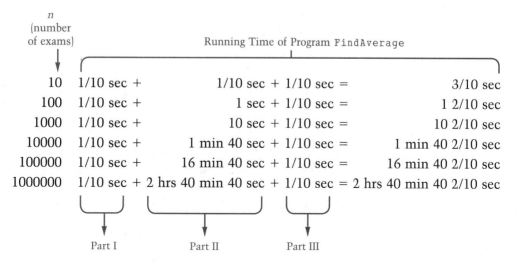

n
(number
of exams)   Running Time of Program FindAverage

10	1/10 sec +	1/10 sec + 1/10 sec =	3/10 sec
100	1/10 sec +	1 sec + 1/10 sec =	1 2/10 sec
1000	1/10 sec +	10 sec + 1/10 sec =	10 2/10 sec
10000	1/10 sec +	1 min 40 sec + 1/10 sec =	1 min 40 2/10 sec
100000	1/10 sec +	16 min 40 sec + 1/10 sec =	16 min 40 2/10 sec
1000000	1/10 sec +	2 hrs 40 min 40 sec + 1/10 sec =	2 hrs 40 min 40 2/10 sec

Part I   Part II   Part III

If there are a million grades to be averaged, then the program runs almost three hours, of which only two-tenths of a second are the running of Parts I and III! In computing the program's running time, the second term is overpowering the others. When n is 10000 or greater, the first and third terms make negligible contributions to the overall formula. So when n is a large number (say, 10000 or greater) then it's safe to say that

$$\text{Running time of Program FindAverage} = \text{the amount of time it takes to run Part II}$$
$$= n * 1/100$$

When n isn't a large number Program FindAverage runs so fast that it takes a negligible amount of the time resource. So we don't have to worry much about the runs where n isn't large. Therefore, we can use $n * 1/100$ as an approximate value of the total time in all the important situations.

But what if we run Program FindAverage on a different computer? On another computer each iteration of the WHILE loop may take 1/1000th of a second to run. In this case, the program's use of the time resource is

$$\text{Running time of Program FindAverage} = n * 1/1000$$

The number that we multiply by n has very little to do with Program FindAverage. It applies only to one particular computer. If we want to describe the behavior of Program FindAverage for all computers, the best we can say is

$$\text{Running time of Program FindAverage} = n * \begin{array}{l}\text{some number that varies from}\\ \text{one computer to another}\end{array}$$

Computer scientists have a special shorthand notation for this. They write

$$\text{Running time of Program FindAverage} = O(n)$$

O(n) time

where "O(n)" is pronounced "order n," "big 'O' of n," "**complexity n**," or just "**linear**." The significance of O(n) time is this: The total running time of the program is proportional to n, where, in this instance, n is the number of grades that are given to the program as input.

Now let's examine Program FindAverage's use of the space resource. The program has four variables, so it uses up four memory spaces of various sizes. Let's say that on a particular computer, grade, sum, and count each take two units of memory space and average takes four units of memory space. Then the total amount of space taken by Program FindAverage is

$$\text{Space consumption of Program FindAverage} = 10 \text{ units}$$

This value doesn't change no matter how many scores have to be averaged. The variable grade, which occupies two units of space, holds each of these scores, one after another.

Of course, the total space used by Program `FindAverage` depends on the particular computer that's running the program. On another computer, `grade`, `sum`, and `count` may take one unit each, and `average` may take four units, in which case

$$\text{Space consumption of Program } \texttt{FindAverage} = 7 \text{ units}$$

So

$$\text{Space consumption of Program } \texttt{FindAverage} = \begin{array}{l}\text{some number that varies} \\ \text{from one computer to another} \\ \text{but doesn't depend on } n\end{array}$$

Once again, computer scientists have a shorthand notation. They write

$$\text{Space consumption of Program } \texttt{FindAverage} = O(1)$$

O(1) space

where $O(1)$ is pronounced "order 1," "big 'O' of 1," "complexity 1," or just "**constant**." The significance of $O(1)$ space is this: the total amount of memory space used to run the program doesn't depend on n where, in this instance, n is the number of grades that are given to the program as input.

Program `FindAverage` has time complexity n and space complexity 1. In other sections, we'll see programs that run more slowly and programs that run faster than Program `FindAverage`. We'll also see programs that consume more space and programs that consume less space than Program `FindAverage`.

Testing and Debugging

Once again let's modify Program `FindAverage` by adding a semicolon after the word `DO`:

```
WHILE grade <> sentinel DO;
```

If we try to run the program the cursor just sits there. The program doesn't seem to do anything. To find out what we've done wrong we insert `WriteLns` in the program in strategic spots.

adding
`WriteLns` for
debugging

```
PROGRAM FindAverage (gradeFil, output);
{Finds the average of several grades.}
  CONST
    sentinel = -1;
  TYPE
    gradeType = -1..100;
    natural   = 0..MAXINT;
  VAR
    grade        : gradeType;
    sum, count   : natural;
    average      : REAL;
    gradeFil     : TEXT;
```

```
BEGIN {FindAverage}
  WriteLn ('I''ve begun executing');
  Reset (gradeFil);
  count := 0;
  sum   := 0;
  ReadLn (gradeFil, grade);

  WriteLn ('I''m about to enter the loop');
  WHILE grade <> sentinel DO;
    BEGIN
      count := count + 1;
      sum   := sum + grade;
      WriteLn ('I''m executing the loop');
      ReadLn (gradeFil, grade)
    END;

  WriteLn ('I''m finished with the loop');
  average := sum / count;
  WriteLn ('The average of the grades is ', average:6:2)
END.  {FindAverage}
```

Now when we run FindAverage, we get

```
I've begun executing
I'm about to enter the loop
```

and nothing more. This tells us that the computer gets up to

```
WHILE grade <> sentinel
```

but it never gets as far as the second ReadLn and never makes it to

```
average := sum / count
```

So we ask whether any of the statements inside the loop ever get executed. To answer this question, we add another WriteLn:

```
WriteLn ('I''m about to enter the loop');
WHILE grade <> sentinel DO;
  BEGIN
    WriteLn ('I''m just entering the loop');
    count := count + 1;
    sum   := sum + grade;
    WriteLn ('I''m executing the loop');
    ReadLn (gradeFil, grade)
  END
```

With this method we can find out exactly which statements get executed and which statements are never reached. We do this to narrow down the suspicious code to one or two lines. For instance, we've just concluded that the troublesome code is somewhere between the WriteLns in

```
WriteLn ('I''m about to enter the loop');
WHILE grade <> sentinel DO;
  BEGIN
    WriteLn ('I''m just entering the loop')
```

We wonder about the semicolon after the word DO and ask ourselves if this might be source of the trouble. If we're not sure about it, we can write an experimental program that puts this one aspect of Pascal to the test:

```
PROGRAM TestWhile (input, output);
{What's the output of this program?}
   VAR
      grade : INTEGER;
BEGIN {TestWhile}
   grade := 90;
   WriteLn ('Execution has begun!');
   WHILE grade <> -1 DO;
      WriteLn ('Will I ever get executed?');
   WriteLn ('Will the loop ever end?')
END.  {TestWhile}
```

Once we do this experiment, the source of the difficulty becomes clear.

6.1 Exercises

Key Words to Review

MAXINT	resource	complexity
predefined	time	O(1)
infinite loop	space	constant
GOTO	O(n)	linear
LABEL		

Questions to Answer

QUE 6.1.1 Why will the following program fragment give you an infinite loop?

```
year := 1990;
WHILE year < 1993 DO
   BEGIN
      Write   (year:4, ' - Women''s and men''s salaries: ');
      ReadLn  (womensSal, mensSal);

      MakeBar (womensSal, 'W');
      MakeBar (mensSal  , 'M');
      WriteLn
   END
```

QUE 6.1.2   Why will the following program fragment give you an infinite loop?

```
WHILE NOT Eof(inFile) DO
    BEGIN
        WHILE NOT Eoln(inFile) DO
            BEGIN
                Read (inFile,  ch);
                Write(outFile, ch);
            END;
        WriteLn(outFile);
        WriteLn
    END
```

QUE 6.1.3   Does each of the following programs take O(n) time?
a. Program OneBar (Section 2.6)
b. Program Trucking (Section 3.8)
c. Program Copy (Section 4.1)
d. Program Copy (Section 5.1)
e. Program Minimum (Section 5.4)
Give an explanation for each program.

QUE 6.1.4   Does each of the following programs take O(1) space?
a. Program HalfPriceSale (Section 2.1)
b. Program Scores (Section 2.3)
c. Program OneBar (Section 2.6)
d. Program Minimum (Section 5.4)
Give an explanation for each program.

QUE 6.1.5   Let's say I have a particular program that takes three seconds to run on a computer made by the Fast Computer Company. The same program takes ten seconds to run on another computer made by the Slow Computer Company. How can I justify talking about the running time of this program without referring to the computer on which it's being run?

Things to Check in a Manual

MAN 6.1.1   Find out how to stop execution of a program that's in an infinite loop. (Note: This is a repeat of Exercise Man.2.6.2.)

MAN 6.1.2   Find out if, in your implementation, there's a way that a program can obtain the time of day from the computer's internal clock. If so, it will be useful when you try this section's Experiments.

Experiments to Try

EXP 6.1.1   Devise an experiment to find the value of MAXINT in your implementation.

EXP 6.1.2   Does your implementation allow you to have an INTEGER variable with a value that's smaller than −MAXINT (such as −MAXINT − 1)?

EXP 6.1.3   Use the information you learned in Exercise Man.6.1.1 to stop execution of a program containing the line

```
WHILE grade <> -1 DO;
```

EXP 6.1.4   Run Program FindAverage several times with gradeFiles of various sizes. For each run, note the size of the gradeFile and the amount of time the program takes to run. (Use the system-clock-time technique that you found in Exercise Man.6.1.2. Have the program print the time twice—immediately before Resetting the gradeFile and immediately after writing the average.) After doing several runs, look over the data you've collected. Is it true that the amount of time the program takes to run increases linearly with the size of the gradeFile?

EXP 6.1.5   In Program FindAverage move sum := 0 inside the WHILE loop.

EXP 6.1.6   In Program FindAverage move average := sum / count inside the WHILE loop.

EXP 6.1.7   Change Program FindAverage so that it has only one ReadLn (grade). Make that statement be the first statement to be executed inside the WHILE loop.

EXP 6.1.8   In Program FindAverage move count := count + 1 so that it's the last statement in the WHILE loop.

EXP 6.1.9   Run Program FindAverage, giving it the number −1 as its first and only input value.

Changes to Make

CHA 6.1.1   Modify Program FindAverage so that each line of input contains two grades—a quiz and an exam for one student. In the end the program reports the average of all the quiz grades and the average of all the exam grades.

CHA 6.1.2   Redo Exercise Cha.6.1.1, this time putting the exam grades after all of the quiz grades in the gradeFile.

CHA 6.1.3   Modify Program FindAverage so that it does something sensible when given input of the kind described in Exercise Exp.6.1.9.

Programs and Subprograms to Write

WRI 6.1.1   Write a program that reads several letters, all of them ws or ms. Each w stands for a woman; each m stands for a man. Have the program write two percentages—the percentage of women and the percentage of men.

WRI 6.1.2   Experimental evidence shows that a person who's not doing any exercise burns about 90 calories per hour. This is called the person's *metabolic rate*. (These figures apply to a person who weighs approximately 70 kilograms, about 155 pounds. Also note that we use the lay person's notion of the term calorie. That is, what we call a calorie is what scientists normally call a kilocalorie.) For each kilometer-per-hour faster that a runner runs, the runner burns up an extra 25 calories per hour. This is expressed in the formula

$$calories = 25.0 * speed + 90.0$$

Write a program that reads a maximum running speed and makes a table showing the metabolic rate for the speeds 0 (standing still), 2, 4, 6, . . . up to the maximum speed.

WRI 6.1.3   Write a program that reads, for each of several drivers, the driver's license number (four digits), state code (two uppercase letters), sex (F or M), age, number of parking violations, and number of moving violations. Then it writes the

- percentage of drivers in California who are under 21
- the license numbers of all drivers with more than three moving violations
- the license number of the driver with the largest number of violations (parking plus moving)
- the number of male drivers whose parking violations outnumber their moving violations

WRI 6.1.4   *(Try this exercise if you've taken calculus.)* One way to find the approximate area under a curve is to use the *Trapezoidal Rule:*

$$(\Delta x/2)[f(x_0) + 2f(x_1) + 2f(x_2) + \cdots + 2f(x_{n-1}) + f(x_n)]$$

Write and test a function Area that accepts a starting value for x, a stopping value for x, and a value for n and returns an approximate value for the area under the curve $f(x) = x^2$ from the starting value to the stopping value. Then try Function Area on some other curves, such as $\sin(x)$, $\ln(x)$, etc.

Things to Think About

THI 6.1.1   Have you ever taken a computer programming course in which the use of GOTO statements was permitted? Look back at some of the programs you wrote for that course. Rewrite these programs (perhaps changing them from another language into Pascal) without using any GOTO statements. Does the prohibition against GOTOs make your new programs easier to understand? Can you give any general guidelines to help you convert your old programs, with GOTOs, into new programs without GOTOs?

6.2

The FOR Statement

You may have noticed that many of the examples given so far have WHILE loops that look like this:

```
counter := initialValue;
WHILE counter < finalValue DO
   BEGIN
      .
      .
      counter := counter + 1
   END
```

This pattern is so common that there's a special statement for it in Pascal. It's called the FOR statement.

Specifications

Input: An INTEGER value, n

Output: The value n!: the product of all INTEGERs from 1 to n (Note: n! is pronounced "n factorial.")

Designing a Program

Remember how we found the sum of several student grades in Program FindAverage (Section 6.1):

```
sum := 0;
   .
   .
WHILE ... DO
  BEGIN
     .
     .
    sum := sum + grade
     .
     .
  END
```

In Program FindAverage, the variable sum served as an *accumulator*. It kept a running tally of the values of grade. When the loop stopped iterating, we had

sum = first grade + second grade + · · · + last grade

Now when we're done computing n! we want

n! = 1 * 2 * 3 * · · · · * n

It's very much like finding a sum except we need to multiply numbers into the accumulator, instead of adding them. So we want something like this:

```
WHILE ... DO
  BEGIN
     .
     .
    product := product * i
     .
     .
  END
```

Now if we give product the initial value 0, then the first loop iteration will give us

product := 0 * 1 (= 0)

and the next iteration will give us

product := 0 * 2 (= 0)

and the next will give us

product := 0 * 3 (= 0)

and product will never be anything but 0. Instead we have to give product the initial value 1. Then in the first loop iteration we'll get

```
product := 1 * 1 ( = 1)
```

and in the next iteration we'll get

```
product := 1 * 2 ( = 2)
```

and in the next iteration

```
product := 2 * 3 ( = 6)
```

and so on. This is how we'll write the program, except that we'll make one change. We won't use a WHILE statement. Instead we'll use something called a FOR statement.

Program Example

```
PROGRAM Factorial (input, output);
{Computes n factorial, for a given value of n.}
  TYPE
    natural  = 0..MAXINT;
    countType = 2..MAXINT;
  VAR
    n, product : natural;
    i          : countType;
BEGIN {Factorial}
  Write ('Number: ');
  ReadLn (n);
  product := 1;

  FOR i := 2 TO n DO
    product := product * i;

  WriteLn (n:2, ' factorial is ', product:12)
END.  {Factorial}
```

Sample Runs

```
Number: 0
 0 factorial is           1
 _____

Number: 1
 1 factorial is           1
 _____

Number: 2
 2 factorial is           2
 _____

Number: 3
 3 factorial is           6
 _____

Number: 4
 4 factorial is          24
 _____

Number: 5
 5 factorial is         120
```

Observations

FOR statement

•
```
FOR i := 2 TO n DO
    product := product * i
```
This FOR statement has (almost[1]) the same effect as

```
i := 2;
WHILE i <= n DO
  BEGIN
    product := product * i;
    i := i + 1
  END
```

When we use a FOR statement, we don't need the statements

```
i := 2
```

or

```
i := i + 1
```

All this is done for us by the FOR statement.

Further Discussion

Here's the syntax diagram of the FOR statement:

FOR *statement*:

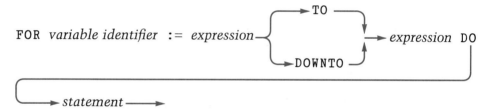

the FOR statement in detail

A **variable identifier** is any identifier that stands for a variable. The *variable identifier* in a FOR statement is often called a **loop counter**. The first *expression* is called the **initial value** of the loop, and the second *expression* is called the **final value** of the loop.

Now notice that in a FOR statement, you can use either of the words TO or DOWNTO. When we use TO we expect the loop's initial value to be less than its final value. If it isn't, as in

```
FOR i := 3 TO 1 DO
    WriteLn ('I never get written.')
```

then the loop is never iterated. If the initial and final values are equal, then the loop is iterated only once. So the output of

---

[1]To find out why we're careful to include the word "almost," see the Programming Style subsection.

```
FOR i := 3 TO 3 DO
   WriteLn ('I appear only once.')
```

is just

```
I appear only once.
```

Here's another technical point: A loop's counter variable has to be declared in the VAR declarations of the program or subprogram that contains the FOR statement. So, for instance,

```
PROCEDURE Loop (VAR i          : countType ;
                     n          : natural   ;
                     VAR product : natural  );
{This procedure won't compile!}
BEGIN {Loop}
   product := 1;
   FOR i := 2 TO n DO
      product := product * i
END;   {Loop}
```

would be incorrect, because the control variable i is a *formal parameter* of Procedure Loop.

When the execution of a FOR loop is finished, the loop's control variable has no useful value. This will come as a surprise to a programmer who tries something like:

```
FOR i := 2 TO 10 DO
   product := product * i;
WriteLn (i)
```

The question here is, When we execute WriteLn (i) what's the value of i? On some implementations it may be 10 or 11, but on others, i may have a very strange value—a value that's not even close to 10 or 11. It's not a good idea to use the control variable outside the FOR loop, even if your implementation lets you get away with it.

Look again at the syntax diagram for the FOR statement. It says you can use TO or DOWNTO. The difference between TO and DOWNTO is simple: With DOWNTO the control variable goes from the initial value DOWNTO the final value, in steps of −1. We say that the control variable is being **decremented**.

Here's a simple example:

```
PROGRAM Countdown (output);
   VAR
      i : 1..10;
BEGIN {Countdown}
   FOR i := 10 DOWNTO 1 DO
      WriteLn (i, ' bottles of beer on the wall')
END.   {Countdown}
```

In a Pascal FOR loop, the computer adds 1 or −1 to the control variable for each loop iteration. (It adds 1 when TO is used; −1 when DOWNTO is used.) In many languages there are statements like the FOR statement that add any number (2, −2, 0.1, etc.) to the control variable for each iteration. In BASIC, for instance, you might have

```
10 FOR I = 2 TO 100 STEP 2
20    PRINT I
30 NEXT I
```

which would make I take on the values 2, 4, 6, . . . , 100. Pascal's FOR loop has no built-in mechanism for making steps other than 1 or −1. To do this in Pascal, you need to have an additional variable:

```
FOR j := 1 TO 50 DO
  BEGIN
    i := 2 * j;
    WriteLn (i:3)
  END
```

or to use a WHILE statement instead of a FOR statement:

```
i := 2;
WHILE i <= 100 DO
  BEGIN
    WriteLn (i:3);
    i := i + 2
  END
```

Programming Style

FOR vs. WHILE

Throughout this discussion we've been careful to say that each FOR loop is almost the same as some WHILE loop. There are a few important differences that make the FOR loop safer to use than the WHILE loop. To see why this is so, we'll compare the FOR loop in Program Factorial with the WHILE loop whose behavior it simulates.

```
FOR i := 2 TO n DO
  product := product * i
```
→ The FOR loop

```
i := 2;
WHILE i <= n DO
  BEGIN
    product := product * i;
    i := i + 1
  END
```
→ The corresponding WHILE loop

In a WHILE loop, the programmer must write a statement like

```
i := i + 1
```

which explicitly **increments** the value of the counter. If the programmer forgets to include this statement (and it's not uncommon for programmers to forget) then the condition i <= n never stops being TRUE, so we have an infinite loop.

The situation is precisely the opposite with a FOR loop. The programmer *must not* write a statement in the loop that changes the value of the loop's counter. The loop's control variable is changed only once per iteration, by the FOR statement itself. This is a safety measure, because it takes control of the number of loop iterations out of the hands of the programmer.

In older programming languages it was common to force a FOR-like loop to end its execution by assigning the final value to the control variable, like this:

```
product := 1;
FOR i := 2 TO n DO
   BEGIN
      product := product * i;
      IF product > 10000 THEN
         i := n
   END
```

This is not permissible in Pascal. The Pascal compiler checks each FOR loop to make sure there are no statements in it like

```
i := n
```

Another outdated way to end a loop's execution is to try to change its final value, like this:

```
product := 1;
FOR i := 2 TO n DO
   BEGIN
      product := product * i;
      IF product > 10000 THEN
         n := i
   END
```

In this code, the statement

```
n := i
```

isn't illegal, but it won't end the execution of the loop. When i is first given the value 2, the computer compares 2 with the value of n and determines exactly how many times the loop will be iterated. Even if the value of n is changed somewhere inside the loop, the computer still iterates the loop that predetermined number of times. Here, again, we have a safety measure. Control of the number of loop iterations has been taken out of the hands of the programmer.

Another safety measure built into the FOR statement is the enhanced ability to use subranges. Let's do a part of Program BarGraph again, this time defining year's subrange so that it contains the years 1990 to 1992—exactly the years we want graphed:

```
VAR
   year : 1990..1992;   {Notice the change from 1993 to 1992!}
      .
      .
year := 1990;
WHILE year < 1993 DO
   BEGIN
      .
      .
      year := year + 1
   END
```

This loop won't work. When `year` has the value 1992, the `WHILE` loop is iterated one last time. But then the computer executes

```
   year := year + 1
```

and adds 1 to `year`, making it 1993. This sends `year` outside of its declared subrange.

This difficulty is solved with a `FOR` loop:

```
VAR
   year : 1990..1992;   {Notice the change from 1993 to 1992!}
      .
      .
FOR year := 1990 TO 1992 DO
   BEGIN
      Write    (year:4, ' - Women''s and men''s salaries: ');
      ReadLn   (womensSal, mensSal);

      MakeBar  (womensSal, 'W');
      MakeBar  (mensSal  , 'M');
      WriteLn
   END
```

When the computer executes this `FOR` loop, it takes special care to keep the values of `year` inside the range 1990 to 1992, so the variable `year` stays inside its declared subrange.

There are special names to express the differences between `FOR` loops and `WHILE` loops. A `FOR` loop is an example of **definite iteration**, and a `WHILE` loop is an instance of **indefinite iteration**. A `FOR` loop is called "definite" because as soon as we know the loop's initial and final values, we know exactly how many iterations the loop will have. Nothing like this is true of a `WHILE` loop.

definite vs. indefinite iteration

In general, a `FOR` statement is safer than a `WHILE` statement because there's less for the programmer to do. When a programmer writes a `FOR` statement, many of the details of counter incrementing and loop iterating are done automatically.

In addition to being safer, definite iteration is often more *efficient* than indefinite iteration; that is, a `FOR` loop will execute faster than the corresponding `WHILE` loop. This happens because the computer can take advantage of the added information given to it by the `FOR` statement; for example, the fact that the counter will have exactly 1 added to it each time.

Structure

An NS chart for a FOR statement is very much like the NS chart for the corresponding WHILE statement.

PROGRAM Factorial:

NS chart for a FOR statement

Write ('Number: ')
ReadLn (n)
product := 1
FOR i := 2 TO n DO
product := product * i
WriteLn (n:2, ' factorial is ', product:12)

Testing and Debugging

How should we test Program Factorial? Let's run it several times, each time with a different value of n.

```
FOR i := 2 TO n DO
   product := product * i
```

But what values of n should we try? Well, n can be a "small" number or a "large" number. By a "small" number we probably mean "a number that makes the loop undergo the *smallest* possible number of iterations." By a "large" number we mean "a number that makes the loop undergo the largest possible number of iterations." These are called **extreme values** of n because they're extremes of what the program is meant to handle. Perhaps these values are larger than the computer can handle, or perhaps they're the smallest values that make any sense in the "real-life" problem that the program is attempting to solve.

extreme values

Now what are the extreme values for the loop in Program Factorial? Well, one extremely small number that comes to mind is 2—the loop's initial value. If we give n the value 2

```
ReadLn (n);        ◄──── The user types the number 2 for n
   .
   .
FOR i := 2 TO n DO
   product := product * i
```

or

```
FOR i := 2 TO 2 DO
   product := product * i
```

then the loop is iterated only once. But there are even smaller numbers we can try. For instance, with the number 1, the loop won't be iterated at all.

```
FOR i := 2 TO 1 DO
  product := product * i
```

It's always important to see how the program behaves when there are no loop iterations. And since extreme values can be so troublesome (that's where most of the bugs in programs tend to occur), we should also test Program Factorial with n being one more than our "small" value of 2.

```
FOR i := 2 TO 3 DO
  product := product * i
```

Now what about the extremely large values of n? Here's what we got when we ran Program Factorial under Turbo Pascal version 6.0, using the input values 7 and 8:

```
Number: 7
  7 factorial is          5040
  _____

Number: 8
  8 factorial is         -25216
```

In Turbo Pascal, the value of MAXINT is 32767, but in "real life" when you multiply 1 * 2 * 3 * 4 * 5 * 6 * 7 * 8 you get 40320. So the computer can't handle the product of the numbers 1 through 8. This means that 7 is an extreme value for Program Factorial running under certain implementations. Once again, since most of the bugs in programs tend to occur at or near the extreme values, we should test Program Factorial by making n be 6, 7, and 8.

Remember: We should never try to hide or gloss over a program's limitations.

---

loop testing

So here are some general guidelines to follow: When testing a program with a loop in it, it's always good to try runs in which the loop is iterated:

1. the *smallest* possible number of times
2. *one more* than the smallest possible number of times
3. *one less* than the smallest possible number of times
4. *zero* times
5. some *"middle"* number of times
6. the *largest* possible number of times
7. *one less* than the largest possible number of times
8. *one more* than the largest possible number of times

In addition, if the problem suggests some number of times that the loop will often be iterated, try that.

6.2 Exercises

Key Words to Review

FOR	variable identifier	decrement
TO	initial value	definite iteration
DOWNTO	final value	indefinite iteration
loop counter	increment	extreme values

Questions to Answer

QUE 6.2.1 Why, in Program Factorial, do we initialize the variable product to 1 instead of to 0?

QUE 6.2.2 In what sense is a FOR statement safer than a WHILE statement?

QUE 6.2.3 In what sense is a FOR statement more efficient than a WHILE statement?

QUE 6.2.4 In Section 3.1 we introduced the notion of procedural abstraction. In what sense is the FOR statement a form of abstraction? What details are being hidden in a FOR loop that aren't hidden with a WHILE loop?

Experiments to Try

EXP 6.2.1 Run Program Factorial with n equal to 0. What answer do you get? Is this consistent with the "meaning" of factorial? Is it consistent with the value given for 0! in an algebra textbook?

EXP 6.2.2 Write a test driver for this section's Procedure Loop. Does the program compile without error diagnostics on your implementation? Does it run?

EXP 6.2.3 Run a program containing the code

```
FOR i := 2 TO 10 DO
   product := product * i;
WriteLn (i)
```

Changes to Make

CHA 6.2.1 Modify Program Factorial so that its output is the sum of the numbers from 1 to n. Test your program with the formula

$$\text{sum of the numbers from 1 to } n = \frac{n(n + 1)}{2}$$

Mathematicians use the *sigma notation* to represent sums of this sort. The sigma notation for the sum of the integers from 1 to n is

$$\sum_{i=1}^{n} i$$

CHA 6.2.2   Modify Program `Factorial` so that it writes a warning message if it's being asked to find a value that's larger than `MAXINT`. (Hint: No `INTEGER`'s value can ever become larger than `MAXINT`, so don't try to test the condition `product >MAXINT`.)

Programs and Subprograms to Write

WRI 6.2.1   Write a program that does the following: Reads in the yearly earnings of 50 families and prints the number of families that earn 50K or more, the average income of such families, and the average income of all 50 families.

WRI 6.2.2   How much will I make in a month (31 days) if I make one cent on the first day, and then each day I make double the amount that I made the previous day? When you write this program, is it possible for your `amountEarned` variable to be of type `INTEGER`?

WRI 6.2.3   Reconsider your solutions to the Programs and Subprograms to Write exercises in Section 2.6, given what you now know about the FOR statement.

WRI 6.2.4   Write a program that reads a number n and computes the sum $1 + 1/2 + 1/3 + \cdots + 1/n$. In sigma notation this sum is

$$\sum_{i=1}^{n} 1/i$$

WRI 6.2.5   Write a program that reads a number n and computes the sum $1 + 1/4 + 1/9 + \cdots + 1/n^2$. In sigma notation this sum is

$$\sum_{i=1}^{n} 1/i^2$$

WRI 6.2.6   *(A formula from a theory called Combinatorics)* We have three awards (first-, second-, and third-place awards) to give out and six students who are deserving of awards. We want to know how many ways there are to pick three students for the three awards. Here's a formula that will answer the question:

$$P(6,3) = \frac{6!}{(6-3)!}$$

More generally, this formula gives us the number of ways we can arrange *r*-many objects if we have *n*-many objects from which we can choose:

$$P(n,r) = \frac{n!}{(n-r)!}$$

Write a program that reads the number of awards and the number of deserving students and then writes the number of ways to choose students to win the awards.

WRI 6.2.7   *(A continuation of Exercise Wri.6.2.6)* What if, instead of having first-, second-, and third-place awards, we simply have three "honorable mentions"—all the same as one another—none better than the other. We want to know how many ways there are to choose three students for the three identical "honorable mentions." Here's the formula:

$$C(6,3) = \frac{6!}{3! \star (6-3)!}$$

More generally, this formula gives us the number of ways we can choose r-many objects without regard to the way in which they're arranged if we have n-many objects from which we can choose:

$$C(n,r) = \frac{n!}{r! \, * \, (n-r)!}$$

Write a program that reads the number of "honorable mentions" and the number of deserving students and then writes the number of ways to choose students.

Things to Think About

THI 6.2.1   Compare these excerpts from two recipes:

"Stir the batter one hundred times."
"Stir the batter until it's thick."

Which of these instructions uses *definite* iteration? Which uses *indefinite* iteration? Explain your answer.

6.3

FOR Statements—Another Example

Specifications In a population growth experiment, there are four kinds of rabbits: immature males (m), immature females (f), mature Males (M), and mature Females (F). Each month two things happen:

1. Each pair of mature rabbits produces a pair of immature rabbits. For simplicity we'll assume that they produce one immature male and one immature female. (In real experiments, with large rabbit populations, this turns out to be a reasonable assumption.)

2. Each immature rabbit becomes mature.

So here's a diagram showing the number of rabbits we have each month:

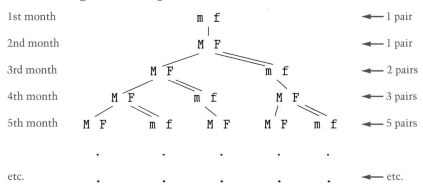

We start with two immature rabbits (m, f). In the second month, the two immature rabbits have become mature (M, F). In the third month, there are two pairs of rabbits, because the original rabbits are still alive (M, F), and they've produced a new pair of rabbits (m, f).[2] Notice the pattern: If you add the number of pairs in the third row to the number of pairs in the fourth row, you get the number of pairs in the fifth row. This is no accident. Keep adding more rows to the family tree until you figure out why it works this way.

The sequence

1 1 2 3 5 8 13 21 . . . etc.

gives the number of pairs of rabbits in each month of the experiment. It's called the *Fibonacci sequence*. It's defined as follows:

The first two terms of the Fibonacci sequence are ones; thereafter, each term is the sum of the two previous terms.

Many things in nature follow the pattern of this sequence. So let's write a program that lists the terms in the Fibonacci sequence.

Input: A number, called `termsNeeded`

Output: Several terms in the Fibonacci sequence (as many `terms` as are `Needed`)

Designing a Program

Here's our first draft of an algorithm:

Find out how many `terms` are `Needed`.
Do the following `termsNeeded`-many times:
    Add the two previous terms to get the next term.
    Write this "next" term.

This first draft needs quite a bit of work. The main difficulty is, What do we mean by "the two previous terms"?

First we'll give these "two previous terms" some names:

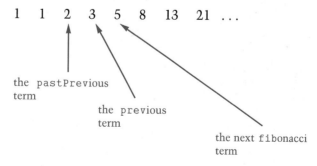

1   1   2   3   5   8   13   21 . . .

the `pastPrevious` term

the `previous` term

the next `fibonacci` term

---

[2]In the diagram, we use a double line to highlight the birth of a new pair of rabbits.

Since each term in the sequence is the sum of the two previous terms, our loop will need a statement like:

```
fib := pastPrev + prev
```

Of course `pastPrev` and `prev` need to be assigned values somewhere. To see how this is done, let's look at the way the terms in the Fibonacci sequence change from one iteration to the next:

In one iteration:

| the
pastPrevious
term | the
previous
term | the next
fibonacci
term |

In the next iteration:

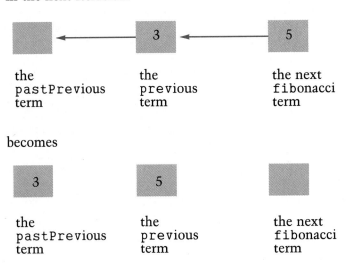

becomes

The arrows in this diagram suggest two more assignment statements:

```
pastPrev := prev;
prev     := fib
```

So now our pseudocode might look like this:

Find out how many `terms` are `Needed`.
Do the following `termsNeeded` times:
    pastPrev := prev
    prev   := fib
    fib   := pastPrev + prev
    Write fib

Of course the first few 1's in the Fibonacci sequence will need special handling.

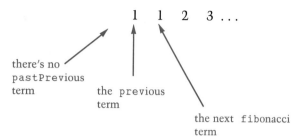

We'll need to assign some initial values before the first iteration of the loop.

```
prev := 1;
fib  := 1
```

The code follows.

Program Example

```
PROGRAM Fibonacci (input, output);
{Lists terms in the Fibonacci sequence.}
  TYPE
    natural = 0..MAXINT;
  VAR
    pastPrev, prev, fib, termsNeeded, count : natural;
BEGIN {Fibonacci}
  WriteLn ('How many terms in the');
  Write   ('Fibonacci sequence do you need? ');
  ReadLn  (termsNeeded);

  prev := 1;
  WriteLn (prev:12);

  fib  := 1;
  WriteLn (fib:12);

  FOR count := 3 TO termsNeeded DO
    BEGIN
      pastPrev := prev;
      prev     := fib;
      fib      := pastPrev + prev;
      WriteLn (fib:12)
    END
END.  {Fibonacci}
```

Sample Runs

```
How many terms in the
Fibonacci sequence do you need? 11
                  1
                  1
                  2
                  3
                  5
                  8
                 13
                 21
                 34
                 55
                 89
```

Observations

storing values
from one
iteration to
another

The Fibonacci sequence problem is typical of many programming problems in which you find yourself storing values in preparation for the next iteration. In this program we take two terms (prev and fib) whose values are calculated in one iteration

```
    prev        := fib;
    fib         := pastPrev + prev;
    WriteLn (fib:12)
END
```

and then we use those values at the beginning of the next iteration.

```
BEGIN
    pastPrev := prev;
    prev     := fib
```

You can liken the situation to a person who needs to write down some "things-to-do-tomorrow" reminders at the end of each day. Each loop iteration is like a day in a person's life. At the end of each day, the program makes itself a note: "I used 8 for the value of prev today; and I used 13 for the value of fib today." On the next day the program reminds itself "Two days ago I used the value 8; and yesterday I used the value 13."

6.3   Exercises

Questions to Answer

QUE 6.3.1   Explain why, in the rabbit population experiment, the number of pairs in each row turns out to be equal to the sum of the numbers of pairs in the two previous rows.

QUE 6.3.2   How are the two variables prev and pastPrev used in Program Fibonacci?

Experiments to Try

EXP 6.3.1   Run Program Fibonacci several times to find out how many terms your implementation can compute. What does the computer do when the terms get to be larger than MAXINT?

Changes to Make

CHA 6.3.1   Modify Program `Fibonacci` so that it writes only one term in the Fibonacci sequence (the last of the `termsNeeded`).

CHA 6.3.2   Modify Program `Fibonacci` so that

```
pastPrev := prev;
prev     := fib
```

are the last statements in each iteration. What other changes have to be made as a result of this change?

CHA 6.3.3   Here's a variation on the Fibonacci sequence: the first three numbers are 1's, and each number after the first three is the sum of the `previous` number and the "pastPastPrevious" number:

1 1 1 2 3 4 6 9 13 . . . etc.

Modify Program `Fibonacci` so that it computes values in this revised "Fibonacci" sequence.

Scales to Practice

PRA 6.3.1   Write a program that reads in five `INTEGER` values. Whenever it reads a positive value it writes the sum of the values that have been read in so far. Whenever it reads a negative value, it writes a zero. Whenever it reads a zero it writes whatever value was written during the previous iteration.

PRA 6.3.2   Write a program that keeps reading values (until the user says to stop) and after each value (beyond the second) writes the largest of the three most recent values.

Programs and Subprograms to Write

WRI 6.3.1   The *moving average* of a sequence of values is the average of the three previous values in the sequence. Write a program that keeps reading values (until the user says to stop) and after each value (beyond the second) writes the moving average.

WRI 6.3.2   Write a program that reads 52 sales amounts—one for each week of the year—and for each week except the first, writes the percentage increase or decrease compared with the previous week's sales.

6.4

Nested FOR Loops

In this section we see what the computer does when we have a FOR loop that contains another FOR loop.

Specifications   Input: A number, n

Output: The multiplication table, for numbers from 1 to n

Designing a Program

Here's some pseudocode:

> For each of n-many rows,
>   for each of n-many columns,
>   write the product of the row number times the column number

The problem seems to beg for nested loops, and we're going to solve it with nested FOR loops.

Program Example

```
PROGRAM MultiplicationTable (input, output);
{Writes a multiplication table for the numbers 1 to n.}
  TYPE
    positive = 1..MAXINT;
  VAR
    n, row, column : positive;
BEGIN {MultiplicationTable}
  Write ('Multiplication table for 1 to what number? ');
  ReadLn (n);
  WriteLn;
  WriteLn;

  FOR row := 1 TO n DO
    BEGIN
      FOR column := 1 TO n DO
        Write (row * column:4);
      WriteLn
    END
END.   {MultiplicationTable}
```

Sample Runs

```
Multiplication table for 1 to what number? 12
  1    2    3    4    5    6    7    8    9   10   11   12
  2    4    6    8   10   12   14   16   18   20   22   24
  3    6    9   12   15   18   21   24   27   30   33   36
  4    8   12   16   20   24   28   32   36   40   44   48
  5   10   15   20   25   30   35   40   45   50   55   60
  6   12   18   24   30   36   42   48   54   60   66   72
  7   14   21   28   35   42   49   56   63   70   77   84
  8   16   24   32   40   48   56   64   72   80   88   96
  9   18   27   36   45   54   63   72   81   90   99  108
 10   20   30   40   50   60   70   80   90  100  110  120
 11   22   33   44   55   66   77   88   99  110  121  132
 12   24   36   48   60   72   84   96  108  120  132  144
```

Observations

outer and inner loop

Program MultiplicationTable has a FOR loop within another FOR loop. One loop (the loop with counter row) is called the **outer loop**, and the other loop (the loop with counter column) is called the **inner loop**. The two loops taken together, are called **nested loops**. Nested loops can be confusing if you're not completely familiar with the way they work. To see how the counters are incremented in this program, look carefully at the Traces subsection that follows.

Traces

```
┌── MultiplicationTable ───────┐
│                              │
│   n   row   column   output  │
│  12                          │
│           1        1       1 │
│                    2       2 │
│                    3       3 │
│                    .       . │
│                    .       . │
│                   12      12 │
│           2        1       2 │
│                    2       4 │
│                    3       6 │
│                    .       . │
│                    .       . │
│                   12      24 │
│           3        1       3 │
│           .        .       . │
│           .        .       . │
│          12        1      12 │
│                    2      24 │
│                    3      36 │
│                    .       . │
│                    .       . │
│                   12     144 │
│                              │
└──────────────────────────────┘
```

Notice how the value of column changes faster than the value of row. You can memorize this fact: The inner loop's counter changes faster than the outer loop's counter. But it's better to *understand* why it happens.

how nested loops work

Program MultiplicationTable has two FOR statements: an outer statement and an inner statement. If we scan the program from top to bottom, we see the outer FOR statement first, so execution of the outer statement starts first. row is given the value 1.

```
┌── MultiplicationTable ───────┐
│                              │
│   n   row   column   output  │
│  12                          │
│         1                    │
│                              │
└──────────────────────────────┘
```

What has to happen for one iteration of this outer loop (with row equal to 1) to be completed? The inner FOR statement has to be executed, and then a WriteLn has to be executed. In executing the inner FOR statement, the value of column goes from 1 to 12. So the value of column changes while the value of row stays at 1.

```
┌─ MultiplicationTable ─────┐
│                                   │
│   n   row   column   output       │
│                                   │
│   12                              │
│                                   │
│         1       1         1       │
│                 2         2       │
│                 3         3       │
│                 .         .       │
│                 .         .       │
│                 .         .       │
│                12        12       │
│                                   │
└───────────────────────────┘
```

Then it's time for the outer loop's second iteration. row gets the value 2. The inner FOR statement and the WriteLn have to be executed again. In executing the inner FOR statement, column again goes from 1 to 12.

```
┌─ MultiplicationTable ─────┐
│                                   │
│   n   row   column   output       │
│                                   │
│   12                              │
│                                   │
│         1       1         1       │
│                 2         2       │
│                 3         3       │
│                 .         .       │
│                 .         .       │
│                 .         .       │
│                12        12       │
│                                   │
│         2       1         2       │
│                 2         4       │
│                 3         6       │
│                 .         .       │
│                 .         .       │
│                 .         .       │
│                12        24       │
│                                   │
└───────────────────────────┘
```

And so on.

Structure

How much of the time resource does Program MultiplicationTable take? Once again, we divide the body of the program into parts as shown on the top of the next page.

Notice that Part I isn't inside either of the FOR loops. But Part II is inside the inner FOR loop, and Part III is in the outer FOR loop, but not the inner FOR loop.

Now let's say that on a particular computer,

Part I takes t_I seconds to run

each execution of Part II takes t_{II} seconds to run

each execution of Part III takes t_{III} seconds to run

As we saw in Section 6.1, the numbers t_I, t_{II}, and t_{III} can vary significantly from one computer to another.

Since Part II is inside the inner FOR loop, it gets executed more times than the other two parts. For instance, if the variable n has the value 12,

```
BEGIN {MultiplicationTable}

    Write  ('Multiplication table ...
    ReadLn (n);                              ——➤ Part I
    WriteLn;
    WriteLn;

    FOR row := 1 TO n DO
      BEGIN
        FOR column := 1 TO n DO

          Write (row * column:4);            ——➤ Part II


          WriteLn                            ——➤ Part III

      END
END.  {MultiplicationTable}
```

then Part I gets executed once, Part II gets executed 144 times, and Part III gets executed 12 times. These numbers make a lot of sense if you remember that each execution of Part II writes a single entry in the table, and that each execution of Part III starts a new row of the table.

In general (for any value of the variable n)

Part I gets executed once

Part II gets executed n^2 times

Part III gets executed n times

So the total amount of time for Program `MultiplicationTable` to run is

$$\text{Running time of Program MultiplicationTable} = t_I + (n^2 * t_{II}) + (n * t_{III})$$

Now make up some values for t_I, t_{II}, and t_{III}, and compute the program's running time for several values of n. You'll discover something like what we discovered in Section 6.1: that when n becomes large, the t_I and t_{III} terms contribute negligible amounts to the total. This is because, when n gets to be very large, n^2 gets to be so much larger than anything else in the formula. In particular, n^2 gets to be so much larger than n. So it's safe to say that

$$\text{Running time of Program MultiplicationTable} = n^2 * t_{II}$$

Of course t_{II} varies from one implementation to another, so the best we can say is

$$\text{Running time of Program MultiplicationTable} = n^2 * \text{some number that varies from one computer to another}$$

O(n^2) time

The shorthand notation for this is

$$\text{Running time of Program } \texttt{MultiplicationTable} = O(n^2)$$

where "O(n^2)" is pronounced "order n^2," "big 'O' of n^2," "complexity n^2," or just "quadratic."

Now let's see how O(n^2) time compares to O(n) time and O(1) time. Let's say we have three programs, called Constant, Linear, and Quadratic. These programs all have the same specifications. They all solve the same problem, but each program solves the problem in its own unique way. (Each program implements a different algorithm.) Because of these differences

Program `Constant` runs in O(1) time

Program `Linear`   runs in O(n) time

Program `Quadratic` runs in O(n^2) time

The number n represents some value that differs from one run to the next (like the highest number in the multiplication table or the number of grades to be averaged). Which program runs "fastest" and which runs "slowest"?

First we'll use simple numbers. Let's say that

Program `Constant` takes 1 second to run

Program `Linear`   takes n seconds to run

Program `Quadratic` takes n^2 seconds to run

Here's a chart showing running times:

	Running time (in seconds) of Programs		
n	Constant	Linear	Quadratic
1	1	1	1
2	1	2	4
3	1	3	9
4	1	4	16
5	1	5	25
6	1	6	36
7	1	7	49
8	1	8	64
9	1	9	81
10	1	10	100

Program `Constant` runs fastest and Program `Quadratic` runs the slowest. Program `Linear` is somewhere in between. In terms of time, we might say that Program `Constant` is the most efficient of the three programs, and Program `Quadratic` is the least efficient.

Do these conclusions depend on the numbers we picked for the running times of the three programs? Not really. Let's change our numbers. Let's assume that

Program `Constant` takes 1000 seconds to run

Program `Linear` takes $100 + (n * 100)$ seconds to run

Program `Quadratic` takes $2 * n^2$ seconds to run

Notice that the running time for Program `Constant` is still O(1), the running time for Program `Linear` is still O(n), and the running time for Program `Quadratic` is still O(n^2). Here's the chart for the running times of the programs:

	Running time (in seconds) of Programs		
n	Constant	Linear	Quadratic
1	1000	200	3
5	1000	600	75
10	1000	1100	300
15	1000	1600	675
20	1000	2100	1200
25	1000	2600	1875
30	1000	3100	2700
35	1000	3600	3675
40	1000	4100	4800
45	1000	4600	6075
50	1000	5100	7500

For small values of n, Program `Constant` is the slowest and Program `Quadratic` is the fastest. But this is an anomaly, brought on because we used small values of n. As n gets larger and larger, and the running time for the three programs becomes more consequential, the old pattern emerges once again: Program `Constant` is fastest, Program `Quadratic` is the slowest, and Program `Linear` is somewhere in between. This pattern will hold for any three programs that run in O(1), O(n), and O(n^2) time.

6.4 Exercises

Key Words to Review

outer loop

inner loop

O(n^2)

quadratic

Questions to Answer

QUE 6.4.1   Explain the way in which the two loop counters change their values when nested FOR loops are being executed.

QUE 6.4.2   Can you find any other Program Examples (besides MultiplicationTable) that we've done up to this point that take $O(n^2)$ time? Explain.

Experiments to Try

EXP 6.4.1   In Program MultiplicationTable, add an INTEGER variable x and replace the two lines

```
    Write (row * column:4);
  WriteLn
```

with

```
  x := x DIV 2 * 2
```

This will eliminate most of the program's output, but still give it something to do each time through the loop. Run the new version of the program several times with various large values of n. For each run, note the value of n and the amount of time the program takes to run. (Use the system-clock-time technique that you found in Exercise Man.6.1.2. Have the program print the time twice—immediately before it starts executing any FOR loops and just before the program ends its run.) After doing several runs, look over the data you've collected. Is it true that the amount of time the program takes to run is proportional to the square of n?

Changes to Make

CHA 6.4.1   Modify Program MultiplicationTable so that its output contains column headings, row headings, and lines to separate the headings from the table's body:

```
12
 * !  1   2   3   4   5   6   7   8   9  10  11  12
 --!--------------------------------------------------
 1 !  1   2   3   4   5   6   7   8   9  10  11  12
 2 !  2   4   6   8  10  12  14  16  18  20  22  24
 3 !  3   6   9  12  15  18  21  24  27  30  33  36
etc.
```

CHA 6.4.2   Modify Program MultiplicationTable so that it creates a table for *addition modulo n*. Here's how we do addition modulo 3:

$$
\begin{array}{c|ccc}
  & 0 & 1 & 2 \\
\hline
0 & 0 & 1 & 2 \\
1 & 1 & 2 & 0 \\
2 & 2 & 0 & 1 \\
\end{array}
$$

When we add 2 and 2 we get 1, because

$$(2 + 2) \text{ MOD } 3 = 4 \text{ MOD } 3 = 1$$

Notice that when we do addition modulo 3, we use the numbers 0, 1, 2, and no others. The same is true for other ns. For instance, for addition modulo 5 we'd use the numbers 0, 1, 2, 3, 4, and no others.

CHA 6.4.3 Reconsider your solutions to the Changes to Make exercises in Section 5.1, given what you now know about the FOR statement.

CHA 6.4.4

```
Modify Program Copy (Section 5.1) so that it
starts by reading four numbers from the keyboard: a starting
line, a finishing line, a starting column, and a finishing
column.  Then it copies the rectangle described by these line
numbers and column numbers.  For example, if the inFile
contains this paragraph, and the user asks for
```

```
        Starting line:     2
        Finishing line:    4
        Starting column:   8
        Finishing column: 23
```

```
then the outFile contains
```

```
        by reading four
         finishing line,
          Then it copies
```

For simplicity you should assume that each line contains characters up to and including one in the finishing column.

Scales to Practice

PRA 6.4.1 Write a program that displays all the ways to make a four-digit number using the digits 1, 2, 3, and 4.

PRA 6.4.2 Write a program that finds all combinations of three INTEGERs whose sum is equal to ten. (For example, $3 + 2 + 5 = 10$.) Make each INTEGER value be between 0 and 10.

Programs and Subprograms to Write

WRI 6.4.1 Write a program that makes a table showing how much a person has in his or her savings account after one year, two years, three years, . . . , up to five years. The table should give this information for various amounts of principal, from $100.00 up to $1000.00, in increments of $100.00. Assume that the interest on the savings account is 5 percent.

WRI 6.4.2 *(This exercise requires some understanding of music.)* The notes in the middle octave of a piano are called

C3   C#3   D3   D#3   E3   F3   F#3   G3   G#3   A3   A#3   B3

In the octave below this, the notes are named C2, C#2, D2, etc. In the octave above, the notes are named C4, C#4, D4, etc. Now the frequency of C3 (the number of times the string vibrates each second when C3 is played) is 261.6. And as long as we're using an equally tempered tuning system, the frequency of a note is Sqrt (12) more than the frequency of the note just below it. Write a program that makes a chart showing the frequencies of all the notes from Octave 0 to Octave 7.

	C	C#	D	D#	E	F	F#	G	G#	A	A#	B
0	136.9	140.4	143.8	147.3	150.7	154.2	157.7	161.1	164.6	168.1	171.5	175.0
1	178.5	181.9	185.4	188.9	192.3	195.8	199.2	202.7	206.2	209.6	213.1	216.6
2	220.0	223.5	227.0	230.4	233.9	237.4	240.8	244.3	247.7	251.2	254.7	258.1
3	261.6	.. *Etc.*										

6.5

Nested FOR Loops—Another Example

Let's consider the multiplication table problem (from Section 6.4) once again. What if we wanted to write only the *lower half* of the multiplication table? After all, in a square-shaped multiplication table the lower half contains exactly the same information as the upper half.

```
Multiplication table for 1 to what number? 12

          2    3    4    5    6    7    8    9   10   11   12
               6    8   10   12   14   16   18   20   22   24
                   12   15   18   21   24   27   30   33   36
  1                     20   24   28   32   36   40   44   48      ← This
  2    4                     30   35   40   45   50   55   60        half of
  3    6    9                     42   48   54   60   66   72        the table
  4    8   12   16                     56   63   70   77   84        isn't
  5   10   15   20   25                     72   80   88   96        needed.
  6   12   18   24   30   36                     90   99  108
  7   14   21   28   35   42   49                    110  120
  8   16   24   32   40   48   56   64                    132
  9   18   27   36   45   54   63   72   81
 10   20   30   40   50   60   70   80   90  100
 11   22   33   44   55   66   77   88   99  110  121
 12   24   36   48   60   72   84   96  108  120  132  144
```

We can get just the lower triangle of a multiplication table by making a very small modification to the program of Section 6.4.

Specifications

Input: A number, n

Output: The lower triangle of multiplication table, for numbers from 1 to n

Designing a Program

The pseudocode for this problem is almost the same as the pseudocode in Section 6.4. Here's a first draft:

determining the inner loop's final value

For each of n-many rows,
    for some of n-many columns,
        write the product of the row number times the column number

Now what do we mean by "some of n-many columns?" The number of columns we use depends on which row of the table we're creating:

The first row has only one number in it:

For row 1,
  for column 1,
    write the product . . .

The second row has two numbers in it:

For row 2,
  for columns 1 and 2,
    write the product . . .

And the third row has three:

For row 3,
  for columns 1, 2, and 3,
    write the product . . .

In general,

For any particular row,
  for columns 1, 2, 3, up to the number of the row,
    write the product . . .

This suggests the following kind of loop nesting:

```
FOR row := 1 TO n DO
       .
       .
    FOR column := 1 TO row DO
```

The whole program follows.

Program Example

```
PROGRAM HalfMultTable (input, output);
{Writes the lower triangle of a multi-
 plication table for the numbers 1 to n.}
  TYPE
    positive = 1..MAXINT;
  VAR
    n, row, column : positive;
BEGIN {HalfMultTable}
  Write ('Multiplication table for 1 to what number? ');
  ReadLn (n);
  WriteLn;
  WriteLn;
  FOR row := 1 TO n DO
    BEGIN
      FOR column := 1 TO row DO
        Write (row * column:4);
      WriteLn
    END
END.  {HalfMultTable}
```

Sample Runs

```
Multiplication table for 1 to what number? 12
 1
 2    4
 3    6    9
 4    8   12   16
 5   10   15   20   25
 6   12   18   24   30   36
 7   14   21   28   35   42   49
 8   16   24   32   40   48   56   64
 9   18   27   36   45   54   63   72   81
10   20   30   40   50   60   70   80   90  100
11   22   33   44   55   66   77   88   99  110  121
12   24   36   48   60   72   84   96  108  120  132  144
```

6.5 Exercises

Questions to Answer

QUE 6.5.1 Explain the reasoning behind the use of the variable row in the code

```
FOR row := 1 TO n DO
   BEGIN
      FOR column := 1 TO row DO
```

QUE 6.5.2 Look once again at the code in Exercise Que.6.5.1. In Section 6.2 we stated that Pascal doesn't allow us to change a FOR loop's final value with a statement that's inside the loop. Does this code violate that rule with its use of the variable row? Why, or why not?

Experiments to Try

EXP 6.5.1 In Program HalfMultTable change the inner FOR loop to

```
FOR column := 1 TO row - 1 DO
```

EXP 6.5.2 In Program HalfMultTable, wherever the word row appears change it to the word column and wherever the word column appears change it to the word row.

Changes to Make

CHA 6.5.1 Modify Program HalfMultTable so that it writes the upper triangle of the table, instead of the lower triangle.

CHA 6.5.2 Modify Program BarGraph (Section 3.1) so that it uses nested FOR loops.

CHA 6.5.3 Modify Program OnlyBars (Section 4.2) so that it uses nested FOR loops.

Scales to Practice

PRA 6.5.1   Modify the program you wrote for Exercise Pra.6.4.1 to display all four-digit numbers using the digits 1 to 6 (inclusive).

PRA 6.5.2   Modify the program you wrote for Exercise Pra.6.5.1 so that the only numbers displayed are the ones whose digits increase as you go from left to right. For example, the number 1346 gets displayed, but the number 3146 does not.

Programs and Subprograms to Write

WRI 6.5.1   Write a program that uses nested FOR loops to draw a tree with asterisks:

```
          **
         ****
        ******
       ********
      **********
     ************
    **************
   ****************
  ******************
 ********************
          **
          **
          **
```

WRI 6.5.2   Write a program that makes optimal use of nested FOR loops to make

```
*
**
***
****
*****
    *
    **
    ***
    ****
    *****
        *
        **
        ***
        ****
        *****
```

WRI 6.5.3   A *positive rational number* is a fraction—a positive integer divided by a positive integer.

$$\frac{2}{3}\quad\frac{3}{2}\quad\frac{1}{2}\quad\frac{5}{5}\quad\frac{24}{56}\ldots\text{etc.}$$

And here's an order in which we can list the positive rational numbers:

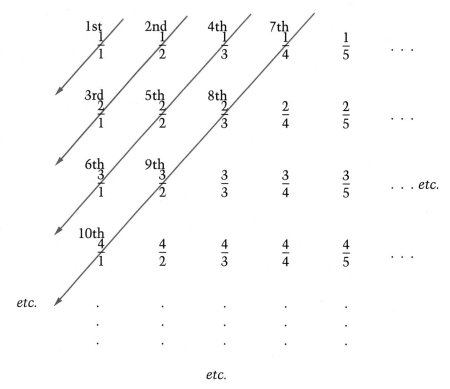

etc.

Write a program that lists positive rational numbers using this ordering.

WRI 6.5.4   Lots of things in computer science and mathematics are named for the seventeenth-century French philosopher Blaise Pascal. For instance, there's Pascal's Triangle:

```
            1
        1       1
    1       2       1
  1     3       3       1
1     4     6     4     1
```

Each number inside the triangle is the sum of the two numbers to the left and the right of it in the row just above it.

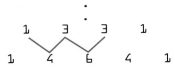

Now look once again at Exercise Wri.6.2.7. The notation $C(n,r)$ is used to mean

$$\frac{n!}{r! * (n - r)!}$$

(Note: The value of 0! is 1.) It turns out that the numbers in Pascal's Triangle can be found by calculating $C(n,r)$ for all values of n and r:

```
                    C(0,0)
               C(1,0 )        C(1,1)
          C(2,0)      C(2,1)       C(2,2)
      C(3,0)      C(3,1 )      C(3,2)       C(3,3)
  C(4,0)      C(4,1)      C(4,2)       C(4,3)       C(4,4)
```

Write a program that draws these five rows of Pascal's Triangle.
Hint: It's easier if you simplify the problem so that the triangle leans toward the left:

```
1
1  1
1  2  1
1  3  3  1
1  4  6  4  1
```

6.6

The REPEAT Statement

A `WHILE` loop's condition is always checked at the "top" of the loop, at the beginning of each iteration, before the execution of the repeated statement. This isn't always convenient. Occasionally there are situations in which testing at the bottom of the loop is more useful. To help us cope with these situations, we have yet another kind of loop. It's called a `REPEAT` statement.

Specifications   In Section 6.4 we had a program that wrote a complete (square-shaped) multiplication table. Then in Section 6.5 we made a slight modification to get a program that wrote a half-sized (triangle-shaped) table. Now what if we want to give the user a choice? Then we probably want to prompt the user to find out what size table is needed. How about an `f` for full-sized table, and an `h` for half-sized table?

Input: A number, n, and a `reply`. (Keep prompting for the `reply` until the user enters the letter f or the letter h.)

Output: If the user entered an f, write the multiplication table, for numbers from 1 to n. If the user entered an h, write the lower triangle of multiplication table, for numbers from 1 to n.

Designing a Program

The words "Keep prompting for the `reply` . . ." suggest a loop. First we'll try a WHILE loop

```
WHILE (reply <> 'f') AND (reply <> 'h') DO
  BEGIN
    Write ('Full table or half table (f or h)?    ');
    ReadLn (reply)
  END
```

Of course we're faced with our usual problem: How can we compare `reply` to f or h if `reply` doesn't already have a value? So we have to give `reply` a value before the WHILE loop is executed. We can use our old trick of doing the first prompt and `ReadLn` before the loop:

```
Write ('Full table or half table (f or h)?      ');
ReadLn (reply);
WHILE (reply <> 'f') AND (reply <> 'h') DO
  BEGIN
    Write ('Full table or half table (f or h)?       ');
    ReadLn (reply)
  END
```

or we can arbitrarily assign an initial value to `reply` to get the loop started:

```
reply := 'x';
WHILE (reply <> 'f') AND (reply <> 'h') DO
  BEGIN
    Write ('Full table or half table (f or h)?       ');
    ReadLn (reply)
  END
```

but either way we get the feeling we're doing something we shouldn't have to do.

Now remember that in a WHILE loop, the condition testing is done at the beginning of each loop iteration. But in this particular problem, we know for sure that we want to read a value for `reply` before the first test is done. What we need is a loop in which the "do more" condition is tested at the end of each loop iteration. As long as we know for sure that it's safe to "leap before we look," we can use a REPEAT statement.

The code follows.

Program Example

```
PROGRAM HalfOrWhole (input, output);
{Writes the lower triangle of a multi-
 plication table for the numbers 1 to n.}
  TYPE
    positive = 1..MAXINT;
  VAR
    n, row, column : positive;
    reply          : CHAR;
```

```
BEGIN {HalfOrWhole}
  Write  ('Multiplication table for 1 to what number? ');
  ReadLn (n);
  REPEAT
    Write  ('Full table or half table (f or h)?          ');
    ReadLn (reply)
  UNTIL (reply = 'f') OR (reply = 'h');
  WriteLn;

  IF reply = 'f' THEN
    FOR row := 1 TO n DO
      BEGIN
        FOR column := 1 TO n DO
          Write (row * column:4);
        WriteLn
      END;
  IF reply = 'h' THEN
    FOR row := 1 TO n DO
      BEGIN
        FOR column := 1 TO row DO
          Write (row * column:4);
        WriteLn
      END
END.  {HalfOrWhole}
```

Sample Runs

```
Multiplication table for 1 to what number? 12
Full table or half table (f or h)?          a
Full table or half table (f or h)?          y
Full table or half table (f or h)?          2
Full table or half table (f or h)?          H
Full table or half table (f or h)?          h
   1
   2   4
   3   6   9
   4   8  12  16
   5  10  15  20  25
   6  12  18  24  30  36
   7  14  21  28  35  42  49
   8  16  24  32  40  48  56  64
   9  18  27  36  45  54  63  72  81
  10  20  30  40  50  60  70  80  90 100
  11  22  33  44  55  66  77  88  99 110 121
  12  24  36  48  60  72  84  96 108 120 132 144
```

Observations

REPEAT statement

A REPEAT statement is very much like a WHILE statement. There are only two differences. First, in a REPEAT statement the condition is tested at the "bottom" of the loop, at the end of each iteration, after the execution of the statements in the loop. Here's what happens in Program HalfOrWhole:

- The lines inside the loop (between REPEAT and UNTIL) are executed.
- The (reply = 'f') OR (reply = 'h') condition is tested.

- If it's FALSE, then the lines inside the loop are executed again.
- The condition is tested again.
- If it's FALSE, then the lines inside the loop are executed again, etc.

Notice that the lines inside the loop are executed once before the condition is ever tested. This is different from the WHILE loop. With a WHILE loop, the repeated statement might never be executed. Here's an example:

```
i := 7;
WHILE i > 100 DO
   BEGIN
      whatever
   END
```

Second, in a WHILE loop, the repeated statement continues to be iterated as long as the condition is TRUE. In a REPEAT loop, the repeated statement is iterated as long as the condition is FALSE; that is, the iteration continues UNTIL the condition is TRUE. This is made very evident by the use of the reserved word UNTIL.

Further Discussion

Here's the syntax diagram for the REPEAT statement:

REPEAT *statement:*

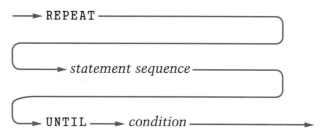

REPEAT
statement
syntax

Now notice that we have a **statement sequence**, not a compound statement, between the words REPEAT and UNTIL. A statement sequence is just a collection of statements, separated from one another by semicolons:

statement sequence:

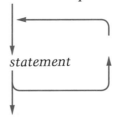

It's like a compound statement without the words BEGIN and END. In a REPEAT statement, we don't need the words BEGIN and END. The statements in the loop are grouped together just by being between the words

REPEAT and UNTIL. Of course, it doesn't hurt anything to put in BEGIN and END:

```
REPEAT
  BEGIN
    Write  ('Full table or half table (f or h)?        ');
    ReadLn (reply)
  END
UNTIL (reply = 'f') OR (reply = 'h')
```

It doesn't change the action of the REPEAT statement. It just means we have only one statement (a compound statement) in the statement sequence.

Programming Style

Notice the two IF statements in Program HalfOrWhole.

```
IF reply = 'f' THEN
    .
    .
    .
IF reply = 'h' THEN
    .
    .
    .
```

Why do we need the second IF? Would it be just as well to turn the second half of the program into an ELSE-part?

```
IF reply = 'f' THEN
  FOR row := 1 TO n DO
    BEGIN
      FOR column := 1 TO n DO
        Write (row * column:4);
      WriteLn
    END
ELSE
  FOR row := 1 TO n DO
    BEGIN
      FOR column := 1 TO row DO
        Write (row * column:4);
      WriteLn
    END
```

After all, we went to all that trouble to make sure that the user gave us an f or an h, so if the value of reply isn't f, what's the sense in testing to see if it's h?

The answer is that sometimes it's best to be doubly safe. Having the computer perform the extra test

```
IF reply = 'h' THEN
```

IF .. IF vs. IF .. ELSE

may seem wasteful at first, but what if another programmer removes your REPEAT loop? Then the ELSE clause becomes the "catch all" for any kind of reply other than f. In some situations this behavior may be acceptable or even desirable. But in others (give the patient half a dose or a full dose) performing some **default action** by accident may prove to be disastrous.

Structure

NS chart for a
REPEAT
statement

Since condition testing is done at the bottom of a REPEAT statement, the NS chart for a REPEAT statement has a right-side-up "L" shape:

Write ('Multiplication table for 1 to what number? ')
ReadLn (n)

<table>
<tr><td rowspan="2"></td><td>Write ('Full table or half table (f or h)? ')</td></tr>
<tr><td>ReadLn (reply)</td></tr>
</table>

UNTIL (reply = 'f') OR (reply = 'h')
WriteLn

.
.
.
Etc.

6.6 Exercises

Key Words to Review

REPEAT	statement sequence	default action
UNTIL		

Questions to Answer

QUE 6.6.1   What are the differences between the REPEAT statement and the WHILE statement?

QUE 6.6.2   Why are the words BEGIN and END not needed to enclose the statements inside a REPEAT statement?

QUE 6.6.3   The REPEAT loop in Program HalfOrWhole is an attempt to make the program more robust. If the user enters a letter other than f or h, the computer still does something sensible. But how robust is Program HalfOrWhole? Can the user still do things to make the program behave in "unacceptable" ways? Explain.

QUE 6.6.4   In Program Minimum (Section 5.4) we had to have two ReadLns—one was immediately before the WHILE loop and another was the first statement inside the WHILE loop. Could we have avoided this apparent duplication by using a REPEAT statement?

Experiments to Try

EXP 6.6.1   Run Program HalfOrWhole and hit the return key when you're prompted for an f or h.

EXP 6.6.2   Add a semicolon after the ReadLn that's inside the REPEAT statement.

EXP 6.6.3   Add a semicolon immediately after the word REPEAT.

Changes to Make

CHA 6.6.1   Modify the programs you wrote for Exercises Cha.5.2.1 and Cha.5.3.4 so that they use REPEAT loops instead of WHILE loops.

CHA 6.6.2   Modify Program Fibonacci (Section 6.3) so that it uses a REPEAT loop instead of a FOR loop. Each time the program writes a term in the Fibonacci sequence, it asks the user whether it should stop or go on and write the next term.

Programs and Subprograms to Write

WRI 6.6.1   Modify the program you wrote for Exercise Wri.6.1.1 so that it uses a REPEAT statement to keep prompting the user until it gets a w or an m.

WRI 6.6.2   Modify the program of Exercise Wri.5.4.3 so that it uses a REPEAT statement instead of a WHILE statement.

WRI 6.6.3   Write a program that looks for the first non-blank character in a disk file and writes that character on the screen.

Chapter Summary

The WHILE statement is only one of several ways to create repetition in a Pascal program. The most important characteristic of the WHILE statement is

> The testing of the condition is done at the "top" of the loop, at the beginning of each iteration, before the execution of the repeated statement.

This means that we can execute a WHILE statement and not perform any iterations. It also means that if a WHILE statement's condition becomes FALSE in the middle of an iteration, the iteration isn't interrupted. Execution of the WHILE loop continues until the beginning of the next iteration.

With a WHILE loop, it's up to the programmer (and possibly the user) to make sure that the loop eventually stops iterating. A loop that can be stopped only by aborting the program is called an *infinite loop*. Infinite loops are, in general, undesirable.

In contrast to a `WHILE` statement, a `FOR` statement cannot cause an infinite loop. A `FOR` statement always stops iterating when the *loop counter* reaches its *final value*. With a `FOR` statement the loop counter is incremented (or decremented) without any extra statements to change the counter's value, such as

```
i := i + 1
```

In a situation where it's possible to use a `FOR` loop (where we know that a counter will need to be stepped from an initial value to a final value), it's better to use a `FOR` statement than a `WHILE` statement. A `FOR` statement is safer and more efficient than the corresponding `WHILE` statement.

Occasionally we find a situation in which, by the very nature of the problem, we're sure that a certain loop will need to be iterated at least once. In such a situation, it's appropriate to use a `REPEAT` statement. In a `REPEAT` statement

> The testing of the condition is done at the "bottom" of the loop, at the end of each iteration, after the execution of the statements in the loop.

This means that we cannot execute a `REPEAT` statement without performing at least one iteration.

7
Simple Types

One of the most fundamental building blocks in programming is the concept of a **type**. A type is a set of values and a set of operations on those values. For instance, Program `RealArithmetic` (Section 2.1) has several variables, and the value stored in each of these variables is a `REAL` number. The word `REAL` is the name of a particular type. It tells us what values can be stored in each of the variables and what operations can be performed on these values. In Program `RealArithmetic`, we store decimal values in each of the variables and perform four operations on these values: addition, multiplication, subtraction, and division.

7.1

Numbers, Variables, and Constants

variables and
constants

We've already seen the use of variables in each of our examples. A **variable** is a place to store a **value**. We refer to the variable by writing its **variable name**. Of course a variable's value can change during the run of the program. That's why it's called a variable.

constants

There are good reasons for having an identifier whose value can't change during the run of a program. An identifier whose value can't change during the run of the program is called a **constant**.[1]

---

[1]Sometimes, for emphasis, we refer to it as a constant identifier.

Program Example

```
PROGRAM Astronomy (input, output);
{This is a program-fragment.}
    CONST
        numberOfPlanets  = 9;
        electronCharge   = -1;
        protonCharge     = +1;
        temperatureOfSun = 11000;
        orbitOf4U182030  = 11.0105;
        ageOfUniverse    = 15.0E9;
        antiprotonCharge = -protonCharge;
        message          = 'Is anyone out there?';

    VAR
        netCharge                : INTEGER;
        velocity, acceleration : REAL;
BEGIN {Astronomy}
    {We'll put statements here later.}
END.  {Astronomy}
```

Observations

In a constant definition, the programmer creates identifiers whose values don't change during the run of the program. For instance, if by accident, the body of Program `Astronomy` contains a statement like

```
ReadLn (numberOfPlanets)
```

the program won't compile. Instead the computer will give you an error diagnostic. The essence of the diagnostic's message will be "You said the value of `numberOfPlanets` should never change, but in the `ReadLn`, you're trying to change it."

- `ageOfUniverse    = 15.0E9;`

mantissa and exponent

In the number 15.0E9, 15.0 is called the **mantissa** and 9 is called the **exponent**. (Of course, the E in 15.0E9 stands for the word *exponent*.) The exponent tells you how many places to move the mantissa's decimal point.

For example, the 9 in 15.0E9 tells the computer to move the decimal point nine places to the right. First you add more zeros (you turn 15.0 into 15.000000000), then you move the decimal point nine places to get 15000000000. So 15.0E9 stands for "fifteen billion."[2]

The fact that 9 is a positive number tells you to move the decimal point in 15.0E9 to the right. If the exponent is negative, you move the decimal point to the left. So 15.0E-9 stands for 0.000000015, which is "fifteen billionths."[3]

A zero exponent means that you shouldn't move the decimal point at all. So 15.0E0 just stands for the number 15.0.

---

[2]British readers will recognize this number as "fifteen thousand million."

[3]In the British system, this number is "fifteen thousand-millionths."

If you're familiar with scientific notation, you'll recognize that `15.0E9` really stands for 15×10^9.

- `antiprotonCharge = -protonCharge;`

preceding a constant with a minus sign

Here's something new: in a `CONST` definition, it's legal to define one constant by putting a minus sign in front of a constant that's defined on an earlier line. In Pascal, we're not allowed to get more elaborate than this with our constant definitions. For instance, a definition like

```
CONST
   numberOfPlanets  = 9;
   morePlanets      = numberOfPlanets + 1;
```

would be illegal.

- `message = 'Is anyone out there?';`

character-string constants

In Pascal, each constant has to be given either a numeric value or a character-string value. In this example, `message` is given a character-string value. If the statement

```
WriteLn (message)
```

appears in the program, the computer will display

```
Is anyone out there?
```

on the screen.

Further Discussion

The syntax diagrams for the **constant definition part** of the program are more complicated than you might expect:

constant definition part:

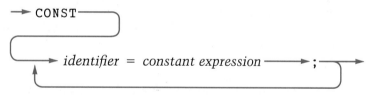

CONST syntax diagrams

The preceding syntax diagram refers to something that it calls a **constant expression**. So here's the syntax diagram for a constant expression:

constant expression:

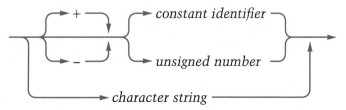

And now we need to know what's meant by **constant identifier, unsigned number**, and **character string**.

Any identifier (starting with a letter and then having only letters and digits in it) becomes a constant identifier when we give it a value in a CONST definition. Once we've done this we can use the constant identifier to form constant expressions. These constant expressions help us in defining other constant identifiers. Here are the diagrams for unsigned number and character string:

unsigned number:

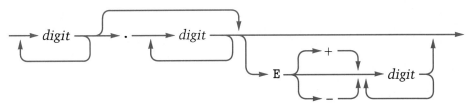

character string:

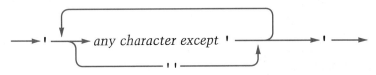

At first these diagrams may seem confusing and unintuitive. You can become familiar with them by trying Exercises Que.7.1.4 to Que.7.1.7. For a really tough exercise, try explaining all the details in the syntax diagrams using ordinary English prose. (It will make you appreciate how useful syntax diagrams really are!)

The Pascal language has one constant identifier that you never need to define. It's called MAXINT. (See Program FindAverage in Section 6.1.) MAXINT is the largest INTEGER value that your implementation can store. On a VAX with an operating system called VMS, no integer variable can store a number bigger than 2147483647, so if we write

MAXINT

```
x := MAXINT
```

then x gets the value 2147483647. On a microcomputer with Turbo Pascal MAXINT has the value 32767. The smallest value that an INTEGER can have is −MAXINT.

Programming Style

Let's add a few statements to Program Astronomy to see how the constants might be used.

Why use constants?

An atom of hydrogen consists of an electron and a proton. Here are two ways to compute the charge of a hydrogen atom:

First way: netCharge := −1 + 1

Second way: netCharge := electronCharge + protonCharge

The first way is the "quick and dirty" way. This first statement is easy to type, but when it's combined with several other statements in a large program, it can be hard to debug. The second way is definitely the preferred way, because it's more self-documenting. The same reasoning gets us to write

```
CONST
    .
    .
    antiprotonCharge = -protonCharge;
```

instead of

```
CONST
    .
    .
    antiprotonCharge = -1;
```

And there's another reason to use constants instead of numbers. Let's say we use the number 9 throughout the program, instead of the constant `numberOfPlanets`. Here are some lines that might appear in the program:

```
bodiesInSolarSystem := 1 + 9
IF planetsWith90PercentWater < 9 THEN
WHILE i < 9 DO
```

But astronomers are gathering evidence that there's a tenth planet in our solar system, which they call Planet X. To make the program useful for the enlarged solar system, we might use our editor to change every 9 to a 10.

```
bodiesInSolarSystem := 1 + 10
IF planetsWith100PercentWater < 10 THEN
WHILE i < 10 DO
```

But that won't quite work, because we'll unintentionally change one of our variable names: `planetsWith90PercentWater` gets changed into `planetsWith100PercentWater`. The problem is easily solved with the constant.

```
CONST
  numberOfPlanets = 9;
        .
        .
bodiesInSolarSystem := 1 + numberOfPlanets
IF planetsWith90PercentWater < numberOfPlanets THEN
WHILE i < numberOfPlanets DO
```

Now we can change from a nine- to a ten-planet solar system by changing just one number in the program: in the constant definition we change the 9 to a 10. After making this simple change, `numberOfPlanets` has the desired value, 10, and the variable name `PlanetsWith90PercentWater` still has 90 in it.

7.1   Exercises

Key Words to Review

type	constant	constant definition part
variable	mantissa	constant expression
value	exponent	constant identifier
variable name	character string	unsigned number

Questions to Answer

QUE 7.1.1   In what ways are constants useful?

QUE 7.1.2   What does `1.23E6` mean? What about `0.3E-2`? What about `5.0E0`?

QUE 7.1.3   Look carefully at the syntax diagram for a character string. What's the reason for the part that says *any character except* `'`? (If you don't know, see Section 3.1.)

QUE 7.1.4   Examine the syntax diagrams in this section and tell which of the following are legal character strings:
a. `'123aBc'`   b. `''''`   c. `''`   d. `'"'`   e. `"Barry Burd"`

QUE 7.1.5   Examine the syntax diagrams in this section and tell which of the following are legal unsigned numbers:
a. `05095709579357729457207239975`   b. `.5`   c. `1.2E345`   d. `0e-0`

QUE 7.1.6   Examine the syntax diagrams in this section and tell which of the following are legal constant expressions:
a. `+warbles`   b. `++warbles`   c. `'Mr. O''Donnell''s pig'`

QUE 7.1.7   Examine the syntax diagrams in this section and tell which of the following are legal constant definition parts:
a. ```
CONST
    -protonCharge = antiprotonCharge;
```
b.  ```
CONST
    one   = 1;
    two   = 2;
    three = 6;
```
c. ```
CONST
    {just a comment here - nothing else}
```

### Things to Check in a Manual

MAN 7.1.1   Look up `MAXINT` in your implementation's manual. What's its value? In what sense is this not an "arbitrary" value? (Compare with Exercise Exp.6.1.1.)

MAN 7.1.2   Is there a section in your manual where all the implementation's limitations, not only `MAXINT`, are listed?
```

Experiments to Try

EXP 7.1.1 Run a program containing the code

```
VAR
  r : REAL;
     .
     .
     .
r := 10.0E1;
WriteLn (r:10:2);
WriteLn (r:10)
```

Changes to Make

CHA 7.1.1 Modify the definition of `orbitOf4U182030` so that a mantissa and exponent are used.

CHA 7.1.2 Modify Program `Factorial` (Section 6.2) to take advantage of the wider range of values that `REAL` numbers provide. Your new Program `RealFactorial` can handle much larger values than the old Program `Factorial`, even though many of these values are only approximate.

CHA 7.1.3 Remove Procedure `PromptAndReadLn` from Program `Points` (Section 5.3). This means having nearly identical `Write/ReadLn` combinations in several parts of the program. To make this more tolerable, create a constant that stores much of the message contained in the prompt.

Programs and Subprograms to Write

WRI 7.1.1 Redo Exercise Wri.5.4.5 using constants to store the values 0 and 1. Then change the specifications so that the two bits used are represented by the letters F (instead of 0) and T (instead of 1).

Things to Think About

THI 7.1.1 Any computer, no matter how large, is ultimately only finite in size and capabilities. That's why the Pascal language has built-in limitations such as the value of MAXINT—the largest INTEGER value allowed by the language. What other limitations have you learned so far that are built into the language? Since a computer is only finite in size, there must be other limitations beyond the ones that you've learned. Can you think of any? Some of these limitations may even be part of the unspoken rules of computer design. They'd be ignored in most of the manuals.

7.2

REALs and INTEGERs

Specifications In this section we'll write programs to solve the quadratic equation

$$x^2 - 5x + 6 = 0$$

Of course it would be easier to solve this equation by hand, but we're interested in seeing how certain computer programs behave.

Here are some formal specs:

Input: None.

Process: Try the values 1.0, 2.0, 3.0, 4.0, and 5.0 for x.

Output: Values of x that satisfy the equation.

Notice the sentence labeled "Process." This gives us some indication of how the program will create the desired output. It's not as detailed as an algorithm written in pseudocode, but it hints at the algorithm that we expect to use. This is especially useful when we have a choice of several possible algorithms.

Program Example

```
PROGRAM IntegerQuadratic (output);
{Finds integer solutions for the
 quadratic equation Sqr(x) - 5*x + 6 = 0}

  VAR
    x, left, right: INTEGER;

BEGIN {IntegerQuadratic}
  WriteLn ('Solutions of Sqr(x) - 5*x + 6 = 0');
  WriteLn;

  FOR x := 1 TO 5 DO
    BEGIN
      left  := Sqr(x) - 5*x + 6;
      right := 0;
      IF left = right THEN
        WriteLn (x:4)
    END
END.   {IntegerQuadratic}


PROGRAM RealQuadratic (output);
{Finds real solutions for the
 quadratic equation Sqr(x) - 5*x + 6 = 0}

  VAR
    x, left, right: REAL;

BEGIN {RealQuadratic}
  WriteLn ('Solutions of Sqr(x) - 5*x + 6 = 0');
  WriteLn;

  x := 1.0;
  WHILE x <= 5.0 DO
    BEGIN
      left  := Sqr(x) - 5*x + 6;
      right := 0.0;
      IF left = right THEN
        WriteLn (x:6:1);
      x := x + 1.0
    END
END.   {RealQuadratic}
```

Sample Runs

Running `IntegerQuadratic`:

```
Solutions of Sqr(x) - 5*x + 6 = 0
    2
    3
```

Running `RealQuadratic`:

```
Solutions of Sqr(x) - 5*x + 6 = 0
    2.0
    3.0
```

Observations

These two programs are almost the same. The only difference is that one uses REAL variables and the other uses INTEGERs.

consistency of types

- `right := 0`

  versus

  `right := 0.0`

  Notice how types are used consistently in each program. For instance, in the first program, `right` is an INTEGER, so it's assigned the value 0. In the second program, `right` is a REAL, so it's assigned the value 0.0.

  If we changed the line in Program `RealQuadratic` to

  `right := 0`

  the program might take a bit longer to run, because the computer would have to convert 0 to 0.0 and then assign 0.0 to `right`. It's easy for a human being to convert 0 to 0.0; but because of the way REAL numbers are stored in a computer, it takes the computer quite a bit of time to do the conversion.

  If we changed the corresponding line in `IntegerQuadratic` to

  `right := 0.0`

  we'd get an error diagnostic. In Pascal it's illegal to assign a REAL value to an INTEGER variable, even if the REAL value ends with .0. If you really need to assign a REAL value to an INTEGER variable, you can use Trunc or Round:

  ```
  VAR
     r : REAL;
     i : INTEGER;
        .
        .
        .
  i := Trunc (r);
        .
        .
        .
  i := Round (r)
  ```

the type of an expression

- left := Sqr(x) - 5*x + 6

Each part of every expression has a type. This statement is copied from Program RealQuadratic. In this statement, 5 is of type INTEGER (because it has no decimal point) and x is REAL (because it's been declared that way). Notice that 5*x is an INTEGER multiplied by a REAL. It's legal to do this in Pascal. When you do it, you get a REAL (because the resulting value may have digits to the right of the decimal point).

At the end of the line we have the INTEGER value 6. We're adding this to a REAL value. When you add an INTEGER to a REAL, you get a REAL.

Further Discussion

types and operations

When we perform an operation, we get a result, and that result has a type. When we add two INTEGER values we get an INTEGER value. When we add two REAL values we get a REAL value. When we add an INTEGER to a REAL, or add a REAL to an INTEGER, we get a REAL. All this information is summarized in the following table:

+	INTEGER	REAL
INTEGER	INTEGER	REAL
REAL	REAL	REAL

The tables for subtraction and multiplication are the same as the table for addition, but division is a bit more complicated. Since there are two ways to do division, / and DIV, there are two tables for division.

/	INTEGER	REAL
INTEGER	REAL	REAL
REAL	REAL	REAL

DIV	INTEGER
INTEGER	INTEGER

Notice that

- When you divide two numbers with /, you always get a REAL result.
- You can only use DIV to divide INTEGERs.

The table for MOD is the same as the table for DIV.

An expression in which REAL and INTEGER values are combined is called a **mixed expression**. The expression

    Sqr(x) - 5*x + 6

from Program RealQuadratic is a mixed expression.

Testing and Debugging

There are several ways to verify that a program runs correctly. For many of our program examples we've done test runs. In Section 5.4 we saw how to do a simple proof of correctness. But let's look at an error that neither test runs nor proofs of correctness will find.

When we first wrote Program `IntegerQuadratic`, its heading looked like this:

```
PROGRAM IntegerQuadratic (input, output);
```

We included `input` in the program's parameter list even though the program reads nothing from the keyboard. The program ran "correctly," but it began its run by creating a link to the keyboard that it didn't need. This link was wasteful and time-consuming. The program still produced the correct answers, so the test runs looked good, and a proof of correctness would have indicated that the program worked. But the program was less than optimal. How do you detect this kind of an "error"?

walkthrough

One way to do it is with a **walkthrough**. A walkthrough is a session in which the programmer, and perhaps several other computer-wise people, go through a program step by step, examining its code and critiquing its design. The programmer knows the program the best. He or she can look at the program with the knowledge of someone who's thought a lot about the design decisions. The other people can examine the program objectively. They see exactly what's been written, not what they think they remember to have been written.

As a new programmer you should do walkthroughs with each of your programs. You should take time to examine each program before you run it. If your instructor permits you to share your work with other students, you should gather for walkthrough sessions, in which they critique your programs and you critique theirs.

7.2 Exercises

Key Words to Review

mixed expression   walkthrough

Questions to Answer

QUE 7.2.1 What's a mixed expression? Why do we need to be aware of the use of mixed expressions?

QUE 7.2.2 Given the following declarations

```
VAR
   a, b, c, x : REAL;
   m, n       : INTEGER;
```

state the type of *each part* of each of the following expressions:

a. `m*x + n`
b. `Trunc(n)`
c. `Round(3*a*n)`
d. `Exp(2.5 * Ln (3))`
e. `Sqr(b) - 4*a*c`
f. `Sqr(m) + Sqr(n)`

Experiments to Try

EXP 7.2.1   Does the following program compile without error diagnostics?

```
PROGRAM TypeCheck (output);
  VAR
    i : INTEGER;
BEGIN {TypeCheck}
  i := 4/2;
  WriteLn (i:3)
END.  {TypeCheck}
```

EXP 7.2.2   In Section 2.4 we convinced you that you need an extra `temp` variable if you want to switch the values stored in two variables `score1` and `score2`. But try running that section's Program `Switcher` with this revised `IF` statement:

```
IF score1 < score2 THEN
  BEGIN
    score1 := score1 + score2;
    score2 := score1 - score2;
    score1 := score1 - score2
  END
```

This new code exploits properties of numbers to do the work of our old `IF` statement without using a `temp` variable. Can you think of a reason not to use the new code?

Now recall our glass of coffee/cup of milk analogy from Section 2.4. We used that analogy to convince you that an extra `temp` variable was needed. What was wrong with the analogy?

Changes to Make

CHA 7.2.1   Modify Program `FindAverage` of Section 6.1 so that it prints an integer value instead of a real value.

CHA 7.2.2   Modify Program `FindAverage` of Section 6.1 so that grades can be REAL numbers.

CHA 7.2.3   Modify Program `Scores` (Section 2.3) so that it writes REAL numbers even though it reads INTEGERs.

7.3

REALs and Numeric Error

From reading Section 7.2 you'd think that careful use of the `INTEGER` and `REAL` types is stylistically wise, but not absolutely necessary. In this section we'll convince you that it's absolutely necessary. We'll do it with an experimental program that compares $(1/x)x$ with 1.

Program Example

```
PROGRAM RealIdentity (input, output);
{Illustrates the inaccuracy of REAL arithmetic.}
   VAR
      x, limit, left, right : REAL;
   BEGIN {RealIdentity}
      Write ('Enter starting value for x: ');
      ReadLn (x);
      Write ('Enter upper limit for x:    ');
      ReadLn (limit);
      WHILE x <= limit DO
         BEGIN
            left  := (1.0 / x) * x;
            right := 1.0;
            IF left <> right THEN
               WriteLn ('Not equal when x is ', x:5:1);
            x := x + 1.0
         END
   END.  {RealIdentity}
```

Sample Runs

Running `RealIdentity` on a VAX with VMS:

```
Enter starting value for x:  1.0
Enter upper limit for x:    55.0
Not equal when x is  41.0
Not equal when x is  47.0
Not equal when x is  55.0
```

Running `RealIdentity` with Turbo Pascal version 6.0:

```
Enter starting value for x:  1.0
Enter upper limit for x:    55.0
Not equal when x is  19.0
Not equal when x is  27.0
Not equal when x is  38.0
Not equal when x is  45.0
Not equal when x is  54.0
```

The cancellation laws of algebra say that $(1/x)x$ is equal to 1. So we'd never expect to get

```
left <> right
```

to be TRUE. But when we run the program on various implementations, we don't get the answer we expect. What's going on here?

If you do the arithmetic with a hand calculator, you'll see what's happening. Divide 1.0 by 3.0, and then multiply the result by 3.0. You might get something like 0.9999999.[4] When you divide 1.0 by 3.0, you lose accuracy. The calculator can't store all the infinitely many digits of the result 0.33333333333333 . . . , so it just stores the first eight of them: 0.3333333. Multiplying this shortened number by 3.0 gives you 0.9999999. It doesn't give you the original answer of 1.0.

The same kind of thing happens when a computer executes Program RealIdentity. There are **roundoff errors** in computing the value of left. So even though the values of left and right are very close, they're not exactly the same. Roundoff errors are examples of a broader class of difficulties known as **numeric errors**.

numeric errors

Look once again at the sample runs of IntegerQuadratic and RealQuadratic in Section 7.2. These runs seem to be correct. In Program IntegerQuadratic there can't be any roundoff error. When the computer does arithmetic on INTEGERs, it doesn't have any decimal digits to deal with. Unless the values we're using become larger than MAXINT or smaller than −MAXINT, calculations with INTEGERs are always correct and exact. In Program RealQuadratic there's no roundoff error because we were lucky—we avoided very large numbers and didn't do any division.

using REALs

The moral of the story is this:

Don't declare a variable to be a REAL if it's possible to make it an INTEGER. INTEGERs are safer to use than REALs. (They also consume less computing time.)

Be skeptical when you compare two REAL numbers for equality. The result you get is often inaccurate.

7.3   Exercises

Key Words to Review

roundoff error   numeric error

Questions to Answer

QUE 7.3.1   Explain how inaccuracies can creep into arithmetic operations when REAL numbers are being used.

---

[4]On the other hand, you may get 1.0. If you do, try this same experiment with other numbers, dividing 1.0 by 55.0, etc.

QUE 7.3.2   Describe the kinds of problems in which REAL numbers should be used. Describe the kinds of problems in which INTEGERs should be used.

Things to Check in a Manual

MAN 7.3.1   How many digits of accuracy do REAL numbers have on your implementation?

MAN 7.3.2   Does your implementation have a pre-defined constant whose value is π (as in the formula πr^2)?

Experiments to Try

EXP 7.3.1   In this section's Sample Runs we saw what two different implementations do when they run the same program with the same input. What does your implementation do? If your implementation never reports

```
Not equal when x is ..
```

try changing the starting and limit values of x.

EXP 7.3.2   When we run the following program

```
PROGRAM Underflow (output);
BEGIN {Underflow}
   WriteLn (1E37);
   WriteLn (0.01/1E37)
END.   {Underflow}
```

the output we get is

```
1.00000E+37
0.00000E+00
```

The value of 0.01/1E37 shouldn't really be zero, but the computer seems to be saying that it is. This is known as *underflow*. Run this program on your computer. What results do you get? Can you explain your results?

EXP 7.3.3   Try running the following program:

```
PROGRAM Ones (output);
   VAR
      x : REAL;
BEGIN {Ones}
   x := 1.0 + 0.000000000000001;
   IF x = 1.0 THEN
      WriteLn ('Equal!')
END.   {Ones}
```

EXP 7.3.4   Try running the following program:

```
PROGRAM Associativity (output);
   VAR
      tiny : REAL;
BEGIN {Associativity}
   tiny := 0.0000000001;
   WriteLn ('(-1.0+1.0)+tiny = ', (-1.0+1.0)+tiny);
   WriteLn ('(-1.0+tiny)+1.0 = ', (-1.0+tiny)+1.0)
END.   {Associativity}
```

Scales to Practice

PRA 7.3.1   Write and test a function subprogram that takes a REAL number, r, and returns the REAL number that's closest to r but has only three digits to the right of the decimal point.

PRA 7.3.2   Write a program that reads REAL numbers from a file until it finds two numbers, one after another, that are no more than epsilon apart in value. The number epsilon is read in when the program begins executing.

Programs and Subprograms to Write

WRI 7.3.1   Write a program that finds the square root of a number using the *Bisection method*. It starts by "guessing" that the square root is between 0 (the smallerGuess) and 10 (the largerGuess). It finds the average of these two numbers and checks to see how the square of this average compares with the number whose square root we're trying to find. If it's larger, then this average becomes the new largerGuess. If it's smaller, then this average becomes the new smallerGuess. The process continues until the square of the average is very close to the given number. (How close is "very close"? That's a value that's given by the user at the beginning of the program's run.)

WRI 7.3.2   a. Find the pattern in the following sequence of fractions:

$$2 * \left(\frac{2}{1} * \frac{2}{3} * \frac{4}{3} * \frac{4}{5} * \frac{6}{5} * \frac{6}{7} * \cdots \right)$$

Then write a program that computes the values of 2/1, 2/3, 4/3, etc. (Have the program prompt the user for the number of fractions desired.)

b. If you don't know the value of π (as in the formula πr^2), then look it up in a book or do Exercise Man.7.3.2. How many fractions do you have to compute before the sequence shown in part a (multiplying the fractions together and then multiplying by 2) comes close to the value of π?

WRI 7.3.3   *Newton's method* provides a way of repeatedly taking better and better "guesses" to find an approximate value of a mathematical function. To find an approximate value for the square root of a number, you

- Take a guess
- Plug it into the right-hand side of the formula to get a new guess:

$$guess = guess - \frac{guess^2 - number}{2 * guess}$$

- Then take this new guess, and plug it into the right-hand side of the same formula, etc.

If you've taken calculus, you'll recognize the denominator 2 * guess as the *derivative* of

    guess² − number

You keep doing this as long as the difference between guess² and the number is larger than some predetermined amount of error tolerance (something that the user decides).

Write a program that uses Newton's method to find approximate values for the square roots of various numbers. Make sure your program writes each guess so you can keep track of the program's progress.

Things to Think About

THI 7.3.1   The study of *numeric errors* began several centuries ago—long before there were calculators or computers. Explain why numeric error is a concern to us even when we do "paper and pencil" calculations.

7.4

Characters

In Section 2.6 we learned that a variable can store a value that's a character rather than a number. That's because there's a type called CHAR in Pascal. In this section we look at a few of the things you can do with variables of type CHAR.

First we need to know exactly what we mean by a character. Clearly the letters A through Z and a through z are characters. But what about the digits 0 through 9 that show up on your screen? They're characters too. And there are other characters, like [and \ and the blank-space character. And then there are characters you can't see on the screen, like the character that tells the cursor to go to a new line.

ASCII
Character Set

All these characters, and more, are members of what's called the **ASCII Character Set**.[5] A complete list of characters in the ASCII Character Set is given in Appendix D. Some of the characters (like A, a, 9, %, blank-space) are **printing characters**, because when they're sent to your screen, a mark of some sort gets displayed. Others (like *go-to-a-new-line* and *make-a-bell-sound*) are **non-printing characters**. Each member of the ASCII Character Set is associated with a number, called an **ASCII code**.

---

[5]ASCII stands for American Standard Code for Information Interchange.

Character	The character's ASCII code	Character	The character's ASCII code
0	48	Y	89
1	49	Z	90
.	.	[	91
.	.	\	92
8	56	.	.
9	57	.	.
.	.	a	97
.	.	b	98
A	65	.	.
B	66	.	.
.	.	y	121
.	.	z	122

In your program, you might have

```
VAR
   x : CHAR;
       .
       .
   x := 'A'
```

This will make the computer put the ASCII code for A into the storage location called x:

```
        x

    ┌─────────┐
    │   65    │
    └─────────┘
```

(Acually, only 0's and 1's can be stored inside a computer. The number 1000001, the *binary representation* of the number 65, is what will be stored. See Section 9.3.)

Now when you write

```
VAR
   x : INTEGER;
       .
       .
   x := 0
```

you're having the computer put the *number zero* into the storage location called x:

```
        x

    ┌─────────┐
    │    0    │
    └─────────┘
```

but when you write

```
VAR
  x : CHAR;
      .
      .
      .
x := '0'
```

you're having the computer put the ASCII code for the character zero into the storage location called x:

x

We have to be careful to use these digits properly. For instance, it's legal to do

```
VAR
  x : INTEGER;
      .
      .
      .
x := 0;
      .
      .
      .
x := x + 1
```

but it's not legal to do

```
VAR
  x : CHAR;
      .
      .
      .
x := '0';
      .
      .
      .
x := x + 1
```

This distinction between character digits and number digits can be a little confusing, so several of this section's exercises will help you sort it out.

EBCDIC
Character Set

We've been referring to the ASCII Character Set as if all computers use it. But actually it's not quite true to say that every computer uses the ASCII Character Set. Many computers use a slightly different way to code characters, called the **EBCDIC Character Set**.[6] The EBCDIC Character Set is very much like the ASCII Character Set. The EBCDIC set is given in detail in Appendix E.[7]

---

[6]EBCDIC stands for Extended Binary Coded Decimal Interchange Code.

[7]Note: Many of the examples in this text tacitly assume the use of the ASCII Character Set. If you're running programs on an IBM mainframe, ask your instructor how to rewrite them so that they run correctly on your machine.

CHAR subranges

Now what can you do with characters? You can make subranges of characters:

```
TYPE
   upperCase = 'A'..'Z';
   lowerCase = 'a'..'z';
VAR
   letter : upperCase;
```

This is usually better than just doing

```
VAR
   letter : CHAR;
```

because the CHAR type includes all the non-printing characters (which, most often, you don't want to use). It's legal to do

```
TYPE
   letterType = 'A..'z';
VAR
   letter : letterType;
```

but it doesn't quite achieve the result you'd expect. Look again at the table of ASCII codes in Appendix D, and notice that the codes for characters like [and \ come between the uppercase letters and the lowercase letters. With letterType and letter defined as above, letter can take on any character value between uppercase A and lowercase z, which unfortunately includes things like [and \.

comparing characters

Now since the characters come in a certain order (the order given by the ASCII codes), you can test to see if one character comes before another. For instance, the condition in

```
IF letter > 'X' THEN
```

is TRUE as long as the value stored in the letter variable comes after X in the ASCII sequence. Look at the table in Appendix D and you'll see that Y and Z come after X. This makes sense. But notice also that the lowercase letters a, b, etc. come after X in the table. (The lowercase letters come after all the uppercase letters.[8]) So a, b, etc. are all greater than X.

characters and FOR loops

You can also make a FOR loop go from one character to another:

```
VAR
   c : CHAR;
      .
      .
      .
FOR c := 'A' TO 'Z' DO
   Write (c)
```

---

[8]In the EBCDIC Character Set it's the other way around: the lowercase letters are all less than the uppercase letters.

or you can make a WHILE loop go from one character to another:

```
VAR
  c : CHAR;
    .
    .
    .
c := 'A';
WHILE c <= 'Z' DO
  BEGIN
    Write (c);
    c := Succ (c)
  END
```

Succ and Pred

In this last code fragment, we change the value of c by calling Pascal's pre-declared function Succ (which stands for Successor). When Succ acts on a character, it returns the next character in the ASCII sequence. So Succ('A') has the value B, and Succ('Z') has the value [.

There's another pre-declared function, Pred, that does the opposite of Succ. (Pred stands for Predecessor.) Pred('B') has the value A, etc. (In mathematics, Pred would be called the **inverse** of Succ.)

Ord and Chr

Now sometimes it's useful for a program to refer to a character's ASCII code. This can be done with Pascal's pre-declared Ord function. (Ord stands for Ordinal.) The Ord of a character is the character's ASCII code.

Character		The character's ASCII code
A	— Ord —→	65
B	— Ord —→	66
	.	
	.	
Y	— Ord —→	89
Z	— Ord —→	90
	.	
	.	
a	— Ord —→	97
b	— Ord —→	98
	.	
	.	
y	— Ord —→	121
z	— Ord —→	122

So Ord(A) is 65, etc.

Another pre-declared function, Chr, does the opposite of Ord. Chr(65) has the value A, etc. (In mathematics, Chr would be called the *inverse* of Ord.)

Character		The character's ASCII code
A	◄— Chr ——	65
B	◄— Chr ——	66
	•	
	•	
Y	◄— Chr ——	89
Z	◄— Chr ——	90
	•	
	•	
a	◄— Chr ——	97
b	◄— Chr ——	98
	•	
	•	
y	◄— Chr ——	121
z	◄— Chr ——	122

These two functions, Ord and Chr, come in handy in a variety of situations. For instance, what if we want to convert an uppercase letter to its lowercase equivalent? Look at the table in Appendix D and you'll see that the ASCII codes for A and a differ by 32, the codes for B and b differ by 32, etc. So to turn a letter to its lowercase equivalent, all we have to do is find the character whose ASCII code is

turning uppercase to lowercase

```
Ord (letter) + 32
```

In other words, we want to find

```
Chr(Ord (letter) + 32)
```

This works fine, but instead of using the number 32, we normally use (Ord ('A') – Ord ('a')), which works even when we're using codes other than the ASCII code.

So here's the function that does the job:[9]

```
FUNCTION LowerCaseEquiv (letter : upperCase) : lowerCase;
{Accepts an uppercase character;
 returns its lowercase equivalent.}
BEGIN {LowerCaseEquiv}
   LowerCaseEquiv := Chr (Ord(letter) + (Ord('a') – Ord('A')))
END;  {LowerCaseEquiv}
```

And here's a trace to show you that Function LowerCaseEquiv really works:

---

[9]For a function that finds the UpperCaseEquivalent of a lowercase letter, see Exercise Que.7.4.5.

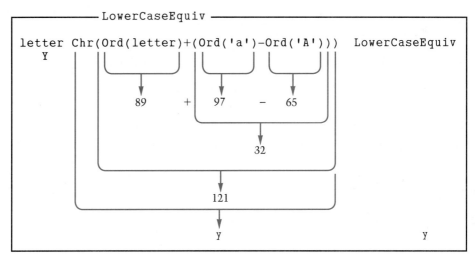

Notice what we've done to make the trace more informative. We've used big braces to show the exact value of each part of the expression `Chr(Ord(letter)+(Ord('a')-Ord('A')))`. It's often very helpful to do this, so we'll do it in many of the examples to come.

Now remember that the digits 0, 1, 2, etc., are in the ASCII Character Set and that they have the unlikely ASCII codes 48, 49, 50, etc. So what if you want to change a digit character into a number? The ASCII code for 0 differs from the value 0 by exactly 48, so to turn `Ord('0')` into 0, all we have to do is subtract 48:

turning digit characters into numbers

```
n := Ord(c) - 48
```

This works fine. But instead of using the number 48, we normally use `Ord ('0')`, which works even when we're using codes other than the ASCII code.

So here's a function that takes a digit character and returns the corresponding digit number:[10]

```
FUNCTION NumericEquiv (c : digitChar) : digitNum;
{Accepts a digit character;
 returns its numeric equivalent.}
BEGIN {NumericEquiv}
   NumericEquiv := Ord(c) - Ord('0')
END;  {NumericEquiv}
```

Function `NumericEquiv` won't work unless the names `digitChar` and `digitNum` have already been defined. (As it says in Section 3.5, they need to be defined before they're used.) The following definitions will work nicely:

---

[10]For a function that takes a digit number and returns the corresponding digit character, see Exercise Que.7.4.6.

```
TYPE
  digitChar = '0'..'9';
  digitNum  =  0 .. 9 ;
```

In these type definitions notice the difference in meaning between '0' and 0.

Now let's put all these ideas together in this section's program example.

Specifications   A typesetter needs to write all the letters of the alphabet, up to a certain letter (for example, A to Q) on a single line. Eventually these letters will be written on a printer that has room for either twenty-four uppercase letters or twenty-six lowercase letters on a single line. (Many printers do **proportional spacing**, in which large letters, like 'L', take up more room on the line than small letters, like 'l'.)

So the typesetter can write all the letters from A to X as capitals. But to write the letters from A to Y, or from A to Z, the typesetter needs to use small letters.

Here are the formal specs:

Input: An uppercase letter, called letterIn.

Output: The alphabet, starting with A and going to letterIn. The alphabet is written in capitals only if fewer than twenty-five letters will be printed. (Otherwise, it's written in small letters.)

The program also "beeps" (makes what's called the **bell** sound) to alert the user when it's done running.

Designing a Program   Here's what has to be done:

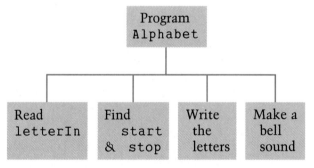

The start letter will always be A or a. The stop letter may be letterIn, or it might be the lowercase equivalent of letterIn. So we may need to call our function that turns letters into their lowercase equivalents:

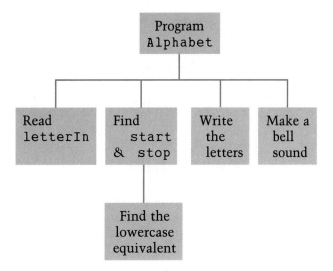

Procedure FindStartAndStop will have an IF statement that calls Function LowerCaseEquiv when more than twenty-four letters need to be printed. Procedure WriteLetters will just have a loop that writes letters, starting with the start letter and ending with the stop letter.

Program Example[11]

```
PROGRAM Alphabet (input, output);
{Displays part of the alphabet.
 Warning!! Works only on implementations
 that use the ASCII Character Set.}
  TYPE
    upperCase = 'A'..'Z';
    lowerCase = 'a'..'z';
  VAR
    letterIn         : upperCase;
    start, stop, c : CHAR;

  {----------}

  PROCEDURE FindStartAndStop (letterIn         : upperCase ;
                              VAR start, stop : CHAR       );
  {Find the first and last letters to be displayed.}

    {----------}

    FUNCTION LowerCaseEquiv (letter : upperCase) : lowerCase;
    {Accepts an uppercase character;
     returns its lowercase equivalent.}
    BEGIN {LowerCaseEquiv}
      LowerCaseEquiv := Chr (Ord(letter) + (Ord('a') - Ord('A')))
    END;  {LowerCaseEquiv}

    {----------}
```

---

[11]Reminder: This program runs correctly on computers that use the ASCII Character Set. IBM mainframes use the EBCDIC Character Set. If you're running programs on an IBM mainframe, ask your instructor how to rewrite the program so that it runs correctly on your machine. In the remainder of this section, we assume an implementation with the ASCII Character Set.

```
BEGIN {FindStartAndStop}
  IF letterIn > 'X' THEN
    BEGIN
      start := 'a';
      stop  := LowerCaseEquiv (letterIn)
    END
  ELSE
    BEGIN
      start := 'A';
      stop  := letterIn
    END
END;  {FindStartAndStop}

{----------}

PROCEDURE WriteLetters (start, stop : CHAR);
{Writes the letters on the screen, from the
 'start' letter to the 'stop' letter.}
  VAR
    c : CHAR;
BEGIN {WriteLetters}
  FOR c := start TO stop DO
    Write (c)
END;  {WriteLetters}

{----------}

BEGIN {Alphabet}
  Write            ('Last letter to be displayed? ');
  ReadLn           (letterIn);
  FindStartAndStop (letterIn, start, stop);
  WriteLetters     (start, stop);
  WriteLn          (Chr (7))
END.  {Alphabet}
```

Sample Runs

```
Last letter to be displayed? X
ABCDEFGHIJKLMNOPQRSTUVWX<bell-sound>
```
_____

```
Last letter to be displayed? Y
abcdefghijklmnopqrstuvwxy<bell-sound>
```

Observations

• `WriteLn (Chr (7))`

This last line of Program `Alphabet` has something we haven't seen before. We're telling the computer to write the character whose ASCII code is 7. If we look in Appendix D we see that the "bell" sound has ASCII code 7. So to "display" this character the computer beeps. That's just what we wanted.

bell sound

7.4 Exercises

Key Words to Review

ASCII Character Set	EBCDIC Character Set	Chr
printing character	Succ	inverse
non-printing character	Pred	proportional spacing
ASCII code	Ord	bell

Questions to Answer

QUE 7.4.1 What's the difference between the digit '2' and the ASCII code 2?

QUE 7.4.2 How is the ASCII code for '0' different from the INTEGER value 0?

QUE 7.4.3 Explain how Function LowerCaseEquiv works.

QUE 7.4.4 In Function LowerCaseEquiv why do we use the expression Ord('a') – Ord('A') instead of the number 32?

QUE 7.4.5 Make a trace to show that

```
FUNCTION UpperCaseEquiv (letter : lowerCase) : upperCase;
{Accepts a lowercase character;
 returns its uppercase equivalent.}
BEGIN {UpperCaseEquiv}
   UpperCaseEquiv := Chr (Ord(letter) – (Ord('a') – Ord('A')))
END;  {UpperCaseEquiv}
```

really does what its prologue comment says it does.

QUE 7.4.6 Make a trace to show that

```
FUNCTION CharacterEquiv (n : digitNum) : digitChar;
{Accepts a numeric digit;
 returns its character equivalent.}
BEGIN {CharacterEquiv}
   CharacterEquiv := Chr (n + Ord('0'))
END;  {CharacterEquiv}
```

really does what its prologue comment says it does.

Experiments to Try

EXP 7.4.1 Write a program that prints the value of Chr(65).

EXP 7.4.2 Write a program that reads a single character and then writes it to the screen. When the program prompts you for input, type in 'A'—the letter A enclosed in single quotes.

EXP 7.4.3 Make your computer "beep" by writing a program that makes the bell sound.

EXP 7.4.4 Try to compile a program with IF 7 < '8' in it.

EXP 7.4.5 Write a program that displays all the "printing" ASCII characters by writing the values of Chr(n), with n going from 32 to 126. Along with each character, have the program display the character's ASCII code.

EXP 7.4.6   Write a test driver for Function LowerCaseEquiv. Run it at least twice—once with an uppercase letter and once in which the letter it receives is already lowercase.

EXP 7.4.7   Run the following program:

```
PROGRAM WriteBox (output);
{Draws a box using the
Extended ASCII Character Set}

BEGIN {WriteBox}
  WriteLn (Chr(218),Chr(196),Chr(191));
  WriteLn (Chr(179),Chr( 32),Chr(179));
  WriteLn (Chr(192),Chr(196),Chr(217))
END.   {WriteBox}
```

to see if it draws a box on your screen:

Changes to Make

CHA 7.4.1   Modify Program Alphabet so that it gives the user several options: (1) print the alphabet as all lowercase letters, (2) print the alphabet as all uppercase letters, (3) before printing the alphabet, prompt the user for up to three letters that are to be printed uppercase. (The rest are to be printed as lowercase letters.)

CHA 7.4.2   Modify Program Copy (Section 5.1) so that as it copies the sentences to another file, it writes all the letters in their uppercase forms. That is, the lowercase letters get changed to uppercase, the uppercase letters don't get changed, and the spaces and punctuation don't get changed.

CHA 7.4.3   A file contains several sentences, all written exclusively with uppercase letters.

    THIS IS A SENTENCE.

Modify Program Copy (Section 5.1) so that while it copies the sentences to another file, it changes all but the first letter of each sentence to lowercase. The program recognizes the first letter of a sentence by looking for the first character in the file and then the first non-blank character after each period.

Scales to Practice

PRA 7.4.1   Write a FOR loop that prints the letters of the alphabet in reverse order (Z through A).

PRA 7.4.2   Modify the program you wrote for Exercise Exp.7.4.5 so that it doesn't use the Chr function.

PRA 7.4.3   Write a loop that prints the letters of the alphabet, alternating between upper- and lowercase.

PRA 7.4.4   Write a loop that prints every alternate letter of the alphabet.

Programs and Subprograms to Write

WRI 7.4.1   Write a program that reads a telephone number, given in the form

    201/555-1932

and writes it in the form

    1(201)555-1932

WRI 7.4.2 Write a program that removes the dashes from a social security number.

WRI 7.4.3 Write a program that prompts the user for a `letter` and then copies a file to the screen leaving blanks in the places where that `letter` does not occur. For example, if the `letter` is f and the file contains the message

    Wheel of Fortune

then the program displays

        f F

It also tells how many times that letter occurred in the file.

WRI 7.4.4 Some telephone answering systems allow you to spell a person's name with the telephone's "keyboard."

1	2 abc	3 def
4 ghi	5 jkl	6 mno
7 pqrs	8 tuv	9 wxyz

When you want to talk to Barry Burd you spell B-u-r-d. The system receives the digits 2-8-7-3 and looks for all the people whose names can be spelled with the 2-8-7-3 keys (Ms. Atre, for instance).

Write a program that translates both ways: Given a digit, it writes all the letters that can be associated with that digit. Given a letter, it writes the digit associated with that letter.

WRI 7.4.5 Write a program that travels around the alphabet. It starts by displaying the uppercase letter A. The letter that's being displayed changes as the user types in various digits. Here's the pattern:

7 go to a or A	8 go to uppercase if not al- ready uppr	9 go to z or Z
4 go back one letter	5 switch case	6 go for- ward one letter
1 go back ten letters	2 go to lowercase if not al- ready lowr	3 go for- ward ten letters

In this scheme, only the numbers 2, 5, and 8 can change the current letter's case. (The other numbers run up against imaginary "boundaries" at A, Z, a, and z.)

7.5

Enumerated Types

Sometimes it's convenient to have variables store values that aren't numbers or characters. Maybe you want a variable named stoplight that holds either green, yellow, or red. You can create a subrange

```
TYPE
   stoplightType = 0..2;
   {0 stands for green; 1 for yellow; 2 for red}
VAR
   stoplight : stoplightType;
     .
     .
stoplight := 0
```

but your program is much more self-documenting if you write

```
TYPE
   stoplightType = (green, yellow, red);
VAR
   stoplight : stoplightType;
     .
     .
stoplight := green
```

The type definition given in the preceding code creates a new type, named stoplightType. A type is a set of values and a collection of operations that can be performed on those values. In this case, the set of values includes only three possible values: green, yellow, and red. And what operations can be performed on those values? The program example in this section shows several possibilities.

Specifications
Input: A day code number representing a day of the week (0 for Sunday, 1 for Monday, . . . , 6 for Saturday).

Output: The number of days 'til the weekend or a message saying It's the weekend.

Designing a Program
All we really have to do to solve this problem is subtract the dayCode number from 6. But we're trying to illustrate the use of enumerated types. So let's represent the days as Sun, Mon, Tue, etc., and see what the program looks like. (In Section 8.6, after we've been introduced to Pascal's CASE statement, we'll see a program that makes more practical use of enumerated types.)

Program Example

```
PROGRAM EnumDemo (input,output);
{Demonstrates several aspects of enumerated types.}
   TYPE
      dayType     = (Sun, Mon, Tue, Wed, Thu, Fri, Sat);
      dayCodeType = 0..6;
      weekdayType = Mon..Fri;
   VAR
      today   : dayType;
      weekday : weekdayType;
      dayCode : dayCodeType;
      count   : INTEGER;

   {----------}

   FUNCTION DayTypeEquiv (dayCode : dayCodeType) : dayType;
   {Converts from a day's code number to the
    corresponding day; 0 gets converted to Sun, etc.}
      VAR
         day  : dayType;
         code : dayCodeType;
   BEGIN {DayTypeEquiv}
      day := Sun;
      WHILE Ord (day) <> dayCode DO
         day := Succ (day);
      DayTypeEquiv := day
   END; {DayTypeEquiv}

   {----------}
```

```
BEGIN {EnumDemo}
  Write  ('Enter a day-number (0 to 6): ');
  ReadLn (dayCode);
  today := DayTypeEquiv (dayCode);
  IF (Mon <= today) AND (today <= Fri) THEN
    BEGIN
      count := 0;
      FOR weekday := today TO Fri DO
        count := count + 1;
      WriteLn (count:1, ' days ''til the weekend')
    END
  ELSE
    WriteLn ('It''s the weekend')
END.  {EnumDemo}
```

Sample Runs

```
Enter a day-number (0 to 6): 0
It's the weekend
```
```
Enter a day-number (0 to 6): 1
5 days 'til the weekend
```
```
Enter a day-number (0 to 6): 3
3 days 'til the weekend
```
```
Enter a day-number (0 to 6): 6
It's the weekend
```

Observations

- ```
TYPE
   dayType = (Sun, Mon, Tue, Wed, Thu, Fri, Sat);
VAR
   today : dayType;
```

*enumerated types*

The programmer creates a new type, called dayType, whose values are Sun, Mon, etc. This is called an **enumerated type**. The name comes from the fact that the programmer "enumerates" (gives a list of) the values in the type.

The variable today can take on any of the seven values: Sun, Mon, etc.

- ```
FUNCTION DayTypeEquiv (dayCode : dayCodeType) : dayType;
```

The result-type of Function DayTypeEquiv is dayType. So the value computed by Function DayTypeEquiv is one of Sun, Mon, Tue, etc.

- ```
TYPE
   weekdayType = Mon..Fri;
VAR
   weekday : weekdayType;
```

*subranges of enumerated types*

The programmer uses subranges to create another new type, called weekdayType. The values of weekdayType range from Mon to Fri.
```

This includes a value like `Wed`, because in the list where `dayType` is defined, `Wed` happens to come between `Mon` and `Fri`.

Note! Pascal programs don't automatically know about the days of the week. If the programmer had listed the `dayType` values in a different order, then the subrange `Mon .. Fri` may not have included `Wed`.

- `day := Succ (day)`

The pre-declared function `Successor` can be used on any enumerated type. Here's how it works:

`Succ and Pred`

```
Sun     ── Succ ─────▶    Mon
Mon     ── Succ ─────▶    Tue
Tue     ── Succ ─────▶    Wed
  .                         .
  .                         .
  .                         .
        etc.
```

The inverse of the successor, called the `Predecessor`, can also be used on enumerated types:

```
Sun     ◀── Pred ─────    Mon
Mon     ◀── Pred ─────    Tue
Tue     ◀── Pred ─────    Wed
  .                         .
  .                         .
  .                         .
        etc.
```

In the definition of `dayType`, `Sun` has no `Predecessor` and `Sat` has no `Successor`. So as long as range checking is turned on, a statement like

```
previousDay := Pred (Sun)
```

will abort the run of the program.

`Ord`

- `Ord (day)`

The pre-declared function `Ordinal` can be used on any enumerated type. Here's how it works:

day	Ord (day)
Sun	0
Mon	1
Tue	2
.	.
.	.
Sat	6

Notice that if we `Ord` the first value in the `dayType` list (the value `Sun`) we get 0, not 1.

In Section 7.4 we saw that the opposite of `Ord` for characters is `Chr`. But `Chr` can't be used on enumerated types.

comparing values of enumerated types

- `IF (Mon <= today) AND (today <= Fri) THEN`

  We can take advantage of the ordering of values in the `dayType` list with the operators `<=`, `<`, `>=`, and `>`. We can also compare `dayType` values with `=` and `<>`. If `today` has the value `Thu`, then `Mon <= today` is `TRUE`, because `Thu` comes after `Mon` in the definition of `dayType`.

  Now notice! If we were perverse enough to define `dayType` with a different ordering:

  ```
  TYPE
      dayType = (Tue, Sun, Wed, Fri, Thu, Sat, Mon);
  ```

  then all our intuitions about the meanings of `Successor`, `Ordinal`, `<=`, etc. would be incorrect. With this new definition, the `Successor` of `Sun` would be `Wed`, and `Mon <= Thu` would be `FALSE`.

enumerated types and FOR loops

- `FOR weekday := today TO Fri DO`

  We can even use an enumerated type in a `FOR` loop. In this loop we go from whatever day `today` is up to `Fri`. Once again we're depending on the order in which the values `Sun`, `Mon`, etc., occur in the type definition for `dayType`.

Further Discussion

It's easy to forget that there are no quote marks in an enumerated type. Beginning programmers are tempted to write

```
TYPE
    stoplightType = ('green', 'yellow', 'red');
```

Enumerated type values are not character strings.

but this is incorrect. The values in an enumerated type are *identifiers,* not character strings. To drive the point home, let's compare

```
WriteLn ('green');
WriteLn ('red')
```

and

```
WriteLn (green);
WriteLn (red)
```

We've seen the first two lines in several examples. As far as the computer is concerned, `'green'` and `'red'` are just character strings, like `'Please enter a number'` or `'Madam I''m Adam'`.

But the next pair of lines don't appear anywhere in our examples because they're risky. They're correct in some implementations and incorrect in others. We'd guess that

```
WriteLn (red)
```

sends the word

```
red
```

to the screen. But the rules say that input and output procedures (such as, ReadLn and WriteLn) for enumerated types are not part of ANSI Standard Pascal. In Section 8.4 we'll see how to get around this, but in the meantime, let's try to get a sense of why the rules were made this way.

We'll compare enumerated types with INTEGERs. An integer like 12 should be thought of as "twelve things," not as "one followed by two." After all if we're using Roman numerals we don't represent it with "one followed by two." If we have a variable whose value is 12, we can write a subprogram to extract the 1 and the 2, but Pascal has no pre-declared subprogram to do this because "one followed by two" isn't really the right way to think of twelve.

By the same token when you see a red light, you think of having to stop. You don't think of the letters 'r'-'e'-'d'. So "redness" is a state that the stoplight can be in. It's the *Please stop!* state. It's not a character string with three letters in it.

In the definition of a new enumerated type we can't do anything to represent the *Please stop!* quality of red, so we don't try. We view red as an atom, an indivisible thing that, as old physics textbooks used to say, has no qualities, no internal structure. It's not until we write subprograms to use the stopLight type that we start treating red as if it has properties of its own.

Now if red is an atom, then the Pascal language shouldn't make it easy for us to view red as a sequence of three letters, and that's exactly what's intended by the rule that says WriteLn(red) won't work.

In Section 4.2 we introduced the notion of *data abstraction*. It means that "the details about the data (the variables and their types) are moved out of conspicuous view." An enumerated type is a form of data abstraction, because details about the codes used to store values like Mon, green, etc., are kept out of view.

You see, with a definition like

```
TYPE
   stoplightType = (green, yellow, red);
```

when the computer sees

```
stoplight := green
```

it stores the value 0 in the variable stoplight. But this isn't obvious when we read the program. In fact, if we don't use Ord we never have to know that anything but green is being stored in the computer's memory. When we create an enumerated type, we're abstracting the details of a type's internal representation and presenting only the details that the programmer needs to know.

Since the values in enumerated type definitions are hard to read and write, it makes sense to think of these values as values that we can't see—the things that are going on inside the program, inside a black box, or inside a machine. When we're driving a car, we usually don't know what positions the pistons are in at any given moment, and this is an example of values that we won't be able to see—values that are often represented as enumerated types. So in Section 8.6, we'll explore this point of view: enumerated values as the hidden values inside a machine.

7.5   Exercises

Key Words to Review

enumerated type	Pred	Ord
Succ		

Questions to Answer

QUE 7.5.1   How do enumerated types help with self-documentation?

QUE 7.5.2   In what sense are enumerated types a form of data abstraction?

QUE 7.5.3   How can a programmer create a "world" in which Wednesday doesn't come between Tuesday and Thursday?

QUE 7.5.4   With colorType and color defined as follows:

```
TYPE
   colorType = (red, orange, yellow, green, blue, indigo, violet);
VAR
   color : colorType;
```

why isn't it legal to write

```
        color := 'blue'
```

Changes to Make

CHA 7.5.1   Modify Program EnumDemo so that it actually writes the names of the days of the week between today and the weekend. Use an IF statement to go from the value of the variable today (for example, Wed) to a day's name (for example, Wednesday). In Section 8.4 we'll see how we can improve on this method of writing day names.

CHA 7.5.2   Modify the definition of dayType so that its values are the *full* names of the days of the week (not just the abbreviations).

Scales to Practice

PRA 7.5.1   Redo Exercises Pra.3.3.1 to Pra.3.3.3 to make use of enumerated types.

Programs and Subprograms to Write

WRI 7.5.1   Modify the program you wrote for Exercise Wri.3.3.2 so that it uses an enumerated type.

WRI 7.5.2 Write and test a function `NextLight` which accepts the previous value of type `stoplightType`

```
TYPE
    stoplightType = (green, yellow, red);
```

and returns the value that would come next on a real-life light. For instance, after `yellow` comes `red`; then after `red` comes `green`, etc.

WRI 7.5.3 Modify the program of Exercise Wri.5.4.5 so that it makes optimal use of the definition

```
TYPE
    parityType = (even, oddd);  {Note the spelling!}
```

WRI 7.5.4 Define two enumerated types, `colorType` and `primaryColorType`. The primary colors are `red`, `blue`, and `yellow`. And here's how they mix to form other colors: `red` and `blue` make `violet`; `red` and `yellow` make `orange`; `blue` and `yellow` make `green`.

Write a function that accepts two arguments of the `primaryColorType` and returns a value of the `colorType`. (Note: The two primary colors may be the same, or they may be different.)

Chapter Summary

One of the most fundamental building blocks in programming is the concept of a *type*. A type is a set of values and a set of operations on those values. Pascal has several pre-defined types. In addition the language gives the programmer the ability to define new types. Among Pascal's pre-defined types are `REAL`, `INTEGER`, and `CHAR`.

`REAL`s and `INTEGER`s can be used together in the same expression (in a so-called *mixed expression*) but whenever possible, this mixing of types should be avoided. Even in an innocent looking statement like

```
right := 0
```

the computer does a time-consuming conversion if `right` is defined to be `REAL`.

A computer can store only finitely many of a real number's infinitely many digits, so the use of Pascal's `REAL` number type can fall victim to *numeric errors*. In general, it's best to follow these guidelines

- Don't declare a variable to be a `REAL` if it's possible to make it an `INTEGER`.

- Be skeptical when you compare two `REAL` numbers for equality.

`CHAR` is another of Pascal's pre-defined types. Values of type `CHAR` belong to the ASCII Character Set (or, for some computers, the EBCDIC Character Set). Each member of the ASCII Character Set is represented by a number, called its *ASCII code*. When we refer to a particular CHARacter in a Pascal program, the number's ASCII code is what's actually stored inside the computer. Using the ASCII codes, we can determine

- the Successor and Predecessor of a character
- the Ord of a character (and the Chr of an ASCII code)
- what characters are within any particular *subrange* of characters
- what values will be included when we do

  ```
  FOR CHAR-type-variable := initial-value TO final-value
  ```

- when a character is <, >, <=, or >= another character
- the lowercase equivalent of an uppercase character
- the uppercase equivalent of a lowercase character
- and so on

Pascal gives a programmer the ability to define new *enumerated types*. Each value of an enumerated type is an identifier. In keeping with the principles of *data abstraction* many details about the representation of an enumerated type value are hidden from the programmer. Even so, we can make use of the order in which identifiers appear in a type definition. Using this order we can determine

- the Successor and Predecessor of a value
- the Ord of a value
- what values are within any particular subrange of the enumerated type
- what values will be included when we do

  ```
  FOR enum-type-variable := initial-value TO final-value
  ```

- when a value is <, >, <=, or >= another value
- and so on

8 Decision Making

The Type BOOLEAN

Why learn two ideas when just one idea will suffice? Why have a programming language that has all kinds of odd, unrelated features, when you can create a language that's tied together by a few simple ideas? In this chapter we'll take one more look at decision making. We'll see how the notion of a *type* can be used to connect decision making with the rest of Pascal. Let's start by looking at a very simple example.

Program Example

```
PROGRAM NOTDemo (output);
{Shows what Pascal's NOT operator does.}
   VAR
      boolVar : BOOLEAN;
BEGIN {NOTDemo}
   boolVar := TRUE;
   WriteLn ('The opposite of TRUE  is ', NOT boolVar:5);
   boolVar := FALSE;
   WriteLn ('The opposite of FALSE is ', NOT boolVar:5)
END.  {NOTDemo}
```

Sample Runs

```
The opposite of TRUE  is FALSE
The opposite of FALSE is  TRUE
```

Observations

the type
BOOLEAN

In Chapter 7 we focused on the notion of a *type*. In Program NOTDemo we introduce a new type, whose name is BOOLEAN. The type BOOLEAN has only two values, TRUE and FALSE. So in Program NOTDemo, we can assign either

```
boolVar := TRUE
```

353

or

```
boolVar := FALSE
```

There are no other values that can be assigned to `boolVar`.

Now a type is a set of values and a set of operations on those values. What operations can be performed on the values `TRUE` and `FALSE`? The operation that's used in Program `NOTDemo` is the operation called `NOT`. Stated simply, `NOT boolVar` is just the opposite of `boolVar`.

NOT

The following program makes a table to illustrate how the `NOT` operator works.

Program Example

```
PROGRAM TruthTableNOT (output);
{Makes a truth table for NOT.}

  VAR
    x : BOOLEAN;

BEGIN {TruthTableNOT}
  WriteLn (' x     !   NOT x  ');
  WriteLn ('--------------------');

  FOR x := FALSE TO TRUE DO
    WriteLn (x:5, '   !  ' ,   NOT x:5)

END.  {TruthTableNOT}
```

Sample Runs

```
  x      !    NOT x
--------------------
FALSE   !     TRUE
 TRUE   !    FALSE
```

Observations The table printed out by this program is called a truth table. It looks very much like a table of values for the minus sign

```
  x   !   -x
-------------
  .   !    .
  .   !    .
  .   !    .
 -3   !    3
 -2   !    2
 -1   !    1
  0   !    0
  1   !   -1
  2   !   -2
  3   !   -3
  .   !    .
  .   !    .
  .   !    .
```

but it deals with `BOOLEAN` values rather than `REAL` or `INTEGER` values.

BOOLEANs in FOR loops

● FOR x := FALSE TO TRUE DO

In Program `TruthTableNOT` we see that BOOLEAN behaves like any of the simple types discussed in Chapter 7.[1] For instance, we can make a FOR loop's control variable range over BOOLEAN values. If we do, we have to remember that FALSE always comes before TRUE. We can go from

FALSE **TO** TRUE

or from

TRUE **DOWNTO** FALSE

Now let's look at some other operations on BOOLEAN values.

Program Example

```
PROGRAM TruthTableAND (output);
{Makes a truth table for AND.}
   VAR
     x, y : BOOLEAN;
BEGIN {TruthTableAND}
   WriteLn ('    x      y  !   x AND y  ');
   WriteLn ('----------------------------');
   FOR x := FALSE TO TRUE DO
     FOR y := FALSE TO TRUE DO
       WriteLn (x:7, y:7, '  !  ',  x AND y:7)
END.  {TruthTableAND}
```

Sample Runs

```
      x       y   !   x AND y
   ----------------------------
   FALSE   FALSE  !    FALSE
   FALSE    TRUE  !    FALSE
    TRUE   FALSE  !    FALSE
    TRUE    TRUE  !     TRUE
```

Observations

The expression x AND y has the value TRUE when *both* x *and* y are TRUE. This truth table is sort of a "multiplication table"

AND

```
      x   y   !   x * y
   --------------------------
      2   1   !      2
      2   2   !      4
      2   3   !      6
      2   4   !      8
      .   .   !      .
      .   .   !      .
```

but instead of showing us how multiplication works, it shows us how AND works.

---

[1]To find out what we mean by a *simple type* see Section 8.7.

Program Example

```
PROGRAM TruthTableOR (output);
{Makes a truth table for OR.}

    VAR
        x, y : BOOLEAN;

    BEGIN {TruthTableOR}
        WriteLn ('      x      y  !    x OR y   ');
        WriteLn ('-------------------------------');

        FOR x := FALSE TO TRUE DO
            FOR y := FALSE TO TRUE DO
                WriteLn (x:7, y:7, '  !  ',  x OR y:7)

    END.   {TruthTableOR}
```

Sample Runs

```
        x       y  !     x OR y
    -----------------------------
    FALSE   FALSE  !     FALSE
    FALSE    TRUE  !     TRUE
     TRUE   FALSE  !     TRUE
     TRUE    TRUE  !     TRUE
```

Observations

OR

The expression x OR y has the value TRUE when *either* x or y *or both* are TRUE. The *or both* part may surprise you a bit, but that's the way the OR operation is defined! To emphasize the fact that the OR operator includes the *or both* possibility, we sometimes call it the **inclusive** OR operator.

Since FALSE comes before TRUE we can even use >, >=, <, and <= as BOOLEAN operators.

Program Example

```
PROGRAM TruthTableLessEqual (output);
{Makes a truth table for <=}

    VAR
        x, y : BOOLEAN;

    BEGIN {TruthTableLessEqual}
        WriteLn ('      x      y  !    x <= y   ');
        WriteLn ('-------------------------------');

        FOR x := FALSE TO TRUE DO
            FOR y := FALSE TO TRUE DO
                WriteLn (x:7, y:7, '  !  ',  x <= y:7)

    END.   {TruthTableLessEqual}
```

Sample Runs

```
        x       y  !    x <= y
    -----------------------------
    FALSE   FALSE  !     TRUE
    FALSE    TRUE  !     TRUE
     TRUE   FALSE  !     FALSE
     TRUE    TRUE  !     TRUE
```

Observations

comparing
BOOLEANs with
<=

- `WriteLn (x:7, y:7, ' ¦ ', x <= y:7)`

When the computer writes the value of x <= y it writes either the word TRUE or the word FALSE, because, after all, even if x and y contain BOOLEAN values, x <= y is a **condition**, which can either be TRUE or FALSE.

Look at the truth table produced by Program `TruthTableLessEqual`. The expression x <= y has the value FALSE only when x is "bigger than" y; that is, when x is TRUE and y is FALSE. What <= seems to be doing for us is this: it's telling us that

```
      x       y    ¦    x <= y
   ---------------------------------
                   ¦
                   ¦
      TRUE   FALSE ¦
                   ¦
```

isn't happening. That is, it's telling us that if x is TRUE, then y is TRUE. Another way to say this: it's telling us that *if* x *then* y. The <= *if . . . then . . .* operator is important in many forms of scientific reasoning.

Now let's see some of these ideas in action.

Specifications

As part of a program to analyze patients' blood types, the user is asked to type in either O, A, B, or AB. People with blood types A and AB are said to have the A antigen, and people with blood types B and AB are said to have the B antigen. People with blood type O have neither the A nor the B antigen.

We want a procedure that accepts two characters (like a B and a blank space) and returns two BOOLEAN values, antigenA and antigenB. antigenA should be TRUE if the patient has the A antigen, and antigenB should be TRUE if the patient has the B antigen.

Designing a Program

We'll be passing two characters to the procedure. Let's call them char1 and char2. Now, assuming that we use the most popular way of labeling the blood types, there will be four possible combinations of values for char1 and char2:

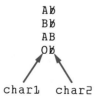

```
      A♭
      B♭
      AB
      O♭
     ╱  ╲
  char1  char2
```

In this example, a ♭ is our way of "picturing" the blank space character.

Now let's label each possible input, to see when the variable `antigenA` should be `TRUE`:

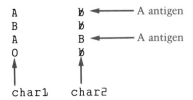

Clearly, the patient has the A antigen as long as the variable `char1` contains the letter A. Now we'll do the same for the B antigen:

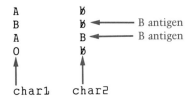

The patient has the B antigen whenever `char1` or `char2` contains the letter B.

So our procedure is likely to have two assignment statements in it:

```
antigenA := char1 = 'A';
antigenB := (char1 = 'B') OR (char2 = 'B')
```

Notice what's going on here in terms of *types:*

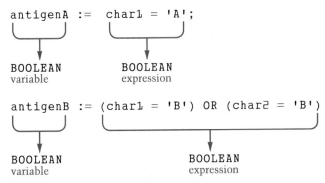

`antigenA` is a `BOOLEAN` variable (a variable that can store the value `TRUE` or `FALSE`), and

```
char1 = 'A'
```

is a `BOOLEAN` expression (an expression that can be either `TRUE` or `FALSE`). The procedure follows.

Program
Example

```
PROCEDURE ComputeAntigensFromChars
                (char1, char2          : CHAR   ;
                 VAR antigenA, antigenB : BOOLEAN);
{Takes two characters and turns them into
 values for antigenA and antigenB.}
BEGIN {ComputeAntigensFromChars}
  antigenA :=  char1 = 'A';
  antigenB := (char1 = 'B') OR (char2 = 'B')
END;  {ComputeAntigensFromChars}
```

Observations   Notice the use of parentheses in

parentheses in
BOOLEAN
expressions

```
(char1 = 'B') OR (char2 = 'B')
```

The parentheses are needed because of Pascal's precedence rules for OR and AND. Recall Precedence Rule 1 from Section 2.2:

Precedence Rule 1: When there are no parentheses, *, /, DIV, and MOD are performed before + and −.

Here's how that rule is expanded to include BOOLEANs:

Precedence Rule 1: When there are no parentheses

   NOT is performed first, then

   *, /, DIV, MOD, and AND are performed, then

   +, −, and OR are performed, and finally

   =, <>, <, >, <=, and >= are performed

So if we write the expression without parentheses

```
char1 = 'B'   OR   char2 = 'B'
```

then the computer will try to check 'B' OR char2 before it checks to see if char1 = 'B'.

```
char1 = 'B'   OR   char2 = 'B'
```

This is unacceptable, since 'B' OR char2 doesn't make sense. The computer can't OR anything with 'B' since 'B' is a character, not a BOOLEAN. You'll get an error diagnostic if you try to compile a program with a line like this in it.

8.1   Exercises

Key Words to Review

BOOLEAN	truth table	inclusive OR
TRUE	AND	condition
FALSE	OR	BOOLEAN expression
NOT		

Questions to Answer

QUE 8.1.1 Give the value (TRUE or FALSE) of each of the following BOOLEAN expressions:
   a. (2 < 6) OR (9 <= 5)
   b. (2 < 6) OR (2 < 10)
   c. (5 = 7) AND (6 <> 6)
   d. NOT FALSE
   e. NOT NOT TRUE

QUE 8.1.2 Translate each of the following English-language phrases into a BOOLEAN expression in Pascal:
   a. "Both a and b are equal to fifteen."
   b. "Neither a nor b is negative."
   c. "a is equal to seven, and b is either greater than 5 or less than −5."
   d. "All three of the variables x, y, and z have values that are divisible by three."
   e. "At least two of the variables x, y, and z have values that are divisible by three."
   f. "Exactly two of the variables x, y, and z have values that are divisible by three."
   g. "None of the variables x, y, and z have values that are divisible by three."

QUE 8.1.3 Translate each of the following BOOLEAN expressions into English that's as smooth and natural-sounding as possible:
   a. 0 <= x
   b. NOT (0 <= x)
   c. (10 <= x) AND NOT (20 <= x)

QUE 8.1.4 Make a truth table for each of the following:
   a. NOT (x OR y)
   b. NOT x AND y

QUE 8.1.5 Explain the difference between

        NOT (x < y) OR (a > b)

   and

        NOT (x < y) AND (a > b)

   In what situation(s) would one of these expressions be TRUE while the other was FALSE?

QUE 8.1.6 Explain why the following expression is TRUE:

        (1 < 10) OR (50 < 55)

QUE 8.1.7   Explain why the following expression is TRUE:

```
(1 > 10) <= (50 > 55)
```

Changes to Make

CHA 8.1.1   Modify any of this section's truth-table-making programs to get truth tables for each of the following BOOLEAN expressions:
a. (NOT x AND y) OR (x AND NOT y)
b. x OR NOT x
c. x AND NOT x

Programs and Subprograms to Write

WRI 8.1.1   In the theory of mathematical logic it's occasionally convenient to define a system with three "boolean" values instead of two. Here are some truth tables for a three-valued system:

```
   x      ¦    NOT x
----------------------------
 LARRY    ¦    CURLY
 CURLY    ¦    LARRY
 MOE      ¦    CURLY


   x      y    ¦   x AND y
----------------------------
 LARRY  LARRY  ¦    LARRY
 CURLY  LARRY  ¦    LARRY
   MOE  LARRY  ¦    LARRY
 LARRY  CURLY  ¦     MOE
 CURLY  CURLY  ¦     MOE
   MOE  CURLY  ¦    LARRY
 LARRY    MOE  ¦    CURLY
 CURLY    MOE  ¦    LARRY
   MOE    MOE  ¦    LARRY
```

Define an enumerated type with the three values LARRY, CURLY, and MOE. Then write and test a function that implements these three-valued versions of NOT and AND.

WRI 8.1.2   *(This is a reworking of Exercise Wri.7.5.4.)* Consider the three primary colors red, green, and blue. If you shine both a red light and a green light together, you get yellow light. This is called the *additive* combining of colors. We'll represent it with a function subprogram named ColorOr. Now if you combine red and green paints, you get black. This is called the *subtractive* combining of colors. We'll represent it with a function subprogram named ColorAnd.

Now here's a diagram of a *color lattice.* It shows the additive and subtractive combinations of various colors:

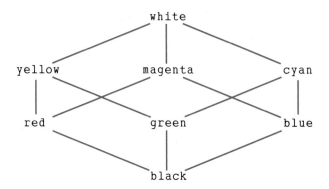

To do `ColorOr` we always follow the lines upward and find the lowest color that's at least as high as the two colors being combined. For instance,

```
ColorOr (red, blue)   is magenta
ColorOr (red, yellow) is yellow
ColorOr (red, cyan)   is white
```

To do `ColorAnd` we follow the lines downward.

Write the two function subprograms `ColorOr` and `ColorAnd`. Each function takes two `colorType` values and returns the resulting `colorType` value. The `colorType` values are `white`, `yellow`, `magenta`, `cyan`, `red`, `green`, `blue`, and `black`.

WRI 8.1.3   In the *binary* number system, the number "two" is represented by 10. So the rules for addition look like this:

$$0 + 0 = 0 \quad 0 + 1 = 1$$
$$1 + 0 = 1 \quad 1 + 1 = 10$$

This is an *addend* ⤴

This is another *addend* ⤴   ⌐This is the *sum*

⌐This is the *carry*

(Note: in all but one of the equations given above, the carry is zero.) If we turn the 0's into FALSEs and the 1's into TRUEs we get

```
F + F = FF   F + T = FT
T + F = FT   T + T = TF
```

Write a procedure that accepts two BOOLEAN addends and computes a sum and a carry.

WRI 8.1.4   When we add two digits in ordinary decimal arithmetic, we sometimes get a carry digit, which gets added into the next column:

```
carry
  1
  17
+ 29
----
  46
```

So one of the columns is the sum of three digits, not just two. This happens in binary arithmetic also:

carry
1
01
+ 01
‾‾‾‾
10

Here we're adding a carry and two addends to get 1.

Here are the rules for binary addition when we're combining a carry and two addends:

$$0 + 0 + 0 = 0 \qquad 0 + 0 + 1 = 1 \qquad 0 + 1 + 0 = 1 \qquad 0 + 1 + 1 = 10$$
$$1 + 0 + 0 = 1 \qquad 1 + 0 + 1 = 10 \qquad 1 + 1 + 0 = 10 \qquad 1 + 1 + 1 = 11$$

(11 is the binary representation for "three")

Redo Exercise Wri.8.1.3 so that your new procedure accepts three values—two addends and a carry—and computes a sum and a carry.

8.2

Using BOOLEANs

Specifications Let's continue our blood types example. Blood types play a part in determining whether one person can donate blood to another person. In particular, if the donor has the A antigen, then the receiver must have it also. The same rule holds for the B antigen. From these two rules, we can build a complete table:

Acceptable donor/receiver pairs:

Receiver Donor	O	A	B	AB
O	yes	yes	yes	yes
A	no	yes	no	yes
B	no	no	yes	yes
AB	no	no	no	yes

Input: The blood types of two people—the potential donor and the potential receiver

Output: The words Don't donate! or Donate!, whichever is appropriate

To write our program, we'll use the procedure from Section 8.1 (Procedure ComputeAntigensFromChars).

Designing a Program

We'll have four BOOLEAN variables:

Variable	will be true as long as
donHasA	the potential donor has the A antigen
recHasA	the receiver has the A antigen
donHasB	the potential donor has the B antigen
recHasB	the receiver has the B antigen

Now quoting from our own explanation of blood type matching: *"If the donor has the A antigen, then the receiver must have it also."* Since <= applied to BOOLEANs means *if . . . then . . .* we get the BOOLEAN expression

```
donHasA <= recHasA
```

The same must be true for the B antigen, so we need

```
(donHasA <= recHasA) AND (donHasB <= recHasB)
```

Now we can have an IF statement that looks like this:

```
IF (donHasA <= recHasA) AND (donHasB <= recHasB) THEN
   WriteLn ('Donate!')
ELSE
   WriteLn ('Don''t donate!')
```

but it's more self-documenting to do the following:

```
compatible := (donHasA <= recHasA) AND (donHasB <= recHasB);
IF compatible THEN
   WriteLn ('Donate!')
ELSE
   WriteLn ('Don''t donate!')
```

a BOOLEAN variable as a condition

Notice what we're doing here: we're using a BOOLEAN variable called compatible as the entire condition in an IF statement. This makes perfect sense, since

- a BOOLEAN variable can be either TRUE or FALSE, and
- the condition in an IF statement is tested to see if it's TRUE or FALSE

In fact, the rule for IF statements in Pascal says that an IF statement's condition has to be a BOOLEAN expression—a combination of variables, operators, parentheses, etc., that, taken together, have the value TRUE or the value FALSE. A BOOLEAN variable is just a simple kind of a BOOLEAN expression.

The program follows.

**Program
Example**

```
PROGRAM BloodTypes (input, output);
{Tells us whether a potential donor can
 give blood to a potential receiver.}
  CONST
    blank = ' ';
  VAR
    donHasA, donHasB, recHasA, recHasB, compatible : BOOLEAN;

  {----------}

  PROCEDURE GetAntigens (VAR donHasA, donHasB,
                             recHasA, recHasB : BOOLEAN);
  {Reads the user's input, and uses it to find the
   antigens of the potential donor and the receiver.}
    VAR
      char1, char2 : CHAR;

    {----------}

    PROCEDURE ReadChars (VAR char1, char2 : CHAR);
    {Reads ONE or TWO characters, and
     always returns TWO characters.}
    BEGIN {ReadChars}
      Read (char1);
      IF Eoln(input) THEN
        char2 := blank
      ELSE
        Read (char2);
      ReadLn
    END;  {ReadChars}

    {----------}

    PROCEDURE ComputeAntigensFromChars
                    (char1, char2              : CHAR    ;
                     VAR antigenA, antigenB : BOOLEAN);
    {Takes two characters and turns them into
     values for antigenA and antigenB.}
    BEGIN {ComputeAntigensFromChars}
      antigenA :=  char1 = 'A';
      antigenB := (char1 = 'B') OR (char2 = 'B')
    END;  {ComputeAntigensFromChars}

    {----------}

  BEGIN {GetAntigens}
    {:::For the donor:::::::}
    Write      ('Enter the blood type of the DONOR:    ');
    ReadChars (char1, char2);
    ComputeAntigensFromChars (char1, char2, donHasA, donHasB);

    {:::For the receiver:::::}
    Write      ('Enter the blood type of the RECEIVER: ');
    ReadChars (char1, char2);
    ComputeAntigensFromChars (char1, char2, recHasA, recHasB)
  END;  {GetAntigens}

  {----------}
```

```
BEGIN {BloodTypes}
  GetAntigens (donHasA, donHasB, recHasA, recHasB);
  compatible := (donHasA <= recHasA) AND (donHasB <= recHasB);
  IF compatible THEN
    WriteLn ('Donate!')
  ELSE
    WriteLn ('Don''t donate!')
END.   {BloodTypes}
```

Sample Runs

```
Enter the blood type of the DONOR:    Bb
Enter the blood type of the RECEIVER: AB
Donate!
```

```
Enter the blood type of the DONOR:    AB
Enter the blood type of the RECEIVER: Ob
Don't donate!
```

Traces

Let's make a drawing to show how we find the value of an expression like

```
(donHasA <= recHasA) AND (donHasB <= recHasB)
```

We'll use the first of our Sample Runs.

evaluating BOOLEAN expressions

Under each BOOLEAN variable, we put the variable's value:

```
(donHasA <= recHasA) AND (donHasB <= recHasB)
  FALSE       TRUE          TRUE         TRUE
```

Then we use the rules for <= (see the table printed out by Program TruthTableLessEqual in Section 8.1) to evaluate the expressions (donHasA <= recHasA) and (donHasB <= recHasB):

```
(donHasA <= recHasA) AND (donHasB <= recHasB)
  FALSE       TRUE          TRUE         TRUE
  └─────┬─────┘              └─────┬─────┘
      TRUE                       TRUE
```

Finally we use the rule for AND to find the value of the whole expression:

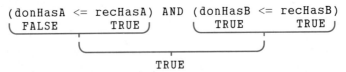

A complicated BOOLEAN expression is easy to evaluate, as long as you do one step at a time and follow the rules given in the truth tables.

Programming Style

Look once again at the IF statement in the main body of Program BloodTypes. It's tempting to write the condition this way:

```
IF compatible = TRUE THEN
```

a BOOLEAN
variable as a
condition

This is legal, but unnecessary. Between the word IF and the word THEN we always put an expression with the value TRUE or FALSE. In a statement like

```
IF A < B THEN ...
```

the expression A < B is TRUE or FALSE. Since compatible is a BOOLEAN variable, compatible is TRUE or FALSE. So between IF and THEN, all we need is the word compatible. With just that one word, the statement reads very much like conversational English:

If [the blood types are] compatible then . . .

Testing and Debugging

At first glance it looks as if we can do exhaustive testing on Program BloodTypes because there are only sixteen possible test cases. (Look at the table in this section's Specifications subsection. The table has sixteen boxes—one for each possible donor/receiver combination.)

Of course we might want to know how the program behaves when it receives "incorrect" input, such as

```
Enter the blood type of the DONOR:    A⊠⊠ ◄── Too many blanks
Enter the blood type of the RECEIVER: BA  ◄── Letters in the
                                              wrong order
```

or

```
Enter the blood type of the DONOR:    AA ◄── Too many As
Enter the blood type of the RECEIVER: ab ◄── Lowercase
```

or

```
                                               ⌠ Hit the S key
                                               | instead of the
                                               ⎰ A key
Enter the blood type of the DONOR:    SB ◄──┘
Enter the blood type of the RECEIVER: A  ◄── Spread AB out
                                             over two lines
    B
```

exceptional test
data

These are all called **exceptional test cases** because the word **exception** is often used to describe an incorrect or unexpected situation during the run of a program. If a program is sufficiently *robust* it can deal sensibly with a wide variety of test data, including exceptional data.

In every program we write we should anticipate exceptional data and make sure that the program will behave in a reasonable way if it ever encounters these data. By doing this we avoid having to debug the program later. Approaching a program this way is called **antibugging** or **defensive programming**. The idea is that we're defending our program against bugs before they occur.

8.2   Exercises

Key Words to Review

exception   antibugging   defensive programming
exceptional test data

Questions to Answer

QUE 8.2.1   Under what circumstances is the statement

```
greater := x > y
```

legal in Pascal?

QUE 8.2.2   Explain how the use of BOOLEANs can help a program to be self-documenting.

QUE 8.2.3   Explain why a line like

```
IF compatible = TRUE THEN
```

is unnecessarily verbose.

Things to Check in a Manual

MAN 8.2.1   As far as the syntax diagrams are concerned is the following condition, without parentheses, legal in Pascal?

```
donHasA <= recHasA   AND   donHasB <= recHasB
```

MAN 8.2.2   First look at Exercise Man.3.1.2. Some implementations have an ASSERT statement or a DEMAND statement, which plays the role of a *conditional halt*. The statement checks the value of a BOOLEAN expression to make sure that it's TRUE. If not, the program is aborted. The use of such a statement is a form of *defensive programming*. Does your implementation support a statement of this kind?

Changes to Make

CHA 8.2.1   Rewrite Program Scores in Section 2.3 so that its IF statement tests the value of a single BOOLEAN variable.

CHA 8.2.2   Rewrite Program OneBar in Section 2.6 so that its WHILE statement tests the value of a single BOOLEAN variable.

CHA 8.2.3   Rewrite Program NoNesting in Section 5.5 so that it has three BOOLEAN variables. Then each of its IF statements tests the value of one of these BOOLEAN variables.

Programs and Subprograms to Write

WRI 8.2.1   Modify the program of Exercise Wri.5.4.5 so that it keeps track of evenness and oddness with two BOOLEAN variables oddDataBits and oddParityBit.

WRI 8.2.2   In the study of genetics, it's convenient to divide people into two categories: dark-eyed and blue-eyed. To determine whether a person is dark-eyed or blue-eyed, we can look at the person's two eye color genes. One of these genes is inherited from the mother, and the other gene is inherited from the father. Here's a chart showing a person's eye color, based on the person's inherited genes:

From the father / From the mother	B	b
B	dark	dark
b	dark	blue

In this chart, uppercase B stands for the dominant dark-eyed gene, and lowercase b stands for the recessive blue-eyed gene. The words *dominant* and *recessive* are meant to remind us that the B gene "dominates" the b gene. A person will be blue-eyed only if both the person's genes are b genes.

Write and test a procedure that accepts a gene from the mother and a gene from the father and writes a message telling whether the child will be dark-eyed or blue-eyed.

WRI 8.2.3   *(This is a continuation of Exercise Wri.8.2.2.)* A mother has two genes, and she can donate a B gene only if one of her genes is the B gene. The same is true of her donating the b gene or of the father's donation, etc. Write and test a procedure that accepts the mother's two genes and the father's two genes and writes all possible pairs of genes that the child can receive. For each possible pair, call the procedure of Exercise Wri.8.2.2 to write a message telling whether the child will be dark-eyed or blue-eyed.

WRI 8.2.4   *(This is a continuation of Exercise Wri.8.2.3.)* We can divide people into two other categories: dark-haired and blond-haired. Just as with eye color, there's a dominant dark-hair gene D and a recessive blond-hair gene d. The chart for D and d works the same way as the chart for B and b. Write a program that reads the eye color and hair color of two adults and the eye color and hair color of a baby and writes a message telling whether or not that baby can possibly be the child of those two adults.

8.3

Another Example

Specifications   Now we have enough equipment to solve an interesting problem. In many of the examples to come we'll want to read in the next item, but we won't know whether that item is a number or a letter. If it's a letter, we'll want it to be stored in a CHAR-type variable; if it's a number we'll want to store it in an INTEGER variable. So we can't just have

```
VAR
  n : INTEGER;
      .
      .
ReadLn (n)
```

or

```
VAR
  c : CHAR;
      .
      .
ReadLn (c)
```

Instead we want a procedure that finds a value for either a CHAR variable or an INTEGER variable and tells us which kind of value it found:

```
TYPE
  kindType = (character, natral);
  natural  = 0..MAXINT;
      .
      .
PROCEDURE ReadLnCharOrNat (VAR c    : CHAR;
                           VAR n    : natural;
                           VAR kind : kindType);
{Reads a value for c OR for n.
 Sets kind to
    character    if a value of c is read;
    natral       if a value of n is read.}
```

Notice how much information we get just by looking at the procedure heading! The name of the procedure tells us roughly what the procedure will do, and the prologue comment makes it more specific. The procedure's parameter list tells us exactly how to call the procedure. (Notice that our procedure will avoid having to deal with plus or minus signs by reading natural numbers, rather than INTEGERs.) If you're writing a program that needs to call ReadLnCharOrNat, then this is all you need to know about the procedure! In a sense this is a complete set of specifications.

Designing a Program

First we design the topmost part of the algorithm:

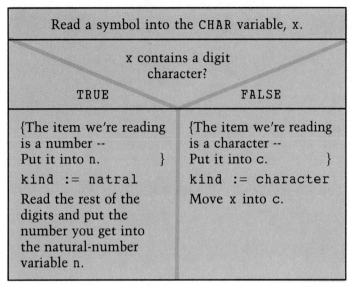

The NS chart suggests that Procedure `ReadLnCharOrNat` has two subprograms:

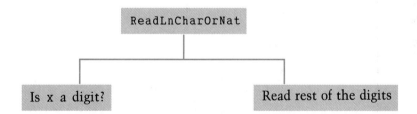

The first subprogram (testing for "digit-ness") is easy to write. (See the Program Example and the Observations that follow it.) As for the second subprogram (reading the rest of the digits), we need a loop that keeps reading symbols and adjusting the value of n:

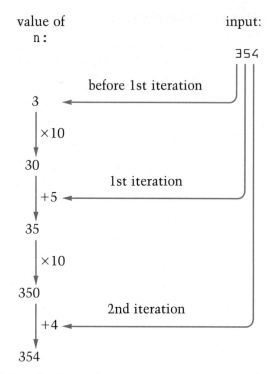

value of
n:

input:

354

before 1st iteration

3

×10

30

1st iteration

+5

35

×10

350

2nd iteration

+4

354

The test driver for Procedure ReadLnCharOrNat has the following specs:

Input: Three items, each on its own line; each "item" is either a natural number or a character

Process: Add 2 to each number, and find the Successor of each character

Output: The new list of items

So here's the code for Procedure ReadLnCharOrNat.

Program Example

```
PROGRAM CharNatTester (input, output);
{A test driver for Procedure ReadLnCharOrNat.}
  TYPE
    kindType = (character, natral);
    natural  = 0..MAXINT;
  VAR
    c     : CHAR;
    n     : natural;
    kind  : kindType;
    count : 1..3;

  {----------}
```

```
PROCEDURE ReadLnCharOrNat (VAR c    : CHAR;
                           VAR n    : natural;
                           VAR kind : kindType);
{Reads a value for c OR for n.
 Sets kind to
   character   if a value of c is read;
   natral      if a value of n is read.}
  VAR
    x : CHAR;
  {----------}

  FUNCTION IsDigit (x : CHAR) : BOOLEAN;
  {Answers the question ''Is x one of the
   digit characters '0' to '9'?''}
  BEGIN {IsDigit}
    IsDigit := ('0' <= x) AND (x <= '9')
  END;  {IsDigit}
  {----------}

  PROCEDURE ReadLnRestNat (x : CHAR; VAR n : natural);
  {Completes the process of reading a natural number.}
    TYPE
      digitChar = '0'..'9';
      digitNum  = 0 .. 9 ;
    {----------}

    FUNCTION NumericEquiv (x : digitChar) : digitNum;
    {Taken from Section 7.4.
     Accepts a digit character;
     returns its numeric equivalent.}
    BEGIN {NumericEquiv}
      NumericEquiv := Ord(x) - Ord('0')
    END;  {NumericEquiv}
    {----------}

  BEGIN {ReadLnRestNat}
    n := NumericEquiv (x);
    WHILE NOT Eoln (input) DO
      BEGIN
        Read (x);
        n := (10 * n) + NumericEquiv (x)
      END;
    ReadLn
  END;  {ReadLnRestNat}
  {----------}

  PROCEDURE ReadLnRestChar (x : CHAR; VAR c : CHAR);
  {Completes the process of reading a character.}
  BEGIN {ReadLnRestChar}
    c := x;
    ReadLn
  END;  {ReadLnRestChar}
  {----------}
```

```
          BEGIN {ReadLnCharOrNat}
            Read (x);
            IF IsDigit (x) THEN
              BEGIN
                kind := natral;
                ReadLnRestNat (x, n)
              END
            ELSE
              BEGIN
                kind := character;
                ReadLnRestChar (x, c)
              END
          END;   {ReadLnCharOrNat}

          {----------}

      BEGIN {CharNatTester}
        FOR count := 1 TO 3 DO
          BEGIN
            Write ('Enter a character or a natural number: ');
            ReadLnCharOrNat (c, n, kind);
            IF kind = character THEN
              WriteLn ('The character after this one is ', Succ(c):1)
            ELSE
              WriteLn ('Add two to this number, you get ',     n+2:3);
            WriteLn
          END
      END.   {CharNatTester}
```

Sample Runs

```
Enter a character or a natural number: 321
Add two to this number, you get 323

Enter a character or a natural number: p
The character after this one is q

Enter a character or a natural number: 5
Add two to this number, you get    7
```

Observations

BOOLEAN-returning functions

• FUNCTION IsDigit (x : CHAR) : BOOLEAN;

A function subprogram can return a BOOLEAN value. When this value gets used, it often appears in the condition part of a WHILE statement, a REPEAT statement, or an IF statement:

```
IF IsDigit (x) THEN
```

Notice how readable this code is! It's easier to understand at a glance than

```
IF ('0' <= x) AND (x <= '9') THEN
```

and, when you read it aloud, it flows more naturally than

```
IF IsDigit (x) = TRUE THEN
```

In many of our earlier programs we used lines like

```
WHILE NOT Eof (inFile) DO
```

and

```
WHILE NOT Eoln (inFile) DO
```

and also

```
IF Odd (number) THEN
```

Now we know what types of values these pre-declared functions return. They return BOOLEAN values.

Programming Style

Recall the style guideline from Section 3.4:

<small>choosing names for BOOLEAN functions</small>

A procedure's name should be a verb or a verb-phrase. A function's name should be a noun or a noun-phrase.

The whole idea was to use names that fit nicely into the pseudocode.

Now for function subprograms that return BOOLEAN values, we need to amend the guideline:

A procedure's name should be a verb or a verb-phrase. A function's name should be
- **a noun or a noun-phrase, if the function's result type is anything except BOOLEAN**
- **an adjective or a phrase that describes a noun,[2] if the function's result type is BOOLEAN**

If we follow this guideline, then it's easy to fit our function names into the pseudocode. For instance, the code

```
IF IsDigit (x) THEN
```

comes easily from the pseudocode

If x is a digit, then

and

```
WHILE HasMoreData (input) DO
```

follows naturally from the pseudocode

While the input file has more data, do

---

[2]My friends in the English Department tell me that the term *adjective-phrase* wouldn't be appropriate here.

8.3 Exercises

Questions to Answer

QUE 8.3.1   Explain the following statement, which is found in Procedure `ReadLnRestNat`:

```
n := (10 * n) + NumericEquiv (x)
```

QUE 8.3.2   Can you think of a situation in which the user enters what he or she *believes* is a character, and Procedure `ReadLnCharOrNat` interprets it as a number? Explain.

QUE 8.3.3   Can you think of a situation in which the user enters what he or she believes is a number, and Procedure `ReadLnCharOrNat` interprets it as a character? Explain.

Experiments to Try

EXP 8.3.1   Write a small program that reads an `INTEGER` value and writes it on the screen. When the program prompts you for the value, type in a character.

EXP 8.3.2   Write a small program that reads a `CHAR` value and writes it on the screen. When the program prompts you for the value, type in a number.

EXP 8.3.3   Write a small program that reads a `REAL` value and writes it on the screen. When the program prompts you for the value, type in an `INTEGER` value.

EXP 8.3.4   Write a small program that reads an `INTEGER` value and writes it on the screen. When the program prompts you for the value, type in a `REAL` value.

EXP 8.3.5   Write a small program that reads an `INTEGER` value and writes it on the screen. When the program prompts you for the value, hit the space bar and the return key several times before typing in the value.

EXP 8.3.6   Write a small program that reads a `CHAR` value and writes it on the screen. When the program prompts you for the value, hit the space bar and the return key several times before typing in the value. Compare with Exercise Exp.8.3.5.

EXP 8.3.7   Write a small program that reads an `INTEGER` value. When it prompts you for the value, type in

```
321a
```

EXP 8.3.8   Write a function that checks to see if two `INTEGER`s are equal to one another and writes a message before returning its `BOOLEAN` value. Then run a program containing the lines

```
IF AreEqual (1, 0) AND AreEqual (3, 3) THEN
    WriteLn ('Both are true')
```

Notice the `AND` between the two calls to Function `AreEqual`. After calling Function `AreEqual` to see if 1 and 0 are equal, does it serve any useful purpose to call Function `AreEqual` again? Does your implementation do it anyway? For more information on this phenomenon, see Section 10.5.

EXP 8.3.9   Run the program of Exercise Exp.8.3.8 and notice the order in which the two function calls are made. If your implementation calls Function `AreEqual` only once, what are the values of x and y in that call? If your implementation calls Function `AreEqual` twice, which of the two calls does it make first?

Changes to Make

CHA 8.3.1 Modify Procedure ReadLnCharOrNat so that it skips over any blank spaces that appear on the line before the character or the natural number.

CHA 8.3.2 Modify Procedure ReadLnCharOrNat to get Procedure ReadLnCharOrInt. The new procedure allows for the possibility that the user may have entered a negative number, or a positive number starting with a plus sign.

CHA 8.3.3 Modify Program Minimum (Section 5.4) so that it doesn't get aborted if the user mistakenly enters a letter instead of a number. (It just "complains" with a warning message and prompts for another number.) For simplicity, you may want to insist that the user never enters a signed number (like −42 or +5).

CHA 8.3.4 Rewrite the program of Exercise Cha.6.2.2 so that it uses BOOLEAN-valued functions.

CHA 8.3.5 Here's an unexpected use for the null statement. Write a function subprogram named CopiedAChar that

- copies the next character (if there is one) from an inFile to an outFile
- displays that same character on the screen, and
- returns TRUE if a character was actually copied and FALSE otherwise

Then the essential code in Program Copy of Section 4.1 is

```
WHILE CopiedAChar (inFile, outFile, output) DO {null statement};
```

In many circles this is considered to be very poor programming style, because Function CopiedAChar has three VAR parameters. Nevertheless, it's an interesting way of thinking about BOOLEAN-returning functions.

Programs and Subprograms to Write

WRI 8.3.1 Add another feature to the program you wrote for Exercises Cha.5.1.1 and Cha.5.1.2. Allow the user to type a number and then the return key. The input

```
--More--10<return>
```

gets the program to display ten more lines, rather than a whole screenful.

WRI 8.3.2 Look over the observations on Program TruthTableOR in Section 8.1. Recall the meaning of the term *inclusive* OR. In contrast to an inclusive OR there's another kind of OR operation called the *exclusive* OR. The rules for exclusive OR are just like the rules for inclusive OR, except when we combine two TRUEs with exclusive OR, we get FALSE.

Write and test a function that accepts two BOOLEAN values and returns the exclusive OR of the two values.

Things to Think About

THI 8.3.1 Discuss the advantages of the technique used in Exercise Cha.8.3.3. Can you think of any other practical uses for Procedure ReadLnCharOrNat?

8.4

The CASE Statement

In so many programming situations, it's perfectly natural to think in terms of IFs:

> IF *some condition is true* THEN
>   *do something*
> ELSE
>   *do another thing*

But there are a number of programming situations where IFs are cumbersome. Take, for instance, the problem, mentioned in Section 7.5, of writing the value of an enumerated type. If we declare

```
TYPE
   dayType = (Sun, Mon, Tue, Wed, Thu, Fri, Sat);
VAR
   day : dayType;
```

then we can certainly do

```
day := Wed
```

But in ANSI Standard Pascal we can't do

```
WriteLn (day)
```

So what do we do? If we try to solve the problem with IF statements, we get a mess:

```
IF day = Sun THEN
   WriteLn ('Sun');
IF day = Mon THEN
   WriteLn ('Mon');
IF day = Tue THEN
   WriteLn ('Tue');
IF day = Wed THEN
   WriteLn ('Wed');
IF day = Thu THEN
   WriteLn ('Thu');
IF day = Fri THEN
   WriteLn ('Fri');
IF day = Sat THEN
   WriteLn ('Sat')
```

This is messy because we're thinking about seven distinct choices that have to be made. It's much better to think in terms of choosing one of seven possibilities. That's how we think of it when we use Pascal's CASE statement:

```
CASE day OF
  Sun: WriteLn('Sun');
  Mon: WriteLn('Mon');
  Tue: WriteLn('Tue');
  Wed: WriteLn('Wed');
  Thu: WriteLn('Thu');
  Fri: WriteLn('Fri');
  Sat: WriteLn('Sat')
END
```

The CASE statement says the same thing as our long collection of IF statements. But the CASE statement says it better because it's a more unified way of thinking about the seven possibilities. The CASE statement is also more concise and less prone to typographical errors.

Further Discussion

END without BEGIN

Notice how a CASE statement has an END but no BEGIN. Instead of being grouped together with BEGIN..END, a CASE statement's alternatives are grouped together with CASE .. OF .. END. This can be confusing when we combine a CASE statement with other statements.

For instance, here's some code to write one of the words none, one, two, or three, depending on the value of an INTEGER variable n:

```
Write ('n is ');
CASE n OF
  0 : WriteLn ('none');
  1 : WriteLn ('one');
  2 : WriteLn ('two');
  3 : WriteLn ('three')
END
```

This is simple enough, but what do we do if n is larger than 3? We can enlarge our CASE statement, but eventually we'll get tired of writing out numbers like 'two-thousand-three-hundred-sixty-four'. One quick fix is to put our CASE statement inside an IF statement:

```
IF (0 <= n) AND (n <= 3) THEN
  BEGIN
    Write ('n is ');
    CASE n OF
      0 : WriteLn ('none');
      1 : WriteLn ('one');
      2 : WriteLn ('two');
      3 : WriteLn ('three')
    END
  END
ELSE
  WriteLn ('not ok')
```

This corresponds to the pseudocode

> If n is between 0 and 3 then
>   write the phrase 'n is', and
>   write the value of n in English
> Otherwise
>   write 'not ok'

In the Pascal code, notice how BEGIN, CASE, and END are used to group statements together:

```
IF (0 <= n) AND (n <= 3) THEN
   BEGIN
      Write ('n is ');
      CASE n OF
         0 : WriteLn ('none');
         1 : WriteLn ('one');
         2 : WriteLn ('two');
         3 : WriteLn ('three')
      END
   END
ELSE
   WriteLn ('not ok')
```

Now here's the syntax diagram for Pascal's CASE statement:

CASE *statement:*

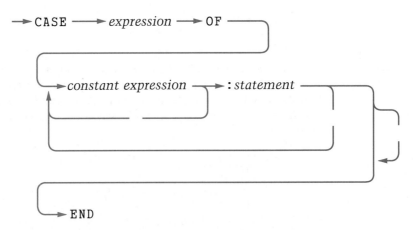

The expression that comes immediately after the word CASE is called a **case index**, and each

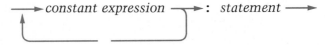

is called an **alternative**. The term *constant expression* comes right out of the syntax diagram in Section 7.1. To see what we mean by a **constant expression**, go back and look at that syntax diagram.

rules
concerning
CASE
statements

The case index, and all the constant expressions in the alternatives, have to belong to an *ordinal* type (see Section 8.7). So something like

```
CONST
   message = 'Is anyone out there?';
      .
      .
CASE message OF
   'Is anyone out there?' : AstronomySubprogram;
   'Madam, I''m Adam.'    : PalindromeSubprogram
```

is illegal, because `message` and `'Madam, I''m Adam.'` don't belong to any ordinal type.

And here's another rule: no two constant expressions in a CASE statement can represent the same value. So an example like

```
CONST
   protonCharge = +1;
   electronCharge = -1;
   antiProtonCharge = -protonCharge;
      .
      .
CASE charge OF
   protonCharge      : protonProcedure;
   electronCharge    : electronProcedure;
   antiProtonCharge  : antiProtonProcedure
END
```

is illegal, because `electronCharge` and `antiProtonCharge` have the same value: −1.

Programming Style

CASE versus IF

In this section we've been emphasizing the virtues of the CASE statement and downplaying the role of IF statements. But notice that there are situations where IF statements are better than CASE statements. Take, for instance, Program `NoNesting` from Section 5.5. The program has three IF statements corresponding to three alternative actions

```
IF (a >= b) AND (a >= c) THEN
   WriteLn (a:5:1);
IF (b >= a) AND (b >= c) THEN
   WriteLn (b:5:1);
IF (c >= a) AND (c >= b) THEN
   WriteLn (c:5:1)
```

but we can't turn this into one CASE statement. We can't do it because we don't have

```
IF expression = one-value THEN
   do one thing
IF expression = another-value THEN
   do another thing
IF expression = a third-value THEN
   do a third thing
etc.
```

The conditions in the program's IF statements are more complicated than that.

```
IF (a >= b) AND (a >= c) THEN
   WriteLn (a:5:1)
```

Even without the AND, a condition like a >= b would be more complicated than

```
expression = one-value
   .
   .
   .
expression = another-value
   .
   .
   .
Etc.
```

which is the only thing a CASE statement can handle.

cascading IFs   If we need to use IF statements and we want to show clearly in the code that we're dealing with three alternative actions, we can do this:

```
PROGRAM Cascade (input, output);
{Finds the largest of three numbers.}
   VAR
      a, b, c : REAL;
BEGIN {Cascade}
   Write  ('Enter three real numbers: ');
   ReadLn (a, b, c);
   Write  ('The largest is ');
   IF      (a >= b) AND (a >= c) THEN
      WriteLn (a:5:1)
   ELSE IF (b >= a) AND (b >= c) THEN
      WriteLn (b:5:1)
   ELSE
      WriteLn (c:5:1)
END.   {Cascade}
```

Notice the way the IF statements are indented in Program Cascade. This is really a pair of nested IFs. It would be quite correct to indent them in the following way:

```
IF      (a >= b) AND (a >= c) THEN
   WriteLn (a:5:1)
ELSE
   IF (b >= a) AND (b >= c) THEN
      WriteLn (b:5:1)
   ELSE
      WriteLn (c:5:1)
```

But sometimes nested IFs are easier to understand if the indentation is adjusted a bit. In this instance we have three possible actions. Our choice of action depends on which of three possible conditions is true. So we indent the nested IFs in a way that emphasizes that there are three parallel actions, with three parallel conditions.

When we indent nested IFs this way we call it **cascading** IFs:

```
IF condition1 THEN
    statement1
ELSE IF condition2 THEN
    statement2
ELSE IF condition3 THEN
    statement3
ELSE IF ...
        .
        .
        .
ELSE
    default statement
```

Cascading IFs are a bit more flexible than CASE statements. Unlike a CASE statement, the last choice in a chain of cascading IFs can be a simple ELSE—a "catchall" statement that's executed when none of the conditions given above it are true. It's convenient to use the word **default** to describe this last alternative.

8.4 Exercises

Key Words to Review

CASE	constant	cascading IFs
case index	OF	default
alternative		

Questions to Answer

QUE 8.4.1 When is a CASE statement preferable to IF statements? When is it better to use IF statements?

QUE 8.4.2 Describe ANSI Standard Pascal's restrictions on the syntax and use of the CASE statement.

QUE 8.4.3 Examine each of the following:
a. 10
b. +warbles
c. ++warbles
d. 'Mr. O''Donnell''s pig'

Which of these can be used as an alternative's constant expression in a CASE statement? Which cannot? Explain.

QUE 8.4.4 Is it legal to have cascading IFs without a default statement? Why, or why not?

Experiments to Try

EXP 8.4.1 What error diagnostic do you get when you add an extra BEGIN to your CASE statement?

```
CASE n OF
   BEGIN
      . . .
```

EXP 8.4.2 What happens when you execute the first CASE statement in our Further Discussion subsection with n having the value 4?

EXP 8.4.3 What happens when you have a variable instead of a constant expression in a CASE statement alternative?

EXP 8.4.4 What happens when you try to run

```
CASE r OF
   1.0 : WriteLn ('one');
      . . .
```

Programs and Subprograms to Write

WRI 8.4.1 Use cascading IFs to redo Exercise Wri.2.3.1, this time with seven levels of commission, as described in the following chart:

Sales up to	Percent commission
$ 1000	5.00
$ 5000	6.00
$ 10000	7.00
$ 12000	7.50
$ 16000	7.75
$ 23000	8.00
above $ 23000	8.25

WRI 8.4.2 Redo Exercise Wri.7.5.1, using a CASE statement to help write the values of the enumerated type.

WRI 8.4.3 Write a program that reads a three-digit number and translates it into words. For instance, if it reads 451, then it writes four hundred fifty-one.

WRI 8.4.4 (A variation on the problem in Exercise Wri.8.4.3.) Write a program that reads a time of day and translates it into words. For instance, if it reads 8 : 19 AM, then it writes Eight nineteen in the morning. You can assume that the user puts a blank space before and after the colon when entering the time of day and puts a blank space before the capital letters AM or PM.

8.5

Using CASE Statements

Specifications We want a program that behaves something like a hand calculator. It accepts simple instructions, like + for "add" and S for "square root" and performs the appropriate operations on numbers that are entered at the keyboard.

The program uses a variable called `register`. The `register` value always starts off at zero. Then if the user types a plus sign and a 5.0

```
Next instruction : +
         operand : 5.0
```

the program adds 5.0 to the register's value. If the user enters an S

```
Next instruction : S
```

the program finds the square root of the value that's currently in the `register` and makes that the `register`'s new value.

In addition to these needed instructions, the program has a few extra instructions for the user's convenience. Lettered instructions (like S for Square root and Q for Quit) can be entered in lower- or uppercase. If the user types H (for Help) the program displays a simple list of available instructions. The program has another way of calling for help, entering a question mark (?), because some users become panic-stricken and can't remember which instruction is the cry for help.

Here are some formal specs:

Input: Numbers (called `operands`) and instructions. The `operands` are all REAL numbers. The instructions are:

Instruction	Name	Action
C or c	Clear	Set the register to 0.0
+	Add	Add the operand to the register
−	Subtract	Subtract the operand from the register
*	Multiply	Multiply the register by the operand
/	Divide	Divide the register by the operand
S or s	Square root	Take the square root of the register
H, h, or ?	Help	Show what instructions are available
Q or q	Quit	Stop running

Output: The output consists of

- prompts (for `instructions` and `operands`)
- the value of the `register` (after each instruction is entered)
- a list of available instructions (when the user asks for "help")

- the error diagnostic **Illegal divide by zero** when the user attempts to divide the register by zero
- the error diagnostic **Illegal Sqrt of negative value** when the register contains a negative number and the user asks for the square root

Designing a Program   Look at the list of instructions in the Input part of the formal specs. When the program reads the next instruction, it has some decision making to do. If we try to handle the decision making with IF statements

```
     .
     .
     .
IF (instruction = '/') THEN
   do division;
IF (instruction = 'S') OR (instruction = 's') THEN
   take square root;
IF (instruction = 'H') OR (instruction = 'h') OR (instruction = '?') THEN
   provide help;
IF
     .
     .
     .
Etc.
```

we then get a very long, clumsy set of conditions, with the variable name instruction repeated over and over again. Instead of using IF statements, we use a CASE statement:

```
     CASE instruction OF
           .
           .
           .
        '/'             : do division;
        'S', 's'        : take square root;
        'H', 'h', '?' : provide help;
           .
           .
           .
        Etc.
```

Even if the program has only two possible courses of action

If the instruction is +, or −, or *, or / then
   read an operand value.
If the instruction is C, or c, or S, or s, or H, or h, or ?, or Q, or q then
   don't read an operand value

a CASE statement can be very useful:

```
  CASE instruction OF
     '+', '-', '*', '/'                                  : GetOperand (operand);
     'C', 'c', 'S', 's', 'H', 'h', '?', 'Q', 'q' : {don't get an operand}
  END
```

Program Example

```
PROGRAM Calculate (input, output);
{Responds to the user's requests to perform calculations.}

  VAR
    instruction : CHAR;
    register    : REAL;

  {----------}

  PROCEDURE GetInstruction (VAR instruction : CHAR);
  {Gets an instruction from the keyboard.}
  BEGIN {GetInstruction}
    Write  ('Next instruction : ');
    ReadLn (instruction)
  END;   {GetInstruction}

  {----------}

  PROCEDURE WriteLnReg (register : REAL);
  BEGIN {WriteLnReg}
    WriteLn ('      register is : ', register:6:2);
    WriteLn;
  END;   {WriteLnReg}

  {----------}

  PROCEDURE React (instruction : CHAR; VAR register : REAL);
  {Executes the user's current instruction.}

    VAR
      operand  : REAL;

    {----------}

    PROCEDURE GetOperand (VAR operand : REAL);
    {Gets an operand from the keyboard.}
    BEGIN {GetOperand}
      Write  ('          operand : ');
      ReadLn (operand)
    END;   {GetOperand}

    {----------}

  BEGIN {React}
    CASE instruction OF
      'C', 'c'     : register := 0.0;
      '+'          : BEGIN
                       GetOperand (operand);
                       register := register + operand
                     END;
      '-'          : BEGIN
                       GetOperand (operand);
                       register := register - operand
                     END;
      '*'          : BEGIN
                       GetOperand (operand);
                       register := register * operand
                     END;
```

```
        '/'               : BEGIN
                              GetOperand (operand);
                              IF operand = 0 THEN
                                WriteLn (Chr (7), '**Illegal divide by zero**')
                              ELSE
                                register := register / operand
                            END;
        'S', 's'          : BEGIN
                              IF register < 0 THEN
                                BEGIN
                                  Write   (Chr (7));
                                  WriteLn ('**Illegal Sqrt of negative value**')
                                END
                              ELSE
                                register := Sqrt (register)
                            END;
        'H', 'h', '?'     : BEGIN
                              WriteLn;
                              WriteLn ('Instructions are: ');
                              WriteLn ('  C : clear        ');
                              WriteLn ('  + : add          ');
                              WriteLn ('  - : subtract     ');
                              WriteLn ('  * : multiply     ');
                              WriteLn ('  / : divide       ');
                              WriteLn ('  S : square root  ');
                              WriteLn ('  H : help         ');
                              WriteLn ('  Q : quit         ');
                              WriteLn
                            END
      END   {CASE}
    END;   {React}
    {----------}

BEGIN {Calculate}
  register := 0.0;
  WriteLnReg (register);
  GetInstruction (instruction);

  WHILE (instruction <> 'Q') AND (instruction <> 'q') DO
    BEGIN
      React           (instruction, register);
      WriteLnReg      (register);
      GetInstruction (instruction)
    END
END.  {Calculate}
```

Sample Runs

```
        register is :    0.00
Next instruction : +
        operand : 5.0
        register is :    5.00

Next instruction : -
        operand : 2.0
        register is :    3.00

Next instruction : /
        operand : 0.0
<bell sound>**Illegal divide by zero**
        register is :    3.00

Next instruction : /
        operand : 2.0
        register is :    1.50

Next instruction : s
        register is :    1.22

Next instruction : q
```

Structure   Here's how we make an NS chart for a CASE statement:

NS chart

A section of the NS chart for Procedure React:

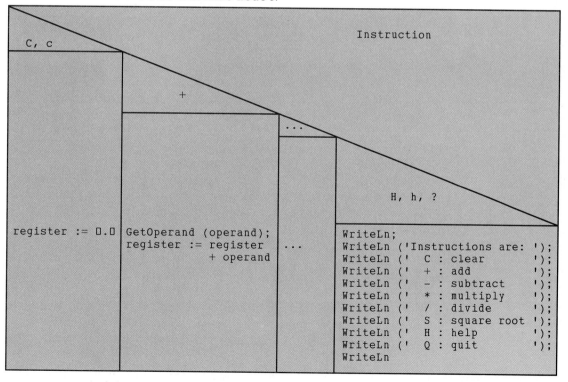

Testing and Debugging

It's legal, but risky, to have a CASE statement that doesn't tell you what to do for all possible values of the case index. For instance, when you write

unexpected case index values

```
VAR
   grade : CHAR;
   .
   .
CASE grade OF
   'A', 'B', 'C' : WriteLn ('Pass     ');
   'D'           : WriteLn ('Marginal');
   'F'           : WriteLn ('Fail     ')
END
```

you're assuming that grade will never be anything other than A, B, C, D, or F. Of course, unforeseen events (like a bug in the program or a typo made by the user) may give grade a different value. An implementation of ANSI Standard Pascal will abort your program if this happens. In situations like this, it's somewhat helpful to create a subrange type:

```
TYPE
   gradeType : 'A'..'F';
VAR
   grade : gradeType;
   .
   .
CASE grade OF
   'A', 'B', 'C' : WriteLn ('Pass                          ');
   'D'           : WriteLn ('Marginal                      ');
   'E'           : WriteLn ('Error - there's no E grade');
   'F'           : WriteLn ('Fail                          ')
END
```

Now the program will send us a nice message if grade gets the value E and will be aborted right away if, at any point in the program, grade gets to be outside the subrange 'A'..'F'. (The computer won't wait until the CASE statement is reached to do the abort. You'll have a better chance of finding where the bad value actually got moved into grade.)

Covering all bases in a CASE statement can be tricky in ANSI Standard Pascal. What happens in Program Calculate if the user types in a code that doesn't represent any of our legal instructions? In our CASE statements we didn't make any provision for unexpected codes (codes other than C, +, -, *, /, S, etc.). It would have been difficult to create a subrange that included all and only the expected characters, and a CASE statement alternative that covered all the unexpected characters would have been long and ugly.

Many implementations of Pascal have extra features that make the CASE statement more versatile. For instance, an ELSE alternative

```
CASE instruction OF
  'C', 'c'      : register := 0.0;
        .
        .
  'H', 'h', '?' : BEGIN
                    WriteLn;
                    WriteLn ('Instructions are: ');
                        .
                        .
                  END
ELSE
    WriteLn (Chr (7), '**Illegal instruction**')
END   {CASE}
```

isn't legal in ANSI Standard Pascal. But if a particular implementation has this feature, it makes it easy to give instructions for unexpected values or for any values in a "catchall" category.

Another feature that's been added to some implementations is a subrange alternative. Here's an example:

```
TYPE
  letterType = 'A'..'z';
  {Unfortunately includes '[', '\', ']', '^', '_', and '`',
    which fall between 'Z' and 'a' in the ASCII Character Set}
VAR
  letter : letterType;
    .
    .
CASE letter OF
  'A', 'E', 'I', 'O', 'U' ,
  'a', 'e', 'i', 'o', 'u'  : WriteLn ('Vowel');

  'B'..'D',   'F'..'H',
  'J'..'N',   'P'..'T',
  'V'..'Z',   'b'..'d',
  'f'..'h',   'j'..'n',
  'p'..'t',   'v'..'z'      : WriteLn ('Consonant');

  '['..'`'                  : WriteLn ('Not a letter')
END
```

Of course, these nice features have their drawbacks. When you use features that are peculiar to one implementation, you're risking having to rewrite your program if you ever need to run it on any other implementation. Rewriting a program so that it runs on a new implementation is called **conversion**. The word *conversion* has a bad connotation among computer professionals, because converting a program tends to be expensive, time-consuming, error-prone, and tedious. It's better to write programs in ANSI Standard Pascal to begin with and avoid using features that are peculiar to your own implementation. When you do this, you're taking the first step in writing programs that are **portable**. A program is portable to the extent that it can be moved from one implementation to another, without any conversion.

portability

8.5   Exercises

Key Words to Review

conversion   portable

Questions to Answer

QUE 8.5.1   Make an NS Chart for Program Calculate. In the chart, show the action of the entire program, not just the CASE statement in Procedure React.

QUE 8.5.2   Would it be possible to rewrite Program ThreeWay (Section 5.5) using a CASE statement? Why, or why not?

Things to Check in a Manual

MAN 8.5.1   In your implementation, is there a way to use subranges instead of just constant expressions in a CASE statement's alternatives?

MAN 8.5.2   In your implementation, is there a way to create a default alternative in a CASE statement?

Changes to Make

CHA 8.5.1   Modify Program Calculate so that the user can enter A or a for addition, M or m for multiplication, etc. What will you do with the S for subtraction?

CHA 8.5.2   Following up on the difficulty in Exercise Cha.8.5.1, modify Program Calculate so that it accepts two-letter instruction codes. That way, Su can be an instruction for subtraction, and Sq can be an instruction for square root.

CHA 8.5.3   Program Calculate, as it's given in this section, will be aborted if you type in a character that doesn't represent a legal instruction. Fix this.

CHA 8.5.4   During a run of Program Calculate the user is always prompted for either an instruction or an operand. The user never has a choice. If we integrate Procedure ReadLnCharOrNat (Section 8.3) into Program Calculate, we can allow the user to enter either a natural number or an instruction at any time.

Let's modify Program Calculate so that the user has this flexibility. Here are a few of the new possibilities:

- The user can ask for help, clear the register, or quit at any time.

- The user can enter two instructions in a row. If the user does this, only the latter instruction is executed.

- The user can enter two natural numbers in a row. If the user does this, the latter number becomes the new value of the register.

CHA 8.5.5   Continuing in the direction we started in Exercise Cha.8.5.4, let's try to make Program Calculate behave more like a hand calculator. Notice, for instance, that a hand calculator displays the result of an instruction immediately after the next instruction is entered. For instance, if you type

    ∃ + 5 - ... etc.

then the number 8 won't be displayed until after the minus sign is entered. Another feature of the hand calculator is the = key, which wasn't used in our original Program Calculate. Modify Program Calculate so that it simulates the behavior of a hand calculator.

Programs and Subprograms to Write

WRI 8.5.1   Redo the program of Exercise Wri.8.1.1 using CASE statements.

WRI 8.5.2   Redo the program of Exercise Wri.8.1.2 using CASE statements.

WRI 8.5.3   My computer system has several classes of users and several different privileges that a user might possess. Here's a table:

Privilege User class	Use e-mail	Run programs	Spawn processes	Read other users' files	Set system parameters
A	Yes	Yes	Yes	Yes	Yes
B	Yes	Yes	Yes	Yes	
M	Yes	Yes		Yes	
P	Yes	Yes	Yes		
X	Yes	Yes			
Z	Yes				

Write a program that reads a user's class and a privilege and decides whether or not the user has that particular privilege.

WRI 8.5.4   *(A continuation of Exercise Wri.6.4.2)* Write a program that reads a sequence of notes from a file and writes the inversion of the sequence on the screen. In the inverted sequence, all pitch changes have been reversed. For instance, if the first three notes of the input tune are F3 G3 G#3, then the first three notes of the output tune are F3 D#3 D3.

WRI 8.5.5   *(In order to do this exercise, it helps to know some algebra.)* Look once again at Exercises Wri.2.1.2 and Wri.2.1.3 in which the Fahrenheit, Celsius, and Kelvin temperature scales were discussed. There's another scale, called the Rankine scale, which is related to the Fahrenheit scale by the following formula:

$$R = F + 459.67$$

So now we have four temperature scales: Fahrenheit, Celsius, Kelvin, and Rankine. Write a program that converts a temperature from any one of these scales to any other. The user determines the source and target scales by entering codes such as F for Fahrenheit and C for Celsius.

8.6

Using Enumerated Types

Now that we've discussed CASE statements and functions that return BOOLEAN values, it's possible to write stylistically sensible programs involving enumerated types.

Specifications It's often handy to think of an enumerated type's values as the various states that a machine can be in. For instance, a stoplight is a machine that, at any given moment, is either in the green state, the yellow state, or the red state. A week is a sort of idealized machine that can be in the Sunday state, the Monday state, etc.

Now what about a person who's reading the sentence

    Cats eat.

This person starts out in the haven't-read-anything-yet state. After reading the word Cats the person might be in the just-saw-a-noun state. Then, after reading the word eat, the person will be in the just-saw-a-complete-sentence state. As the person or machine reads the sentence it makes transitions from one state to another, like this:

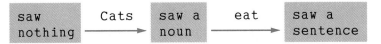

But what about a sentence like Furry black mongrel cats eat? When we consider this example, we see that putting adjectives at the beginning of a sentence doesn't make much of a difference. It's as if reading an adjective has the same effect as not reading anything. Reading one adjective after another just keeps putting us back in the same state over and over again.

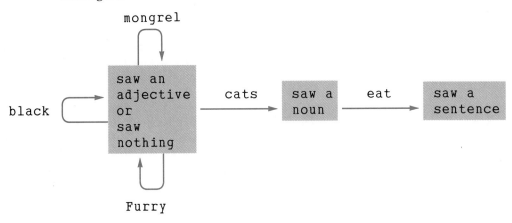

Of course, if we get an ungrammatical combination of words like `Black cats black`, then we'd expect to go into a `bad-grammar` state:

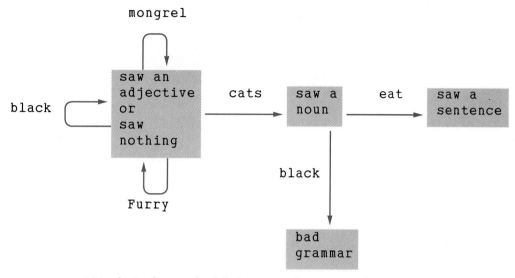

Now let's change the labels on our diagram so that we're using the more "official" terminology:

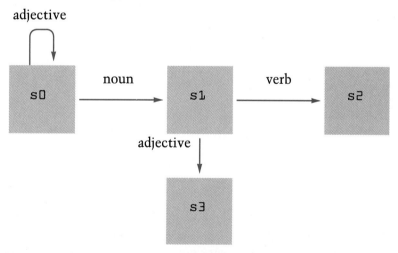

finite-state machines

When we design a machine by making a state diagram, like the one given above, we call our creation a finite-state machine. In this machine `s2` is usually called an accept state because reaching state `s2` means that the machine accepts what's been given to it as being grammatically correct. Similarly, `s3` is called a reject state. Of course, there are more ways to get to the reject state than we showed in our previous diagram.

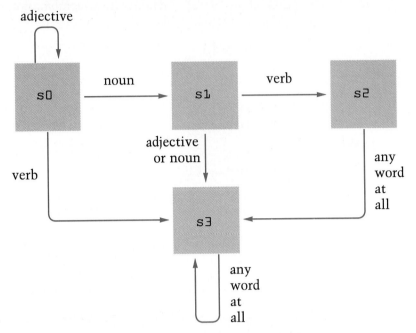

The machine that we've drawn here accepts only the simplest sentences (and in fact we're going to give it letters instead of real words) but it's a very good start at solving the **natural language recognition** problem.

Here are some formal specs:

Input: A sequence of words followed by a period

Output: Either

```
You've typed in a sentence
```

or

```
You haven't typed in a sentence
```

whichever is appropriate.

Designing a Program

We won't write a program that understands the whole English language. That would be too difficult. Instead our program will fulfill a modest goal: It will respond positively when we've typed in a sentence of the form

```
any-number-of-adjectives noun verb.
```

like the sentences

```
Furry black mongrel cats eat.
Black cats eat.
Cats eat.
Etc.
```

To do this, we'll use our most recent machine diagram. This diagram has four states, so we'll need an enumerated type with the four states as its values:

```
TYPE
   stateType = (s0, s1, s2, s3);
```

and a variable `state` to keep track of the current state of the machine. There are three kinds of words in the sample sentences, so we'll have another enumerated type:

```
TYPE
   partOfSpeechType = (adjective, noun, verb);
```

In its broadest outline, the program is very simple:

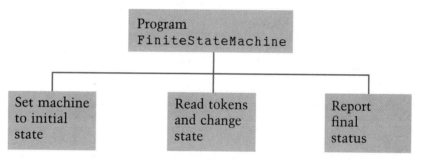

We use the term *token* to refer to any item that we might find as part of a sentence. In this case, an "item" means either a word or a period. Since a typical sentence contains several tokens, the middle box in our hierarchy diagram involves a loop:

```
Read a token.
```
As long as the `token` is a word
    Find what `partOfSpeech` the word belongs to.
    Change the `state` accordingly.
    Read another `token`.

So the hierarchy diagram looks like this:

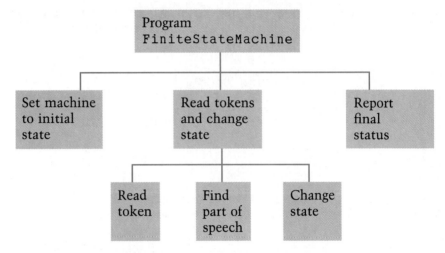

But we need one more component. The subprogram that reports the final status needs to know if the machine is in its accept state s2.

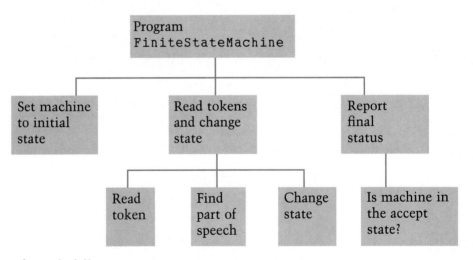

The code follows.

Program Example

```
PROGRAM FiniteStateMachine (input, output);
{Reads a simple sentence and decides
 if it's grammatically correct.}
  CONST
    period = '.';
  TYPE
    stateType = (s0, s1, s2, s3);
  VAR
    state : stateType;
  {----------}
```

```
{parameterless} FUNCTION InitialState : stateType;
{Returns the initial state.}
BEGIN {InitialState}
  InitialState := s0
END;  {InitialState}

{----------}

PROCEDURE ReadAndChange (VAR state : stateType);
{Read a word and change the state appropriately.}
  TYPE
    partOfSpeechType = (adjective, noun, verb);
    tokenType        = CHAR;
    wordType         = CHAR;
  VAR
    partOfSpeech : partOfSpeechType;
    token        : tokenType;
    word         : wordType;

  {----------}

  PROCEDURE ReadToken (VAR fileIn : TEXT       ;
                       VAR token  : tokenType);
  {A stub!  Gets a period; or gets the next *letter* and
   returns this letter as if it's a *whole word*.}
  BEGIN {ReadToken}
    Read (fileIn, token)
  END;  {ReadToken}

  {----------}

  FUNCTION PartOfSpch (word : wordType) : partOfSpeechType;
  {A stub, that interprets letters as words.
   The various letters are suggestive of words, as follows:
   f = furry, b = black, m = mongrel
   d = dogs,  c = cats,
   e = eat,   s = sleep}
  BEGIN {PartOfSpch}
    CASE word OF
      'f', 'b', 'm' : PartOfSpch := adjective;
      'd', 'c'      : PartOfSpch := noun;
      'e', 's'      : PartOfSpch := verb
    END
  END;  {PartOfSpch}

  {----------}

  PROCEDURE ChangeState (VAR s          : stateType       ;
                             partOfSpeech : partOfSpeechType);
  {Changes the state of the machine, given the
   current state and the current word-input.}
```

```
      BEGIN {ChangeState}
        CASE partOfSpeech OF
          adjective : IF s <> s0 THEN
                          s := s3;

          noun      : IF s = s0  THEN
                          s := s1
                        ELSE
                          s := s3;

          verb      : IF s = s1  THEN
                          s := s2
                        ELSE
                          s := s3
        END
      END; {ChangeState}

      {----------}

    BEGIN {ReadAndChange}
      Write ('Enter several words, followed by a period: ');

      ReadToken (input, token);
      WHILE token <> period DO
        BEGIN
          word         := token;
          partOfSpeech := PartOfSpch (word);
          ChangeState (state, partOfSpeech);
          ReadToken   (input, token)
        END
    END;  {ReadAndChange}

    {----------}

    PROCEDURE Report (s : stateType);
    {Prints final message on the screen.}

      {----------}

      FUNCTION IsAcceptState (s : stateType) : BOOLEAN;
      {Returns TRUE if the sentence is grammatically correct;
              FALSE otherwise.}
      BEGIN {IsAcceptState}
        IsAcceptState := s = s2
      END;  {IsAcceptState}

      {----------}

    BEGIN {Report}
      IF IsAcceptState (s) THEN
        WriteLn ('You''ve typed in a sentence')
      ELSE
        WriteLn ('You haven''t typed in a sentence')
    END;  {Report}

    {----------}

  BEGIN {FiniteStateMachine}
    state := InitialState;
    ReadAndChange (state);
    Report        (state)
  END.  {FiniteStateMachine}
```

Sample Runs

```
Enter several words, followed by a period: bfmce.
You've typed in a sentence
```
_____

```
Enter several words, followed by a period: mbds.
You've typed in a sentence
```
_____

```
Enter several words, followed by a period: de.
You've typed in a sentence
```
_____

```
Enter several words, followed by a period: bsd.
You haven't typed in a sentence
```

Observations

- ```
  {parameterless} FUNCTION InitialState : stateType;
  ```
  We could put the machine into its initial state without calling a function, by just setting

  ```
  state := s0
  ```

  a function instead of a constant

  But it's much better to prepare for the possibility that the initial state might not always be s0. We'll have trouble doing this with a CONST definition because of Pascal's rule that the type definition part must come after the CONST definition part. We'd be allowed to do

  ```
  PROGRAM FiniteStateMachine (input, output);
     TYPE
        stateType = (s0, s1, s2, s3);
     {----------}
     PROCEDURE ReadAndChange (VAR state : stateType);
        CONST
           initialState = s0;
     BEGIN {ReadAndChange}
        .
        .
     END;  {ReadAndChange}
     {----------}
  BEGIN {FiniteStateMachine}
     .
     .
  END.   {FiniteStateMachine}
  ```

  because this would put the CONST definition and the type definition in two different subprograms. But we're not permitted to do
  ```

```
┌─ PROGRAM FiniteStateMachine (input, output); ─────────────┐
│    TYPE                                                    │
│      stateType = (s0, s1, s2, s3);                         │
│    CONST                                                   │
│      initialState = s0;                                    │
│    {----------}                                            │
│ ┌─ PROCEDURE ReadAndChange (VAR state : stateType); ─┐     │
│ │  BEGIN {ReadAndChange}                             │     │
│ │    .                                               │     │
│ │    .                                               │     │
│ └─ END;   {ReadAndChange} ──────────────────────────┘     │
│    {----------}                                            │
│ BEGIN {FiniteStateMachine}                                 │
│    state := initialState                                   │
│    .                                                       │
│    .                                                       │
└─ END.    {FiniteStateMachine} ────────────────────────────┘
```

because it puts the CONST definition after a TYPE definition within a single subprogram. And yet we need to define stateType with its s0 state before we define initialState to be equal to s0.

So we create a function called InitialState that has no parameters and always returns the same value, s0. If we ever want to change the initial state, we just have to change one assignment statement inside Function InitialState. We never have to make any changes at the various places where InitialState is called. The same reasoning compels us to create Function IsAcceptState.

- TYPE
    wordType = CHAR;

Since when is a word the same as a single character? We don't know enough Pascal to deal with whole words yet; and even if we did, reading whole words would distract us from the task at hand, which is understanding finite-state machines. So instead of dealing with whole words, our sentences consist of single-letter words. A sentence like

Why create a new type name?

bfmce.

stands for

Black furry mongrel cats eat.

and

bsd.

stands for the ungrammatical "non-sentence"

Black sleep dogs.

The whole "vocabulary" for our finite-state machine is in Function `PartOfSpch`.

Now, having decided that our words are to be of type `CHAR`, we could sprinkle the identifier `CHAR` all over our program, using it wherever we want to refer to words; but this wouldn't be self-documenting, and we'd have no way of distinguishing our words (which are temporarily `CHAR`s) from any honest `CHAR`s in our program. So we create a new type, named `wordType`, that will be the same as the `CHAR` type until we change its definition.

Further Discussion

Notice how the subprograms `ReadToken` and `PartOfSpch` deal specifically with characters rather than whole words. If we ever expand Program `FiniteStateMachine` so that it deals with whole words, we'll have to rewrite these two subprograms. In the meantime, the main program calls these two subprograms, so—whole words or not—these subprograms better have some code in them (or else there would be no way to test the rest of the program). A subprogram that doesn't do everything we'd expect it to do, one that's been created just to help test a larger program, is called a **stub**.

stubs

At first it may seem that stubs are something to be avoided; but this, in fact, is not the case at all. You're encouraged to use stubs in order to keep your attention focused on the broad outline of the problem. After all, in top-down design you create the program in layers. The main program gives an overview of the algorithm, and successive subprograms solve the problem in greater and greater detail. Now what if you want to test the overview before you've dealt with the fine details? This is a reasonable thing to do, since the overview is every bit as important as the details. (In some senses the overview is even more important. If the overall plan isn't correct, the details won't fit together correctly. Conversely, a good start with a nice well-planned outline can help sort out the detail-subprograms in an orderly coherent fashion.)

So now we're planning to run the main program, even though the subprograms it calls haven't been written. Even though you haven't written these detail-subprograms, you need to have subprograms that do something, or else there won't be anything for the main program to call. This is where stubs come in.

We've already seen how top-down design helps us create orderly, coherent programs. When we use stubs to test the program as it's being designed, we're doing **top-down testing**. We're running the broad outline of the program as soon as it's available and using stubs instead of complete subprograms (until the complete subprograms, at the "bottom," are written).

top-down testing

There is, in fact, a technique called **prototyping**, in which a program is intentionally written only with stubs. A program with just stubs can be written very fast. The program is shown to the user, who gets the feel of

prototyping

using it, and critiques it from the user point of view. Based on the user's comments, the program is redesigned. Since stubs were used, the programmer didn't invest a tremendous amount of time in writing the program, and so the program can be reworked to meet the user's needs.

Now let's assume that we've written a version of Program FiniteStateMachine, with our wordType definition and our stubs, and later we're ready to change the program so that it reads whole words. Then we don't have to rip apart the whole fabric of Program FiniteStateMachine. All we have to do is change the definition of wordType and rewrite the two subprograms ReadToken and PartOfSpch. Except for this type definition and these two subprograms, none of the code in Program FiniteStateMachine makes any assumption about words being CHARs or whole words, or whatever. We've managed to narrow the necessary changes to a well-defined part of the program. One can almost say that the single-letter nature of a word has been "hidden" in a small portion of the program.

This notion, of "hiding" (that is, isolating) a type definition, and hiding all the code that makes explicit use of that type definition, is one of the most important ideas in computer programming. In its fully developed form, it's called **information hiding**. If taken to its logical end, information hiding provides a way of sorting out which tasks should be delegated to subprograms and the way in which the subprograms should be grouped. (For more about information hiding, see Sections 3.9, 9.6, and 12.9.)

information hiding

With the features we have in ANSI Standard Pascal, we can't do true information hiding. But we can describe Program FiniteStateMachine as an illustration of *data abstraction*. We can say that details about the wordType, the things that can be done with wordType variables, are placed in Procedure ReadToken and Function PartOfSpch, where they're out of conspicuous view. The rest of the code in Program FiniteStateMachine deals with wordType as an abstract entity—an entity whose broad outline is understood ("call ReadToken if you want to read a word"), but whose details (exactly how to read a word) have been set aside.

data abstraction

Testing and Debugging

There are so many interesting sentences you can use to test Program FiniteStateMachine. For instance

```
Enter several words, followed by a period: ed.
You haven't typed in a sentence
```

tells us that Eat dogs! isn't a sentence (because the machine doesn't expect a verb followed by a noun). But our knowledge of English tells us that it is. What about this next example?

```
Enter several words, followed by a period: bfbfbfce.
You've typed in a sentence
```

Our machine accepts `Black furry black furry black furry cats eat` as a grammatically correct sentence, but it certainly doesn't sound correct.

artificial intelligence

Any program that attempts to understand a **natural language** like English is, of necessity, a simplified program. That's because natural languages are so rich and complex. Programs that work with natural languages belong in a special part of computer science called **artificial intelligence (AI)**. In artificial intelligence, researchers look for ways to "make computers do things, at which, at the moment, people are better."[3] Since AI programs tend to mimic the workings of the human mind, many AI programs implement heuristics rather than algorithms. A **heuristic** is like an algorithm, except that a heuristic isn't guaranteed to produce the desired result every time. Program `FiniteStateMachine` may or may not be able to recognize a grammatically correct sentence. We, the programmers, make no promises. So Program `FiniteStateMachine` implements a heuristic, rather than an algorithm.

heuristics

Of course, some heuristics are better than others. There are computer programs that are capable of handling long and complicated English sentences. Our Program `FiniteStateMachine` is only a very simple illustration of what can be done. The word we'd normally use to describe Program `FiniteStateMachine` is the word **naive**. An algorithm or heuristic that isn't as clever as we'd like it to be, or isn't as clever as one we know we could have written, is usually called naive.

8.6 Exercises

Key Words to Review

finite-state machine	stub	artificial intelligence
accept state	top-down testing	heuristic
reject state	prototyping	naive
natural language recognition	information hiding	

Questions to Answer

QUE 8.6.1 In what sense can a person, listening to another person say a sentence, be compared with a machine?

QUE 8.6.2 Modify the machine diagram that's given in the beginning of this section (with states `s0`, `s1`, `s2`, and `s3`) so that it accepts certain sentences containing adverbs, such as `Dogs eat carefully`.

QUE 8.6.3 Compare finite-state machines with syntax diagrams.

---

[3]Rich, Elaine. *Artificial Intelligence*, Englewood Cliffs, N.J., Prentice-Hall, 1983.

QUE 8.6.4   In what situations is it acceptable to write a "quick and dirty" subprogram that hardly satisfies the specs?

Experiments to Try

EXP 8.6.1   What does Program FiniteStateMachine do when it's given a "sentence" without a period?

EXP 8.6.2   What does Program FiniteStateMachine do when it's given a sentence that begins with a period?

EXP 8.6.3   What does Program FiniteStateMachine do when it encounters a blank space in the middle of an otherwise grammatically correct sentence?

EXP 8.6.4   Try to compile a program containing

```
TYPE
   stateType = (s0, s1, s2, s3);
```

in the main program and

```
CONST
   initialState = s0;
```

in a subprogram.

EXP 8.6.5   Try to compile a program containing the code

```
TYPE
   colorType     = (red, green, blue);
   stopLightType = (green, yellow, red);
```

EXP 8.6.6   Redo Exercise Exp.8.6.5 but this time put the definition of the stopLightType in a subprogram.

Changes to Make

CHA 8.6.1   Modify Program FiniteStateMachine so that it accepts some sentences that have an adjective and a noun coming after the verb, such as Dogs eat furry cats.

CHA 8.6.2   Modify Program FiniteStateMachine so that it accepts some sentences with adverbs.

Programs and Subprograms to Write

WRI 8.6.1   Write a program that reads characters until it reaches a blank space or the end-of-line indicator. Then it writes a message to tell the user if the input was a valid Pascal identifier.

WRI 8.6.2   Find the syntax diagram for a *character string* (in Appendix C). Then write a program that reads characters until it reaches a blank space or the end-of-line indicator. The program writes a message to tell the user if the input was a valid character string.

WRI 8.6.3   Redo Exercise Wri.8.6.2, this time using the syntax diagram for an *unsigned number.*

Things to Think About

THI 8.6.1   Think of some typical (or interesting) sentences in the English language. Then draw diagrams for finite-state machines that accept these sentences as being grammatically correct. Do your machines accept only sentences that are grammatically correct, or do they occasionally end up in their final states when they're given grammatically incorrect sentences? Are there grammatically correct sentences that do not send your machines to their final states?

8.7

Simple Types: A Summary

types

expressions

A lot of ideas about types have been scattered around Chapters 7 and 8. Here's a summary of the most important ideas: A type is a set of values and a set of operations on those values. Anything in a Pascal program that has a value is called an **expression**. If we have a declaration like

```
VAR
   x : REAL;
```

and an assignment such as

```
x := 16.0
```

then $3.0*x$ + Sqrt(x) is an expression (with the value 52.0), and so is $3.0*x$ (because it has the value 48.0), and so is x (with the value 16.0), and so is 3.0 and so is Sqrt(x).

As far as operations go, we have two kinds. There are operations that are denoted as operator symbols (like +) and operations that are denoted as functions (like Sqrt).

Now here's a list giving Pascal's simple types. Along with each type's name, we give the operations on that type (the operations that are built into the Pascal language):

Built-in operations		
	Operator symbols	Pre-declared functions

REAL	`+,-,*,/`
	`unary +, -`
	`=, <>, <, >`
	`<=, >=`
		`Abs, Sqr, Sin`
		`Cos, Exp, Ln,`
		`Sqrt, Arctan,`
		`Trunc, Round`

INTEGER	`+,-,*,/`
	`DIV, MOD`
	`unary +, -`
	`=, <>, <, >`
	`<=, >=`
		`Abs, Sqr, Sin`
		`Cos, Exp, Ln,`
		`Sqrt, Arctan,`
		`Chr, Ord, Succ,`
		`Pred, Odd`

CHAR	`=, <>, <, >,` `<=, >=`	`Ord, Succ, Pred`
Enumerated types	`=, <>, <, >,` `<=, >=`	`Ord, Succ, Pred`

BOOLEAN	`OR, AND, NOT`
	`=, <>, <, >,`
	`<=, >=`
		`Ord, Succ, Pred`

Note that in expressions like $+3.0$ and -4, + and – are being used as **unary** operators. In expressions like $3 + 4$ and $3.5 - 4.2$, + and – are being used as **binary** operators.

simple types   Each of the types listed in the table is called a **simple type**. These are called simple because they're not structured; that is, with the simple types we don't have types within types. (We'll get to the structured types in Chapters 10, 11, and 12.)

ordinal types   All the simple types except REAL are also called **ordinal types**. The word *ordinal* is used to suggest a discrete *ordering*. An ordinal type is one in which values have Successors and Predecessors. For instance, the Successor of the INTEGER value 3 is the INTEGER value 4. The Predecessor of the BOOLEAN value TRUE is the BOOLEAN value FALSE.

In addition to the types listed in the table, you can make up your own simple types. The new types defined in

```
TYPE
    jobPriorityType      = 0..10;
    numberOwnedType      = INTEGER;
    cashValueType        = REAL;
    numberBorrowedType = numberOwnedType;
```

are all simple types. And you can make up your own operations. For instance,

```
FUNCTION Add (c, d : colorType) : colorType;
{Adds two colors together.}
BEGIN {Add}
  IF c = d THEN
    Add := c
  ELSE
    Add := brown
END;  {Add}
```

is a new operation on colors.

8.7   Exercises

Key Words to Review

expression   binary operator   ordinal type
unary operator   simple type

Questions to Answer

QUE 8.7.1   What's *simple* about Pascal's simple types?

QUE 8.7.2   Is the character string

'Pascal by Example'

a value that belongs to a simple type? Why, or why not?

QUE 8.7.3   What's the difference between a simple type and an ordinal type?

QUE 8.7.4   Can you recall any places in a Pascal program where ordinal types must be used?

QUE 8.7.5   Why is REAL not considered to be an ordinal type?

Things to Check in a Manual

MAN 8.7.1   Many implementations have several pre-declared types that are variations on the INTEGER and REAL types. Does your implementation have pre-declared simple types, besides the ones required by the ANSI Standard?

Experiments to Try

EXP 8.7.1   What are the values of Ord (FALSE) and of Ord (TRUE)?

EXP 8.7.2   What happens when you ask for Ord (3.14159)?

EXP 8.7.3   What's the value of Succ (MAXINT − 1)? What about Succ (MAXINT)? What about Pred (−MAXINT)?

EXP 8.7.4   What's the value of Ord (10)?

Chapter Summary

A type is a set of values and a set of operations on those values. Pascal has four predefined simple types. They are REAL, INTEGER, CHAR, and BOOLEAN. The predefined type BOOLEAN has only two values—TRUE and FALSE. There are several operations that can be performed on BOOLEAN values, including the operations NOT, AND, and OR.

In a Pascal program, anything that has a value is called an *expression*, and every expression has a type. *Conditions*, such as the ones found in IF statements, WHILE statements, and REPEAT statements, are expressions of type BOOLEAN.

```
IF condition THEN

WHILE condition THEN

REPEAT .. UNTIL condition
```

A function subprogram can return a BOOLEAN value. When it does, a call to that function is itself a BOOLEAN expression. Like any other BOOLEAN expression, it can be used as the condition in an IF statement, a WHILE statement, or a REPEAT statement. ANSI Standard Pascal has three predeclared functions whose result types are BOOLEAN. They are Eof, Eoln, and Odd.

In addition to the IF statement, Pascal's CASE statement provides a mechanism for making decisions. In a CASE statement, the computer chooses alternative courses of action depending on the value of an expression. The expression is called the *case-index*. Sometimes, when the use of IF statements would lead to very clumsy code, it's still possible to create clear, readable code using a CASE statement. But there are situations involving several alternatives in which the CASE statement is not applicable. In certain of these situations, cascading IFs can be used to enhance a program's readability.

A finite-state machine is an idealized model of a machine. At any given time the machine is in any one of its possible states. The machine makes a transition from one state to another depending on the input that it receives. In Pascal, it's handy to think of the values of an enumerated type as the states in a finite-state machine.

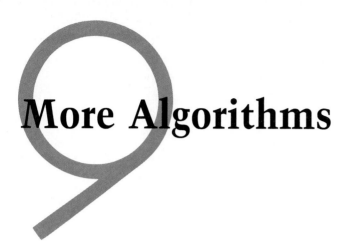

More Algorithms

9.1

Nested Loops with Accumulators

Let's look at an example that combines several of the features of loops that we've been discussing in earlier chapters.

Specifications

Input: Some data from a survey on television viewing habits. The data are divided into several *groups*—each group representing an entire city. A typical city's data look like this:

```
1
3
5
Philadelphia
```

These data tell us that we surveyed three households in Philadelphia. The first household had one television set, the second had three sets, and the third had five sets. The word `Philadelphia` tells us that we're at the end of the data for that city.

Output: For each city in the survey, the average number of television sets per household; for the overall survey, the average number of television sets per household and the average number of households surveyed in each city.

Designing a Program

Reread the description of the input that's given in the specs. We have several cities, and each city has several numbers. This tells us that we want nested loops.

"what goes where" in a loop

For each city do
   For each number within a city do
     . . .

A city's name indicates the end of that city's data, so we'll create a function `AtEndOfCity` that checks to see if we're about to read a city's name. Then we can translate

For each number within a city do

. . .

into

```
WHILE NOT AtEndOfCity DO
   BEGIN
      .
      .
   END
```

We know that we've done all the cities when there are no more data, so we'll translate

For each city do

. . .

into

```
WHILE HasMoreData (input) DO
   BEGIN
      .
      .
      .
   END
```

Putting these two loops together, we get

```
WHILE HasMoreData (input) DO
   BEGIN
      .

      WHILE NOT AtEndOfCity DO
         BEGIN
            .
            .
         END
      .
      .
   END
```

These two `WHILE` loops divide the program into five regions:

```
┌─BEGIN {Cities} ─────────────────────────────────┐
│           I                                      │
├── WHILE HasMoreData (input) DO ──────────────────┤
│      BEGIN                                        │
│              II                                   │
├─────── WHILE NOT AtEndOfCity DO ─────────────────┤
│          BEGIN                                    │
│                  III                              │
├────────── END ───────────────────────────────────┤
│              IV                                    │
├────── END ───────────────────────────────────────┤
│          V                                         │
└─END.   {Cities} ─────────────────────────────────┘
```

Inside the various regions we'll need the usual things: ReadLns, initializations, and increments. The initializations and increments will be for counters and accumulators. The question is, where do all these things go? It's difficult to find rules for this that apply in every situation, so we'll just describe some of the thinking that went into Program Cities.

We can classify each region by the frequency with which its statements are executed:

```
┌─BEGIN {Cities} ─────────────────────────────────┐
│           I   Executed once, before any cities are processed
├── WHILE HasMoreData (input) DO ──────────────────┤
│      BEGIN                                        │
│              II   Executed once for each city, before the
│                   city's households have been processed
├─────── WHILE NOT AtEndOfCity DO ─────────────────┤
│          BEGIN                                    │
│                  III   Executed once for each household
├────────── END ───────────────────────────────────┤
│              IV   Executed once for each city, after the
│                   city's households have been processed
├────── END ───────────────────────────────────────┤
│          V   Executed once, after all cities have been processed
└─END.   {Cities} ─────────────────────────────────┘
```

Let's start with the variable TVsInThisCity. In each region of the program, what do we need to do with the variable TVsInThisCity?

When we read in the number of TVsInThisHousehold, we have to add that number to the running total of the number of TVsInThisCity. This is done for each household, so it has to be done in Region III.

```
┌─ BEGIN {Cities} ──────────────────────────────────────────────────┐
│            I                                                        │
├──── WHILE HasMoreData (input) DO ─────────────────────────────────┤
│        BEGIN                                                        │
│                 II                                                  │
│        ┌──── WHILE NOT AtEndOfCity DO ─────────────────────────────┤
│        │     BEGIN                                                  │
│        │         Accumulate (TVsInThisCity, TVsInThisHousehold)    │
│        │               III                                         │
│        └──── END ──────────────────────────────────────────────────┤
│                 IV                                                  │
├──── END ──────────────────────────────────────────────────────────┤
│            V                                                        │
└─ END.   {Cities} ─────────────────────────────────────────────────┘
```

Accumulate will be the name of one of our procedures. The effect of this call to Accumulate will be to add the value of TVsInThisHousehold to the accumulator TVsInThisCity.

Since TVsInThisCity is an accumulator, it has to be given an initial value somewhere. But where? The tally of the TVsInThisCity has to be restarted *once for each city,* in preparation for the reading of several values for TVsInThisHousehold. So this accumulator needs to be initialized in Region II.

```
┌─ BEGIN {Cities} ──────────────────────────────────────────────────┐
│            I                                                        │
├──── WHILE HasMoreData (input) DO ─────────────────────────────────┤
│        BEGIN                                                        │
│           Initialize (TVsInThisCity);                              │
│                 II                                                  │
│        ┌──── WHILE NOT AtEndOfCity DO ─────────────────────────────┤
│        │     BEGIN                                                  │
│        │         Accumulate (TVsInThisCity, TVsInThisHousehold)    │
│        │               III                                         │
│        └──── END ──────────────────────────────────────────────────┤
│                 IV                                                  │
├──── END ──────────────────────────────────────────────────────────┤
│            V                                                        │
└─ END.   {Cities} ─────────────────────────────────────────────────┘
```

Now where do we use the tally we've made of the `TVsInThisCity`? For any particular city, we have to finish tallying the `TVsInThisCity` before we can use the value. So we can use this value only after the city's households have all been processed. Thus we use `TVsInThisCity` in Region IV. We use it in two ways:

- The specs tell us to find the average number of TVs per household in each city, so we divide `TVsInThisCity` by the number of households in this city.

- The specs tell us to find the average number of TVs per household in the whole survey. In preparing to find that overall average, we add `TVsInThisCity` to the running total `TVsInSurvey`.

```
BEGIN {Cities}
        I
    WHILE HasMoreData (input) DO
        BEGIN
            Initialize (TVsInThisCity);
                    II
            WHILE NOT AtEndOfCity DO
                BEGIN
                    Accumulate (TVsInThisCity, TVsInThisHousehold)
                            III
                    END;
            TVsPerHouseholdInThisCity := TVsInThisCity / householdsInThisCity;
            Accumulate (TVsInSurvey, TVsInThisCity)
                    IV
            END
        V
    END.   {Cities}
```

Of course the grand total `TVsInSurvey` has to be given a starting value somewhere. This is a total for all cities, so it has to be initialized only once, before any of the cities have been processed. So this belongs in Region I.

```
┌─ BEGIN {Cities} ──────────────────────────────────────────────────────┐
│                                                                        │
│     Initialize (TVsInSurvey);                                          │
│              I                                                         │
├──── WHILE HasMoreData (input) DO ──────────────────────────────────────┤
│        BEGIN                                                           │
│           Initialize (TVsInThisCity);                                 │
│                  II                                                   │
│   ┌──── WHILE NOT AtEndOfCity DO ─────────────────────────────────────┤
│   │       BEGIN                                                       │
│   │          Accumulate (TVsInThisCity, TVsInThisHousehold)          │
│   │                III                                               │
│   ├──── END; ───────────────────────────────────────────────────────┤
│   │       TVsPerHouseholdInThisCity := TVsInThisCity / householdsInThisCity; │
│   │       Accumulate (TVsInSurvey, TVsInThisCity)                    │
│   │             IV                                                   │
│   ├──── END ─────────────────────────────────────────────────────────┤
│   │          V                                                       │
└── END.    {Cities} ───────────────────────────────────────────────────┘
```

And after all the cities have been processed there are some overall averages to report—the average number of television sets per household and the average number of households surveyed in each city. These averages depend not on the results from any one city, but on the combined results of all cities. So this reporting is done in Region V, after all the cities have been processed.

```
┌─ BEGIN {Cities} ──────────────────────────────────────────────────────┐
│                                                                        │
│     Initialize (TVsInSurvey);                                          │
│              I                                                         │
├──── WHILE HasMoreData (input) DO ──────────────────────────────────────┤
│        BEGIN                                                           │
│           Initialize (TVsInThisCity);                                 │
│                  II                                                   │
│   ┌──── WHILE NOT AtEndOfCity DO ─────────────────────────────────────┤
│   │       BEGIN                                                       │
│   │          Accumulate (TVsInThisCity, TVsInThisHousehold)          │
│   │                III                                               │
│   ├──── END; ───────────────────────────────────────────────────────┤
│   │       TVsPerHouseholdInThisCity := TVsInThisCity / householdsInThisCity; │
│   │       Accumulate (TVsInSurvey, TVsInThisCity)                    │
│   │             IV                                                   │
├───┴── END; ─────────────────────────────────────────────────────────┤
│     WriteLn (TVsPerHouseholdInSurvey   :6:2);                         │
│     WriteLn (householdsPerCityInSurvey:6:2)                           │
│            V                                                          │
└── END.    {Cities} ───────────────────────────────────────────────────┘
```

The whole program follows.

Program
Example

```
PROGRAM Cities (input, output);
{Tallies data from a survey of television viewing habits.}
  TYPE
    kindType = (character, natral);
    natural  = 0..MAXINT;
  VAR
    c       : CHAR;
    n       : natural;
    kind    : kindType;
    TVsInThisHousehold,
    TVsInThisCity,      householdsInThisCity,
    TVsInSurvey,        householdsInSurvey,   citiesInSurvey : natural;

  {----------}
  PROCEDURE Initialize (VAR v : natural);
  {Initializes to zero.}
  BEGIN {Initialize}
    v := 0
  END;   {Initialize}

  {----------}
  PROCEDURE Increment (VAR counter : natural);
  {Increments by 1.}
  BEGIN {Increment}
    counter := counter + 1
  END;   {Increment}

  {----------}
  PROCEDURE Accumulate (VAR accumulator : natural;
                            newValue     : natural);
  {Adds newValue to the accumulator.}
  BEGIN {Accumulate}
    accumulator := accumulator + newValue
  END;   {Accumulate}

  {----------}
  FUNCTION HasMoreData (VAR aFile : TEXT) : BOOLEAN;
  {Determines whether or not aFile contains more data.}
  BEGIN {HasMoreData}
    HasMoreData := NOT Eof(aFile)
  END;   {HasMoreData}

  {----------}
  FUNCTION AtEndOfCity (kind : kindType) : BOOLEAN;
  {Determines whether processing of a city is completed.}
  BEGIN {AtEndOfCity}
    AtEndOfCity := kind = character
  END;   {AtEndOfCity}

  {----------}
```

```
PROCEDURE ReadLnCharOrNat (VAR c    : CHAR;
                           VAR n    : natural;
                           VAR kind : kindType);
{Straight from Section 8.3}
{----------}
PROCEDURE WriteIntermediate (TVsInThisCity,
                             householdsInThisCity : natural);
{Writes values pertaining to a particular city.}

   VAR
     TVsPerHouseholdInThisCity : REAL;

BEGIN {WriteIntermediate}
   TVsPerHouseholdInThisCity := TVsInThisCity / householdsInThisCity;
   Write   ('Average number of TVs per household in this city:  ');
   WriteLn (TVsPerHouseholdInThisCity:6:2);
   WriteLn
END;  {WriteIntermediate}
{----------}
PROCEDURE WriteFinal (householdsInSurvey,
                      citiesInSurvey,
                      TVsInSurvey        : natural);
{Writes final summary data from the survey.}

   VAR
     householdsPerCityInSurvey,
     TVsPerHouseholdInSurvey   : REAL;

BEGIN {WriteFinal}
   TVsPerHouseholdInSurvey := TVsInSurvey / householdsInSurvey;
   WriteLn;
   Write   ('Average number of TVs per household in all cities: ');
   WriteLn (TVsPerHouseholdInSurvey  :6:2);

   householdsPerCityInSurvey := householdsInSurvey / citiesInSurvey;
   WriteLn;
   Write   ('Average number of households per city:             ');
   WriteLn (householdsPerCityInSurvey:6:2)
END;  {WriteFinal}
{----------}
BEGIN {Cities}
   Initialize (citiesInSurvey);
   Initialize (householdsInSurvey);
   Initialize (TVsInSurvey);
   WriteLn    ('Enter survey data for several cities:');
   WriteLn;
```

```
      WHILE HasMoreData (input) DO
        BEGIN
          Increment   (citiesInSurvey);
          Initialize (householdsInThisCity);
          Initialize (TVsInThisCity);

          ReadLnCharOrNat (c, TVsInThisHousehold, kind);
          WHILE NOT AtEndOfCity (kind) DO
            BEGIN
              Increment        (householdsInThisCity);
              Accumulate       (TVsInThisCity, TVsInThisHousehold);
              ReadLnCharOrNat (c, TVsInThisHousehold, kind)
            END;

          WriteIntermediate (TVsInThisCity, householdsInThisCity);

          Accumulate (householdsInSurvey, householdsInThisCity);
          Accumulate (TVsInSurvey, TVsInThisCity)
        END;

      WriteFinal (householdsInSurvey, citiesInSurvey, TVsInSurvey)
    END.  {Cities}
```

Sample Runs

```
Enter survey data for several cities:
1
3
5
Philadelphia
Average number of TVs per household in this city:    3.00
2
2
Milwaukee
Average number of TVs per household in this city:    2.00
1
2
3
San Diego
Average number of TVs per household in this city:    2.00
<end-of-file indicator>

Average number of TVs per household in all cities:   2.38
Average number of households per city:               2.67
```

Programming Style

when to create a subprogram

It's not uncommon to think of subprograms in the following way: In the main program, we find several lines of code that we think should be separated out. We take these lines out of the main program and use them (with some modifications) to create a new subprogram. Before we've created a subprogram, when this code is still part of the main program, we call it **in-line code**.

When is it appropriate to turn in-line code into a new subprogram? There are several reasonable answers:

- When several lines of code appear together several times in the main program. Instead of typing these lines over and over again, write them once in a subprogram, and call the subprogram several times.
- When the in-line code becomes very large. A hundred-line program is difficult to read, but not if its main program consists of only a few lines, which call several short subprograms.

Neither of these reasons applies very well to our Procedures `Initialize`, `Increment`, and `Accumulate`. When we change

```
TVsInSurvey := 0
```

into a procedure call

```
Initialize (TVsInSurvey)
```

we're not saving any typing effort. These procedures demonstrate some other reasons for creating a new subprogram:

- To make the program more self-documenting. It's easier to understand what a subprogram call does than to read the corresponding in-line code, especially when the subprogram has been given an informative name.
- To ensure that the program is correct. Calling a subprogram can be less prone to error than writing the code in line.

For instance, compare the procedure call

```
Accumulate (TVsInThisCity, TVsInThisHousehold)
```

with the corresponding in-line code:

```
TVsInThisCity := TVsInThisCity + TVsInThisHousehold
```

The procedure call is easier to read than the in-line code, because the word `TVsInThisCity` occurs only once in the procedure call. The human reader has to read the in-line code slowly, to verify that the variable names on either side of the `:=` are the same. (And there's no guarantee that the programmer won't type one of the variable names incorrectly.) If we say in English what these lines do, we might say something like

```
Add TVsInThisHousehold to TVsInThisCity
```

So even in our English-language understanding of this action, the name `TVsInThisCity` occurs only once.

Even when the in-line code has no repeated names, calling a subprogram can make a program more readable. The procedure call

```
Initialize (TVsInThisCity)
```

is a bit easier to understand than

```
TVsInThisCity := 0
```

because the procedure name `Initialize` gives the human reader a hint that the variable is being given the *initial* value of 0. Of course, this depends very heavily on Procedure `Initialize` having an informative name. (Actually, the procedure call tells us only that the variable is given an initial value. We can choose to peek at the body of Procedure `Initialize` itself, to learn what the initial value is, or we can ignore this detail in order to better see the overall action of Program `Cities`.)

Testing and Debugging

simple test data

Here's one approach to black box testing that we haven't discussed yet. Look at the values we used to test Program `Cities` in this section's Sample Runs. This clearly isn't "real-life" data. It's too simple to have been taken from real life. But that's exactly what makes it worthwhile. These data are so simple that it's easy to verify that the output is correct. We can do most of the checking without a calculator or a paper and pencil. Taking the average of the numbers 1, 2, and 3 is that easy.

Such data certainly don't strain Program `Cities` to its limits, but sometimes it's important to be sure that the calculations we do when we check a program's output are absolutely correct. In situations such as these, the very simplest test data may be the best.

9.1 Exercises

Key Words to Review

in-line code

Questions to Answer

QUE 9.1.1   In Designing a Program, we explained the placement of several statements in the body of Program `Cities`. Explain the placement of the other statements in Program `Cities`.

QUE 9.1.2   Create more test data for Program `Cities`, this time with an eye toward "straining the program to its limits."

Experiments to Try

EXP 9.1.1   Run Program `Cities` and have a city in which no households were surveyed.

EXP 9.1.2   Run Program `Cities` with no data at all. That is, give it the end-of-file indicator as soon as it starts running.

Programs and Subprograms to Write

WRI 9.1.1   Write a program that reads lines that look like this:

    M 5 6 125

which means we surveyed a male whose height was 5 feet, 6 inches, and who weighed 125 pounds. The last line of the file has no numbers in it, just the words

    END OF DATA

Your program should report the average height of males, the average weight of males, the average heights and weights of females, and the average heights and weights of all people in the survey.

WRI 9.1.2   The sequence of numbers

    2 7 6 9 5 1 4 3 8

is called a three-by-three *Magic square* because it contains the numbers 1 to 9 and, when you split the sequence into three rows, you get the same sum (15) by adding up the numbers along any row, the numbers along any column, or the numbers along either of the two diagonals.

2	7	6
9	5	1
4	3	8

Here are all the other three-by-three Magic squares:

    2 9 4 7 5 3 6 1 8   4 3 8 9 5 1 2 7 6   4 9 2 3 5 7 8 1 6

    6 1 8 7 5 3 2 9 4   6 7 2 1 5 9 8 3 4   8 1 6 3 5 7 4 9 2

    8 3 4 1 5 9 6 7 2

Write a program that reads a sequence containing the numbers 1 through 9 and writes a message telling whether that sequence is or is not a Magic square.

WRI 9.1.3   Write a program that reads several of a student's grades and finds the student's average grade but, in doing so, ignores the student's lowest grade.

WRI 9.1.4   Read a paragraph and report the following information about the paragraph: the number of letters, the number of words, the number of sentences, the average number of letters in a word, the average number of letters in a sentence, the average number of words in a sentence.

Things to Think About

THI 9.1.1   Discuss the merits of a statement such as

    Accumulate (TVsInThisCity, TVsInThisHousehold)

versus its in-line counterpart

    TVsInThisCity := TVsInThisCity + TVsInThisHousehold

Ask your instructor for an opinion. (Your instructor may not agree with Barry Burd!)

THI 9.1.2   In doing the exercises from this text, how do you decide whether a particular task should be done in a subprogram or with in-line code? What unwritten rules do you find yourself using?

9.2

Holding Values from One Iteration to Another

Specifications

Input: A sequence of non-negative integer values. In the sequence all 0's are lumped together, all 1's are lumped together, all 2's . . . etc. Aside from this "lumping," the values are in no particular order. For example,

```
5
5
10
10
10
2
6
6
6
6
6
3
3
```

Output: The value that appears most often in the sequence and the number of times it appears. For example,

```
The mode is   6
It occurred   5 times
```

The value that appears most often in the sequence is called the *mode* of the sequence.

Designing a Program

One piece of advice that's often given to beginning programmers is to *role-play* being the computer. Instead of thinking about

role-play the computer

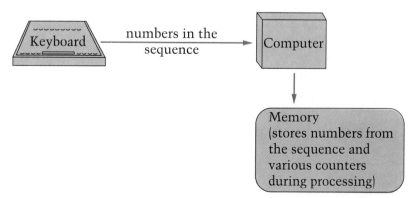

think about

At first this may seem to be a silly analogy, but actually it illustrates a very important point; namely, that *the computer does nothing more than execute an algorithm.* If another person is calling out numbers to you, and you're keeping track of things on a piece of paper, then you're doing the same thing—executing an algorithm, following instructions that you decided on in advance.

Now let's get back to the problem at hand. How will you keep track of the numbers the other person reads to you? At first you're tempted to copy down every number that the other person gives you, but this is wasteful. All you ever need to remember is

the number that's appeared most often in the sequence so far (the mode), and

how many times this number has appeared (the modeCount)

To illustrate this, let's look at the sample input given in the Specifications. The other person shows you a 5, then another 5. On your sheet of paper you note that you've seen two 5's:

Then the person shows you three 10's, so you no longer need to keep track of the 5's. You can erase the 5 on your scratch pad and just keep track of the 10's:

Here's some pseudocode:

Algorithm `FindMode`:

In a loop, do the following:
    Read a number; call it `valueIn`.
    Update `valueInCount`, the count of how many times you've seen this number
    Update `mode` and `modeCount`

Now, how do you update the variables `valueInCount`, `mode`, and `modeCount`? Let's look at `valueInCount` first. This variable keeps track of how many times the current `valueIn` has been read:

As we read these valuesIn:		This is what happens to valueInCount:
5	⟶	set valueInCount to 1
5	⟶	increment valueInCount to 2
10	⟶	drop valueInCount back down to 1
10	⟶	increment valueInCount to 2
10	⟶	increment valueInCount to 3

So here's the algorithm:

Algorithm `UpdateCount`:

If this `valueIn` equals the `previousValueIn` then
    add 1 to `valueInCount`
otherwise
    `valueInCount := 1`

And what about updating `mode` and `modeCount`? We should change `mode` and `modeCount` whenever we find that the current number occurs more times than the number we thought was the mode; that is, whenever `valueInCount` gets to be larger than `modeCount`:

Algorithm `UpdateMode`:

If `valueInCount` has grown to be larger than `modeCount`, make
```
mode       := valueIn
modeCount := valueInCount
```

This is the thinking that went into this section's program example.

Program Example

```
PROGRAM FindMode (input, output);
{Finds the mode of a collection of numbers.}
  TYPE
    natural = 0..MAXINT;
  VAR
    valueIn, valueInCount, mode, modeCount, prevValueIn : natural;

  {----------}
  PROCEDURE Initialize (VAR valueIn     , valueInCount,
                            mode         , modeCount,
                            prevValueIn                 : natural);
  {Initializes all variables to zero.}
  BEGIN {Initialize}
    valueIn       := 0;
    valueInCount := 0;
    mode          := 0;
    modeCount     := 0;
    prevValueIn   := 0
  END;   {Initialize}

  {----------}
  PROCEDURE UpdateCount (valueIn         : natural ;
                         VAR valueInCount : natural ;
                             prevValueIn  : natural);
  {Keeps count of how many times the valueIn has appeared.}
  BEGIN {UpdateCount}
    IF prevValueIn = valueIn THEN
      valueInCount := valueInCount + 1
    ELSE
      valueInCount := 1
  END;   {UpdateCount}

  {----------}
```

```
PROCEDURE UpdateMode (valueIn , valueInCount : natural ;
                         VAR mode, modeCount    : natural);
{Keeps the 'mode' up to date.}
BEGIN {UpdateMode}
  IF valueInCount > modeCount THEN
    BEGIN
      mode      := valueIn;
      modeCount := valueInCount
    END
END;  {UpdateMode}

{----------}

PROCEDURE UpdatePrev (valueIn : natural; VAR prevValueIn : natural);
{Stores the valueIn from the previous iteration.}
BEGIN {UpdatePrev}
  prevValueIn  := valueIn
END;  {UpdatePrev}

{----------}

BEGIN {FindMode}
  Initialize (valueIn, valueInCount, mode, modeCount, prevValueIn);
  WriteLn ('Enter several numbers: ');

  WHILE NOT Eof (input) DO
    BEGIN
      ReadLn      (valueIn);
      UpdateCount (valueIn, valueInCount, prevValueIn);
      UpdateMode  (valueIn, valueInCount, mode, modeCount);
      UpdatePrev  (valueIn, prevValueIn)
    END;

  WriteLn;
  WriteLn ('The mode is ', mode:2);
  WriteLn ('It occurred ', modeCount:2, ' times')
END.  {FindMode}
```

Sample Runs

```
Enter several numbers:
5
5
10
10
10
2
6
6
6
6
6
3
3
<end-of-file indicator>

The mode is  6
It occurred  5 times
```

```
Enter several numbers:
5
5
10
10
10
2
3
3
6
6
6
6
6
<end-of-file indicator>

The mode is   6
It occurred   5 times
```

Testing and Debugging   The algorithm that we used in Program FindMode has a serious deficiency—the value of mode is updated far too often. Look at the first of the two input sequences given in the Sample Runs. Just before the fourth 6 is read, we have

UpdateMode					
valueIn	valueInCount	valueInCount > modeCount		mode	modeCount
·	·		·		
6	3	FALSE		10	3

At that point we still think the number 10 might be the mode, because it's occurred 3 times in the sequence (and so has the number 6). Now when the fourth 6 is read, valueInCount gets to be larger than modeCount:

UpdateMode					
valueIn	valueInCount	valueInCount > modeCount		mode	modeCount
·	·		·		
6	3	FALSE		10	3
6	4	TRUE			

so Procedure UpdateMode changes the values of mode and modeCount:

UpdateMode					
valueIn	valueInCount	valueInCount > modeCount		mode	modeCount
·	·		·		
6	3	FALSE		10	3
6	4	TRUE		6	4

But then when the fifth 6 is read, Procedure `UpdateMode` changes `mode` and `modeCount` again:[1]

valueIn	valueInCount	valueInCount > modeCount	mode	modeCount
.	.		.	
	.		.	
6	3	FALSE	10	3
6	4	TRUE	6	4
6	**5**	**TRUE**	**6**	**5**

UpdateMode

Wouldn't it be faster to wait until *all* the 6's have been read and *then* update `mode` and `modeCount`? Let's try it that way:

```
BEGIN {FindMode}
  Initialize (valueIn, valueInCount, mode, modeCount, prevValueIn);
  WriteLn ('Enter several numbers: ');

  WHILE NOT Eof (input) DO
    BEGIN
      ReadLn       (valueIn);
      IF prevValueIn <> valueIn THEN                          {Changed}
        UpdateMode (prevValueIn, valueInCount, mode, modeCount);  {Changed}
      UpdateCount (valueIn, valueInCount, prevValueIn);
      UpdatePrev  (valueIn, prevValueIn)
    END;

  WriteLn;
  WriteLn ('The mode is ', mode:2);
  WriteLn ('It occurred ', modeCount:2, ' times')
END.  {FindMode}
```

The new strategy is to call Procedure `UpdateMode` only when we discover a brand new number in the sequence—that is, when `valueIn` is different from `prevValueIn`. With the sequence just given, we don't change the `mode` to 6 until we read in the first of the two 3's.

Now before we become too elated, we should check our new code on the sequences given in this section's Sample Runs. Here's what we get:

---

[1] Actually, Procedure `UpdateMode` doesn't really change the value of `mode`—it just assigns `mode` the value 6 again.

```
Enter several numbers:
5
5
10
10
10
2
6
6
6
6
6
3
3
<end-of-file indicator>

The mode is   6
It occurred   5 times
```

```
Enter several numbers:
5
5
10
10
10
2
3
3
6
6
6
6
6
<end-of-file indicator>

The mode is 10
It occurred  3 times
```

The new code works fine with the first sequence, but with the second
sequence, it tells us that the mode is 10 when the mode is really 6. What's
going wrong?

adding
WriteLns

Let's borrow our technique of adding WriteLns from Section 6.1.

```
PROGRAM FindMode (input, output);
{Finds the mode of a collection of numbers.}
   CONST
      debugging = TRUE;
   TYPE
      natural = 0..MAXINT;
   VAR
      valueIn, valueInCount, mode, modeCount, prevValueIn : natural;

   {----------}
```

```
PROCEDURE Initialize (VAR valueIn      , valueInCount,
                           mode         , modeCount,
                           prevValueIn               : natural);
{Initializes all variables to zero.}
BEGIN {Initialize}
  valueIn      := 0;
  valueInCount := 0;
  mode         := 0;
  modeCount    := 0;
  prevValueIn  := 0
END;  {Initialize}

{----------}

PROCEDURE UpdateCount (valueIn            : natural ;
                       VAR valueInCount : natural ;
                           prevValueIn    : natural);
{Keeps count of how many times the valueIn has appeared.}
BEGIN {UpdateCount}
  IF prevValueIn = valueIn THEN
    valueInCount := valueInCount + 1
  ELSE
    valueInCount := 1
END;  {UpdateCount}

{----------}

PROCEDURE UpdateMode (valueIn , valueInCount : natural ;
                      VAR mode, modeCount    : natural);
{Keeps the 'mode' up to date.}
BEGIN {UpdateMode}
  IF valueInCount > modeCount THEN
    BEGIN
      mode      := valueIn;
      modeCount := valueInCount
    END
END;  {UpdateMode}

{----------}

PROCEDURE UpdatePrev (valueIn : natural; VAR prevValueIn : natural);
{Stores the valueIn from the previous iteration.}
BEGIN {UpdatePrev}
  prevValueIn  := valueIn
END;  {UpdatePrev}

{----------}
```

```
BEGIN {FindMode}
  Initialize (valueIn, valueInCount, mode, modeCount, prevValueIn);
  WriteLn ('Enter several numbers: ');
  WHILE NOT Eof (input) DO
    BEGIN
      ReadLn (valueIn);
      IF prevValueIn <> valueIn THEN                          {Changed}
        UpdateMode (prevValueIn, valueInCount, mode, modeCount);  {Changed}

      IF debugging THEN
        WriteLn ('Possible mode update - the mode is now ', mode:2);

      UpdateCount (valueIn, valueInCount, prevValueIn);
      UpdatePrev  (valueIn, prevValueIn)
    END;
  WriteLn;
  WriteLn ('The mode is ', mode:2);
  WriteLn ('It occurred ', modeCount:2, ' times')
END.  {FindMode}
```

```
Enter several numbers:
5
Possible mode update - the mode is now  0
5
Possible mode update - the mode is now  0
10                                          ◄──── valueIn is no longer 5
Possible mode update - the mode is now  5◄──── the mode becomes 5
10
Possible mode update - the mode is now  5
10
Possible mode update - the mode is now  5
2                                           ◄──── valueIn is no longer 10
Possible mode update - the mode is now 10◄──── the mode becomes 10
3
Possible mode update - the mode is now 10
3
Possible mode update - the mode is now 10
6
Possible mode update - the mode is now 10
6
Possible mode update - the mode is now 10
6
Possible mode update - the mode is now 10
6
Possible mode update - the mode is now 10
6
Possible mode update - the mode is now 10
6                                           ◄──── Oops! valueIn is still 6
Possible mode update - the mode is now 10
<end-of-file indicator>

The mode is 10
It occurred  3 times
```

If we look at the bottom of the sample run and think carefully about our new strategy, we can see what's going on. Our new strategy tells us to call Procedure UpdateMode only after discovering a brand new number in the input sequence. But in this sequence there are no "brand new numbers" after the last 6. So the value of mode never gets updated to 6.

What we need to do is add one more call to Procedure UpdateMode. We add it after the program's main WHILE loop:

```
PROGRAM FindMode (input, output);
{Finds the mode of a collection of numbers.}
  CONST
    debugging = FALSE;
  TYPE
    natural = 0..MAXINT;
  VAR
    valueIn, valueInCount, mode, modeCount, prevValueIn : natural;
  {----------}
  PROCEDURE Initialize (VAR valueIn     , valueInCount,
                            mode         , modeCount,
                            prevValueIn               : natural);
  {Initializes all variables to zero.}
  BEGIN {Initialize}
    valueIn      := 0;
    valueInCount := 0;
    mode         := 0;
    modeCount    := 0;
    prevValueIn  := 0
  END;  {Initialize}

  {----------}

  PROCEDURE UpdateCount (valueIn            : natural ;
                         VAR valueInCount : natural ;
                         prevValueIn        : natural);
  {Keeps count of how many times the valueIn has appeared.}
  BEGIN {UpdateCount}
    IF prevValueIn = valueIn THEN
      valueInCount := valueInCount + 1
    ELSE
      valueInCount := 1
  END;  {UpdateCount}

  {----------}

  PROCEDURE UpdateMode (valueIn , valueInCount : natural ;
                        VAR mode, modeCount    : natural);
  {Keeps the 'mode' up to date.}
  BEGIN {UpdateMode}
    IF valueInCount > modeCount THEN
      BEGIN
        mode      := valueIn;
        modeCount := valueInCount
      END
  END;  {UpdateMode}

  {----------}
```

```
PROCEDURE UpdatePrev (valueIn : natural; VAR prevValueIn : natural);
{Stores the valueIn from the previous iteration.}
BEGIN {UpdatePrev}
  prevValueIn  := valueIn
END;  {UpdatePrev}

{----------}
```

```
BEGIN {FindMode}
  Initialize (valueIn, valueInCount, mode, modeCount, prevValueIn);
  WriteLn ('Enter several numbers: ');

  WHILE NOT Eof (input) DO
    BEGIN
      ReadLn (valueIn);
      IF prevValueIn <> valueIn THEN                          {Changed}
        UpdateMode (prevValueIn, valueInCount, mode, modeCount);  {Changed}

      IF debugging THEN
        WriteLn ('Possible mode update - the mode is now ', mode:2);

      UpdateCount (valueIn, valueInCount, prevValueIn);
      UpdatePrev  (valueIn, prevValueIn)
    END;
  UpdateMode (prevValueIn, valueInCount, mode, modeCount);       {Changed}

  WriteLn;
  WriteLn ('The mode is ', mode:2);
  WriteLn ('It occurred ', modeCount:2, ' times')
END.   {FindMode}
```

We need this extra call to UpdateMode to cover the possibility that the mode is the very last number appearing in the sequence. It's easy to miss this possibility when testing Program FindMode. This is a nice illustration **extreme values** of the need to test our program with **extreme values** (see Section 6.2). Notice how, in this instance, the word extreme doesn't mean that we're typing in "large" numbers or "small" numbers. It means that the position of the mode in the input sequence is "large."

turning debugging on and off   Now before we bid a fond farewell to Program FindMode let's take one last look at the final version of the program. Notice the lines

```
CONST
  debugging = FALSE;
    .
    .
    .
IF debugging THEN
  WriteLn ('Possible mode update - the mode is now ', mode:2)
```

Instead of removing the extra WriteLns, we've left them in the program for future debugging needs. We don't need to hunt through the code, picking out just those WriteLns that were added at the last minute. Instead we turn a whole set of debugging statements on and off by changing just one word in the code (the value of the debugging constant).

9.2 Exercises

Key Words to Review

extreme values

Questions to Answer

QUE 9.2.1 Compare the roles of the two variables—prev in Program Fibonacci (Section 6.3) and prevValueIn in Program FindMode.

QUE 9.2.2 Make a trace of our last version of Program FindMode but leave off that final call to Procedure UpdateMode and trace the program with a list of numbers in which the last number occurs most often.

QUE 9.2.3 In this section we had to think carefully about the behavior of Program FindMode when the mode is the very last number appearing in the sequence. Do any of our versions of FindMode have difficulties when the mode is the first number in the sequence?

QUE 9.2.4 Write a proof of correctness for Program FindMode (assuming that the user supplies at least one input value before indicating end-of-file).

Changes to Make

CHA 9.2.1 Modify Program FindMode so that it does something sensible if the user supplies no input (that is, if the user's first response is to indicate end-of-file).

CHA 9.2.2 Modify Program FindMode so that its run ends when the user types in a sentinel value.

CHA 9.2.3 Modify Program FindMode so that it finds the number that appears least often in the sequence (excluding numbers that don't appear at all). Can you make this modification in such a way that, for some runs, the new program does less work than the old program would do?

CHA 9.2.4 Modify Program FindMode so that it handles lists of numbers that are bimodal. A list is *bimodal* if there are two numbers that each occur most often in the list. For instance the list

1 1 2 2 2 2 3 5 5 5 5 6 6

is bimodal because the numbers 2 and 5 occur four times each. The numbers 2 and 5 are both called the *modes* of the list.

CHA 9.2.5 Modify Program FindMode so that it finds the number that appears most often in the sequence and the number that appears next-to-most often.

Programs and Subprograms to Write

WRI 9.2.1   Write a program whose input looks like this:

```
95  A
88  A
88  A
73  C
84  B
84  B
84  B
87  B
51  E
```

Each line of input contains an exam score followed by the corresponding letter grade. Notice that the grades are "curved" so that the program has no way of matching up letter grades with scores unless it reads this input. The program should report the letter grade that appears most often, the exam score that appears most often, the letter grade that corresponds to the score that appears most often, and the average of the exam scores. And what about an "average" letter grade? An A counts as 4.0, a B counts as 3.0, etc. Then if the "average" of all the letters is 3.50 or greater we'll call this an "average letter grade" of A. Similarly, an average between 2.50 and 3.50 makes an "average letter grade" of B, etc.

Things to Think About

THI 9.2.1   In Designing a Program to find the mode we imagined that we'd use our scratch pad to keep track of only a few numbers at once. What if we lift this restriction and decide that it's all right to copy down every number that the other person gives us? Does that change the algorithm we can use to find the mode? In Chapter 10 we'll see algorithms in which we deal with large collections of values.

9.3

Binary Numbers

There are many ways to represent whole numbers. Here's the **decimal representation** of the number one hundred five:

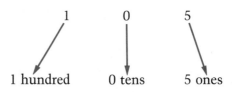

The decimal representation of one hundred five has three digits: 1, 0, and 5. They go in the hundreds column, the tens column, and the ones column.

Now here's what's going on mathematically in this decimal representation:

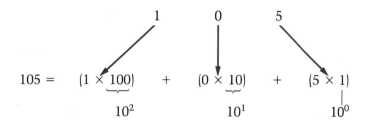

$$105 = (1 \times 100) + (0 \times 10) + (5 \times 1)$$
$$\; 10^2 \qquad\qquad 10^1 \qquad\qquad 10^0$$

Each digit gets multiplied by a power of ten, because a "hundred" is 10^2, a "ten" is 10^1, and a "one" is 10^0.

Now here's the **binary representation** of one hundred five:

$$105 = (1 \times 64) + (1 \times 32) + (0 \times 16) + (1 \times 8) + (0 \times 4) + (0 \times 2) + (1 \times 1)$$
$$2^6 \qquad 2^5 \qquad 2^4 \qquad 2^3 \qquad 2^2 \qquad 2^1 \qquad 2^0$$

The binary representation of one hundred five has seven **bits**. Each bit is either a 1 or a 0. The bits go in the sixty-fours column, the thirty-twos column, the sixteens column, etc. In the binary representation of a number, the columns are powers of two instead of powers of ten.

how to find a binary representation

Now let's say we're given a decimal number, like 105. Here's how we find its binary representation:

- *First iteration:*

  $1 = 105 \text{ DIV } 64$ So 64 "goes once" into 105.

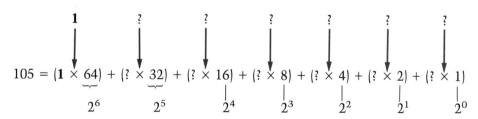

$$105 = (1 \times 64) + (? \times 32) + (? \times 16) + (? \times 8) + (? \times 4) + (? \times 2) + (? \times 1)$$
$$2^6 \qquad 2^5 \qquad 2^4 \qquad 2^3 \qquad 2^2 \qquad 2^1 \qquad 2^0$$

$41 = 105 - 64$ We've accounted for 64 of the original 105 with the leftmost 1 bit. The rest of the bits have to represent the 41 that remains. (Notice that $105 \text{ MOD } 64$ is also 41. We could have used MOD instead of subtraction.)

$32 = 64 \text{ DIV } 2$ So now we'll think about what goes in the 32's column.

- *Next iteration:*

$1 = 41$ `DIV` 32 So 32 "goes once" into 41.

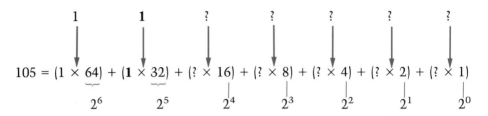

$9 = 41 - 32$ We've accounted for 32 more of the original 105. The rest of the bits have to represent the 9 that remains. (Notice that 41 `MOD` 32 is also 9. We could have used `MOD` instead of subtraction.)

$16 = 32$ `DIV` 2 So now we'll think about what goes in the 16's column.

- *Next iteration:*

$0 = 9$ `DIV` 16 So there are no 16's in 9.

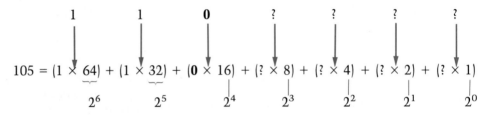

This 0 bit doesn't account for anything, so don't subtract 16 from 9. The rest of the bits have to represent the 9 that remains. (Notice that 9 `MOD` 16 is still 9. Once again `MOD` would give us the correct result!)

$8 = 16$ `DIV` 2 So now we'll think about what goes in the 8's column.

.
.

(Finish it! It'll help you understand how it works!)
Now we have our work cut out for us.

Specifications Input: A `decimal` number

Output: The binary equivalent of the `decimal` number

Designing a Program Look once more at the example we just went through. We performed a few iterations of four separate steps:

```
1)    1 = 105 DIV 64
2) Make the first bit be 1
3) 41 = 105 MOD 64
4) 32 =   64 DIV  2
```

```
1)   1 =  41 DIV 32
2) Make the next bit be 1
3)   9 =  41 MOD 32
4) 16 =  32 DIV  2
1)   0 =   9 DIV 16
2) Make the next bit be 0
         .
         .
         .
Etc.
```

Now we won't always be using these particular numbers 105, 64, etc. In our Pascal code we'll need to refer to variables that can store numbers like these. So let's make up variable names for some of the numbers in the first iteration:

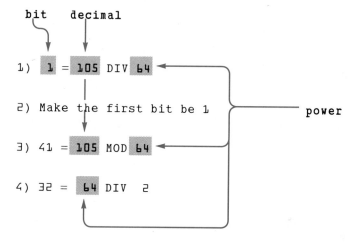

This gives us

```
bit = decimal DIV power;
Write (bit:1);
41  = decimal MOD power;
32  = power DIV 2
```

And what about the remaining numbers 41 and 32?

- 41 gets used as the decimal value in the second iteration
- 32 gets used as the power value in the second iteration

So let's set it up that way in our code:

```
bit      := decimal DIV power;
Write (bit:1);
decimal := decimal MOD power;
power    := power DIV 2
```

This, then, is the code that gets iterated in a loop.

Program
Example

```pascal
PROGRAM BinaryTest (input, output);
{Test driver for Procedure WriteBinary.}
  TYPE
    natural = 0..MAXINT;
  VAR
    decimal, nBits : natural;
    count          : 1..8;

  {----------}

  FUNCTION IntegerExp (base : INTEGER; exponent : natural) : INTEGER;
  {Raises the 'base' to the 'exponent' power.}
    VAR
      pow, i : INTEGER;
  BEGIN {IntegerExp}
    pow := 1;
    FOR i := 1 TO exponent DO
      pow := base * pow;
    IntegerExp := pow
  END;  {IntegerExp}

  {----------}

  PROCEDURE WriteBinary (decimal, nBits : natural);
  {Using nBits-many bits, writes the binary
   equivalent of the 'decimal' number.}

    VAR
      power : natural;
      bit   : 0..1;

  BEGIN {WriteBinary}
    power := IntegerExp (2, nBits) DIV 2;
    WHILE power > 0  DO
      BEGIN
        bit     := decimal DIV power;
        Write (bit:1);
        decimal := decimal MOD power;
        power   := power DIV 2
      END
  END;  {WriteBinary}

  {----------}

BEGIN {BinaryTest}
  FOR count := 1 TO 8 DO
    BEGIN
      Write  ('Decimal number:     ');
      ReadLn (decimal);
      Write  ('How many bits?:     ');
      ReadLn (nBits);
      Write  ('Binary equivalent: ');

      WriteBinary (decimal, nBits);
      WriteLn;
      WriteLn
    END
END.  {BinaryTest}
```

**Sample
Runs**

```
Decimal number:     0
How many bits?:     1
Binary equivalent:  0

Decimal number:     1
How many bits?:     1
Binary equivalent:  1

Decimal number:     1
How many bits?:     3
Binary equivalent:  001

Decimal number:     2
How many bits?:     2
Binary equivalent:  10

Decimal number:     3
How many bits?:     2
Binary equivalent:  11

Decimal number:     105
How many bits?:     7
Binary equivalent:  1101001

Decimal number:     1024
How many bits?:     11
Binary equivalent:  10000000000

Decimal number:     32767
How many bits?:     25
Binary equivalent:  0000000000111111111111111
```

Observations Look back at the beginning of this section, where we computed the binary representation of 105. You'll see that 64 was the first number we "DIVed" into 105. But in that discussion, we never said where the number 64 came from. We actually got it by plugging 7 into the formula

$$2^{\text{number-of-bits-required}} \text{ DIV } 2$$

So in the program, before we start the first iteration, we have to find the value of

$$2^{\text{nBits}} \text{ DIV } 2$$

To find 2^{nBits} we call Function IntegerExp:

```
power := IntegerExp (2, nBits) DIV 2
```

Function IntegerExp has two formal parameters, base and exponent. It takes base to the exponent power. That is, it multiplies the base by itself exponent-many times.

Structure How much time does Procedure WriteBinary take to run? The procedure's WHILE loop writes one bit during each iteration. We can say that the running time of Procedure WriteBinary is O(n), where n is the number of bits that will be written. This is important information. We'll make use of it when we look at the next program example.

9.3   Exercises

Key Words to Review

decimal representation   binary representation   bit

Questions to Answer

QUE 9.3.1   Give the binary representation of each of the following decimal numbers:
a. 42   b. 0   c. 64   d. 15

QUE 9.3.2   Give the decimal representation of each of the following binary numbers:
a. 101010   b. 111

QUE 9.3.3   What happens to a number's binary representation when you multiply the number by 2?

QUE 9.3.4   Explain why the binary number system, which is based on powers of 2 rather than powers of 10, needs only two bits (0 and 1) for representing numbers.

QUE 9.3.5   Are there any positive integers that can be represented using decimal notation, but can't be represented using binary notation? Why, or why not?

Experiments to Try

EXP 9.3.1   Modify Program WriteBinary so that it writes the binary values of Ord ('A') and Ord ('a'). Does this tell you anything about the reasoning behind the codes used in the ASCII Character Set?

EXP 9.3.2   Run Program BinaryTest with the input

```
Decimal number:    2
How many bits?:    1
```

EXP 9.3.3   Run Program BinaryTest with the input

```
Decimal number:    -2
```

Changes to Make

CHA 9.3.1   Modify Procedure WriteBinary so it writes the *one's complement* of the number it receives. In the one's complement representation all the 0's in a binary representation are changed to 1's and vice versa.

CHA 9.3.2   To find the 8-bit *two's complement* of a number, subtract the number from 2^8 and find the binary representation of the result. Modify Procedure WriteBinary so it writes the two's complement of the number it receives.

CHA 9.3.3   Modify Procedure WriteBinary so that it writes the *octal* representation of the number it receives. The octal numbering system uses the eight digits 0 through 7. The octal representation of the number one hundred five is 151 because:

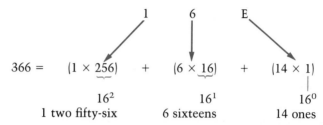

$$105 = (1 \times 64) + (5 \times 8) + (1 \times 1)$$

$$8^2 \qquad\qquad 8^1 \qquad\qquad 8^0$$

1 sixty-four   5 eights   1 one

CHA 9.3.4 Modify Procedure `WriteBinary` so that it writes the hexadecimal representation of the number it receives. The hexadecimal numbering system uses the sixteen digits 0, 1, 2, 3, 4, 5, 6, 7, 8, 9, A, B, C, D, E, and F. The letters A through F stand for the values ten through fifteen. The hexadecimal representation of the number three hundred sixty-six is `16E` because:

$$366 = (1 \times 256) + (6 \times 16) + (14 \times 1)$$

$$16^2 \qquad\qquad 16^1 \qquad\qquad 16^0$$

1 two fifty-six   6 sixteens   14 ones

CHA 9.3.5 Modify Procedure `WriteBinary` so that it writes the *left shift* of the number that's given to it. When you left shift a number, you move each of its bits to the left by one position. In so doing, the leftmost bit gets eliminated ("pushed off the edge") and a 0 enters as the rightmost bit. For example:

```
Decimal number:    105
How many bits?:    7
Binary equivalent: 1101001
Left shift:        1010010
```

CHA 9.3.6 Modify Procedure `WriteBinary` so that it accepts two numbers and writes the *bitwise* `AND` of the two numbers. When you combine two binary numbers with the bitwise `AND`, you get 1 in the positions where both the first number and the second number have a 1. You get 0 in all the other positions.

CHA 9.3.7 Modify Program `BinaryTest` to include code that computes the number of bits needed in the binary representation of the `decimal` number. This new version of the program doesn't need to prompt the user for a value of `nBits`.

Scales to Practice

PRA 9.3.1 Use `MOD` to write a function subprogram that accepts an `INTEGER` between 1 and 10 and returns the integer plus 1, if the integer isn't 10, and 1, if the integer is 10.

PRA 9.3.2 Look again at Program `WriteLnDemo` in Section 3.6. With the techniques illustrated in that program, create a procedure that writes any `INTEGER` using the minimum possible number of places on the screen.

Programs and Subprograms to Write

WRI 9.3.1   When we *fold* a decimal number we add some of the number's digits to its other digits. For instance, if we fold 2391 in half we get 23 + 91, which equals 114. Write and test a function that folds four-digit numbers in half. (Note: Folding is actually good for something! You'll see folding again when you learn about *hashing* in a later course.)

WRI 9.3.2   *(A memory page problem)* A computer's memory is divided into many *bytes*. Roughly speaking, a byte's worth of memory can hold one character, such as the letter a. These bytes are grouped together into *pages*.

For instance, our computer's memory may be divided into ten pages, each page having 1024 bytes. Within each page, the bytes will typically be numbered 0 to 1023, and the pages themselves will be numbered 0 to 9.

Taking all these pages together, the computer memory has 10240 (= 10 times 1024) bytes for storing information. The bytes can be numbered 0 through 10239.

Now let's say that the information that you need is located in byte number 2222. Write a program that tells us what page it's on and what number byte it is in within that page.

9.4

An Exponential Example

In Section 8.1, we made truth tables for AND, OR, and NOT. Here's a truth table for (a AND b) OR (NOT c):

a	b	c	!	(a AND b)	(NOT c)	(a AND b) OR (NOT c)
T	T	T	!	T	F	T
T	T	F	!	T	T	T
T	F	T	!	F	F	F
T	F	F	!	F	T	T
F	T	T	!	F	F	F
F	T	F	!	F	T	T
F	F	T	!	F	F	F
F	F	F	!	F	T	T

left side
of the
truth table

To make the table easier to read, we've used the letters T and F instead of the words TRUE and FALSE.

Since (a AND b) OR (NOT c) has three variables in it, the truth table has eight rows. This is because there are eight different ways to assign TRUE or FALSE to each of three variables. The left side of the truth table lists all eight ways.

Specifications   Input: A number `nBoolVars`—the number of BOOLEAN variables

Output: The left side of a truth table with `nBoolVars`-many BOOLEAN variables

Designing a Program   What we really want is to read a number like 3 and then figure out all the ways `TRUE` and `FALSE` (or T and F) can be written three in a row. Here's one thing we could try:

the connection between truth tables and binary numbers

```
FOR i := FALSE TO TRUE DO
   FOR j := FALSE TO TRUE DO
      FOR k := FALSE TO TRUE DO
         Write (i, j, k)
```

The problem with this approach is that we need a different number of nested FORs for each value of `nBoolVars`. The pseudocode

Read `nBoolVars`
Execute `nBoolVars`-many nested FOR statements.

is difficult to implement in Pascal.

But look at the binary representations of the numbers 0 to 7:

Decimal numbers	Binary numbers (0's and 1's)	BOOLEAN values (F's and T's)		
7	111	T	T	T
6	110	T	T	F
5	101	T	F	T
4 ⟶	100 ⟶	T	F	F
3	011	F	T	T
2	010	F	T	F
1	001	F	F	T
0	000	F	F	F

Each binary representation is a way of writing 1's and 0's three in a row. So if we change 1's to Ts and 0's to Fs we get the left side of a truth table.

Now how did we know to start with the number 7 and work our way down to 0? Here's a chart to show what's going on:

If nBoolVars is	we go from
1	1
2	3
3	7
4	15
	down to 0

.

.

Etc.

But where do the numbers in the right half of the chart come from?

If nBoolVars is	we go from	
1	1	$= 2^1 - 1$
2	3	$= 2^2 - 1$
3	7	$= 2^3 - 1$
4	15	$= 2^4 - 1$
	down to 0	

.

.

Etc.

If we want a truth table with three BOOLEAN variables, we just find $2^3 - 1$. In other words,

```
topRow := IntegerExp (2, nBoolVars) - 1
```

and

```
CONST
  bottomRow = 0;
```

And while we're examining the chart, let's take note of something that will be useful later on. When we write the numbers from 7 down to 0, we actually write eight numbers.

If nBoolVars is	we go from		This gives us a truth table with
1	1	$= 2^1 - 1$	2
2	3	$= 2^2 - 1$	4
3	7	$\mathbf{= 2^3 - 1}$	**8**
4	15	$= 2^4 - 1$	16
	down to 0		**rows**

.

.

Etc.

Here's another way to say the same thing: When we write the numbers $2^3 - 1$ down to 0, we actually write 2^3 numbers.

The program follows.

Program Example

```
PROGRAM TruthTable (input, output);
{Writes all possible combinations of nBoolVars-many T's and F's.}
  CONST
    bottomRow = 0;
  TYPE
    natural = 0..MAXINT;
  VAR
    start, topRow, decimal, nBoolVars : natural;
  {----------}

  FUNCTION IntegerExp (base : INTEGER; exponent : natural) : INTEGER;
  {Same as in Program BinaryTest, Section 9.3.}
  {----------}

  PROCEDURE WriteBinary (decimal, nBits : natural);
  {Same as in Program BinaryTest, Section 9.3, except here it writes
   'F' instead of 0; 'T' instead of 1}
  {----------}

BEGIN {TruthTable}
  Write  ('How many boolean variables?: ');
  ReadLn (nBoolVars);
  WriteLn;
  topRow := IntegerExp (2, nBoolVars) - 1;

  FOR decimal := topRow DOWNTO bottomRow DO
    BEGIN
      WriteBinary (decimal, nBoolVars);
      WriteLn
    END
END.   {TruthTable}
```

Sample Runs

```
How many boolean variables?: 3
     T   T   T
     T   T   F
     T   F   T
     T   F   F
     F   T   T
     F   T   F
     F   F   T
     F   F   F
```

Structure

How much time does Program `TruthTable` take to run? Each time the `FOR` loop in the main body is iterated, it calls Procedure `WriteBinary`. So the time required for Program `TruthTable` to run is

number of `FOR` loop iterations   multiplied by   time required for each call to Procedure `WriteBinary`

Let's think about each of these quantities separately:

- number of `FOR` loop iterations

  Remember what we said when we were doing the design of Program `TruthTable`. To write all combinations of three `BOOLEAN` values, we go from 7 down to 0, which is a total of eight combinations. We get the number 8 by finding 2^3. In other words

  number of `FOR` loop iterations $= 2^{\text{nBoolVars}}$

- time required for each call to Procedure `WriteBinary`

  We figured this out in Section 9.3. It's $O(n)$. In Section 9.3, n was the number of bits that would be written. In this section, it's the number of `BOOLEAN` variables whose values will be written. In other words

  time required for each call to Procedure `WriteBinary` $= \text{nBoolVars}$

Now putting this all together, we get: The time required for Program `TruthTable` to run is

number of `FOR` loop iterations   multiplied by   time required for each call to Procedure `WriteBinary`

which equals

$2^{\text{nBoolVars}}$ multiplied by nBoolVars

In other words, the time required for Program `TruthTable` to run is

$O(2^n n)$

which is pronounced "order 2^n times n," "big 'O' of 2^n times n," "complexity 2^n times n," or just "exponential."[2]

Notice that in computing the complexity of Program `TruthTable` we've ignored all but the `FOR`-loop and `WHILE`-loop parts of the program. The only reason we can do this is because the other parts of the program make negligible contributions to the amount of time the program takes to run. This happens because $O(2^n n)$ time is so large compared with $O(1)$, $O(n)$, and $O(n^2)$. To see this, let's enlarge the chart we made in Section 6.4. Recall that we had three programs, called `Constant`, `Linear`, and `Quadratic`, that ran in $O(1)$, $O(n)$, and $O(n^2)$ times, respectively. To this group we'll add a new program, called Program `Exponential`, that takes $O(2^n n)$ time. Let's assume that Program `Exponential` always takes $2^n n$ seconds to run, where n is some value that differs from one run to the next. Here's the chart for the running times of the four programs:

	Running time (in seconds) of Programs			
n	Constant	Linear	Quadratic	Exponential
1	1	1	1	2
2	1	2	4	8
3	1	3	9	24
4	1	4	16	64
5	1	5	25	160
6	1	6	36	384
7	1	7	49	896
8	1	8	64	2048
9	1	9	81	4608
10	1	10	100	10240

An exponential program (or an exponential part of a program) takes much more time to run than an $O(1)$, $O(n)$, or $O(n^2)$ program.

Programming Style
In computer science, the **problem domain** (or **application domain**) is the field of endeavor from which we derive our particular problem. In Program `Trucking` (Section 3.8), we derived a problem ("print a table showing mileage versus profit") from the *business* problem domain. In this section, we've derived the problem ("print the left side of a truth table") from a problem domain called *logic*.

As programmers, we have to be aware of the rules and conventions in each problem domain. We must take care to respect these rules and conventions when we write our programs. For example, in Program

---

[2]Strictly speaking, the word "exponential" refers to programs of order 2^n.

Trucking we printed the profit with two digits to the right of the decimal point, because money comes in units of one-hundredth of a dollar.

In the logic problem domain, it's not uncommon to associate 0's and 1's with the values FALSE and TRUE, but 0 is always associated with FALSE and 1 with TRUE. The left side of a truth table commonly starts with a row of TRUEs and ends with a row of FALSEs:

```
T   T   T
T   T   F
        .
        .
        .
F   F   F
```

So in order to follow the conventions in the problem domain, Program TruthTable needs to write numbers from binary 111 down to binary 000. That's why the main program's FOR loop is a DOWNTO loop.[3]

Of course, as a programmer, you can't know everything about every problem domain. That's why you have to study the problem carefully and make sure that the user has given you all the information you need. The user will often assume that you understand the problem domain's unwritten rules; and it's up to you, the programmer, to make sure that you do. You must search through the problem to find any points of uncertainty and ask the user for clarification on any parts of the specifications that are unclear.

9.4   Exercises

Key Words to Review

exponential time   problem domain   application domain

Questions to Answer

QUE 9.4.1   Explain the following claim: The problem of writing the left side of a truth table is the same as the problem of writing all binary numbers from a certain number down to zero.

QUE 9.4.2   Describe a scenario in which we have an exponential-time program and a linear-time program, and the linear time program actually takes longer (by ordinary clock time) to run.

Experiments to Try

EXP 9.4.1   Run Program TruthTable several times with various values of nBoolVars. Is it true that the amount of time the program takes to run is proportional to $2^{\text{nBoolVars}}$nBoolVars? For hints on performing this experiment, see Exercise Exp. 6.4.1.

---

[3]Each of our truth tables in Section 8.1 started with a row of FALSEs and ended with a row of TRUEs. We violated the conventions of the logic problem domain in order to simplify the introduction of the type BOOLEAN.

Changes to Make

CHA 9.4.1   Modify Procedure WriteBinary so that it writes Fs and Ts instead of 0's and 1's.

CHA 9.4.2   Modify Program TruthTable so that its output includes the horizontal and vertical lines that one normally sees on a truth table.

CHA 9.4.3   If x and y are BOOLEAN variables, and x and y are both FALSE, then the expression x = y is TRUE (because x and y have the same value). Now let z be another BOOLEAN variable with the value FALSE. At first you might guess that since x, y, and z all have the same value, the expression (x = y) = z is TRUE. But it's not! (Why not?)

Modify Program TruthTable so that it makes a truth table for the "equal signs" expression that has nBoolVars-many BOOLEAN variables.

Programs and Subprograms to Write

WRI 9.4.1   When we write a number with our usual decimal representation, we say that the *base* (or the *radix*) for the representation is 10. When we use the binary representation, we say we're using base 2. Now look back at the work you did for Exercise Cha.9.3.3. In that exercise, the base of the representation was 8.

Write a program that reads values, from 2 to 10, for baseIn and baseOut. Then it reads a number in the baseIn representation and writes the same number in the baseOut representation.

WRI 9.4.2   Write a program that reads a number n and writes all *subsets* of the set {0, 1, 2, 3, . . ., n−1}. For instance, if n is 3, then the program writes

```
{}    { 0}    { 1}    { 1, 0}    { 2}    { 2, 0}    { 2, 1}
{ 2, 1, 0}
```

To find out what it means to be a subset, see Section 12.7.

9.5

A Pseudorandom Number Generator

Many problems in computer science and a huge collection of problems from "real life" involve the use of **random** numbers. A program that plays chess may generate numbers randomly in order to determine its next move. A program that simulates the servicing of customers at a bank might make a random guess about the number of customers who will arrive at the bank in the next three hours.

So a function subprogram that returns a "random number" is a very useful thing to have. But what's a "random number"? And what do we do to get one? Answers to these questions aren't easy. Let's start with some formal specs.

Specifications

Input: Function Random has one formal parameter—an INTEGER called seed.

Output: The result-value of Function Random is a REAL number between 0.0 and 1.0. When the function is called over and over again, these result-values tend to be uniformly distributed over the range 0.0 to 1.0, without being distributed in any easily observable pattern.

In addition, Function Random modifies the value of the seed (so we'll make seed be a VAR parameter).

random versus pseudorandom

There's one sentence in the specs that's a real mouthful: ". . . uniformly distributed over the range 0.0 and 1.0, without being distributed in any easily observable pattern." It would take quite a bit of mathematical equipment to make this sentence more precise. We won't attempt it here. Instead we'll give a warning about something the specs don't say.

The specs don't say that the values produced by calls to Function Random are independent of one another. This means that the values produced by one call to Function Random depend on the values produced by the previous call. This isn't quite the same as tossing a coin. When you toss a coin two times the result you get on the second toss has nothing to do with the result you got on the first toss. Coin tosses are independent of one another; calls to Function Random are not.

Since the values generated by successive calls to our function are not independent, we won't say that they're being generated "randomly." Instead we'll say we're generating a **pseudorandom** sequence of numbers. Because of its long history, Function Random violates certain rules of programming style. It goes by the misleading name Random instead of the more appropriate name Pseudorandom. It's also a function with a VAR parameter! But as part of this long history, Function Random and other functions like it have undergone an enormous amount of study and fine-tuning. The version we present here is the result of years of careful investigation by many researchers.

Program Example

```
PROGRAM DisplayRandom (input, output);
{Displays several numbers in a pseudorandom sequence.
 Runs correctly if MAXINT is 2147483647 (= 2 to the 31st power - 1) or
 larger -- When running under Turbo Pascal, change INTEGER to LONGINT.}
  CONST
    numsPerPage = 5;
  VAR
    seed                            : INTEGER;
    numCount, pageCount, pageLimit : INTEGER;

  {----------}
```

```
FUNCTION Random (VAR seed : INTEGER) : REAL;
{Pseudorandom number generator.
 Adapted (with some stylistic modifications) from the paper
 "Random Number Generators: Good ones are hard to find",
 (S. Park and K. Miller, Communications of the Association
 for Computing Machinery, Vol. 31, No. 10, October 1988)
 and from subsequent work by the same two authors.}
    CONST
      a = 48271;
      m = 2147483647;
      q = 44488;        {= m DIV a}
      r = 3399;         {= m MOD a}
    VAR
      lo, hi, test : INTEGER;
  BEGIN {Random}
    hi   := seed DIV q;
    lo   := seed MOD q;
    test := a * lo - r * hi;
    IF test > 0 THEN
      seed := test
    ELSE
      seed := test + m;
    Random := seed / m
  END;  {Random}

  {----------}
BEGIN {DisplayRandom}
  Write  ('How many pages?            ');
  ReadLn (pageLimit);
  Write  ('Starting value for the seed: ');
  ReadLn (seed);

  FOR pageCount := 1 TO pageLimit DO
    BEGIN
      Write ('Hit <return> to see ', numsPerPage:2, ' numbers... ');
      ReadLn;
      FOR numCount := 1 TO numsPerPage DO
        WriteLn ( Random(seed) : 9:7 );
      WriteLn
    END
END.   {DisplayRandom}
```

Sample Runs

Running Program `DisplayRandom` on a VAX 6310 with VMS version 5.3:

```
How many pages?            4
Starting value for the seed: 2014083620
Hit <return> to see  5 numbers...
0.4427294
0.9883826
0.2141361
0.5646501
0.2224590
```

```
Hit <return> to see  5 numbers...
0.3167565
0.1517116
0.2696532
0.4304633
0.8911584
Hit <return> to see  5 numbers...
0.1077134
0.4322487
0.0792525
0.5988271
0.9836267
Hit <return> to see  5 numbers...
0.6466160
0.8010284
0.4427105
0.0782060
0.0802054
```

Observations

calling Function Random

Notice how Function `Random` is used:

- First the user is asked to supply an initial value for `seed`. Any positive integer value will do. The first call to Function `Random` uses this seed to produce the function's result-value—a "random number" between 0.0 and 1.0—and a new value for `seed`.

- The second call to Function `Random` takes the value of `seed` produced by the first call, and produces another result-value between 0.0 and 1.0 and another value for `seed`.

- The third call to Function `Random` takes the value of `seed` produced by the second call, etc.

If need be, the initial value of `seed` can come from some anonymous source, like the computer system's internal clock, rather than the user. In any case the initial value of `seed` determines all the values produced by subsequent calls to Function `Random`. If we run Program `DisplayRandom` twice, giving it the same initial value for `seed` each time, then the two runs will produce exactly the same sequence of "random" numbers. This makes a convincing argument for the use of the term pseudorandom. The pseudo prefix makes it sound as if our code is somehow less than adequate. But in many applications the predictable behavior of Function `Random` is an advantage. There are many problems in computer science and in other fields in which it's necessary to produce the same sequence of "random" numbers more than once.

- ```
  {Displays several numbers in a pseudorandom sequence.
     Runs correctly if MAXINT is 2147483647
     (= 2 to the 31st power - 1) or
     larger -- When running under Turbo
     Pascal, change INTEGER to LONGINT.}
  ```
  ```

portability

With pseudorandom number generators like Function Random, portability is a serious issue. Our subprogram doesn't work if an implementation's MAXINT is too small. We can change the function so that it works for implementations with smaller values of MAXINT (see Exercise Exp.9.5.1), but then there will *still* be some implementations on which the function doesn't run correctly. This difficulty with portability is one that we can never entirely avoid.

• Write ('Hit <return> to see ', numsPerPage:2, ' numbers... ');
  ReadLn;

ReadLn
without
parameters

Here's a useful trick. Remember how, in Section 2.2, we said that when the computer executes a ReadLn ". . . the user is expected to press the 'return' key. The computer will not resume execution of the program until the user presses this key." So when the computer executes a ReadLn with no parameter list, it doesn't read any *values* from the keyboard—it just waits for the user to hit the return key. This can be used to put a pause in the program. The user gets a chance to stare at one screenful of output before it gets replaced by the next screenful.

Further Discussion

You may notice that we haven't explained any of the calculations done in the body of Function Random. That's because the technical details are beyond the scope of this text. As far as we're concerned Function Random is a black box. But there's one thing we should call to your attention: The algorithm implemented by Function Random depends heavily on an area of mathematics known as *Number Theory*. In particular, the notion of a *prime number* (see Exercises Wri.9.5.5, Wri.9.5.6, and Wri.10.2.4) plays an important role. This is a good example of a highly theoretical study that has very far-reaching practical implications.

Testing and Debugging

testing a
pseudorandom
number
generator

How would you test a subprogram like Function Random? All you can discover by staring at a sample run is that the numbers don't appear to be distributed in any simple pattern. Clearly you need to search the literature for some appropriate mathematical tools. If you do, you'll probably find something called the Chi-square test. Once again, we'll bypass the mathematical details in favor of the moral lessons. In this case the lessons are as follows:

1. We can't check the correctness of Function Random by comparing its output with the "right answers." In this problem, there isn't one special set of "right answers." The Chi-square test doesn't compare the output of Function Random against another sequence of numbers. Instead it analyzes Function Random's sequence to see if the numbers tend to cluster into one place or another between 0.0 and 1.0. This is clearly different from most of our other testing situations, in which we match up a program's results with the results we get from hand calculations, deductive reasoning, etc.

2. The Chi-square test isn't a short calculation. When we actually perform the test, we'll probably do it with a computer program. This means that when the test is completed we'll still be one level removed from the answer. That is, we'll still need to convince ourselves that the program that performs the Chi-square test is correct and that the data from Function Random have been fed to it correctly. This is typical of many complex testing situations. For many real-life problems, we can determine the correctness of a program only with a long series of tests. As the testing process progresses, we evaluate each of the tests individually. But when the testing process is complete, we must also examine the entire chain of tests to make sure that the sheer length of the process hasn't introduced any subtle errors of its own.

9.5   Exercises

Key Words to Review

random   pseudorandom   Chi-square test

Questions to Answer

QUE 9.5.1   What's the difference between *random* and *pseudorandom*?

QUE 9.5.2   Explain why the statement ReadLn (seed) is executed only once during a run of Program DisplayRandom.

QUE 9.5.3   Each time Function Random is called it modifies the value of the variable seed. Explain what happens if, during a run of Program DisplayRandom, the value of seed returns to the value originally entered by the user.

QUE 9.5.4   We named this section's program DisplayRandom. Why didn't we name it TestRandom?

Experiments to Try

EXP 9.5.1   Does Function Random seem to work correctly on your implementation? Does it work if you change INTEGER to some other INTEGER-like type? (Turbo Pascal users—see the program's prologue comment. Other users—see Exercise Man.8.7.1.) If not, try the following variation:

```
FUNCTION Random (VAR seed : REAL) : REAL;
{Another pseudorandom number generator.
 Adapted (with some stylistic modifications) from the paper
 "Random Number Generators: Good ones are hard to find",
 (S. Park and K. Miller, Communications of the Association
 for Computing Machinery, Vol. 31, No. 10, October 1988)
 and from subsequent work by the same two authors.}
```

```
CONST
   a = 48271.0;
   m = 2147483647.0;
   q = 44488.0;          {= m DIV a}
   r = 3399.0;           {= m MOD a}
VAR
   lo, hi, test : REAL;
BEGIN {Random}
   hi   := Trunc (seed / q);
   lo   := seed - q * hi;
   test := a * lo - r * hi;
   IF test > 0.0 THEN
      seed := test
   ELSE
      seed := test + m;
   Random := seed / m
END;  {Random}
```

This version of Function Random implements the same algorithm as our earlier version. There are only two differences:

- Some implementations can't run the earlier version because their value of MAXINT isn't large enough. This version tries using REAL variables instead of INTEGER variables.

- Since DIV and MOD can't be used on REAL variables, a few arithmetic operations had to be changed. The new version uses the REAL-type equivalents of DIV and MOD.

EXP 9.5.2   Think of all numbers less than a half as meaning "the coin flip gave us heads" and all numbers bigger than or equal to one half as meaning "the coin flip gave us tails." Then modify Program DisplayRand so that, as it calls Function Random several times, it counts the number of heads and the number of tails. Are there equally as many heads as tails?

Do the counts get closer to half heads and half tails when you increase the number of pages produced by Program DisplayRandom?

EXP 9.5.3   Change the experiment you did in Exercise Exp.9.5.2 so that you're flipping an imaginary "three-sided coin" (heads, tails, and *feet*??).

EXP 9.5.4   Devise an experiment to find out how many times Function Random needs to be called before the seed assumes the value that it started with.

Changes to Make

CHA 9.5.1   Function Random always gives you a REAL number between 0.0 and 1.0. How can you call Function Random if you want a REAL number between 0.0 and 10.0? An INTEGER between 1 and 10? A REAL number between 5.0 and 10.0?

Programs and Subprograms to Write

WRI 9.5.1   If there's a lottery in your home state, find out what its rules are. If not, use these (simple) rules: The player chooses a five-digit number, and the computer (using Function Random) creates another five-digit number. If the two numbers have fewer than three digits in common

```
Player:    07940
Computer:  87049

2 digits in common
```

then the player loses a dollar (the cost of the lottery ticket). If the two numbers have three digits in common, then the player wins $100. With four digits in common, the player wins $1,000. With five digits in common, the player wins $10,000.

Write a program that plays the lottery with the user. As it plays, it keeps track of how much the user has lost and/or won. (Warning: This game may get boring! You may want to add an amount the player wins if the two numbers have only one digit in common.)

WRI 9.5.2   (A continuation of Exercise Wri.9.5.1) Write a lottery program that simulates the actions of both the computer and the player and thus determines a typical player's earnings after many years of playing the lottery.

WRI 9.5.3   Write a program that plays the paper-scissors-stone game ten times with the user. The program decides which kind of hand to make by calling Function Random.

WRI 9.5.4   Modify the program you wrote for Exercise Wri.5.4.3 so that the numbers being rolled are generated ramdomly by the program (and reported in the program's output). Remember: There are more ways to roll a 7(1 +6, 2 + 5, 3 + 4) than there are to roll a 2 (1 + 1), so not all numbers from 2 to 12 are equally likely to be rolled!

WRI 9.5.5   A positive integer is called a *prime* number if it's evenly divisible only by itself and by 1. All other numbers are called *composite* numbers. For instance, the number 7 is prime, because 1 and 7 divide evenly into 7, but 2, 3, 4, 5, and 6 don't divide evenly into 7. The number 6 is composite, because 2 divides evenly into 6 (and so does 3). Write and test a function subprogram that accepts a positive integer, and returns 0 if the integer is composite and 1 if the integer is prime. (*Hint:* To see if a number is prime, you only need to try dividing it by all the numbers that are less than or equal to the number's square root.)

WRI 9.5.6   The *greatest common divisor (gcd)* of two positive integers is the largest number that divides evenly into both of them. Here's a way to find the gcd of the numbers 8 and 27:

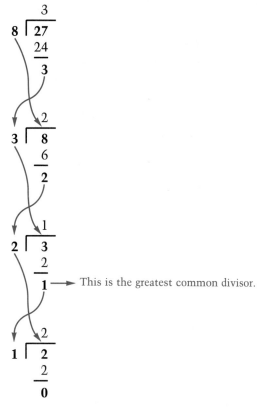

Each time through a loop, you take the remainder and the divisor from the previous iteration and make them the divisor and dividend for the current iteration. You keep doing this as long as the remainder isn't zero. This is called the *Euclidean algorithm.* First get some practice with the Euclidean algorithm by finding the gcd of 8 and 12. (*Hint:* It's 4.) Then write a program that reads two numbers and uses the Euclidean algorithm to find the greatest common divisor.

9.6

Another Look at Object-Oriented Programming (Supplementary)

In Section 3.9 we decomposed the time-amounts problem using *information hiding.* Here's a quick review: First, we find the naturally occurring *classes of data* in the problem. (In the time-amounts problem, we had hours, minutes, and times.) Then for each class of data we create a Turbo Pascal UNIT, which *encapsulates* all details about the data class in its code. It's as if we're hiding a data class's detail inside a unit. The unit's code describes the operations that can be performed on a class of data.

Each Turbo Pascal UNIT has two sections: an INTERFACE section and an IMPLEMENTATION section.

The INTERFACE section describes exactly what we need to know in order to make use of the facilities (operations, etc.) provided by the unit. For instance, the INTERFACE section in the HoursUnit contains the *heading* of Function SumOfHours. In the code of another unit, we'll find the "sum" of two hour-amounts by calling Function SumOfHours, using the heading in this INTERFACE section as a guide.

The IMPLEMENTATION section gives details about the way in which the unit's facilities are implemented. These are details that we don't need to know if we're just making use of the facilities that the unit provides. For example, the IMPLEMENTATION section of HoursUnit contains the entire *body* of Function SumOfHours. If we look inside this body, it becomes clear that hours start at 1, go up to 12, and then back to 1 again. This is the kind of detail that we don't need to know when we call Function SumOfHours. It's a detail about hours that's hidden inside the HoursUnit. If another unit needs to know the "sum" of two hour-amounts it just calls Function SumOfHours, which does the needed calculations and returns an answer of the appropriate type.

Back in Section 3.9 we had only a handful of Pascal features at our disposal. Now that we have a few more features, like type definitions and BOOLEAN-returning functions, we can do a more rigorous example. In this section we'll redo the minimum problem from Section 5.4 using an object-oriented approach. First let's review the specs:

Input: Several values (each of type INTEGER)

Output: The smallest of these values

Designing a Program

First we look for the naturally occurring classes of data in the problem. In this particular problem we're trying to find the smallest of several integer values. So the integer *value* is a data class. We'll have a Turbo Pascal unit to define what we mean by an integer value and to describe the operations that can be performed on such values.

So what operations will we need to perform in this problem? Certainly we'll need to ReadLnValues and WriteLnValues, but we'll also need to compare two values to see if one of them is LessThan the other. And if we find that the value we just read is smaller than the minimum value so far, we'll have to Assign this new value to min. Here's a diagram:

```
valueType
  LessThan
  AssignValue
  ReadLnValue
  WriteLnValue
```

The code follows.

**Program
Example**

```
UNIT ValueU;
{Provides definition of, and operations on, valueType.}
INTERFACE

  TYPE
    valueType = INTEGER;

  FUNCTION  LessThan    (v1, v2    : valueType) : BOOLEAN;
  PROCEDURE AssignValue (VAR v1    : valueType ;
                             v2     : valueType);
  PROCEDURE ReadLnValue (VAR value : valueType);
  PROCEDURE WriteLnvalue (value    : valueType);

IMPLEMENTATION

  FUNCTION LessThan (v1, v2 : valueType) : BOOLEAN;
  {Determines whether valueType variable 'v1'
   is less than valueType variable 'v2'.}
  BEGIN {LessThan}
    LessThan := v1 < v2
  END;   {LessThan}

  {----------}

  PROCEDURE AssignValue  (VAR v1    : valueType ;
                              v2     : valueType);
  {Assigns the value stored in v2 to the variable v1.}
  BEGIN {AssignValue}
    v1 := v2
  END;   {AssignValue}

  {----------}

  PROCEDURE ReadLnValue (VAR value : valueType);
  {Reads a valueType.}
  BEGIN {ReadLnValue}
    ReadLn (value)
  END;   {ReadLnValue}

  {----------}

  PROCEDURE WriteLnValue (value : valueType);
  {Writes a valueType.}
  BEGIN {WriteLnValue}
    WriteLn (value:5)
  END;   {WriteLnValue}

END. {ValueU}
```

```
PROGRAM Minimum (input, output);
{Writes the smallest of the
 values given to it as input.}
  USES ValueU;
  VAR
    min, n : valueType;
BEGIN {Minimum}
  WriteLn ('Enter one or more values.');
  WriteLn ('(Terminate by indicating end-of-file): ');

  ReadLnValue (min);
  WHILE NOT Eof(input) DO
    BEGIN
      ReadLnValue (n);
      IF LessThan (n, min) THEN
        AssignValue (min, n)
    END;
  WriteLn       ('The smallest is ');
  WriteLnValue (min)
END.   {Minimum}
```

**Sample
Runs**

```
Enter one or more values.
(Terminate by indicating end-of-file):
10
-1
5
3
-2
8
The smallest is
  -2
```

Observations Once again we have a main program that does all its work by calling subprograms. In this case the subprograms all come from the ValueUnit. Unlike the units in Section 3.9, this ValueUnit contains a type definition.

```
TYPE
  valueType = INTEGER;
```

This is one more way in which we encapsulate details about the valueType in the ValueUnit. In fact, we have solid evidence to support the claim that all details about the valueType are encapsulated in the ValueUnit. To see the evidence, let's try changing the problem's specs:

Input: Several values, each a letter of the alphabet

Output: The smallest of these values—where our notion of "smallest" is **case-insensitive**; that is, both A and a come before B and b, which in turn come before C and c, etc.

Program
Example

```
UNIT NewValU;
{Provides another definition of, and operations on, valueType.}
INTERFACE
   TYPE
      valueType = CHAR;

   FUNCTION  LessThan      (v1, v2    : valueType) : BOOLEAN;
   PROCEDURE AssignValue   (VAR v1    : valueType ;
                                v2    : valueType);
   PROCEDURE ReadLnValue   (VAR value : valueType);
   PROCEDURE WriteLnvalue  (value     : valueType);
IMPLEMENTATION
   FUNCTION IsUpperCase (letter : valueType) : BOOLEAN;
   {Determines whether a character is an uppercase letter.}
   BEGIN {IsUpperCase}
     IsUpperCase := ('A' <= letter) AND (letter <= 'Z')
   END;  {IsUpperCase}

   {----------}

   FUNCTION LowerCaseEquiv (letter : valueType) : valueType;
   {Accepts a character; returns its lowercase equivalent.}
   BEGIN {LowerCaseEquiv}
     IF IsUpperCase (letter) THEN
       LowerCaseEquiv := Chr (Ord(letter) + (Ord('a') - Ord('A')))
     ELSE
       LowerCaseEquiv := letter
   END;  {LowerCaseEquiv}

   {----------}

   FUNCTION LessThan (v1, v2 : valueType) : BOOLEAN;
   {Determines whether valueType variable 'v1'
    is less than valueType variable 'v2'.}
   BEGIN {LessThan}
     LessThan := LowerCaseEquiv (v1) < LowerCaseEquiv (v2)
   END;  {LessThan}

   {----------}

   PROCEDURE AssignValue  (VAR v1    : valueType ;
                               v2    : valueType);
   {Assigns the value stored in v2 to the variable v1.}
   BEGIN {AssignValue}
     v1 := v2
   END;  {AssignValue}

   {----------}

   PROCEDURE ReadLnValue (VAR value : valueType);
   {Reads a valueType.}
   BEGIN {ReadLnValue}
     ReadLn (value)
   END;  {ReadLnValue}

   {----------}
```

```
PROCEDURE WriteLnValue (value : valueType);
{Writes a valueType.}
BEGIN {WriteLnValue}
  WriteLn (value:5)
END;  {WriteLnValue}

END. {NewValU}
```

Sample Runs

```
Enter one or more values.
(Terminate by indicating end-of-file):
J
e
N
b
U
r
D
The smallest is
    b
```

Observations Now notice what we've done. We've created a new unit to describe the valueType but we haven't written a new main program Minimum. We didn't need to. The only change we needed to make in Program Minimum was to tell the compiler that we'd be using the definitions and declarations provided by the new unit:

```
USES NewValU;
```

Since the main Program Minimum contains no details about valueType we don't need to change the main program's code when we suddenly decide that values should be characters. We make changes only in the unit that describes the valueType. If we decided on some new and unusual way to ReadLnValues or WriteLnValues, these changes would also take place in the unit, not the main program.

Have we really hidden the details?

Our decomposition has passed a crucial test. We've shown that all information about a certain class of data, the valueType, is hidden in the ValueU and NewValU units. In contrast, the main program knows no details about the valueType. Given an appropriate unit to use, the main program works correctly whether the values are INTEGERs, CHARs, weekdayTypes, or whatever.

Unit NewValU has one interesting feature that we didn't find in Section 3.9. The two functions IsUpperCase and LowerCaseEquiv are declared in the IMPLEMENTATION section but not in the INTERFACE section. This means that these two function subprograms cannot be called by the main program. They're not part of the NewValU unit's interface to the "outside world." We do this to protect the main program from accidentally making calls to these subprograms. After all, the main program's only job is to provide an algorithm that finds the minimum of several values. The main program has no business knowing any details about values (like the fact that values come in two flavors, lower- and uppercase).

no INTERFACE section declaration

9.6   Exercises

Key Words to Review

case-insensitive

Questions to Answer

QUE 9.6.1   Can there be items in the IMPLEMENTATION section that are not revealed in any way in the INTERFACE section? Explain.

QUE 9.6.2   Can there be items in the INTERFACE section for which no further detail is given in the IMPLEMENTATION section? Explain.

QUE 9.6.3   Test the code given in Section 3.9 to see if the hours class of data is completely encapsulated inside the HoursUnit. (Hint: It's not.)

QUE 9.6.4   Rethink each of the decompositions you gave for Exercise Que.3.9.9 in light of what you now know about object-oriented programming.

Changes to Make

CHA 9.6.1   Modify the ValueUnit so that Program Minimum finds the earliest day of the week that's given to it. Use the enumerated type dayType as described in Section 7.5.

Programs and Subprograms to Write

WRI 9.6.1   Write an object-oriented version of Program FindMode from Section 9.2.

WRI 9.6.2   Redo Exercise Wri.5.1.4, this time writing an object-oriented version of the program.

Things to Think About

THI 9.6.1   In this section we performed a test to show that all details about the valueType are encapsulated in the ValueUnit. Did the test provide conclusive airtight proof of that fact? Why, or why not?

Chapter Summary

In this chapter we presented several techniques, each deserving special attention. These techniques make ample use of the Pascal features that we've covered thus far.

The first of these techniques is the placing of statements in a program with several levels of nested looping. The proper placement of statements can be determined by the following method:

1. Recognize that a program divides naturally into *regions* along the boundaries of its loops.

2. Determine the frequency with which each region is executed.

3. Analyze each statement to determine the frequency with which it must be executed.

4. Combine steps 2 and 3 to place each statement into its proper region.

Another technique used in this chapter is to hold a value from one iteration to another. In the case of Program FindMode the variable prevValueIn holds the previous iteration's input value. This previous input value can then be compared with the current input value. The same technique was used in Program Fibonacci (Section 6.3) to store values from two previous iterations.

In Procedure WriteBinary we used DIV and MOD to find the binary representation of a number. We obtained the code by

1. writing down the steps in a sample calculation

2. dividing the steps into several iterations

3. observing similar steps from one iteration to the next

4. substituting variable names for the numbers in one of the iterations

In the next section we extended our work on binary numbers to obtain all possible combinations of the values TRUE and FALSE for a given number of BOOLEAN variables. When we analyzed the running time of our algorithm, we found it to be exponential.

Then we looked at a function that generates numbers in a pseudorandom fashion. We treated the body of Function Random like a black box, talking about the algorithm without saying much about why it works. However we did make the following observations:

- Function Random actually generates a *pseudorandom* sequence of numbers. That is, the numbers are not independent of one another.

- Pseudorandom number generators, like Function Random, can be highly non-portable. Great care must be taken to ensure that a particular subprogram runs correctly on a particular implementation.

- The algorithm implemented by Function Random depends heavily on an area of mathematics known as *Number Theory*. In particular, the notion of a *prime number* plays an important role.

Finally we revisited *information hiding*, an important aspect of object-oriented programming. We encapsulated all details about a particular class of data into a unit, and in so doing we "hid" these details from the main program. We also performed a test to make sure that all details about a particular class of data had been hidden. The test is

1. Change several details in the specs about this class of data.

2. Implement these changes by making the necessary changes in the code.

3. Check to make sure that all changes were made in the unit that (we claim) encapsulates this class of data.

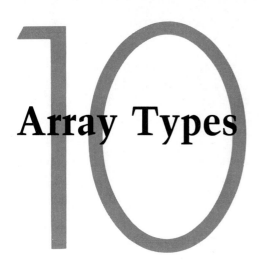

Array Types

What Is an Array?

In everyday life, it's often handy to collect several things together and refer to them individually as "the first thing," "the second thing," "the third," etc. When we do this in a computer program, we get what's called an **array**.

A few examples can illustrate the point. We'll start with an analogy from algebra. In algebra we can have a variable x with subscripts 1, 2, and 3. The subscripted versions of the variable look like this:

x_1 x_2 x_3

We can give these variables values by writing:

Let $x_1 = 5.67$, $x_2 = 7.17$, and $x_3 = 4.13$

Creating an array in Pascal is like creating a variable with subscripts. We can declare an **array variable** named x by writing:

```
VAR
   x : ARRAY [1..3] OF REAL;
```

The "subscripted" versions of x will look like this:

```
x[1]    x[2]    x[3]
```

and we'll assign values to x by writing:

```
x[1] := 5.67;
x[2] := 7.17;
x[3] := 4.13
```

To take an analogy from "everyday life," let's say that our office has three workers—Alice, Bob, and Carol—and our office mailroom has three mailboxes:

467

Alice	Bob	Carol

One morning each person receives a letter announcing his or her salary for next year. So each person's mailbox contains a letter, with an important number on the letter.

Alice	Bob	Carol
$32,000	$32,000	$35,000

Now we have three names and three numbers. Each name has a number associated with it.

In plain English, we might say

"the mailbox marked Alice has the number 32000.00 in it."

In Pascal we can create an enumerated type:

```
TYPE
   worker = (Alice, Bob, Carol);
```

and declare an array variable named mailbox by writing:

```
VAR
   mailbox : ARRAY [worker] OF REAL;
```

Then we assign values to mailbox by writing

```
mailbox[Alice] := 32000.00;
mailbox[Bob]   := 32000.00;
mailbox[Carol] := 35000.00
```

Notice that, in each assignment statement, we make reference to three items:

the word mailbox

the name of a worker (Alice, Bob, or Carol)

a salary value

Now we might describe Alice's situation by saying

"the Alice component of the array variable mailbox has been assigned the value 32000.00."

This section has several experiment-type programs to show you how to manipulate arrays. The first program follows.

**Program
Example**

```
PROGRAM ThreeValues (output);
{Stores three REAL values in an
 array, and then writes the values.}
   VAR
      x : ARRAY [1..3] OF REAL;
BEGIN {ThreeValues}
   x[1] := 5.67;
   x[2] := 7.17;
   x[3] := 4.13;

   WriteLn (x[1]:5:2, x[2]:5:2, x[3]:5:2)
END.  {ThreeValues}
```

**Sample
Runs**

```
5.67 7.17 4.13
```

Observations

**declaring an
array**

- ```
  VAR
      x : ARRAY [1..3] OF REAL;
  ```

x is a single variable that contains three values. The letter x refers to all three of these values. In addition, each of the three values has its own individual name. These names are x[1], x[2], and x[3]. The numbers 1 through 3 come from the subrange 1..3.

**indices, values,
and components**

The variable x is called an array. The numbers 1 through 3 are called **indices** of the array.[1]

We can visualize a "simple" variable, like

```
VAR
   i : INTEGER;
```

as a single memory location with a name.

i

When that variable is assigned a value, the value becomes the content of the variable's memory location.

i

16

---

[1]The singular form of the word *indices* is *index*. Thus, 2 is an *index* of the array x.
```

In contrast, an array variable represents several memory locations, each with its own name.

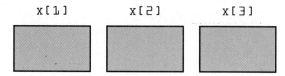

The whole collection of memory locations has the name x. Each of these locations is called a **component** of the array x. When a component of x is assigned a value, with a statement like

```
x[1] := 5.67
```

that value becomes the content of one of the variable's memory locations.

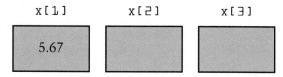

In Program `ThreeValues`, the value stored in each component of x is of type REAL, because of the word REAL in the VAR declaration.

Program Example

```
PROGRAM OtherIndices (output);
{Shows that an array's indices
 don't have to begin with 1.}

  VAR
    x : ARRAY [-1..1] OF REAL;
BEGIN {OtherIndices}
  x[-1] := 5.67;
  x[ 0] := 7.17;
  x[+1] := 4.13;

  WriteLn (x[-1]:5:2, x[0]:5:2, x[1]:5:2)
END.  {OtherIndices}
```

Sample Runs

```
5.67 7.17 4.13
```

Observations

• VAR

    x : ARRAY [-1..1] OF REAL;

In many programming languages, array indices have to begin with the number 1. But in Pascal, if it's convenient to have an array whose indices begin with some other number, we can do it easily. In Program `OtherIndices` we have an array x with three components whose indices are −1, 0, and 1. Notice that the indices we chose for the

indices need not start with 1

components of the array have nothing to do with the values that we store in the array. This array's values are the same as the values we stored in the array of Program `ThreeValues`.

Program Example

```
PROGRAM EnumeratedRange (output);
{Shows that an array's indices
 don't have to be INTEGERs:}
    TYPE
       worker = (Alice, Bob, Carol);
    VAR
       mailbox : ARRAY [worker] OF REAL;
BEGIN {EnumeratedRange}
   mailbox[Alice] := 32000.00;
   mailbox[Bob]   := 32000.00;
   mailbox[Carol] := 35000.00;

   WriteLn ('Alice: $', mailbox[Alice]:8:2);
   WriteLn ('Bob  : $', mailbox[Bob]  :8:2);
   WriteLn ('Carol: $', mailbox[Carol]:8:2)
END.  {EnumeratedRange}
```

Sample Runs

```
Alice: $32000.00
Bob  : $32000.00
Carol: $35000.00
```

Observations

indices need not be INTEGERs

In this program we have an array `mailbox` whose indices aren't integers. They're enumerated values. In Pascal, the name of any ordinal type (such as the name `worker`) can be used to define the indices of an array.[2] Subranges of ordinal types will work too. For instance

```
TYPE
   worker = (Alice, Bob, Carol);
VAR
   mailbox : ARRAY [Alice..Carol] OF REAL;
```

or even

```
TYPE
   worker = (Alice, Bob, Carol);
VAR
   mailbox : ARRAY [Bob..Carol] OF REAL;
```

are legal array declarations. This flexibility, being able to use enumerated values for array indices, was one of the features that originally made Pascal stand out from other programming languages.

---

[2] In case you've forgotten what an ordinal type is, see Section 8.7.

Program Example

```
PROGRAM Zeros (output);
{Fills an array with zeros.}
   VAR
     x : ARRAY [1..3] OF REAL;
   BEGIN {Zeros}
     x[1] := 0.0;
     x[2] := 0.0;
     x[3] := 0.0;
     WriteLn (x[1]:5:2, x[2]:5:2, x[3]:5:2)
   END.   {Zeros}
```

Sample Runs

```
0.00 0.00 0.00
```

Observations   This program just fills an array with zeros. And here's where arrays really come in handy. Instead of filling the array this way, we can loop through the array, as in the next example.

Program Example

```
PROGRAM ArrayLooping (output);
{Shows how to loop through the
 components of an array.}
   TYPE
     rangeType = 1..3;
   VAR
     x : ARRAY [rangeType] OF REAL;
     i : rangeType;
   BEGIN {ArrayLooping}
     FOR i := 1 TO 3 DO
       x[i] := 0.0;

     FOR i := 1 TO 3 DO
       Write (x[i]:5:2);
     WriteLn
   END.   {ArrayLooping}
```

Sample Runs

```
0.00 0.00 0.00
```

Observations   The new program, ArrayLooping, does exactly the same thing as Program Zeros, but it uses loops. This is an enormous advantage. If we were dealing with one hundred values instead of just three, Program Zeros would have one hundred assignment statements, while Program ArrayLooping would still have only two small FOR loops. What's more, you can't do this without arrays.

looping through an array

```
VAR
    a1, a2, a3 : REAL;
BEGIN
       .
       .
    FOR i := 1 TO 3 DO
       ai := 0.0
       .
       .

END
```

Notice how the second FOR loop in Program ArrayLooping works. The Write is executed three times, putting all three values on the same line. After the loop, the WriteLn finishes off the line.[3] If we'd wanted to put the three values on three different lines, we would have done it with

```
FOR i := 1 TO 3 DO
    WriteLn (x[i]:5:2)
```

Program Example

```
PROGRAM ArrayReading (input, output);
{Shows one way to read values
 into an array.}
   TYPE
      rangeType = 1..3;
   VAR
      x : ARRAY [rangeType] OF REAL;
      i : rangeType;
BEGIN {ArrayReading}
   WriteLn ('Enter three values on three separate lines:');
   FOR i := 1 TO 3 DO
      ReadLn (x[i]);
   WriteLn;
   WriteLn ('The values are:');
   FOR i := 1 TO 3 DO
      Write (x[i]:5:2);
   WriteLn
END.   {ArrayReading}
```

Sample Runs

```
Enter three values on three separate lines:
4.1
3.2
2.7
The values are:
 4.10 3.20 2.70
```

---

[3]On some implementations, a final WriteLn at the end of the program is unnecessary.

Observations

reading values
into an array

This program just shows how to read an array with a FOR loop. Since we're using a ReadLn, we expect the array's three values to be typed in on three separate lines. If the three values are typed all on one line, we use

```
FOR i := 1 TO 3 DO
   Read (x[i])
```

Note that in Pascal, you need to read each value of an array individually. You usually do this with a loop. It's not legal to do anything like

```
VAR
   x : ARRAY [rangeType] OF REAL;
      .
      .
ReadLn (x)
```

where you try to read an entire array with one Read or one ReadLn.

Program Example

```
PROGRAM Reverse (input, output);
{Reads three REAL numbers and
 writes them in reverse order.}
   TYPE
      rangeType = 1..3;
   VAR
      x : ARRAY [rangeType] OF REAL;
      i : rangeType;
BEGIN {Reverse}
   WriteLn ('Enter three values on three separate lines:');
   FOR i := 1 TO 3 DO
      ReadLn (x[i]);
   WriteLn;
   WriteLn ('The same values in reverse are:');
   FOR i := 3 DOWNTO 1 DO
      Write (x[i]:5:2);
   WriteLn
END.  {Reverse}
```

Sample Runs

```
Enter three values on three separate lines:
4.1
3.2
2.7

The same values in reverse are:
 2.70 3.20 4.10
```

Observations

other kinds of
looping

- FOR i := 3 DOWNTO 1 DO
     Write (x[i]:5:2)

  You can use all kinds of loops (FOR loops, WHILE loops, REPEAT loops) with arrays. In this example we use a FOR loop with DOWNTO.

**Program
Example**

```
PROGRAM ArrayParameters (output);
{Shows how arrays can be supplied
 as parameters to subprograms.}
  TYPE
    rangeType = 1..3;
    arrayType = ARRAY [rangeType] OF REAL;
  VAR
    x : arrayType;

  {----------}

  PROCEDURE FillWithZeros (VAR x : arrayType);
  {Fills the array x with zeros.}

    VAR
      i : rangeType;
  BEGIN {FillWithZeros}
    FOR i := 1 TO 3 DO
      x[i] := 0.0
  END;  {FillWithZeros}

  {----------}

  PROCEDURE WriteArray (y : arrayType);
  {Writes the array's values to the screen.}

    VAR
      i : rangeType;
  BEGIN {WriteArray}
    FOR i := 1 TO 3 DO
      Write (y[i]:5:2);
    WriteLn
  END;  {WriteArray}

  {----------}

BEGIN {ArrayParameters}
  FillWithZeros (x);
  WriteArray     (x)
END.  {ArrayParameters}
```

**Sample
Runs**

```
0.00 0.00 0.00
```

Observations   This program shows that array-type variables can be parameters to subprograms.

**arrays and
subprogram
parameters**

- `PROCEDURE FillWithZeros (VAR x : arrayType);`

  Procedure `FillWithZeros` "changes" the values stored in the array (it makes these values be zeros), so the array `x` is declared as a `VAR` parameter.

- `PROCEDURE WriteArray (y : arrayType);`

  Procedure `WriteArray` doesn't change any of the values in the array (it just writes them to the screen), so `WriteArray`'s formal parameter is declared as a value parameter.

An actual parameter name can be the same as the name of the corresponding formal parameter:

```
PROCEDURE FillWithZeros (VAR x : arrayType);
   .
   .
FillWithZeros (x)
```

or the two names can be different:

```
PROCEDURE WriteArray (y : arrayType);
   .
   .
WriteArray (x)
```

```
• TYPE
   rangeType = 1..3;
   arrayType = ARRAY [rangeType] OF REAL;
      .
      .
PROCEDURE FillWithZeros (VAR x : arrayType);
```

Here's where a named type is more than just useful. In this example, it's absolutely necessary. A declaration like

```
PROCEDURE FillWithZeros(VAR x:ARRAY [rangeType] OF REAL);
```

isn't legal in ANSI Standard Pascal. In order to pass an array to Procedure FillWithZeros, you have to create a new type name (such as arrayType).

Creating a new type name gives us a different perspective on the meaning of the word *array*. In the earlier examples we thought of an array as a particular variable with more than one component. But here we see that *array* is a property that a type can possess; that is, certain types, like the new type named arrayType, can be described as **array types**.

array types

structured types

Until this chapter, each of the types we've used has been a *simple type*. In contrast, an array type, like the one used in Program ArrayParameters, is an example of a **structured type**. As the words suggest, a structured type is one that has structure. It's created by combining other types. In Program ArrayParameters, we created the type arrayType by combining three values, each of type REAL. We indexed these values with the numbers 1 to 3. In other examples and in other chapters, we'll create different kinds of structured types.

Program Example

```
PROGRAM MoreArrayParameters (input, output);
{Demonstrates certain aspects of supplying
 arrays as parameters to subprograms.}
```

```
        TYPE
          rangeType = 1..3;
          arrayType = ARRAY [rangeType] OF REAL;
        VAR
          x   : arrayType;
          sum : REAL;
        {----------}
        PROCEDURE ReadArray (VAR x : arrayType);
        {Reads values into the array x, from the keyboard.}
          VAR
            i : rangeType;
        BEGIN {ReadArray}
          FOR i := 1 TO 3 DO
            ReadLn (x[i])
        END;  {ReadArray}
        {----------}
        FUNCTION ArraySum (x : arrayType) : REAL;
        {Finds the sum of the values in the array.}
          VAR
            i     : rangeType;
            local : REAL;
        BEGIN {ArraySum}
          local := 0.0;
          FOR i := 1 TO 3 DO
            local := local + x[i];
          ArraySum := local
        END;   {ArraySum}
        {----------}
      BEGIN {MoreArrayParameters}
        WriteLn   ('Enter three values on three separate lines:');
        ReadArray (x);

        sum := ArraySum (x);

        WriteLn;
        Write   ('The sum of the values is ');
        WriteLn (sum:8:2)
      END.   {MoreArrayParameters}
```

**Sample
Runs**

```
      Enter three values on three separate lines:
      4.1
      3.2
      2.7

      The sum of the values is    10.00
```

Observations   In Procedure `ReadArray` we see how to read an array with a subprogram. Here's how *not* to read an array with a subprogram:

functions cannot return structured types

```
FUNCTION BadArrayRead : arrayType;
{This function doesn't work.}
   VAR
      temp : arrayType;
      i    : rangeType;
BEGIN {BadArrayRead}
   FOR i := 1 TO 3 DO
      ReadLn (temp[i]);
   BadArrayRead := temp
END;  {BadArrayRead}
```

Function BadArrayRead won't work because in ANSI Standard Pascal it's illegal to have a function return an array as its result. For now, let's make things easy and say that only simple types can be the result types of functions. In Chapter 14, we'll see one more type that can be the result type of a function.

Of course this doesn't mean that arrays and functions can't be used together. In Function ArraySum, we pass an array as a formal parameter. It's perfectly legal, as long as the result type of the function isn't an array. In Program MoreArrayParameters the result type of Function ArraySum is REAL.

Program Example

```
PROGRAM StillMoreArrayParameters (output);
{Shows various ways in which an array, or part of an
 array, can be supplied as a parameter to a subprogram.}
   TYPE
      rangeType = 1..3;
      arrayType = ARRAY [rangeType] OF REAL;
   VAR
      x : arrayType;
      i : rangeType;
   {----------}

   PROCEDURE Initialize (VAR x : arrayType);
   {Fills the array with some "miscellaneous" values.}

   BEGIN {Initialize}
      x[1] := 5.67;
      x[2] := 7.17;
      x[3] := 4.13
   END;  {Initialize}
   {----------}

   PROCEDURE Increment (VAR r : REAL);
   {Adds 1.0 to a REAL number.}

   BEGIN {Increment}
      r := r + 1.0
   END;  {Increment}
   {----------}
```

```
        PROCEDURE WriteLnComponent (x : arrayType; i : rangeType);
        {Writes just one component of the array x.}
        BEGIN {WriteLnComponent}
           WriteLn ('x[', i:1, '] = ', x[i]:5:2)
        END;   {WriteLnComponent}
        {----------}
  BEGIN {StillMoreArrayParameters}
     Initialize (x);

     Increment (x[2]);
     Increment (x[3]);

     WriteLnComponent (x, 1);
     i := 2;
     WriteLnComponent (x, i)
  END.   {StillMoreArrayParameters}
```

Sample Runs

```
     x[1] =   5.67
     x[2] =   8.17
```

Observations

arrays and subprogram parameters

There are several ways for a subprogram to handle an array. In Procedure `Initialize`, the entire array is passed as a parameter. In Procedure `Increment`, only one component at a time is passed. Notice that there's nothing in Procedure `Increment`'s heading or body that says anything about arrays. Since each component of x is REAL, Procedure `Increment` simply deals with REALs. In Procedure `WriteLnComponent`, the whole array is passed, along with the index of one component. The procedure uses the index to find the value of the particular component.

Program Example[4]

```
PROGRAM ArrayAssign (input, output);
{Shows that a single assignment statement can be used
 to copy values from one array into another array.}
  TYPE
     rangeType = 1..3;
     arrayType = ARRAY [rangeType] OF REAL;
  VAR
     x, y : arrayType;
  {----------}

  PROCEDURE ReadArray (VAR x : arrayType);
  {Put Procedure ReadArray (from
   Program MoreArrayParameters) right here.}
  {----------}

   PROCEDURE WriteArray (y : arrayType);
   {Put Procedure WriteArray (from
    Program ArrayParameters) right here.}
   {----------}
```

---

[4]In this program, and in some of the programs that follow, we've left out parts of certain subprograms. You should put these parts back in before you run the programs.

```
BEGIN {ArrayAssign}
  WriteLn   ('Enter three values on three separate lines:');
  ReadArray (x);

  y := x;

  WriteLn;
  WriteLn      ('The values are:');
  WriteArray (y)
END.  {ArrayAssign}
```

Sample Runs

```
Enter three values on three separate lines:
4.1
3.2
2.7

The values are:
 4.10 3.20 2.70
```

Observations

• VAR

```
    x, y : arrayType;
              .
              .
```

```
y := x
```

array assignment

Look! You can move all the values from one array into another array with just one assignment statement. Of course, two arrays must have the same type before you can do an assignment this way. Even two arrays with "similar" types can't be used. For instance, if we declare

```
TYPE
  rangeType  = 1..3;
  arrayType  = ARRAY [rangeType] OF REAL;
  arrayType2 = ARRAY [rangeType] OF REAL;
VAR
  x : arrayType;
  y : arrayType2;
```

then

```
y := x
```

is illegal in ANSI Standard Pascal. Instead, you have to do the assignment one component at a time:

```
FOR i := 1 TO 3 DO
  y[i] := x[i]
```

Program Example

```
PROGRAM MoreArrayAssign (input, output);
{Moves some values from one array into another.}
  TYPE
    rangeType = 1..3;
    arrayType = ARRAY [rangeType] OF REAL;
  VAR
    x, y : arrayType;
```

```
     {----------}
     PROCEDURE ReadArray (VAR x : arrayType);
     {Put Procedure ReadArray (from
      Program MoreArrayParameters) right here.}
     {----------}
     PROCEDURE WriteArray (y : arrayType);
     {Put Procedure WriteArray (from
      Program ArrayParameters) right here.}
     {----------}
 BEGIN {MoreArrayAssign}
     WriteLn    ('Enter three values on three separate lines:');
     ReadArray (x);

     y[1] := 0.0;
     y[2] := x[1];
     y[3] := x[2];

     WriteLn;
     WriteLn    ('After shifting, the values are: ');
     WriteArray (y)
 END.   {MoreArrayAssign}
```

Sample Runs

```
Enter three values on three separate lines:
4.1
3.2
2.7

After shifting, the values are:
0.00 4.10 3.20
```

Observations

component-by-component assignment

In Program `MoreArrayAssign` we move values from one array into another array, but we don't match up the components "one by one." The first component of x becomes the second component of y, etc.

Program Example

```
PROGRAM IndexVersusValue (output);
{Obtains a value for each component of an array
  by multiplying the component's index by 2.}
   TYPE
      rangeType = 1..3;
      arrayType = ARRAY [rangeType] OF REAL;
   VAR
      x : arrayType;
      i : rangeType;
BEGIN {IndexVersusValue}
   FOR i := 1 TO 3 DO
      x[i] := 2 * i;

   FOR i := 1 TO 3 DO
      WriteLn ('x[', i:1, '] = ', x[i]:5:2);
END.   {IndexVersusValue}
```

Sample Runs

```
x[1] =   2.00
x[2] =   4.00
x[3] =   6.00
```

Observations

keeping track of indices and values

We've already seen lots of examples that use array indices and array values. Here's a program that emphasizes the difference between indices and values. The indices in this program are the numbers 1, 2, and 3. The values in this program are the numbers 2.0, 4.0, and 6.0. Here's a picture:

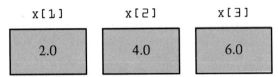

The indices 1, 2, and 3 are used to *distinguish between* the various components of the array. The indices are "in order." In contrast, the values are *stored* in the array.

• x[i] := 2 * i

On this line we stretch your understanding of arrays by using the indices to assign values. If we translate this statement into pseudocode, it says

the ith component of the array x is assigned the value 2 * i.

So, for instance, the 2nd component of x is assigned the value 2 * 2, which is 4. Since the values in x are REAL, the 4 gets converted into 4.00.

• WriteLn ('x[', i:1, '] = ', x[i]:5:2)

In this statement the first i stands for an index (either 1, 2, or 3) and x[i] stands for the value stored in a particular component of the array x.

For instance, if i is 2, then x[i] must mean x[2], so x[i] stands for the value 4.0.

Program Example

```
PROGRAM IndexExpressions (input, output);
{Shows what happens when an index is more complicated
  than just a number, or just a variable name.  Contains
  a statement which may cause the run to be aborted.}
  TYPE
    rangeType = 1..3;
    arrayType = ARRAY [rangeType] OF REAL;
  VAR
    x : arrayType;
    i : rangeType;
  {----------}
```

```
        PROCEDURE ReadArray (VAR x : arrayType);
        {Put Procedure ReadArray (from
         Program MoreArrayParameters) right here.}

        {----------}

        PROCEDURE WriteArray (y : arrayType);
        {Put Procedure WriteArray (from
         Program ArrayParameters) right here.}

        {----------}

  BEGIN {IndexExpressions}
        WriteLn    ('Enter three values on three separate lines:');
        ReadArray (x);

        i          := 1;
        x[i]       := x[i] + 1;
        x[i + 1]  := x[i];
        i          := i + 2;
        x[i]       := x[Trunc(x[i])];   {The run might be aborted here!}
        WriteLn;
        WriteLn    ('After several changes, the values are: ');
        WriteArray (x)
  END.  {IndexExpressions}
```

Sample Runs

```
        Enter three values on three separate lines:
        4.1
        3.2
        2.7

        After several changes, the values are:
         5.10 5.10 5.10
        _____


        Enter three values on three separate lines:
        4.1
        3.2
        5.7

        After several changes, the values are:
         5.10 5.10 0.50
        _____


        Enter three values on three separate lines:
        4.1
        3.2
        51.3

        After several changes, the values are:
         5.10 5.1084183571180000000000000000000.00
```

Observations

evaluating
expressions
involving arrays

Expressions like the ones in this example can be confusing if you're not careful. The best way to be careful is to use braces to show the value of each part of every expression. Let's assume that the user types in the values 4.1, 3.2, and 2.7 for x[1], x[2], and x[3], as in the first sample run given above. Here's how the computer evaluates each of the expressions in the body of the program:

- i   := 1;
  x[i] := x[i] + 1

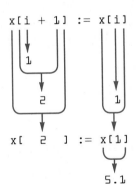

So when these statements are executed, x[1] gets the value 5.1.

- x[i + 1] := x[i]

When this statement is executed, x[2] gets the value 5.1.

```
•  i     := i + 2;
   x[i] := x[Trunc(x[i])];   {The run might be aborted here!}
```

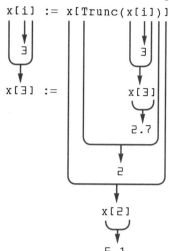

When these statements are executed, x[3] gets the value 5.1.

index out of range

Now why did we put the big comment on this last line of code? It's because we won't always be lucky enough to have Trunc(x[i]) turn out to be a number between 1 and 3. In the second and third of the Sample Runs, Trunc(x[i]) is a number outside this range.

In the second sample run, Trunc(x[i]) is 5 (check this!) so

```
x[i] := x[Trunc(x[i])]
```

means

```
x[3] := x[5]
```

and the computer either aborts your program or looks for whatever garbage value is in the fifth position from x[1]:

The computer's memory:

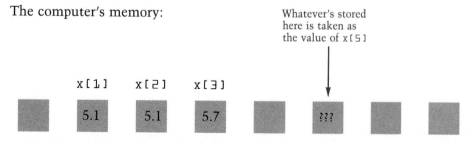

In the second of the Sample Runs this garbage value happens to be 0.50. In the third of the Sample Runs, our computer looked for x[50] and found an awful value with dozens of digits.

All things considered, it's better if the computer just aborts your program when the indices are out of range. On most implementations, when you compile a program there's a way to tell the computer whether it should abort the program or "look for garbage" when it encounters an array index that's outside the expected range of values.[5] If the program is aborted, the

index checking

computer is doing what's called **index checking**.

When you're testing a new program, it's best to compile it with index checking. If any of the program's array indices become too high or too low, the computer will abort your program immediately. Once you're reasonably sure that your program works correctly, you may want to recompile it without index checking. It takes time for the computer to do index checking. Your program will run faster without it.

Program Example

```
PROGRAM ChangeVariables (input, output);
{Shows how x[i] and x[j] can both stand for the same thing.}
  TYPE
    rangeType = 1..3;
  VAR
    x    : ARRAY [rangeType] OF REAL;
    i, j : rangeType;
BEGIN {ChangeVariables}
  WriteLn ('Enter three values on three separate lines:');

  FOR i := 1 TO 3 DO
    ReadLn (x[i]);

  WriteLn;
  WriteLn ('The values are:');

  FOR j := 1 TO 3 DO
    Write (x[j]:5:2);
  WriteLn
END.  {ChangeVariables}
```

Sample Runs

```
Enter three values on three separate lines:
4.1
3.2
2.7

The values are:
4.10 3.20 2.70
```

Observations

using different variables for the index

In the call to ReadLn, components of x are referred to as x[i], but in the call to Write, the same components are referred to as x[j]. The choice of i over j, or j over i, makes absolutely no difference. In the call to ReadLn, when i has the value 1, x[i] means x[1] (the first component of x). In the call to WriteLn, when j has the value 1, x[j] means x[1] (the same first

---

[5]Recall a similar discussion in Section 3.1. In many implementations, we have the option of forcing the computer to check for either array indices being out of bounds or subrange values being out of bounds or both.

component of x).[6] Look at the sample run for this program. You'll see that the `ReadLn` loop makes the computer read values for `x[1]`, `x[2]`, and `x[3]`, and the `Write` loop makes the computer write exactly the same values.

Beginning programmers commonly make the mistake of associating the array's index with a particular variable name. But in this last Program Example we see that any variable with an `INTEGER` value from 1 to 3 can be used as an index for x. We can change from one such variable to another in the middle of the program.

10.1   Exercises

Key Words to Review

array	component	structured type
array variable	array type	index checking
index, indices		

Questions to Answer

QUE 10.1.1   Let's say we execute `WriteLn (x[i]:2, x[j]:2)` and the numbers 4 4 show up on the screen. Can we conclude from this that the variables i and j have the same value? Why, or why not?

QUE 10.1.2   If we know that `x[2 + 1]` has the value 4.00, then can we conclude that `x[2] + x[1]` has the value 4.00? Why, or why not?

QUE 10.1.3   Trace the following fragment of code:

```
i := 3;
j := 2;
a[2] := 3;
a[3] := 5;
a[5] := 3;
WriteLn (a[i] : 3);
WriteLn (a[i+2] : 3);
WriteLn (a[i]+2 : 3);
WriteLn (a[i]+a[j] : 3);
WriteLn (a[i+j] : 3);
WriteLn (a[a[2]] : 3);
WriteLn (a[a[a[3]]] + a[j] + j : 3)
```

Things to Check in a Manual

MAN 10.1.1   Does your implementation provide a way for you to specify whether or not you want it to do index checking? If so, how?

---

[6]It's as if John were the first person waiting in line. We could say "Grab the *i*th person in line, where *i* is 1," or "Grab the *j*th person in line, where *j* is 1." Either way, we're still going to grab John.

Experiments to Try

EXP 10.1.1   With the declarations

```
VAR
  a : ARRAY [1..5] OF REAL;
  i : INTEGER;
  j : 5..10;
```

run the following fragment of code:

```
i    := 5;
a[i] := 3.14;
j    := 5;
WriteLn (a[j]:4:2)
```

Do a[i] and a[j] have the same value?

EXP 10.1.2   Declare an array a : ARRAY [1..5] OF REAL; and try executing the statements

```
a[6] := 49.0;
WriteLn (a[6]:4:1)
```

EXP 10.1.3   Try declaring an array whose indices are the numbers 1 to MAXINT.

EXP 10.1.4   What happens if you declare an array with index range 1..1?

EXP 10.1.5   What happens if you declare an array with index range 1..0?

EXP 10.1.6   Run Program ArrayAssign but use arrayType and arrayType2 as in the Observations which follow the Program Example.

EXP 10.1.7   With Procedure Change declared as follows:

```
PROCEDURE Change(VAR i, x : INTEGER);
BEGIN {Change}
  i := i + 1;
  x := x + 1
END;  {Change}
```

find out what happens when you call Change   (i, a[i])

EXP 10.1.8   With Procedure Change declared as follows:

```
PROCEDURE Change (VAR i : INTEGER; VAR a : arrayType);
BEGIN {Change}
  i    := i + 1;
  a[i] := a[i] + 1
END;  {Change}
```

find out what happens when you call Change   (i, a)

Scales to Practice

PRA 10.1.1   Read ten values into an array. Then write the same values on the screen—first write them two on each line, then write them again with five on each line.

PRA 10.1.2   Read ten values into an array. Then go through the array to find the sum of the even-indexed values.

PRA 10.1.3 Read several numbers into an array. Then write all the numbers in the array that are larger than the average of the numbers in the array.

PRA 10.1.4 Read ten values into an array. Then reverse the values in the array by switching the first and the tenth values, the second and the ninth values, etc. Then write the reversed array. (To see once again how we switch values, look back at Sections 2.4 and 2.5.)

PRA 10.1.5 Read ten values into an array x and another ten values into an array y. Write a list of positions where the arrays x and y contain the same values. That is, write a list of indices, i, such that x[i] is equal to y[i].

PRA 10.1.6 Read ten values into an array. Then shift the values in the array so that what used to be the first value becomes the second value, what used to be the second value becomes the third value, etc. At the end, the first component of the array gets what used to be the tenth value. Write the values in the new array.

PRA 10.1.7 Read a list of ten values into an array. Then go through the array to find the smallest value stored in the array. To do this, use our Minimum algorithm (Section 5.4).

PRA 10.1.8 Read in a list of numbers and write them out in increasing order. Even if you know about sorting, you don't need to use it. Use our Minimum algorithm (Section 5.4).

PRA 10.1.9 Use the function you wrote for Exercise Pra.9.3.1 to create a *circular array*. A circular array is one for which there's a NextIndex function that accepts an index of the array and returns either

- the index of the next component, if there is a next component
- the index of the first component, otherwise

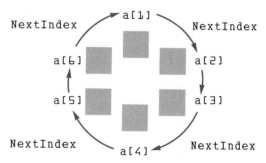

10.2

Using Arrays

Specifications An instructor gives a make-up exam to three students. The *average* grade on the exam is 67 out of 100. That doesn't sound very good. What about the *median* grade? The median grade is the "middle" grade. If the three grades were 5, 96, and 100, then the median grade is 96, even though the average of the three grades is only 67. The average and the median are two very different statistical ways of measuring "middle-ness."

It turns out that it's easiest to find the median of a list of grades when the grades are given to you in order, starting with the smallest grade (for example, 5) and going up to the highest grade (for example, 100). In this case we'll say that the list of grades is **non-decreasing** because the values in the list never decrease. At worst they stay the same (for example, 6, 88, 95, 95, 95, 100).[7]

Input: Several grades, given in non-decreasing order

Output: The median of the grades

Now here's a detail we need to think about: What if there are an even number of grades: 5, 80, 96, and 100? Is 80 the middle, or is 96 the middle? Some statisticians take the average of 80 and 96 (= 88) to be the median of such a list. In our program, we'll just report both numbers, 80 and 96, as the "median."

Designing a Program

Here's the pseudocode:

Read in all the grades, and `count` them as you read them.
Find `count DIV 2`.
If `count` is odd,
    write the (`count DIV 2 + 1`)st grade;
If `count` is even,
    write the (`count DIV 2`)nd and (`count DIV 2 + 1`)st grades

Why do we need an array?

Now why do we need an array to do this? We need an array because we have to examine some of the grades more than once. If we write code that looks like:

```
VAR
   grade : 1..100;

WHILE NOT Eof DO
   BEGIN
      ReadLn (grade);
      {Do whatever you have to do with this grade}
   END
```

then the variable `grade` always stores the most recent grade that we've read. The other grades aren't stored in any variable. So, after we've read the third grade and decided that there are three of them (and that the second grade is the one in the middle), we can't go back and find the second grade to print out its value. That's why we need an array: We need to store all the grades at once, so we can find the middle grade in order to print out its value.

---

[7]A sequence of values is said to be *increasing* if each value is larger than the one that comes before it (for example, 81 83 86 89 100). A sequence of values is said to be *decreasing* if each value is smaller than the one that comes before it (for example, 100 89 86 83 81). A sequence of values is said to be *non-decreasing* if each value is at least as large as the one that comes before it (for example, 81 83 83 89 89). A sequence of values is said to be *non-increasing* if each value is at least as small as the one that comes before it (for example, 89 89 83 83 81).

Program Example

```
PROGRAM Median1 (fInput, output);
{Finds the median of up to fifty students' grades.
 Requires the grades to be entered in non-decreasing order.}
   TYPE
      gradeType = 0..100;
      indexType = 1..50;
      arrayType = ARRAY [indexType] OF gradeType;
   VAR
      stu    : arrayType;
      count  : 0..50;
      fInput : TEXT;
BEGIN {Median1}
   Reset (fInput);
   count := 0;
   WHILE NOT Eof (fInput) DO
      BEGIN
         count := count + 1;
         ReadLn (fInput, stu[count])
      END;
   IF Odd(count) THEN
      WriteLn ('The median is ', stu[(count DIV 2) + 1]:3)
   ELSE
      BEGIN
         Write   ('The median is between ');
         WriteLn (stu[count DIV 2]:3, ' and ', stu[(count DIV 2) + 1]:3)
      END
END.   {Median1}
```

Sample Runs

Here's an fInput file with an odd number of grades in it:

```
70
75
78
78
80
83
84
84
85
89
90
94
95
96
96
99
100
```

The output of the program for this fInput is:

```
The median is  85
```

Here's an `fInput` file with an even number of grades in it:

```
70
75
78
78
80
83
84
84
85
89
90
94
95
96
96
99
```

The output of the program for this `fInput` is:

```
The median is between  84 and  85
```

10.2 Exercises

Key Words to Review

non-decreasing

Questions to Answer

QUE 10.2.1 Explain, in your own words, why an array is needed in Program `Median1`.

QUE 10.2.2 The average, median, and mode are three ways statisticians talk about the "middle" of all the values. Why wouldn't we need an array to find the average of several grades? Why didn't we need an array in Section 9.2 to find the mode of several values?

Changes to Make

CHA 10.2.1 Modify Program `Median1` so that it does something sensible when the `fInput` file is empty.

CHA 10.2.2 There's another way to talk about the median of a collection of grades. We can say that the median is larger than about 50 percent of the grades and smaller than the other 50 percent of the grades. Then we can get more ambitious and divide the grades not in half, but into four groups:

- A number that's larger than 25 percent of the grades and smaller than 75 percent of the grades is called Q_1—the *first quartile*.
- The median also goes by the name Q_2—the *second quartile*.

- A number that's larger than 75 percent of the grades and smaller than 25 percent of the grades is called Q_3—the *third quartile.*

Modify Program `Median1` so that it prints the first, second, and third quartiles of a collection of grades.

CHA 10.2.3   Modify the program of Exercise Cha.10.2.2 by having the computer write all the grades, with arrows written immediately below each of the three quartile numbers. (Note: You can make something that looks like an upward arrow with the caret ^ character that appears as a "shift-6" on most keyboards.)

Programs and Subprograms to Write

WRI 10.2.1   You're given two lines of input. The first line has ten prices (the prices of items 1 through 10). The second line has ten quantities (the quantities of items 1 through 10). Write a program that reads the prices and quantities and prints the total cost of buying all the items.

WRI 10.2.2   On each line of a file there are ten test scores. Write a program that does the following, for each line of the file:

Read all ten test scores.
Drop the lowest score.
Write the nine remaining scores on the screen.

WRI 10.2.3   Write a program that

reads ten REAL numbers,
writes them on the screen,
writes the sum of the numbers,
asks the user which of the ten numbers should be changed, and what the new value should be,
refreshes the screen (that is, writes all ten numbers again, having made the desired change),
asks the user for another change,
Etc.

WRI 10.2.4   Review the definition of a *prime* number in Exercise Wri.9.5.5. We can find all the prime numbers between, say, 1 and 100, with an algorithm known as the *Sieve of Erastostheses:*

Eliminate all the numbers that are multiples of 2;
Eliminate all the numbers that are multiples of 3;
Eliminate all the numbers that are multiples of 5;
Etc.

Notice that multiples of 4 don't have to be eliminated. They were already eliminated when we eliminated all multiples of 2. The same is true for multiples of 6, etc.

Write a program that uses the Sieve of Erastostheses to find all prime numbers from 1 to 100.

WRI 10.2.5   Rewrite the bar graph program from Section 4.2, this time making the bars grow vertically rather than horizontally.

WRI 10.2.6 Modify the program of Exercise Cha.9.2.4 so that it handles a sequence of numbers with up to ten modes. As the program runs, the various modes are stored in an array.

WRI 10.2.7 Write a program that reads several students' test scores and writes each of the scores on the screen. Next to each score, the program writes the *percentile rank* of that score. A score's percentile rank is the percentage of scores that are *less than or equal to* that score. For instance, the percentile rank of the median score is 50 percent.

WRI 10.2.8 Write a program that reads the test grades of several students and writes the average of the test grades and the *standard deviation* of the test grades. To compute the standard deviation of several grades, use the formula

$$standard\ deviation = \sqrt{\frac{\sum_{i} (grade_i - average)^2}{n - 1}}$$

where n is the number of student grades. (For a review of the $\sum$ notation, see Exercises Cha.6.2.1, Wri.6.2.4, and Wri.6.2.5.)

WRI 10.2.9 Modify the program of Exercise Wri.10.2.8 so that it also writes each student's *z*-score. To compute a student's *z*-score, use the formula

$$z\text{-}score = \frac{grade_i - average}{standard\ deviation}$$

Things to Think About

THI 10.2.1 Are there problems that are best solved using simple types, rather than arrays? Can you devise a general rule to decide what sorts of problems should be solved using arrays and what sorts of problems should be solved using only simple types?

10.3

Another Way to Solve the Same Problem

Program Median1 is nice, but it has a few serious deficiencies. Let's think about what happens when our instructor gives an exam to a large lecture class of five hundred students.

First, the list of grades needs to be given to Program Median1 in non-decreasing order. This means the instructor has to sort the five hundred grades by hand before typing them in. This is inconvenient.

Next, we have to change indexType so that it ranges from 1 to 500. We're not offended that we have to change indexType. That part is unavoidable. What bothers us is having to make so large an array when (as we're about to learn) a smaller array will do.

Designing a Program

In Program Median1 we stored all the grades by creating an array stu whose indices were students (the first to the five-hundredth student) and whose values were grades. We'd rearrange the students so that their grades were in non-decreasing order.

The array in Program Median1:

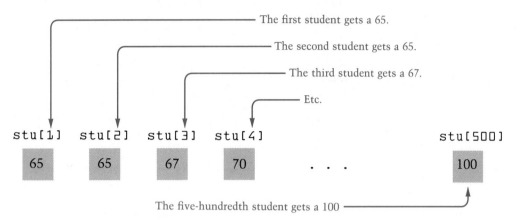

The first student gets a 65.

The second student gets a 65.

The third student gets a 67.

Etc.

stu[1]   stu[2]   stu[3]   stu[4]   stu[500]

| 65 | 65 | 67 | 70 | . . . | 100 |

The five-hundredth student gets a 100

storing the same information in a different way

In Program Median2 we'll store the same grades in a different form. We'll create an array named howMany. The indices of the howMany array will be grades. Each value stored in the howMany array will be the number of students who have a particular grade.

The array in Program Median2:

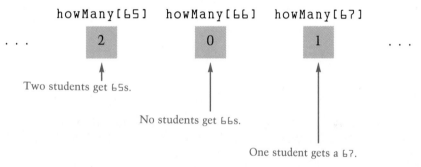

howMany[65]   howMany[66]   howMany[67]

. . . | 2 | 0 | 1 | . . .

Two students get 65s.

No students get 66s.

One student gets a 67.

Now to find the median grade in Program Median2, we keep adding up the values in the howMany array until we get to half the number of students.

Program Example

```
PROGRAM Median2 (fInput, output);
{Finds the median of the students' grades.  Doesn't
 require the grades to be entered in non-decreasing
 order; however, this version works only when the
 number of grades is odd.  See Exercise Cha.10.3.3.}
```

```
      TYPE
        cardinal  =  0..MAXINT;
        gradeType = -1..100;
        arrayType = ARRAY [gradeType] OF cardinal;
      VAR
        howMany : arrayType;
        grade   : gradeType;
        count,
        recount : cardinal;
        fInput  : TEXT;
    BEGIN {Median2}
      Reset (fInput);
      FOR grade := 0 TO 100 DO
        howMany[grade] := 0;

      count := 0;
      WHILE NOT Eof (fInput) DO
        BEGIN
          WHILE NOT Eoln (fInput) DO
            BEGIN
              count := count + 1;
              Read (fInput, grade);
              howMany[grade] := howMany[grade] + 1
            END;
          ReadLn (fInput)
        END;

      recount := 0;
      grade   := -1;
      WHILE recount < (count DIV 2) + 1 DO
        BEGIN
          grade   := grade + 1;
          recount := recount + howMany[grade]
        END;
      WriteLn ('The median is ', grade:3)
    END.  {Median2}
```

Sample Runs

If the fInput file contains

```
70 75 78 78 80 83 84 84 85 89 90 94 95 96 96 99 99
```

then the output of Program Median2 is

```
The median is  85
```

Now here's an fInput file with some data taken from real life:

```
49 56 51 91 50 44 48 91 77 14 64 50 66 78 42 95 97 36 60 73 71
71 70 68 20 57 58 80 88 72 56 48 80 79 56 97 75 59 92 90 88 81
79 63 91
```

Here's the output of Program Median2:

```
The median is  70
```

Here's a run with extreme data. In this case the word *extreme* means that all students receive the same grade: The fInput file:

```
90 90 90 90 90
```

The corresponding output:

```
The median is   90
```

Here's another extreme situation—only one student: The fInput file:

```
95
```

The corresponding output:

```
The median is   95
```

10.3 Exercises

Questions to Answer

QUE 10.3.1 If you're given all the values in the stu array from Program Median1, can you use them to create the howMany array in Program Median2? Why, or why not?

QUE 10.3.2 If you're given all the values in the howMany array from Program Median2, can you use them to create an exact copy of the stu array in Program Median1? Why, or why not?

Experiments to Try

EXP 10.3.1 Redo the experiments in Exercise Exp.9.5.3 with a ten-sided coin. Use an array to store the ten tallies that you need to keep.

Changes to Make

CHA 10.3.1 Add code to Program Median2 so that it uses the howMany array to compute the *average* of the scores in the fInput file.

CHA 10.3.2 Add code to Program Median2 so that it uses the howMany array to print a copy of all the scores in the fInput file. In this copy, the scores should appear in non-decreasing order.

CHA 10.3.3 To simplify Program Median2 we never had it write

```
The median is between ...
```

the way Program Median1 did. Whenever the user enters an even number of students' grades, Program Median2 writes only one of the two grades in the middle. Modify Program Median2 so that, like Median1, it writes both middle grades when the number of grades is even.

Programs and Subprograms to Write

WRI 10.3.1   Write a program that reads a paragraph and tallies the number of times each letter of the alphabet occurs in the paragraph.

WRI 10.3.2   In Section 6.3 we saw an interesting but rather complicated program to compute terms of the Fibonacci sequence. The program can be made much simpler if we use arrays. Just declare an array called `fib`, and store the first term in the sequence in `fib[1]`, the second term in `fib[2]`, etc. Whenever you calculate the next term in the sequence, you use terms you've already stored in the array. Write a program to compute terms in the Fibonacci sequence using this method.

WRI 10.3.3   In Section 9.2 we found the mode of a sequence of numbers without storing anything in an array. Without having arrays, we had to assume that numbers were "lumped" together in the sequence. Write a program, using arrays, that finds the mode of a list of numbers. Don't assume that numbers in the sequence are lumped together.

Things to Think About

THI 10.3.1   Now we've seen two ways to solve the same problem: find the median of a collection of grades. Which is "better"? Is the first way better in some situations and worse in other situations? If so, describe the situations. (First, describe the situations by giving examples. Then, describe the situations by making up a general rule.) Can you devise a general rule to decide what sorts of problems should be solved using the first method, and what sorts of problems should be solved using the second method?

10.4

Character Arrays

Until now, most of our arrays have had indices and components with numeric values

```
VAR
   x : ARRAY [1..3] OF REAL;
```

but we can also have arrays of BOOLEANs, arrays of colors, arrays whose indices are CHARacters, etc. In this section we focus our attention on arrays that handle CHARacter values.

Specifications   A cryptogram is a message that's been translated into a "secret code." Only those who know the coding scheme can read and understand the message. For instance, if we take the successor of each letter in Barry Burd, we get the cryptogram Cbssz Cvse. To go back to Barry Burd, we take each letter's predecessor.

Now let's use the correct terminology: We start with a message, written in ordinary English, like the name Barry Burd. This is called the *plain text.* The plain text gets *encrypted*—that is, turned into a cryptogram.

Another name for a cryptogram is *encrypted text*. In order to understand the cryptogram, one needs to *decrypt it*—that is, turn it back into plain text.

Of the many methods for encrypting messages, one of the easiest is called a *simple substitution cipher.* In a simple substitution cipher, letters are systematically replaced by other letters. A simple substitution cipher uses a *cipher alphabet*—a table that gives the hidden meaning of each letter. In the example with successors and predecessors, the cipher alphabet would look like this:

    b   stands for a

    c   stands for b

    d   stands for c

    .

    .

    etc.

Another way of encrypting a message is to apply a *transposition cipher.* With a transposition cipher we rearrange the letters in a message. For instance we could simply reverse the letters in the message

```
you do not know right from left
```

to get

```
tfel morf thgir wonk ton od uoy
```

In this program we'll have

> Input: A cryptogram and a cipher alphabet
>
> Process: Decrypt the cryptogram by reversing it and then finding each letter's equivalent in the cipher alphabet
>
> Output: The original plain text message

Designing a Program

In its barest essence, there are four things that Program `CryptoDriver` must do:

> Read the `cipherAlphabet` from the `cipherFile`.
> Read the `cryptogram`.
> `Decrypt` the `cryptogram`, using the `cipherAlphabet`, to get the `plainText`.
> Write the `plainText` message on the screen.

To this bare essence we add a few details:

First, each subprogram needs to know how many characters are contained in the `cryptogram` (and in the resulting `plainText`). We store this in a variable called `messageSize` and pass it back and forth from one subprogram to another.

Next, the final `plainText` is displayed on the screen by a procedure called `WriteLnMessage` that writes not only the `plainText`, but also a brief `explanation` to tell the user what's being written.

Here's some more detailed pseudocode:

Read the `cipherAlphabet` from the `cipherFile`.
Read the `cryptogram` and determine its `messageSize`.
`Decrypt` the `cryptogram`, using the `cipherAlphabet`, to get a `plainText` with `messageSize`-many characters.
Write this `plainText` containing `messageSize`-many characters, along with a brief `explanation`.

So here's an outline of the code of Program `CryptoDriver`:

```
PROGRAM CryptoDriver (cipherF, input, output);
{A test driver for Procedure Decrypt.}
   PROCEDURE ReadCrypto (VAR cryptogram  : messageType ;
                         VAR messageSize : indexType   );

   PROCEDURE ReadCipher (VAR cipherF     : TEXT         ;
                         VAR cipherAlph  : cipherAlphType);

   PROCEDURE Decrypt (cryptogram      : messageType   ;
                      cipherAlph      : cipherAlphType ;
                      VAR plainText : messageType     ;
                      messageSize     : indexType      );

   PROCEDURE WriteLnMessage (explanation : explainType ;
                             message     : messageType ;
                             messageSize : indexType    );
BEGIN {CryptoDriver}
   ReadCipher     (cipherF, cipherAlph);
   ReadCrypto     (cryptogram, messageSize);

   Decrypt        (cryptogram, cipherAlph, plainText, messageSize);

   WriteLn;
   WriteLnMessage ('Plain text: ', plainText, messageSize)
END.  {CryptoDriver}
```

Now recall how we do the `Decrypt`ing. To get our first draft of the `plainText` message, we reverse all the letters in the `cryptogram`. Then we find each letter's equivalent in the cipher alphabet. This suggests two new subprograms within Procedure `Decrypt`:

```
PROGRAM CryptoDriver (cipherF, input, output);
{A test driver for Procedure Decrypt.}
   PROCEDURE ReadCrypto (VAR cryptogram  : messageType ;
                         VAR messageSize : indexType   );

   PROCEDURE ReadCipher (VAR cipherF     : TEXT         ;
                         VAR cipherAlph  : cipherAlphType);

   PROCEDURE Decrypt (cryptogram      : messageType   ;
                      cipherAlph      : cipherAlphType ;
                      VAR plainText : messageType     ;
                      messageSize     : indexType      );
```

```
         PROCEDURE Transpose (cryptogram     : messageType ;
                              VAR plainText : messageType ;
                              messageSize   : indexType  );
         PROCEDURE Substitute (cipherAlph     : cipherAlphType ;
                               VAR plainText : messageType     ;
                               messageSize   : indexType       );
      BEGIN {Decrypt}
        Transpose  (cryptogram, plainText, messageSize);
        Substitute (cipherAlph, plainText, messageSize)
      END;  {Decrypt}
      PROCEDURE WriteLnMessage (explanation : explainType ;
                               message     : messageType ;
                               messageSize : indexType  );
   BEGIN {CryptoDriver}
     ReadCipher      (cipherF, cipherAlph);
     ReadCrypto      (cryptogram, messageSize);

     Decrypt         (cryptogram, cipherAlph, plainText, messageSize);

     WriteLn;
     WriteLnMessage ('Plain text: ', plainText, messageSize)
   END.  {CryptoDriver}
```

Now notice what we've done. We've gone from the pseudocode to a collection of subprogram headings. This collection of subprogram headings forms an outline for the completed program. This is very good, because the part of the program we've included in our outline is the most important part. In creating the subprogram headings we've actually shown how the pieces of the program are going to fit together.

We can think of the outline we've created in more than one way. We can think of it as

- a step beyond the pseudocode—the beginning of the implementation of the pseudocode
- a kind of hierarchy diagram—using indentation instead of lines and boxes to show which subprograms are subordinate to which other subprograms
- a piece of code that can almost be compiled

compiling an early outline of the program

This last way of looking at the outline is the most important. If we add definitions and declarations at the top of the outline and add stub bodies to the subprograms, we get a program that can actually be compiled.

```
PROGRAM CryptoDriver (cipherF, input, output);
{A test driver for Procedure Decrypt.}
  CONST
    maxMessageSize = 50;
  TYPE
    lowerType      = 'a'..'z';
    indexType      = 1..maxMessageSize;
    cipherAlphType =          ARRAY [lowerType] OF lowerType;
    messageType    =          ARRAY [indexType] OF CHAR;
    explainType    = PACKED ARRAY [1..12]      OF CHAR;
  VAR
    cipherAlph  : cipherAlphType;
    cryptogram,
    plainText   : messageType;
    messageSize : indexType;
    cipherF     : TEXT;

  {----------}

  PROCEDURE ReadCrypto (VAR cryptogram  : messageType ;
                        VAR messageSize : indexType  );

  BEGIN {ReadCrypto}
    messageSize := 1
  END;  {ReadCrypto}

  {----------}

  PROCEDURE ReadCipher (VAR cipherF    : TEXT           ;
                        VAR cipherAlph : cipherAlphType);

  BEGIN {ReadCipher}
  END;  {ReadCipher}

  {----------}

  PROCEDURE Decrypt (cryptogram    : messageType    ;
                     cipherAlph    : cipherAlphType ;
                     VAR plainText : messageType    ;
                     messageSize   : indexType      );

    {----------}

    PROCEDURE Transpose (cryptogram    : messageType ;
                         VAR plainText : messageType ;
                         messageSize   : indexType  );

    BEGIN {Transpose}
    END;  {Transpose}

    {----------}

    PROCEDURE Substitute (cipherAlph    : cipherAlphType ;
                          VAR plainText : messageType    ;
                          messageSize   : indexType      );

    BEGIN {Substitute}
    END;  {Substitute}

    {----------}

  BEGIN {Decrypt}
    Transpose  (cryptogram, plainText, messageSize);
    Substitute (cipherAlph, plainText, messageSize)
  END; {Decrypt}

  {----------}
```

```
          PROCEDURE WriteLnMessage (explanation : explainType ;
                                    message     : messageType ;
                                    messageSize : indexType   );
       BEGIN {WriteLnMessage}
       END;  {WriteLnMessage}

       {----------}
   BEGIN {CryptoDriver}
      ReadCipher      (cipherF, cipherAlph);
      ReadCrypto      (cryptogram, messageSize);

      Decrypt         (cryptogram, cipherAlph, plainText, messageSize);

      WriteLn;
      WriteLnMessage ('Plain text: ', plainText, messageSize)
   END.  {CryptoDriver}
```

Of course, if we go on and run this skeletal program we get no output, but we still get some very important information. We learn that the subprograms we plan to use, with their various parameter lists, will fit together correctly. This is very useful information, especially in a large project where one team of programmers writes specs for the main program, another team writes specs for Procedure Decrypt, etc. Compiling the outline is a tangible test to ensure that each team's vision of the project is consistent with that of the other teams.

Program Example

```
       PROGRAM CryptoDriver (cipherF, input, output);
       {A test driver for Procedure Decrypt.}
         CONST
           maxMessageSize = 50;
         TYPE
           lowerType       = 'a'..'z';
           indexType       = 1..maxMessageSize;
           cipherAlphType  =         ARRAY [lowerType] OF lowerType;
           messageType     =         ARRAY [indexType] OF CHAR;
           explainType     = PACKED ARRAY [1..12]      OF CHAR;
         VAR
           cipherAlph  : cipherAlphType;
           cryptogram,
           plainText   : messageType;
           messageSize : indexType;
           cipherF     : TEXT;

         {----------}
```

```
PROCEDURE ReadCrypto (VAR cryptogram  : messageType ;
                      VAR messageSize : indexType  );
{Reads a cryptogram of maxMessageSize
 or fewer lowercase letters.}

  VAR
    i : 0..maxMessageSize;
BEGIN {ReadCrypto}
  Write  ('Enter a cryptogram (');
  Write  (maxMessageSize:2);
  Write  (' or fewer lowercase letters): ');
  WriteLn;

  i := 0;
  WHILE NOT Eoln (input) AND (i < maxMessageSize) DO
    BEGIN
      i := i + 1;
      Read (cryptogram[i])
    END;

  messageSize := i
END;  {ReadCrypto}
{----------}
PROCEDURE ReadCipher (VAR cipherF    : TEXT            ;
                      VAR cipherAlph  : cipherAlphType);
{Reads the cipher alphabet.}

  VAR
    letter : lowerType;
BEGIN {ReadCipher}
  Reset (cipherF);
  FOR letter := 'a' TO 'z' DO
    Read (cipherF, cipherAlph[letter])
END;  {ReadCipher}
{----------}
PROCEDURE Decrypt (cryptogram     : messageType    ;
                   cipherAlph     : cipherAlphType ;
                   VAR plainText  : messageType    ;
                   messageSize    : indexType      );
{Turns encrypted text into plain text.}

  VAR
    plainInd : indexType;

  {----------}

  PROCEDURE Transpose (cryptogram     : messageType ;
                       VAR plainText  : messageType ;
                       messageSize    : indexType   );
  {Reverses the letters in the cryptogram to
   get a temporary version of the plain text.}

    VAR
      cryptIndex : 0..maxMessageSize;
      plainIndex : indexType;
```

```
   BEGIN {Transpose}
     cryptIndex := messageSize;
     FOR plainIndex := 1 TO messageSize DO
       BEGIN
         plainText[plainIndex] := cryptogram[cryptIndex];
         cryptIndex         := cryptIndex - 1
       END
   END; {Transpose}

   {----------}

   PROCEDURE Substitute (cipherAlph    : cipherAlphType ;
                         VAR plainText : messageType    ;
                         messageSize   : indexType       );
   {Substitutes letters in the plainText
    using the cipher alphabet.}

      VAR
        i : indexType;

      {----------}

      FUNCTION IsLowerCase (ch : CHAR) : BOOLEAN;
      {Determines whether a character is a lowercase letter.}
      BEGIN {IsLowerCase}
        IsLowerCase := ('a' <= ch) AND (ch <= 'z')
      END;   {IsLowerCase}

      {----------}

   BEGIN {Substitute}
     FOR i := 1 TO messageSize DO
       IF IsLowerCase (plainText[i]) THEN
         plainText[i] := cipherAlph[plainText[i]]
   END;   {Substitute}

   {----------}

BEGIN {Decrypt}
  Transpose  (cryptogram, plainText, messageSize);
  Substitute (cipherAlph, plainText, messageSize)
END;  {Decrypt}

{----------}

PROCEDURE WriteLnMessage (explanation : explainType ;
                          message     : messageType ;
                          messageSize : indexType   );
{Writes a message, along with a brief explanation.}

   VAR
     i : indexType;

BEGIN {WriteLnMessage}
  Write (explanation);

  FOR i := 1 TO messageSize DO
    Write (plainText[i]:1);
  WriteLn
END;  {WriteLnMessage}

{----------}
```

```
BEGIN {CryptoDriver}
   ReadCipher   (cipherF, cipherAlph);
   ReadCrypto   (cryptogram, messageSize);

   Decrypt      (cryptogram, cipherAlph, plainText, messageSize);

   WriteLn;
   WriteLnMessage ('Plain text: ', plainText, messageSize)
END.  {CryptoDriver}
```

**Sample
Runs**

With the following `cipher`File:

```
qwertyuiopasdfghjklzxcvbnm
```

a run of Program `CryptoDriver` might look like this:

```
Enter a cryptogram (50 or fewer lowercase letters):
ygn lh oyhzzkdoidj

Plain text: programming is fun
```

Observations   First notice how we read and write most of the arrays in this program:

```
FOR letter := 'a' TO 'z' DO
  Read (cipherF, cipherAlph[letter])
     .
     .
FOR i := 1 TO messageSize DO
  Write (plainText[i]:1);
WriteLn
```

Then look at the way we write the `explanation` array:

```
Write (explanation)
```

Here's why we can write the `explanation` array by just naming it in a `Write`:

- TYPE
     ```
     explainType = PACKED ARRAY [1..12] OF CHAR;
        .
        .
     ```

PACKED arrays

```
PROCEDURE WriteLnMessage (explanation : explainType ;
                           message      : messageType ;
                           messageSize : indexType   );
```

The word PACKED tells the compiler to store the values of the explanation array in a way that *saves space*. In this section, we won't go into details about what it means to save space. We'll only say that when an array type is defined

```
PACKED ARRAY [1..something-or-other] OF CHAR
```

string types

then it's called a **string type**. And there are lots of nice things we can do with string-type arrays that we can't do with other arrays, such as

```
Write (explanation)
```

or

```
explanation := 'Plain text: '
```

or

```
WriteLnMessage ('Plain text: ', plainText, messageSize)
```

or

```
IF explanation < 'Plainest    ' THEN
```

For more information on string types and what it means for an array to be PACKED, see Section 10.9.

Programming Style

Take another look at the code for Procedure Substitute:

```
FOR i := 1 TO messageSize DO
   IF IsLowerCase (plainText[i]) THEN
      plainText[i] := cipherAlph[plainText[i]]
```

creating extra variables for efficiency

We'll assume for a moment that i has the value 4. In order to find the location in memory where plainText[4] is stored, the computer has to do what's called an **indexing** calculation. It does this calculation to find out what memory location is 3 positions beyond plainText[1].

1 position from plainText[1]	2 positions from plainText[1]	**3 positions from plainText[1]**	4 positions from plainText[1]

plainText[1]	plainText[2]	plainText[3]	**plainText[4]**	plainText[5]

This indexing calculation is done three times during each iteration of the FOR loop in Procedure Substitute.

```
FOR i := 1 TO messageSize DO
   IF IsLowerCase (plainText[i]) THEN
      plainText[i] := cipherAlph[plainText[i]]
```

Each indexing calculation takes a bit of time—not an enormous amount of time, but time the computer could use to do other things.

Now let's see what happens when we declare a new variable temp and use it to store values of plainText[i]:

```
FOR i := 1 TO messageSize DO
   BEGIN
      temp := plainText[i];
      IF IsLowerCase (temp) THEN
         plainText[i] := cipherAlph[temp]
   END
```

Then the indexing calculation is done only two times during each iteration of the FOR loop in Procedure Substitute. This should save a bit of time, since the added time for moving a value into a new temp variable is fairly small.

So should we make the change? Some authors say *yes*; others say *no*. We say it depends on the situation:

- If adding a new variable detracts from the program's readability, don't do it. Some code is easier to read with an extra variable, but in some code an extra variable just gets in the way. By far the best time-saving measure you can take is to make your code readable so that no one ever has to spend extra time figuring out how your program works.

- In Procedure Substitute the difference between using temp and not using temp was one fewer indexing calculation. So the difference in running time between the two versions of Program CryptoDriver would be very small. But if you have a very large loop, with many indexing calculations on an array like plainText, adding an extra variable may speed up your program execution quite a bit. Most likely it will also enhance the program's readability.

- If a compiler does something called *optimizing*, then it creates an extra variable like temp whether you declare it or not! As your code is being translated, the compiler analyzes it for any subtle points that can be made more efficient. These points are corrected behind your back! The only way you can see that an extra variable has been added is to look at the machine language code—the result of the translation. So, if you're using an **optimizing compiler**, then adding temp probably doesn't change the running time of the program. Once again, the primary consideration is readability.

optimizing compilers

10.4 Exercises

Key Words to Review

PACKED	indexing
string type	optimizing compiler

Questions to Answer

QUE 10.4.1 Explain why, in Program CryptoDriver, it's useful to have the indices of the cipherAlph array be the letters 'a' through 'z'.

QUE 10.4.2 Look again at the outline for Program CryptoDriver, given at the end of the Designing a Program subsection. Some authors refer to this as "compilable pseudocode." Explain why this phrase makes sense.

QUE 10.4.3 In Procedure Substitute, when we declare a new variable temp, we reduce the number of indexing calculations to plainText[i] by just one calculation. This saves us some time, but not a lot of time. Write a fragment of code in which this same trick saves us from making a large number of indexing calculations.

Experiments to Try

EXP 10.4.1   Compile and run the final outline of Program `CryptoDriver`, given in the Designing a Program subsection.

EXP 10.4.2   Redo Exercise Exp.10.4.1, this time with an incorrect procedure call

```
Decrypt (cryptogram, plainText, cipherAlph, messageSize)
```

in the main body of the outline. Does the outline still compile successfully? If not, what does this tell us about the usefulness of attempting to compile the outline?

Changes to Make

CHA 10.4.1   Modify Procedure `Decrypt` so that, instead of a simple letter reversal, it uses a *rail-fence transposition*. With a rail-fence transposition the original message is divided into two halves and the characters in the two halves appear in alternating fashion in the cryptogram.

```
pnrgo girsa mfmuin
```

CHA 10.4.2   Rewrite Program `BloodTypes` from Section 8.2 so that it uses an array type

```
ARRAY ['A'..'B'] OF BOOLEAN
```

Programs and Subprograms to Write

WRI 10.4.1   Write and test a procedure that reads a line containing a person's name and stores it in an eighty-character array. In the array, an asterisk tells us that we've reached the end of the name.

WRI 10.4.2   Using the asterisk technique described in Exercise Wri.10.4.1, write and test a procedure that *concatenates* two character arrays. That is, it takes "first-name" and "last-name" arrays and creates a "full-name" array by putting the two single-name arrays together, one after the other. In the big array, an asterisk tells us that we've reached the end of the full name.

WRI 10.4.3   Redo Exercise Wri.7.4.3 using the array

```
VAR
   contestantGuessed : ARRAY ['a'..'z'] OF BOOLEAN;
```

In this version the user chooses several letters. When the user chooses the letter f the value `contestantGuessed['f']` becomes TRUE. Once again, only the letters that have been guessed by the user appear on the screen. The other letters appear as blank spaces.

WRI 10.4.4   Write and test a procedure that accepts an INTEGER value and sends back an array containing that integer's digit characters.

WRI 10.4.5   Write and test a procedure that does the opposite of what's done in Exercise Wri.10.4.4; that is, accepts an array containing an integer's digit characters and sends back the INTEGER value. (Compare with Procedure `ReadLnCharOrNat` in Section 8.3.)

WRI 10.4.6   Write and test a procedure that accepts a character array and sends back the same array after doing a *case-rotation*. What happens in a case-rotation depends on the word that's being rotated:

- `program` gets changed to `Program`
- `Program` gets changed to `PROGRAM`
- `PROGRAM` gets changed to `program`

WRI 10.4.7   A *palindrome* is a sentence that reads the same way backwards and forwards. Here are some well-known palindromes:

```
Madam, I'm Adam.
Able was I ere I saw Elba.
A man, a plan, a canal, Panama!
Doc, note, I dissent!  A fast never prevents a fatness; I diet on cod.
```

Write a program that reads in a sequence of up to 50 letters and prints out a message telling whether or not that sequence is a palindrome. If you like you can assume that the sequence has no punctuation, no blank spaces, and no capitals (`madamimadam`).

WRI 10.4.8   Suppose you call directory assistance because you'd like to congratulate the author of *Pascal by Example*. The operator is likely to type something like `Barie Byrd` into the computer, because few people know the correct spelling. If the computer is "smart" it should look for all names whose spelling is similar to this incorrect spelling. The question is, how can we make the computer be "smart"?

The answer is something called the *Soundex method*. (The Soundex method was developed by Margaret K. Odell and Robert C. Russell. For more information, see U.S. Patents 1261167 [1918] and 1435665 [1922].) Here's how it's done:

- Remove all the vowels and all occurrences of h, w, and y, except the letters at the beginning of a first or last name. So `Barie Byrd` becomes `Br Brd` and `Barry Burd` becomes `Brr Brd`.

- Change all letters to digits (except the letters at the beginning of a first or last name). Use the following table to make the change:

Letter	gets changed to
b f p v	1
c g j k q s x z	2
d t	3
l	4
m n	5
r	6

So `Br Brd` becomes `B6 B63` and `Brr Brd` becomes `B66 B63`.

- Eliminate any duplicating digits that come next to one another, as long as these digits come from letters that were next to one another in the original name. So `B6 B63` is still `B6 B63` but `B66 B63` becomes `B6 B63`.

- Add extra zeros or cut off the rightmost digits to ensure that each code has exactly three digits. So `Barie Byrd` finally becomes `B600 B630` and `Barry Burd` is also `B600 B630`.

- Since `Barie Byrd` and `Barry Burd` have the same Soundex codes, the computer will offer one spelling as an alternative for the other.

Write and test a function subprogram that accepts two words and returns a `BOOLEAN` value indicating whether or not the words have identical Soundex codes.

WRI 10.4.9   Here's a list of all the letters in the Roman alphabet (paraphrased from *Collier's Encyclopedia*, 1984, Vol. 7, p. 529):

a 0.074	f 0.028	k 0.003	o 0.075	s 0.061	w 0.016
b 0.010	g 0.016	l 0.036	p 0.027	t 0.092	x 0.005
c 0.031	h 0.034	m 0.025	q 0.003	u 0.026	y 0.019
d 0.042	i 0.074	n 0.079	r 0.076	v 0.015	z 0.001
e 0.130	j 0.002				

Along with each letter, we've given the *frequency* with which that letter is used in common English prose. A frequency of 0.074 for the letter a means that 74 out of 1000 letters are as. Write a program that reads a cryptogram, counts how many times each letter is used in the cryptogram, and uses that count (along with our list) to make up a cipher alphabet for the cryptogram.

10.5

Linear Search

In the next few sections we'll examine a few useful and commonly used algorithms. We'll implement these algorithms as Pascal programs, but the main goal will not be to study Pascal programs per se. Rather the goal will be to study the algorithms on which the programs are based.

searching, merging, and sorting

We'll examine algorithms that search, merge, and sort. **Searching** for a particular value in an array means finding that value in the array (that is, finding the index of the component where that value is stored). *Sorting* an array means rearranging the values in the array so that they're in order, either increasing or decreasing (perhaps non-increasing, or non-decreasing). *Merging* two arrays means combining them into one array so that the new array is sorted.

Searching, sorting, and merging are done so often in computing that some programming languages, like COBOL, have built-in `SEARCH`, `SORT`, and `MERGE` statements. Many *operating systems* have their own built-in programs that do searching, sorting, and merging. A program that's "built into" an operating system is called a **utility**. Normally you can run a utility by typing an operating system command. (See Section 1.4 to review operating system *commands*.)

In the next few sections and in Sections 13.5, 14.11, and 14.13, we'll try to impress you with the wide variety of algorithms that can be used to solve the searching, merging, and sorting problems. We'll start with algorithms that do searching.

Specifications

linear search

The **linear search** algorithm is the simplest (the most naive) way to search for a value in an array. We just examine the array's values from the first to the last until we find the value we're looking for.

In this section's program example, the linear search is implemented as a subprogram, and the subprogram is called by a test driver. We do it this way to emphasize that a subprogram that does searching can be used in many applications and could be inserted into many different main programs.

Input (to the test driver): Ten INTEGER values, to be stored in an array a, and another INTEGER value, to be stored in a variable named searchFor.

Process (performed by Procedure LinearSearch): Find the index of the first component in a where searchFor is stored.

Output (of the test driver): The index where searchFor is stored or a message indicating that searchFor isn't stored anywhere in a.

Designing a Program

adding an extra value

Without too much work we can improve on the simple strategy of "just examining the array's values from the first to the last until we find the value we're looking for." After all, in this simple strategy we need a loop that continues until *either* we've found the value we're looking for *or* we've reached the end of the array. So each time through the loop we have to test two conditions to see if we should do another iteration.

But if we're clever we'll start by putting an extra value into the array. In the last component of the array we'll put the value that we're searching for. Then we never need to test the second condition, because when we get to the end of the array, the first condition will stop us.

Program Example

```
PROGRAM LinSearchDriver (fInput, input, output);
{Test driver for Procedure LinearSearch.}
   CONST
      lo = 1;
      hi = 11;
   TYPE
      anyType   = INTEGER;
      indexType = lo..hi;
      arrayType = ARRAY [indexType] OF anyType;
   VAR
      a                : arrayType;
      i, whereFound : indexType;
      searchFor     : anyType;
      fInput        : TEXT;
      {----------}
```

```
      PROCEDURE LinearSearch (a         : arrayType ;
                              searchFor : anyType   ;
                              VAR i     : indexType);
      {Implements the linear search algorithm.}

      BEGIN {LinearSearch}
        a[hi] := searchFor;
        i := lo;

        WHILE a[i] <> searchFor DO
          i := i + 1
      END;   {LinearSearch}

      {----------}

   BEGIN {LinSearchDriver}
     Reset (fInput);
     FOR i := lo TO hi-1 DO
       ReadLn (fInput, a[i]);

     Write  ('Value to be searched for: ');
     ReadLn (searchFor);

     LinearSearch (a, searchFor, whereFound);

     IF whereFound < hi THEN
       WriteLn ('Found in position ', whereFound:2)
     ELSE
       WriteLn ('Not found')
   END.   {LinSearchDriver}
```

Sample Runs

With the following f I n p u t file:

```
35
51
12
29
36
60
23
34
89
100
```

we can have two runs that look like this:

```
Value to be searched for: 12
Found in position  3
```

```
Value to be searched for: 63
Not found
```

Traces

With searchFor equal to 12, the algorithm proceeds as follows:

```
a[1] a[2] a[3] a[4] a[5] a[6] a[7] a[8] a[9] a[10] a[11]
 35   51   12   29   36   60   23   34   89   100   12
  ↑
TRUE
```

```
a[1] a[2] a[3] a[4] a[5] a[6] a[7] a[8] a[9] a[10] a[11]
 35   51   12   29   36   60   23   34   89   100   12
       ↑
     TRUE
```

```
a[1] a[2] a[3] a[4] a[5] a[6] a[7] a[8] a[9] a[10] a[11]
 35   51   12   29   36   60   23   34   89   100   12
            ↑
         FALSE
```

For each line in the trace:

- the arrow points from the value of a[i] <> searchFor (TRUE or FALSE) to the value of a[i]
- the values *not* in bold are the ones that the program has already examined (the values that the program will ignore from this point on)

Programming Style

- TYPE
     anyType = INTEGER;

Why create a new type name?

Throughout this LinearSearch procedure, the name anyType stands for the type INTEGER, so why don't we just use the word INTEGER? It's because we want to emphasize that in some problems you'll be searching for non-INTEGER values, and the linear search algorithm will work for these other values. For instance, to search for letters, we just change the definition of anyType to

```
TYPE
  anyType = CHAR;
```

We don't have to make any other changes to Procedure LinearSearch or Program LinSearchDriver!

We'll use the word **polymorphic** to describe an algorithm or program that can be applied, without modification, to several different types of values.

staying within the index range

In order to simplify the loop's condition we added an extra value at the end of the array a. We put it in the eleventh component. So if we don't add an extra value and we use a more complicated condition

```
(i <= 10) AND (a[i] <> searchFor)
```

we may be tempted to change hi to 10. After all, if we're not putting anything into a[11], why even have an a[11] component?

The problem with this reasoning is as follows: Let's say that when i gets to be 10, we have

Searching for 63:

```
a[1] a[2] a[3] a[4] a[5] a[6] a[7] a[8] a[9] a[10]
 35   51   12   29   36   60   23   34   89   100
                                               ↑
```

```
(i <= 10)  AND  (a[i] <> searchFor)
    ‿                    ‿
  TRUE                 TRUE
         ‿
        TRUE
```

Since the condition is TRUE we iterate the loop again, adding 1 to i. Then we test the condition again

Searching for 63:

```
a[1] a[2] a[3] a[4] a[5] a[6] a[7] a[8] a[9] a[10]  i is 11
 35   51   12   29   36   60   23   34   89   100        ↑
```

```
(i <= 10)  AND  (a[i] <> searchFor)
    ‿                    ‿
 FALSE                   ?
         ‿
```

Since (i <= 10) is FALSE, this whole condition *must* be FALSE

Without even looking at (a[i] <> searchFor), we know that the whole condition must be FALSE. The condition (a[i] <> searchFor) doesn't need to be tested.

Now it would be nice if we could say that, since (a[i] <> searchFor) doesn't need to be tested, it won't be tested. But we can't be sure that the computer will avoid doing the (a[i] <> searchFor) test. Some implementations avoid it; others don't. Implementations that avoid testing a condition like this are said to be doing **short-circuit evaluation** of BOOLEAN expressions.

short-circuit evaluation of BOOLEAN expressions

If the computer does the (a[i] <> searchFor) test, then the program might abort when the computer makes reference to a[11]. That's why a still needs an eleventh component.

Structure

How much time does Procedure LinearSearch take to run? To answer this question, we'll distinguish between two ways of measuring time consumption:

- **worst-case time:** What's the *largest* number of times the WHILE loop can be iterated in any particular run?
- **average time:** On the average, how many times is the WHILE loop iterated?

average time vs. worst-case time

First let's consider worst-case time: The worst situation is when every component of a is examined, and searchFor is never found (or at least it's never found until that last "extra" component is reached). In this case, the WHILE loop does ten complete iterations—one for each regular component in the array.

If we change the type definitions so that a has 101 components, then, in the worst case, the WHILE loop is iterated 100 times. In other words, the WHILE loop does $n - 1$ complete iterations, where n is the number of components in the array a. Thus, the worst-case time of Procedure LinearSearch is $O(n)$.

Now let's consider the average time. We'll assume that searchFor can occur anywhere in a with equal probability. That is, searchFor isn't more likely to occur at the beginning of a than at the end of a.

If a[4] has the value searchFor, then the WHILE loop does three complete iterations. If a[8] has the value searchFor, then the WHILE loop does seven complete iterations. So, depending on where searchFor lies in the array, the WHILE loop is iterated any number of times, from 0 to 10.

The average of the numbers 0 to 10 is 5. So on the average, the WHILE loop does five iterations. In general, if the array a is declared as having n components, then the WHILE loop is iterated an average of $(n - 1)/2$ times.

So notice this: the average number of loop iterations is smaller than the worst-case number of loop iterations, but not significantly smaller. Both the average and worst-case running times are $O(n)$.

In the next section we'll compare this $O(n)$ algorithm with another algorithm that does searching.

10.5   Exercises

Key Words to Review

searching	polymorphic	worst-case time
utility	short-circuit evaluation	average time
linear search		

Questions to Answer

QUE 10.5.1   Do the numbers in the linear search program's input file have to be sorted (either non-increasing or non-decreasing) in order for the linear search algorithm to work? Why, or why not?

QUE 10.5.2   Find two lines of code in Program `LinSearchDriver` that express the "essence" of the linear search algorithm.

QUE 10.5.3   Does "average case" mean "the average of all cases" or "the single case which is the average"? Explain.

QUE 10.5.4   Write a proof of correctness for Procedure `LinearSearch`.

Things to Check in a Manual

MAN 10.5.1   Does your implementation have an option that lets you decide whether or not short-circuit evaluation of `BOOLEAN` expressions will be used?

Experiments to Try

EXP 10.5.1   In the beginning of Program `LinSearchDriver`, change

```
TYPE
    anyType   = INTEGER;
```

to

```
TYPE
    anyType   = CHAR;
```

Run the new program to verify that it now searches through lists of `CHAR`-type values, without needing any other modifications.

Changes to Make

CHA 10.5.1   Modify Procedure `LinearSearch` so that it finds the *last* component of a that contains the `searchFor` value.

CHA 10.5.2   Modify Procedure `LinearSearch` so that it finds the indices of *every* component of a containing the `searchFor` value.

CHA 10.5.3   Two values are said to be *adjacent* if they're right next to one another in an array. Modify Procedure `LinearSearch` so that it finds the first pair of *adjacent* `searchFor` values in the array a. For example, if a contains the values

7 8 9 9 6 7 7 8 4 3 3 7 7 7 2 3

and `searchFor` is 7, then your modified procedure should find

7 8 9 9 6 7 7 8 4 3 3 7 7 7 2 3
          ↑ ↑

CHA 10.5.4   Assume that the numbers in the `fInput` file are in non-decreasing order. Modify Procedure `LinearSearch` so that it takes advantage of this assumption.

CHA 10.5.5   Modify Program `CryptoDriver` (Section 10.4) so that it tries using three different cipher alphabets to decrypt the cryptogram. After trying a particular cipher alphabet, the program "guesses" whether this cipher alphabet was correct by looking through the decrypted text for the words `the`, `The`, `I`, `a`, `an`.

Programs and Subprograms to Write

WRI 10.5.1 Write a program to handle customer information in the following way: Read each customer's identification number, zip code, and balance due from a disk file into three arrays.

id	zip	bal
305	07940	1000.00
452	55455	12.53
226	19149	0.00
.	.	.
.	.	.

Etc.

Then have the user type in an identification number, which identifies a particular customer. The program writes the customer's zip code and balance. (For example, Customer 305's zip code is 07940, and 305's balance is 1000.00 dollars.)

WRI 10.5.2 Modify the program of Exercise Wri.10.5.1 so that the user types in a zip code and a balance, and the program prints the identification numbers of all customers in that zip code with a balance over that amount.

WRI 10.5.3 Here's an enhanced version of Exercise Wri.5.1.1. A disk file contains several lines. Each line contains an eight-letter user name, followed by the encryption of a six-letter password. The user is prompted for a name and a password. The program looks for the user's name in the disk file. If it finds the user's name, then it looks on the remainder of the line for the encryption of a password. The program encrypts the password given to it by the user and compares this with the encryption that it found in the disk file. If they match, the program sends to the screen the message

```
You are now logged on.
```

Otherwise, it sends the message

```
Incorrect password.
```

Notice that at no time does the program *decrypt* a password. This is a typical security measure. The only one who knows the password's plain text form is the user. Neither the computer system, the system's users, nor the system's managers know how to decrypt an encrypted password.

10.6

Binary Search

The strategy used in a linear search is simple: Examine the elements of the array in order, starting with the first and working your way toward the last. As natural as this strategy is, it's not always the best. You'd never use a

What is a
binary search?
linear search to find a name in a phone book. It would be silly to start on
page 1, with Aaacon Plumbing, and work your way toward Jeffrey Smith!
Instead you open the book roughly in the middle, and check to see if you've
reached the S's or not. If you've opened only to the M's, you thumb forward.
You can ignore the earlier pages because they can't possibly contain a Smith.

The **binary search** works roughly like a person searching through a
telephone book. Even before we examine the code in detail, we can make a
few preliminary observations:

1. The telephone book search strategy wouldn't work if the names weren't
   in alphabetical order. When you open to the M's you know you can ignore
   everything that comes earlier, because Jeffrey Smith comes after the M
   listings. Translating this into the jargon of computing: the array input to
   the binary search algorithm must already be sorted. The values in the
   array must be in non-decreasing or non-increasing order.

2. Right at the beginning of the search you decide to ignore half the names
   in the book. As long as you continue to search for Jeffrey Smith, you'll
   never bother with these earlier pages. The next thing you'll do is to look
   in the middle of the remaining pages, and decide to ignore half of these.
   You'll keep dividing the list of remaining names in half, until you find
   Jeffrey Smith.

   Surely the binary search runs faster than the linear search. In a binary
   search, you decide to ignore half the names in the book without even
   examining them. In the linear search, you "ignore" a name only after
   you've examined it and determined that it's not the one you're looking
   for.

Specifications The formal specs for the binary search are the same as the specs for the
linear search, except that the array a must be sorted before the search
begins. We'll assume that the values in fInput are sorted in non-
decreasing order.

**Program
Example**

```
PROGRAM BinSearchDriver (fInput, input, output);
{Test driver for Procedure BinarySearch.}
   CONST
      loConst = 1;
      hiConst = 16;
   TYPE
      anyType   = INTEGER;
      indexType = loConst..hiConst;
      arrayType = ARRAY [indexType] OF anyType;
   VAR
      a                 : arrayType;
      i, whereFound : indexType;
      searchFor        : anyType;
      fInput           : TEXT;
      {----------}
```

```
              PROCEDURE BinarySearch (a            : arrayType ;
                                      lo, hi        : indexType ;
                                      searchFor     : anyType   ;
                                      VAR middle    : indexType);
              {Implements the binary search algorithm.}
              BEGIN {BinarySearch}
                middle := (hi + lo) DIV 2;
                WHILE (a[middle] <> searchFor) AND (hi > lo) DO
                  BEGIN
                    IF searchFor < a[middle] THEN
                      hi := middle - 1
                    ELSE
                      lo := middle + 1;
                    middle := (hi + lo) DIV 2
                  END
              END;  {BinarySearch}

              {----------}

            BEGIN {BinSearchDriver}
              Reset (fInput);
              FOR i := loConst TO hiConst DO
                ReadLn (fInput, a[i]);

              Write  ('Value to be searched for: ');
              ReadLn (searchFor);

              BinarySearch (a, loConst, hiConst, searchFor, whereFound);

              IF a[whereFound] = searchFor THEN
                WriteLn ('Found in position ', whereFound:2)
              ELSE
                WriteLn ('Not found')
            END.   {BinSearchDriver}
```

Sample Runs

With the following fInput file:

```
5
7
8
12
15
15
23
29
34
35
36
51
55
60
89
90
```

we can have two runs that look like this:

```
Value to be searched for: 15
Found in position  6
```

```
Value to be searched for: 100
Not found
```

Traces

As in the trace of the linear search, we'll use bold typeface for the values that haven't yet been eliminated. In this trace we write a new copy of the array whenever the value of lo, hi, or middle changes. First let's search for the value 15:

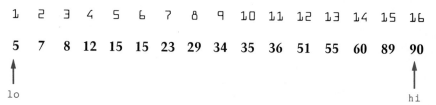

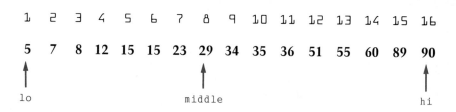

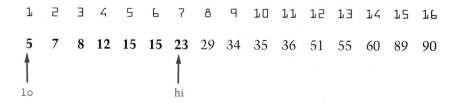

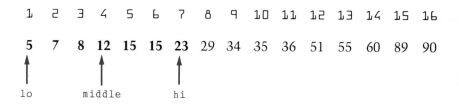

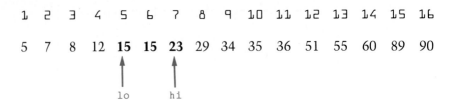

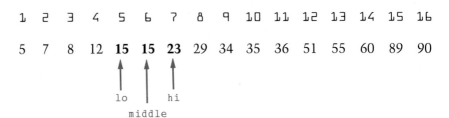

Notice: The binary search finds 15 in a[b]. In contrast, the linear search would have started from the leftmost end of the array and would have kept moving rightward until it found 15 in a[5].

Now we'll search for the value 100:

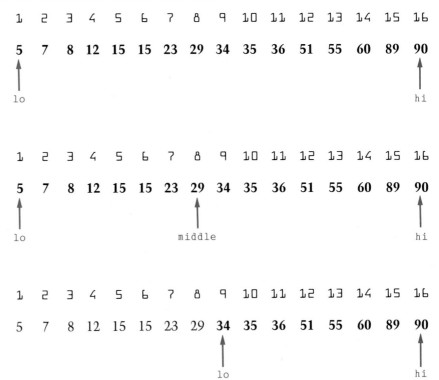

1   2   3   4   5   6   7   8   9   10   11   12   13   14   15   16

5   7   8   12   15   15   23   29   **34**   **35**   **36**   **51**   **55**   **60**   **89**   **90**

                                 lo   middle   hi

1   2   3   4   5   6   7   8   9   10   11   12   13   14   15   16

5   7   8   12   15   15   23   29   34   35   36   51   **55**   **60**   **89**   **90**

                       lo   hi

1   2   3   4   5   6   7   8   9   10   11   12   13   14   15   16

5   7   8   12   15   15   23   29   34   35   36   51   **55**   **60**   **89**   **90**

                     lo   hi

                            middle

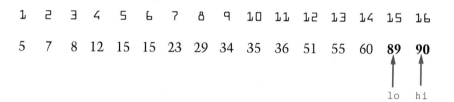

1   2   3   4   5   6   7   8   9   10   11   12   13   14   15   16

5   7   8   12   15   15   23   29   34   35   36   51   55   60   **89**   **90**

                             lo hi

1   2   3   4   5   6   7   8   9   10   11   12   13   14   15   16

5   7   8   12   15   15   23   29   34   35   36   51   55   60   **89**   **90**

                             lo hi

                            middle

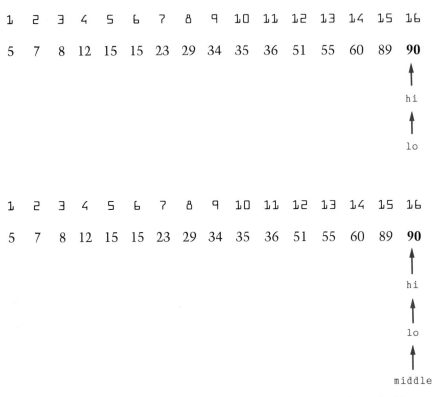

In this situation, Procedure `BinarySearch` goes to quite a bit of effort, only to find that the number 100 occurs nowhere in the array a.

Structure   What's the worst-case time for a run of Procedure `BinarySearch`? Of course the worst happens when `searchFor` isn't one of the values in a. This is the situation in the second of the two traces we've just given. We start with an array of 16 components. At the end of the first iteration, eight of these are eliminated and half of them (a[9] to a[16]) are remaining. In the next iteration, the list of remaining components is divided in half and only four components (a[13] to a[16]) remain. During each iteration, the number of remaining components is cut in half:

start   →   16 components
1st iteration → $16/2 = 8$ components
2nd iteration→ $(16/2)/2 = 4$ components
3rd iteration → $((16/2)/2)/2 = 2$ components
4th iteration → $(((16/2)/2)/2)/2 = 1$ component

The numbers look a bit different if we begin with an odd number of components or if we chop off the right half of the array instead of the left half. But the general rule is still the same: the number of iterations is roughly equal to the number of times the array size can be divided by 2. Mathematicians have a name for this number: it's called the **logarithm with base 2**. If the array a has n components, then the largest possible number of loop iterations in Procedure `BinarySearch` is $\log_2 n$. We call this **logarithmic time** or $O(\log n)$. Let's extend the chart we made in Section 9.4 to compare logarithmic time with constant, linear, quadratic, and exponential time:

logarithmic time

Running time (in seconds) of Programs

n	Constant	Log	Linear	Quadratic	Exponential
1	1	1	1	1	2
2	1	1	2	4	8
3	1	2	3	9	24
4	1	2	4	16	64
5	1	3	5	25	160
6	1	3	6	36	384
7	1	3	7	49	896
8	1	3	8	64	2048
9	1	4	9	81	4608
10	1	4	10	100	10240

In terms of size, the numbers in the `Log` column come between the numbers in the `Constant` and `Linear` columns. This reflects the fact that an $O(\log n)$-time algorithm is slower than an $O(1)$-time algorithm, but faster than $O(n)$-, $O(n^2)$-, and $O(2^n)$-time algorithms.

A binary search takes at most $O(\log n)$ time, and a linear search takes at most $O(n)$ time. So if we're lucky enough to be given a sorted array, a binary search will usually be faster than a linear search. Of course "usually" doesn't mean "always." To find the value 5 in the list

5   7   8   12   15   15   23   29   34   35   36   51   55   60   89   90

a linear search takes only one step (one loop iteration), and a binary search takes three. It all depends on the input data. But if we don't know much about the data, except that it's a sorted array, we're best off trying a binary search.

10.6   Exercises

Key Words to Review

binary search	logarithmic time
logarithm with base 2	$O(\log n)$

Questions to Answer

QUE 10.6.1   Write a trace of Procedure BinarySearch when a is

$$-54 \quad -49 \quad -21 \quad -18 \quad -5 \quad 0 \quad 0 \quad 0 \quad 3 \quad 6 \quad 18 \quad 22 \quad 44$$

and searchFor is −49.

QUE 10.6.2   Write a trace of Procedure BinarySearch when a is

$$-54 \quad -49 \quad -21 \quad -18 \quad -5 \quad 0 \quad 0 \quad 0 \quad 3 \quad 6 \quad 18 \quad 22 \quad 44$$

and searchFor is −51.

QUE 10.6.3   In the linear search we added an extra value to the array to make the program run a bit faster. Why doesn't it help to do this with the binary search?

QUE 10.6.4   Describe the behavior of Program BinSearchDriver if the numbers in the fInput file are all equal.

QUE 10.6.5   Describe the behavior of Program BinSearchDriver if, by accident, the numbers in the fInput file are in *decreasing* order.

Experiments to Try

EXP 10.6.1   In Procedure BinarySearch, try changing searchFor < a[middle] to searchFor <= a[middle].

EXP 10.6.2   In Procedure BinarySearch, change (hi > lo) to (hi >= lo).

EXP 10.6.3   In Procedure BinarySearch, try changing (hi + lo) DIV 2 to ((hi + lo) DIV 2) + 1.

Changes to Make

CHA 10.6.1   Modify Procedure BinarySearch so that it finds *the smallest number that's greater than* searchFor.

CHA 10.6.2   Modify Procedure BinarySearch so that it always finds the *earliest* occurrence of the searchFor value in the array.

Programs and Subprograms to Write

WRI 10.6.1   Repeat Exercise Wri.10.5.1, this time assuming that values in the id array are in increasing order. (Customer 305's zip code is still 07940, and 305's balance is still 1000.00 dollars, but now these values might be in the second components of the id, zip, and bal arrays, rather than the first.)

WRI 10.6.2   Write a program that reads a file containing names and telephone numbers, as if from a telephone book, looks for a particular name, and prints the corresponding telephone number.

Things to Think About

THI 10.6.1   Imagine that you've lost your keys and you need to find them in a hurry. Even though you're not aware of it, you use some kind of a search method to find them.

Can you describe the method? Is it anything like the linear search or the binary search? If not, how is it different? Can you use these ideas to create a new method for searching through a list of numbers?

10.7

Merging Arrays

Let's look at an abstract problem that has many applications in real-life programming. Imagine that we have three arrays—two small arrays and one large array. The two small arrays have five components each, and the large array has ten components (enough room to store the values from both of the small arrays). Assume also that the values in each of the small arrays are stored in non-decreasing order:

The first small array:

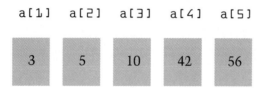

The second small array:

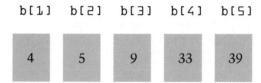

We want to combine the values in the two small arrays so that they're stored in the large array in non-decreasing order:

The large array:

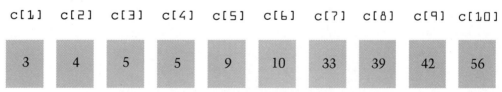

Combining the two small arrays into one large array is called *merging*. Merging is a very useful thing to do. For instance, a company has two lists of names and addresses. The first list has this year's new customers on it; the second list has customers from all previous years. Each list is arranged

merging

alphabetically, by last name. At the end of this year the company wants to merge the first list into the second list. This kind of activity is an example of *year-end processing.*

Specifications

Input: The values to be stored in two smaller arrays. Each array's values are in non-decreasing order.

Process: Merge the two smaller arrays into one large array.

Output: The values in the large array.

Designing a Program

Let's role-play the computer the way we did in Section 9.2. Imagine a card game in which two players contribute to a common pile. The first player has the hand

role-playing the computer

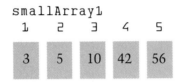

and the second player has

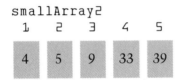

(Each player's hand is an array. We're giving our cards integer values, not the ordinary card values like "king of spades," etc.)

Each player singles out the lowest card in his or her hand.

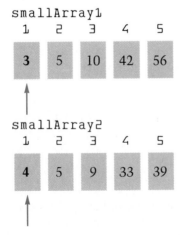

(Singling out these two cards is like setting two index variables each to 1.)

The player with the lowest card contributes to the common pile and then singles out the next lowest card in his or her hand.

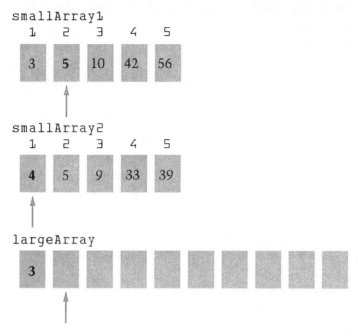

smallArray1

smallArray2

largeArray

(In the computer program the corresponding action is to increment the index of one of the small arrays. The index of the larger array is also incremented. This prepares us for the next iteration.)

So far we've described an algorithm that looks something like this:

```
sm1 := 1;
sm2 := 1;
lg  := 1;
WHILE (sm1 <= 5) AND (sm2 <= 5) DO
    IF smallArray1[sm1] < smallArray2[sm2] THEN
        Move smallArray1[sm1] to largeArray[lg]
        Increment sm1
        Increment lg
    ELSE
        Move smallArray1[sm2] to largeArray[lg]
        Increment sm2
        Increment lg
```

The question is: what to do when you've moved all the values from either of the smallArrays into the largeArray? You have to "jump" to either

```
{Move the rest of the smallArray1 values into largeArray.}
WHILE sm1 <= 5 DO
  Move smallArray1[sm1] to largeArray[lg]
  Increment sm1
  Increment lg
```

or

```
{Move the rest of the smallArray2 values into largeArray.}
WHILE sm2 <= 5 DO
  Move smallArray1[sm2] to largeArray[lg]
  Increment sm2
  Increment lg
```

to move the remaining elements in the other smallArray over to the largeArray. But this "jumping" can be clumsy, and it forces you to have three pieces of code (represented by the three preceding pieces of pseudocode) that are almost identical.

adding extra values

To fix this, we'll add an extra value to the end of each small array, just like the extra value that we added at the end of the array in Procedure LinearSearch. In this program, our extra values will be MAXINTs.

Now a slight modification of the original pseudocode works just fine:

```
sm1 := 1;
sm2 := 1;
lg  := 1;
WHILE (sm1 <= 5) OR (sm2 <= 5) DO
   IF smallArray1[sm1] < smallArray2[sm2] THEN
       Move smallArray1[sm1] to largeArray[lg]
       Increment sm1
       Increment lg
   ELSE
       Move smallArray1[sm2] to largeArray[lg]
       Increment sm2
       Increment lg
```

Because of the change to the word OR, this loop doesn't stop iterating until all the values of both of the small arrays have been moved. When you've moved all the regular values in, say, smallArray1, this loop keeps comparing the remaining values in smallArray2 with the MAXINT in smallArray1. Since MAXINT is so large, the smallArray2 values are always the ones that are placed into largeArray. So smallArray2 is "cleansed" of its remaining values.

Program Example

```
PROGRAM Merge (input, output);
{Merges two arrays of equal size.}
   CONST
     smallMax = 6;
     largeMax = 10;
   TYPE
     smallType = ARRAY [1..smallMax] OF INTEGER;
     largeType = ARRAY [1..largeMax] OF INTEGER;
     positive  = 1..MAXINT;
   VAR
     smallArray1, smallArray2 : smallType;
     largeArray               : largeType;
     sm1, sm2, lg             : positive;

   {----------}

   PROCEDURE ReadArray(VAR smallArray : smallType);
   {Reads values into either of the two small arrays.}

     VAR
        i : 1..smallMax;
   BEGIN {ReadArray}
     Write ('Enter ', smallMax-1 : 1, ' integers: ');

     FOR i := 1 TO smallMax-1 DO
       Read (smallArray[i]);

     smallArray[smallMax] := MAXINT;
     WriteLn
   END;  {ReadArray}

   {----------}

   PROCEDURE Move (VAR largeArray  : largeType;
                       smallArray  : smallType;
                   VAR lg, sm      : positive);
   {Moves a value from one of the small arrays into
    the large array, and adjusts indices as needed.}

   BEGIN {Move}
     largeArray[lg] := smallArray[sm];
     lg := lg + 1;
     sm := sm + 1
   END;  {Move}

   {----------}

   PROCEDURE WriteArray (largeArray : largeType);
   {Writes the values in the large array.}

     VAR
        i : 1..largeMax;
   BEGIN {WriteArray}
     Write ('After merging, the values are: ');

     FOR i := 1 TO largeMax DO
       Write (largeArray[i]:3);
     WriteLn
   END;  {WriteArray}

   {----------}
```

```
                BEGIN {Merge}
                  ReadArray (smallArray1);
                  ReadArray (smallArray2);
                  sm1 := 1;
                  sm2 := 1;
                  lg  := 1;
                  WHILE (sm1 < smallMax) OR (sm2 < smallMax) DO
                    IF smallArray1[sm1] < smallArray2[sm2] THEN
                      Move (largeArray, smallArray1, lg, sm1)
                    ELSE
                      Move (largeArray, smallArray2, lg, sm2);
                  WriteArray (largeArray)
                END.  {Merge}
```

Sample
Runs

```
Enter 5 integers: 3 5 10 42 56
Enter 5 integers: 4 5  9 33 39
After merging, the values are:  3  4  5  5  9 10 33 39 42 56
```

Traces

To see how Program Merge works we'll envision the array indices as arrows (M stands for MAXINT) as shown on the facing page.

Dealing with several array indices at once, as in Program Merge, can be tricky. Notice that the lg arrow always points to "nothing." The lg index always stays one step ahead of the contents of largeArray. That is, lg is always being incremented so that largeArray[lg] is the first component of largeArray whose value is undefined. Similarly, sm1 is always being incremented so that smallArray1[sm1] is the first component of smallArray1 that hasn't yet been put into largeArray. This practice of keeping indices "one step ahead" is very common. It's used in many programs that manipulate arrays.

how the indices
change

Now notice that no details of the procedure calls are portrayed in the trace. This keeps the trace down to a manageable size, but more importantly it eliminates details that would keep us from seeing the forest for the trees. After all, the purposes of writing a trace are to help us understand

top-down
tracing

- how the program works
- why it does what the programmer intended it to do
- why it solves the problem that the programmer intended it to solve

or to help us debug the program, if it's not working correctly. We should put in exactly enough detail to fulfill these purposes, and no more.

But how do we know how much detail is enough? The general rule of thumb is that too much detail is better than too little detail. When in doubt, put in the details. Never leave out details that you're unsure about. If you can't figure out why your program isn't running correctly, there's a chance that you've omitted important details from your trace. Put the details back in.

One way to approach trace writing is to create your traces in a top-down fashion. That is, begin with a trace that has very little detail, and add details

```
─────────────────────── Merge ───────────────────────
smallArray1          smallArray2          largeArray
1  2  3  4  5  6     1  2  3  4  5  6     1  2  3  4  5  6  7  8  9  10
---ReadArray-------ReadArray----
3  5  10 42 56  M    4  5  9  33 39  M
↑                    ↑                    ↑
sm1                  sm2                  lg
------------------------------Move--------------------------------
3  5  10 42 56  M    4  5  9  33 39  M    3
   ↑                    ↑                    ↑
   sm1                  sm2                  lg
------------------------------Move--------------------------------
3  5  10 42 56  M    4  5  9  33 39  M    3  4
   ↑                       ↑                    ↑
   sm1                     sm2                  lg
------------------------------Move--------------------------------
3  5  10 42 56  M    4  5  9  33 39  M    3  4  5
   ↑                       ↑                       ↑
   sm1                     sm2                     lg
------------------------------Move--------------------------------
3  5  10 42 56  M    4  5  9  33 39  M    3  4  5  5
      ↑                    ↑                          ↑
      sm1                  sm2                        lg
------------------------------Move--------------------------------
3  5  10 42 56  M    4  5  9  33 39  M    3  4  5  5  9
      ↑                       ↑                          ↑
      sm1                     sm2                        lg
------------------------------Move--------------------------------
3  5  10 42 56  M    4  5  9  33 39  M    3  4  5  5  9  10
         ↑                    ↑                             ↑
         sm1                  sm2                           lg
------------------------------Move--------------------------------
3  5  10 42 56  M    4  5  9  33 39  M    3  4  5  5  9  10 33
         ↑                          ↑                          ↑
         sm1                        sm2                        lg
------------------------------Move--------------------------------
3  5  10 42 56  M    4  5  9  33 39  M    3  4  5  5  9  10 33 39
         ↑                          ↑                             ↑
         sm1                        sm2                           lg
------------------------------Move--------------------------------
3  5  10 42 56  M    4  5  9  33 39  M    3  4  5  5  9  10 33 39 42
            ↑                       ↑                                ↑
            sm1                     sm2                              lg
------------------------------Move--------------------------------
3  5  10 42 56  M    4  5  9  33 39  M    3  4  5  5  9  10 33 39 42 56
            ↑                       ↑                                   ↑
            sm1                     sm2                                 lg
-----------------------------WriteArray----------------------------
```

to the trace as they're needed. Instead of cluttering up the old trace, add the new details on a separate page—a page that traces just one subprogram call.

Look again at the trace for Program `Merge`. The portion of the trace that deals with Procedure `ReadArray` has no detail at all. So here's a detailed trace that deals exclusively with Procedure `ReadArray`:

```
 ┌────────── ReadArray ──────────────────────┐
 │                                            │
 │  i  smallArray                             │
 │       [1]   [2]   [3]   [4]   [5]   [6]     │
 │                                            │
 │  ─────────Write {prompt}──────────         │
 │                                            │
 │  1      3                                   │
 │  2            5                             │
 │  3                  10                      │
 │  4                        42                │
 │  5                              56   MAXINT │
 │                                            │
 └────────────────────────────────────────────┘
```

Notice that in this trace, the writing of a prompt is represented by a line. In an even more detailed trace we'd show the prompt message that actually gets written to the screen.

In most of the examples thus far we've been designing algorithms and programs in a top-down fashion. Now in this section, we see that *tracing* an existing program can also be done from the top, downward.

10.7 Exercises

Key Words to Review

merge

Questions to Answer

QUE 10.7.1 Explain the purpose of `MAXINT` in Program `Merge`.

QUE 10.7.2 Describe the behavior of Program `Merge` when each `smallArray` contains five 10's.

QUE 10.7.3 Describe the behavior of Program `Merge` when one of the `smallArrays` accidentally contains values that are not in non-decreasing order.

QUE 10.7.4 Describe the behavior of Program `Merge` when one of the `smallArrays` accidentally contains six values in non-decreasing order, and the sixth value isn't `MAXINT`.

QUE 10.7.5 Write a proof of correctness for Program `Merge`.

Experiments to Try

EXP 10.7.1 In the main body of Program Merge, change the WHILE loop's condition to

```
(sm1 < smallMax) AND (sm2 < smallMax)
```

without making any other changes.

Changes to Make

CHA 10.7.1 Rewrite Program Merge so that it doesn't use any extra (MAXINT) values.

CHA 10.7.2 In the Traces subsection we explained how the array indices in Program Merge are always staying one step ahead of the action. Rewrite Program Merge so that the array indices are always "where the action is."

Scales to Practice

PRA 10.7.1 Let's say we have two arrays, smallArray1 and smallArray2, and that the values in each of these arrays are in non-decreasing order. If the two arrays contain the same values, we'll say that smallArray1 and smallArray2 are *similar*, even though some values may occur more often in one array than in the other array. For instance,

```
smallArray1
1 5 5 6 8 9 9 9
smallArray2
1 1 5 6 6 8 8 9
```

are similar arrays. Write a function subprogram that accepts two arrays and returns a BOOLEAN value indicating whether or not the two arrays are similar.

Programs and Subprograms to Write

WRI 10.7.1 Here's a variation on Exercise Wri.10.5.1: We have six arrays idA, zipA, balA, idB, zipB, and balB. The identification numbers in array idA are in increasing order, and so are the numbers in array idB. Write a program that merges idA and idB into one big array id, and combines the other four arrays accordingly.

WRI 10.7.2 Two teachers, Teacher x and Teacher y, rank the same students (from best to worst). Teacher x puts the students' identification numbers into an array x, listing the students from best to worst, and Teacher y does the same with an array called y:

		Teacher x's opinion	Teacher y's opinion
Best student	→	101 = x[1]	101 = y[1]
2nd best student	→	152 = x[2]	125 = y[2]
3rd best student	→	806 = x[3]	806 = y[3]
4th best student	→	125 = x[4]	152 = y[4]
5th best student	→	301 = x[5]	301 = y[5]

Write a program that divides the students into the largest possible number of groups. Student A cannot be in a higher group than Student B unless both teachers think that Student A is better than Student B.

10.8

Selection Sort

sorting algorithms

The literature on computer science contains over a hundred different algorithms for **sorting**. Each algorithm uses its own unique strategy for arranging values in non-decreasing order. Some algorithms take more time to run than others. Some work well for large files (the so-called **external sorting** algorithms); others work well for small arrays (the **internal sorting** algorithms). Some sorting algorithms are called **stable**, because if they find two 5's next to one another in an array, they never switch the two 5's. Other sorting algorithms are **unstable**. It's quite surprising to see that there are so many completely different ways of solving the same problem. In this section we examine one of the simplest sorting algorithms: the **selection sort**.

Specifications

Input: A file with several INTEGER values in it

Output: The INTEGER values, in non-decreasing order

Designing a Program

selection sort

The strategy for the selection sort is simple:

Selection sort for the array a:

Find the component of the array where the smallest value is stored. Switch the value stored in that component with whatever is stored in a[1]. Now the smallest value in the array is stored in a[1]. Find the component of the array where the second smallest value is stored. Switch the value stored in that component with whatever is stored in a[2]. Now the second smallest value in the array is stored in a[2].

Etc.

We've already written code to do most of the work. In Section 2.5 we created Procedure Switch. We can use it here to "Switch the value stored in a component with whatever is stored in. . . ." And in Section 5.4 we created Program Minimum. The same Minimum algorithm will help us find "the smallest value in the array, the second smallest value in the array, etc." The code follows.

Program
Example

```
PROGRAM SelectionSortDriver (fInput, output);
{Test driver for Procedure SelectionSort.}
  CONST
    lo =  1;
    hi = 10;
  TYPE
    anyType   = INTEGER;
    indexType = lo..hi;
    arrayType = ARRAY [indexType] OF anyType;
  VAR
    a      : arrayType;
    fInput : TEXT;

  {----------}

  PROCEDURE ReadArray (VAR fInput : TEXT; VAR a : arrayType);
  {Reads unsorted values.}

    VAR
      i : indexType;

  BEGIN {ReadArray}
    Reset (fInput);
    FOR i := lo TO hi DO
      Read (fInput, a[i]);
    ReadLn (fInput)
  END;  {ReadArray}

  {----------}

  PROCEDURE SelectionSort (VAR a : arrayType);
  {Implements the selection sort algorithm.}

    VAR
      start, minIndex : indexType;

    {----------}

    FUNCTION IndexOfSmallest (a             : arrayType;
                              start, finish : indexType) : indexType;
    {Returns the index of the smallest value in the array
     'a', between the 'start' and 'finish' components.}

      VAR
        minIndex, thisIndex : indexType;

    BEGIN {IndexOfSmallest}
      minIndex := start;

      FOR thisIndex := start+1 TO finish DO
        IF a[thisIndex] < a[minIndex] THEN
          minIndex := thisIndex;

      IndexOfSmallest := minIndex
    END;  {IndexOfSmallest}

    {----------}
```

```
      PROCEDURE Switch (VAR x, y : anyType);
      {Switches two values, x and y.}
        VAR
          temp : anyType;
      BEGIN {Switch}
        temp := x;
        x    := y;
        y    := temp
      END;  {Switch}

      {----------}

  BEGIN {SelectionSort}
    FOR start := 1 TO hi-1 DO
      BEGIN
        minIndex := IndexOfSmallest (a, start, hi);
        Switch (a[start], a[minIndex])
      END
  END;  {SelectionSort}

  {----------}

  PROCEDURE WriteArray (a : arrayType);
  {Writes sorted values.}

    VAR
      i : indexType;

  BEGIN {WriteArray}
    WriteLn ('The values in non-decreasing order are: ');

    FOR i := lo TO hi DO
      Write (a[i]:5);
    WriteLn
  END;  {WriteArray}

  {----------}

BEGIN {SelectionSortDriver}
  ReadArray      (fInput, a);
  SelectionSort (a);
  WriteArray      (a)
END.  {SelectionSortDriver}
```

Sample Runs

Here's an fInput file:

```
31 95 62 56 10 43 43 12 22 83
```

And here's the corresponding output:

```
The values in non-decreasing order are:
   10   12   22   31   43   43   56   62   83   95
```

Traces

a[1]	a[2]	a[3]	a[4]	a[5]	a[6]	a[7]	a[8]	a[9]	a[10]	
31	95	62	56	10	43	43	12	22	83	
31	95	62	56	**10**	43	43	12	22	83	← 10 is the smallest
10	95	62	56	**31**	43	43	12	22	83	← switch 10 with a[1]
10	**95**	62	56	31	43	43	**12**	22	83	← 12 is the next smallest
10	**12**	62	56	31	43	43	**95**	22	83	← switch 12 with a[2]
10	12	**62**	56	31	43	43	95	**22**	83	Etc.
10	12	**22**	56	31	43	43	95	**62**	83	
10	12	22	**56**	**31**	43	43	95	62	83	
10	12	22	**31**	**56**	43	43	95	62	83	
10	12	22	31	**56**	**43**	43	95	62	83	
10	12	22	31	**43**	**56**	43	95	62	83	
10	12	22	31	43	**56**	**43**	95	62	83	
10	12	22	31	43	**43**	**56**	95	62	83	
10	12	22	31	43	43	**56**	95	62	83	← 56 gets switched
10	12	22	31	43	43	**56**	95	62	83	with itself!
10	12	22	31	43	43	56	**95**	**62**	83	
10	12	22	31	43	43	56	**62**	**95**	83	
10	12	22	31	43	43	56	62	**95**	**83**	
10	12	22	31	43	43	56	62	**83**	**95**	
10	12	22	31	43	43	56	62	83	95	

Structure

running time of the selection sort

It's easy to calculate the running time of the selection sort. Procedure SelectionSort contains a FOR loop, and inside that FOR loop is a call to Procedure IndexOfSmallest, which contains its own FOR loop. Whenever we have a loop within a loop we start to suspect a running time of $O(n^2)$. Let's check this $O(n^2)$ guess by tracing the values of start and thisIndex in several calls to Procedure IndexOfSmallest as shown on the top of the next page. In this trace we've assumed that our array's indices range from 1 to 5. With 5 values to sort, the trace has $4 + 3 + 2 + 1$ rows, and notice that $4 + 3 + 2 + 1$ is 10, which happens to be same as

$$\frac{5^2 - 5}{2}$$

More generally, mathematicians can prove that the sum

$$(n - 1) + (n - 2) + \cdots + 2 + 1$$

is the same as

$$\frac{n^2 - n}{2}$$

```
┌────────────────── SelectionSort ──────────────────────────────────────────┐
│  start   hi                                                                 │
│    1      5                                                                 │
│                      ┌──────────────────────── IndexOfSmallest ─┐          │
│                      │  start  finish  thisIndex                 │          │
│                      │    1       5        2                     │          │
│                      │                     3                     │          │
│                      │                     4                     │          │
│                      │                     5                     │          │
│                      └───────────────────────────────────────────┘          │
│    2                 ┌──────────────────────── IndexOfSmallest ─┐          │
│                      │  start  finish  thisIndex                 │          │
│                      │    2       5        3                     │          │
│                      │                     4                     │          │
│                      │                     5                     │          │
│                      └───────────────────────────────────────────┘          │
│    3                 ┌──────────────────────── IndexOfSmallest ─┐          │
│                      │  start  finish  thisIndex                 │          │
│                      │    3       5        4                     │          │
│                      │                     5                     │          │
│                      └───────────────────────────────────────────┘          │
│    4                 ┌──────────────────────── IndexOfSmallest ─┐          │
│                      │  start  finish  thisIndex                 │          │
│                      │    4       5        5                     │          │
│                      └───────────────────────────────────────────┘          │
└────────────────────────────────────────────────────────────────────────────┘
```

So if we have n values to sort, the selection sort will take $(n^2 - n)/2$ steps to sort them. When n becomes large, the size of n^2 will dwarf everything else in the formula, so the running time of a selection sort is $O(n^2)$.

10.8   Exercises

Key Words to Review

sorting	internal sort	unstable sort
external sort	stable sort	selection sort

Questions to Answer

QUE 10.8.1   Describe the behavior of the selection sort algorithm when the array starts with its values already in non-decreasing order.

QUE 10.8.2   Describe the behavior of the selection sort algorithm when the array starts with its values in decreasing order (and the selection sort puts them in *non*-decreasing order).

QUE 10.8.3   Assume you have an array containing INTEGERs in no particular order. You want to search for the number 42 in this array. Since a binary search is faster than a linear search, you decide on a binary search. But then you remember that a binary search works only when the values are sorted (in non-decreasing order, for instance). So you decide to sort the values with the selection sort and then search for 42 with the binary search. Does this strategy really save time over doing a linear search? Why, or why not?

QUE 10.8.4   Write a proof of correctness for Procedure `SelectionSort`.

Changes to Make

CHA 10.8.1   Make a very small change to Program `SelectionSortDriver` so that it sorts an array of `CHAR`acters instead of an array of numbers.

CHA 10.8.2   Change Program `SelectionSortDriver` so that it sorts an array of characters, but have one character be "less than" another if it comes before the other on a typewriter keyboard. For instance, q is less than w, which is less than e, which is less than r, etc. By this definition, the "smallest" character is q (in the upper left-hand corner) and the "largest" character is m.

CHA 10.8.3   Add `WriteLns` to Program `SelectionSortDriver` so that it writes its own trace. (See the Traces subsection.)

Programs and Subprograms to Write

WRI 10.8.1   Take the three arrays from Exercise Wri.10.5.1. Assume that the numbers in the `id` array are not in any particular order. Rearrange the values in the three arrays so that, after the rearranging has been done,
a. zip codes and balances follow their respective identification numbers (customer 305 still has zip code 07940 and balance $1000.00)
b. the values in the `id` array are in increasing order

WRI 10.8.2   Redo Exercise Wri.10.8.1 so that the user can choose from among three options: the identification numbers are in increasing order, the zip codes are in non-decreasing order, or the balances are in non-increasing order.

WRI 10.8.3   Consider the table of letters in Exercise Wri.10.4.9. Write a program that reads the table and rearranges it so that the letters occur in order of decreasing frequency of use.

WRI 10.8.4   Write and test a function subprogram that returns a value in the enumerated type

```
TYPE
    slopeType = (decreasing, nonIncreasing, nonDecreasing,
                 increasing, noneOfTheAbove);
```

depending on which of these values properly describes the array that's passed to it.

WRI 10.8.5   Write a program that does a *replacement-selection sort*. Here's the algorithm:

Go through the array looking for values that are smaller than a[1]. Each time you find such a value, switch it with the a[1] value, and continue looking for values smaller than the new a[1] value until you reach the end of the array.
Then go through the array, starting at a[3], looking for values that are smaller than a[2]. Each time you find such a value, switch it with the a[2]

value and continue looking for values smaller than the new a[2] value until you reach the end of the array.

. . . Etc.

WRI 10.8.6   Write a program that reads several students' test scores and prints them out in decreasing order, with dashed lines enclosing the scores whose percentile rank is between 90 and 100, between 80 and 90, between 70 and 80, etc. For an explanation of *percentile ranks*, see Exercise Wri.10.2.7.

Things to Think About

THI 10.8.1   Shuffle a deck of playing cards and then put the cards back in order (ace, two, three, etc., with all the spades first, then all the diamonds, then clubs, then hearts). You probably didn't use anything like a selection sort to get the cards back in order. What kind of an algorithm did you use? Can you describe the algorithm in pseudocode? Can you turn the pseudocode into a program that sorts a list of numbers?

10.9

String Types in ANSI Standard Pascal (Supplementary)

In Section 10.4 we briefly mentioned PACKED arrays and string types. In this section, we'll discuss these ideas in depth.[8]

Program Example

```
PROGRAM CharArray (output);
{Creates an array whose values are of type CHAR.}
  TYPE
    indexType = 1..5;
    arrayType = ARRAY [indexType] OF CHAR;
  VAR
    letters : arrayType;
    i       : indexType;
BEGIN {CharArray}
  letters[1] := 'B';
  letters[2] := 'A';
  letters[3] := 'R';
  letters[4] := 'R';
  letters[5] := 'Y';

  FOR i := 1 TO 5 DO
    Write (letters[i]:1);
  WriteLn
END.   {CharArray}
```

[8]Note: Turbo Pascal's handling of string types differs considerably from the ANSI Standard. If the implementation you're using is Turbo Pascal you should compare the material in this section with the material on arrays and strings in your Turbo manual. You'll find some important differences.

Sample Runs

    BARRY

Observations This program is pretty easy to understand, but notice how long and tedious it is, compared with the next program.

Program Example

```
PROGRAM PackedCharArray (output);
{Creates a PACKED array whose values are of type CHAR.
 Since the array is packed, we can do five assignments
 in one statement, and write five components in one
 call to 'WriteLn'.}
  TYPE
    indexType  = 1..5;
    packedType = PACKED ARRAY [indexType] OF CHAR;
  VAR
    word : packedType;
BEGIN {PackedCharArray}
  word := 'BARRY';
  WriteLn (word)
END.   {PackedCharArray}
```

Sample Runs

    BARRY

Observations

PACKED arrays

With the addition of the word PACKED in the VAR declaration, we've been able to shorten the program by many lines. What does the word PACKED actually do? Here's the story:

In Program CharArray we define an array type whose components are characters. Here's what the array letters might look like:

letters[1] letters[2] letters[3] letters[4] letters[5]

B	A	R	R	Y

Recall from Section 7.4 that when characters are stored inside the computer, they're encoded as numbers. Here's how the letters values just given might be stored:

letters[1] letters[2] letters[3] letters[4] letters[5]

0066	0065	0082	0082	0089

We've put zeros in front of the numbers to emphasize a point: to store the numeric code for a character, some computers will use more digits than the

few that are required. This is wasteful. It would be better to store these
numbers using only two digits for each:

but some computers can only store or retrieve four digits at once.[9] For such
a computer, a two-digit number is too small a unit to handle conveniently.

In Program `PackedCharArray` we force the computer to store the
values of `word` in a way that isn't wasteful. We do this with the word
`PACKED`. This word tells the computer to pack two characters into one
memory location.[10] The values in the array `word` will be stored this way:

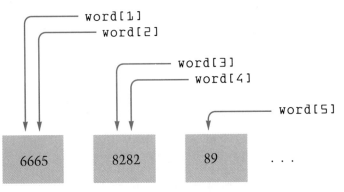

The codes 66 and 65, for the characters B and A, will be stored in the first
location; codes for two Rs will be stored in the second location, etc. Now if
we instruct the computer to

```
Write (word[1]:1)
```

the computer will have to retrieve 6665 from its memory location, separate
the 66 from the 65, and write the letter corresponding to 66, which is B.
Notice what's happened—by using `PACKED` we've saved some storage
space, but we've made the computer take more time to retrieve the first
component of `word`. Without using `PACKED`, the computer wouldn't have
to take time to separate the 66 from the 65.

With packed arrays, you save space; with unpacked arrays you save
time. It's a trade-off. In fact, it's a trade-off that permeates all of computing.
It even has analogs in our daily lives. Here's an example: Every year in April
I put my winter clothes in a box and store them in the attic. I bring my
summer clothes down from the attic and spread them out in the closet. In
May, my summer shirts take up lots of closet space, but it takes very little

[9]A computer that's not *byte addressable* can only store or retrieve four digits at once.

[10]This is only true of some implementations. Many implementations store `PACKED` arrays and
unpacked arrays exactly the same way.

time to pick one. Meanwhile, my winter shirts are folded up in the attic. They're out of the way where they're not wasting space, but it would take a while to find them if I needed them.

We'll see more examples of the time-versus-space trade-off in the chapters to come.

what you can do with PACKED arrays

Now once you've declared `word` to be a `PACKED ARRAY`, there are certain things you can do with it that you couldn't have done with an unpacked array.

```
word := 'BARRY';
WriteLn (word)
```

You can't use a single assignment statement to assign `'BARRY'` to an unpacked array, and you can't write all the components of an unpacked array with just one array name inside a `WriteLn`.

You see, when you write something like `'BARRY'` in your program (several characters enclosed in quotes), the computer stores this string as a `PACKED` array. And it's illegal to do the following because you're not allowed to mix `PACKED` and unpacked arrays:

```
TYPE
   indexType    = 1..5;
   packedType   =            ARRAY [indexType] OF CHAR;
   unpackedType = PACKED ARRAY [indexType] OF CHAR;
VAR
   unpackedArray : unpackedType;
   packedArray   : packedType;
      .
      .
BEGIN
   {These assignments are illegal:}
   unpackedArray := packedArray;
   unpackedArray := 'BARRY'
      .
      .
```

This is the same as not being able to assign `REAL`s to `INTEGER`s:

```
VAR
   r : REAL;
   i : INTEGER;
      .
      .
BEGIN
   {This assignment is illegal:}
   i := r
```

strong typing

It's called **strong typing**. Roughly speaking, strong typing means not mixing different types in assignment statements, parameter passing, etc. Packed and unpacked arrays are different enough that they shouldn't be mixed.

So what do you do if you want to move characters from a `PACKED` array to an unpacked array? There's a pre-declared procedure in Pascal that does it for you:

Program Example

```
PROGRAM UsingUnpack (output);
{Demonstrates use of Procedure Unpack.  Moves values
 from two packed arrays into an unpacked array.}

  TYPE
    arrayType       =        ARRAY [1..10] OF CHAR;
    packedArrayType = PACKED ARRAY [1.. 5] OF CHAR;
  VAR
    unpackedWhole             : arrayType;
    packedFirst, packedLast : packedArrayType;
    i                         : 1..10;
BEGIN {UsingUnpack}
  packedFirst := 'BARRY';
  packedLast  := ' BURD';

  Unpack (packedFirst, unpackedWhole, 1);
  Unpack (packedLast , unpackedWhole, 6);

  FOR i := 1 TO 10 DO
    Write (unpackedWhole[i]:1);
  WriteLn
END.  {UsingUnpack}
```

Sample Runs

```
BARRY BURD
```

Observations

Unpack

Calling Procedure Unpack is very much like executing an assignment statement. Here's a diagram that shows what happens when we execute the statement

```
Unpack (packedFirst, unpackedWhole, 1)
```

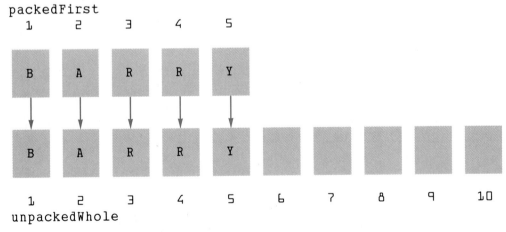

And when we execute

```
Unpack (packedLast , unpackedWhole, 6)
```

we get

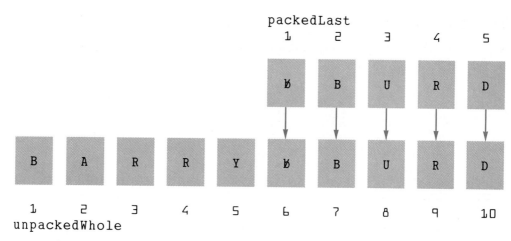

(The ƀ symbol is our way of "picturing" the blank space character in the drawing.) Notice the role played by the third parameter (1 and then 6) in the call to Procedure Unpack. It's the point in the unpacked array where the assignment starts.

Pascal has a pre-declared procedure Pack that does the opposite of Unpack.

Program
Example

Pack

```
PROGRAM UsingPack (input, output);
{Demonstrates use of Procedure Pack.  Moves values
 from an unpacked array into two packed arrays.}
   TYPE
      arrayType       =        ARRAY [1..10] OF CHAR;
      packedArrayType = PACKED ARRAY [1.. 5] OF CHAR;
   VAR
      unpackedWhole            : arrayType;
      packedFirst, packedLast  : packedArrayType;
      i                        : 1..10;
BEGIN {UsingPack}
   Write ('Enter ten characters: ');
   FOR i := 1 TO 10 DO
      Read (unpackedWhole[i]);
   ReadLn;

   Pack (unpackedWhole, 1, packedFirst);
   Pack (unpackedWhole, 6, packedLast );

   Write   ('The characters are:   ');
   WriteLn (packedFirst:5, packedLast:5)
END.   {UsingPack}
```

Sample
Runs

```
Enter ten characters: BARRY BURD
The characters are:   BARRY BURD
```

Observations Procedure Pack also behaves very much like an assignment statement:

• Pack (unpackedWhole, 1, packedFirst)

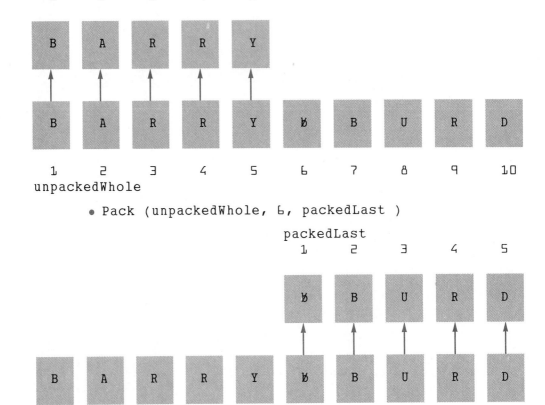

• Pack (unpackedWhole, 6, packedLast)

In this instance notice the role played by the middle parameter (1 and then 6).

Using Procedures Unpack and Pack can be a little confusing. Here are some rules to help you remember how they work:

proper use of Pack and Unpack

1. In each procedure, there's a *source* and a *target*. Values from the source are getting copied to the target. In each procedure's parameter list, the source is listed before the target.

2. In addition to a source and a target, each procedure's parameter list has an *index*. This is always an index in the unpacked array. It's the place in the unpacked array where the assignment begins.

3. The PACKED array is always used in its entirety; that is,

   a. In Procedure Pack some portion of the unpacked array must fill the entire PACKED array.

   b. In Procedure Unpack, the entire packed array must be moved to a portion of the unpacked array.

Further Discussion

Packed and unpacked arrays obey certain rules. For instance, the following code isn't legal:

```
TYPE
   packedArrayType = PACKED ARRAY [1..5] OF CHAR;
VAR
   packedArray : packedArrayType;

   PROCEDURE ChangeChar (VAR c : CHAR);
      .
      .

ChangeChar (packedArray[i])
```

A component of a packed array cannot match up with a VAR parameter in a call to a subprogram.[11]

Some packed array types are specially useful and are called **string types** An array type is called a string type as long as

What is a string type?

- it's PACKED

- its indices are integers

- its lowest index is 1

- its highest index is greater than 1

- its components are of type CHAR (or of any new type, defined by the programmer by renaming CHAR)

In addition, the objects that we call character strings like

```
'BARRY'
'Madam, I''m Adam'
'!#$%&'
```

are of string type.

Be careful how you interpret the rules in the definition of a string type. Notice in particular that the array types in

---

[11]Note: For technical reasons, the call

```
Read (packedArray[i])
```

is legal!

```
TYPE
   worker             = (Alice, Bob, Carol);
   upperCase          = 'A'..'Z';
   nonIntegerIndices  = PACKED ARRAY [worker] OF CHAR;
   doesntStartWith1   = PACKED ARRAY [0..6] OF CHAR;
   notCharComponents  = PACKED ARRAY [1..5] OF upperCase;
```

aren't string types.

What can you do with a string type?

Several convenient things can be done with string types:

- An entire string can be written as a single item in a `Write` or `WriteLn`.

- A single `:=` can be used to copy a character string into a string-type array, as long as the character-string and the string-type array have the *same number of components.*

- The operators `<`, `>`, `<=`, `>=`, `=`, and `<>` can be used to compare strings, as long as the strings being compared have the same number of components.

The second item tells us that we have a little more leeway with strings than with other arrays. If `word` belongs to a string type, we can do something like

```
word := 'BARRY'
```

But notice the emphasis in the second item on the phrase *same number of components.* An assignment such as

```
TYPE
   packedArrayType = PACKED ARRAY [1..5] OF CHAR;
VAR
   packedArray : packedArrayType;
      .
      .
   packedArray := 'abc'
```

is illegal, since `packedArray` has five components, and `'abc'` has only three components.

When you compare two strings with `<`, `>`, `<=` or `>=`, the comparison is always done **lexicographically**. This means it's done almost the way it would be done in a dictionary. For instance, if we compare `'Procedure'` to `'Protector'` by doing

```
'Procedure' < 'Protector'
```

the computer sees that the first three letters of `'Procedure'` are identical to the first three letters of `'Protector'`. Then it notes that `'c' < 't'` and gives the comparison the value `TRUE`.

But recall from Section 7.4 that the result of comparing two characters with `<`, `>`, `<=`, or `>=` depends on the implementation. The same is true about comparing strings. An implementation whose character set is ASCII will find that

```
'Procedure' < 'protector'
```

is TRUE, since uppercase P comes before lowercase p in the ASCII Character Set. In contrast, an EBCDIC implementation will get the value FALSE when it encounters the very same comparison, because uppercase P comes after lowercase p in the EBCDIC Character Set. In general, it's dangerous to rely on <, >, <=, and >= to compare characters and strings.

10.9 Exercises

Key Words to Review

PACKED	string type	Pack
strong typing	Unpack	lexicographic comparison

Questions to Answer

QUE 10.9.1   Which of the following things are legal in ANSI Standard Pascal?
   a. Using an assignment statement to copy values from a PACKED array into an unpacked array.
   b. Using an assignment statement to put 'abc' into a string variable that has three components.
   c. Using an assignment statement to put 'abc' into an unpacked array that has three components.

QUE 10.9.2   With the declarations

```
VAR
    unpArray :         ARRAY [1..10] OF CHAR;
    pacArray : PACKED ARRAY [1.. 5] OF CHAR;
```

write code to do each of the following:
   a. Copy all the characters from pacArray into unpArray starting from the first component of unpArray.
   b. Copy five characters from unpArray into pacArray starting from the sixth component of unpArray.
   c. Copy two characters from pacArray into unpArray starting from the eighth component of unpArray.

Things to Check in a Manual

MAN 10.9.1   Does your implementation use different methods to store values of PACKED and unpacked arrays?

MAN 10.9.2   Are there any rules about the use of PACKED and unpacked arrays that are marked in your manual as "not adhering to the ANSI standard"?

Experiments to Try

EXP 10.9.1   With the definition and declarations given here:

```
TYPE
   subChar = 'a'..'e';
VAR
   arr1, arr3 :         ARRAY [1..3] OF CHAR;
   arr2         :         ARRAY [5..7] OF CHAR;
   pArr1      : PACKED ARRAY [1..3] OF CHAR;
   pArr2      : PACKED ARRAY [5..7] OF CHAR;
   pArr3      : PACKED ARRAY [1..3] OF subChar;
```

which of the following statements actually work (compile successfully and make the expected assignment):

a. arr1   := 'xyz'   b. arr2   := arr1   c. arr3   := arr1
d. pArr1 := 'xyz'   e. pArr1 := 'ab'   f. pArr1 := 'ab '
g. pArr1 := 'abcd'   h. pArr2 := 'xyz'   i. pArr3 := 'xyz'
j. pArr2 := pArr1   k. pArr3 := pArr2   l. Pack (arr1, 1, pArr1)
m. Pack (arr1, 2, pArr1)   n. Unpack (pArr1, arr1, 1)
o. Unpack (pArr1, arr1, 3)   p. Unpack (arr1, pArr1, 1)
q. Unpack ('abc', arr1, 1)

Programs and Subprograms to Write

WRI 10.9.1   Write a function that receives a string that's potentially eighty characters long and returns the length of the string—the number of characters that come before the first blank space in the string.

WRI 10.9.2   Let's say we have two strings, called smallStr and largeStr. We'll say that smallStr is a *substring* of largeStr as long as all the characters in smallStr occur, one after another, inside largeStr. For instance, if smallStr is 'ith comput' and largeStr is 'Down with computer nerds!', then smallStr is a substring of largeStr. Write and test a function subprogram that accepts two strings, smallStr and largeStr, and determines whether or not smallStr is a substring of largeStr. If it is, then the function returns the position number in largeStr where smallStr starts. Otherwise, the function returns 0.

WRI 10.9.3   Modify the program you wrote for Exercise Wri.10.9.2 so that the user can put wild cards in smallStr. A *wild card* is a symbol that stands for several possible characters. For instance the *pound sign, #,* can stand for any single digit character. If smallStr is 'x##' then the program should look, in largeStr, for x11, x12, x85, etc. Other wild cards you might use are ? to stand for any character, and * to stand for any sequence of characters. Examples:

a?b stands for aab, abb, acb, a1b, etc.

(*) stands for (1), (xyz), ( ), etc.

WRI 10.9.4   Write a program to solve the *word wrap* problem: Read a paragraph from a file and write it to the screen in such a way that no line is more than fifty characters long and no word is broken in the middle by the end of a line.

Things to Think About

THI 10.9.1   Review the description of *strong typing* that's given in this section. Some programming languages don't have strong typing. So in those languages you can mix types together more freely than you can in Pascal. For instance, you may be able to do ch := ch + 1 to get the successor of a character.

Think about the advantages of using a language with strong typing. What might be some of the disadvantages?

Chapter Summary

An *array* is a single variable that contains several values. Each value is stored in one of the array's *components*. We refer to a particular component of the array by giving the name of the array variable, along with an *index*.

```
array-name[index]
```

Each array is said to belong to a particular *array type*. We can define an array type in a TYPE definition

```
TYPE
    array-name = ARRAY [index-type] OF value-type;
```

or we can create the array type in the VAR declaration when we declare the array:

```
VAR
    array-name : ARRAY [index-type] OF value-type;
```

In any case, the *index type* tells us the *range* of indices (such as 1..10), and the *value type* tells us what values can be stored in the array's components. All the values that are stored in the array must belong to this *value type*.

An array type is called a *structured type* because it's created by combining other types. (An array type is created by combining several components, and each component has the *value type*.) In contrast to a structured type, a *simple type* is one that's not created by combining other types.

Searching for a particular value in an array means finding that value in the array. *Sorting* an array means rearranging the values in the array so that they're in order, either non-decreasing or non-increasing. *Merging* two arrays means combining them into one array so that the new array is sorted.

In a *linear search* we examine the array's values from the first to the last, until we find the value we're looking for. In a *binary search* we look at the middle of the array and decide whether we should

- stop, because we've found the value we're searching for

- eliminate the upper half of the array, because we've found a value that's larger than what we're searching for
- eliminate the lower half of the array, because we've found a value that's smaller than what we're searching for

In a *selection sort* we look for the smallest value in an array and switch it with the array's first component. Then we look for the second smallest value in the array and switch it with the array's second component. We continue this way until the array has been sorted.

Wherever we declare an array type, we can use the word PACKED:

```
TYPE
    array-name = PACKED ARRAY [index-type] OF value-type;
```

or

```
VAR
    array-name : PACKED ARRAY [index-type] OF value-type;
```

This tells the computer to store the array's values in a way that doesn't waste space. When an array is created without the word PACKED, we say that the array is *unpacked.*

Some array types are called *string types.* An array type is called a string type as long as

- it's PACKED
- its indices are integers
- its lowest index is 1
- its highest index is greater than 1
- its components are of type CHAR (or of any new type, defined by the programmer by renaming CHAR)

In addition, the objects that we call *character strings* are of string type. In Pascal, there are several things we can do with string types that we can't do with other array types:

```
WriteLn (string-type array)
string-type array := 'Hello'
string-type array <= 'Hello'
```

More on Arrays

11.1

Introducing Two-Dimensional Arrays

The arrays we studied in Chapter 10 are called **one-dimensional arrays** because, in those arrays, each component has *one index*. It's usually helpful to think of a one-dimensional array as a "row" of information. For instance, we can think of the `stu` array in Program `Median1` (Section 10.2) as a row of grades

Contents of the `stu` array:

70	75	78	78	80	83	84	84	85	89	90	94	95	96	96	99	100

For many problems, one-dimensional arrays work well. But for other problems, it's better to think of the data as a rectangular table, consisting of several rows and columns. The Pascal types that we use to represent rectangular tables are **two-dimensional** array types.

Program Example

```
PROGRAM TwoByThreeArray (output);
{Introduces two-dimensional arrays.}
    VAR
        x : ARRAY [1..2, 1..3] OF REAL;
BEGIN {TwoByThreeArray}
    x[1,1] := 5.67;
    x[1,2] := 7.17;
    x[1,3] := 4.13;

    x[2,1] := 6.91;
    x[2,2] := 4.03;
    x[2,3] := 5.80;

    WriteLn (x[1,1]:5:2, x[1,2]:5:2, x[1,3]:5:2);
    WriteLn (x[2,1]:5:2, x[2,2]:5:2, x[2,3]:5:2)
END.  {TwoByThreeArray}
```

**Sample
Runs**

```
5.67 7.17 4.13
6.91 4.03 5.80
```

Observations

declaring a two-
dimensional
array

• VAR
```
    x : ARRAY [1..2, 1..3] OF REAL;
```
Here's a picture of the array x created in Program TwoByThreeArray:

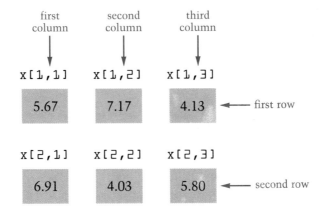

The array has two rows (numbered 1 and 2), and three columns (numbered 1, 2, and 3). Notice that in the array's declaration, the range of row indices comes first, then comes the range of column indices.

```
x : ARRAY [1..2, 1..3] OF REAL;
            rows    cols
```

When we want to refer to a component of the array, we give the component's row number first, then its column number.

```
x[2,3] := 5.80;
```
2nd row   3rd column

**Program
Example**

```
PROGRAM LoopingInTwoDimensions (input, output);
{Shows how to step through a two-dimensional array.}
    TYPE
        rowRange = 1..2;
        colRange = 1..3;
    VAR
        x   : ARRAY [rowRange, colRange] OF REAL;
        row : rowRange;
        col : colRange;
```

```
BEGIN {LoopingInTwoDimensions}
  WriteLn ('Enter six numbers - one on each line: ');
  FOR row := 1 TO 2 DO
    FOR col := 1 TO 3 DO
      ReadLn ( x[row,col] );
  WriteLn;
  WriteLn ('The numbers are: ');
  FOR row := 1 TO 2 DO
    FOR col := 1 TO 3 DO
      Write ( x[row,col]:5:2 );
  WriteLn
END.  {LoopingInTwoDimensions}
```

Sample Runs

```
Enter six numbers - one on each line:
3.21
4.34
5.67
2.81
2.90
1.00

The numbers are:
 3.21 4.34 5.67 2.81 2.90 1.00
```

Observations

looping
through a
two-dimensional
array

• ```
  FOR row := 1 TO 2 DO
    FOR col := 1 TO 3 DO
  ```

In order to "loop" through a two-dimensional array you usually need nested FOR statements. Notice the order in which these nested loops travel through x. When row has the value 1, col goes from 1 to 3:

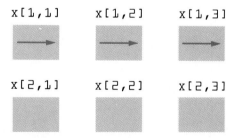

Then when row has the value 2, col goes from 1 to 3 again:

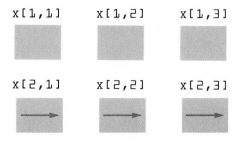
  ```

Now look at Program `LoopingInTwoDimensions` with its `ReadLn` and `Write` loops. Each time through the `ReadLn` loop, the computer reads a whole line to get the value of one component of the array (because of the `Ln`). Each time through the `Write` loop, the computer only uses *part of* a line to write a value, so all the values in the array get written on a single line. (The `WriteLn` isn't executed until all six values have been written.)

Program Example

```
PROGRAM MoreLooping (input, output);
{Shows how to loop through a two-
 dimensional array row by row.}
  TYPE
    rowRange = 1..2;
    colRange = 1..3;
  VAR
    x   : ARRAY [rowRange, colRange] OF REAL;
    row : rowRange;
    col : colRange;
BEGIN {MoreLooping}
  WriteLn ('Enter two rows of numbers - ');
  WriteLn (' three numbers on each row: ');
  FOR row := 1 TO 2 DO
    BEGIN
      FOR col := 1 TO 3 DO
        Read ( x[row,col] );
      ReadLn
    END;
  WriteLn;
  WriteLn ('The numbers are: ');
  FOR row := 1 TO 2 DO
    BEGIN
      FOR col := 1 TO 3 DO
        Write ( x[row,col]:5:2 );
      WriteLn
    END
END.   {MoreLooping}
```

Sample Runs

```
Enter two rows of numbers -
 three numbers on each row:
3.21 4.34 5.67
2.81 2.90 1.00

The numbers are:
 3.21 4.34 5.67
 2.81 2.90 1.00
```

Observations

```
• FOR row := 1 TO 2 DO
    BEGIN
      FOR col := 1 TO 3 DO
        Write ( x[row,col]:5:2 );
      WriteLn
    END
```

row-by-row looping

These loops are a little more complicated than the ones in Program LoopingInTwoDimensions. In executing

```
FOR col := 1 TO 3 DO
  Write ( x[row,col]:5:2 )
```

the computer writes three components. (It changes the column number while the row number stays fixed. So it writes the three that are stored in a single row of the array.)

Taken as a whole the nested write loops have the following effect:

```
FOR row := 1 TO 2 DO
  BEGIN
    Write the row;
    WriteLn
  END
```

So each row is written on a separate line.

Program Example

```
PROGRAM ArrayParameters (input, output);
{Shows how two-dimensional arrays
 can be passed as parameters.}
  TYPE
    rowRange  = 1..2;
    colRange  = 1..3;
    arrayType = ARRAY [rowRange, colRange] OF REAL;
  VAR
    x : arrayType;
  {----------}
  PROCEDURE ReadArray (VAR x : arrayType);
  {Reads a two-by-three array of real numbers.}
    VAR
      row : rowRange;
      col : colRange;
  BEGIN {ReadArray}
    FOR row := 1 TO 2 DO
      BEGIN
        FOR col := 1 TO 3 DO
          Read ( x[row,col] );
        ReadLn
      END
  END;  {ReadArray}
  {----------}
```

```
            PROCEDURE WriteArray (y : arrayType);
            {Writes a two-by-three array of real numbers.}
              VAR
                 row : rowRange;
                 col : colRange;
            BEGIN {WriteArray}
              FOR row := 1 TO 2 DO
                BEGIN
                  FOR col := 1 TO 3 DO
                    Write ( y[row,col]:5:2 );
                  WriteLn
                END
            END;   {WriteArray}

            {----------}

         BEGIN {ArrayParameters}
            WriteLn     ('Enter two rows of numbers - ');
            WriteLn     (' three numbers on each row: ');

            ReadArray   (x);

            WriteLn;
            WriteLn     ('The numbers are: ');

            WriteArray (x)
         END.   {ArrayParameters}
```

Sample Runs

```
Enter two rows of numbers -
 three numbers on each row:
3.21 4.34 5.67
2.81 2.90 1.00

The numbers are:
3.21 4.34 5.67
2.81 2.90 1.00
```

Observations

two-dimensional arrays and subprogram parameters

This program shows how two-dimensional arrays can be passed as parameters. Notice that Procedure ReadArray has a VAR parameter and Procedure WriteArray has a *value* parameter. Notice also the names of the formal parameters:

```
PROCEDURE ReadArray (VAR x : arrayType);
          .
          .
          .
PROCEDURE WriteArray (y : arrayType);
          .
          .
          .
ReadArray  (x);
WriteArray (x)
```

In ReadArray the formal parameter has the same name as the actual parameter. In WriteArray the two names are different. We can choose to do it either way. (Of course we should always do it the way that makes the program most readable.)

Program Example

```
PROGRAM Transpose (input, output);
{Reads a "rectangle" of real numbers and writes the
 same numbers, flipped along the diagonal of the rectangle.}
   TYPE
     rowRange  = 1..2;
     colRange  = 1..3;
     arrayType = ARRAY [rowRange, colRange] OF REAL;
   VAR
     x   : arrayType;
     row : rowRange;
     col : colRange;
BEGIN {Transpose}
   Write   ('Enter a two-by-three '          );
   WriteLn ('"rectangle" of real numbers: ');

   FOR row := 1 TO 2 DO
     BEGIN
       FOR col := 1 TO 3 DO
         Read ( x[row,col] );
       ReadLn
     END;

   WriteLn;
   Write   ('After being flipped along '     );
   WriteLn ('the diagonal, the numbers are: ');

   FOR col := 1 TO 3 DO
     BEGIN
       FOR row := 1 TO 2 DO
         Write ( x[row,col]:5:2 );
       WriteLn
     END
END.   {Transpose}
```

Sample Runs

```
Enter a two-by-three "rectangle" of real numbers:
3.00 4.00 5.00
2.00 7.00 1.00

After being flipped along the diagonal, the numbers are:
 3.00 2.00
 4.00 7.00
 5.00 1.00
```

Observations

switching counters

Program Transpose shows what happens when we switch counters. In the Read loops, the outer loop counter is row and the inner loop counter is col—the way it was in all our previous examples.

But in the Write loops it's the other way around—the outer loop counter is col and the inner loop counter is row. You should make a trace of this program to make sure you understand why it gives us the Sample Run pictured above.

Program Example

```
PROGRAM ChangeVariables (input, output);
{Shows how x[row,col] and x[i,j]
 can both stand for the same thing.}
   TYPE
     rowRange  = 1..2;
     colRange  = 1..3;
     arrayType = ARRAY [rowRange, colRange] OF REAL;
   VAR
     x        : arrayType;
     row, i : rowRange;
     col, j : colRange;
BEGIN {ChangeVariables}
   WriteLn ('Enter two rows of numbers - ');
   WriteLn (' three numbers on each row: ');

   FOR row := 1 TO 2 DO
     BEGIN
       FOR col := 1 TO 3 DO
         Read ( x[row,col] );
       ReadLn
     END;

   WriteLn;
   WriteLn ('The numbers are: ');

   FOR i := 1 TO 2 DO
     BEGIN
       FOR j := 1 TO 3 DO
         Write ( x[i,j]:5:2 );
       WriteLn
     END

END.   {ChangeVariables}
```

Sample Runs

```
Enter two rows of numbers -
 three numbers on each row:
3.21 4.34 5.67
2.81 2.90 1.00

The numbers are:
 3.21 4.34 5.67
 2.81 2.90 1.00
```

Observations

• Read (x[**row,col**]);

      .

      .

Write (x[**i,j**]:5:2)

This program emphasizes a point we made in Section 10.1. The choice of one variable over another for the indices of an array makes *absolutely no difference*. Any variable with an INTEGER value from 1 to 2 can be used as the first index for x, and any variable with an INTEGER value from 1 to 3 can be used as the second index of x. We can even change variables in the middle of a program.

using different variables for the indices

11.1   Exercises

Key Words to Review

one-dimensional array   two-dimensional array

Questions to Answer

Exercises Que.11.1.1 to Que.11.1.4 pertain to an array x with declaration

```
VAR
  x : ARRAY [1..2, 1..3] OF REAL;
```

QUE 11.1.1   Does x[1,2] always have the same value as x[2,1]? Why, or why not?

QUE 11.1.2   Can x[1,2] ever have the same value as x[2,1]? Why, or why not?

QUE 11.1.3   Discuss the placement of Write and WriteLn in the following code:

```
FOR row := 1 TO 2 DO
  BEGIN
    FOR col := 1 TO 3 DO
      Write ( x[row,col]:5:2 );
    WriteLn
  END
```

QUE 11.1.4   Make a trace of the following fragment:

```
FOR row := 1 TO 2 DO
  FOR col := 1 TO 3 DO
    x[row,col] := row + col;
row := 1;
col := 2;
WriteLn ( x[Trunc(x[row,row]) , Round(x[row,col])] :5:2 )
```

Experiments to Try

EXP 11.1.1   In Program TwoByThreeArray change the first assignment statement to

```
x[1] := 5.67
```

EXP 11.1.2   In Program TwoByThreeArray change the last assignment statement to

```
x[3,2] := 5.80
```

EXP 11.1.3   Run Program MoreLooping several times, moving the WriteLn to various places inside and outside the loop.

EXP 11.1.4   Try the following variations on the Write loop in Program Transpose:
```
a.  FOR col := 1 TO 3 DO
      BEGIN
        FOR row := 1 TO 2 DO
          Write ( x[col,row]:5:2 );
        WriteLn
      END
```

b. FOR **row** := 1 TO 3 DO
      BEGIN
        FOR **col** := 1 TO 2 DO
          Write (x[col,row]:5:2);
        WriteLn
      END

EXP 11.1.5   Add the definition

```
TYPE
    arrayType2 = ARRAY [1..3, 1..2] OF REAL;
```

to Program ArrayParameters and try passing an array of type arrayType2 to the (unmodified) version of Procedure ReadArray.

EXP 11.1.6   Modify Program ChangeVariables so that, before reading a value of x[row,col], it writes the values of row and col. Also before writing a value of x[i,j], it writes the values of i and j.

EXP 11.1.7   With OneHigher declared as follows:

```
FUNCTION OneHigher (VAR i : indexType) : indexType;
BEGIN {OneHigher}
    i           := i + 1;
    OneHigher := i
END;   {OneHigher}
```

run a program containing the lines

```
i := 1;
WriteLn (a[OneHigher(i),OneHigher(i)] : 2)
```

Scales to Practice

PRA 11.1.1   Write a program that reads values into a three-by-three array and then writes all the values along the array's diagonal. For instance, with the input

```
1 2 3
4 5 6
7 8 9
```

the output is

```
1 5 9
```

PRA 11.1.2   Write a program that fills the perimeter of a rectangular array with 1's and the rest of the array with 0's. Then it displays all the values in the array.

Programs and Subprograms to Write

WRI 11.1.1   In this exercise, we'll use the word *matrix* to mean roughly the same thing as a *two-dimensional array*. Let m be a matrix with two rows and two columns. To find the *determinant* of m, we multiply the values along each diagonal, and then subtract one product from another:

$$\text{determinant of } \begin{bmatrix} 1 & 3 \\ 5 & 4 \end{bmatrix} \text{ is } 1*4 - 3*5 = 4 - 15 = -11$$

Write a program that reads the values of a two-by-two matrix and computes the determinant of the matrix.

WRI 11.1.2 Here's a way of multiplying two "arrays" together, called *matrix multiplication*:

$$\begin{bmatrix} 1 & 6 & 3 \\ 0 & 4 & 1 \\ 2 & 0 & 1 \end{bmatrix} \times \begin{bmatrix} 5 & 8 & 1 \\ 2 & 0 & 1 \\ 7 & 4 & 1 \end{bmatrix} = \begin{bmatrix} 38 & & \\ & & \\ & & \end{bmatrix} \qquad 1*5 + 6*2 + 3*7 = 38$$

$$\begin{bmatrix} 1 & 6 & 3 \\ 0 & 4 & 1 \\ 2 & 0 & 1 \end{bmatrix} \times \begin{bmatrix} 5 & 8 & 1 \\ 2 & 0 & 1 \\ 7 & 4 & 1 \end{bmatrix} = \begin{bmatrix} 38 & 20 & \\ & & \\ & & \end{bmatrix} \qquad 1*8 + 6*0 + 3*4 = 20$$

$$\begin{bmatrix} 1 & 6 & 3 \\ 0 & 4 & 1 \\ 2 & 0 & 1 \end{bmatrix} \times \begin{bmatrix} 5 & 8 & 1 \\ 2 & 0 & 1 \\ 7 & 4 & 1 \end{bmatrix} = \begin{bmatrix} 38 & 20 & 10 \\ & & \\ & & \end{bmatrix} \qquad 1*1 + 6*1 + 3*1 = 10$$

$$\begin{bmatrix} 1 & 6 & 3 \\ 0 & 4 & 1 \\ 2 & 0 & 1 \end{bmatrix} \times \begin{bmatrix} 5 & 8 & 1 \\ 2 & 0 & 1 \\ 7 & 4 & 1 \end{bmatrix} = \begin{bmatrix} 38 & 20 & 10 \\ 15 & & \\ & & \end{bmatrix} \qquad 0*5 + 4*2 + 1*7 = 15$$

and so on, until you get

$$\begin{bmatrix} 1 & 6 & 3 \\ 0 & 4 & 1 \\ 2 & 0 & 1 \end{bmatrix} \times \begin{bmatrix} 5 & 8 & 1 \\ 2 & 0 & 1 \\ 7 & 4 & 1 \end{bmatrix} = \begin{bmatrix} 38 & 20 & 10 \\ 15 & 4 & 5 \\ 17 & 20 & 3 \end{bmatrix}$$

Write a program that reads two arrays, performs matrix multiplication, and then writes the result.

11.2

Two-Dimensional Arrays as Tables

What is a table?   We can think of a **table** as a rectangular array of values, with row headings and column headings.

For instance, my day care center has several classrooms. Each classroom has kids of a certain age group. In addition, each classroom emphasizes either academics or play. (The "play" emphasis includes social skills, esteem building, etc.) This makes ten classrooms in all. Here's a table giving the number of kids in each of the ten classrooms:

Emphasis \ Age	0	1	2	3	4
Academic A	7	9	12	4	13
Play B	8	9	16	9	10

This can be viewed as an array:

howMany['A',0] howMany['A',1] howMany['A',2] howMany['A',3] howMany['A',4]

7	9	12	4	13

howMany['B',0] howMany['B',1] howMany['B',2] howMany['B',3] howMany['B',4]

8	9	16	9	10

Specifications

Input: The number of children in each classroom

We want three procedures to produce three separate reports:

Output: Given a classroom (an emphasis and an age), report how many kids are in that classroom.

Output: Report the number of kids in each age group.

Output: Given a cutoff for the number of kids in a class, report which classrooms are above the cutoff.

Designing a Program

Clearly we need an array to hold the values in the table

```
TYPE
  emphasisType = 'A'..'B';
  ageType      = 0 .. 4 ;
  cardinal     = 0 .. MAXINT;
  howManyType  = ARRAY [emphasisType, ageType] OF cardinal;
VAR
  howMany : howManyType;
```

Each component of the two-dimensional array howMany tells us how many kids are in a particular classroom.

Then we'll have three procedures, as requested in the specs:

Output: Given a classroom (an emphasis and an age), report how many kids are in that classroom. In this first procedure, we take two *indices* (emphasis and age) and we report the *value* stored in the component that has those indices.

```
Read emphasis
Read age
WriteLn (howMany[emphasis,age])
```

Output: Report the number of kids in each age group. In the second procedure we let the two indices vary. After choosing a particular age we let emphasis go from A to B, summing up the numbers of kids in the A and B groups. Then we choose the next age and do the same thing.

```
For each age category
   total := howMany['A',age] + howMany['B',age]
```

Output: Given a `cutoff` **for the number of kids in a class, report which classrooms are above the** `cutoff`**.** In the third procedure, we read the `cutoff` value and look for indices (`emphasis` and `age`) of components containing numbers greater than that `cutoff` value.

```
Read cutoff
For each emphasis
   For each age
      IF howMany[emphasis,age] > cutoff THEN
         Write emphasis and age
```

In addition to the procedures just mentioned, we'll need a procedure that reads values into the `howMany` array.

Program Example

```
PROGRAM DayCareToday (kidsFile, input, output);
{Gives several tallies on the population of a day care center.}
   CONST
      youngest = 0;
      oldest   = 4;
      mostAcad = 'A';
      mostPlay = 'B';
   TYPE
      cardinal     = 0..MAXINT;
      emphasisType = mostAcad..mostPlay;
      ageType      = youngest..oldest;
      howManyType  = ARRAY [emphasisType, ageType] OF cardinal;
   VAR
      howMany  : howManyType;
      kidsFile : TEXT;
{I/O SUBROGRAMS::::::::::::::::::::::::::::::::::::::::::::::}
{:::::::::::::::::::::::::::::::::::::::::::::::::::::::::::::}

{INPUT SUBPROGRAMS::::::::::::::::::::::::::::::::::::::::::::}

   PROCEDURE ReadArray (VAR kidsFile : TEXT        ;
                        VAR howMany  : howManyType);
   {Reads values into the 'howMany' array.}

      VAR
         emphasis : emphasisType;
         age      : ageType;
   BEGIN {ReadArray}
      Reset (kidsFile);
      FOR emphasis := mostAcad TO mostPlay DO
         FOR age := youngest TO oldest DO
            Read (kidsFile, howMany[emphasis,age]);
      ReadLn (kidsFile)
   END;  {ReadArray}

   {----------}
```

```
      PROCEDURE ReadLnEmph (VAR emphasis : emphasisType);
      {Prompts user and reads an emphasisType value.}
      BEGIN {ReadLnEmph}
        Write  ('Emphasis to report (');
        Write  (mostAcad:1, ' to ', mostPlay:1, ')? ');
        ReadLn (emphasis)
      END;   {ReadLnEmph}

      {----------}

      PROCEDURE ReadLnAge (VAR age : ageType);
      {Prompts user and reads an ageType value.}
      BEGIN {ReadLnAge}
        Write  ('Age to report (');
        Write  (youngest:1, ' to ', oldest:1, ')?        ');
        ReadLn (age)
      END;   {ReadLnAge}

      {----------}

      PROCEDURE ReadLnCut (VAR cutoff : cardinal);
      {Prompts the user and reads a class size cutoff.}
      BEGIN {ReadLnCut}
        Write  ('Cutoff? ');
        ReadLn (cutoff)
      END;   {ReadLnCut}

  {OUTPUT SUBPROGRAMS::::::::::::::::::::::::::::::::::::::}

      PROCEDURE WriteLnHowMany (howMany  : howManyType ;
                                emphasis : emphasisType;
                                age      : ageType     );
      {Writes the number of kids in a particular class.}

      BEGIN {WriteLnHowMany}
        Write  ('There are ', howMany[emphasis,age]:2    );
        WriteLn (' kids in class ', emphasis:1, '-', age:1)
      END;   {WriteLnHowMany}

      {----------}

      PROCEDURE WriteLnAgeTotal (howMany : howManyType ;
                                 age     : ageType     );
      {Writes the number of kids of a particular age.}

        VAR
          total : cardinal;
          emphasis : emphasisType;

      BEGIN {WriteLnAgeTotal}
        total := 0;
        FOR emphasis := mostAcad TO mostPlay DO
          total := total + howMany[emphasis,age];

        Write  ('There are ', total:2    );
        WriteLn (' children of age ', age:1)
      END;   {WriteLnAgeTotal}
```

```
{REPORT SUBPROGRAMS:::::::::::::::::::::::::::::::::}
{:::::::::::::::::::::::::::::::::::::::::::::::::::::}
   PROCEDURE ReportHowMany (howMany : howManyType);
   {Writes the number of children in a classroom.}
      VAR
        emphasis : emphasisType;
        age      : ageType;
   BEGIN {ReportHowMany}
      WriteLn         ('Reporting number of kids in a class: ');
      ReadLnEmph      (emphasis);
      ReadLnAge       (age);

      WriteLnHowMany (howMany, emphasis, age);
      WriteLn
   END;  {ReportHowMany}

   {----------}

   PROCEDURE ReportAgeTotals (howMany : howManyType);
   {Writes the number of children of each age.}
      VAR
        age   : ageType;
        total : cardinal;
   BEGIN {ReportAgeTotals}
      WriteLn ('Reporting age totals:');

      FOR age := youngest TO oldest DO
        WriteLnAgeTotal (howMany, age);
      WriteLn
   END;  {ReportAgeTotals}

   {----------}

   PROCEDURE ReportOverCutoff (howMany : howManyType);
   {Writes which classes have more than 'cutoff'-many kids.}
      VAR
        emphasis : emphasisType;
        age      : ageType;
        cutoff   : cardinal;
   BEGIN {ReportOverCutoff}
      WriteLn   ('Reporting classes in excess of cutoff: ');
      ReadLnCut (cutoff);

      FOR emphasis := mostAcad TO mostPlay DO
        FOR age := youngest TO oldest DO
          IF howMany[emphasis,age] > cutoff THEN
            WriteLnHowMany (howMany, emphasis, age);
      WriteLn
   END;  {ReportOverCutoff}
{MAIN PROGRAM:::::::::::::::::::::::::::::::::::::::}
BEGIN {DayCareToday}
   ReadArray        (kidsFile, howMany);
   ReportHowMany    (howMany);
   ReportAgeTotals  (howMany);
   ReportOverCutoff (howMany)
END.  {DayCareToday}
```

Sample Runs

With the following kidsFile

```
7 9 12 4 13
8 9 16 9 10
```

a run of Program DayCareToday might look like this:

```
Reporting number of kids in a class:
Emphasis to report (A to B)? B
Age to report (0 to 4)? 3
There are  9 kids in class B-3

Reporting age totals:
There are 15 children of age 0
There are 18 children of age 1
There are 28 children of age 2
There are 13 children of age 3
There are 23 children of age 4

Reporting classes in excess of cutoff:
Cutoff? 10
There are 12 kids in class A-2
There are 13 kids in class A-4
There are 16 kids in class B-2
```

Further Discussion

One way to think of a two-dimensional array is to imagine a one-dimensional array in which each component is a whole row; that is, a two-dimensional array can be thought of as an "array of arrays":

an array of arrays

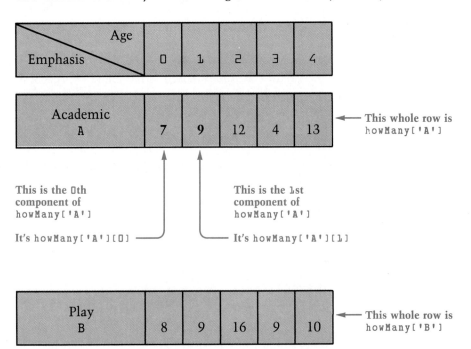

This is more than just a useful analogy. A two-dimensional array is *the same as* an array of one-dimensional arrays. In Program DayCareToday we could have defined howManyType like this:

```
TYPE
   howManyType  = ARRAY [emphasisType] OF
                              ARRAY [ageType] OF cardinal;
```

And whether we use the old definition or the new definition, we can refer to a component of howMany as if howMany is an array of arrays. In other words, we can freely change back and forth between

```
WriteLn (howMany[emphasis,age])
```

and

```
WriteLn (howMany[emphasis][age])
```

The array type howManyType in Program DayCareToday is called a *two-dimensional array type.* An array type with three indices would be called a *three-dimensional array type,* and so on. If we further divided our howMany groups by the number of years children have been at our day care center, we'd have a three-dimensional array:

three-dimensional arrays

```
TYPE
   cardinal        = 0..MAXINT;
   emphasisType    = mostAcad..mostPlay;
   ageType         = youngest..oldest;
   yrsEnrolledType = 0..4;
   howManyType     = ARRAY [emphasisType, ageType, yrsEnrolledType]
                                                    OF cardinal;
VAR
   howMany : howManyType;
```

Then howMany would be a three-dimensional array. To represent howMany pictorially, we'd have several "planes." Each plane would have two rows and five columns. (See the next page.) A one-dimensional array is like a "row"; a two-dimensional array is like a "rectangle"; a three-dimensional array is like a "rectangular solid"; a four-dimensional array is like a "hyper solid"; etc.

We gave Program TenDim to a VAX with ANSI Standard Pascal, and it ran correctly:

Emphasis \ Age	0	1	2	3	4
Academic A	0	0	0	0	3
Play B	0	0	0	0	4

← enrolled 4 years

.

.

.

Emphasis \ Age	0	1	2	3	4
Academic A	0	4	5	1	2

← enrolled 1 year

Emphasis \ Age	0	1	2	3	4
Academic A	7	5	6	2	13
Play B	8	3	10	2	10

← enrolled 0 years

```
PROGRAM TenDim (output);
{Demonstrates the use of a ten-dimensional array!}
   TYPE
      rg = 1..3;
      arrayType = ARRAY [rg,rg,rg,rg,rg,rg,rg,rg,rg,rg] OF INTEGER;
   VAR
      arr : arrayType;
BEGIN {TenDim}
   arr[1,1,1,1,1,1,1,1,1,1] := 0;
   WriteLn (arr[1,1,1,1,1,1,1,1,1,1])
END.   {TenDim}
```

multi-
dimensional
arrays

In Program TenDim the variable arr is a ten-dimensional array. Even though we put a value in only one component of arr, this array has 59049 components. Although it's impossible to visualize an array like this, there are many applications in which **multi-dimensional arrays** beyond three dimensions are very useful. For instance, we may want to tally income versus age versus job satisfaction versus region of the country. Or we might want to keep track of a particle's position in Einstein's four-dimensional space-time.

Programming Style

grouping subprograms using comments

Notice how the subprograms in Program `DayCareToday` are divided into two groups—I/O SUBPROGRAMS and REPORT SUBPROGRAMS. The I/O SUBPROGRAMS group is further divided into a group of INPUT SUBPRO-GRAMS and a group of OUTPUT SUBPROGRAMS. We use some very noticeable comments to separate the groups from one another. It's very valuable to think in terms of "groups" of subprograms. As you can see in Program `DayCareToday`, it tends to make the overall organization of the program a bit clearer.

logical cohesion

But how do we decide which subprograms belong in which groups? The style shown in Program `DayCareToday` is an example of something called **logical cohesion** because the subprograms in each group are "logically" related to one another. As attractive as it seems, logical cohesion is not the latest word in subprogram grouping. It's quickly being replaced by a much more powerful notion called *object-oriented programming*. For discussions of object-oriented programming, see Sections 3.9, 9.6, and 12.9.

11.2   Exercises

Key Words to Review

table	multi-dimensional array	logical cohesion
multi-dimensional array	type	

Questions to Answer

QUE 11.2.1   What's the connection between the headings of a table and the indices of an array?

QUE 11.2.2   In certain other programming languages all arrays have index ranges that begin with 1. Why would that restriction be inconvenient when dealing with this section's day care problem?

QUE 11.2.3   Describe ways in which this section's Procedure `ReportOverCutoff` and Procedure `LinearSearch` (from Section 10.5) are similar. Could we modify Procedure `ReportOverCutoff` to take advantage of an extra value in the array, the way we did for Procedure `LinearSearch`? Why, or why not?

Changes to Make

CHA 11.2.1   The specs in this section gave Program `DayCareToday` three problems to solve. Make the program more flexible by having the user decide, during a run of the program, which of the three problems should be solved. (Solve the second? Solve all three? Solve the first several times, with various values for emphasis and age?) What other kinds of information might you make the program capable of reporting?

CHA 11.2.2   Modify Program DayCareToday so that it does various kinds of reporting using the three-dimensional array type mentioned in this section's Further Discussion subsection.

CHA 11.2.3   Modify Program SelectionSortDriver (Section 10.8) so that it sorts arrays of names instead of arrays of numbers.

Scales to Practice

PRA 11.2.1   Write a program that reads values into a two-dimensional array and then goes through the array to find (a) the smallest value stored in the array and (b) the indices of this smallest value. Then the program writes this smallest value and its indices.

PRA 11.2.2   Write a function called SumColumn that sums up the values in one column of an array. Write a main program that reads a two-dimensional array and calls Function SumColumn several times once for each column in the two-dimensional array.

PRA 11.2.3   *(A continuation of Exercise Pra.11.2.2)* Modify Function SumColumn (if necessary) and modify the main program so that you get not only the sums of all the columns but also the sums of all the rows.

PRA 11.2.4   Read values into a two-dimensional array and test to see if there's a row in this array with the following property: For each number in that row there's another value in that number's column that's smaller than that number.

Programs and Subprograms to Write

WRI 11.2.1   Read values into a two-dimensional array of CHARacters. This array has thirty rows and two columns. Each row represents a voter in an election. The first column contains the voter's sex (F or M) and the second column contains the voter's candidate preference (a or b). Give percentages telling how each candidate will do among voters of each sex.

WRI 11.2.2   Have a two-dimensional array of grades. The first row is the quiz grades for Student #1; the second row is the quiz grades for Student #2; etc. Read in a student number and print out all quiz grades for that student and the average for that student. Input a quiz grade and print the numbers of all students whose average was at least that high (after dropping each student's lowest grade). Find the class average for each quiz and the average of all quizzes for all students.

WRI 11.2.3   Redo Exercise Wri.11.2.2, this time using the following unusual rule: A grade of −1 in the two-dimensional array indicates that the student missed the quiz and that the next quiz the student takes should count double. Similarly, missing two quizzes in a row means that the next quiz the student takes should count triple, etc. (Instructors: Don't try this rule! It can be very unpopular with students.)

WRI 11.2.4   Redo Exercise Wri.11.2.3. This time, if a student misses a quiz, then all the quizzes for the rest of the semester count more to take up the slack.

11.3

Two-Dimensional Arrays as Tableaus

In Section 11.2 we saw how a table of values can be implemented using a two-dimensional array. We showed how the table's row headings and column headings help us choose components of the array.

But there are certain problems in which row and column headings are of limited use, even though we're dealing with a rectangular array of values. In these situations, row and column headings may be cumbersome to use, and other ways of thinking about the rectangle's values may be more natural or more convenient.

What is a tableau?

Let's use the word **tableau** to describe a rectangle of values that doesn't have row or column headings. The three-by-three board in a game of tic-tac-toe is a good example of a tableau.

Specifications   First we represent a tic-tac-toe board as a two-dimensional array of Xs, Os, and blanks. Then we want a function with

> Parameters: The board array (that is, the Xs, Os, and blanks on the tic-tac-toe board in the middle of a game) and a player's mark (either an X for the X-player, or an O for the O-player)
>
> Result value: TRUE if the player has already won on this board; FALSE otherwise

Designing a Program

so many ways to write a tic-tac-toe program!

We'll need code to define the types and variables described in the specs:

```
TYPE
   indexType  = 1..3;
   markType   = (X, O, blank);
   playerType = X..O;
   boardType  = ARRAY [indexType, indexType] OF markType;
VAR
   board : boardType;
```

and a function IsAWin that has the required parameters and result type:

```
FUNCTION IsAWin (board  : boardType;
                 player : playerType) : BOOLEAN;
```

Now the tic-tac-toe board is an array that looks like this:

board[1,1]	board[1,2]	board[1,3]
board[2,1]	board[2,2]	board[2,3]
board[3,1]	board[3,2]	board[3,3]

To check for a win, we'll look for all Xs or all Os in each row, each column, and each diagonal. But how do we step through the array indices? There are so many ways to do it. First we'll look at a **brute force approach**:

```
FUNCTION IsAWin1 (b        : boardType;
                  player : playerType) : BOOLEAN;
{Decides if board 'b' is a win for this player.}
BEGIN {IsAWin1}
   {Check the three rows:}
   IF      (b[1,1] = player) AND (b[1,2] = player) AND
           (b[1,3] = player) THEN
      IsAWin1 := TRUE
   ELSE IF (b[2,1] = player) AND (b[2,2] = player) AND
           (b[2,3] = player) THEN
      IsAWin1 := TRUE
   ELSE IF (b[3,1] = player) AND (b[3,2] = player) AND
           (b[3,3] = player) THEN
      IsAWin1 := TRUE

   {Check the three columns:}
   ELSE IF (b[1,1] = player) AND (b[2,1] = player) AND
           (b[3,1] = player) THEN
      IsAWin1 := TRUE
   ELSE IF (b[1,2] = player) AND (b[2,2] = player) AND
           (b[3,2] = player) THEN
      IsAWin1 := TRUE
   ELSE IF (b[1,3] = player) AND (b[2,3] = player) AND
           (b[3,3] = player) THEN
      IsAWin1 := TRUE

   {Check the two diagonals:}
   ELSE IF (b[1,1] = player) AND (b[2,2] = player) AND
           (b[3,3] = player) THEN
      IsAWin1 := TRUE
   ELSE IF (b[1,3] = player) AND (b[2,2] = player) AND
           (b[3,1] = player) THEN
      IsAWin1 := TRUE

   {If no win is found:}
   ELSE
      IsAWin1 := FALSE
END;   {IsAWin1}
```

There's something aesthetically unappealing about Function IsAWin1 even though IsAWin1 works and is fairly easy to read. (Actually, not everyone would agree that IsAWin1 is easy to read. It's easy to see the overall idea of Function IsAWin1, but it's hard to check all the array indices to make sure that they're correct.)

So what can we do to improve on Function IsAWin1? One thing we can do is make more use of BOOLEAN expressions:

```
FUNCTION IsAWin2 (b       : boardType;
                  player : playerType) : BOOLEAN;
{Decides if board 'b' is a win for this player.}
BEGIN {IsAWin2}
  IsAWin2 :=

  {Check the three rows:}
  (b[1,1] = player) AND (b[1,2] = player) AND (b[1,3] = player)
  OR
  (b[2,1] = player) AND (b[2,2] = player) AND (b[2,3] = player)
  OR
  (b[3,1] = player) AND (b[3,2] = player) AND (b[3,3] = player)
  OR

  {Check the three columns:}
  (b[1,1] = player) AND (b[2,1] = player) AND (b[3,1] = player)
  OR
  (b[1,2] = player) AND (b[2,2] = player) AND (b[3,2] = player)
  OR
  (b[1,3] = player) AND (b[2,3] = player) AND (b[3,3] = player)
  OR

  {Check the two diagonals:}
  (b[1,1] = player) AND (b[2,2] = player) AND (b[3,3] = player)
  OR
  (b[1,3] = player) AND (b[2,2] = player) AND (b[3,1] = player)
END;  {IsAWin2}
```

Function IsAWin2 is still a maze of indices, but at least the maze isn't obscured by IFs and ELSEs. In certain situations, IsAWin2 runs faster than IsAWin1, because when IsAWin1 does a test and an assignment

```
      test

        │
        ▼
  IF        (b[1,1] = player) AND (b[1,2] = player) AND
            (b[1,3] = player) THEN
        IsAWin1 := TRUE
                      ▲
                      │

            assignment
```

IsAWin2 just does an assignment

```
      assignment

          │
          ▼

IsAWin2 :=
(b[1,1] = player) AND (b[1,2] = player) AND (b[1,3] = player)
```

But if your implementation doesn't do short-circuit evaluation of BOOLEAN expressions (Section 10.5), IsAWin2 will run much more slowly than IsAWin1. If our player has a win along the first row, then IsAWin1 will check only that first row.

```
{Check the three rows:}
IF      (b[1,1] = player) AND (b[1,2] = player) AND
        (b[1,3] = player) THEN
   IsAWin1 := TRUE
ELSE ...
```
nothing beyond this point will be checked

But every part of the BOOLEAN expression in IsAWin2 will be evaluated,
so IsAWin2 will check every row, every column, and both diagonals.

Here's a version of Function IsAWin that does a compromise between
IFs and BOOLEAN expressions:

```
FUNCTION IsAWin3 (b      : boardType;
                  player : playerType) : BOOLEAN;
{Decides if board 'b' is a win for this player.}
   VAR
     w : BOOLEAN;
BEGIN {IsAWin3}
   {Check the three rows:}
   w :=   (b[1,1] = player) AND (b[1,2] = player) AND
          (b[1,3] = player);
   IF NOT w THEN
      w := (b[2,1] = player) AND (b[2,2] = player) AND
           (b[2,3] = player);
   IF NOT w THEN
      w := (b[3,1] = player) AND (b[3,2] = player) AND
           (b[3,3] = player);
   {Check the three columns:}
   IF NOT w THEN
      w := (b[1,1] = player) AND (b[2,1] = player) AND
           (b[3,1] = player);
   IF NOT w THEN
      w := (b[1,2] = player) AND (b[2,2] = player) AND
           (b[3,2] = player);
   IF NOT w THEN
      w := (b[1,3] = player) AND (b[2,3] = player) AND
           (b[3,3] = player);
   {Check the two diagonals:}
   IF NOT w THEN
      w := (b[1,1] = player) AND (b[2,2] = player) AND
           (b[3,3] = player);
   IF NOT w THEN
      w := (b[1,3] = player) AND (b[2,2] = player) AND
           (b[3,1] = player);

   IsAWin3 := w
END;  {IsAWin3}
```

On an implementation that doesn't do short-circuit evaluation, Function
IsAWin3 is probably faster than IsAWin2 but slower than IsAWin1.
(Why?) Function IsAWin3 looks a little nicer than IsAWin1 but it's more
clumsy than IsAWin2.

One way to avoid that clumsy look is to move some repetitive text into
a subprogram:

```
FUNCTION IsAWin4 (b         : boardType;
                  player : playerType) : BOOLEAN;
{Decides if board 'b' is a win for this player.}
   VAR
     win : BOOLEAN;

   {----------}

   FUNCTION Expansion (b                   : boardType;
                       r1,c1,r2,c2,r3,c3 : indexType;
                       p                   : playerType) : BOOLEAN;
   {Expands row and column numbers into
    a test for a win for player 'p'.}
   BEGIN {Expansion}
     Expansion :=
       (b[r1,c1] = p) AND (b[r2,c2] = p) AND (b[r3,c3] = p)
   END;  {Expansion}

   {----------}

BEGIN {IsAWin4}
  {Check the three rows:}
  win :=    Expansion (board, 1,1, 1,2, 1,3, player);
  IF NOT win THEN
    win := Expansion (board, 2,1, 2,2, 2,3, player);
  IF NOT win THEN
    win := Expansion (board, 3,1, 3,2, 3,3, player);
  {Check the three columns:}
  IF NOT win THEN
    win := Expansion (board, 1,1, 2,1, 3,1, player);
  IF NOT win THEN
    win := Expansion (board, 1,2, 2,2, 3,2, player);
  IF NOT win THEN
    win := Expansion (board, 1,3, 2,3, 3,3, player);
  {Check the two diagonals:}
  IF NOT win THEN
    win := Expansion (board, 1,1, 2,2, 3,3, player);
  IF NOT win THEN
    win := Expansion (board, 1,3, 2,2, 3,1, player);
  IsAWin4 := win
END;  {IsAWin4}
```

In Function IsAWin4 we avoid all the b[,]s by writing Function Expansion, which does the b[,]s once and for all. We can carry this idea further, to get an even shorter program:

```
FUNCTION IsAWin5 (b         : boardType;
                  player : playerType) : BOOLEAN;
{Decides if board 'b' is a win for this player.}
   VAR
     win : BOOLEAN;

   {--------}
```

```
PROCEDURE Expand (b                    : boardType ;
                  r1,c1,r2,c2,r3,c3 : indexType ;
                  p                    : playerType;
                  VAR w                : BOOLEAN  );
{Expands row and column numbers into
 a test for a win for player 'p'.}
BEGIN {Expand}
  IF NOT w THEN
    w := (b[r1,c1] = p) AND (b[r2,c2] = p) AND (b[r3,c3] = p)
END;  {Expand}

{--------}

BEGIN {IsAWin5}
  win := FALSE;

  {Check the three rows:}
  Expand (board, 1,1, 1,2, 1,3, player, win);
  Expand (board, 2,1, 2,2, 2,3, player, win);
  Expand (board, 3,1, 3,2, 3,3, player, win);

  {Check the three columns:}
  Expand (board, 1,1, 2,1, 3,1, player, win);
  Expand (board, 1,2, 2,2, 3,2, player, win);
  Expand (board, 1,3, 2,3, 3,3, player, win);

  {Check the two diagonals:}
  Expand (board, 1,1, 2,2, 3,3, player, win);
  Expand (board, 1,3, 2,2, 3,1, player, win);

  IsAWin5 := win
END;   {IsAWin5}
```

All these examples leave us with the nagging feeling that there must be
a more uniform way to handle all these indices. The notion of a "win" in
tic-tac-toe is so simple. So why are we forced to clutter up all our functions
with 1's, 2's, and 3's?

Instead of thinking of the board as having three rows, three columns,
and two diagonals, let's try thinking in terms of eight routes, where each
route has three positions:

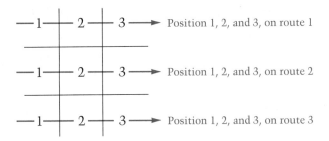

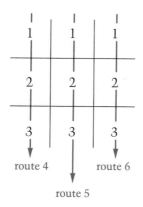
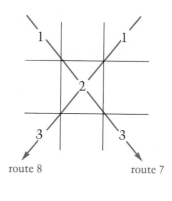

route 4   route 6   route 8   route 7

route 5

To check for a win we can have a loop

```
route := 1
REPEAT
    Check to see if this route is a WinningRoute for the player
    route := route + 1
UNTIL finding a winning route or running out of routes
```

Now since we have this nice pseudocode that deals with routes, we need a way to go from talk about routes to talk about array indices. One way to do this is with Functions RowNum and ColNum:

```
FUNCTION RowNum (route : routeType;
                 pos   : positionType) : indexType;
{Takes a route number (1 to 8) and a position along that
 route (1 to 3), and returns a row number (1 to 3).}
FUNCTION ColNum (route : routeType;
                 pos   : positionType) : indexType;
{Takes a route number (1 to 8) and a position along that
 route (1 to 3), and returns a column number (1 to 3).}
```

For example, RowNum (7,3) should have the value 3, because the third position in the seventh route is in row 3.

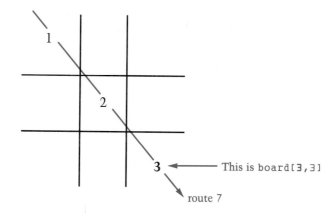

3 ← This is board[3,3]

route 7

ColNum (7,3) should also be equal to 3.

Now our algorithm is quite simple. In the main body of Function IsAWin6 we do

```
route := 1;
REPEAT
  win := IsWinningRoute (board, route, player);
  route := route + 1
UNTIL win OR (route = 9)
```

And to find out if a particular route IsWinningRoute for our player we just plug calls to Functions RowNum and ColNum into our usual BOOLEAN expression:

```
IsWinningRoute :=
  (board[ RowNum(route,1), ColNum(route,1) ] = player) AND
  (board[ RowNum(route,2), ColNum(route,2) ] = player) AND
  (board[ RowNum(route,3), ColNum(route,3) ] = player)
```

This BOOLEAN expression checks for our player's mark in positions 1, 2, and 3 of the desired route. That's just what we want.

We seem to have devised a readable algorithm that's also quite elegant. Of course, we've left off an important detail: the bodies of Functions RowNum and ColNum. It's inside these functions that we've buried the ugly details about the indices of the board array.

```
FUNCTION IsAWin6 (b       : boardType;
                  player : playerType) : BOOLEAN;
{Decides if board 'b' is a win for this player.}
  TYPE
    routeType    = 1..9;
    positionType = 1..3;
  VAR
    route : routeType;
    win   : BOOLEAN;
  {----------}

  FUNCTION IsWinningRoute (board  : boardType;
                           route  : routeType;
                           player : playerType) : BOOLEAN;
  {Checks this route on the board to
   see if it's a win for this player.}
    {----------}

    FUNCTION RowNum (route : routeType;
                     pos   : positionType) : indexType;
    {Takes a route number (1 to 8) and a position along that
     route (1 to 3), and returns a row number (1 to 3).}
    BEGIN {RowNum}
      IF route <= 3 THEN
        RowNum := route
      ELSE
        RowNum := pos
    END;  {RowNum}
    {----------}
```

```
      FUNCTION ColNum (route : routeType;
                       pos   : positionType) : indexType;
      {Takes a route number (1 to 8) and a position along that
       route (1 to 3), and returns a column number (1 to 3).}
      BEGIN {ColNum}
        CASE route OF
          1, 2, 3 : ColNum := pos;
          4, 5, 6 : ColNum := route - 3;
          7       : ColNum := pos;
          8       : ColNum := 4 - pos
        END
      END;  {ColNum}

      {----------}

    BEGIN {IsWinningRoute}
      IsWinningRoute :=
        (board[ RowNum(route,1), ColNum(route,1) ] = player) AND
        (board[ RowNum(route,2), ColNum(route,2) ] = player) AND
        (board[ RowNum(route,3), ColNum(route,3) ] = player)
    END;   {IsWinningRoute}

    {----------}

  BEGIN {IsAWin6}
    route := 1;
    REPEAT
      win := IsWinningRoute (board, route, player);
      route := route + 1
    UNTIL win OR (route = 9);
    IsAWin6 := win
  END;   {IsAWin6}
```

Functions RowNum and ColNum are quite cryptic, but at least they form a very small, isolated part of the program. If we like, we can get rid of them by creating two new arrays—rowNum and colNum. These arrays store the information contained in the bodies of Functions RowNum and ColNum.

```
TYPE
  indexType    = 1..3;
  routeType    = 1..9;
  positionType = 1..3;
  rowColNum    = ARRAY [routeType, positionType] OF indexType;
VAR
  rowNum, colNum : rowColNum;
```

The rowNum array:

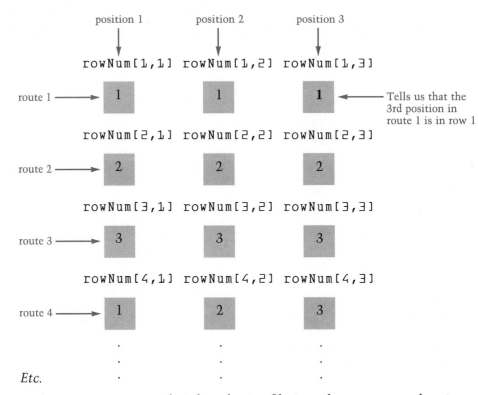

Etc.

The main program reads values from a file into the rowNum and colNum arrays. Then, whenever the main program calls Function IsAWin, it passes these arrays to the function. The function uses these arrays instead of referring to RowNum and ColNum functions:

```
FUNCTION IsAWin? (board             : boardType ;
                  player            : playerType;
                  rowNum, colNum : rowColNum) : BOOLEAN;
{Decides if board 'b' is a win for this player.}
   VAR
     route : routeType;
     win   : BOOLEAN;

   {----------}

   FUNCTION IsWinningRoute (board             : boardType ;
                            route             : routeType ;
                            player            : playerType;
                            rowNum, colNum : rowColNum) : BOOLEAN;
   {Checks this route on the board to
    see if it's a win for this player.}
```

```
      BEGIN {IsWinningRoute}
        IsWinningRoute :=
          (board[ rowNum[route,1], colNum[route,1] ] = player) AND
          (board[ rowNum[route,2], colNum[route,2] ] = player) AND
          (board[ rowNum[route,3], colNum[route,3] ] = player)
      END;  {IsWinningRoute}

      {----------}
    BEGIN {IsAWin?}
      route := 1;
      REPEAT
        win    := IsWinningRoute (board, route, player, rowNum, colNum);
        route := route + 1
      UNTIL win OR (route = 9);
      IsAWin? := win
    END;  {IsAWin?}
```

Function IsAWin? may be the best of all the versions that we've created. But beware—the story doesn't end here. There are many more ways to check for a win in tic-tac-toe. Some of them are extraordinarily clever. Tic-tac-toe is a fine example of a problem that is easy to describe, but endlessly interesting to program.

Testing and Debugging

automated testing

How would we go about testing our various versions of Function IsAWin? First we'd write a test driver, and we'd run each version with a few tic-tac-toe boards. But with seven different versions of Function IsAWin, and several tic-tac-toe boards for each, we'd quickly run out of patience and energy.

Perhaps we can automate the testing process. We can create a file with several tic-tac-toe boards in it:

```
XXX
OOX
OO

OOX
XXX
OO

 .
 .
 .
etc.
```

Each version of Function IsAWin should read this file and give its opinion on each of the boards in the file. Here's the pseudocode for our test driver:

Repeat several times:
  Read a board array from the testFile,
  Call IsAWin and write a message telling whether X wins or O wins (or neither).
  (The user compares the message that's been written with the board that's in the testFile to see if the program is working.)

We've taken the drudgery out of testing by automating our testing process. We've created a test driver that steps Function IsAWin through a file of tic-tac-toe boards. Now why don't we take this idea of **automated testing** one step further? In the test file along with each tic-tac-toe board, let's include the answer that we expect to get from Function IsAWin.

```
XXX
OOX
OO
TF  ◄─── it's TRUE that X wins; it's FALSE that O wins
OX
O X
O
FT  ◄─── it's FALSE that X wins; it's TRUE that C wins
  .
  .
  .
etc.
```

Then the test driver can compare the result it gets from Function IsAWin with the answer we expect to get.

Repeat several times:
Read a board array from the testFile,
Read xWins and oWins from the testFile.
    These are the correct answers for this board
    (xWins = T means that player X wins on this board; etc.)
Call IsAWin and compare the results with the values xWins and oWins. If there's a discrepancy, write an error message on the screen.

Here's a test driver that does this for the first six versions of Function IsAWin:

```
PROGRAM WinTestDriver (testFile, output);
  TYPE
    indexType   = 1..3;
    markType    = (X, O, blank);
    playerType  = X..O;
    boardType   = ARRAY [indexType, indexType] OF markType;
  VAR
    board              : boardType;
    count              : INTEGER;
    xWins, oWins : BOOLEAN;
    testFile           : TEXT;

  {----------}

  PROCEDURE ReadBoard (VAR testFile : TEXT        ;
                       VAR board    : boardType);
  {Reads characters 'X', 'O', and blank,
   converts them into enumerated markType
   values, and fills the board with them.}
    VAR
      row, col : indexType;
      ch       : CHAR;
```

```
        BEGIN {ReadBoard}
          FOR row := 1 TO 3 DO
            BEGIN
              FOR col := 1 TO 3 DO
                BEGIN
                  Read (testFile, ch);
                  IF ch = 'X' THEN
                    board[row,col] := X
                  ELSE IF ch = 'O' THEN
                    board[row,col] := O
                  ELSE IF ch = ' ' THEN
                    board[row,col] := blank
                  ELSE
                    WriteLn (Chr(7), 'Error reading testFile.')
                END;
              ReadLn (testFile)
            END
        END;  {ReadBoard}
        {----------}

        PROCEDURE ReadBools (VAR testFile    : TEXT    ;
                             VAR xWins, oWins : BOOLEAN);
        {Converts 'T' to TRUE and 'F' to FALSE;
         Reads two such letters -
           the first tells if we expect X to win
           the second tells if we expect O to win}

          VAR
            xChar, oChar : CHAR;

        BEGIN {ReadBools}
          ReadLn (testFile, xChar, oChar);
          xWins := xChar = 'T';
          oWins := oChar = 'T'
        END;  {ReadBools}
        {----------}

        FUNCTION IsAWin (b      : boardType;
                         player : playerType) : BOOLEAN;
        {Put any of the IsAWin functions here.}

        {----------}

      BEGIN {WinTestDriver}
        Reset (testFile);

        FOR count := 1 TO 12 DO
          BEGIN
            ReadBoard (testFile, board);
            ReadBools (testFile, xWins, oWins);
          · IF (IsAWin(board,X) <> xWins) OR
               (IsAWin(board,O) <> oWins) THEN
                  WriteLn (Chr(7), 'Error: test #', count:1)
          END;

        WriteLn ('Test concluded')
      END.  {WinTestDriver}
```

We ran the first six versions of `IsAWin` with the test driver and with the following `testFile`:

```
XXX    X wins with route 1
OOX
OO
TF
OOX    X wins with route 2
XXX
OO
TF
OOX    O wins with route 3

OOO
FT
OX     O wins with route 4
O X
O
FT
XO     O wins with route 5
XO
OO
FT
X O    O wins with route 6
XXO
O O
FT
XO     X wins with route 7
 XO
 OX
TF
XXO    O wins with route 8
 OX
O
FT
XXO    Neither player wins
XXO
OO
FF
       No moves made


FF
XXX    X wins all possible ways
XXX
XXX
TF
OOO    Both X and O win
XXX

TT
```

placing
"comments" in
the data file In addition to the tic-tac-toe boards and the `T` and `F` answers, the `testFile` contained a comment for each board. These comments didn't get read by `WinTestDriver` because the program's `ReadLns` skipped over them. But the comments were quite useful in helping us keep track of the various boards that we were testing.

None of the runs of the `WinTestDriver` produced any error messages. Each run just gave us the message

```
Test concluded
```

Things looked good, but it bothered us that the test driver was hiding so many details of the testing process. How did we know that the test driver program was correct?

We made Function `IsAWin6` incorrect by changing one number:

```
IsWinningRoute :=
    (board[ RowNum(route,2), ColNum(route,1) ] = player) AND
    (board[ RowNum(route,2), ColNum(route,2) ] = player) AND
    (board[ RowNum(route,3), ColNum(route,3) ] = player)
```

and ran the test driver again. This time we got

```
Error: test #1
Error: test #7
Error: test #8
Test concluded
```

bebugging

So at least we knew that the test driver was capable of finding an error. This trick we used, of intentionally putting bugs into a program to make sure the program doesn't work with the bugs added, goes by the name **bebugging**.

11.3 Exercises

Key Words to Review

tableau	automated testing
brute force approach	debugging

Questions to Answer

QUE 11.3.1 Why do we use the term *brute force* to describe the approach taken in Function `IsAWin1`?

QUE 11.3.2 Explain how we got Function `IsAWin5` as a natural extension of the thinking that went into Function `IsAWin4`.

QUE 11.3.3 In Function `IsAWin4` we had a subprogram called `Expansion`, but in Function `IsAWin5` we gave the corresponding subprogram the name `Expand`. What style rule compelled us to change the name this way?

QUE 11.3.4 To what extent can the technique of bebugging convince us that a program runs correctly?

Changes to Make

CHA 11.3.1 Modify Function `IsAWin6` so that `routeType` is an enumerated type.

CHA 11.3.2   Write a test driver for Function IsAWin?.

CHA 11.3.3   Choose one of the earlier versions of IsAWin and modify it for a four-by-four tic-tac-toe board.

CHA 11.3.4   Choose one of the later versions of IsAWin and modify it for a four-by-four tic-tac-toe board.

CHA 11.3.5   Expand on the work we did in this section to create a program that keeps track of two users playing tic-tac-toe. The program repeatedly prompts the users for moves and displays the current state of the board. When one of the players wins, the program makes an appropriate announcement.

CHA 11.3.6   Modify the program you wrote for Exercise Cha.11.3.5 so that the computer is one of the two players. Use Function Random from Section 9.5 to help the computer decide on each of its moves. This is indeed an interesting problem. You'll find that the computer seldom wins unless it uses some clever heuristic for filtering out some of the more senseless moves.

Programs and Subprograms to Write

WRI 11.3.1   Write and test a subprogram that prompts the user for the coordinates of a checker piece that's to be moved and the coordinates of the place where the piece should be moved. Then it modifies the checker board array accordingly.

WRI 11.3.2   Write a program that takes input from two users playing *Nim*. After each move it displays the remaining sticks. When one of the players removes the last stick, it announces who won, and ends the game.

WRI 11.3.3   Modify the program of Exercise Wri.11.3.2 so that the computer plays against only one player. The computer decides on its next move by calling Function Random from Section 9.5.

WRI 11.3.4   Write a program that deals cards to two players (users) by calling Function Random from Section 9.5. As the program deals, the users play the card game called *twenty-one*. Can you think of some cute way to make it so that a user doesn't see the other's face-down card?

WRI 11.3.5   The program of Exercise Wri.11.3.4 is more interesting if the computer hesitates before it shows each card and hesitates a bit more before it shows who won. Call Function Random (Section 9.5) to keep varying the amount of delay time in an unpredictable way. Can you fine-tune the length of delays to heighten the excitement?

WRI 11.3.6   Redo Exercise Wri.9.1.2, using what you now know about two-dimensional arrays.

Things to Think About

THI 11.3.1   Of all the versions of Function IsAWin that we presented in this section, which one do you *really* like the best? Why?

THI 11.3.2   Can you think of yet another way to solve the problem posed in this section? Create your own IsAWin8 function.

11.4

Three-Dimensional Arrays and Beyond

Specifications

seven-segment code

A calculator normally displays digits using the **seven-segment code**. In the seven-segment code a digit is composed of several segments, with seven possible segments in all.

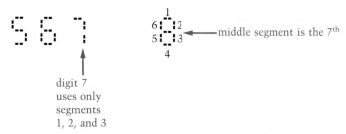

digit 7
uses only
segments
1, 2, and 3

Input: A number of up to five digits, such as 09876

Output: The same number, printed using the seven-segment code, for example,

Designing a Program

One approach to this problem is to put the seven-segment representation for each digit right in the Pascal code:

```
CASE digit OF
   'O' : BEGIN
            WriteLn ('  _  ');
            WriteLn ('| |');
            WriteLn ('|_|')
         END;
   '1' : BEGIN
            WriteLn ('     ');
            WriteLn ('   |');
            WriteLn ('   |')
         END;
   '2' : BEGIN
            WriteLn ('  _  ');
            WriteLn ('  _|');
            WriteLn ('|_  ')
         END
{Etc.}
```

This approach works well enough for displaying one digit, but modifying it to display many digits side by side is very cumbersome:

```
FOR place := 1 TO 5 DO {write the 1st row of all five digits}
   BEGIN
      digit := number[place];
      CASE digit OF
         '0' : Write (' __ ');
         '1' : Write ('    ');
         '2' : Write (' __ ');
         {Etc.}
      END
   END;
WriteLn;
FOR place := 1 TO 5 DO {write the 2nd row of all five digits}
   BEGIN
      digit := number[place];
      CASE digit OF
         '0' : Write ('| |');
         '1' : Write ('  |');
         '2' : Write (' __|');
         {Etc.}
      END
   END;
WriteLn;
FOR place := 1 TO 5 DO {write the 3rd row of all five digits}
   BEGIN
      digit := number[place];
      CASE digit OF
         '0' : Write ('|__|');
         '1' : Write ('   |');
         '2' : Write ('|__ ');
         {Etc.}
      END
   END;
WriteLn
```

We'd need three very similar-looking loops that differ only by the content of their WriteLns. Notice also that in this latest version the original digits' Writes have to be scrambled, so we can't glance at the Writes and immediately understand that they're meant to write digits. In fact, it's very hard to write this last bit of code correctly, because when you're putting underscores and vertical bars in the Writes, it's difficult to keep track of what you're doing.

put information in the data, not the code

Instead of putting all the alternatives in the code, it's much better to put them in the data. We create a file (digitFil) that contains the seven-segment code representation of each digit:

and we read this file into a three-dimensional array (called display), with three rows, three columns, and ten planes:

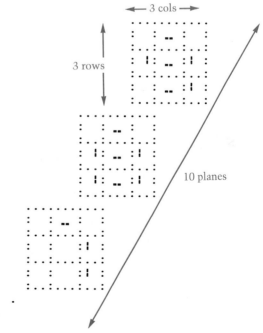

```
For each digit
  For each row
    For each column
      Read display[digit, row, col]
    ReadLn (to go to the next row).
```

Notice how the loops are nested: the `digit` loop is the outer loop so the `digit` counter is the slowest to change. This makes sense, because in the `digitFile`, we read all the rows and all the columns of a single digit before we change to another digit.

To print the seven-segment code for a single digit, say 8, we just print one of the planes in the `display` array:

> For each `row`
>   For each `column`
>   Write display[8, row, col]
>   WriteLn (to go to the next row).

And now it's easy to print several digits side by side. We just create a "For each `digit`" loop, and make sure to put it in the right place:

> For each `row`
>   **For each `digit`**
>   For each `column`
>   Write display[**digit**, row, col]
>   Write a blank space between digits.
>   WriteLn (to go to the next row).

Program Example

```
PROGRAM SevenSegmentCode (digitFil, input, output);
{Reads up to five digits and displays
 them using the seven-segment code.}
  TYPE
    digitType  = '0'..'9';
    placeType  = 1..6;
    numberType = ARRAY [placeType] OF digitType;
    rowType    = 1..3;
    colType    = 1..3;
    threeArray = ARRAY [digitType, rowType, colType] OF CHAR;
  VAR
    display  : threeArray;
    number   : numberType;
    last     : placeType;
    digitFil : TEXT;

  {----------}

  PROCEDURE ReadDisplay (VAR digitFil : TEXT        ;
                         VAR display  : threeArray);
  {Reads the display array from the digitFil(e).}

    VAR
      dig : digitType;
      row : colType;
      col : rowType;
```

```
BEGIN {ReadDisplay}
  Reset (digitFil);
  FOR dig := '0' TO '9' DO
    FOR row := 1 TO 3 DO
      BEGIN
        FOR col := 1 TO 3 DO
          Read (digitFil, display[dig,row,col]);
        ReadLn (digitFil)
      END
END;  {ReadDisplay}
{----------}

PROCEDURE ReadNumber (VAR number : numberType;
                      VAR last   : placeType);
{Reads a number of up to five digits.}

  VAR
    place : placeType;
BEGIN {ReadNumber}
  place := 1;
  WHILE NOT Eoln DO
    BEGIN
      Read (number[place]);
      place := place + 1
    END;
  ReadLn;
  last := place - 1
END;  {ReadNumber}
{----------}

PROCEDURE WriteNumber (number  : numberType ;
                       last    : placeType  ;
                       display : threeArray);
{Writes the number (of up to five digits)
 using the seven-segment code.}

  VAR
    place  : placeType;
    row    : colType;
    col    : rowType;
BEGIN {WriteNumber}
  FOR row := 1 TO 3 DO
    BEGIN
      FOR place := 1 TO last DO
        BEGIN
          FOR col := 1 TO 3 DO
            Write ( display[number[place],row,col] );
          Write (' ')
        END;
      WriteLn
    END
END;  {WriteNumber}
{----------}
```

```
BEGIN {SevenSegmentCode}
  ReadDisplay (digitFil, display);

  Write       ('Enter a number of up to five digits: ');
  ReadNumber  (number, last);

  WriteLn;
  WriteLn     ('The seven-segment code for this number:');
  WriteLn;
  WriteNumber (number, last, display)
END.   {SevenSegmentCode}
```

Sample Runs

Enter a number of up to five digits; 0
The seven-segment code for this number:

Enter a number of up to five digits: 456
The seven-segment code for this number:

Enter a number of up to five digits: 09876
The seven-segment code for this number:

Programming Style

There's a general principle of programming style that goes something like this:

Whenever you have a choice of putting information in the code, or putting it in the data, put the information in the data. Make the code as general as it can be.

Why shouldn't we put information in the code?

We saw this principle in action as we designed the SevenSegmentCode program. Instead of putting our display digits in CASE statements, we put them into the digitFile and had the code simply read the digitFile.

There are several reasons for following this principle. Perhaps the most important reason is this:

It's easy to modify data, but it's hard to modify code.

Generally speaking, programs are very rigid structures. Each part of a program depends on many other parts. When you modify one part, it often forces you to modify other parts. So if you put information into the code (for example, write a big CASE statement with all the digits displayed in it), then in all probability you'll have a delicate operation to perform when you need to change that information.

On the other hand, data tend to be very flexible. When you put ReadLns in your program, you expect to be reading different data each time the program runs. You usually design the program to handle all kinds of data. So a data file is a very flexible and changeable entity.

11.4   Exercises

Key Words to Review

seven-segment code

Questions to Answer

QUE 11.4.1 Explain why it's difficult to display digits side by side when the seven-segment codes of the digits are "stored" in a CASE statement.

QUE 11.4.2 In the pseudocode that immediately precedes this section's Program Example, why is For each digit sandwiched in between For each row and For each column?

Changes to Make

CHA 11.4.1 To Program SevenSegmentCode's abilities, add printing letters of the alphabet.

CHA 11.4.2 Program SevenSegmentCode reads the displays of all ten of the digits, even though it may need to display only a few of them. Modify the program so that it reads only the displays that it needs (and skips the others).

CHA 11.4.3 Rewrite the program fragments in the beginning of Section 8.4 (the ones that write the days of the week and the words none, one, two, etc.). Instead of using CASE statements, use arrays.

CHA 11.4.4 Modify Procedure ChangeState in Section 8.6 so that it uses an array type with the definition

```
ARRAY [stateType, partOfSpeechType] OF stateType
```

instead of a CASE statement.

CHA 11.4.5 Rewrite Program BloodTypes from Section 8.2 so that it uses

```
TYPE
   patientType   = (donor, receiver);
   antigenType   = 'A'..'B';
   bloodCompType = ARRAY [patientType, antigenType] OF BOOLEAN;
```

Compare this with Exercise Cha.10.4.2.

Programs and Subprograms to Write

WRI 11.4.1   In a certain kind of computer game, when you specify a direction (N, S, E, W, NE, NW, etc.) the computer "moves" you one step in that direction and describes where you are when you make that step.

```
N
You're in the cave of the frebus seloneus bear.
N
You're in the inner cave.  The bear is angry.
S
You're in the cave of the frebus seloneus bear.
```

Write a program that displays a message each time the user enters one or two letters, specifying a direction. To represent the imaginary world in which the user is traveling, use a two-dimensional array of character strings.

WRI 11.4.2   Redo Exercise Wri.8.4.1, this time storing the table of commissions as data in an array, rather than as code in a cascading IF.

Things to Think About

THI 11.4.1   Can you think of any reasons, other than the one we gave at the end of this section, for representing information in the data rather than in the code?

THI 11.4.2   Can you think of any situations in which it's better to put information in the code than in the data?

11.5

Conformant Array Parameters (Supplementary)

Look once again at Program Merge in Section 10.7. This program has one very important deficiency: smallArray1 and smallArray2 need to have the same number of components. Procedure ReadArray's formal parameter smallArray is of type smallType, so in the call to ReadArray, the actual parameter corresponding to smallArray has to be of type smallType. And every array of type smallType has six components.

But in many real-life problems, the two arrays being merged do not have the same number of components.

There's no satisfactory solution to this problem in ANSI Standard Pascal. If you have two arrays, one with a thousand components and the other with five thousand components, you can "cheat" and give them both five thousand components. You can pad the smaller array with four thousand MAXINTs. But that seems wasteful, and indeed it is.

However, there's another version of Pascal called the ISO Standard.[1] ISO Standard Pascal has a feature, called **conformant array parameters**, that allows a subprogram to accept arrays of many different sizes.

Instead of creating a new problem to illustrate the ideas of this section, we'll rewrite Program Merge so that it uses conformant array parameters.

The new program (called Program Conformant) may not run on your computer. Many older implementations of Pascal have no mechanism for passing varying-sized arrays to subprograms or have their own mechanisms that are different from those in the ISO Standard. Consult your manual to find out if your implementation has conformant array parameters or some other feature that serves the same purpose.

Since conformant array parameters are not yet implemented on many computers, we cover them only briefly in this section.

Specifications Our new program's specs are the same as the specs for Program Merge, except the two "smaller" arrays are now one small array and one medium-sized array. The small- and medium-sized arrays don't necessarily have the same index ranges.

Program Example

```
PROGRAM Conformant (input, output);
{Merges two arrays of unequal size.}
   CONST
     smallMax = 6;
     medMax   = 8;
     largeMax = 12;
   TYPE
     smallType = ARRAY [1..smallMax] OF INTEGER;
     medType   = ARRAY [1..medMax  ] OF INTEGER;
     largeType = ARRAY [1..largeMax] OF INTEGER;
     positive  = 1..MAXINT;
   VAR
     smallArray : smallType;
     medArray   : medType;
     largeArray : largeType;
     sm, md, lg : positive;

   {----------}

   PROCEDURE ReadArray(VAR anArray :
                        ARRAY [lo..hi:INTEGER] OF INTEGER);
   {Reads values into a one-dimensional array of integers.}
     VAR
        i : positive;
   BEGIN {ReadArray}
     Write ('Enter ', hi - lo : 1, ' integers: ');
     FOR i := lo TO hi-1 DO
       Read (anArray[i]);

     anArray[hi] := MAXINT;
     WriteLn
   END;  {ReadArray}

   {----------}
```

_____
[1]ISO stands for International Standards Organization.

```
            PROCEDURE Move (VAR largeArray : largeType;
                           anArray         :
                             ARRAY [lo..hi:INTEGER] OF INTEGER;
                           VAR lg, anIndex : positive);
            {Moves a value from the small or medium array into
             the large array, and adjusts indices as needed.}
            BEGIN {Move}
              largeArray[lg] := anArray[anIndex];
              lg             := lg + 1;
              anIndex        := anIndex + 1
            END;   {Move}

            {----------}

            PROCEDURE WriteArray (largeArray : largeType);
            {Writes the values in the large array.}

              VAR
                i : 1..largeMax;
            BEGIN {WriteArray}
              Write ('After merging, the values are: ');

              FOR i := 1 TO largeMax DO
                Write (largeArray[i]:3);
              WriteLn
            END;   {WriteArray}

            {----------}

          BEGIN {Conformant}
            ReadArray (smallArray);
            ReadArray (medArray);
            sm := 1;
            md := 1;
            lg := 1;

            WHILE (sm < smallMax) OR (md < medMax) DO
              IF smallArray[sm] < medArray[md] THEN
                Move (largeArray, smallArray, lg, sm)
              ELSE
                Move (largeArray, medArray, lg, md);

            WriteArray (largeArray)
          END.   {Conformant}
```

Sample Runs

```
    Enter 5 integers: 3 5 10 42 56
    Enter 7 integers: 4 5 9 33 39 50 60
    After merging, the values are:   3  4  5  5  9 10 33 39 42 50 56 60
```

Observations

In ANSI Standard Pascal we'd need to declare

```
        PROCEDURE ReadArray(VAR anArray : array-type-identifier);
```

that is, anArray would have to be declared using a one-word type name. But in the ISO standard, a formal parameter name like anArray can be declared using a **conformant array schema**.

conformant
array schema

```
      PROCEDURE ReadArray(VAR anArray :
                    ARRAY [lo..hi:INTEGER] OF INTEGER);
```

This makes anArray a conformant array parameter.

According to our new procedure heading, ReadArray's formal parameter is a one-dimensional array whose indices and values are INTEGERs. Within the body of Procedure ReadArray, the lowest and highest indices of anArray go by the names lo and hi. The procedure heading doesn't give us specific values for lo and hi, so the values of lo and hi can change from one call of ReadArray to the next.

We also declare anArray to be a conformant array parameter in Procedure Move.

- CONST
    ```
      smallMax = 6;
      medMax   = 8;
    TYPE
      smallType = ARRAY [1..smallMax] OF INTEGER;
      medType   = ARRAY [1..medMax  ] OF INTEGER;
    VAR
      smallArray : smallType;
      medArray   : medType;
               .
               .
               .
    ReadArray (smallArray);
    ReadArray (medArray)
    ```

how to use conformant array parameters

The first time Procedure ReadArray is called, lo has the value 1 and hi has the value 6. The second time ReadArray is called, lo has the value 1 and hi has the value 8. Notice that the values of lo and hi don't appear in the calls to Procedure ReadArray. Instead, when Procedure ReadArray is called, values for lo and hi are obtained from the definitions of smallType and medType.

- ```
    Write ('Enter ', hi - lo : 1, ' integers: ');
    FOR i := lo TO hi-1 DO
            .
            .
            .
    ```

Here's where we use lo and hi in the body of Procedure ReadArray.

- ```
    PROCEDURE ReadArray(VAR anArray :
                   ARRAY [lo..hi:INTEGER] OF INTEGER);
      VAR
        i : positive;
    ```

It's tempting to declare i with a subrange:

```
VAR
  i :  lo..hi;
```

but this isn't legal. Since the values of lo and hi can change from one call of ReadArray to another, these names can't be used to define a variable's subrange.

- CONST
    smallMax = 6;
  TYPE
    smallType = ARRAY [1..smallMax] OF INTEGER;
  VAR
    smallArray : smallType;

only a
parameter
can be
"conformant"

smallArray isn't a formal parameter; it's a variable in the main program's VAR declaration. Since it's not a formal parameter, it *cannot* be defined using a conformant array schema. The smallArray indices can range from 1 to 6. The only way to change this, even in ISO Standard Pascal, is to change the value of smallMax in the CONST definition. You can do this when you edit Program Conformant, but since smallMax is a constant, its value can't be changed during a run of Program Conformant. So, unlike the situation with a conformant array schema, the index range of smallArray can't be decided during the run of the program.

11.5   Exercises

Key Words to Review

    conformant array   conformant array schema
      parameter

Questions to Answer

QUE 11.5.1   Describe the role of the identifiers lo and hi in Procedure ReadArray.

QUE 11.5.2   Describe the role of the identifiers lo and hi in Procedure Move.

QUE 11.5.3   In what sense can Procedures ReadArray and Move be described as *polymorphic?*

QUE 11.5.4   Why have we taken care to avoid the term *conformant array* in this section?

Things to Check in a Manual

MAN 11.5.1   Does your implementation have features for accomplishing what conformant array parameters accomplish in ISO Standard Pascal?

MAN 11.5.2   Does your implementation give you the option of choosing among various standards (ANSI Standard Pascal, ISO Standard Pascal, or possibly some other version)?

Experiments to Try

EXP 11.5.1   Add the statement

```
ReadArray (largeArray)
```

to Program Conformant.

EXP 11.5.2   Change

```
lo..hi   to   1..smallMax
```

in the heading of Procedure ReadArray.

Changes to Make

CHA 11.5.1   Modify Procedure WriteArray in Program Conformant so that the procedure uses a conformant array parameter.

CHA 11.5.2   Modify Program BinSearchDriver (Section 10.6) so that it uses conformant array parameters.

CHA 11.5.3   Modify Program Median2 (Section 10.3) so that it finds the median grade on a ten-point quiz or a hundred-point exam, whichever the instructor chooses.

Programs and Subprograms to Write

WRI 11.5.1   Look at the program you wrote for Exercise Wri.11.2.2. First make sure that you used a subprogram to accomplish each of the tasks described in the exercise. Then rewrite the subprograms so that they can handle arrays of various sizes (various numbers of students and various numbers of quizzes).

WRI 11.5.2   Modify the code you wrote for Exercise Wri.10.4.2 to make optimal use of conformant array parameters.

Chapter Summary

We began this chapter with a study of *two-dimensional arrays*. A two-dimensional array is an array with two indices.

Two-dimensional arrays are used to solve problems in which the data fall naturally into a rectangular shape. Very often we use a two-dimensional array to store the information contained in a *table*. When we do this, the row and column headings of the table can often become the indices of the array. For problems of this kind, we usually move through the table with nested loops. The outer loop steps from one row to another, and the inner loop steps from one column to another.

For some other problems (which we've called *tableau* problems) the usual kind of nested looping does not provide the most useful way to step through the array. In this kind of a problem, we can be very creative in discovering the simplest, most readable, most natural way to move from one component of the array to another.

For some problems the data takes the shape of several rectangular planes. To solve this kind of problem we use a three-dimensional array. We can also find problems that require four-dimensional arrays, five-dimensional arrays, and so on.

In ANSI Standard Pascal, each dimension of a subprogram's formal array parameter has a particular range of indices. The only way to "change" an index range of a formal array parameter is to create another subprogram with a different index range. But in ISO Standard Pascal a subprogram can have *conformant array parameters*. A range of indices for a conformant array parameter is not specified in a subprogram parameter list. A subprogram with a conformant array parameter can be called many times, each time with an actual parameter of a different size.

12 Records and Sets

12.1

What Is a Record?

An array type is called a *structured type,* because an array has many parts. Each part of an array is called a *component.* In this chapter we'll explore another structured type, called a **record type**. Like an array type, a record type is a structured type. Each part of a record is called a **field**.

Arrays and records differ in an important way:

- In an array, each component has the same type. For instance, if we declare array a with

```
VAR
    a : ARRAY [1..5] OF INTEGER;
```

then each component of a is an INTEGER.

- In a record, the various fields can have different types.

In addition to this, the syntax of records is a bit different from the syntax of arrays.

Specifications A company's employeeFile contains four lines for each employee in the company. Each group of four lines looks like this:

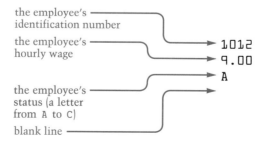

the employee's identification number
the employee's hourly wage

1012
9.00
A

the employee's status (a letter from A to C)

blank line

We want to read lines from the empFile and, for each employee, write two lines on the screen such as

```
Employee id: 1012
Hourly wage: 9.45
```

Type A employees get 5 percent raises; type B employees get 7 percent raises; type C employees get 10 percent raises.

Our first version of Program Raises follows.

Program Example (Version 1)

```
PROGRAM Raises1 (empFile, output);
{Reports new hourly wages for
 employees listed in the empFile.}
  TYPE
    idType     = 0000..9999;
    wageType   = REAL;
    statusType = 'A'..'C';

  VAR
    id      : idType;
    wage    : wageType;
    status  : statusType;
    rate    : REAL;
    empFile : TEXT;

BEGIN {Raises1}
  Reset (empFile);
  WHILE NOT Eof (empFile) DO
    BEGIN
      ReadLn (empFile, id);
      ReadLn (empFile, wage);
      ReadLn (empFile, status);
      ReadLn (empFile);

      CASE status OF
        'A' : rate := 1.05;
        'B' : rate := 1.07;
        'C' : rate := 1.10
      END;

      wage := wage * rate;

      WriteLn ('Employee id: ', id  :4  );
      WriteLn ('Hourly wage: ', wage:4:2);
      WriteLn
    END
END.  {Raises1}
```

**Sample
Runs**

With the following empFile:

```
1012
9.00
A

3490
6.00
B

6600
7.00
C
```

the output looks like this:

```
Employee id: 1012
Hourly wage: 9.45

Employee id: 3490
Hourly wage: 6.42

Employee id: 6600
Hourly wage: 7.70
```

This first version of Program Raises works well but lacks a certain elegance. We treat id, wage, and status as if they're three entirely separate entities, when we know perfectly well that they're all part of the same bundle of information—the information about an employee. Things still look clumsy when we create a separate procedure to ReadEmployeeInfo.

**Program
Example
(Version 2)**

```
PROGRAM Raises2 (empFile, output);
{Reports new hourly wages for
 employees listed in the empFile.}
  TYPE
    idType     = 0000..9999;
    wageType   = REAL;
    statusType = 'A'..'C';

  VAR
    id      : idType;
    wage    : wageType;
    status  : statusType;
    rate    : REAL;
    empFile : TEXT;

  {----------}

  PROCEDURE ReadEmpInfo (VAR empFile : TEXT       ;
                         VAR id      : idType     ;
                         VAR wage    : wageType   ;
                         VAR status  : statusType);
  {Reads information for one employee from the empFile.}

  BEGIN {ReadEmpInfo}
    ReadLn (empFile, id);
    ReadLn (empFile, wage);
    ReadLn (empFile, status);
    ReadLn (empFile)
  END;  {ReadEmpInfo}

  {----------}
```

```
BEGIN {Raises2}
  Reset (empFile);
  WHILE NOT Eof (empFile) DO
    BEGIN
      ReadEmpInfo (empFile, id, wage, status);
      CASE status OF
        'A' : rate := 1.05;
        'B' : rate := 1.07;
        'C' : rate := 1.10
      END;

      wage := wage * rate;
      WriteLn ('Employee id: ', id  :4  );
      WriteLn ('Hourly wage: ', wage:4:2);
      WriteLn
    END
END.   {Raises2}
```

Observations

- ```
PROCEDURE ReadEmpInfo (VAR empFile : TEXT   ;
                       VAR id   : idType   ;
                       VAR wage   : wageType   ;
                       VAR status : statusType);
```

Our formal parameter list looks cluttered and unwieldy, when it should really be conveying a simple idea:

```
PROCEDURE ReadEmpInfo (VAR empFile                        : TEXT ;
                       VAR one parameter that stores all
                           the information for an employee : ... );
```

Clearly we need to create a new type that stores a combination of what was in our old id, wage, and status variables. Here's how we do it:

- ```
TYPE
   empRecType = RECORD
                   id   : idType;
                   wage   : wageType;
                   status : statusType
                END;
VAR
   empRec : empRecType;
```

empRec is a variable of type empRecType. So empRec has three

creating records   fields:

empRec.id   empRec.wage   empRec.status

| 1012 | | 9.00 | | A |

The three empRec fields are called empRec.id, empRec.wage, and empRec.status. If we had an empArray instead of an empRec, then the various components might be called empArray[id], empArray[wage], and empArray[status]. But with a record type we use a dot instead of square brackets. For instance, to multiply the wage field of empRec by the value of rate, we do

```
empRec.wage := empRec.wage * rate
```

and to write the id and wage fields of empRec we do

```
WriteLn ('Employee id: ', empRec.id  :4  );
WriteLn ('Hourly wage: ', empRec.wage:4:2)
```

Another version of the complete program, using our new record type empRecType follows.

Program Example (Version 3)

```
PROGRAM Raises3 (empFile, output);
{Reports new hourly wages for
 employees listed in the empFile.}
   TYPE
      idType     = 0000..9999;
      wageType   = REAL;
      statusType = 'A'..'C';

      empRecType = RECORD
                     id     : idType;
                     wage   : wageType;
                     status : statusType
                   END;
   VAR
      empRec  : empRecType;
      rate    : REAL;
      empFile : TEXT;
   {----------}

PROCEDURE ReadRecord (VAR empFile : TEXT;
                      VAR empRec   : empRecType);
{Reads information for one employee from the empFile.}

BEGIN {ReadRecord}
   ReadLn (empFile, empRec.id);
   ReadLn (empFile, empRec.wage);
   ReadLn (empFile, empRec.status);
   ReadLn (empFile)
END;   {ReadRecord}

   {----------}
```

```
BEGIN {Raises3}
  Reset (empFile);
  WHILE NOT Eof (empFile) DO
    BEGIN
      ReadRecord (empFile, empRec);

      CASE empRec.status OF
        'A' : rate := 1.05;
        'B' : rate := 1.07;
        'C' : rate := 1.10
      END;

      empRec.wage := empRec.wage * rate;

      WriteLn ('Employee id: ', empRec.id  :4  );
      WriteLn ('Hourly wage: ', empRec.wage:4:2);
      WriteLn
    END
END.  {Raises3}
```

Observations   To call Procedure `ReadRecord` we just do

```
ReadRecord (empFile, empRec)
```

a record as a
parameter

This passes all three of `empRec`'s fields to Procedure `ReadRecord`. Now our code manages to convey the idea that three pieces of information about an employee (`id`, `wage`, and `status`) are all part of one bundle of information called the `employeeRecord`.

But with all the dotted names the code is still cumbersome, especially when compared with our original program `Raises1`. We can trim our code down, using a new kind of statement called a `WITH` statement.

**Program
Example
(Version 4)**

```
PROGRAM Raises4 (empFile, output);
{Reports new hourly wages for
 employees listed in the empFile.}
  TYPE
    idType     = 0000..9999;
    wageType   = REAL;
    statusType = 'A'..'C';

    empRecType = RECORD
                    id     : idType;
                    wage   : wageType;
                    status : statusType
                 END;
  VAR
    empRec  : empRecType;
    rate    : REAL;
    empFile : TEXT;

  {----------}
```

```
      PROCEDURE ReadRecord (VAR empFile : TEXT;
                            VAR empRec  : empRecType);
      {Reads information for one employee from the empFile.}
      BEGIN {ReadRecord}
        WITH empRec DO
          BEGIN
            ReadLn (empFile, id);
            ReadLn (empFile, wage);
            ReadLn (empFile, status)
          END;
        ReadLn (empFile)
      END;  {ReadRecord}

      {----------}

   BEGIN {Raises4}
      Reset (empFile);
      WHILE NOT Eof (empFile) DO
        BEGIN
          ReadRecord (empFile, empRec);

          WITH empRec DO
            BEGIN
              CASE status OF
                'A' : rate := 1.05;
                'B' : rate := 1.07;
                'C' : rate := 1.10
              END;
              wage := wage * rate;
              WriteLn ('Employee id: ', id  :4  );
              WriteLn ('Hourly wage: ', wage:4:2);
              WriteLn
            END
        END
   END.  {Raises4}
```

Observations

```
• WITH empRec DO
    BEGIN

      .
      .
      .

    END
```

The new Program Raises4 does exactly the same thing as Raises3, but in Raises4 we don't use the dot notation. We achieve the same effect using WITH statements.

WITH statements

For instance, all three of empRec's field names occur in the following code:

```
WITH empRec DO
  BEGIN
    ReadLn(empFile, id);
    ReadLn(empFile, wage);
    ReadLn(empFile, status)
  END
```

Because of the WITH statement, the computer treats this code as if it says

```
ReadLn(empFile, empRec.id);
ReadLn(empFile, empRec.wage);
ReadLn(empFile, empRec.status)
```

More precisely, the line

```
WITH empRec DO
```

says: In the statement following this line, the programmer has the option of referring to a field of this empRec variable simply by writing the field name without putting empRec. in front of it. Now remember that the programmer's option applies to the statement following the WITH empRec DO line. As always, we need to be careful when we use the words "statement following." The statement following the WITH empRec DO line can be a compound statement, as in Procedure ReadRecord, but it can also be a simple statement or a structured statement.

12.1   Exercises

Key Words to Review

record type	RECORD
field	WITH

Questions to Answer

QUE 12.1.1   What's the most important difference between arrays and records?

QUE 12.1.2   Should you always create a record type whenever you want to avoid having a long parameter list? Why not?

QUE 12.1.3   A RECORD type definition is one place in Pascal where we use an END without a BEGIN. Can you think of another place?

Experiments to Try

EXP 12.1.1   In any of the programs of this section, change definition of empRecType so that the fields id, wage, and status are listed in a different order.

EXP 12.1.2   Add another empRecType variable, called empRec2, to Program Raises4. Then try to do

```
empRec2 := empRec
```

EXP 12.1.3   Add another empRecType variable, called empRec2, to Program Raises4. Then try to do

```
IF empRec2 = empRec THEN
   WriteLn ('Equal')
```

Changes to Make

CHA 12.1.1 Modify Program `Raises4` so that almost all the work is done with subprograms; that is, the employee's `wage` is calculated by a subprogram and the output is produced by a subprogram.

Programs and Subprograms to Write

WRI 12.1.1 Redo Exercise Wri.9.1.1, using a record with four fields to store the letter `M` or `F`, the "feet" part of a person's height, the "inches" part of a person's height, and the person's weight.

WRI 12.1.2 Redo Exercise Wri.6.1.3, using a record to store the information about a driver. For the sake of simplicity, use numeric code (1 to 50) for the state.

WRI 12.1.3 A travel company offers custom-made tours at the following rates:

	Cost per day	
	For each adult	For each child
Guided	$110	$55
Unguided	$ 95	$45

Write a program that reads the information about a tour (number of adults, number of children, guided or unguided, number of days) into a record variable and writes the price of the tour.

12.2

Using Records

Specifications On June 30, 1978, the author of this text celebrated his 10000-days "birthday." He made such a fuss over it that his friends started asking him for presents when they'd turn 15-million-minutes old or 1-billion-seconds old. In this section and the next section, we'll develop a program to get you started playing the "how-long-have-I-been-alive?" game.

Designing a Program First, we want a procedure that reads a date, which the user enters in the form

```
mm dd yyyy
```

In other words, the user enters two digits for the month, two digits for the day, and four digits for the year.

We could define

```
TYPE
   monthType = 1..12;
```

but it's more self-documenting to do

```
TYPE
   monthType  = (Jan, Feb, Mar, Apr, May, Jun,
                 Jul, Aug, Sep, Oct, Nov, Dec);
```

When you're writing a program, it's easier to think in terms of month abbreviations than month numbers. Compare the following two CASE statements for readability:[1]

```
CASE month OF
   1, 3, 5, 7,
   8, 10, 12  : DaysInMonth := 31;
   4, 6, 9, 11 : DaysInMonth := 30;
   2          : IF IsLeapYear (year) THEN
                   DaysInMonth := 29
                ELSE
                   DaysInMonth := 28
END
```

versus

```
CASE month OF
   Jan, Mar, May, Jul,
   Aug, Oct, Dec      : DaysInMonth := 31;
   Apr, Jun, Sep, Nov : DaysInMonth := 30;
   Feb                : IF IsLeapYear (year) THEN
                          DaysInMonth := 29
                       ELSE
                          DaysInMonth := 28
END
```

Now we could declare Procedure ReadDate as follows:

```
PROCEDURE ReadDate (VAR month : monthType;
                    VAR day   : dayType  ;
                    VAR year  : yearType);
```

but it's much more elegant to do

```
PROCEDURE ReadDate (VAR date : dateType);
```

where dateType is a combination of monthType, dayType, and yearType.

What we need to do is define a record type:

```
TYPE
   monthType  = (Jan, Feb, Mar, Apr, May, Jun,
                 Jul, Aug, Sep, Oct, Nov, Dec);
   dayType    = 1..31;
   yearType   = 1900..2050;
   dateType   = RECORD
                   month : monthType;
                   day   : dayType;
                   year  : yearType
                END;
```

---

[1]A few months before this book was printed we caught a nasty error in the manuscript. The first of these CASE statements had the month number 2 where the month number 3 should be. But the second CASE statement with abbreviations for month names was correct. What does this say about subtle differences in readability?

Then date becomes a variable with three fields:

date.month   date.day   date.year

Feb   13   1951

and each field contains a value of a different type.
Procedure ReadDate follows.

Program Example

```
PROCEDURE ReadDate (VAR date : dateType);
{Reads a date from the keyboard.}
  VAR
    monthNumber : monNumType;

  {----------}

  FUNCTION MonthFromMonNum (monthNumber : monNumType) : monthType;
  {Turns a month number (1 to 12) into a month (Jan to Dec).}
    VAR
      m        : monthType;
      monthOrd : 0..11;
  BEGIN {MonthFromMonNum}
    m        := Jan;
    monthOrd := monthNumber - 1;

    WHILE Ord(m) < monthOrd DO
      m := Succ(m);

    MonthFromMonNum := m
  END;  {MonthFromMonNum}

  {----------}

BEGIN {ReadDate}
  WITH date DO
    BEGIN
      Write  ('Enter a date (mm dd yyyy): ');
      ReadLn (monthNumber, day, year);
      month := MonthFromMonNum (monthNumber)
    END
END;  {ReadDate}
```

Observations

Recall that the programmer has the option of not prefacing field names with date. in the statement following the line

WITH and a simple or compound statement

```
WITH date DO
```

In Procedure ReadDate, the statement following this line is a compound statement. But in the next subprogram, Function DaysInMonthAfter, the statement following the WITH line is a simple statement.

Program Example

```
FUNCTION DaysInMonthAfter (date : dateType) : natural;
{Finds the number of days left in
  the month (after a particular date).}

BEGIN {DaysInMonthAfter}
  WITH date DO
    DaysInMonthAfter := DaysInMonth (month, year) - day
END;  {DaysInMonthAfter}
```

Observations In this subprogram we call another function named DaysInMonth, which is easy to write. The statement

```
CASE month OF
  Jan, Mar, May, Jul,
  Aug, Oct, Dec          : DaysInMonth := 31;
  Apr, Jun, Sep, Nov     : DaysInMonth := 30;
  Feb                    : IF IsLeapYear (year) THEN
                              DaysInMonth := 29
                           ELSE
                              DaysInMonth := 28
END
```

forms most of the function's body.

When we call Function DaysInMonthAfter with the date February 13, 1996, the call to DaysInMonth (month, year) gives us 29, so for DaysInMonthAfter we get 29 − 13 (= 16). Indeed in 1996 there are 16 days in February after the 13th of the month.

In the next example the statement following the WITH line is a structured statement.

WITH and a structured statement

Program Example

```
FUNCTION DaysInYearAfter (date : dateType) : natural;
{Finds the number of days left in
  the year (after a particular date).}

  VAR
    dayCount : natural;
    m        : monthType;
BEGIN {DaysInYearAfter}
  dayCount := DaysInMonthAfter (date);

  WITH date DO
    IF month < Dec THEN
      FOR m := Succ (month) TO Dec DO
        dayCount := dayCount + DaysInMonth (m, year);

  DaysInYearAfter := dayCount
END;  {DaysInYearAfter}
```

Observations Function DaysInYearAfter achieves its result by tallying up the values returned by Function DaysInMonth for each month from the current date onward.

Further Discussion

WITH doesn't directly cause an action

We can divide Pascal's statements into two kinds: statements that directly cause some action to occur and others that don't. For instance, an IF statement directly causes the checking of a condition and possibly the execution of a THEN-part or an ELSE-part. But a compound statement, formed with BEGIN and END, is just a way of grouping other statements together. The words BEGIN and END certainly have an effect on the action of the program, but they don't directly cause any action. The same is true of a WITH statement. A WITH statement doesn't directly cause any action to occur—it just plays a role in determining the meanings of certain field names. The action that's taken using those field names depends on the other statements in the program (such as assignments, IFs, FORs, etc.).

12.2 Exercises

Questions to Answer

QUE 12.2.1 Why do we say that it's more elegant to have

```
PROCEDURE ReadDate (VAR date : dateType);
```

than

```
PROCEDURE ReadDate (VAR month : monthType;
                    VAR day   : dayType ;
                    VAR year  : yearType);
```

QUE 12.2.2 Why do we say that the WITH statement doesn't directly cause any action to occur?

Experiments to Try

EXP 12.2.1 If rec1 has two fields i and c, and rec2 has two fields r and b, run a program containing the code

```
WITH rec1 DO
  WITH rec2 DO
    WriteLn (i, b)
```

EXP 12.2.2 Redo Exercise Exp.12.2.1 using the following code:

```
WITH rec1, rec2 DO
  WriteLn (i, b)
```

EXP 12.2.3 If rec1 has two fields i and c, and rec2 also has two fields i and c, run a program containing the code

```
WITH rec2 DO
  WITH rec1 DO
    WriteLn (i, c)
```

EXP 12.2.4 Redo Exercise Exp.12.2.3 using the following code:

```
WITH rec1 DO
  WITH rec2 DO
    WriteLn (i, c)
```

Changes to Make

CHA 12.2.1   Rewrite Function `MonthFromMonNum` so that it doesn't contain a loop.

Programs and Subprograms to Write

WRI 12.2.1   Redo Exercise Wri.9.2.1, using a record type to store a number grade along with its letter grade.

WRI 12.2.2   Redo Exercise Cha.3.3.1, this time storing the information as a record type. The record includes fields for the principal, the interest rate, and the number of years of compounding.

12.3

Using Records (Continued)

Specifications   Now we're ready to write a program that tells you how many days you've been alive.

> Input: Two dates, a `startDate` and a `stopDate`
>
> Output: The number of days between the `startDate` and the `stopDate`

Designing a Program   The main body of Program `Days` is very simple. We have

```
ReadDate (startDate);
ReadDate (stopDate);
WriteLn  (DaysBetween (startDate, stopDate))
```

where `startDate` and `stopDate` are two separate record variables:

```
VAR
   startDate, stopDate : dateType;
```

Looking at this little fragment of code, we see that Program `Days` will need to have two subprograms:

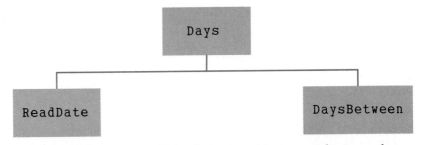

In Section 12.2 we saw Procedure `ReadDate` with its subprogram `MonthFromMonNum`. What about Function `DaysBetween`? To calculate the number of days between two dates, we'll use the following strategy:

Step 1: Find the number of days in this year
that come after the `startDate`:

Step 2: Add the number of days in the years
between `startDate` and the `stopDate`:

Step 3: Subtract the number of days remaining
in the year after the `stopDate`:

In Steps 1 and 3 we'll use a function named `DaysInYearAfter`. For Step 2 we'll use another function named `DaysInYearsBetween`.

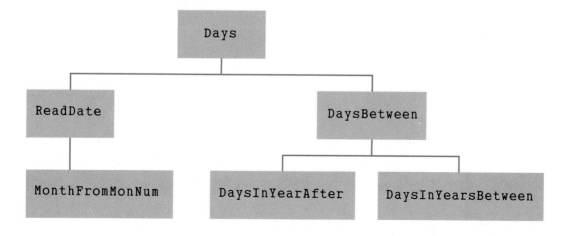

We already wrote Function `DaysInYearAfter` in Section 12.2. If we look carefully at the code, we find out what other functions our program needs.

Calling Subprogram		Called Subprogram
`DaysInYearAfter`	calls	`DaysInMonthAfter`
`DaysInYearAfter`	calls	`DaysInMonth`

Our program needs Functions `DaysInMonthAfter` and `DaysInMonth`, which also appeared in Section 12.2. And what subprograms did those two functions call? When we look at the code in Section 12.2, we see that

Calling Subprogram		Called Subprogram
`DaysInMonthAfter`	calls	`DaysInMonth`
`DaysInMonth`	calls	`IsLeapYear`

Now we can use this information to make a complete hierarchy diagram for Program `Days`:

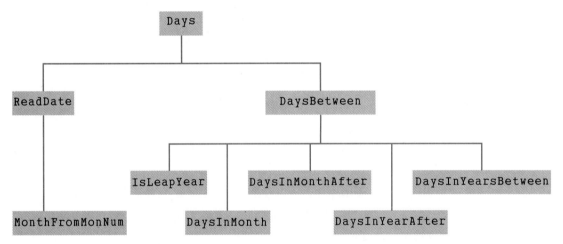

When we first glance at the hierarchy diagram, it looks as if we have lots of work ahead of us. But if we look more carefully, we see that each of these functions, except Function `IsLeapYear`, was already written in Section 12.2!

Program Example

```
PROGRAM Days (input, output);
{Finds the number of days between two dates.}
  CONST
    loYear = 1900;
    hiYear = 2050;
  TYPE
    monthType   = (Jan, Feb, Mar, Apr, May, Jun,
                   Jul, Aug, Sep, Oct, Nov, Dec);
    monNumType = 1..12;
    dayType    = 1..31;
    yearType   = loYear..hiYear;
    natural    = 0..MAXINT;
    dateType   = RECORD
                   month : monthType;
                   day   : dayType;
                   year  : yearType
                 END;
  VAR
    startDate, stopDate : dateType;

  {----------}

  PROCEDURE ReadDate (VAR date : dateType);
  {Reads a date from the keyboard.}
    VAR
      monthNumber : monNumType;

    {----------}

    FUNCTION MonthFromMonNum (monthNumber : monNumType) : monthType;
    {Turns a month number (1 to 12) into a month (Jan to Dec).}
      VAR
        m        : monthType;
        monthOrd : 0..11;
    BEGIN {MonthFromMonNum}
      m        := Jan;
      monthOrd := monthNumber - 1;

      WHILE Ord(m) < monthOrd DO
        m := Succ(m);

      MonthFromMonNum := m
    END;   {MonthFromMonNum}

    {----------}

  BEGIN {ReadDate}
    WITH date DO
      BEGIN
        Write  ('Enter a date (mm dd yyyy): ');
        ReadLn (monthNumber, day, year);
        month := MonthFromMonNum (monthNumber)
      END
  END;   {ReadDate}

  {----------}
```

```
FUNCTION DaysBetween (startDate,
                      stopDate : dateType) : natural;
{Finds the number of days between two dates.}

  VAR
    dayCount : natural;

  {----------}

  FUNCTION IsLeapYear (y : yearType) : BOOLEAN;
  {Determines whether year 'y' is a leap year.}
  BEGIN {IsLeapYear}
    IsLeapYear := (y MOD 4 = 0) AND
                   NOT((y MOD 100 = 0) AND (y MOD 400 <> 0))
  END;  {IsLeapYear}

  {----------}

  FUNCTION DaysInMonth (m : monthType;
                        y : yearType ) : dayType;
  {Finds the number of days in a month.}
  BEGIN {DaysInMonth}
    CASE m OF
      Jan, Mar, May, Jul,
      Aug, Oct, Dec       : DaysInMonth := 31;
      Apr, Jun, Sep, Nov  : DaysInMonth := 30;
      Feb                 : IF IsLeapYear (y) THEN
                               DaysInMonth := 29
                            ELSE
                               DaysInMonth := 28
    END
  END;  {DaysInMonth}

  {----------}

  FUNCTION DaysInMonthAfter (date : dateType) : natural;
  {Finds the number of days left in
   the month (after a particular date).}
  BEGIN {DaysInMonthAfter}
    WITH date DO
      DaysInMonthAfter := DaysInMonth (month, year) - day
  END;  {DaysInMonthAfter}

  {----------}

  FUNCTION DaysInYearAfter (date : dateType) : natural;
  {Finds the number of days left in
   the year (after a particular date).}
    VAR
      dayCount : natural;
      m        : monthType;
  BEGIN {DaysInYearAfter}
    dayCount := DaysInMonthAfter (date);

    WITH date DO
      IF month < Dec THEN
        FOR m := Succ (month) TO Dec DO
          dayCount := dayCount + DaysInMonth (m, year);

    DaysInYearAfter := dayCount
  END;  {DaysInYearAfter}
```

```
      {----------}
      FUNCTION DaysInYearsBetween (startDate,
                                   stopDate : dateType) : natural;
      {Finds the number of days in any
       years that come between two dates.}
         VAR
           dayCount : natural;
           y          : yearType;
      BEGIN {DaysInYearsBetween}
         dayCount := 0;

         FOR y := startDate.year + 1 TO stopDate.year DO
           IF IsLeapYear (y) THEN
             dayCount := dayCount + 366
           ELSE
             dayCount := dayCount + 365;

         DaysInYearsBetween := dayCount
      END;  {DaysInYearsBetween}

      {----------}

   BEGIN {DaysBetween}
     dayCount      := DaysInYearAfter (startDate);
     dayCount      := dayCount + DaysInYearsBetween (startDate, stopDate);
     dayCount      := dayCount - DaysInYearAfter (stopDate);
     DaysBetween := dayCount
   END;  {DaysBetween}

   {----------}

BEGIN {Days}
  ReadDate (startDate);
  ReadDate (stopDate);

  Write     (DaysBetween (startDate, stopDate) : 10);
  WriteLn  (' days between these two dates'        )
END.  {Days}
```

Sample Runs

```
Enter a date (mm dd yyyy): 02 13 1951
Enter a date (mm dd yyyy): 06 15 2000
      18020 days between these two dates
```
_____

```
Enter a date (mm dd yyyy): 05 01 1995
Enter a date (mm dd yyyy): 05 02 1995
      1 days between these two dates
```

Observations

- IsLeapYear := (y MOD 4 = 0) AND
  NOT((y MOD 100 = 0) AND (y MOD 400 <> 0))

Most people think there's a leap year every four years, but it's a bit more complicated than that. Plug numbers into this expression to see exactly when leap years do and do not occur. Then you can try to explain the leap year rule in plain English. (See Exercise Que.12.3.2.)

- `FOR y := startDate.year + 1 TO stopDate.year DO`

  In this loop we refer to the `year` fields of `startDate` and `stopDate` without making any reference to the `month` and `day` fields of these records. That's certainly an acceptable thing to do. Since `startDate` and `stopDate` are two different record variables, a `WITH` statement wouldn't be of much use here.

using dots instead of WITH

Programming Style

When you write a program the size of `Days`, you have many style decisions to make. Several of these decisions involve serious trade-offs. Let's trace the action of Program `Days` when the `startDate` and `stopDate` are one day apart (as in the first of our Sample Runs):

Step 1: Find `DaysInYearAfter (startDate)`

Step 2: Add `DaysInYearsBetween (startDate, stopDate)` (0 days)

Step 3: Subtract `DaysInYearAfter (stopDate)`

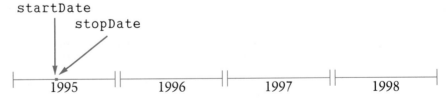

All that work just to find out that May 2 comes one day after May 1! We could have put `IF` statements in our program to judiciously avoid calls to `DaysInYearAfter`. But this would have made more paths of execution in our program. Our program might have become cluttered up with exceptions and special cases. We decided to keep our program simple. The price we paid was to have a program that takes a bit longer to run.

readability and efficiency

It's a classic trade-off—readable programs generally take more pages to code and take longer to run than unreadable programs. Sometimes, when you want a program to run very fast, you resolve the dilemma in favor of the unreadable program. But years of experience have shown that unreadable programs can also be time-consuming. When a program isn't readable, it takes an enormous amount of time to maintain the program.

program maintenance

The process of making changes to a program, either to fix bugs or make improvements, is called **program maintenance**. Debugging is one part of program maintenance, but it's certainly not the whole story. Changes are often made to improve the way a program runs, to add new ways for the user to interact with the program, or to anticipate future needs.

Structure

One way to classify the changes we make to programs is differentiate between changes to the body and changes to the definitions and declarations.

For instance, we could add IF statements to Program Days and avoid calls to DaysInYearAfter when these calls aren't needed. This would change the program's body.

Or we could change monthType to a subrange of the INTEGERs. This would change the program's definitions, but in turn it would force us to change the subprogram bodies, because so much of Program Days makes use of the definition of monthType. A change like this would have many more far-reaching effects than adding a few IF statements. Function DaysInMonth would have to be rewritten; the reference to Dec in Function DaysInYearAfter would have to be changed. Function MonthFromMonNum would no longer be needed, so Procedure ReadDate would be rewritten, etc. Any subprogram that refers to the month field of startDate or stopDate would need to be examined and possibly changed. Of course the effort would be simpler if we could keep the number of subprograms that deal with month or with any of the other fields of dateType, to a minimum.

data abstraction

This is where *data abstraction* comes in handy. Look at the main body of Program Days.

```
ReadDate (startDate);
ReadDate (stopDate);

Write    (DaysBetween (startDate, stopDate) : 10);
WriteLn  (' days between these two dates'        )
```

You can read these lines and understand what they're meant to do without knowing anything about records or record types. That's because there's no reference in any of these lines to the *fields* of startDate or stopDate. The same is true of the body of Function DaysBetween. The function treats dateType as an **abstract data type**. It doesn't deal with any details about dateType. Instead of dissecting startDate and stopDate into the fields month, day, and year, the function passes the startDate and stopDate records to its subprograms DaysInYearAfter and

DaysInYearsBetween. It's only in these subprograms that the individual fields of startDate and stopDate are used.

The goal, then, is to bury the details of dateType's internal structure in as small a portion of the program as possible. If we could put all references to dateType's internal structure in only one part of the program, we would be practicing *information hiding*. Of course, "one part" of the program doesn't necessarily mean "one subprogram." It could mean a group of subprograms collected together in the text of the program.

information hiding

Pascal was created in the late sixties and early seventies, right around the time the first paper on information hiding was written.[2] So Pascal wasn't developed with information hiding in mind. Information hiding and, to some extent data abstraction, are difficult to do in Pascal. Newer languages (like Ada, Modula-2, C++) have features that help the programmer collect subprograms together. Then the programmer can create a data type whose internal structure can be used only within this collection of subprograms.

12.3   Exercises

Key Words to Review

program maintenance   abstract data type

Questions to Answer

QUE 12.3.1   Describe the method (or methods) we used to create the hierarchy diagram for Program Days. Did we create Program Days from the top downward?

QUE 12.3.2   Look carefully at the assignment statement in Function IsLeapYear and tell, in simple English, exactly when leap years do and do not occur.

QUE 12.3.3   What's the difference between program maintenance and program debugging?

QUE 12.3.4   How does the use of abstract data types help with the task of maintaining a program?

Experiments to Try

EXP 12.3.1   Run Program Days with both the startDate and the stopDate in the year 2050.

EXP 12.3.2   Run Program Days, giving it a startDate that comes after the stopDate.

EXP 12.3.3   Run Program Days, giving it various dates that don't exist, like February 29, 1995. Are there any that the program accepts without being aborted?

Changes to Make

CHA 12.3.1   Rewrite Program Days so that the user types the startDate and the number of days, and the program writes the stopDate.

---

[2] D. L. Parnas, "On the criteria used in decomposing systems into modules," *Communications of the ACM*, Vol. 15, 1972, pp. 1053–1058.

CHA 12.3.2   Modify Program Days to answer the efficiency criticism in this section's Programming Style subsection. That is, have the program skip any nonessential steps when calculating the number of days between May 1, 1995, and May 2, 1995.

CHA 12.3.3   Take a look at the work you did for Exercise Wri.3.5.1. Then modify Program Days to get Programs Hours, Minutes, and Seconds. Perhaps there's a 200,000-hours or a 10,000,000-minutes celebration for you in the near future!

Programs and Subprograms to Write

WRI 12.3.1   Call your local pizza joint and find out how they figure their prices. Chances are, they consider the size of the pizza (small, medium, or large), the crust (thin or thick), the number of toppings, and whether or not the customer has a coupon. Write a program that reads information about an order and writes a bill. The program stores information about the order in a record variable.

WRI 12.3.2   Redo Exercise Wri.6.4.2, using a record type to store the notes. A record of this type has three fields. The first field stores a letter (A to G), the second field stores a BOOLEAN value that determines if the note is a sharp, and the third field stores an octave number.

12.4

Homogeneous Records

Recall from Section 12.1 that

- In an array, each component has the same type
- In a record, the various fields can have different types.

Why use homogeneous records?

But sometimes it's convenient to define a record type whose fields all have the same type. Here's why: When you define an array type, you're telling the computer that you should be allowed to perform indexing on the type. This is a fancy way of saying that you can do

```
ReadLn (i);
a[i] := 10
```

That is, you can use the value of a variable (like i) to decide which component of the array should be referenced. The value of a variable like i can be decided during the run of the program with an assignment, a ReadLn, etc. So it's not until the run of the program that we know which component of a will get the value 10.

On the other hand, when you define a record type, you can't do indexing. For instance, with

```
TYPE
   monthType  = (Jan, Feb, Mar, Apr, May, Jun,
                 Jul, Aug, Sep, Oct, Nov, Dec);
   dayType    = 1..31;
   yearType   = 1900..2050;
   dateType   = RECORD
                   month : monthType;
                   day   : dayType;
                   year  : yearType
                END;
VAR
   date : dateType;
```

you cannot do

```
ReadLn (fieldName);
date.fieldName := 1951
```

The idea here is that the three fields of dateType aren't very similar. You might assign the value 1951 to a year, but you'd never want to assign the value 1951 to a month. So when you write the code, you're not allowed to have a statement that could assign 1951 to just any old field of the date record.

This illustrates one of the important features of a record type: You have several fields whose values aren't "similar." Since you can't do indexing with a record, it's hard to write a statement that treats all the fields in a similar way.

But once in a while you have a problem that involves "non-similar" fields that all happen to be of the same type. Then you need to create a record type in which all the fields have the same type. A record type in which all fields have the same type is called a **homogeneous record type**. This section provides an example.

Specifications A *rational number* is a fraction whose numerator and denominator are both integers. For instance

$$\frac{5}{6} \quad \frac{-20}{5} \quad \frac{1}{1} \quad \frac{0}{5} \quad \frac{6}{-3} \quad \frac{-1}{-1}$$

are all rational numbers. Of course

$$\frac{6}{0} \quad \frac{0}{0}$$

aren't rational because denominators should never be zero.

In Section 7.3 we saw that the computer can't find a completely accurate REAL value for an expression like 1.0/3.0. This is a limitation we learn to live with when we're dealing with REAL numbers.

But what if we create a new type rational? Then the value of 1.0/3.0 might be accurately represented by the rational number

$$\frac{1}{3}$$

First we need to tell the computer what we mean by a rational number:

```
TYPE
   rational = RECORD
                 num, denom : INTEGER
              END;
```

With this definition, we tell the computer that a rational number has a numerator and a denominator. We don't tell the computer that when we write rationals, we usually write the numerator on top of the denominator. The computer doesn't need to know that until much later.

Now remember that a type is a set of values and a set of operations that we can perform on those values. In the type definition, we describe the values that a rational number can have. (The value of a rational is made up of two INTEGER values.) But this information is incomplete unless we describe the operations that can be performed on rationals. After all, it's nice to know that 1.0/3.0 is accurately represented by

```
r.num   := 1;
r.denom := 3
```

but if we can't add this to anything or multiply it by anything, then the representation is useless.

So now we have to describe the operations that can be performed on rationals. We need subprograms that can add two rationals, subtract rationals, multiply and divide rationals, read rationals, write rationals, etc. In this section we create just a few of these subprograms.

The easiest is the procedure that multiplies rationals.

Program Example

```
PROCEDURE MultRats (r1, r2   : rational ;
                         VAR rProd : rational);
{Multiplies two rationals.}

BEGIN {MultRats}
   rProd.num   := r1.num   * r2.num;
   rProd.denom := r1.denom * r2.denom
END;  {MultRats}
```

Observations

$$\frac{3}{4} \star \frac{5}{6} = \frac{15}{24}$$

To multiply two fractions (two rationals), we multiply the two numerators together, and multiply the two denominators together. Doing this in Procedure MultRats gives us a rational called rProd. The num and denom fields of rProd are calculated in two separate assignment statements.

A function cannot return a record.

Notice that MultRats can't be a function subprogram, since a function's result type can't be a structured type, like rational.

Program Example

```
FUNCTION EqualRats (r1, r2 : rational) : BOOLEAN;
{Checks to see if two rationals are equal.}

BEGIN {EqualRats}
  EqualRats := (r1.num * r2.denom) = (r1.denom * r2.num)
END;  {EqualRats}
```

Observations

$$\frac{1}{2} = \frac{3}{6}$$

because

$$1 * 6 = 2 * 3$$

Program Example

```
PROCEDURE AddRats (r1, r2  : rational ;
                      VAR rSum : rational);
{Adds two rationals.}

BEGIN {AddRats}
  rSum.num   := (r1.num * r2.denom) + (r1.denom * r2.num);
  rSum.denom := r1.denom * r2.denom
END;  {AddRats}
```

Observations

$$\frac{1}{2} + \frac{3}{4} = \frac{(1*4) + (2*3)}{(2*4)} = \frac{10}{8}$$

Program Example

```
PROCEDURE ReadLnRat (VAR r : rational);
{Reads a rational number.}

  VAR
    charIn : CHAR;

BEGIN {ReadLnRat}
  Read (r.num);
  REPEAT
    Read (charIn)
  UNTIL charIn = '/';
  ReadLn (r.denom);

  IF r.denom = 0 THEN
    WriteLn (Chr(7), 'Warning : zero denominator');
END;  {ReadLnRat}

{----------}

PROCEDURE WriteLnRat (r : rational);
{Writes a rational number.}

BEGIN {WriteLnRat}
  WriteLn (r.num:2, ' /', r.denom:2)
END;  {WriteLnRat}
```

Observations   It's not until Procedures `ReadLnRat` and `WriteLnRat` that we "tell" the computer about the numerator being "on top of" the denominator or about the numerator and denominator being separated by a slash. This comes as a surprise to people who think that the slash plays a central role in deciding what the word *fraction* means.

In fact, a fraction is just

- two numbers, a numerator and a denominator, and
- a set of operations that we can perform on this pair of numbers (`MultRats`, `EqualRats`, `AddRats`, `ReadLnRat`, `WriteLnRat`, etc.)

Two of these operations, `ReadLnRat` and `WriteLnRat`, determine what a fraction "looks like" if we choose to display it on the screen, but the other operations are equally important (if not more important) in defining what we mean by a fraction (a `rational` number).

A test driver for our `rational` number subprograms follows.

Program Example

```
PROGRAM Rationals (input, output);
{Performs simple operations on rational numbers.}
  TYPE
    rational = RECORD
                     num, denom : INTEGER
                   END;
  VAR
    ra, rb, rc : rational;
  {----------}
  PROCEDURE ReadLnRat (VAR r : rational);
  {Reads a rational number.}
    VAR
      charIn : CHAR;
  BEGIN {ReadLnRat}
    Read (r.num);
    REPEAT
      Read (charIn)
    UNTIL charIn = '/';
    ReadLn (r.denom);
    IF r.denom = 0 THEN
      WriteLn (Chr(7), 'Warning : zero denominator');
  END;   {ReadLnRat}
  {----------}
  FUNCTION EqualRats (r1, r2 : rational) : BOOLEAN;
  {Checks to see if two rationals are equal.}
  BEGIN {EqualRats}
    EqualRats := (r1.num * r2.denom) = (r1.denom * r2.num)
  END;   {EqualRats}
  {----------}
```

```
PROCEDURE MultRats (r1, r2    : rational ;
                         VAR rProd : rational);
{Multiplies two rationals.}
BEGIN {MultRats}
   rProd.num   := r1.num   * r2.num;
   rProd.denom := r1.denom * r2.denom
END;   {MultRats}
{----------}
PROCEDURE AddRats (r1, r2   : rational ;
                       VAR rSum : rational);
{Adds two rationals.}
BEGIN {AddRats}
   rSum.num   := (r1.num * r2.denom) + (r1.denom * r2.num);
   rSum.denom := r1.denom * r2.denom
END;   {AddRats}
{----------}
PROCEDURE WriteLnRat (r : rational);
{Writes a rational number.}
BEGIN {WriteLnRat}
   WriteLn (r.num:2, ' /', r.denom:2)
END;   {WriteLnRat}
{----------}
BEGIN {Rationals}
   Write      ('Enter a rational called "ra": ');
   ReadLnRat (ra);
   Write      ('Enter a rational called "rb": ');
   ReadLnRat (rb);

   MultRats   (ra, rb, rc);
   Write      ('Product: ');
   WriteLnRat (rc);

   AddRats    (ra, rb, rc);
   Write      ('Sum:      ');
   WriteLnRat (rc);

   IF EqualRats (ra, rb) THEN
      WriteLn ('ra and rb are equal')
   ELSE
      WriteLn ('ra and rb are not equal')
END.   {Rationals}
```

Sample Runs

```
Enter a rational called "ra": 1 / 2
Enter a rational called "rb": 2 / 3
Product:  2 / 6
Sum:      7 / 6
ra and rb are not equal
```

_____

```
Enter a rational called "ra": 1 / 2
Enter a rational called "rb": 2 / 4
Product:  2 / 8
Sum:      8 / 8
ra and rb are equal
```

```
Enter a rational called "ra": -1 / -1
Enter a rational called "rb":  2 /  3
Product: -2 /-3
Sum:       -5 /-3
ra and rb are not equal
```

```
Enter a rational called "ra": 0 / 2
Enter a rational called "rb": 2 / 0
<beep>Warning : zero denominator
Product:  0 / 0
Sum:      4 / 0
ra and rb are not equal
```

Programming Style

an abstract data type

Nowhere in the main body of Program `Rationals` do we ever refer to a field of `ra`, `rb`, or `rc`. There's nothing in this part of the program that makes any reference to a `RECORD` of any sort. This means that, in the main body of our program, the type `rational` is treated entirely as an abstract data type. In the main body of the the program, the only things we do with the `rational` variables `ra`, `rb`, and `rc` are to pass them as parameters to subprograms `MultRats`, `EqualRats`, `AddRats`, `ReadLnRat`, and `WriteLnRat`.

This makes the program's main body clean, uncluttered, and readable. It keeps the essential features of `rational` numbers (that is, the operations) separate from the picky details (the fact that `rationals` are implemented as records). It also gives us some flexibility: if we decide later to redefine the `rationals` as an array type

```
TYPE
   part     = (num, denom);
   rational = ARRAY [part] OF INTEGER;
```

then the main body of Program `Rationals` still works, without making a single change!

12.4   Exercises

Key Words to Review

indexing   homogeneous record type

Questions to Answer

QUE 12.4.1   You have a problem in which there are three pieces of information that always seem to go together. Each of them is a REAL value. How do you decide whether to create an array with three components or a record with three fields?

QUE 12.4.2   Function MultRats is actually used to find a single value—a rational number stored as a record. So why can't Procedure MultRats be turned into a function subprogram?

QUE 12.4.3   When we talk about the fraction one-third we often say "one over three." What role does the word *over* play in the definition of rational numbers?

Experiments to Try

EXP 12.4.1   Change the definition of type rational so that the fields num and denom are declared on two different lines:

```
TYPE
   rational = RECORD
                 num   : INTEGER;
                 denom : INTEGER
              END;
```

Does this make any difference in the way the program runs?

EXP 12.4.2   Create a record type that has only one field, and write a short program to see if that record type is treated the way you would expect it to be treated.

Changes to Make

CHA 12.4.1   Rewrite the code in this section using the definition

```
TYPE
   part     = (num, denom);
   rational = ARRAY [part] OF INTEGER;
```

CHA 12.4.2   Modify Program FindMode in Section 9.2 as follows: Combine the variables prev, curr, and ctCurr into a record called valuesReadRec. Combine the variables mode and ctMode into a record called modeRec. How do these changes affect the rest of Program FindMode? Has any safety been lost in parameter passing?

CHA 12.4.3   Redo Exercise Cha.12.4.2 with Program FindMode2, also from Section 9.2.

CHA 12.4.4   Modify Program Days in Section 12.3 so that all three fields of a dateType record are of the same type (the type INTEGER).

Programs and Subprograms to Write

WRI 12.4.1   Write and test a procedure that subtracts one rational number from another.

WRI 12.4.2   Write and test a procedure that divides one rational number by another.

WRI 12.4.3   Write and test a procedure that adds an integer to a rational number; for example, 1/2 + 1 = 3/2

WRI 12.4.4   Write and test a procedure that reduces a fraction to its lowest terms; for example, it takes 3/6 and turns it into 1/2.

WRI 12.4.5   Write and test a procedure that eliminates the so-called improper fractions; for example, it takes 7/2 and turns it into 3 and 1/2. This requires creation of a new type, because our old `rational` type doesn't have a field to store the 3.

WRI 12.4.6   Redo Exercise Wri.6.5.3, using the representation for rational numbers that we developed in this section.

WRI 12.4.7   An *equilateral triangle* is a triangle with three equal sides. Let's say we have two such triangles. One of them is "nailed" to the table so it can't move. The other triangle can move, and it needs to be placed on top of the first triangle. There are six ways to put the second triangle on top of the first one:

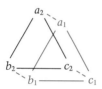

Leave the second triangle alone

Rotate the second triangle counterclockwise

Rotate the second triangle clockwise

Flip the second triangle

Flip the second triangle and rotate it counterclockwise

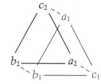

Flip the second triangle and rotate it clockwise

Each of these placements is called a *symmetry of the triangle*. Write a program that finds all the symmetries of the triangle. In the program's output, represent the six symmetries this way:

```
        a2              c2
    b2    c2        a2    b2        etc.
```

WRI 12.4.8   Redo Exercise Wri.12.4.7, this time finding the *symmetries of the square*. (Hint: There are eight of them.)

WRI 12.4.9   Look up *imaginary numbers* in an algebra textbook. Find out how to multiply two imaginary numbers, and what happens when you multiply a real number by an imaginary number. Write and test a subprogram that accepts two such numbers and returns their product.

WRI 12.4.10   Look up *complex numbers* in an algebra textbook. Find out how to add, subtract, multiply, and divide two complex numbers. Then write a program that does arithmetic for complex numbers.

WRI 12.4.11   *(Double precision arithmetic)* Write and test a procedure that can add two very large numbers together. Each number, potentially larger than `MAXINT`, is stored in a record with two `INTEGER` fields. By combining the two `INTEGER` fields we get the digits of the large number.

WRI 12.4.12   *(Quad precision arithmetic)* Modify the procedure you wrote for Exercise 12.4.11 so that each record has four fields. Test your new procedure by redoing Exercise Wri.6.2.2.

WRI 12.4.13   Repeat Exercise Wri.12.4.12 for subtraction, multiplication, and division.

12.5

The Nesting of Structured Types

Once again we want to look at nesting—that is, "things within other things."

Each sack had seven cats,
Each cat had seven kits;

In this instance we'll look at defining structured types within structured types. We'll create a record type, vStringType, one of whose fields is an array. Then we'll think about having an array of such records and having record types that contain other record types.

Specifications   In Pascal, every one-dimensional array has a fixed number of components. For instance, if we have

```
CONST
  maxMessageSize = 50;
TYPE
  indexType     = 1..maxMessageSize;
  messageType   = ARRAY [indexType] OF CHAR;
VAR
  plainText : messageType;
```

then plainText is an array with 50 components—no more, no less. We might not use all 50 of these components, but they're still part of the array.

Now what about people's names? Not all names have the same length. There are short names like Burd and long names like Nepomnyashchiy. And even though we can't have arrays whose lengths vary, perhaps we can devise some elegant mechanism for handling differences in the lengths of names.

Here's an idea: We can have an array called content; but along with that array, we can have a variable called length that stores the number of components in the array that contain useful information.

```
CONST
  maxLength = 80;
TYPE
  indexType  = 1..maxLength;
  bigIndType = 0..maxLength;
VAR
  content : ARRAY [indexType] OF CHAR;
  length  : bigIndType;
```

If we store the name Burd in the array, then we have

content[1]   content[2]   content[3]   content[4]   content[5]   content[6]

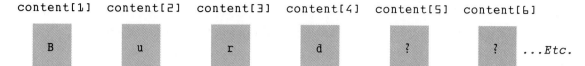

...Etc.

length

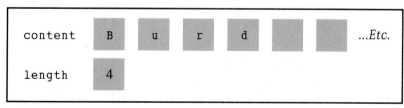

Of course, wherever we refer to the content array, we also need to refer to its length. For instance, to write the name Burd on the screen, we need to write the values stored in all the components from content[1] up to content[length] (which is the same as content[4]). So since the length of this array is so intimately connected with the array itself, why not create a record type?

```
CONST
   maxLength = 80;
TYPE
   indexType   = 1..maxLength;
   bigIndType  = 0..maxLength;
   vStringType = RECORD
                    content : ARRAY [indexType] OF CHAR;
                    length  : bigIndType
                 END;
VAR
   lastName : vStringType;
```

Now the variable lastName contains two fields. One field, called content, is an array of CHARacters. The other field, called length, is a number from 0 to 80.

lastName:

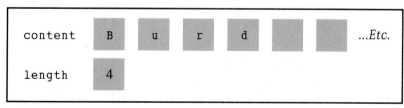

If we go on to declare several variables of this vStringType record type, we get several content arrays, each with its own length.

```
VAR
   firstName, lastName, fullName : vStringType;
```

firstName:

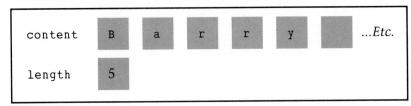

lastName:

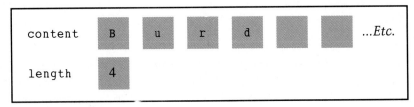

fullName:

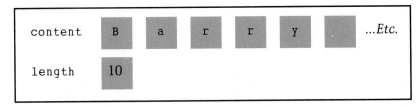

Notice how we don't have to make up extra names for the various lengths.

Once we've defined our vStringType we need a collection of subprograms to deal with it. In particular, we'd like to have

Procedure ReadVString: Reads characters from the keyboard until it reaches a **whitespace** character. As the procedure reads characters, it places them into a vString. (Note: Several of the characters in the ASCII Character Set are considered to be whitespace characters, but our procedure will look for only two of them—the blank space and the end-of-line indicator.)

Procedure WriteVString: Writes a vString to the screen.

Procedure MakeABlank: Makes a vString that contains just one character—the blank space character.

Procedure Concatenate: **Concatenates** two vStrings—that is, makes a new vString by putting two old vStrings together, one after another.

There are many more things we could do with vStrings, like

- cut off the first character
- search for the characters of one vString inside another vString
- make a vString with no characters in it

and so on. But for simplicity we'll stick to the subprograms mentioned in our first list.

Our main program will have the following specs:

Input: A last name and a first name, on two separate lines

Output: A full name (the first name, then a blank space, then the last name) all on one line

It wouldn't be hard to write a main program that did all this without using vStrings, but then we wouldn't be using this versatile and elegant tool that we've just created. As long as we've got vStringType, and we know it's going to be useful for dealing with all kinds of problems that involve words of varying length, we might as well use it.

Program Example

```
PROGRAM VStringTester (input, output);
{Performs simple operations on varying-length strings.}
CONST
   maxLength = 80;
   blank     = ' ';
TYPE
   indexType   = 1..maxLength;
   bigIndType  = 0..maxLength;
   vStringType = RECORD
                    content : ARRAY [indexType] OF CHAR;
                    length  : bigIndType
                 END;
VAR
   firstName, lastName, fullName, oneBlank : vStringType;
{----------}

PROCEDURE ReadVString (VAR vStr : vStringType);
{Reads a vString from the keyboard.  Keeps reading until
 it finds the end-of-line or a blank space.  For a more
 robust version, try Exercises Cha.12.5.2 and Cha.15.2.4.}
   VAR
      index  : bigIndType;
      charIn : CHAR;
```

```
BEGIN {ReadVString}
  index := 0;

  REPEAT
    Read (charIn);
    IF charIn <> blank THEN
      BEGIN
        index                 := index + 1;
        vStr.content[index] := charIn
      END
  UNTIL Eoln (input) OR (charIn = blank);

  vStr.length := index;
  IF Eoln (input) THEN
    ReadLn
END;  {ReadVString}
{----------}

PROCEDURE MakeABlank (VAR vStr : vStringType);
{Makes vStr be the vString containing a single blank space.}

BEGIN {MakeABlank}
  WITH vStr DO
    BEGIN
      content[1] := blank;
      length     := 1
    END
END;  {MakeABlank}
{----------}

PROCEDURE Concatenate (vStr1, vStr2 : vStringType ;
                       VAR vStr3    : vStringType);
{Concatenates vStr1 and vStr2 giving vStr3.}

  VAR
    i1, i2 : indexType;
    i3     : bigIndType;

BEGIN {Concatenate}
  i3 := 0;

  FOR i1 := 1 TO vStr1.length DO
    BEGIN
      i3 := i3 + 1;
      vStr3.content[i3] := vStr1.content[i1]
    END;

  FOR i2 := 1 to vStr2.length DO
    BEGIN
      i3 := i3 + 1;
      vStr3.content[i3] := vStr2.content[i2]
    END;

  vStr3.length := i3
END;   {Concatenate}
{----------}
```

```
PROCEDURE WriteVString (vStr : vStringType);
{Writes a vString to the screen.}

   VAR
     i : indexType;
BEGIN {WriteVString}
   WITH vStr DO
     FOR i := 1 TO length DO
       Write (content[i])
END;  {WriteVString}

{----------}

BEGIN {VStringTester}
   WriteLn      ('Enter last-name and first-name');
   Write        ('(separated by a space, '      );
   WriteLn      ('or on two separate lines):'   );
   ReadVString  (lastName);
   ReadVString  (firstName);
   WriteLn;

   MakeABlank   (oneBlank);
   Concatenate  (firstName, oneBlank, firstName);
   Concatenate  (firstName, lastName, fullName);

   Write        ('The full name is: ');
   WriteVString (fullName);
   WriteLn
END.  {VStringTester}
```

Sample Runs

```
Enter last-name and first-name
(separated by a space, or on two separate lines):
Burd
Barry

The full name is: Barry Burd
```

_____

```
Enter last-name and first-name
(separated by a space, or on two separate lines):
Ritter Harriet

The full name is: Harriet Ritter
```

_____

```
Enter last-name and first-name
(separated by a space, or on two separate lines):
Nepomnyashchiy
J.

The full name is: J. Nepomnyashchiy
```

Observations

```
• PROCEDURE Concatenate (vStr1, vStr2 : vStringType ;
                            VAR vStr3    : vStringType);
      .
      .
   vStr3.content[i3] := vStr1.content[i1]
```

evaluating
nested
expressions

The best way to understand an expression like vStr1.content[i1] is to make a drawing showing the types of its various parts. Since vStr1 is of type vStringType, its content field is an array:

```
TYPE
    indexType   = 1..maxLength;
    bigIndType  = 0..maxLength;
    vStringType = RECORD
                    content : ARRAY [indexType] OF CHAR;
                    length  : bigIndType
                  END;
```

So we get

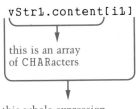

vStr1.content[i1]

this is an array
of CHARacters

Then when we choose the i1st component of that array, we get

vStr1.content[i1]

this is an array
of CHARacters

this whole expression
is a single CHARacter

* PROCEDURE Concatenate (**vStr1**, **vStr2** : **vStringType** ;
                                        VAR **vStr3**   : **vStringType**);

.
.
.

Concatenate   (**firstName**, oneBlank, **firstName**)

two formal
parameters—
one actual
parameter

Two different formal parameters get the same actual parameter passed to them. Is this going to work? Yes, it is. If we think once again about pass by reference and pass by value, the picture at the top of the next page shows how it works. In the call to Procedure Concatenate, both firstName parameters refer to the same memory location—the location where this first name is stored. This name is passed by value to vStr1, so a *copy* of it is placed into a memory location that's used exclusively by vStr1.

But this same name is passed by reference to vStr3. This means the computer makes vStr3 refer to the same memory location as firstName.

Inside Procedure Concatenate, when the statement

vStr3.content[i3] := vStr1.content[i1]

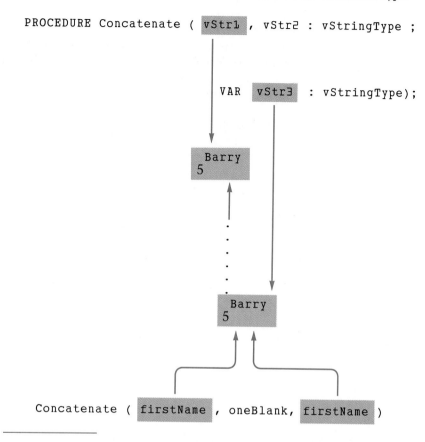

is executed, characters from vStr1's own memory location are being copied to the memory location referred to by vStr3. In other words, characters are copied from vStr1's memory location to firstName's memory location. That's just what we want.

Further Discussion

deeper nesting

What if we need to sort a collection of one thousand names? Perhaps we can do it with an array of vStrings. First we declare

```
CONST
  maxLength = 80;
TYPE
  indexType    = 1..maxLength;
  bigIndType   = 0..maxLength;
  vStringType  = RECORD
                   content : ARRAY [indexType] OF CHAR;
                   length  : bigIndType
                 END;
  vStrArrayType = ARRAY [1..1000] OF vStringType;
VAR
  namesArray : vStrArrayType;
```

This gives us a very elaborate structure for the `namesArray` variable:

namesArray[1]

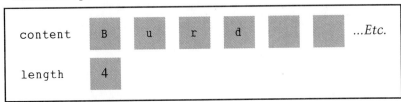

namesArray[2]

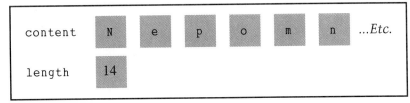

namesArray[3]

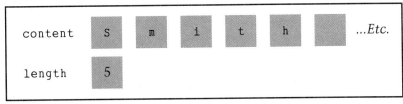

.
.
.
Etc.

`namesArray[3]` refers to the third name in our collection of names. It's actually a whole record, with `content` and `length` fields. So what if we want to refer the second letter of this third name? First we select the `content` field of the third name:

`namesArray[3].content`

Then we pick the second letter of that `content` field:

`namesArray[3].content[2]`

This makes sense because of the following diagram:

namesArray[3].content[2]

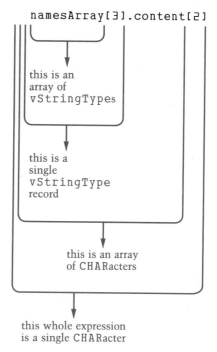

this is an
array of
vStringTypes

this is a
single
vStringType
record

this is an array
of CHARacters

this whole expression
is a single CHARacter

And here's one more idea: What if we want to add full names to our employeeRecType of Section 12.1? We could do it this way:

```
CONST
  maxLength = 80;
TYPE
  indexType   = 1..maxLength;
  bigIndType  = 0..maxLength;
  vStringType = RECORD
                  content : ARRAY [indexType] OF CHAR;
                  length  : bigIndType
                END;
  idType     = 0000..9999;
  wageType   = REAL;
  statusType = 'A'..'C';

  empRecType = RECORD
                 name   : vStringType;
                 id     : idType;
                 wage   : wageType;
                 status : statusType
               END;
VAR
  empRec  : empRecType;
```

Then name is a *record within a record!* Here's a picture of the structure we're creating:

An `empRec` value:

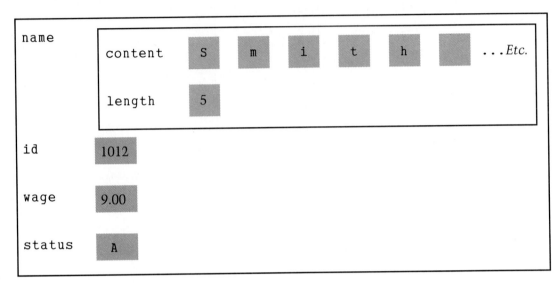

An expression such as

`empRec.name.content[2]`

refers to

the second component of
the `content` array of
the `name` field of
the `empRec` record.

12.5   Exercises

Key Words to Review

      whitespace   concatenate

Questions to Answer

QUE 12.5.1   Suppose we have an array of `vStrings`.
- a. Write an expression that refers to the third letter of the tenth `vString` in the array.
- b. Write an expression that refers to the length of the eighth `vString` in the array.

QUE 12.5.2   Consider the definition of an `empRecType` given at the end of this section.
- a. Write an expression that refers to an employee's identification number.
- b. Write an expression that refers to the first letter of an employee's name.

QUE 12.5.3   Consider the definition of an `empRecType` given at the end of this section, and imagine that we have an array of such employee records:

```
VAR
   empArray : ARRAY [1..100] OF empRecType;
```

a. Write an expression that refers to the identification number of the sixty-seventh employee.

b. Write an expression that refers to the first letter of that sixty-seventh employee's name.

Experiments to Try

EXP 12.5.1   Here's something you'll find useful when you get to Exercises Wri.12.5.5 and Wri.12.5.6. Run the following program:

```
PROGRAM Suits (output);
{Displays the four suits
 in a deck of cards.}
   VAR
      i : 3..6;
BEGIN {Suits}
   FOR i := 3 TO 6 DO
      Write (Chr(i));
   WriteLn
END.   {Suits}
```

Depending on various characteristics of your implementation, it may or may not display little letter-size symbols for the four suits in a deck of cards.

EXP 12.5.2   With the following definitions and declarations:

```
TYPE
   recType1 = RECORD
                 i : INTEGER;
                 c : CHAR
              END;
   recType2 = RECORD
                 r   : REAL;
                 b   : BOOLEAN;
                 rec : recType1
              END;

VAR
   rec1 : recType1;
   rec2 : recType2;
```

run a program containing the code

```
WITH rec2.rec DO
   WriteLn (i, c)
```

EXP 12.5.3   Redo Exercise Exp.12.5.2 using the following code:

```
WITH rec1 DO
   WITH rec2 DO
      WriteLn (i, c)
```

EXP 12.5.4   Redo Exercise Exp.12.5.2 using the following code:

```
WITH rec2 DO
  WITH rec1 DO
    WriteLn (i, c)
```

EXP 12.5.5   With Procedure ChangeTwice declared as follows:

```
PROCEDURE ChangeTwice (VAR a, b : INTEGER);
BEGIN {ChangeTwice}
  a := a + 1;
  b := b - 1
END.   {ChangeTwice}
```

run a program containing the call ChangeTwice (x, x).

Changes to Make

CHA 12.5.1   Write test drivers for the definitions of empRecType and vStrArrayType as given in this section.

CHA 12.5.2   Rewrite Procedure ReadVString so that it skips over any whitespace that comes before the name. Then you'll have a much more robust (and realistic) version of the procedure than the one we've given in this section.

CHA 12.5.3   Modify Function IsAWin? in Section 11.3 so that the board, rowNum, and colNum arrays are all passed to the function as one large gameDescription record. Then redo Exercise Cha.11.3.2 in which you write a test driver for Function IsAWin?.

CHA 12.5.4   Modify Procedure LinearSearch from Section 10.5 so that it searches through an array of records. Each record has the following form:

```
TYPE
  personType = RECORD
                 id      : 0000..9999;
                 balance : REAL
               END;
```

The user enters a person's id number and the program writes that person's balance. In the terminology of searching, the field on which the search is conducted (in this case the id field) is called the *search key*.

CHA 12.5.5   Modify Program Merge from Section 10.7 so that it merges two "smaller" vStrings into one larger vString.

CHA 12.5.6   Modify Procedure SelectionSort from Section 10.8 so that it sorts an array of records. Each record has the following form:

```
TYPE
  personType = RECORD
                 name  : vStringType;
                 phone : phoneType
               END;
```

where phoneType is a record with three fields:

(201) 555-1212

area code   exchange   number line

The main program can ask Procedure `SelectionSort` to sort either alphabetically by name or numerically by telephone number. The number (201) 555-1212 comes right before the number (201) 555-1213. In the terminology of sorting, the field on which the sort is conducted (either the `name` field or the `phone` field) is called the *sort key*.

CHA 12.5.7   Take the program of Exercise Cha.12.5.6, and add the ability to sort partly on `phone` and partly on `name`. That is, the records are sorted so that the area codes are non-decreasing from one record to another. Within each area code, the records are sorted so that the names are in alphabetical order.

Programs and Subprograms to Write

WRI 12.5.1   Write a function subprogram that accepts a `vString` and returns the `vString`'s length. (Easy, isn't it?)

WRI 12.5.2   Write a subprogram that makes a `vString` with no characters in it.

WRI 12.5.3   Write a subprogram called `Cdr` that cuts the first character off of a `vString`. (To find out where the name `Cdr` comes from, look in any book on the Lisp programming language.)

WRI 12.5.4   In Exercise Wri.11.3.1 you've probably defined some sort of a `checkerPieceType`. Modify the definition of a `checkerPieceType` so that it becomes a record type. One of the fields in the record is `king : BOOLEAN`.

WRI 12.5.5   Modify the program you wrote for Exercise Wri.11.3.4 so that each card is represented by a record. One field stores the card's "number" (ace through king) and the other field stores the card's suit (heart, diamond, club, or spade). For help in displaying the various suits, try Experiment Exp.12.5.1.

WRI 12.5.6   Write a program that reads a disk file containing the numbers and suits of the fifty-two cards in a deck. The cards aren't necessarily stored in order (the way you'd find them in a brand new pack). The program uses the record representation described in Exercise Wri.12.5.5 to store each card. The output of the program, written to another disk file, is the same deck of cards after a "perfect" shuffle has been done. In a perfect shuffle, the deck is divided exactly in half and the two halves are merged together, with cards from each half alternating to form the new deck.

12.6

Variant Records

When it seems natural to combine several pieces of dissimilar data, we use a record type. In Program `Raises3` (Section 12.1), each employee's record was a combination of the employee's identification number, wage, and status. To this we could have added the employee's name, address, social security number, etc.

Occasionally we find a problem in which the pieces that need to be combined *vary* from one record to another. Say, for instance, we're keeping track of the people connected with a college or university. The record for each person contains that person's identification number, but in addition to this the students' records might contain fields for year of anticipated graduation, grade-point average, and dollar-amount owed in tuition and fees. At the same time, the faculty members' records should have fields for academic rank and yearly salary. And each person on the university's staff should have a record containing that person's employment level and hourly rate of pay. (A staff member's level might be a number between 1 and 5. The least experienced staff members are hired at level 1, while the most senior staff members are level 5.)

What we need is a record type that allows different categories of people to share certain fields but not others.

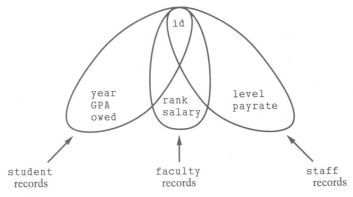

Pascal provides a mechanism for doing exactly what we've just described. It's called a **variant record type**.

```
TYPE
   statusType = (student, faculty, staff);
   idType    = 000..999;
   yearType  = 1990..2010;
   rankType  = (assistant, associate, full);
   levelType = 1..5;
   personType =
      RECORD
         id : idType;
         CASE status : statusType OF
            student: (year   : yearType  ;
                      gpa    : REAL       ;
                      owed   : REAL      );
            faculty: (rank   : rankType   ;
                      salary : REAL      );
            staff  : (level  : levelType ;
                      payrate : REAL      )
         END;
   VAR
      p : personType;
```

This code says that the information stored in p can be broken into fields in three different ways:

p (of type `personType`):

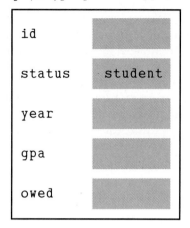

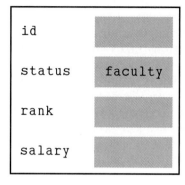

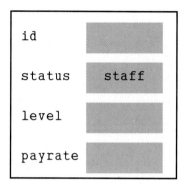

referring to a variant record's fields

The status field is special—it's called the tag field. The value that's stored in the tag field (in this case, either student, faculty, or staff) decides how the rest of the information gets divided into fields. For a student we might have

```
WITH p DO
  BEGIN
    status := student;
    id     := 483;
    year   := 1996;
    gpa    := 3.50;
    owed   := 10000.91
  END
```

but for a faculty member we'd have

```
WITH p DO
  BEGIN
    status := faculty;
    id     := 333;
    rank   := assistant;
    salary := 25000.00
  END
```

Specifications Look again at Procedure ReadLnCharOrNat in Section 8.3.

```
PROCEDURE ReadLnCharOrNat (VAR c    : CHAR;
                           VAR n    : natural;
                           VAR kind : kindType);
{Reads a value for c OR for n.
 Sets kind to
   character   if a value of c is read;
   natral      if a value of n is read.}
```

Notice the big word OR in the prologue comment. This procedure has three VAR parameters, but it never assigns meaningful values to all three of them. What a waste! Even if the space that's wasted isn't such a big deal, it's so inelegant.

Well this is where variant records are handy. We can use a variant record to store either a character or a natural number in one memory location. That memory location takes the place of both c and n in Procedure ReadLnCharOrNat. With this new record type the procedure always places a meaningful value into the same memory location. Sometimes it notes that the kind of value stored in this location is a character, and other times it notes that the kind of value stored there is a natral.

So let's rewrite Program CharNatTester (again from Section 8.3) to make use of this new variant record type. If you compare the new version with the old version, you'll see that there are very few changes.

Program Example

```
PROGRAM CharNatTester (input, output);
{A test driver for Procedure ReadLnCharNatRec.}
  TYPE
    kindType    = (character, natral);
    natural     = 0..MAXINT;
    charNatType = RECORD
                    CASE kind : kindType OF
                      character : (c : CHAR);
                      natral    : (n : natural)
                  END;
  VAR
    charNat : charNatType;
    count   : 1..3;
  {----------}
  PROCEDURE ReadLnCharNatRec (VAR charNat : charNatType);
  {Reads a value for c OR for n.
   Sets kind to
      character    if a value of c is read;
      natral       if a value of n is read.}
    VAR
      x : CHAR;
    {----------}
    FUNCTION IsDigit (x : CHAR) : BOOLEAN;
    {Answers the question "Is x one of the
     digit characters '0' to '9'?"}
    BEGIN {IsDigit}
      IsDigit := ('0' <= x) AND (x <= '9')
    END; {IsDigit}
    {----------}
```

```
PROCEDURE ReadLnRestNat (x : CHAR; VAR n : natural);
{Completes the process of reading a natural number.}
   TYPE
      digitChar = '0'..'9';
      digitNum  = 0 .. 9 ;

   {----------}

   FUNCTION NumericEquiv (x : digitChar) : digitNum;
   {Taken from Section 7.4.
    Accepts a digit character;
    returns its numeric equivalent.}
   BEGIN {NumericEquiv}
      NumericEquiv := Ord(x) - Ord('0')
   END;   {NumericEquiv}

   {----------}

BEGIN {ReadLnRestNat}
   n := NumericEquiv (x);
   WHILE NOT Eoln (input) DO
      BEGIN
         Read (x);
         n := (10 * n) + NumericEquiv (x)
      END;
   ReadLn
END;   {ReadLnRestNat}

{----------}

PROCEDURE ReadLnRestChar (x : CHAR; VAR c : CHAR);
{Completes the process of reading a character.}
BEGIN {ReadLnRestChar}
   c := x;
   ReadLn
END;   {ReadLnRestChar}

{----------}

BEGIN {ReadLnCharNatRec}
   WITH charNat DO
      BEGIN
         Read (x);
         IF IsDigit (x) THEN
            BEGIN
               kind := natral;
               ReadLnRestNat (x, n)
            END
         ELSE
            BEGIN
               kind := character;
               ReadLnRestChar (x, c)
            END
      END
END;   {ReadLnCharNatRec}

{----------}
```

```
BEGIN {CharNatTester}
  FOR count := 1 TO 3 DO
    BEGIN
      Write ('Enter a character or a natural number: ');
      ReadLnCharNatRec (charNat);
      WITH charNat DO
        IF kind = character THEN
          WriteLn ('The character after this one is ', Succ(c):1)
        ELSE
          WriteLn ('Add two to this number, you get ',    n+2:3);
      WriteLn
    END
END.   {CharNatTester}
```

Sample Runs

A run of this program looks the same as a run of Program `CharNatTester` in Section 8.3.

Observations

- ```
  TYPE
    kindType    = (character, natral);
    natural     = 0..MAXINT;
    charNatType = RECORD
                      CASE kind : kindType OF
                          character : (c : CHAR);
                          natral    : (n : natural)
                  END;
  VAR
    charNat : charNatType;
  ```

the fields of a variant record

This code says that the information stored in `charNat` can be broken into fields in two different ways:

`charNat`

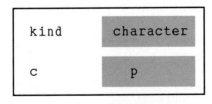

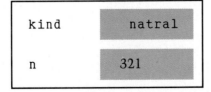

The value stored in the `kind` field decides what field name we use to refer to the rest of the record.
  ```

* PROCEDURE ReadLnCharNatRec (VAR charNat : . . .);
    .
    .
    .

  ReadLnCharNatRec (charNat);

  Instead of passing three separate variables (c, n, and kind) to the procedure, we pass just one record variable called charNat. This record variable contains two fields that are used to store either a character or a natural number, and a kind value.

* WITH charNat DO
    IF kind = character THEN
      WriteLn ('The character . . . ', Succ(c):1)
    ELSE
      WriteLn ('Add two to   . . . ',   n+2:3)

  The IF statement is identical to the one in the old version of Program CharNatTester. The difference is that in this version, we put it inside a WITH statement. That's because kind, c, and n are now field names of the record variable called charNat.

Further Discussion

Be careful when using variant records.

When we first wrote the new version of Program CharNatTester, it contained the following incorrect code:

```
WITH charNat DO
  BEGIN
    WriteLn ('The character after this one is ', Succ(c):1);
    WriteLn ('Add two to this number, you get ',      n+2:3)
  END
```

Instead of writing either the c field or the n field, we wrote both fields. When we ran the program on a VAX with VMS we got

```
Enter a character or a natural number: 321
The character after this one is B
Add two to this number, you get 323

Enter a character or a natural number: p
The character after this one is q
Add two to this number, you get 370

Enter a character or a natural number: 5
The character after this one is
Add two to this number, you get    7
```

Using Turbo Pascal we got almost the same thing, but the last part of the run looked like this:

```
Enter a character or a natural number: 5
The character after this one is ♠
Add two to this number, you get    7
```

The ♠ was a little picture that looked a lot like the spade on a deck of cards. This is what the implementation displays when it writes the ASCII character whose code number is 6.

The important thing to notice is that neither implementation gave us any error diagnostics when we used the wrong field name. Variant records give us a way of bypassing Pascal's strong typing mechanisms. (See Section 10.9.) For that reason, variant records should be used with an enormous amount of care.

12.6   Exercises

Key Words to Review

variant record type   tag field

Questions to Answer

QUE 12.6.1 Find every change that we made to Procedure ReadLnCharOrNat in order to get Procedure ReadLnCharNatRec.

QUE 12.6.2 Find every change that we made to Program CharNatTester in order for it to call the new procedure ReadLnCharNatRec.

QUE 12.6.3 With the personType definition given at the beginning of this section, describe what would happen if you tried

```
WITH p DO
  BEGIN
    status := student;
    id     := 483;
    year   := 1996;
    gpa    := 3.50;
    owed   := 10000.91
  END;
WriteLn (payrate)
```

Things to Check in a Manual

MAN 12.6.1 In this section we barely scratched the surface in discussing Pascal's rules on variant record types. Find the section in your manual on variant records to find out what kinds of rules and restrictions we skipped.

Experiments to Try

EXP 12.6.1 Change the definition of kindType to

```
TYPE
    kindType = (character, natral, someOtherKind);
```

Then try to compile Program CharNatTester without making any other changes.

EXP 12.6.2 Run the following program and examine its output carefully:

```
PROGRAM VarRecExp (input, output);
  TYPE
    varRecType = RECORD
                   CASE bool : BOOLEAN OF
                     FALSE : ( int1, int2 : INTEGER;
                               cha1, cha2 : CHAR     );
                     TRUE  : (arr : ARRAY [1..3] OF INTEGER)
                 END;
  VAR
    varRec : varRecType;
    i      : 1..3;
BEGIN {VarRecExp}
  WITH varRec DO
    BEGIN
      bool := FALSE;
      Write   ('Enter two integers:    ');
      ReadLn  (int1, int2);
      Write   ('Enter two characters: ');
      ReadLn  (cha1, cha2);
      Write   ('You entered:          ');
      FOR i := 1 TO 3 DO
        Write (arr[i]:10);
      WriteLn;
      WriteLn;

      bool := TRUE;
      Write   ('Enter three integers: ');
      FOR i := 1 TO 3 DO
        Read (arr[i]);
      ReadLn;
      Write   ('You entered:          ');
      WriteLn (int1:10, int2:10, cha1:10, cha2:10)
    END
END.  {VarRecExp}
```

Changes to Make

CHA 12.6.1 Modify Program CharNatTester so that it maintains an array of charNatType records. What we'll have, then, will be a kind of "heterogeneous array." Some of its components will contain CHAR values and others will contain natural values.

CHA 12.6.2 Modify Program Days from Section 12.3 so that it uses

```
TYPE
  dateType = RECORD
               year : yearType;
               CASE month : monthType OF
                 Jan, Mar, May, Jul,
                 Aug, Oct, Dec      : (day31 : 1..31);
                 Apr, Jun, Sep, Nov : (day30 : 1..30);

                 Feb : (  CASE leapYear : BOOLEAN OF
                            FALSE : (day28 : 1..28);
                            TRUE  : (day29 : 1..29)   )
             END;
```

Programs and Subprograms to Write

WRI 12.6.1   Write a program that answers questions, posed by the user, about various people at a university. You can use some of the code from the beginning of this section. The program gets information about people from a disk file.

WRI 12.6.2   Redo Exercises Wri.12.5.5 and Wri.12.5.6, this time using a variant record type. The record type's tag field is a BOOLEAN that determines whether the card is a number card or a picture card. If it's a number card, the record has a field with subrange type 1..10. If it's a picture card, the record has a field with enumerated type (jack, queen, king).

Things to Think About

THI 12.6.1   In the Further Discussion subsection we "accidentally" wrote the c field of a charNat record without having explicitly assigned a value to that field. Think again about our last bit of output (the ♠ character). Was it just "random garbage" or did it somehow make sense? Does this suggest any relationship between the way variant records work and the way Chr and Ord work? See if you can find support for your theory by looking at the ASCII Character Set (Appendix D) and examining the rest of the output from that particular run.

12.7

Sets

What is a set?   The most fundamental building block of modern mathematics is the **set**. A set is simply a collection of things. The things can be numbers, people, other sets, whatever. And sets can be combined in various ways to form other sets. Here are a few examples:

elements
union

- Let Set_1 be {Harriet, Barry, Sam, Jennie}, and let Set_2 be {Alan, Barry, Ed, Norma, Phil}. Set_1 has four **elements** and Set_2 has five elements.

- The **union** of Set_1 and Set_2 is the new set {Harriet, Barry, Sam, Jennie, Alan, Ed, Norma, Phil}. Anything that's an element of either Set_1 or Set_2 is an element of the union. Notice that Barry appears only once in the union. An element can't appear twice in one set.

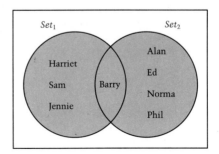

intersection

- The **intersection** of Set_1 and Set_2 is the new set {Barry}. Anything that's an element of both Set_1 and Set_2 is an element of the intersection.

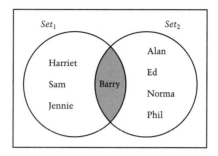

difference

- The **difference** between Set_1 and Set_2 (Set_1 minus Set_2) is the new set {Harriet, Sam, Jennie}. Anything that's an element of Set_1 but not Set_2 is an element of the difference.

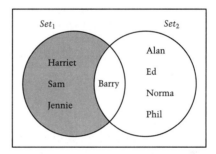

There are also interesting ways to compare sets with one another:

subsets and supersets

- Let Set_3 be {Norma, Alan, Barry}. Then Set_3 is a **subset** of Set_2. This is true because each of the elements in Set_3 is also an element of Set_2. Another way of saying the same thing is to say that Set_2 is a **superset** of Set_3.

- We can even say that Set_3 is a subset of itself. Even though it seems a bit redundant to say it, each element of Set_3 is, in fact, an element of Set_3.

empty set and singleton set

In this book we'll be interested in two special kinds of sets. The first is the **empty set**. The empty set is the set with no elements in it. Mathematicians usually refer to the empty set by writing $\varnothing$. The other "special" set that's of interest is a **singleton set**. A singleton set is a set with only one element in it, like the set {Barry}.

Specifications The program in this section just demonstrates how to use Pascal's set types and shows what results you'll get when you use them.

Program Example

```
PROGRAM SetsDemo (input, output);
{Demonstrates operations on set types.}
   TYPE
      digitType = 0..9;
      setType   = SET OF digitType;
   VAR
      s1, s2, s3 : setType;

   {----------}

   PROCEDURE ReadLnSet (VAR s : setType);
   {Reads a set's elements from the keyboard.}

      VAR
         d : digitType;
   BEGIN {ReadLnSet}
      s := [];
      WHILE NOT Eoln DO
         BEGIN
            Read (d);
            s := s + [d]
         END;
      ReadLn
   END;   {ReadLnSet}

   {----------}

   PROCEDURE WriteLnSet (s : setType);
   {Writes a set's elements to the screen.}

      VAR
         d : digitType;
   BEGIN {WriteLnSet}
      FOR d := 0 TO 9 DO
         IF d IN s THEN
            Write (d:2);
      WriteLn
   END;   {WriteLnSet}

   {----------}

BEGIN {SetsDemo}
   Write      ('Enter the elements of the set s1: ');
   ReadLnSet (s1);
   s2 := [0..2, 6];

   WriteLn;
   WriteLn;
   Write      ('s1 contains: ');
   WriteLnSet (s1);
   Write      ('s2 contains: ');
   WriteLnSet (s2);
   WriteLn;

   s3 := s1 + s2;
   Write      ('The union is:          ');
   WriteLnSet (s3);
```

```
      s3 := s1 * s2;
      Write      ('The intersection is: ');
      WriteLnSet (s3);

      s3 := s1 - s2;
      Write      ('The difference is:    ');
      WriteLnSet (s3);
      WriteLn;

      IF s2 <= s1 THEN
         WriteLn ('s2 is a subset of s1')
      ELSE
         WriteLn ('s2 is not a subset of s1')
   END.  {SetsDemo}
```

Sample Runs

```
Enter the elements of the set s1: 2 3 5 7
s1 contains:  2 3 5 7
s2 contains:  0 1 2 6

The union is:         0 1 2 3 5 6 7
The intersection is:  2
The difference is:    3 5 7

s2 is not a subset of s1
```

Observations

• ```
  TYPE
     digitType = 0..9;
     setType   = SET OF digitType;
  VAR
     s1, s2, s3 : setType;
  ```

**creating a set**

This tells the compiler that each of the sets s1, s2, and s3 contains digits. digitType is called the **base type** for these sets. The base type of a set must be an *ordinal type.* Instead of

```
TYPE
   digitType = 0..9;
   setType   = SET OF digitType;
```

we can have

```
TYPE
   intSetType = SET OF 0..255;
```

or

```
TYPE
   dayType    = (Sun, Mon, Tue, Wed, Thu, Fri, Sat);
   daySetType = SET OF dayType;
```

Of course, we *cannot* have

limitations on base types

```
TYPE
   badSetType = SET OF REAL;
```
```

nor can we have

```
TYPE
   arrayType  = ARRAY [1..3] OF INTEGER;
   badSetType = SET OF arrayType;
```

since REALs and array types aren't ordinal types.

Along with the overall limitation to ordinal types, most implementations put additional restrictions on the values that can be in a set's base type. For instance, a definition like

```
TYPE
   intSetType = SET OF 0..256;
```

isn't legal on many implementations either because base types can't contain more than 256 values or because base types can't contain INTEGER values outside the range 0 to 255. The reason for having these restrictions is efficiency. It would be difficult for an implementation to perform set operations very quickly if it didn't have some restrictions of this kind.

- s2 := [0..2, 6]

specifying the elements of a set

This statement puts the elements 0, 1, 2, and 6 into the set that's stored in the variable s2. In mathematics the notation for this set is

{0, 1, 2, 6}

Notice that in Pascal we use square brackets [and], instead of curly braces, to enclose the elements of a set.

- ```
  s3 := s1 + s2;
  Write         ('The union is:           ')
  ```
       .
       .
  ```
  s3 := s1 * s2;
  Write         ('The intersection is: ');
  ```
       .
       .
  ```
  s3 := s1 - s2;
  Write         ('The difference is:   ')
  ```

set operations

+ is the Pascal symbol for union, * is the symbol for intersection, and − is the symbol for difference.

- ```
  WHILE NOT Eoln DO
     BEGIN
        Read (d);
        s := s + [d]
     END
  ```

Here's the loop that reads new elements into the set s. Notice, in particular, how the assignment statement works: Each time through the loop, the assignment statement uses the union operator + to put the new value of d into s. If s already has this value in it, the assignment statement doesn't add anything to s (because no element can appear more than once in a set).

It's easy to make a mistake and write

```
s := s + d
```

for this assignment statement. This is incorrect, because you can only apply the union operation + to two sets. You can't apply it to a set s and a digit d.

In this loop, the variable s is an accumulator. It accumulates the values that are read into d. We've already seen that accumulators need to be initialized, and this accumulator is no exception. As usual, it's done at the top of the loop.

- `s := [ ]`

[ ] is Pascal's symbol for the empty set. Initializing s as the empty set is very much like initializing an INTEGER or REAL accumulator with the value 0.

IN

- `IF d IN s THEN`

In Pascal, the word IN means "is an element of."

- `IF s2 <= s1 THEN`

comparing sets

In Pascal, you can compare two sets with the operators =, <=, >=, or <>. If you do, = means "has exactly the same elements as" and <= means "is a subset of."

Of course >= means "is a superset of," and <> means "does not have exactly the same elements as." In ANSI Standard Pascal, it's not legal to compare sets with < or >.

Further Discussion

What if we change the IF statement in Procedure WriteLnSet to

```
IF NOT d IN s THEN
```

precedence rules

This won't work. To show you why it won't work, we have to add IN to our precedence rules:

Precedence Rule 1: When there are no parentheses

NOT is performed first, then

*, /, DIV, MOD, and AND are performed, then

+, −, and OR are performed, and finally

=, <>, <, >, <=, >=, and IN are performed

So in the expresssion

```
NOT d IN s
```

the computer first tries to find `NOT d` and then checks to see if `NOT d` is in the set `s`. But `NOT d` doesn't make sense, because `d` isn't of type `BOOLEAN`. Unless you add parentheses

```
IF NOT (d IN s) THEN
```

the compiler will give you an error diagnostic.

12.7   Exercises

Key Words to Review

set	difference	singleton set
element	subset	SET
union	superset	IN
intersection	empty set	base type

Questions to Answer

QUE 12.7.1   What's wrong (or at least misleading) in the following description of a set? {Pascal, COBOL, C, Pascal, English, England}

QUE 12.7.2   Give an example, not explicitly mentioned in this section, of a type that cannot be the base type of a Pascal set.

QUE 12.7.3   Give an example, not explicitly mentioned in this section, of a type that can be the base type of a Pascal set.

QUE 12.7.4   Consider the use of the Pascal statement

```
s := []
```

and explain how the empty set isn't the same as "nothing."

Things to Check in a Manual

MAN 12.7.1   Beyond the overall limitation to ordinal types, what restrictions does your implementation place on the values that can be in a set's base type?

MAN 12.7.2   Some implementations provide operations on SETs in addition to the ones required by ANSI Standard Pascal. Does yours?

Experiments to Try

EXP 12.7.1   In Program SetsDemo change

```
s2 := [0..2, 6]
```

to

```
s2 := [6, 0..2]
```

EXP 12.7.2   In Program SetsDemo change

```
s2 := [0..2, 6]
```

to

```
s2 := [0..2, 1, 6, 6]
```

EXP 12.7.3   What happens when you try to define

```
TYPE
   intSetType = SET OF INTEGER;
```

Programs and Subprograms to Write

WRI 12.7.1   One way to avoid using Pascal's SET feature is to create an array of BOOLEANs:

```
TYPE
   intSetType = ARRAY [1..10] OF BOOLEAN;
VAR
   intSet : intSetType;
```

The value TRUE in intSet[3] would mean that the number 3 is an element of intSet.

Write and test subprograms that implement the various set operations (union, intersection, subset, etc.) for this representation of a set.

WRI 12.7.2   Write and test a function that accepts a set s of INTEGERs between 0 and 30 and returns the largest value in s.

WRI 12.7.3   Write and test a function that accepts a set s of INTEGERs between 0 and 30 and another INTEGER value n. It returns the largest value in s that's smaller than n.

12.8

Using Sets

Specifications   In this section we'll use sets to write a program that identifies letters of the alphabet. It does this by posing questions to the user. Each question helps the program narrow the possibilities until it either finds a single letter, eliminates all the letters, or runs out of questions.

The task isn't as straightforward as it might first seem. Different people have different ways of describing letters. Even if we use a very rigorous classification scheme, the one that linguists use, we run into difficulties. (How do we classify the letter c? Do we group it with the letter k because of words like "**cat**", or with the letter s because of words like "pro**c**eed"?)

In a particular branch of Artificial Intelligence called **Expert Systems**, computers are programmed to "address problems normally thought to require human specialists for their solution."[3] The program in this section is an "expert" on the letters of the alphabet.

---

[3]Michaelsen, R. H., Michie, D., and Boulanger, A. "The Technology of Expert Systems," *BYTE* 10, No. 4, p. 303, April (1985).

Input: The input to Program `LettersExpert` comes from two files:

- One file has twenty lines. Each pair of lines looks like:

```
CONSONANT                doesn't include the GLIDESs y & w
bcdfghjklmnpqrstvxz
```

The first line has a word describing an **attribute** that certain letters possess and possibly a comment about the nature of that attribute. The next line has a list of letters possessing that attribute. The file containing this information is called `attribF`.

- The other input file is the standard keyboard file `input`. On the keyboard the user types Y or N in response to questions about letters, like the question

```
CONSONANT (Y or N)?:
```

Process: The variable `remaining` stores a set of letters. At first this set contains all the letters of the alphabet. Each time the user replies to a question, the computer eliminates, from `remaining`, any letters that don't match the user's reply.

Output: For each attribute in the `attribFile` the computer writes

- a question about that attribute (such as `CONSONANT (Y or N)?:`)
- a list of the letters possessing that attribute
- and, after the user's reply has been used to eliminate some letters, the list of the letters that are still `remaining`.

Designing a Program

Let's add more detail to the "process" part of the specs: At first, the set `remaining` stores all the letters of the alphabet:

```
remaining := ['a'..'z']
```

Then to ask the user questions about letters, the computer needs to repeatedly execute the following pseudocode:

Read (from `attribFile`) the name of an attribute and the list of letters possessing that attribute. Store this list of letters in the set-type variable `haveAttribute`.
Write the name of the attribute on the screen, and ask the user if the letter she's thinking about possesses that attribute.
    If `Yes`, then take all the letters out of `remaining` except the ones in the `haveAttribute` set.
    If `No`, then take, from `remaining`, all the letters in the `haveAttribute` set.

To take all the letters out of `remaining` except the ones in the `haveAttribute` set, we do

```
remaining := remaining * haveAttribute
```

To take, from remaining, all the letters in the haveAttribute set, we do

```
remaining := remaining - haveAttribute
```

Program Example

```
PROGRAM LettersExpert (attribF, input, output);
{Identifies letters of the alphabet.}
  TYPE
    attributeType = PACKED ARRAY [1..10] OF CHAR;
    lowerCaseType = 'a'..'z';
    letterSetType = SET OF lowerCaseType;
    cardinal      = 0..26;
  VAR
    attribute     : attributeType;
    remaining,
    haveAttribute : letterSetType;
    reply         : CHAR;
    attribF       : TEXT;

  {----------}

  FUNCTION IsEmpty (s : letterSetType) : BOOLEAN;
  {Determines whether the set 's' is empty.}

  BEGIN {IsEmpty}
    IsEmpty := s = []
  END;   {IsEmpty}

  {----------}

  FUNCTION IsSingleton (s : letterSetType) : BOOLEAN;
  {Determines whether the set 's' is a singleton.}

    VAR
      elt   : lowerCaseType;
      count : cardinal;

  BEGIN {IsSingleton}
    count := 0;
    FOR elt := 'a' TO 'z' DO
      IF elt IN s THEN
        count := count + 1;
    IsSingleton := count = 1
  END;   {IsSingleton}

  {----------}

  PROCEDURE ReadLnAttrib (VAR attribF    : TEXT        ;
                          VAR attribute : attributeType);
  {Reads a ten-character attribute (possibly
   padded with blanks) from the attribF file.}

    VAR
      i : 1..10;

  BEGIN {ReadLnAttrib}
    FOR i := 1 TO 10 DO
      Read (attribF, attribute[i]);
    ReadLn (attribF)
  END;   {ReadLnAttrib}

  {----------}
```

```
PROCEDURE ReadLnSet (VAR attribF       : TEXT            ;
                     VAR haveAttribute : letterSetType);
{Reads a set's elements from the attribF file.}
  VAR
    elt : lowerCaseType;
BEGIN {ReadLnSet}
  haveAttribute := [];
  WHILE NOT Eoln (attribF) DO
    BEGIN
      Read (attribF, elt);
      haveAttribute := haveAttribute + [elt]
    END;
  ReadLn (attribF)
END;  {ReadLnSet}

{----------}

PROCEDURE WriteLnSet (remaining : letterSetType);
{Writes a set's elements to the screen.}
  VAR
    elt : lowerCaseType;
BEGIN {WriteLnSet}
  FOR elt := 'a' TO 'z' DO
    IF elt IN remaining THEN
      Write (elt:1)
    ELSE
      Write (' ');
  WriteLn
END;  {WriteLnSet}

{----------}

BEGIN {LettersExpert}
  Reset (attribF);
  remaining := ['a'..'z'];
  Write      ('Initially the set contains: ');
  WriteLnSet (remaining);
  WriteLn;
  REPEAT
    ReadLnAttrib (attribF, attribute);
    ReadLnSet    (attribF, haveAttribute);

    REPEAT
      Write (attribute, '(Y or N)?: ');
      ReadLn (reply)
    UNTIL (reply = 'Y') OR (reply = 'N');

    IF reply = 'Y' THEN
      BEGIN
        remaining := remaining * haveAttribute;
        Write      ('Eliminate all but            ');
        WriteLnSet (haveAttribute)
      END
```

```
      ELSE
        BEGIN
          remaining := remaining - haveAttribute;
          Write      ('Eliminate                        ');
          WriteLnSet (haveAttribute)
        END;
      Write ('Letters remaining:            ');
      IF IsEmpty (remaining) THEN
        Write ('NONE!', Chr(7))
      ELSE
        WriteLnSet (remaining);
      WriteLn
    UNTIL IsEmpty (remaining) OR IsSingleton (remaining) OR
        Eof (attribF)
  END.  {LettersExpert}
```

Sample Runs

With the following attributeFile:

```
VOWEL
aeiou
CONSONANT          doesn't include the GLIDEs y & w
bcdfghjklmnpqrstvxz
VOICELESS          don't make the vocal chords vibrate
ptkfsh
STOP               can't be drawn out when spoken
ptkbdg
FRICATIVE          produce friction when spoken
fsvz
NASAL              make breath pass through nose
mn
LABIAL             involves use of lips
pbfvmw
VELAR              involves use of soft palate
kg
```

a run might look like this:

```
Initially the set contains: abcdefghijklmnopqrstuvwxyz
VOWEL       (Y or N)?: N
Eliminate               a   e   i    o    u
Letters remaining:        bcd fgh jklmn pqrst vwxyz

CONSONANT (Y or N)?: Y
Eliminate all but         bcd fgh jklmn pqrst v x z
Letters remaining:        bcd fgh jklmn pqrst v x z

VOICELESS (Y or N)?: Y
Eliminate all but           f h k     p st
Letters remaining:          f h k     p st

STOP        (Y or N)?: Y
Eliminate all but       b d g   k     p   t
Letters remaining:              k     p   t

FRICATIVE (Y or N)?: N
Eliminate                   f         s v   z
Letters remaining:              k     p   t
```

```
NASAL       (Y or N)?: N
Eliminate                                      m n
Letters remaining:                        k      p      t

LABIAL      (Y or N)?: Y
Eliminate all but                  b    f     m   p      v w
Letters remaining:                                p
```

or like this:

```
Initially the set contains: abcdefghijklmnopqrstuvwxyz

VOWEL       (Y or N)?: Y
Eliminate all but                  a    e    i       o       u
Letters remaining:                 a    e    i       o       u

CONSONANT (Y or N)?: Y
Eliminate all but                   bcd fgh jklmn pqrst v x z
Letters remaining:                 NONE!<beep>
```

12.8 Exercises

Key Words to Review

> Expert Systems   attribute

Questions to Answer

QUE 12.8.1   Explain why we use the intersection operator when the user replies that the letter has a particular attribute.

QUE 12.8.2   Explain why we use the difference operator when the user replies that the letter does not have a particular attribute.

QUE 12.8.3   Can you describe a scenario related to the LettersExpert problem in which we'd use the union operator (other than just reading elements into the haveAttribute set)?

Things to Check in a Manual

MAN 12.8.1   Does your implementation provide a feature by which a FOR statement can iterate through the elements of a SET? In something called ANSI Extended Pascal it's legal to write

```
FOR letter IN ['A', 'E', 'I', 'O', 'U'] DO
```

For more information, see reference in Appendix H.

Scales to Practice

PRA 12.8.1   Write a program that reads a letter and decides whether the letter is in a vowelSet or a consonantSet.

PRA 12.8.2   Write a program that reads a character and uses sets to decide whether that character is or isn't a letter.

PRA 12.8.3   Write a program that reads a character and decides whether the character is one of the four operator symbols +, −, *, or /.

PRA 12.8.4   Write a program that reads the attribFile used by Program LettersExpert and then reads a letter from the keyboard. The program writes the names of all the attributes possessed by the letter.

Programs and Subprograms to Write

WRI 12.8.1   Write and test a function subprogram called Strspn that accepts a string of characters and a set. It finds the index of the earliest component in the string containing a character that's not in the set. The function returns a number that is one less than this index value.

WRI 12.8.2   Write a program that reads values into a set, in no particular order, and then moves them one by one into an array so that they appear in the array in non-decreasing order.

WRI 12.8.3   Redo Exercise Wri.10.4.3, using a Pascal set type to store the letters that the contestant has guessed.

WRI 12.8.4   We have an elevator in a building with five floors plus a basement. The elevator's memory chip maintains a SET of floors that need to be visited. When the elevator visits a floor, it removes that floor from the set. Then for one instant while the elevator is moving from one stop to another, it accepts some new floors into the set.

  Write a program that simulates the behavior of the elevator. Requests for visits to floors are typed in at the keyboard. When the elevator visits a floor, the program just writes the floor number on the screen. Remember that at any moment in time, the elevator is either going up or down. If it's going up, then the next floor it visits will be the nearest floor that's above the elevator's current position. If it's going down, then the next floor it visits will be the nearest floor that's below the elevator's current position.

WRI 12.8.5   Modify Exercise Wri.12.8.4 for a building with three elevators. Remember that there's still only one set of floor requests.

12.9

Object Types (Supplementary)

Now that we've covered record types we can examine some of the richness of object-oriented programming. The idea behind what we'll do is fairly simple.

A Pascal RECORD can bring various fields of data together into a single type. But a type should be more than just data. Along with the data is a collection of operations that can be performed on the data. Why don't we extend the notion of a record type so that it encapsulates the operations as well as the data?

```
TYPE
   indexType   = 1..maxLength;
   bigIndType  = 0..maxLength;
   vStringObj  = OBJECT
                   content : ARRAY [indexType] OF CHAR;
                   length  : bigIndType;
                   PROCEDURE ReadVString;
                   PROCEDURE MakeABlank;
                   PROCEDURE Concatenate (vStr1, vStr2 : vStringObj);
                   PROCEDURE WriteVString;
                 END;
```

What is an object type?

This is the definition of an **object type** called vStringObj. It's a modification of the record type that we defined in Section 12.5. This object type contains two data fields—content and length—and four procedure headings—ReadVString, MakeABlank, Concatenate, and WriteVString. These four procedures are so intimately related to the vStringObj type that they're included here as part of the type's definition. In OOP terminology it's common to refer to these subprograms **methods**

not so much as procedures, but rather as **methods**. It suggests that vStringObj is providing the rest of the code with four methods for dealing with its values.

So now let's look at the code for our object-oriented solution to the vString problem.

Program Example

```
UNIT VStringU;
{Provides simple operations on varying-length strings.}
INTERFACE
   CONST
      maxLength = 80;
      blank     = ' ';
   TYPE
      indexType   = 1..maxLength;
      bigIndType  = 0..maxLength;
      vStringObj  = OBJECT
                      content : ARRAY [indexType] OF CHAR;
                      length  : bigIndType;
                      PROCEDURE ReadVString;
                      PROCEDURE MakeABlank;
                      PROCEDURE Concatenate (vStr1, vStr2 : vStringObj);
                      PROCEDURE WriteVString;
                    END;
```

```
IMPLEMENTATION
    PROCEDURE vStringObj.ReadVString;
    {Reads a vString from the keyboard.  Keeps reading until
     it finds the end-of-line or a blank space.  For a more
     robust version, try Exercises Cha.12.5.2 and Cha.15.2.4.}
       VAR
          index : bigIndType;
          charIn : CHAR;
    BEGIN {ReadVString}
       index := 0;

       REPEAT
         Read (charIn);
         IF charIn <> blank THEN
           BEGIN
             index          := index + 1;
             content[index] := charIn
           END
       UNTIL Eoln (input) OR (charIn = blank);

       length := index;
       IF Eoln (input) THEN
         ReadLn
    END;   {ReadVString}
    {----------}

    PROCEDURE vStringObj.MakeABlank;
    {Makes a vString contain a only single blank space.}

    BEGIN {MakeABlank}
       content[1] := blank;
       length     := 1
    END;   {MakeABlank}
    {----------}

    PROCEDURE vStringObj.Concatenate (vStr1, vStr2 : vStringObj);
    {Concatenates vStr1 and vStr2.}

       VAR
          i1, i2 : indexType;
          i3     : bigIndType;
    BEGIN {Concatenate}
       i3 := 0;

       FOR i1 := 1 TO vStr1.length DO
         BEGIN
           i3 := i3 + 1;
           content[i3] := vStr1.content[i1]
         END;

       FOR i2 := 1 to vStr2.length DO
         BEGIN
           i3 := i3 + 1;
           content[i3] := vStr2.content[i2]
         END;

       length := i3
    END;   {Concatenate}
```

```
{----------}
PROCEDURE vStringObj.WriteVString;
{Writes a vString to the screen.}
   VAR
      i : indexType;
BEGIN {WriteVString}
   FOR i := 1 TO length DO
      Write (content[i])
END;   {WriteVString}
END. {VStringU}
```

Observations

- IMPLEMENTATION
        PROCEDURE vStringObj.ReadVString;

the syntax of methods

The syntax of methods is a bit different from the syntax of ordinary subprograms. Procedure `ReadVString` doesn't need to have a formal parameter of type `vStringObj`. Instead, we view `ReadVString` as a "field" of the `vStringObj` type, and we refer to it as such using the dot notation.

Now in the body of `ReadVString` we don't use dots or WITH to refer to the data fields of `vStringObj`.

```
BEGIN {ReadVString}
  index := 0;

  REPEAT
    Read (charIn);
    IF charIn <> blank THEN
      BEGIN
        index          := index + 1;
        content[index] := charIn
           .
           .
```

We don't need dots or WITH because `ReadVString`, being a field of `vStringObj`, is inextricably tied to the data fields of `vStringObj`.

- PROCEDURE vStringObj.Concatenate (vStr1, vStr2 : vStringObj);
         .
         .

   content[i3] := vStr1.content[i1]
         .
         .

   content[i3] := vStr2.content[i2]

The `Concatenate` method deals with three `vStrings`, not just one.

Two of these `vStrings`—`vStr1` and `vStr2`—are treated as formal parameters in `Concatenate`'s heading. These are the two smaller `vStrings` that we're trying to paste together when we call the method. Notice what we have to do in `Concatenate`'s body to refer to the content fields of `vStr1` and `vStr2`—we have to use the dot notation, just as we would with any ordinary record type. Indeed, Concatenate has no special relationship with either vStr1 or vStr2. They're just formal parameters.

In contrast there's a third vString that's intimately related to Concatenate. It's the result we get when we've pasted vStr1 and vStr2 together. This vString doesn't go by any particular name in Concatenate's code. The Concatenate method is one of its fields. When we simply refer to content[i] with no dot in the body of Concatenate, we're referring to the content field of this third vString. We don't need a dot because Concatenate is inextricably tied to the content field, and all the other fields, of this third vString.

More on this in a moment. First we give the main program that uses our new VStringUnit:

Program Example

```
PROGRAM VStrPro (input, output);
{Performs simple operations on varying-length strings.}
   USES VStringU;

   VAR
      firstName, lastName, fullName, oneBlank : vStringObj;
BEGIN {VStrPro}
   WriteLn ('Enter last-name and first-name');
   Write   ('(separated by a space, '      );
   WriteLn ('or on two separate lines):'   );
   lastName.ReadVString;
   firstName.ReadVString;
   WriteLn;

   oneBlank.MakeABlank;
   firstName.Concatenate (firstName, oneBlank);
   fullName.Concatenate  (firstName, lastName);

   Write ('The full name is: ');
   fullName.WriteVString;
   WriteLn
END.   {VStrPro}
```

Sample Runs

A run of VStrPro looks the same as a run of Program VStringTester (Section 12.5).

Observations

- VAR
      firstName, lastName, fullName, oneBlank : vStringObj;

objects and instances

In this VAR declaration we declare four individual **objects**. Each object is called an **instance** of the object type whose name is vStringObj.

Now notice the way we use these two terms—*object* and *object type*. They're not the same. An object type is a template that we use to create one or more objects. Stated more simply, an object type is defined in the TYPE definition part of the program, and an object is declared in the VAR declaration part of the program.

- lastName.ReadVString;
  firstName.ReadVString

  messages

  Here we have two calls to Procedure ReadVString. In OOP terminology we refer to these as **messages** to the objects lastName and firstName. Once again, the terminology reflects a certain point of view. We think of each object as a complete, self-contained package, which not only contains data, but also contains the methods by which those data are to be manipulated. We can think of lastName and firstName as two **actors** in a play. Each actor works independently, receiving messages from the other actors and from the director. When an actor receives a message, she responds by following a predetermined method—whichever method is appropriate for the message that she's received. This comparison with actors is used quite often in the literature on OOP.

  Notice, once again, the use of the dot. Since lastName is of type vStringObj, it has several fields. One of the fields is called ReadVString. Since ReadVString is a field of the lastName object, we use

  lastName.ReadVString

  to refer to it.

- fullName.Concatenate (firstName, lastName)

  If you think about it carefully, you'll realize that there are, in effect, four different Concatenates in Program VStrPro. There's one for each of the four objects declared in the program's VAR declaration. One of these Concatenates belongs to the fullName object. It's referred to as fullName.Concatenate. What we've done here is to call fullName.Concatenate and pass two parameters to it—the parameters firstName and lastName.

  Of course firstName and lastName have Concatenates of their own, but those particular Concatenates aren't being used here. Only fullName.Concatenate is being called upon to do the work.

Why create object types?

So much for the syntax of objects and object types. Now we're ready for a very important point. One of the most important goals of computer programming is to develop code that's **reusable**. It's not good enough to create a VStringUnit that works with one main program but not with any others. We want code that, once written, can be extended to help solve a variety of problems. We want our VStringUnit to help us solve problems dealing with names, telephone numbers, sentences, reserved words in a computer program, algebraic formulas, and more. And we don't want to modify any code in the VStringUnit when we do this. Since the VStringUnit isn't broken, we shouldn't try to fix it.

What we need is a syntax that permits our object types to be **extensible**. When we have a problem that's "bigger" than the vString problem, we won't modify our VStringUnit. Instead we'll create a new object type that **inherits** the data fields and methods of the vStringObj type.

Let's say we want a program that does various things with people's names. For one thing, it keeps track of a first name and a last name, and it deals with both parts individually. In spite of our claims about reusability we need to keep this discussion simple. So let's assume that everyone has the same uncomplicated kind of name—a first name, then a blank space, and then a last name.

content[1] content[2] content[3] content[4] content[5] content[6] content[7]

With this "uncomplicated" kind of name, we always have a blank space in the middle. So why bother storing something that we know for sure is always there? Instead, let's think of a full name as a vString with a special place holder in the middle of it to keep track of where the first name ends and the last name begins.

content[1] content[2] content[3] content[4] content[5] content[6]

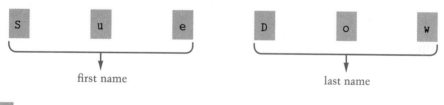

the midSpace
place holder

At first it might seem that the purpose of the place holder is to save space—to be able to store a full name without using up an extra blank space in the middle. But that's not really true. The midSpace variable stores an index value, which is bound to take up as much room in our computer's memory as a blank space. More realistically, the midSpace place holder helps us go immediately to the start of a person's last name, without having to search through the first name until we reach the blank space in the middle. This might save us some time if we're displaying the last names of fifty thousand people.

Now let's stop and think about what we've got:

A full name *is a* vString with a midSpace place holder to keep track of where the first name ends and the last name begins.

Object-oriented programmers would say that there's an **is a** relationship between full names and vStrings. This can be contrasted with a **has a** relationship:

A mailing label *has a* full name. It also *has a* street address, *has a* city, *has a* state, and *has a* zip code.

In Section 12.5 we nested a record type inside another record type to represent the "has a" relationship between a whole employee record and the employee's name. That's the right way to represent "has a" relationships. But for "is a" relationships we need objects. In particular, we create a new object type that inherits the data fields and methods of an old object type. The next program shows how it works.

**Program
Example**

```
UNIT NamesU;
{Provides simple operations on names.}
INTERFACE
  USES VStringU;
  TYPE
    nameObj  = OBJECT (vStringObj)
                  midSpace : bigIndType;
                  PROCEDURE ReadName;
                  PROCEDURE WriteFirst;
                  PROCEDURE WriteLast;
                  PROCEDURE WriteName;
               END;
IMPLEMENTATION
  PROCEDURE nameObj.ReadName;
  {Reads a name and stores it as a nameObj.  Won't
   work if it encounters end-of-line before blank space.}
    VAR
      fName, lName : vStringObj;
  BEGIN {ReadName}
    fName.ReadVString;
    lName.ReadVString;
    midSpace := fName.length + 1;
    Concatenate (fName, lName)
  END;   {ReadName}
  {----------}
  PROCEDURE nameObj.WriteFirst;
  {Writes the first-name half of a name.}
    VAR
      index : indexType;
```

```
BEGIN {WriteFirst}
  FOR index := 1 TO midSpace-1 DO
    Write (content[index]:1)
END;   {WriteFirst}

{----------}

PROCEDURE nameObj.WriteLast;
{Writes the last-name half of a name.}
  VAR
    index : indexType;
BEGIN {WriteLast}
  FOR index := midSpace TO length DO
    Write (content[index]:1)
END;   {WriteLast}

{----------}

PROCEDURE nameObj.WriteName;
{Writes a name on the screen.}
  VAR
    index : indexType;
BEGIN {WriteName}
  WriteFirst;
  Write (' ');
  WriteLast
END;   {WriteName}
END. {NamesU}
```

Observations

- ```
  TYPE
    nameObj   = OBJECT (vStringObj)
                  midSpace : bigIndType;
                  PROCEDURE ReadName;
                  PROCEDURE WriteFirst;
                  PROCEDURE WriteLast;
                  PROCEDURE WriteName;
                END;
  ```

Notice the word vStringObj in parentheses. This type definition tells the compiler that a nameObject *is a* vStringObject with an extra data field called midSpace and four extra methods called

inheritance

ReadName, WriteFirst, WriteLast, and WriteName. This means that a nameObject really has three data fields—two that it inherits from vStringObj and a new one of its own. It also has eight methods—four that it inherits from vStringObj and four new ones of its own. The body of Procedure WriteLast uses all three data fields:

```
FOR index := midSpace TO length DO
  Write (content[index]:1)
```
```

The body of Procedure `ReadName` uses two of the methods the `nameObj` inherits from `vStringObj`:

```
fName.ReadVString;
lName.ReadVString;
midSpace := fName.length + 1;
Concatenate (fName, lName)
```

And the body of Procedure `WriteName` uses two of the new methods that belong just to `nameObj`:

```
WriteFirst;
Write (' ');
WriteLast
```

So there you have it. Without making a single change to the code of the `VStringUnit`, we've managed to extend the `vStringObject` type to deal with names.

Now here's a simple main program that uses our `NamesUnit`:

```
PROGRAM NamesPro (input, output);
{Performs simple operations on names.}

  USES NamesU;

  VAR
    name : nameObj;

BEGIN {NamesPro}
  WriteLn ('Enter a full name: ');
  name.ReadName;
  WriteLn;

  WriteLn ('The name is: ');
  name.WriteName;
  WriteLn;

  WriteLn;
  WriteLn ('Written another way: ');
  name.WriteLast;
  Write (', ');
  name.WriteFirst;
  WriteLn
END.   {NamesPro}
```

Sample Runs

```
Enter a full name:
Susan Dow

The name is:
Susan Dow

Written another way:
Dow, Susan
```

Objects and object types are the basic building blocks of object-oriented programming, but of course there's more. OOP gives us a whole new way of thinking about data and operations. It suggests strategies for problem decomposition that can't be implemented with the old Pascal syntax. But even when we're programming in ANSI Standard Pascal, thinking about objects gives us new insight into the nature of algorithms and their data.

12.9   Exercises

Key Words to Review

object type	message	inherit
method	actor	is a
object	reusability	has a
instance	extensibility	

Questions to Answer

QUE 12.9.1   What's the difference between an object and an object type? How does this correspond to the relationship between a variable and its type?

QUE 12.9.2   Why do we use the term *method* to talk about a procedure or function that's part of an object type definition?

QUE 12.9.3   Summarize the use (and absence) of dots in the syntax of objects, methods, and messages.

QUE 12.9.4   In what sense is an object something like an actor in a play?

QUE 12.9.5   Compare the two procedures named Concatenate from this section and Section 12.5. Explain why one of them has two formal parameters and the other has three.

QUE 12.9.6   Is code truly reusable if we have to modify it (even slightly) to make it work in a new situation? Why, or why not?

QUE 12.9.7   Suppose we wanted to add name handling (with a midSpace) capabilities to the code of Section 12.5. Why would we be forced to make changes to Program VStringTester with our editor?

QUE 12.9.8   Why don't we need to change this section's VStringUnit or VStrProgram when we add name handling capabilities to the specs?

Things to Check in a Manual

MAN 12.9.1   If you don't use Turbo Pascal, find out if your implementation has anything corresponding to the notion of an object type. If the phrase *object type* isn't in your manual's index, you might want to look up the word *class*.

MAN 12.9.2   Does your implementation's manual say anything about something called *separate compilation?*

MAN 12.9.3   If you use Turbo Pascal, read your manual to find out about virtual methods.

MAN 12.9.4   If you use Turbo Pascal, read your manual to find out about the PRIVATE section of an object type definition.

MAN 12.9.5   Does your implementation's manual discuss *polymorphism* in connection with object-oriented programming?

Experiments to Try

EXP 12.9.1   Add a call to Procedure WriteVString from the main body of Program NamesPro.

Changes to Make

CHA 12.9.1   Write code to handle more complicated names than the ones that can be handled by our NamesUnit—names like F. Scott Fitzgerald, Lorette Ellane Petersen Archer Cheswick, Chris Van Wyk, Malcolm X, and Cher.

CHA 12.9.2   Rewrite the code in Section 12.4 to obtain an object-oriented version of Program Rationals.

CHA 12.9.3   Write an object-oriented version of Program Median1 (Section 10.2).

CHA 12.9.4   Write an object-oriented version of Program LinSearchDriver (Section 10.5).

CHA 12.9.5   Write an object-oriented version of Program BinSearchDriver (Section 10.6).

Programs and Subprograms to Write

WRI 12.9.1   Redo Exercise Wri.12.8.2 using the tools of this section.

Things to Think About

THI 12.9.1   Several times in this text we've emphasized that a type is a collection of values and a collection of operations on those values. Summarize whatever evidence you've collected from the text that supports this claim.

Chapter Summary

A record, like an array, is formed by combining values. But unlike an array, the values stored in a record might not all have the same type. Thus a record is used to combine dissimilar values that, by virtue of the problem being solved, are related to one another.

Each portion of a record is called a *field*. To refer to a particular field of record we follow the record name with a dot and then the field name. Another way of accomplishing the same thing is to put the statement containing the field name inside a WITH statement.

Although the various fields of a record need not have the same type, they can have the same type. A record in which all the fields are of the same type is called a *homogeneous record*. A homogeneous record is used when the various fields have the same type, but are still dissimilar in the kind of information they contain. We can do indexing on an array, but not on a record. Therefore, the use of a homogeneous record prevents us from easily choosing among various pieces of information. This is a safety device.

Many problems involve the nesting of records within records, arrays within records, records within arrays, etc. The syntax of an expression involving such a type can always be discovered by making a drawing, showing the types of larger and larger portions of the expression.

A *variant record* is a record that can be viewed in various ways, with various collections of fields, depending on the value of a special field called the *tag field*. Variant records give us a way of bypassing Pascal's strong typing mechanisms. For that reason, variant records should be used with an enormous amount of care.

In mathematics and in Pascal a *set* is a collection of things. In mathematics these "things" can be numbers, people, other sets, etc. In Pascal the "things" must be values in a particular ordinal type. This ordinal type is called the *base type* of the set. In Pascal we can perform many operations on sets, just as we can in mathematics. Here's a table showing Pascal's built-in operations on sets:

Name	Symbol	Meaning	
element of	IN	`(e IN x)`	means e is an element of x
intersection	*	`(e IN x*y)`	means `(e IN x) AND (e IN y)`
union	+	`(e IN x+y)`	means `(e IN x) OR (e IN y)`
difference	–	`(e IN x-y)`	means `(e IN x) AND NOT (e IN y)`
equality	=	`(x = y)`	means x and y have the same elements
inequality	<>	`(x <> y)`	means `NOT (x = y)`
subset of	<=	`(x <= y)`	means every element of x is an element of y
superset of	>=	`(x >= y)`	means every element of y is an element of x

An *object type* is very much like a record type, but in addition to its data fields, an object type contains *methods*. A method is like an ordinary subprogram except that a method is part of a particular type. The object type, with its data fields and methods, is said to *encapsulate* a particular class of data. Once we've created an object type we can extend it by creating another object type. The new object type inherits the old object type's data fields and methods. Thus a unit containing object type definitions is truly a *reusable* piece of software.

In this chapter we studied two kinds of structured types: records and sets. New programmers often avoid records and sets in favor of arrays and simple types. A person solving the `Raises` problem of Section 12.1 might settle for the first version, `Raises1`, instead of delving deeper to get the third and fourth versions.

In Section 11.4 we talked about putting information into the *data* rather than the *code*. When we combine several variables into a structured type, we're giving "shape" to the data. This "shape" makes it easier to understand the problem, because it helps us think about the big picture (the whole employeeRecordType) instead of the small details (a four-digit identification number, a REAL wage type, and a one-letter status type). We're also helping to create an abstract data type, which is a good thing to do.

In theory, we can take any program that uses records or sets and rewrite it so that it doesn't use these structured types. But even though records and sets don't add power to the Pascal language, they influence the way we think about a problem. This is important, because when we do elegant thinking we write elegant code.

More on Subprograms

13.1

Recursive Functions

"The first sentence in Section 13.1 of *Pascal by Example* is *false.*"

Self-reference is a very strange thing. Take, for instance, the first sentence of this section—the one in quotes. That sentence automatically contradicts itself. It can't be true, and it can't be false. Here's why:

- If the sentence were true, then it would truthfully claim its own falsehood. That can't be right.

- If the sentence were false, then it would be making a *false* claim about its own *falsehood*, which would make it true. That can't be right either!

Either way, true or false, there's something bizarre about the sentence.

Subprograms can also make reference to themselves. When they do, they're called **recursive**; and instead of being bizarre and contradictory, they're often very powerful and extremely elegant.

Specifications
Input: A number, called termNeeded.

Output: One term in the Fibonacci sequence (whichever value appears in the termNeededth position of the sequence).

These are almost the same as the specs for Program Fibonacci in Section 6.3; but instead of writing several terms, our new program writes just one term. We made this change because the new program won't be finding terms of the Fibonacci sequence in the same order as the old program (the first term, then the second, then the third, etc.). Even so, it will be interesting to compare the new program with the old program.

Designing a Program

Let's look again at Program Fibonacci in Section 6.3 and recall the definition of the Fibonacci sequence:

> The first two terms of the Fibonacci sequence are ones; thereafter, each term is the sum of the two previous terms.

Each term in the sequence (except the first and second) is defined in terms of the earlier terms; that is, the sequence is defined by making reference to its own terms. The situation is ripe for self-reference. This is illustrated in concrete terms in our new program Fibonacci2.

Program Example

```
PROGRAM Fibonacci2 (input, output);
{Finds a term in the Fibonacci sequence.}
   TYPE
      natural = 0..MAXINT;
   VAR
      termNeeded : natural;
   {----------}

   FUNCTION Fib (i : natural) : natural;
   {Recursively finds the i-th
    term in the Fibonacci sequence.}
   BEGIN {Fib}
      IF (i = 1) OR (i = 2) THEN
         Fib := 1
      ELSE
         Fib := Fib (i - 1) + Fib (i - 2)        {R}
   END;  {Fib}
   {----------}

BEGIN {Fibonacci2}
   WriteLn ('Which term in the');
   Write   ('Fibonacci sequence do you need? ');

   ReadLn  (termNeeded);

   WriteLn;
   WriteLn;
   Write   ('Term number ', termNeeded:2, ' is ');
   WriteLn (Fib(termNeeded) : 12)
END.   {Fibonacci2}
```

Sample Runs

```
Which term in the
Fibonacci sequence do you need? 1

Term number  1 is             1
```
_____

```
Which term in the
Fibonacci sequence do you need? 2

Term number  2 is             1
```
_____

```
Which term in the
Fibonacci sequence do you need? 3
Term number  3 is              2
```

```
Which term in the
Fibonacci sequence do you need? 4
Term number  4 is              3
```

```
Which term in the
Fibonacci sequence do you need? 5
Term number  5 is              5
```

```
Which term in the
Fibonacci sequence do you need? 6
Term number  6 is              8
```

```
Which term in the
Fibonacci sequence do you need? 23
Term number 23 is             28657
```

Observations

recursion

First notice how short Program Fibonacci2 is, compared to the original Program Fibonacci (Section 6.3). The original program uses iteration (looping), and this new program uses recursion. A **recursive program** (a program that contains a **recursive subprogram**) can be surprisingly brief.

- ```
  IF (i = 1) OR (i = 2) THEN
     Fib := 1
  ELSE
     Fib := Fib (i - 1) + Fib (i - 2)     {R}
  ```

going from a definition

This code is, with very little modification, a rewording of the definition of a Fibonacci sequence.

The first two terms of the Fibonacci sequence are
   ones;
thereafter, each term is
   the sum of the two previous terms.

- ```
  Fib := Fib (i - 1) + Fib (i - 2)     {R}
  ```

recursive function calls

This line is so important that we'll need to refer to it over and over again in our discussion of Program Fibonacci2. To make it easy to refer back to this line, we'll give it a name. We'll call it *line R*. (Of course the *R* stands for *recursive*.)

The name Fib appears three times on line R. The leftmost appearance isn't new or unusual. Inside a function, the function's name normally appears on the left side of at least one assignment statement. But on the right side of line R we have, within Function `Fib`, two calls to Function `Fib` itself. This is new and unusual.

For the sake of concreteness, let's assume that i has the value 5. Then if we read line R aloud, it seems to say

The value of `Fib (5)` is `Fib (5 - 1) + Fib (5 - 2)`.

which means that

The value of `Fib (5)` is `Fib ( 4 ) + Fib ( 3 )`.

Just as we stated in the definition of the Fibonacci sequence, the value of `Fib(5)` is the sum of the values of the two previous terms. We cannot overemphasize this point: *the code in a recursive function is often a very close rewording of a definition.* Line R mirrors the definition of a Fibonacci sequence, even to the point of containing a self-reference.

Definitions are nice, but does line R actually work? In terms of calls to subprograms, it seems to be saying

The result that should be returned by this call to `Fib` := The result returned by calling `Fib(4)` + The result returned by calling `Fib(3)`

When line R is executed, two new runs of Function `Fib` are created:

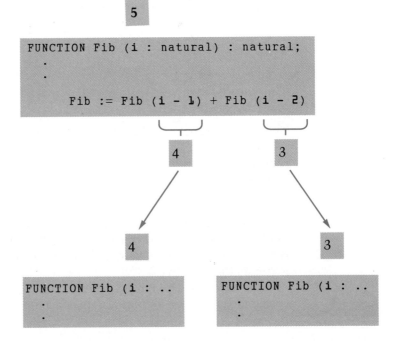

The formal parameter in each of these new runs is still called i, but in one of the runs, i has the value 4, and in the other run, i has the value 3.

The trick is to realize that these two new runs of Function Fib have line R's of their own. Each of these runs creates two more runs of Function Fib. Where does it all end? To see the whole picture, step by step, read the Traces subsection of this section.

Traces

We'll trace Program Fibonacci2 using two different graphic techniques—the conventional trace with subprograms in boxes and a tree-like trace. First the tree-trace:

tree trace of a recursive program

Let's assume that the ReadLn in the main body of the program gets the value 5 for termNeeded.

Fibonacci2
termNeeded = 5

When Function Fib is called from the main body of the program, the formal parameter i in Function Fib gets the value 5.

Fibonacci2
termNeeded = 5

|

Fib
i = 5

Inside this call to Function Fib, line R is executed. Since i is 5, i-1 is 4 and i-2 is 3. So line R creates two new calls to Function Fib. The formal parameter has the value 4 in one of these calls, and the value 3 in the other call.

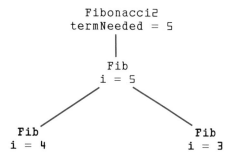

So in executing line R in the i=5 version of Function Fib, the computer has to call an i=4 version of Fib and an i=3 version of Fib. Of course, the i=5 version of Fib isn't finished yet. The i=4 version and the i=3 version have to complete their runs and return their result values before execution of line R in the i=5 version of Fib can be completed.

But the i=4 and i=3 versions of `Fib` have their own line R's:

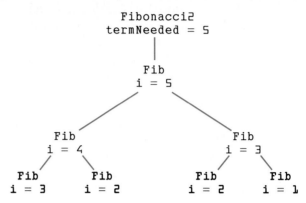

Now there are seven versions of Function `Fib`, all running at the same time! And it doesn't stop here. Our new i=3 version has a line R, which calls two more `Fib`s:

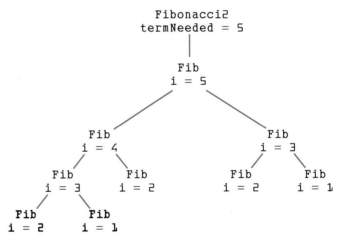

But now we've finally hit rock bottom.

```
IF (i = 1) OR (i = 2) THEN
   Fib := 1
      .
      .
```

In any version of `Fib` that has 1 or 2 for its value of i, line R isn't executed. Instead

```
Fib := 1
```

is executed, and the value 1 is returned. This happens in several of the `Fib`s that we've created.

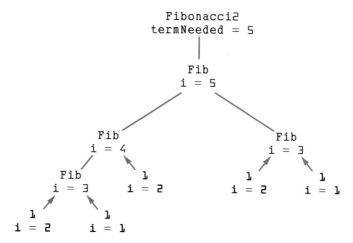

The line

    Fib := 1

is much simpler than line R, because it doesn't contain any self-reference. A "rock bottom" statement that's executed instead of a self-referencing statement is called the **base** of the recursion. It represents the final step, where we stop creating new runs of Function Fib, and start returning from the runs that we've created. Every recursive subprogram must have a base statement. Without a base, the creating of more and more versions of the subprogram would never end.

Now let's look at an i=3 version of Fib. Its line R called two other Fibs:

    Fib := Fib (2) + Fib (1)

which have both returned values of 1:

    Fib :=   1   +   1

So in an i=3 version, the function name Fib gets the value 2. This means that an i=3 version of Fib will return the value 2.

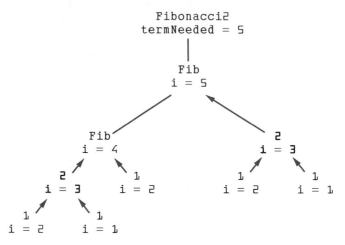

And what about an i=4 version of Fib? Its line R calls two other Fibs:

```
Fib := Fib ( 3 ) + Fib ( 2 )
```

which return values of 2 and 1:

```
Fib :=      2      +      1
```

So an i=4 version adds 2 and 1, gets 3, and assigns this result to the function name Fib. This means that an i=4 version of Fib returns the value 3.

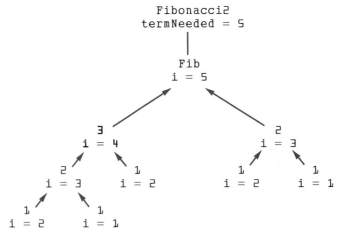

And finally the i=5 version adds 3 and 2, to get its result, 5:

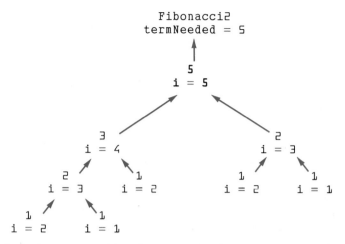

Thus the value returned by the original call to Function Fib, in the main body of Program Fibonacci2, is 5.

All this function calling for such a small program! Recursive function calling can make the computer do a lot of work with very few lines of code.

Now here's the conventional box-trace of Program Fibonacci2. As you might imagine, making a box-trace of this program means drawing boxes within boxes within boxes.

box trace of a recursive program

The main program calls an i=5 version of Fib, which in turn calls two more versions—an i=4 version and an i=3 version.

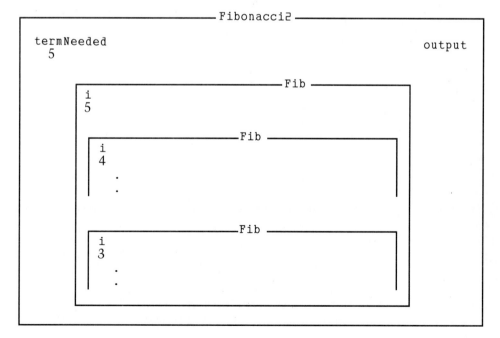

The i=4 version calls an i=3 version and an i=2 version

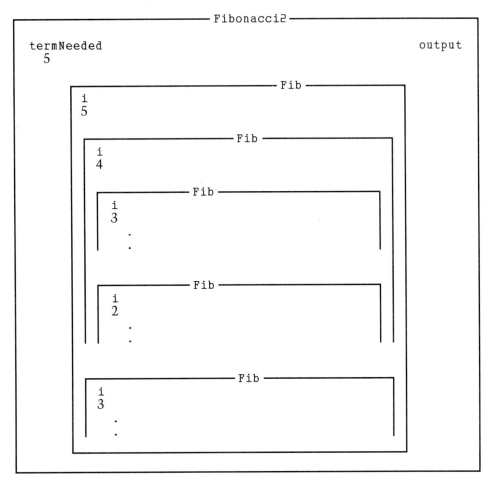

and so on. The complete trace is shown on page 695.

Structure

recursion and efficiency

Look again at the iterative Fibonacci program, in Section 6.3. It had a FOR loop that, during each iteration, calculated one new term in the Fibonacci sequence. So the running time for this program was proportional to termsNeeded—the number of terms that were being calculated. In other words, the running time of the iterative Fibonacci program was O(n). The program's space consumption was even more modest. No matter how many elements were to be calculated, Program Fibonacci used only five variables. The total amount of space required to run the iterative Program Fibonacci was O(1).

Now look at the tree-trace of the recursive Fibonacci2 program. Each version of Function Fib takes a certain fixed amount of time and space to

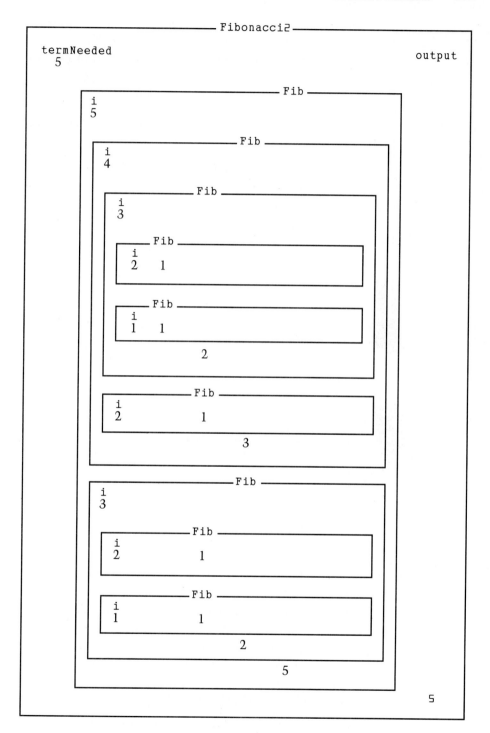

execute. So the number of Fibs on the tree is a fair measure of the program's overall time and space usage. Now here's a chart that shows, among other things, how the number of Fibs on the tree grows as termNeeded becomes larger and larger:

n	Iterative program time	Iterative program space	Recursive program (time and space)
↓	↓	↓	↓
termsNeeded or termNeeded	Number of iterations:	Number of variables:	Number of calls to Function Fib on the tree:
1	1	4	1
2	2	4	1
3	3	4	3
4	4	4	5
5	5	4	9
6	6	4	15
7	7	4	25
.	.	.	.
.	.	.	.

We got the numbers in the *Recursive program* column by making several traces of Program Fibonacci2.

Now look at the numbers in the *Recursive program* column. The amount of time and space consumed by the recursive program grows by leaps and bounds as the value of termNeeded increases![1] This isn't even a time-versus-space trade-off. The iterative Fibonacci program is clearly better, in terms of both time and space.

Why, then, do we bother writing recursive programs? There are two reasons:

1. Since recursive programs are very much like definitions, they tend to be very elegant.

2. Some recursive programs are as efficient, and even more efficient, than their iterative counterparts.

Recursive programs can, in fact, be quite efficient and extremely elegant. But often they're difficult to write because it's hard to "think recursively." That's why we'll do several more examples of recursive programs in the sections to come.

---

[1]With some hard work it's possible to show that the number of calls to Fib grows exponentially with termNeeded.

13.1   Exercises

Key Words to Review

recursive   recursive program
recursive subprogram   base of recursion

Questions to Answer

QUE 13.1.1   Critique the following definitions:

A programmer is a person who writes programs.

A program is something that's written by a programmer.

QUE 13.1.2   Explain how the body of Function `Fib` is a rewording of the definition of the Fibonacci sequence.

QUE 13.1.3   Read Exercise Man.3.3.1 on inline subprogram calling. Can a recursive function be called inline? Why, or why not?

Experiments to Try

EXP 13.1.1   In Function `Fib` change line R to

```
Fib := Fib + Fib      {R}
```

EXP 13.1.2   In Function `Fib` change line R to

```
Fib (i) := Fib (i - 1) + Fib (i - 2)     {R}
```

EXP 13.1.3   At the beginning of Function `Fib`'s body, add a statement that writes the value of `i`.

EXP 13.1.4   Further modify the code of Exercise Exp.13.1.3 so that `termNeeded` is of type `INTEGER` and gets a value of zero when the program begins running.

Changes to Make

CHA 13.1.1   Was it unfair to compare this section's Program `Fibonacci2` with Program `Fibonacci` of Section 6.3? After all, Program `Fibonacci` wrote all terms of the Fibonacci sequence, up to and including the `termsNeeded`th term. Program `Fibonacci2` writes only one term—the `termNeeded` term. Modify Program `Fibonacci` of Section 6.3 so that each time it runs it writes only the `termNeeded` term. Now how do the two programs compare in terms of running time and space?

CHA 13.1.2   What kinds of modifications would it take to make the recursive program `Fibonacci2` write all terms in the Fibonacci sequence, up to and including the `termNeeded`th term?

CHA 13.1.3   Modify this section's Function `Fib` so that it computes values in the variation on the Fibonacci sequence, as described in Exercise Cha.6.3.3.

Programs and Subprograms to Write

WRI 13.1.1 Review the meaning of the phrase "greatest common divisor" from Exercise Wri.9.5.6. Here's a recursive definition of the gcd of two numbers a and b (with a being the larger of the two):

> If b divides evenly into a then
>   the gcd of a and b is b
> otherwise
>   the gcd of a and b is the same as the gcd of a MOD b and b

Plug in a few numbers to make sure this definition is correct. Then use the definition to write a recursive program that finds the greatest common divisor of two numbers.

WRI 13.1.2 Redo Exercise Wri.6.2.6 using the formulas

$$P(n, r) = (n - r + 1) * P(n, r - 1)$$
$$P(n, 1) = n$$

Test your program by comparing its results with those of the program you wrote for Exercise Wri.6.2.6.

WRI 13.1.3 Redo Exercise Wri.6.2.7 using the formulas

$$C(n, r) = \frac{(n - r + 1)}{r} * C(n, r - 1)$$
$$C(n, 1) = n$$

Test your program by comparing its results with those of the program you wrote for Exercise Wri.6.2.7.

WRI 13.1.4 *(Another way to do Exercise Wri.13.1.3)* Look at Exercise Wri.6.5.4 and notice that

$$C(4, 1) = C(3, 0) + C(3, 1)$$

and

$$C(4, 2) = C(3, 1) + C(3, 2)$$

In general, if r isn't 0, and r isn't equal to n, then

$$C(n, r) = C(n - 1, r - 1) + C(n - 1, r)$$

Use this last formula to write a recursive program that computes the value of $C(n, r)$, for any two INTEGER values n and r.

13.2

Recursive Procedures

In Section 13.1 we looked at a program with a **recursive function**. In this section we'll see a program with a **recursive procedure**.

Specifications Program Reverse in Section 10.1 reads a few values, stores them in an array, and writes them to the screen in reverse order. If we use recursion, we can solve the same problem without an array.

Designing a Program

Our old Program Reverse stored values in an array. More specifically, it stored each value in a separate *array component*

x[1]   x[2]   x[3]

4.1   3.2   2.7

and then wrote the array components in reverse order.

Now let's say we have a recursive Procedure ReadAndWrite that has a local REAL variable r.

```
PROCEDURE ReadAndWrite (VAR fInput : TEXT);
   VAR
     r : REAL;
```

Since ReadAndWrite is recursive, it creates many versions of itself when it runs. Each of these versions has its own local variable r. So we can store each value that we read in a separate local variable r.

```
PROCEDURE ReadAndWrite (VAR fInput : TEXT);
   VAR
     r : REAL;
   4.1
```

calls

```
PROCEDURE ReadAndWrite (VAR fInput : TEXT);
   VAR
     r : REAL;
   3.2
```

calls

```
PROCEDURE ReadAndWrite (VAR fInput : TEXT);
   VAR
     r : REAL;
   2.7
```

When one version of a recursive subprogram is finished running, it returns control to the version that called it. This means that we return from the various versions of Procedure ReadAndWrite in reverse order.

```
PROCEDURE ReadAndWrite (VAR fInput : TEXT);
  VAR
    r : REAL;
   4.1
```

calls

returns to

```
PROCEDURE ReadAndWrite (VAR fInput : TEXT);
  VAR
    r : REAL;
   3.2
```

calls

returns to

```
PROCEDURE ReadAndWrite (VAR fInput : TEXT);
  VAR
    r : REAL;
   2.7
```

We can use this pattern to get the values written in reverse order.

**Program
Example**

```
PROGRAM RecReverse (input, output);
{Reads several real numbers and
 writes them in reverse order.}

  {--------}

  PROCEDURE ReadAndWrite (VAR fInput : TEXT);
  {Reads a real value and, after calling
   itself recursively, writes the real value.}

    VAR
      r : REAL;

  BEGIN {ReadAndWrite}
    IF NOT Eof (fInput) THEN
      BEGIN
        ReadLn         (fInput, r);
        ReadAndWrite (fInput);
        Write          (r:5:2)
      END
  END;   {ReadAndWrite}

  {--------}

BEGIN {RecReverse}
  WriteLn ('Enter several real values, one to a line:');
  ReadAndWrite (input);
  WriteLn
END.   {RecReverse}
```

**Sample
Runs**

```
Enter several real values, one to a line:
4.1
3.2
2.7
<end-of-file indicator>
2.70 3.20 4.10
```

Observations

calling a
recursive
procedure

• ReadAndWrite (input)

The syntax for a recursive procedure call is simple. We don't have to
worry about names appearing on different sides of an := sign. Whenever
the name of a procedure appears inside the procedure's own body, that
name represents a recursive call; that is, it's a statement in which the
procedure is calling a new version of itself.

Traces

postponement

Here's a good way to understand how Procedure ReadAndWrite works:
Without recursion, the body of ReadAndWrite might look something
like this:

```
Do the following several times:
    ReadLn (fInput, r);
    Write  (r:5:2)
```

It would read a number, then write the number, then read another number,
etc. Of course, the values wouldn't be written in reverse order—they'd be
written in the same order in which they're read.
Now instead of looping, we put a recursive call in the code

```
ReadLn         (fInput, r);
ReadAndWrite (fInput);
Write          (r:5:2)
```

and we make sure to put it before the Write. The effect of this is to
postpone the writing of a number until after the other versions of
ReadAndWrite have been run and the latter numbers have been written.

```
ReadLn (fInput, r);
Read and write the numbers that get typed in after r, and then finally
Write  (r:5:2)
```

Postponement is a frequently used trick in recursive subprograms. You
can see postponement when you look at a trace of Program RecReverse:

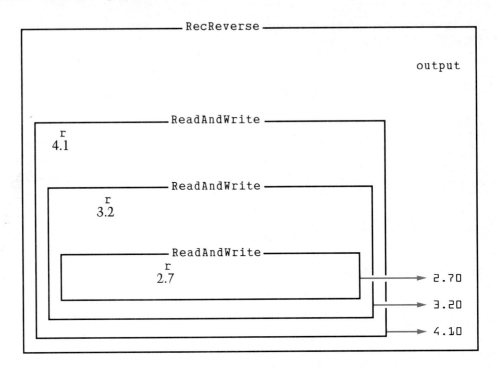

13.2   Exercises

Key Words to Review

recursive function   recursive procedure   postponement

Questions to Answer

QUE 13.2.1   Explain the way(s) in which recursive procedures are different from recursive functions.

QUE 13.2.2   In what sense does Program RecReverse postpone the writing of a number?

QUE 13.2.3   Compare this section's Program RecReverse with the iterative Program Reverse of Section 10.1. How do they compare in terms of time and space usage?

Experiments to Try

EXP 13.2.1   In Procedure ReadAndWrite move the ReadLn so that it comes after the recursive call to ReadAndWrite.

EXP 13.2.2   In Procedure ReadAndWrite move the WriteLn so that it comes before the recursive call to ReadAndWrite.

EXP 13.2.3   Add the statement

```
WriteLn ('The same values in reverse are:');
```

to Program `RecReverse`. Here are three different places to try adding it:

a. in the main program, before the call to Procedure `ReadAndWrite`
b. in Procedure `ReadAndWrite`, before the `IF` statement
c. in Procedure `ReadAndWrite`, anywhere inside the `IF` statement

EXP 13.2.4 Can a program call itself?

Changes to Make

CHA 13.2.1 Modify Program `RecReverse` so that it reverses a line of `CHAR`acters. It stops when it reaches the end-of-line indicator in the `fInput` file.

CHA 13.2.2 Modify the program you wrote for Exercise Cha.13.2.1 so that it works for more than one line of input; that is, it reads a line of input, prints it out in reverse order, then reads another line of input, prints it out in reverse order, etc.

CHA 13.2.3 Modify the program of Exercise Cha.13.2.2 so that it prints some lines in their original order and prints others in reverse order.

Here's how it decides: Each line of input either has all its characters in alphabetical order or has all its characters in reverse alphabetical order. In either case, the program prints the line so that its characters are in alphabetical order.

Programs and Subprograms to Write

WRI 13.2.1 *(A continuation of Exercise Wri.6.4.2)* Write a program that reads a sequence of notes from a file and writes the *retrograde* sequence on the screen. In the retrograde sequence, the notes are played in reverse order. (Hey! Why isn't this exercise one of our Scales to Practice?)

13.3

Another Recursive Procedure

using postponement

In Section 13.2 we saw a bare-bones postponement program. All the program did was reverse the order in which values were printed. In this section we'll combine postponement with some arithmetic calculations to get a new program that converts numbers from decimal to binary.

Specifications The specifications are the same as those for Program `BinaryTest` in Section 9.3.

Designing a Program Let's say we start with `decimal` equal to 13, and several times we do

```
Write (decimal MOD 2 : 1);  ◄—— write the rightmost binary bit
decimal := decimal DIV 2    ◄—— chop off that rightmost bit
```

Then here's what happens:

What gets written:

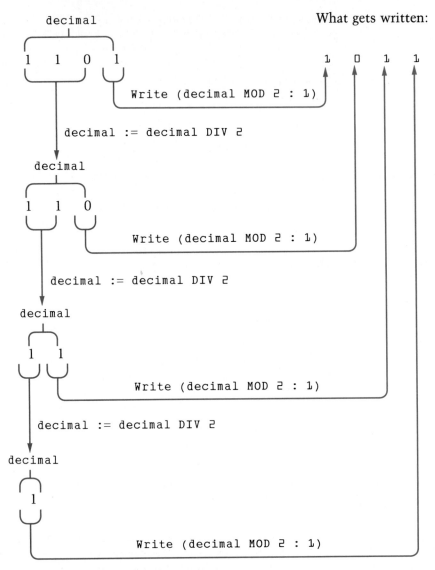

We write all the bits in the binary representation of 13, but we write them in the wrong order. The first one to be written is the rightmost, then the next-to-rightmost, etc. The output is 1011, when it should really be 1101.

So we need to reverse the order in which the Writes are executed. We can do this with recursive postponement. Instead of doing

```
Write (decimal MOD 2 : 1);    ◄──── write the rightmost binary bit
decimal := decimal DIV 2      ◄──── chop off that rightmost bit
```

we postpone writing the rightmost with a recursive procedure call.

```
WriteBin (decimal DIV 2);    ◄──── write the other bits first, and then
Write (decimal MOD 2 : 1)    ◄──── write the rightmost bit
```

With this code the rightmost bit doesn't get written until we've returned from the call to WriteBin. By that time, all the other bits have been written. We know that WriteBin writes all the "other" bits of the decimal value, because it receives decimal DIV 2 as its actual parameter. Passing decimal DIV 2 to WriteBin is like chopping off decimal's rightmost bit. It achieves much the same effect as the statement

```
decimal := decimal DIV 2
```

Here's a picture to show what happens:

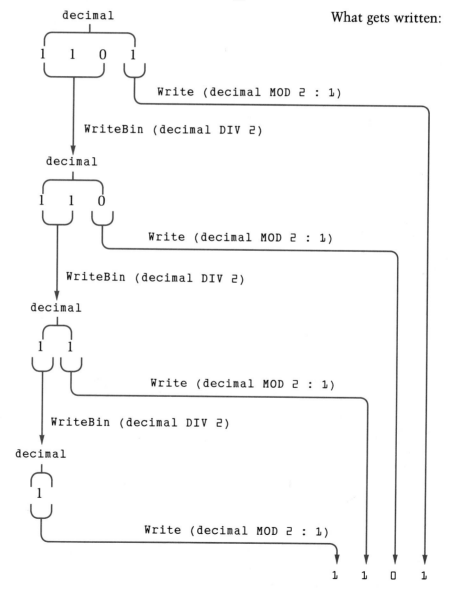

Look over the Traces subsection to see another picture of the same action.

Program Example

```
PROGRAM BinaryTest2 (input, output);
{Test driver for Procedure WriteBin.}
   TYPE
     natural = 0..MAXINT;
   VAR
     decimal : natural;

   {----------}

   PROCEDURE WriteBin (decimal : natural);
   {Writes the binary equivalent of the 'decimal' number.}

   BEGIN {WriteBin}
     IF decimal > 1 THEN
       WriteBin (decimal DIV 2);
     Write (decimal MOD 2 : 1)
   END;   {WriteBin}

   {----------}

BEGIN {BinaryTest2}
   Write  ('Decimal number:      ');
   ReadLn (decimal);

   Write     ('Binary equivalent: ');
   WriteBin (decimal);
   WriteLn
END.   {BinaryTest2}
```

Sample Runs

```
Decimal number:    13
Binary equivalent: 1101
```

Observations Notice again how short Program BinaryTest2 is, compared with its iterative counterpart (Program BinaryTest in Section 9.3). The code for a recursive procedure can be very brief when compared with the code for an iterative procedure.

In Designing a Program we used the notion of postponement to design Procedure WriteBin. But in Section 13.1 we emphasized that the code in a recursive subprogram is often a very close rewording of a definition. So *going from a definition* let's look at the definition of a number's binary representation:

We'll take the number 13. Its binary representation is 1101. We can view 1101 as having two parts:

This is the *binary* representation of 6; ⟶ 110 | 1 ◂─── This is 13 MOD 2
and 6 is 13 DIV 2

So we can write the binary representation of 13 by

- writing the binary representation of `13 DIV 2`, and then
- writing the value of `13 MOD 2`

We can turn this into pseudocode

```
How to WriteBin (13):
  First WriteBin (13 DIV 2)
  and then Write (13 MOD 2)
```

and then it's easy to translate the pseudocode into Pascal:

```
PROCEDURE WriteBin (decimal : natural);

BEGIN {WriteBin}
  WriteBin (decimal DIV 2);
  Write (decimal MOD 2)
END;   {WriteBin}
```

So we've managed to get a recursive subprogram from a definition. Of course, the definition that we used is hardly the most obvious definition of a binary number:

The binary representation of a number, called `decimal`, is the binary representation of `decimal DIV 2`, followed by the value of `decimal MOD 2`.

The only case we've failed to consider is the *base* case. When `decimal` is 0 or 1, we don't want to divide the problem into two parts—it's small enough already. Instead we can just `Write (decimal MOD 2)`.[2] So if `decimal` is 0 or 1, we'll skip the recursive call to `WriteBin`:

```
PROCEDURE WriteBin (decimal : natural);

BEGIN {WriteBin}
  IF decimal > 1 THEN
    WriteBin (decimal DIV 2);
  Write (decimal MOD 2)
END;   {WriteBin}
```

---

[2]In fact, it would be sufficient to just `Write (decimal)`, but this would make the code more complicated.

Traces

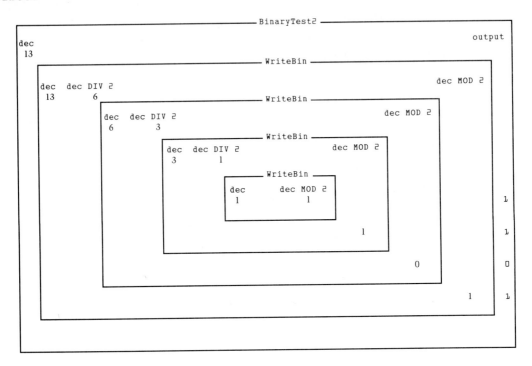

Structure

recursion and efficiency

Let's compare the time consumption of our two programs that convert from decimal to binary. In Section 9.3 we showed that the running time of the iterative procedure WriteBinary is O(n), where n is the number of bits that are written. What about the recursive procedure WriteBin that we developed in this section?

A run of Program BinaryTest2 makes several calls to Procedure WriteBin. Almost every time the procedure is called it performs exactly three steps:

```
IF decimal > 1 THEN          ◄——— compare decimal with 1
   WriteBin (decimal DIV 2); ◄——— call another WriteBin
   Write (decimal MOD 2 : 1) ◄——— write a bit
```

So the amount of time it takes to perform each of these calls is the same, no matter how many bits are eventually written. Now if we look at a trace of Program BinaryTest2 we see that there's a call to Procedure WriteBin for each bit that's written. Then the overall running time of Program BinaryTest2 is

the number of	$\star$	some fixed amount of time it takes for
bits written		each recursive call to Procedure WriteBin

Once again this is O(n), where n is the number of bits that are written. The recursive procedure WriteBin is just as efficient as its iterative counterpart.

What's more, in the iterative procedure WriteBinary, we chose to prompt the user for the number of bits to be used, instead of doing an extra calculation based on the size of the decimal number. (See Exercise Cha.9.3.7.) With the recursive procedure WriteBin we can avoid both of these clumsy devices. Procedure WriteBin simply reaches the base of recursion when the correct number of recursive calls have been made (that is, when decimal > 1 is no longer true). Procedure WriteBin is much more elegant than its iterative counterpart.

13.3   Exercises

Questions to Answer

QUE 13.3.1   Explain how the body of Procedure WriteBin is a rewording of one of the definitions of a number's binary representation.

QUE 13.3.2   In Section 13.1 we saw that the recursive Function Fib takes much more time to run than its iterative counterpart. Why isn't the recursive procedure WriteBin much less efficient than its iterative counterpart?

QUE 13.3.3   Why doesn't the recursive program BinaryTest2 need to prompt the user for the number of bits required in a number's binary representation?

Experiments to Try

EXP 13.3.1   Add a few WriteLns to Procedure WriteBin as follows:

```
WriteLn (decimal : 4);
IF decimal > 1 THEN
   WriteBin (decimal DIV 2);
Write (decimal MOD 2 : 1);
WriteLn;
WriteLn (decimal : 4)
```

Changes to Make

CHA 13.3.1   Redo Exercise Cha.9.3.3, using a recursive procedure.

CHA 13.3.2   Redo Exercise Cha.9.3.4, using a recursive procedure.

CHA 13.3.3   Write a recursive version of Function IntegerExp from Section 9.3.

Scales to Practice

PRA 13.3.1   We have a rectangular pattern of numbers stretching leftward and downward indefinitely:

1	1	1	1	1	1
1	2	3	4	5	6
1	3	6	10	15	21 ... *Etc.*
1	4	10	20	35	56
1	5	15	35	70	126

.
.
.

Etc.

The rectangle's top row and the leftmost column contain 1's. And every number "inside" the rectangle is the sum of the number above it and the number to its left. Write and test a recursive function that takes a point on this rectangle (a `row` and a `column`) and returns the number which appears at that point.

PRA 13.3.2   Redo Exercise Pra.13.3.1 but this time have a three-dimensional box that's composed of several rectangular planes. The box's first plane (the frontmost plane) contains 1's. The top row and the leftmost column of every other plane contains 1's also. And every number "inside" the box is the sum of three numbers: the number above it on the same plane, the number to its left on the same plane, and the number right next to it on the previous plane. Write and test a recursive function that takes a point in the box (a `plane`, a `row`, and a `column`) and returns the number which appears at that point.

Programs and Subprograms to Write

WRI 13.3.1   Look once again at the last array of numbers in Exercise Wri.6.5.4.

1				
1	1			
1	2	1		
1	3	3	1	
1	4	6	4	1

Here's a recursive way to describe the numbers in this array:

If a number appears in column 1, it's a 1.
If a number appears in row x and column x, it's a 1.
If a number appears in row r and column c, where r and c aren't the same, then it's the sum of two other numbers:
the number which appears in row r−1 and column c−1, and
the number which appears in row r−1 and column c.

Use this description to write a recursive program that takes the row and column of a component and writes the number stored in that particular component.

WRI 13.3.2   We have three awards (first-, second-, and third-place awards) to give out and three students (called Students 1, 2, and 3) who are deserving of awards. We want a list of all possible ways to give the awards to the three students. (first place to Student 1, second to Student 2, third to Student 3; or first place to Student 1, second to Student

3, third to Student 2, etc.). We do it with a recursive procedure called `FillArray` that repeatedly

fills the nth component of a `student` array with an award number, `num`, from an `awardSet`, and then either

writes the values in the array, if all three students have been given awards, or calls itself recursively, to fill the n–1st component of the array with award numbers from `awardSet` – `[num]`

WRI 13.3.3   *(This problem requires some understanding of the mathematical notion of a function.)* There's a mathematical formula known as *Ackermann's function* whose values are given by the following rules:

$A(0,y) = y + 1$ for any y (rule 1)
$A(x,0) = A(x - 1,1)$ if $x > 0$ (rule 2)
$A(x,y) = A(x - 1, A(x,y - 1))$ if $x > 0$ and $y > 0$ (rule 3)

Here are some examples to show how these rules are applied:

$A(0,1) = 1 + 1$ by rule 1
$\quad\quad = 2$
$A(1,0) = A(0,1)$ by rule 2
$\quad\quad = 2$
$A(2,0) = A(1,1)$ by rule 2
$\quad\quad = A(0, A(1,0))$ by rule 3
$\quad\quad = A(0, 2)$
$\quad\quad = 2 + 1$ by rule 1
$\quad\quad = 3$

Write a recursive program that reads two non-negative integers, x and y, and writes the value of $A(x,y)$. Test the program with the following values for x and y:

x	y	A(x,y)
0	1	2
1	0	2
2	0	3
2	1	5
3	1	?

Beware! Testing Ackermann's function can take an enormous amount of time, even for some very small values of x and y. For instance A(4,2) takes much more than 20 billion years to compute, and our universe is less than 20 billion years old.

13.4

Recursion vs. Iteration

Recall, from Chapters 1 and 2, that every algorithm can be implemented using only decision making and looping. Where, then, does recursion fit in? It turns out that recursion is an alternative to looping. We can turn any iterative algorithm into a recursive algorithm and vice versa. Of course, there are some problems that naturally seem to call for recursion and others that have the "feel" of iteration about them.

In this section we'll explore the iteration/recursion connection by writing two programs to solve the same simple problem. One program will be iterative, and the other will be recursive.

Specifications

Input: Two numbers, start and stop

Output: The sum of the numbers from start to stop

Designing a Program

The iterative code is easy to write.

```
sum := 0;
FOR i := start TO stop DO
    sum := sum + i
```

Of course, if we have the iterative code, we can look at some rules for translating iterative code into recursive code, but it's better to *understand concepts* than to memorize rules. So once again let's try to think recursively.

going from a definition

We want to compute the sum of the numbers from 1 to 5. We'll divide the computation into two parts:

> The *sum* of the numbers from 1 to 5 is:
> the *sum* of the numbers from 1 to 4,
> plus
> the number 5.

Here's a picture:

To get the *sum* of the numbers from 1 to 5:

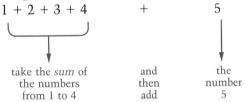

Now notice that our instructions for finding the sum of the numbers 1 to 5 involve finding the sum of the numbers 1 to 4. This self-reference is what recursion is all about. To find the sum of the numbers from 1 to 4, we'll again break the problem into two parts:

To get the *sum* of the numbers from 1 to 4:

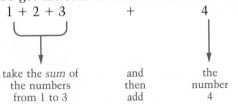

In each of these pictures we're doing the same thing:

To get the *sum* of the numbers from `start` to `stop`:

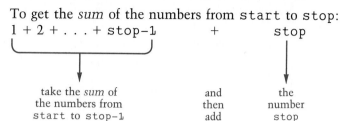

$$1 + 2 + \ldots + \texttt{stop-1} \qquad + \qquad \texttt{stop}$$

take the *sum* of   and   the
the numbers from   then   number
`start` to `stop-1`   add   `stop`

Now we can turn the words in the diagram into pseudocode:

The *sum* equals
    the *sum* of the numbers from `start` to `stop-1`
      +
   `stop`

and then turn this pseudocode into Pascal code:

```
RecurSum := RecurSum (start, stop-1) + stop
```

And what about the base case? If we keep subtracting 1 from `stop`, then eventually `stop` will become smaller than `start`, at which point there are no numbers to sum up between `start` and `stop`. At that point we just do

```
RecurSum := 0
```

Putting everything together, we get

```
IF start > stop THEN
  RecurSum := 0
ELSE
  RecurSum := RecurSum (start, stop-1) + stop
```

The complete program follows.

Program
Example

```
PROGRAM Iterative (input, output);
{Reads two numbers, 'start' and 'stop', and writes
 the sum of the numbers from 'start' to 'stop'.}
  VAR
    start, stop : INTEGER;
  {----------}
  FUNCTION IterSum (start, stop : INTEGER) : INTEGER;
  {Finds the sum of the numbers from 'start' to 'stop'.}
    VAR
      i, sum : INTEGER;
  BEGIN {IterSum}
    sum := 0;
    FOR i := start TO stop DO
      sum := sum + i;
    IterSum := sum
  END;  {IterSum}
  {----------}
```

```
BEGIN {Iterative}
  Write   ('Enter start and stop: ');
  ReadLn  (start, stop);

  WriteLn;
  WriteLn;
  Write   ('The sum of the numbers from ' );
  Write   (start:2, ' to ', stop:2, ' is ');
  WriteLn (IterSum (start, stop) : 4)
END.  {Iterative}
```

```
PROGRAM Recursive (input, output);
{Reads two numbers, 'start' and 'stop', and writes
 the sum of the numbers from 'start' to 'stop'.}

  VAR
    start, stop : INTEGER;

  {----------}

  FUNCTION RecurSum (start, stop : INTEGER) : INTEGER;
  {Finds the sum of the numbers from 'start' to 'stop'.}

  BEGIN {RecurSum}
    IF start > stop THEN
      RecurSum := 0
    ELSE
      RecurSum := RecurSum (start, stop-1) + stop
  END;  {RecurSum}

  {----------}

BEGIN {Recursive}
  Write   ('Enter start and stop: ');
  ReadLn  (start, stop);

  WriteLn;
  WriteLn;
  Write   ('The sum of the numbers from ' );
  Write   (start:2, ' to ', stop:2, ' is ');
  WriteLn (RecurSum (start, stop) : 4)
END.  {Recursive}
```

Sample Runs

If we give both programs the same input, their runs will be identical. Each of the following runs comes from both programs—Iterative and Recursive:

```
Enter start and stop: 1 5
The sum of the numbers from  1 to  5 is    15
_____

Enter start and stop: 5 5
The sum of the numbers from  5 to  5 is     5
_____

Enter start and stop: 3 6
The sum of the numbers from  3 to  6 is    18
_____
```

```
Enter start and stop: 6 3
The sum of the numbers from  6 to  3 is    0
```

Observations

*comparing
iteration and
recursion*

We have two programs that solve the same problem. So let's take each program apart, piece by piece. Then we can try to match up the pieces. We'll see what part of the recursive program corresponds to what part of the iterative program.

So let's begin with the iterative program. Function `IterSum` has

1. an assignment statement, which gives `sum` its initial value
2. a loop, with
   a. a counter, `i`
   b. an accumulator, `sum`

And what about Function `RecurSum`? It has different building blocks.

1. Function `RecurSum` doesn't have a `sum` variable so it doesn't give any `sum` variable an initial value. But the statement

   ```
   RecurSum := 0
   ```

   serves a similar purpose. Since `RecurSum` is a recursive function, it's helpful to think of 0 as a **base value** rather than an initial value. After all, this assignment statement doesn't get executed at the beginning of a loop; it gets executed at the base of the recursion, when `RecurSum` has called itself so many times that `stop` has become smaller than `start`.

2. Function `RecurSum` has no explicit loop, but `RecurSum`'s calling itself creates a kind of repetition that plays the role of a loop as seen in the diagram at the top of page 716.

   a. Function `RecurSum` has no counter, but notice how the name `stop` is used to "count down" from 5 to 0. The value of `stop` is 1 less each time `RecurSum` is called anew, and it's 1 more again each time we return from a call to `RecurSum`. This is a commonly used trick in recursive programs. Remember it, so you can use it when you need it.

   b. In Function `RecurSum`, the role of the accumulator is taken on by the function name itself in the statement

      ```
      RecurSum := RecurSum (start, stop-1) + stop
      ```

      In fact this statement looks very much like its counterpart in Function `IterSum`

      ```
      sum := sum + i
      ```

      The only difference is that `RecurSum` is the name of a function, so on the right side of the assignment, `RecurSum` has parameters.

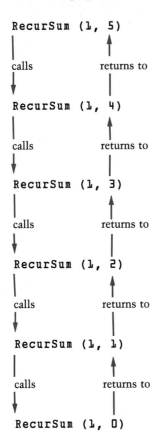

Recursive "repetition" that plays the role of a loop

13.4 Exercises

Key Words to Review

base value

Questions to Answer

QUE 13.4.1 In what sense is recursion an "alternative to looping"?

QUE 13.4.2 Write a trace of this section's Program Recursive.

QUE 13.4.3 In this section's Observations we compared an Iterative program with its Recursive counterpart, piece by piece. Do the same analysis with Programs Fibonacci and Fibonacci2, from Sections 6.3 and 13.1.

Experiments to Try

EXP 13.4.1 Add the statement

        WriteLn (start, stop)

to the body of Function RecurSum. This helps you see how the function is being called.

EXP 13.4.2   Redo Exercise Exp.13.4.1, this time with

```
IF start = stop THEN
   RecurSum := start
ELSE
   RecurSum := RecurSum (start, stop-1) + stop
```

in the body of Function RecurSum. Redo each of this section's Sample Runs with the new code. Note: Running the revised program with 6 for start and 3 for stop will cause an infinite loop, so be prepared to abort your program, as in Exercise Man.6.1.1.

EXP 13.4.3   Redo Exercise Exp.13.4.2, but replace IF start = stop with IF start >= stop.

Changes to Make

CHA 13.4.1   Modify Function RecurSum so that the value of start increases by 1 for each new call (instead of having the value of stop decrease by 1 with each call).

CHA 13.4.2   Rewrite Program FindAverage, Section 6.1, so that it uses recursion instead of iteration.

CHA 13.4.3   Write and test a recursive function that accepts a non-negative integer n and returns the value of *n factorial*. (See Section 6.2.)

CHA 13.4.4   Rewrite Program Proof1 (from Exercise Que.5.4.5) so that it uses recursion instead of iteration.

CHA 13.4.5   Rewrite Program Proof2 (from Exercise Que.5.4.6) so that it uses recursion instead of iteration.

CHA 13.4.6   In Procedure WriteBinary (Section 9.3) the user is prompted for the number of bits used in a particular binary representation. But Procedure WriteBin (Section 13.3) figures the number of bits on its own. Modify the recursive procedure WriteBin so that it prompts the user for a number of bits. Thus, if the user asks for 6 bits in the representation of 13, the program writes

```
Binary equivalent: 001101
```

Programs and Subprograms to Write

WRI 13.4.1   Redo Exercise Wri.10.4.7 using recursion instead of iteration. When the program begins running, the first thing it does is prompt the user for the exact number of characters in the proposed palindrome. Then it reads this number of characters and reports its decision (palindrome or no palindrome).

WRI 13.4.2   In Section 9.4 we wrote an iterative program to display the left side of a truth table with nBoolVars-many BOOLEAN variables. Now we can do it with a recursive procedure called FillArray which

fills the nth component of an array with a BOOLEAN value, and then either writes the values in the array, if all the values from the first to the

nBoolVars component have been filled, or
recursively calls itself twice:

once to fill the n−1st component of the array with TRUE, and
once to fill the n−1st component of the array with FALSE

WRI 13.4.3   Review the definition of the determinant of a two-by-two matrix, given in Exercise Wri.11.1.1. Here's a way of finding a determinant that works for any "square" matrix (any *n*-by-*n* array):

The determinant of a one-by-one matrix is just the value contained in the matrix:

determinant of [3] is 3

To find the determinant of an *n*-by-*n* matrix, multiply each value in the first row by the *determinant* of the matrix you get by eliminating the first row and the column containing that value:

$$\text{determinant of } \begin{bmatrix} 1 & 3 \\ 5 & 4 \end{bmatrix} \text{ is } 1 * \text{ determinant of } \begin{bmatrix} 1 & 3 \\ 5 & 4 \end{bmatrix} - 3 * \text{ determinant of } \begin{bmatrix} 1 & 3 \\ 5 & 4 \end{bmatrix}$$

which equals $1 * 4$ $- 3 * 5$

which is $4 - 15 = -11$.

Compare this with the result we obtained in Exercise Wri.11.1.1. Notice here how we *add* the first term and then *subtract* the second term in order to compute the determinant. The same alternation of signs is used to find the determinant of a three-by-three matrix:

$$\text{determinant of } \begin{bmatrix} 1 & 3 & 6 \\ 5 & 4 & 8 \\ 2 & 7 & 9 \end{bmatrix} \text{ is}$$

$$+ 1 * \begin{matrix} \det \\ \text{of} \end{matrix} \begin{bmatrix} 1 & 3 & 6 \\ 5 & 4 & 8 \\ 2 & 7 & 9 \end{bmatrix} - 3 * \begin{matrix} \det \\ \text{of} \end{matrix} \begin{bmatrix} 1 & 3 & 6 \\ 5 & 4 & 8 \\ 2 & 7 & 9 \end{bmatrix} + 6 * \begin{matrix} \det \\ \text{of} \end{matrix} \begin{bmatrix} 1 & 3 & 6 \\ 5 & 4 & 8 \\ 2 & 7 & 9 \end{bmatrix}$$

which equals

$$+ 1 * \begin{matrix} \det \\ \text{of} \end{matrix} \begin{bmatrix} 4 & 8 \\ 7 & 9 \end{bmatrix} \quad - 3 * \begin{matrix} \det \\ \text{of} \end{matrix} \begin{bmatrix} 5 & 8 \\ 2 & 9 \end{bmatrix} \quad + 6 * \begin{matrix} \det \\ \text{of} \end{matrix} \begin{bmatrix} 5 & 4 \\ 2 & 7 \end{bmatrix}$$

Etc. (The final answer is 55.)

Write a program that reads the values of a matrix and computes the determinant of the matrix using this recursive method.

Things to Think About

THI 13.4.1   Is is true that *every* iterative program can be turned into a recursive program? Explain.

13.5

Recursive Binary Search

Recall the binary search from Section 10.6. Here's another way to think about binary searching:

How to *look for* a value in the array a:

If the value is smaller than whatever's stored in the middle component of a, then
   look for the value in the lower half of a
otherwise
   look for the value in the upper half of a.

Notice the use of self-reference—we describe how to *look for* a value in an array by saying we should *look for* the value in a part of the array. Here's what the pseudocode looks like when it's translated into Pascal:

```
PROCEDURE BinarySearch (from lo to hi);
    .
    .
BEGIN {BinarySearch}
    .
    .
  IF searchFor < a[middle] THEN
     hi := middle - 1
  ELSE
     lo := middle + 1;
  BinarySearch (from the new lo to the new hi)
END;  {BinarySearch}
```

It's very natural to think of the binary search as a recursive algorithm, and so in this section we present a recursive version of the binary search.

Program Example

```
PROGRAM BinSearchDriver (fInput, input, output);
{Test driver for Procedure BinarySearch.}
  CONST
    loConst = 1;
    hiConst = 16;
  TYPE
    anyType   = INTEGER;
    indexType = loConst..hiConst;
    arrayType = ARRAY [indexType] OF anyType;
  VAR
    a                 : arrayType;
    i, whereFound : indexType;
    searchFor     : anyType;
    fInput        : TEXT;
  {----------}
```

```
PROCEDURE BinarySearch (a           : arrayType ;
                        lo, hi      : indexType ;
                        searchFor   : anyType   ;
                        VAR middle  : indexType);
{Implements the binary search algorithm.}
BEGIN {BinarySearch}
  middle := (hi + lo) DIV 2;
  IF (a[middle] <> searchFor) AND (hi > lo) THEN      {**}
    BEGIN
      IF searchFor < a[middle] THEN
        hi := middle - 1
      ELSE
        lo := middle + 1;
      BinarySearch (a, lo, hi, searchFor, middle)     {**}
    END
END;   {BinarySearch}

{----------}

BEGIN {BinSearchDriver}
  Reset (fInput);
  FOR i := loConst TO hiConst DO
    ReadLn (fInput, a[i]);

  Write  ('Value to be searched for: ');
  ReadLn (searchFor);

  BinarySearch (a, loConst, hiConst, searchFor, whereFound);

  IF a[whereFound] = searchFor THEN
    WriteLn ('Found in position ', whereFound:2)
  ELSE
    WriteLn ('Not found')
END.   {BinSearchDriver}
```

Observations   To go from the iterative to the recursive version, we change only two lines! They're marked with {**} comments. An IF statement in this recursive program replaces a WHILE statement in the iterative program. A recursive call to BinarySearch replaces an assignment statement in the iterative version.

In this example, the last thing Procedure BinarySearch does is to call itself, and that's how something resembling looping is achieved. This is a
tail recursion   commonly used technique, called **tail recursion**. The word *tail* refers to the fact that calling itself is the last thing the procedure does.

13.5   Exercises

Key Words to Review

tail recursion

Questions to Answer

QUE 13.5.1   Write traces for both versions of Procedure `BinarySearch`—the iterative version in Section 10.6 and the recursive version in this section. How are the traces similar? In what ways are they different?

QUE 13.5.2   To go from the iterative to the recursive `BinarySearch` procedure, we changed only two lines of code. Explain why we made each of these changes. Why were no other changes necessary?

QUE 13.5.3   Check the program examples in previous sections of this chapter to see if we used tail recursion without mentioning it explicitly.

Experiments to Try

EXP 13.5.1   Change

```
IF (a[middle] <> searchFor) AND (hi > lo) THEN    {**}
```

back to the WHILE statement we had in our iterative version of Procedure `BinarySearch` (Section 10.6).

Changes to Make

CHA 13.5.1   Rewrite Program `Minimum` from Section 5.4 so that it uses recursion instead of iteration.

CHA 13.5.2   Rewrite Program `Points` from Section 5.3 so that it uses only recursion, no iteration.

CHA 13.5.3   Rewrite Program `Copy` from Section 5.1 so that it uses only recursion, no iteration.

CHA 13.5.4   Rewrite Program `MultiplicationTable` from Section 6.4 so that it uses only recursion, no iteration.

CHA 13.5.5   Rewrite Procedure `LinearSearch` from Section 10.5 so that it uses only recursion, no iteration.

Things to Think About

THI 13.5.1   Is it true that every recursive program can be turned into an iterative program? Explain.

13.6

Evaluating Prefix Expressions

When you write an arithmetic expression to add two numbers, there are only three places you can put the plus sign:

- in the middle:

  2 + 3

- before the numbers:

  $+$ ᒋ ∃

- after the numbers:

  ᒋ ∃ $+$

Until now, you may have seen only the ᒋ $+$ ∃ version. When you do it this way you're using **infix** notation. Infix notation is the one that's most commonly used; but in some ways, it's the worst. If you use **prefix** notation (putting the operator before the numbers) or **postfix** notation (putting the operator after the numbers), then—no matter how complicated an expression is—you never need to use parentheses. Here's a table, showing several infix expressions and their corresponding prefix and postfix forms:

Prefix	Infix	Postfix	Value
$-$ 10 1	10 $-$ 1	10 1 $-$	9
$*$ 6 5	6 $*$ 5	6 5 $*$	30
$+$ 9 $-$ 3 2	9 $+$ (3 $-$ 2)	9 3 2 $-$ $+$	10
$+$ $-$ 9 3 2	(9 $-$ 3) $+$ 2	9 3 $-$ 2 $+$	8
$*$ $-$ 1 2 $-$ 3 4	(1 $-$ 2) $*$ (3 $-$ 4)	1 2 $-$ 3 4 $-$ $*$	1

Notice that no parentheses are needed in any of the prefix or postfix expressions.

Specifications

Input: A prefix expression, containing natural numbers (integers without signs) and operators ($+$, $-$, $*$, and $/$). Each item in the expression (a number or a sign) is separated from its neighbors by at least one blank space. The symbols $+$, $-$, and $*$ have their usual meanings. The symbol $/$ stands for INTEGER division (DIV).

Output: The value of the prefix expression.

Designing a Program

How do we interpret a prefix expression to get a numeric result? We read from left to right. Whenever we see an operator, we apply it to the next two numbers. We just have to be careful when we say *the next two numbers*. Let's look at the prefix expression $+$ $-$ 9 ∃ ᒋ:

When we see the plus sign, we start looking for two numbers:

We keep reading and we see the minus sign. So we *postpone* looking for the plus sign's numbers. We put the plus sign on the back burner, and we look for two numbers following the minus sign:

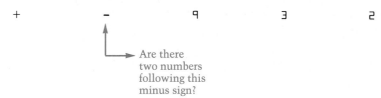

Are there
two numbers
following this
minus sign?

After the minus sign we find 9 and 3.

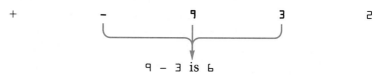

9 − 3 is 6

Now we can take the plus sign off the back burner, because it's followed by the two numbers, 6 and 2. As it happens, the 6 comes from having applied the minus sign:

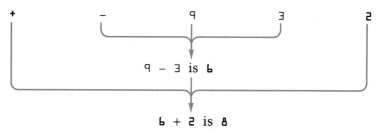

9 − 3 is 6

6 + 2 is 8

The same thing happens when we evaluate + 9 − 3 2. The plus sign gets put on the back burner while the minus sign looks for two numbers:

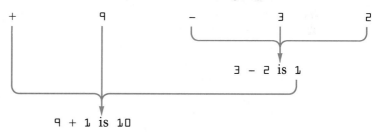

3 − 2 is 1

9 + 1 is 10

Now here's some pseudocode:

How to *get a value:*
Read an item (a number or an operator).
If the item is an operator character then
   get two more values, and
   apply the operator to those values.

The fact that we *get a value* by *getting two more values* tells us that this pseudocode describes a recursive subprogram.

Program
Example

```
PROGRAM Prefix (input, output);
{Evaluates a prefix expression.}
  TYPE
    kindType = (character, natral);
    natural  = 0..MAXINT;

  {----------}

  PROCEDURE ReadCharOrNat (VAR c    : CHAR;
                           VAR n    : natural;
                           VAR kind : kindType);
  {Reads a value for c OR for n.
   Sets kind to
     character    if a value of c is read;
     natral       if a value of n is read.}

    VAR
      x : CHAR;

    {----------}

    FUNCTION IsDigit (x : CHAR) : BOOLEAN;
    {Answers the question "Is x one of the
     digit characters '0' to '9'?"}
    BEGIN {IsDigit}
      IsDigit := ('0' <= x) AND (x <= '9')
    END;  {IsDigit}

    {----------}

  PROCEDURE ReadRestNat (x : CHAR; VAR n : natural);
  {Completes the process of reading a natural number.}

    TYPE
      digitChar = '0'..'9';
      digitNum  = 0 .. 9 ;

    {----------}

    FUNCTION NumericEquiv (x : digitChar) : digitNum;
    {Taken from Section 7.4.
     Accepts a digit character;
     returns its numeric equivalent.}
    BEGIN {NumericEquiv}
      NumericEquiv := Ord(x) - Ord('0')
    END;  {NumericEquiv}

    {----------}

  BEGIN {ReadRestNat}
    n := NumericEquiv (x);
    Read (x);
    WHILE IsDigit (x) DO    {This loop has been reorganized.}
      BEGIN
        n := (10 * n) + NumericEquiv (x);
        Read (x)
      END
    {A ReadLn has been removed}
  END;   {ReadRestNat}
```

```
{----------}
  PROCEDURE ReadRestChar (x : CHAR; VAR c : CHAR);
  {Completes the process of reading a character.}
  BEGIN {ReadRestChar}
    c := x
    {A ReadLn has been removed}
  END;  {ReadRestChar}

{----------}
BEGIN {ReadCharOrNat}
  REPEAT                      {.......................}
    Read (x)                  {Skip any leading blanks}
  UNTIL x <> ' ';             {.......................}

  IF IsDigit (x) THEN
    BEGIN
      kind := natral;
      ReadRestNat (x, n)
    END
  ELSE
    BEGIN
      kind := character;
      ReadRestChar (x, c)
    END
END;  {ReadCharOrNat}

{----------}
FUNCTION Value (VAR fInput : TEXT) : INTEGER;
{Obtains a value (recursively) from fInput.}

  VAR
    c            : CHAR;
    n            : natural;
    kind         : kindType;
    left, right  : INTEGER;
BEGIN {Value}
  ReadCharOrNat (c, n, kind);

  IF kind = character THEN
    BEGIN
      left  := Value (fInput);
      right := Value (fInput);
      CASE c OF
        '+' : Value := left + right;
        '-' : Value := left - right;
        '*' : Value := left * right;
        '/' : Value := left DIV right
      END
    END

  ELSE
    Value := n

END;  {Value}

{----------}
```

```
      BEGIN {Prefix}
        WriteLn ('Enter a prefix expression: '                       );
        WriteLn (Value(input) : 5, ' is the value of this expression')
      END.  {Prefix}
```

Sample Runs

```
        Enter a prefix expression:
        + - 9 3 2
                8 is the value of this expression
        _____

        Enter a prefix expression:
            +   9   -   3   2
           10 is the value of this expression
        _____

        Enter a prefix expression:
        9
                9 is the value of this expression
        _____

        Enter a prefix expression:
        9 9
                9 is the value of this expression
        _____

        Enter a prefix expression:
        - 100 101
              -1 is the value of this expression
```

Observations The most important part of Program Prefix is Function Value—the recursive subprogram that gets two values and combines them with an arithmetic operator. But the bulk of the code in Program Prefix is taken up by Procedure ReadCharOrNat, which bears a striking resemblance to our old Procedure ReadLnCharOrNat from Section 8.3. In fact, this ReadCharOrNat is copied quite faithfully from Section 8.3 with only a few modifications. The modifications are needed because we want to type a prefix expression, with its various CHARacters and natural numbers, all on one line. We don't want to do a ReadLn every time we get a character or a natural number from the keyboard. Instead, after reading one of these items, we want to get the next item *from the same line*.

It's not difficult to make this change. First we have to remove the ReadLns that finished off the two procedures ReadLnRestNat and ReadLnRestChar. Then, since it no longer makes sense to have

```
      WHILE NOT Eoln (input) DO
```

we need to change the loop in Procedure ReadRestNat:

```
n := NumericEquiv (x);
Read (x);
WHILE IsDigit (x) DO      {This loop has been reorganized.}
  BEGIN
    n := (10 * n) + NumericEquiv (x);
    Read (x)
  END
```

Instead of reading until we get to the end of a line, we're now reading until we reach a character that Isn't a Digit. In the specifications for Program Prefix we insisted that at least one blank space come after each item in the expression. That's good, because it means that this character which Isn't a Digit is just a harmless blank space. We can ignore it and go on to read more items.

This insistence on blank spaces is a bit artificial. After all, an expression containing items that aren't followed by blank spaces

```
+9-3 2
```

can be a meaningful prefix expression. The reason why we want blank spaces is because we can't do without them until we get to file windows in Section 15.2.

Of course if it's artificial to insist on blank spaces between items, the least we can do is to allow the user to enter any number of blank spaces (not just one) between items. That's why we make one more change to Procedure ReadCharOrNat.

```
REPEAT              {......................}
  Read (x)          {Skip any leading blanks}
UNTIL x <> ' '      {......................}
```

Procedure ReadCharOrNat skips over any leading blank spaces—spaces that come before the next natural number or the next operator.

13.6 Exercises

Key Words to Review

      infix   prefix   postfix

Questions to Answer

QUE 13.6.1   Find the value of each of the following prefix expressions:
a. + * 5 6 − 2 3
b. + − * 3 4 / 8 2 5
c. − 3 − 4 1

QUE 13.6.2   Turn each of the following prefix expressions into an equivalent infix expression:
a. / * / * 1 2 3 4 5
b. + 9 − − 3 5 8

QUE 13.6.3   Turn each of the following infix expressions into an equivalent prefix expression:
   a. (2 * 3) / (4 - 5)
   b. (6 + ((3/4) - (5/6))) * 9
   c. 8

QUE 13.6.4   Explain the output in each of this section's Sample runs.

Experiments to Try

EXP 13.6.1   Run Program Prefix with each of the following inputs:
   a. 9 + 5
   b. 9 3 2 - -
   c. + -
        9 3 2
   d. +
   e. % % 9 3 2

EXP 13.6.2   In an effort to reduce the size of Program Prefix (and the number of pages in this book!) we change the body of Procedure Value as follows:

```
ReadCharOrNat (c, n, kind);
IF kind = character THEN
   CASE c OF
     '+' : Value := Value (fInput) + Value (fInput);
     '-' : Value := Value (fInput) - Value (fInput);
     '*' : Value := Value (fInput) * Value (fInput);
     '/' : Value := Value (fInput) DIV Value (fInput)
   END
ELSE
   Value := n
```

Does this work?

Changes to Make

CHA 13.6.1   Modify Program Prefix so that it's robust enough to skip over characters that are neither digits nor operator symbols.

CHA 13.6.2   Modify Program Prefix so that it can read a prefix expression from a disk file.

Programs and Subprograms to Write

WRI 13.6.1   (The Towers of Hanoi—a solution using iteration) A puzzle consists of three pegs, labeled A, B, and C, and three rings, labeled 1, 2, and 3.

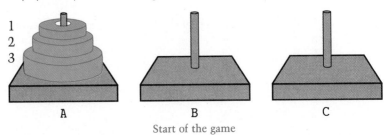

1
2
3

A   B   C

Start of the game

The ring numbers are meant to suggest sizes—with 1 being the smallest and 3 being the largest. The rings have to be placed on the pegs so that a small ring is never underneath a larger ring.

At first all three rings are on the A peg. The object of the puzzle is to move all three rings to another peg, by repeatedly taking the top ring of one peg and moving it onto another peg. For instance, with the game starting as shown, the only allowable moves are to move ring 1 to peg B or to move ring 1 to peg C.

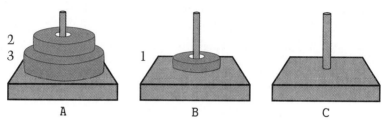

Player moves ring 1 to peg B

Notice how the "small ring never underneath a larger ring" rule constantly restricts the allowable moves. After moving ring 1 to peg B, the player can only move ring 1 again or move ring 2 to peg C.

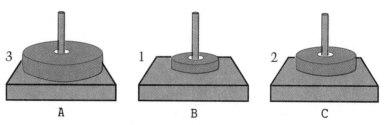

Player moves ring 2 to peg C

Write a program that "solves" the Towers of Hanoi puzzle. Your program should write the sequence of moves leading from having all rings on peg A to having all rings on peg B or all on peg C.

```
Move ring 1 to peg B.
Move ring 2 to peg C.
Etc.
```

Here's how your program will work: Think of the pegs as being arranged in a small circle

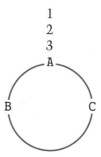

Then perform the following loop:

> As long as you haven't moved all the rings to a different peg do:
> Move ring 1 counterclockwise by one letter (one peg).
> Find the largest ring that can be moved and make any allowable move with it.

Before you try writing the program, trace the action of this algorithm on the puzzle as pictured, to make sure that the algorithm will work.

WRI 13.6.2   *(A continuation of Exercise Wri.13.6.1)* Here's a recursive algorithm to solve the Towers of Hanoi problem:

> Move *three* rings from peg A to peg B by
> moving *two* rings from peg A to peg C,
> moving ring 3 from peg A to peg B, and then
> moving the *two* rings from peg C to peg B.

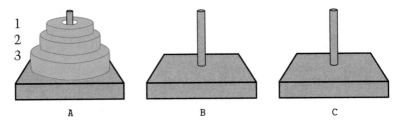

Start of the game

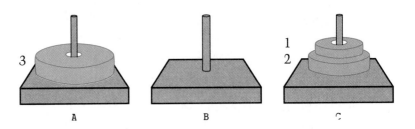

Moving *two* rings from peg A to peg C

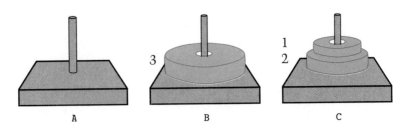

Moving ring 3 from peg A to peg B

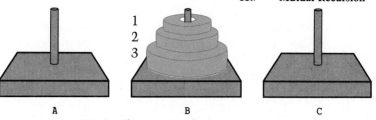

Moving the *two* rings from peg C to peg B

This algorithm is recursive, since moving *two* rings from peg `whatever` to peg `whatever-else` is really more than can be done in one allowable move and thus requires a call to the same algorithm:

Move *two* rings from peg A to peg C by
    moving *one* ring from peg A to peg B,
    moving ring 2 from peg A to peg C, and then
    moving the *one* ring from peg B to peg C.

Things to Think About

THI 13.6.1   In Section 13.4 we said that "there are some problems that naturally seem to call for recursion and others that have the 'feel' of iteration about them." Which category does this section's prefix expression problem fall into? What about the sum of numbers from the `start` to `stop` problem of Section 13.4? And what about the other problems in this chapter? Can you classify the kind of problem that "naturally seems to call for recursion"?

13.7

Mutual Recursion

So far in this chapter we've seen several subprograms that call themselves. What about a subprogram that calls itself indirectly? In this section we'll have a subprogram call another subprogram, which in turn calls the first subprogram again. This is called **mutual recursion**. Besides being an interesting tangle of subprogram calls, mutual recursion is a useful way to think about certain problems.

Specifications   Consider the following diagram:

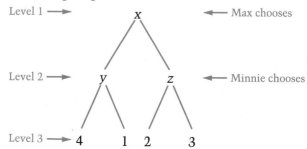

game trees

We can think of this as a **tree**. The tree grows upside down with the **root** at point x (at Level 1). As we scan downward, we see the tree fanning out until it gets to the **leaves** at the very bottom (Level 3).

We can also think of this as a drawing of a **game** for two players. (We'll call the players "Max" and "Minnie.") At the start of the game, the playing piece is at the root (point x). Max must move the playing piece to Level 2. In so doing, Max must decide to move the playing piece either to point y or to point z. Then Minnie must move the playing piece to a point on Level 3.

The outcome of the game is this: Whatever number the playing piece lands on at Level 3, Minnie must pay Max that many dollars. Clearly it's in Minnie's best interest to land on as small a number as possible. The question is, which way should Max move? To point y or to point z?

To help answer this question let's add two more assumptions: the assumptions that the game has perfect information and certainty. **Perfect information** means that a player always knows exactly where the playing piece is on the tree. **Certainty** means that each player has full knowledge of the possible moves along the tree and where they'll lead. Among other things, this means that if the playing piece is at point y, Minnie knows enough to move to the 1. So if Max moves from x to y, he'll get only \$1. On the other hand, if he moves to z, he'll get \$2.

In fact, using our assumptions, we can see exactly how this game will be played. At Level 2, Minnie will always go toward the *minimum* number. Knowing this, Max can predict what will happen if he moves to point y or to point z:

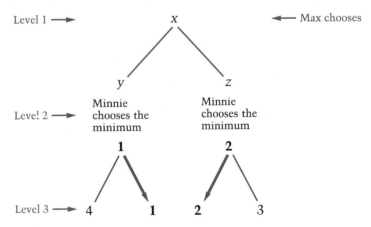

And Max, knowing all this, will pick the *maximum* of the two possibilities:

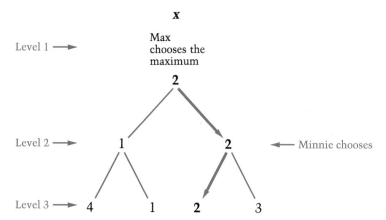

So at the end of this game, Minnie will always owe two dollars to Max.

Now let's make a few observations about this kind of a game:

1. Because of our perfect information and certainty assumptions, the game always gets played the same way; and the result (what Minnie owes Max) is always the same amount. None of the games we play in real life works this way, for two reasons:

    a. Many real-life games don't have perfect information and certainty.

    b. Real-life games that do have perfect information and certainty (like chess) are so complex that it's impossible for the players to make effective use of all the information that, in theory, they could possess.

2. Numbers on the tree seem to trickle up from the leaves to the root. (In the example just given, the number 2 started on one of the leaves and worked its way to the root.) We write a number like 2 at a particular point on the tree once we've determined that the game would naturally proceed from that point down to a leaf with the number 2. In the example, the number 2 written at the root means that the game will always proceed to the leaf that's got a 2 on it.

3. Look again at our example, in which Minnie goes toward the *minimum* number and Max goes toward the *maximum* number. In any game of this kind, with any number of levels on the tree, we end up flipping back and forth this way between minimum and maximum. Here's an example with four levels:

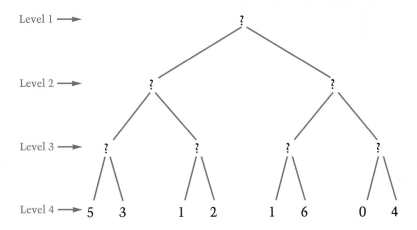

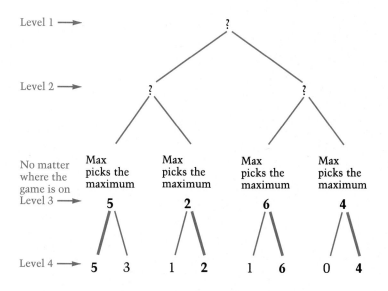

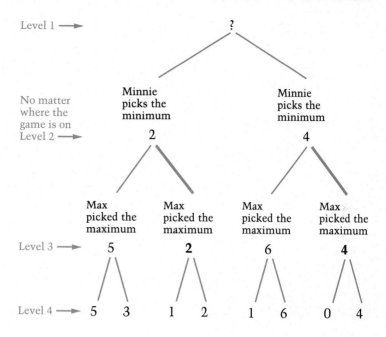

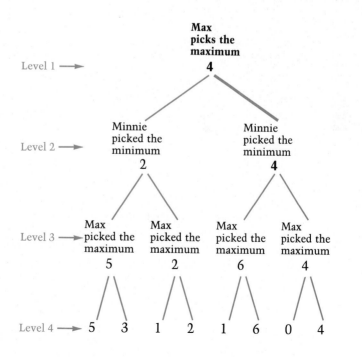

Here are some formal specs for Program `Minimax`:

Input: A game tree

Output: The amount of money Minnie will pay to Max at the end of the game

Designing a Program

representing a tree with an expression

First we have to be more specific in describing how we're going to input "a game tree." We can't draw the tree with all its lines (at least not with the Pascal features we already know). Instead we'll use a clever trick that takes open parenthesis to mean "go down one level" and close parenthesis to mean "go up one level." Here's the way we'll represent a tree with only two levels:

    is represented by the expression (4 1)

and

    is represented by the expression (2 3)

To represent more complicated trees, we just combine these simpler expressions:

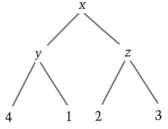   is represented by the expression
((4 1) (2 3))

Why do we use mutual recursion?

Now we need a program to read these expressions and use them to find the amount that Minnie pays to Max. Our Pascal program can't have real live players, so instead it has two functions, called `Max` and `Min`. Function `Max` finds the larger of two numbers:

```
IF left > right THEN
   Max := left
ELSE
   Max := right
```

and `Min` finds the smaller of two numbers:

```
IF left < right THEN
   Min := left
ELSE
   Min := right
```

Now if we look at one of our earlier tree diagrams, we can see where `Max` and `Min` are called:

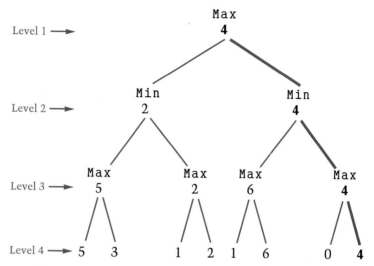

The trees that we've been creating are actually diagrams of recursive functions calling one another! At the top of the tree we have Function `Max`.

Level 1 ⟶   **Max**
4

So our main program has to call Function `Max`. Now `Max` needs to get two values and take the maximum of them. It gets these values by making two calls to Function `Min`.

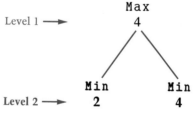

```
left   := Min;
right  := Min;
IF left > right THEN
   Max := left
ELSE
   Max := right
```

And each of the two `Min`s, in turn, gets its values by making two calls to `Max`.

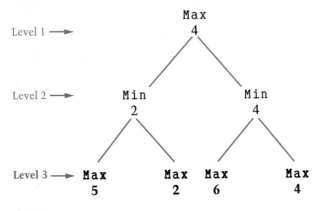

```
left   := Max;
right  := Max;
IF left < right THEN
   Min := left
ELSE
   Min := right
```

This is where mutual recursion comes in. Function `Max` calls Function `Min`, and likewise Function `Min` calls Function `Max`.

And what about the parentheses in the expression used to represent a tree? Those need to be read too. In fact, they help guide the calling of one function by another. Whenever `Max` is called, it reads an item from the keyboard and checks to see if that item is a number or an open parenthesis. If the item is an open parenthesis, then `Max` calls two versions of Function `Min` to obtain values from two smaller trees:

Reading open parenthesis:

((4 1) (2 3))

```
ReadCharOrNat (c, n, kind);

IF kind = character THEN
   IF c = '(' THEN
      BEGIN
         left  := Min;
         right := Min
         .
         .
         .
       Etc.
```

If the item is a natural number, then `Max` recognizes that it's reached a leaf of the tree and simply returns that number:

$$(\ (\ 4 \ 1 \ ) \ (\ 2 \ 3 \ ) \ )$$

```
            ReadCharOrNat (c, n, kind);
                       .
                       .
   IF kind = natral THEN
     Max := n
```

The complete code follows.

Program Example

```
PROGRAM Minimax (input, output);
{Finds the value of a game tree.}
   TYPE
     kindType      = (character, natral);
     natural       = 0..MAXINT;
   {----------}
   PROCEDURE ReadCharOrNat (VAR c    : CHAR;
                            VAR n    : natural;
                            VAR kind : kindType);
   {Copy Procedure ReadCharOrNat
    (from Section 13.6) here.}
   {----------}
   FUNCTION Max : INTEGER;
     FORWARD;
   {----------}
   FUNCTION Min : INTEGER;
   {Finds the smaller of the next two values on the tree.}
     VAR
       c             : CHAR;
       n             : natural;
       kind          : kindType;
       left, right   : INTEGER;
       closeParens   : CHAR;
   BEGIN {Min}
     ReadCharOrNat (c, n, kind);

     IF kind = character THEN
       IF c = '(' THEN
         BEGIN
           left  := Max;
           right := Max;
           IF left < right THEN
             Min := left
           ELSE
             Min := right;
           ReadCharOrNat (closeParens, n, kind)
         END;
     IF kind = natral THEN
       Min := n
   END;  {Min}
```

```
{----------}
FUNCTION Max;
{Finds the larger of the next two values on the tree.}
   VAR
      c            : CHAR;
      n            : natural;
      kind         : kindType;
      left, right  : INTEGER;
      closeParens  : CHAR;
BEGIN {Max}
   ReadCharOrNat (c, n, kind);

   IF kind = character THEN
      IF c = '(' THEN
         BEGIN
           left  := Min;
           right := Min;
           IF left > right THEN
             Max := left
           ELSE
             Max := right;
           ReadCharOrNat (closeParens, n, kind)
         END;

      IF kind = natral THEN
         Max := n

END;   {Max}

{----------}

BEGIN {Minimax}
   WriteLn ('Enter an expression to represent the tree: ');
   WriteLn (Max:5, ' is the value of this game tree.'    )
END.   {Minimax}
```

Sample Runs

```
Enter an expression to represent the tree:
( 4 1 )
    4 is the value of this game tree.
```

```
Enter an expression to represent the tree:
( 2 3 )
    3 is the value of this game tree.
```

```
Enter an expression to represent the tree:
( ( 4 1 ) ( 2 3 ) )
    2 is the value of this game tree.
```

```
Enter an expression to represent the tree:
(   ( ( 5 3 ) ( 1 2 ) )    ( ( 1 6 ) ( 0 4 ) )   )
    4 is the value of this game tree.
```

```
Enter an expression to represent the tree:
( ( 4 1 ) ( ( 2 0 ) 3 ) )
        2 is the value of this game tree.
```

Observations

Recall from Section 3.5 the rule in Pascal that no identifier can be used before it's declared. When it comes to mutual recursion, this rule presents a bit of a problem. If Functions Max and Min are to call one another, they both need to be declared above one another, which is impossible. To fix this, Function Max's declaration is divided into two parts.

FORWARD declarations

* ```
  FUNCTION Max : INTEGER;
     FORWARD;
  ```

  The first part is called a FORWARD declaration. It's a heading without a body. Instead of a body, we use the word FORWARD. The word FORWARD is called a **compiler directive**. It tells the compiler that the body of Function Max is to be found later in the text of the program.

* ```
  FUNCTION Max;
        .
        .
  BEGIN {Max}
     ReadCharOrNat (c, n, kind);
        .
        .
  ```

  The second part of Max's declaration has a heading and a body. But notice that the heading is missing its result type! The function's result type : INTEGER appears only in the earlier FORWARD declaration. If Function Max had formal parameters, they too would appear only in the FORWARD declaration.

  This is the way we set up a pair of mutually recursive subprograms in Pascal. Function Min is sandwiched between the two parts of Function Max (as shown on this page and the next):

```
FUNCTION Max : INTEGER;
   FORWARD;
{----------}
FUNCTION Min : INTEGER;
      .
      .
BEGIN {Min}
      .
      .
   left  := Max;
   right := Max
      .
      .
END; {Min}
{----------}
```

```
FUNCTION Max;
       .
       .
BEGIN {Max}
       .
       .
    left  := Min;
    right := Min
       .
       .
  END;   {Max}
```

So Min is declared above the body of Max, and Max's FORWARD declaration appears above Min. This means that Max can call Min, and Min can call Max.

13.7   Exercises

Key Words to Review

mutual recursion	leaf	certainty
tree	game	FORWARD
root	perfect information	compiler directive

Questions to Answer

QUE 13.7.1   Draw two levels of the game tree for tic-tac-toe.

QUE 13.7.2   Explain the results obtained in the first and second of this section's Sample Runs.

QUE 13.7.3   Explain why the expression

$$(((5 3) (1 2))   ((1 6) (0 4))   )$$

represents the four-level tree that's pictured in this section's Specifications subsection.

QUE 13.7.4   Draw a picture of the tree that is represented by the following expression:

$$((4 1) ((2 0) 3))$$

QUE 13.7.5   Write a trace of Program Minimax.

QUE 13.7.6   What kinds of FORWARD declarations do you need to create a program with *three* mutually recursive subprograms? Try out your answer by writing a program with three subprogram stubs.

Experiments to Try

EXP 13.7.1   Add a result type to the second heading of Function Max.

EXP 13.7.2   Look once again at the placement of subprogram headings in Program Minimax. It's somewhat similar to the placement of code we'd have if Min were simply a subprogram declared within Function Max. Modify the program so that Min is a subprogram within Max, and see if the program still works.

Changes to Make

CHA 13.7.1   Turn the mutual recursion of Program `Minimax` into ordinary recursion. Have a single Function `MaxOrMin` with a formal parameter of type `BOOLEAN`. When this parameter is `TRUE`, the function behaves like our Function `Max`. When the parameter is `FALSE`, it behaves like our Function `Min`.

CHA 13.7.2   Modify Program `Prefix` of Section 13.6 so that it uses mutual recursion. To do this, turn the `THEN`-part of Procedure `Value`'s `IF` statement into a separate subprogram.

CHA 13.7.3   Modify Program `Minimax` so that it uses a `levelCount` variable to decide when it's reached the base of recursion. A run of the new Program `Minimax` might look like this:

```
How many levels? 4
Enter the values on the leaves:
5 3  1 2    1 6  0 4
      4 is the value of this game tree.
```

In this example, `levelCount` starts off at 4. Whenever one subprogram calls the other, it sends the called subprogram a value of `levelCount` that's one smaller than the value it received. When a subprogram receives a sufficiently small value of `levelCount`, it reads leaf values from the keyboard instead of making recursive calls. Notice that no parentheses are needed in the input. (We're assuming the game tree is completely filled. A tree like the one in the last of our Sample Runs cannot be represented in this scheme.)

Programs and Subprograms to Write

WRI 13.7.1   A *bill of materials* is a list that looks something like this:

```
( room ( floor     (boards carpeting)
         walls     (lathe plaster wallpaper)
         ceiling (Sheetrock paint)        ) )
```

To read this aloud, we'd probably say "A room has a floor, some walls, and a ceiling. A floor has boards and carpeting. A wall has . . ." Of course we don't have to stop at boards and carpeting.

```
( room ( floor     (boards ( wood ) carpeting ( nylon polyester ) )
         walls     ... etc.
```

At the outermost edge of this list we have a *product* (a room). At the innermost core of the list we have *raw materials* (wood, nylon, etc.). In the middle we have *semi-finished goods* (floor, ceiling, carpeting, etc.).

Write a program that reads a bill of materials from a disk file and reads an item from the keyboard. The program searches for the item in the bill of materials and displays a new list, indented as in outline form, that tells what materials are needed to manufacture the particular item. For instance, if the user enters the word `floor` then the program writes

```
floor
  boards
    wood
  carpeting
    nylon
    polyester
```

13.8

Passing Subprograms as Parameters (Supplementary)

Why pass a subprogram?

Until this point in the book, the formal parameters of subprograms have always been the names of variables.[3] For instance, we may have a procedure declared as follows:

```
PROCEDURE Plot (lowerLimit, upperLimit, increment : REAL);
{Plots points on a trigonometric Sine curve.}

  VAR
    x : REAL;
BEGIN {Plot}
  x := lowerLimit;
  WHILE x <= upperLimit DO
    BEGIN
      Draw (Sin (x));
      x := x + increment
    END
END;  {Plot}
```

Each time we call Procedure `Plot` we can supply new values for the variables `lowerLimit`, `upperLimit`, and `increment`. The action of Procedure `Plot` depends on the actual values that are supplied when `Plot` is called.

Now what if we want to call `Plot` several times, having it plot values of `Sin (x)` the first time, `Cos (x)` the second time, $4*x + 2$ the third time, etc.?

Occasionally it's convenient to pass a function or a procedure as a parameter to another subprogram. That's exactly what we do in this section's program example.

Specifications

functional parameters

In Section 10.8 we sorted an array of INTEGERs using an algorithm called selection sort. Instead of using the name INTEGER throughout the program, we defined a new type

```
TYPE
  anyType   = INTEGER;
```

and used `anyType` in the program's declarations. We did this to emphasize that, by changing the word INTEGER in this one type definition

```
TYPE
  anyType   = CHAR;
```

---

[3]The material described in this section conforms to ANSI Standard Pascal, but it doesn't conform to many older Pascal implementations. See your implementation's manuals for more details.

we could make the selection sort algorithm work for types other than the INTEGERs. In this section we'll sort letters of the alphabet. But as soon as we consider doing this, a question arises. What does it mean for one letter to be "less than" another? Do we mean alphabetically, or do we intend to use the ASCII ordering in which all the uppercase letters come first, and all the lowercase letters come later? And what about the EBCDIC code? In the EBCDIC code, all the *lower*case letters come before the *upper*case letters.

So here's what we can do: We can change just *one line* in Procedure SelectionSort from

```
IF a[thisIndex] < a[minIndex] THEN
```

to

```
IF LessThan (a[thisIndex], a[minIndex]) THEN
```

This change means that when we compare two letters, we do it with a function call instead of with Pascal's < comparison operator. Then we can have several different versions of Function LessThan—one for the ASCII ordering, another for the EBCDIC ordering, and a third for **case insensitive** ordering. (When we say *case insensitive* we mean the ordinary alphabetical ordering in which uppercase versus lowercase doesn't matter. That is, both A and a come before B and b, which in turn come before C and c, etc.)

How do we switch from one version of LessThan to another? We can change the code before each run of the program, but it's better to pass the name of a *function* to Procedure SelectionSort whenever we call it.

Here are some formal specs for Procedure SelectionSort:

Input (via the formal parameter list): An array of letters (CHAR values) and a LessThan function to describe what it means for one letter to be less than another

Process: Sort the array of letters using the LessThan function

Output (as a VAR parameter in the formal parameter list): The array of letters, in non-decreasing order

Program Example

```
PROGRAM SelectionSortDriver (fInput, output);
{Test driver for Procedure SelectionSort.}
   CONST
     lo =  1;
     hi = 10;
   TYPE
     anyType   = CHAR;
     indexType = lo..hi;
     arrayType = ARRAY [indexType] OF anyType;
   VAR
     a       : arrayType;
     fInput : TEXT;
```

```
{----------}
FUNCTION IsUpperCase (ch : CHAR) : BOOLEAN;
{Determines whether a character is an uppercase
 letter. Works on ASCII and EBCDIC implementations.}
BEGIN {IsUpperCase}
  IsUpperCase := ch IN ['A'..'I', 'J'..'R', 'S'..'Z']
END;  {IsUpperCase}
{----------}
FUNCTION IsLowerCase (ch : CHAR) : BOOLEAN;
{Determines whether a character is a lowercase
 letter. Works on ASCII and EBCDIC implementations.}
BEGIN {IsLowerCase}
  IsLowerCase := ch IN ['a'..'i', 'j'..'r', 's'..'z']
END;  {IsLowerCase}
{----------}
FUNCTION LowerCaseEquiv (ch : CHAR) : CHAR;
{Accepts a character; returns its lowercase equivalent.}
BEGIN {LowerCaseEquiv}
  IF IsUpperCase (ch) THEN
    LowerCaseEquiv := Chr (Ord(ch) + (Ord('a') - Ord('A')))
  ELSE
    LowerCaseEquiv := ch
END;  {LowerCaseEquiv}
{----------}
FUNCTION AsciiLessThan (ch1, ch2 : CHAR) : BOOLEAN;
{ch1 is less than ch2 if ch1 has a smaller
 ASCII code than ch2 (without assuming that
 the implementation uses ASCII codes).}
BEGIN {AsciiLessThan}
  IF IsUpperCase (ch1) AND IsLowerCase (ch2) THEN
    AsciiLessThan := TRUE
  ELSE IF IsLowerCase (ch1) AND IsUpperCase (ch2) THEN
    AsciiLessThan := FALSE
  ELSE
    AsciiLessThan := ch1 < ch2
END;  {AsciiLessThan}
{----------}
FUNCTION EbcdicLessThan (ch1, ch2 : CHAR) : BOOLEAN;
{ch1 is less than ch2 if ch1 has a smaller
 EBCDIC code than ch2 (without assuming that
 the implementation uses EBCDIC codes).}
BEGIN {EbcdicLessThan}
  IF IsLowerCase (ch1) AND IsUpperCase (ch2) THEN
    EbcdicLessThan := TRUE
  ELSE IF IsUpperCase (ch1) AND IsLowerCase (ch2) THEN
    EbcdicLessThan := FALSE
  ELSE
    EbcdicLessThan := ch1 < ch2
END;  {EbcdicLessThan}
```

```
{----------}
FUNCTION CaseInsLessThan (ch1, ch2 : CHAR) : BOOLEAN;
{ch1 is less than ch2 if ch1 is alphabetically
 earlier than ch2, regardless of case.}
BEGIN {CaseInsLessThan}
  CaseInsLessThan := LowerCaseEquiv (ch1) < LowerCaseEquiv (ch2)
END;   {CaseInsLessThan}
{----------}
PROCEDURE ReadArray (VAR fInput : TEXT; VAR a : arrayType);
{Reads unsorted values.}
  VAR
    i : indexType;
BEGIN {ReadArray}
  Reset (fInput);
  FOR i := lo TO hi DO
    Read (fInput, a[i]);
  ReadLn (fInput)
END;   {ReadArray}
{----------}
PROCEDURE SelectionSort (VAR a : arrayType;
                           FUNCTION LessThan (ch1,ch2:anyType) : BOOLEAN);
{Implements the selection sort algorithm.}
  VAR
    start, minIndex : indexType;

  {----------}
  FUNCTION IndexOfSmallest
            (a             : arrayType;
             start, finish : indexType;
             FUNCTION LessThan (ch1,ch2:anyType) : BOOLEAN) : indexType;
  {Returns the index of the smallest value in the array
   'a', between the 'start' and 'finish' components.}
    VAR
      minIndex, thisIndex : indexType;
  BEGIN {IndexOfSmallest}
    minIndex := start;

    FOR thisIndex := start+1 TO finish DO
      IF LessThan (a[thisIndex], a[minIndex]) THEN
         minIndex := thisIndex;

    IndexOfSmallest := minIndex
  END;   {IndexOfSmallest}

  {----------}
```

```
    PROCEDURE Switch (VAR x, y : anyType);
    {Switches two values, x and y.}
      VAR
        temp : anyType;
    BEGIN {Switch}
      temp := x;
      x    := y;
      y    := temp
    END;   {Switch}
    {----------}

  BEGIN {SelectionSort}
    FOR start := 1 TO hi-1 DO
      BEGIN
        minIndex := IndexOfSmallest (a, start, hi, LessThan);
        Switch (a[start], a[minIndex])
      END
  END;   {SelectionSort}
  {----------}

  PROCEDURE WriteArray (a : arrayType);
  {Writes sorted values.}

    VAR
      i : indexType;
  BEGIN {WriteArray}
    WriteLn ('The values in non-decreasing order are: ');

    FOR i := lo TO hi DO
      Write (a[i]:5);
    WriteLn
  END;   {WriteArray}
  {----------}
BEGIN {SelectionSortDriver}
  ReadArray      (fInput, a);

  SelectionSort (a, AsciiLessThan);
  WriteLn        ('ASCII: ');
  WriteArray     (a);
  WriteLn;

  SelectionSort (a, EbcdicLessThan);
  WriteLn        ('EBCDIC: ');
  WriteArray     (a);
  WriteLn;

  SelectionSort (a, CaseInsLessThan);
  WriteLn        ('Case insensitive: ');
  WriteArray     (a)
END.   {SelectionSortDriver}
```

Sample Runs

With the following fInput file:

```
    BullWinKle
```

the output of Program SelectionSortDriver is

```
ASCII:
The values in non-decreasing order are:
    B    K    W    e    i    l    l    l    n    u

EBCDIC:
The values in non-decreasing order are:
    e    i    l    l    l    n    u    B    K    W

Case insensitive:
The values in non-decreasing order are:
    B    e    i    K    l    l    l    n    u    W
```

Observations

formal functional parameters

```
• FUNCTION IndexOfSmallest
       (a               : arrayType;
        start, finish : indexType;
        FUNCTION LessThan (ch1,ch2:anyType) : BOOLEAN)
                                      : indexType;
```

When we call Function IndexOfSmallest we should pass it a FUNCTION that has two anyType arguments and returns a BOOLEAN result. Then when we use the word LessThan inside the body of Procedure IndexOfSmallest

```
IF LessThan (a[thisIndex], a[minIndex]) THEN
```

we're referring to whatever function has been passed. LessThan is called a **functional parameter**.

Look at the body of Function IndexOfSmallest and notice that ch1 and ch2 don't appear anywhere in this body. This happens when we pass functions (or procedures) to subprograms. The names ch1 and ch2 are just placeholders. They tell the compiler to expect a function with two formal parameters to be passed. This function that's passed will use its two formal parameters, but IndexOfSmallest won't use them. Function IndexOfSmallest just calls whatever function is passed to it.

```
• PROCEDURE SelectionSort (VAR a : arrayType;
       FUNCTION LessThan (ch1,ch2:anyType) : BOOLEAN);
       .
       .
       .
minIndex := IndexOfSmallest(a, start, hi, LessThan)
```

actual functional parameters

This is how IndexOfSmallest gets a function passed to it. Procedure SelectionSort calls IndexOfSmallest and passes it a function name. In this instance the name that's passed to IndexOfSmallest is still the name LessThan. That's because SelectionSort is just passing on a name that it got from being called itself.

```
FUNCTION IndexOfSmallest
         (a                : arrayType;
          start, finish : indexType;
          FUNCTION LessThan (ch1,ch2:anyType) : BOOLEAN) : indexType;
     .
     .
IF LessThan (a[thisIndex], a[minIndex]) THEN
        ↑

      IndexOfSmallest calls the function
```

```
PROCEDURE SelectionSort (VAR a : arrayType;
                         FUNCTION LessThan (ch1,ch2:anyType) : BOOLEAN);
     .
     .
minIndex := IndexOfSmallest (a, start, hi, LessThan)
                                              ↑

                    Procedure SelectionSort passes
                    the function on to IndexOfSmallest
```

```
SelectionSort (a, AsciiLessThan)
                  ↑
                  The main program passes an actual
                  function to Procedure SelectionSort
```

```
 •  SelectionSort (a, AsciiLessThan);
     .
     .
    SelectionSort (a, EbcdicLessThan);
     .
     .
    SelectionSort (a, CaseInsLessThan)
```

The main program has three calls to Procedure SelectionSort with three different function names given as actual parameters. Look at the headings of Functions AsciiLessThan, EbcdicLessThan, and CaseInsLessThan. Each of these functions has two anyType parameters (CHAR parameters, actually) and returns a BOOLEAN result. So each of these functions can serve as the actual parameter for the formal name LessThan.

So far we've seen a program in which functions are being passed as parameters. But procedures can be parameters too. An example follows.

Specifications

procedural parameters

Let's look again at Program LettersExpert in Section 12.8. It has two procedures, IsSingleton and WriteLnSet, whose bodies look quite similar. The essential work in both procedures is

```
FOR elt := 'a' TO 'z' DO
   IF elt IN the set THEN
      do something or other
```

So here's what we propose: we'll make a single procedure, called StepThru, out of the little fragment of code just given. In this code we will replace the words *do something or other* with a call to doSomething.

```
PROCEDURE StepThru
               (   .
                   .
               PROCEDURE doSomething (elt      : lowerCaseType;
                                      VAR count : cardinal     ));
{Steps through a set and 'does something' with each element.}
   .
   .
BEGIN {StepThru}
   FOR elt := 'a' TO 'z' DO
      IF elt IN s THEN
         doSomething (elt, count)
END;   {StepThru}
```

The name doSomething will be a **procedural parameter**. So each time we call StepThru we'll be supplying the name of an actual procedure:

```
StepThru (... , CountElement);
   .
   .
StepThru (... , WriteElement)
```

In other words, each time we call StepThru, we tell it exactly what *something* it's supposed to do as it steps through the set.

We could rewrite Program LettersExpert with this idea, but to keep the example simple, we'll just use the idea to write a program that counts the number of elements in a particular set and then writes the elements in the set to the screen.

Program Example

```
PROGRAM SetOps (input, output);
{Counts a set's elements and
 then writes the set's elements.}
   TYPE
      lowerCaseType = 'a'..'z';
      letterSetType = SET OF lowerCaseType;
      cardinal      = 0..26;
```

```
     VAR
       s     : letterSetType;
       count : cardinal;

     {----------}
     PROCEDURE CountElement (elt        : lowerCaseType;
                             VAR count : cardinal     );
     {Counts an element of a set.}

     BEGIN {CountElement}
       count := count + 1
     END;  {CountElement}

     {----------}
     PROCEDURE WriteElement (elt        : lowerCaseType;
                             VAR count : cardinal     );
     {Writes an element of a set.}

     BEGIN {WriteElement}
       Write (elt:3)
     END;   {WriteElement}

     {----------}
     PROCEDURE StepThru
                  (s           : letterSetType;
                   VAR count : cardinal;
                   PROCEDURE doSomething (elt        : lowerCaseType;
                                          VAR count : cardinal     ));
     {Steps through a set and 'does something' with each element.}

        VAR
          elt : lowerCaseType;
     BEGIN {StepThru}
       FOR elt := 'a' TO 'z' DO
         IF elt IN s THEN
           doSomething (elt, count)
     END;   {StepThru}

     {----------}
   BEGIN {SetOps}
     s      := ['a'..'d', 'g'..'j', 'q'];
     count := 0;

     StepThru (s, count, CountElement);
     WriteLn  ('The set has ', count:2, ' elements');

     WriteLn;
     Write    ('The set''s elements are: ');
     StepThru (s, count, WriteElement)
   END.  {SetOps}
```

**Sample
Runs**

```
The set has  9 elements
The set's elements are:   a  b  c  d  g  h  i  j  q
```

Observations Notice that Procedure WriteElement does nothing more than plain old Write. Why do we need to create a new Procedure WriteElement? There are two reasons. Here's the first one:

making
parameter lists
that match

In Procedure `StepThru`, we always *do something or other*. Sometimes we do it with a set element (. . . we `Write` the element . . .), and sometimes we do it with a counter (. . . we increment `count` . . .). So in the heading of `StepThru`, the procedural parameter `doSomething` has to have *two* formal parameters, `elt` and `count`.

```
PROCEDURE StepThru
             (s            : letterSetType;
              VAR count : cardinal;
              PROCEDURE doSomething (elt        : lowerCaseType;
                                     VAR count : cardinal       ));
```

This means that any actual procedure that we pass to `StepThru` has to have two parameters, and they have to have the same types as `elt` and `count`.

```
    PROCEDURE CountElement (elt        : lowerCaseType;
                            VAR count : cardinal       );
        .
        .
        .
    PROCEDURE WriteElement (elt        : lowerCaseType;
                            VAR count : cardinal       );
```

Since the pre-declared `Write` doesn't have quite these parameters, we make up our own Procedure `WriteElement`. The variable `count` isn't used in the body of `WriteElement` because a `count` isn't useful for writing a set's elements. That's OK.

restrictions

Now even if we didn't have this difficulty with the parameters of `Write`, we'd still need to create our own Procedure `WriteElement`. In ANSI Standard Pascal it's illegal to pass a pre-declared subprogram as a parameter.

```
    StepThru (s, count, Write)
```

13.8 Exercises

Key Words to Review

case insensitive   functional parameter   procedural parameter

Questions to Answer

QUE 13.8.1   The names `ch1` and `ch2` appear in the heading of Function `IndexOfSmallest` but not in the function's body. Explain why.

QUE 13.8.2   In Procedure `SelectionSort` the name `LessThan` appears in a parameter list

```
    minIndex := IndexOfSmallest (a, start, hi, LessThan)
```

but in Procedure `IndexOfSmallest` the same name appears before a parameter list

```
IF LessThan (a[thisIndex], a[minIndex]) THEN
```

Explain this.

QUE 13.8.3 Let's say we needed a procedure that changed all the lowercase letters in a set into their uppercase equivalents. Would it help to use Procedure StepThru? Why, or why not?

Things to Check in a Manual

MAN 13.8.1 Does your implementation allow procedures as parameters to subprograms? If so, does it use the same syntax that we described here, or does it use some slightly different syntax?

MAN 13.8.2 Does your implementation allow functional or procedural *types?* Can you do something like

```
TYPE
    LessThanType = FUNCTION (ch1,ch2:anyType) : BOOLEAN;
```

Experiments to Try

EXP 13.8.1 Modify Function AsciiLessThan so it's a stub with only one formal CHAR parameter. Does the program still compile?

EXP 13.8.2 Move AsciiLessThan so that it's declared after Procedure SelectionSort and immediately before the main body of Program SelectionSortDriver.

EXP 13.8.3 Let's say we have a subprogram Sub that accepts another subprogram Accepted as one of its parameters. Can Accepted also have a subprogram as one of its parameters?

EXP 13.8.4 Let's say we have a subprogram Sub that accepts another subprogram Accepted as one of its parameters. When Sub is called from the main program, can we pass Sub to itself?

EXP 13.8.5 Let's say we have a subprogram Sub that accepts another subprogram Accepted as one of its parameters. When Sub calls Accepted, can it pass itself (Sub) to Accepted?

Changes to Make

CHA 13.8.1 Instead of doing all three sorts, have the SelectionSortDriver prompt the user to choose one of the three possibilities. Then extend the number of possibilities to six. (For each of the three ordering methods, the user can choose to sort in non-decreasing or non-increasing order.)

CHA 13.8.2 Redo Exercise Cha.13.7.1. This time the BOOLEAN value helps decide whether to pass a function LessThan or another function GreaterThan to the next MaxOrMin.

Scales to Practice

PRA 13.8.1   Write and test a BOOLEAN-valued function called FnsAreEqual. It takes two functional parameters, F1 and F2, and two INTEGER parameters, start and stop. It checks to see if F1 and F2 are equal for all INTEGER values from start to stop.

PRA 13.8.2   Write and test a function subprogram called MinInRange that has as its formal parameters two INTEGERs, start and stop, and a function f, which accepts an INTEGER and returns an INTEGER. Function MinInRange returns the smallest value that f will ever return if it's given an INTEGER between start and stop.

Programs and Subprograms to Write

WRI 13.8.1   Look again at Exercises Wri.10.5.1, Wri.10.8.1, and Wri.10.8.2. Combine these exercises using a record type to store a customer's identification number, zip code, and balance due. Have a single sort procedure that works for any of the three options that can be chosen by the user. The sort procedure gets a different LessThan function passed to it for each of the three options.

WRI 13.8.2   Let's say we have a function that accepts two BOOLEAN values and returns a BOOLEAN result. This function is called a *tautology* if it always returns TRUE, no matter what values it accepts. For example, the function

```
FUNCTION AlwaysTrue (a, b : BOOLEAN) : BOOLEAN;
BEGIN {AlwaysTrue}
  AlwaysTrue := (a OR NOT a) AND (b OR NOT b)
END;  {AlwaysTrue}
```

is a tautology. A function is called a *contradiction* if it always returns FALSE, no matter what values it accepts. For instance, the function

```
FUNCTION NeverTrue (a, b : BOOLEAN) : BOOLEAN;
BEGIN {NeverTrue}
  NeverTrue := (a AND NOT a) OR (b AND NOT b)
END;  {NeverTrue}
```

is a contradiction. A function is *indeterminate* if it's neither a tautology nor a contradiction. Write and test a function WhatKind that accepts a function f. Function f has two BOOLEAN parameters and returns a BOOLEAN result. Function WhatKind returns one of the enumerated values taut, contra, or indet, depending on what kind of function f is.

WRI 13.8.3   *(Trapezoidal Rule)* Rewrite Function Area from Exercise Wri.6.1.4 so that it accepts a REAL-valued function, f, with one REAL parameter, x; a starting value for x; a stopping value for x; and a value for n; and returns an approximate value for the area under f from the starting value to the stopping value.

WRI 13.8.4   *(This problem requires some knowledge of analytic geometry.)* Write and test a procedure that accepts a function subprogram as one of its parameters and makes a rough plot of that function, using asterisks (or some other appropriate character) to represent points on the function's graph.

Chapter Summary

In this chapter we covered recursive functions and procedures. A subprogram is *recursive* if it calls itself. The sequence of calls in the execution of a recursive subprogram forms a chain or a tree. At the bottom of this chain or tree we find the *base* of the recursion. The code in a recursive subprogram is often a very close rewording of a definition.

In one section we discussed the strategy of *postponement*. With recursive postponement, an action in a subprogram gets delayed by a recursive call to the subprogram itself. The overall effect is to reverse the order in which these actions take place.

In another section we showed that recursive subprograms are very much like their iterative counterparts. To turn an iterative subprogram into a recursive subprogram we exploit the fact that a recursive chain of calls is somewhat like an iterative loop.

In yet another section we described the technique known as *mutual recursion*. In mutual recursion we have one subprogram calling another subprogram and this other subprogram in turn calling the first subprogram. Mutual recursion is a useful way to think about certain problems.

Finally we reached the Chapter Summary, in which we stated that this chapter covers recursive functions and procedures. We reminded the reader that a subprogram is recursive if it calls itself. The sequence of calls in the execution of a recursive subprogram forms a chain or a tree. At the bottom of this chain or tree . . .

Pointers

14

In previous chapters we combined values using arrays, records, and sets. In this chapter, we'll examine one more way to combine values. This new way of combining values, using **pointers**, has several advantages and several disadvantages over the other methods. We'll do some comparisons later in the chapter.

What Is a Pointer?

When we create an array of integers, we line up values in memory, one next to another, like this:

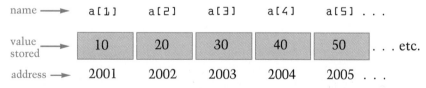

The computer knows each memory location by a number called the location's **address**. The numbers on the bottom row of the diagram are typical memory addresses. When values are stored next to one another in an array, their memory addresses are consecutive. That is, the values are stored in **adjacent** memory locations. To find the value of a[4], the computer examines the value that's stored three locations beyond a[1].

But this isn't always the best way to collect values together. Sometimes it's better not to store integers in adjacent memory locations. Here's how the same integers might be stored in memory locations that are not adjacent:

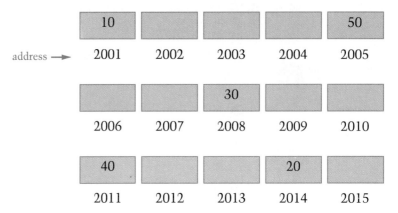

But then we have a problem: the integers aren't stored right next to one another, so we need a new way to find these various integers that we've stored. One way to do it is to store, along with each integer, the address of the next integer:

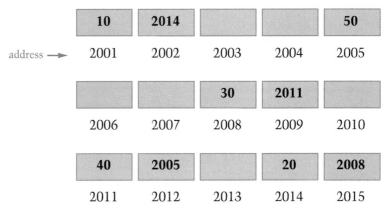

linked lists and cells

Now, instead of an array, we have what's called a **linked list**. A linked list consists of several **cells**. A typical cell in the linked list given above looks like this:

It contains two things:

- a useful value (a value that's pertinent to a particular problem — 10 employees, 10 months, 10 planets, whatever)
- an address (the address where the next useful value can be found)

visualizing a linked list

So our last diagram shows a linked list with five cells. It's a nice diagram, but in a certain sense it isn't very helpful in the study of linked lists. The diagram contains much more detail about linked lists than we need to know. For one thing, the actual numbers used as addresses aren't particularly important. The important thing is that certain memory locations contain information that points to other locations. Let's say that these memory locations contain pointer values and represent the pointing pictorially with arrows:

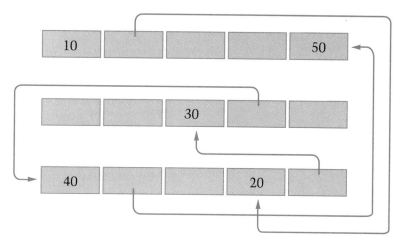

That's a bit better. The arrows help us visualize the work done by numbers like 2014, 2011, etc. But now we've got an intricate tangle of arrows! So when we're fully accustomed to the notion that the integers aren't stored in adjacent memory locations, we can simplify the diagram even more. We can untangle the arrows and draw the cells in a row, even though they don't necessarily come one after another in memory:

Now it's easy to see what's going on. The diagram gives us all the relevant information we had in the earlier diagrams, but it doesn't clutter up the visual scene with memory addresses or crisscrossing arrows. This is the kind of diagram we use when we trace a program that has a linked list.

14.1   Exercises

Key Words to Review

pointer	adjacent locations	cell
address	linked list	

Questions to Answer

QUE 14.1.1   Explain how pointers provide a way of connecting non-adjacent memory locations together.

QUE 14.1.2   Look once again at the memory diagrams we've been making in this section. After each integer value except 50 we've stored a pointer value. Now imagine that one location after the 50 there's some kind of an "end of list" indicator—a pointer that points nowhere. Write pseudocode to tell how one finds all the numbers that are stored in a linked list.

QUE 14.1.3   We want to find all the numbers in a linked list. What if we start with the first memory location (in this section, location 2000) and examine all the locations that come after it (2001, 2002, 2003, etc.)? In this section's examples, we'd find all the linked list's values by the time we got to memory location 2015. Why is this not a good way to find all the values stored in a linked list?

QUE 14.1.4   In this section we said that "the actual numbers used as addresses in a linked list aren't particularly important." Justify this claim.

Things to Check in a Manual

MAN 14.1.1   How is an address actually stored in your implementation? If we could look inside the computer, would we find that an address is the same as an INTEGER value?

Scales to Practice

PRA 14.1.1   The diagrams we've been making in this section are reminiscent of arrays, and in fact they can be implemented using arrays. Write a program with an array that mimics the diagrams in the section. The array contains INTEGER values and has indices ranging from 2001 to 2015. Assign values to certain locations in the array:

10	2014			50
2001	2002	2003	2004	2005

		30	2011	
2006	2007	2008	2009	2010

40	2005		20	2008
2011	2012	2013	2014	2015

Then write code that jumps around in the array by following the four-digit numbers. As it jumps, it prints the two-digit numbers on the screen. Thus, the output of this program is

    10 20 30 40 50

Note: Your code will need a way of deciding when it's reached the last two-digit number. Refer to Exercise Que.14.1.2 for some ideas.

Things to Think About

THI 14.1.1 Following the pointers in a linked list is something like taking part in a treasure hunt. You're given a clue (a pointer) that you follow until you get to another place (another cell) where you find a further clue. As you go, you pick up certain goodies (food, coins, etc. . . . or, in the case of linked lists, "useful" values like the numbers 10, 20, 30, etc.). Can you think of any other real-life situations that are anything like linked lists?

14.2

Pointers in Pascal

Pointers can be confusing the first time you see them, but they're really pretty simple if you remember a few important ideas. We'll state these ideas here and then explain them with some examples:

caret
- When a **caret** symbol ^ is used in a type definition, it means *is a pointer to. . . .*
- When a caret symbol ^ is used in the body of a program or subprogram, it means *the thing pointed to by. . . .*
- If we have two variables, say `ptr` and `temp`, in which pointers are stored, and we execute

```
ptr := temp
```

this makes `ptr` point to the same place that `temp` points to.

Remember to look for these ideas as you read through the examples.

Program Example

```
PROGRAM PointDemo (output);
{Creates one cell.}
   TYPE
      ptrType  = ^cellType;
      cellType = RECORD
                       info : INTEGER;
                       next : ptrType
                    END;
   VAR
      ptr : ptrType;
BEGIN {PointDemo}
   New (ptr);
   ptr^.info := 50;
   ptr^.next := NIL;
   Write (ptr^.info:3)
END.   {PointDemo}
```

Sample Runs

```
50
```

Observations   First we look at the program's TYPE definitions and VAR declarations:

- ```
  TYPE
     ptrType  = ^cellType;
  ```

<span style="float:left">defining a
pointer type</span>
ptrType is the name of a new type. When the caret symbol ^ is used in a type definition it means *pointer to*.[1] So this type definition says that the value stored in a ptrType variable is a *pointer to* a cellType value.

- ```
  VAR
     ptr : ptrType;
  ```

declaring a
pointer
The VAR declaration says that ptr is a ptrType variable, so

ptr

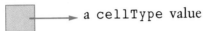
a cellType value

Remember what "pointer" actually means: it means an *address*. So the value stored in the variable ptr will actually be a number—it will be the address where a cellType value is stored:

ptr

		a
2135	. . . many memory locations later . . .	cellType value

2001   2135

Now what's this cellType value that's being pointed to?

- ```
  TYPE
     cellType = RECORD
                   info : INTEGER;
                   next : ptrType
                END;
  ```

<span style="float:left">defining a cell</span>
A cellType value has two fields. The first field contains information that's useful in solving some problem. In Program PointDemo we chose, when defining cellType, to put an ordinary INTEGER in this field.

ptr   a cellType value

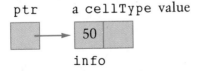

info

The second field contains a value of type ptrType. If we look again at the definition of type ptrType, we see that a ptrType is a pointer to a cellType value.

---

[1]Some implementations use an up-arrow ↑ instead of a caret.
  ```

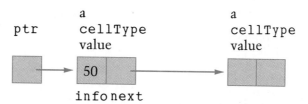

So the second field of each cellType points to another cellType. This is something new.

We've examined the type definitions at the top of Program PointDemo, and we've shown how the definitions lend themselves to the creation of a linked list, but we haven't shown how the linked list actually comes to be created. After all, the declaration of the variable ptr creates just one storage location:

ptr

At this point there are no cells and no list—just one variable that will eventually contain a ptrType value. To see how a list is created, we have to look at each line in the program's body:

- New (ptr)

creating a cell

New is a pre-declared procedure in Pascal. New makes a pointer variable point to something. When New is applied to the variable ptr, it puts the address of a cellType into the variable ptr.

ptr

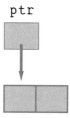

info next

We're oversimplifying a bit when we just say "puts the address of a cellType into ptr." It's more accurate to say it this way: When New is applied to the variable ptr, the computer finds some adjacent memory locations—enough locations to store a cellType record. It puts the address of the first of these locations in the variable ptr. So, by calling New, we make ptr point to memory locations where a cellType record can be stored.

- ptr^.info := 50

referring to a
field in a cell

When the caret symbol ^ is used in the body of a program it means *the value pointed to by. . . .* So ptr^ means *the cellType record pointed to by* ptr.

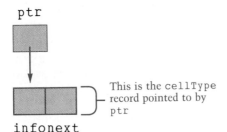

This is the `cellType` record pointed to by `ptr`

We've already seen that a `cellType` record has two fields—an `info` field and a `next` field. So `ptr^.info` means *the* `info` *field of the record pointed to by* `ptr`.

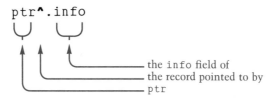

the `info` field of
the record pointed to by
`ptr`

In `PointDemo`'s first assignment statement we put 50 in this `info` field:

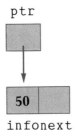

You should stop and make sure you understand why `ptr^.info` means *the* `info` *field of the record pointed to by* `ptr`. It's very important because in this chapter you'll see expressions of the form

```
something^.something-else
```

over and over again.

- `ptr^.next := NIL`

  `ptr^.next` means *the* `next` *field of the record pointed to by* `ptr`. In `PointDemo`'s second assignment statement, we put the value `NIL` into this field:

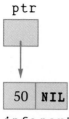

info next

NIL

NIL is a special pointer value in Pascal. It's the pointer that points nowhere. Giving next the value NIL is like saying "next doesn't point anywhere" and "next doesn't contain the address of any cellType value."

- Write (ptr^.info:3)

ptr^.info is still *the* info *field of the record pointed to by* ptr. The number 50 is stored in that info field. So this statement writes 50 to the screen.

Now let's rewrite the program so that it uses two pointers.

Program Example

```
PROGRAM TwoPointers (output);
{Creates one cell with two
 pointers to point to it.}
   TYPE
      ptrType  = ^cellType;
      cellType = RECORD
                      info : INTEGER;
                      next : ptrType
                  END;
   VAR
      ptr, temp : ptrType;
BEGIN {TwoPointers}
   ptr := NIL;

   New (temp);
   temp^.info := 50;
   temp^.next := ptr;
   ptr        := temp;

   Write (ptr^.info:3)
END.   {TwoPointers}
```

Sample Runs

50

Traces

- VAR
     ptr, temp : ptrType;

This VAR declaration creates two variables named ptr and temp:

- `ptr := NIL;`
  `New (temp);`
  `temp^.info := 50`

  The `NIL` value is stored in `ptr`, and `temp` gets the address of a memory location where a `cellType` record can be stored. Then 50 is placed in the cell's `info` field.

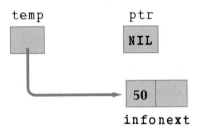

- `temp^.next := ptr`

  The `NIL` value that's currently stored in `ptr` is also placed into `temp^.next`:

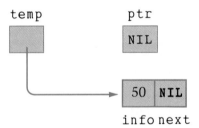

- `ptr := temp`

pointer assignment If you have two variables, `ptr` and `temp`, in which pointers are stored, and you execute this assignment statement, *it makes `ptr` point to the same place that `temp` points to.* There's actually nothing mysterious about this rule. The computer is just taking the address that's in `temp` and putting it into `ptr`:

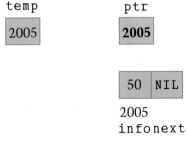

If we replace the addresses with arrows, it looks like this:

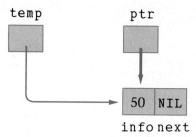

temp　　　　　　　　ptr

50　NIL

info next

- `Write (ptr^.info:3)`

The number 50, stored in `ptr^.info`, is written on the screen.

So far we've managed only to make storage of the value 50 a bit more complicated. But soon we'll see that we've taken some very useful steps.

In the next program example we take the four statements in the middle of Program `TwoPointers`'s body and execute them twice.

Program Example

```
PROGRAM BiggerList (output);
{Creates a linked list with two cells.}
   TYPE
      ptrType  = ^cellType;
      cellType = RECORD
                    info : INTEGER;
                    next : ptrType
                 END;
   VAR
      ptr, temp : ptrType;
BEGIN {BiggerList}
   ptr := NIL;

   New (temp);
   temp^.info := 50;
   temp^.next := ptr;
   ptr        := temp;

   New (temp);
   temp^.info := 40;
   temp^.next := ptr;
   ptr        := temp;

   Write (temp^.info:3);
   temp := temp^.next;
   Write (temp^.info:3)
END.  {BiggerList}
```

Sample Runs

```
40 50
```

Traces

Let's go step by step through the action of Program BiggerList. The first five statements in Program BiggerList are copied right from Program TwoPointers, so to start off, we get

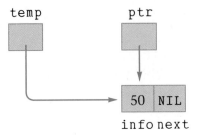

Then in Program BiggerList we execute four of these statements again. Here's what happens:

- New (temp);
  temp^.info := 40

  temp is made to point to a newly found memory location—the location where a cellType record can be stored. Then the value 40 is assigned to the info field of the record pointed to by temp:

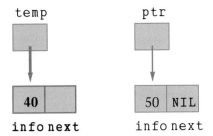

- temp^.next := ptr

  temp^.next means *the* next *field of the record pointed to by* temp.

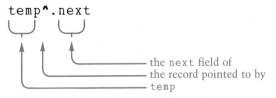

When the assignment statement is executed, temp^.next is made to point to the same record that ptr points to:

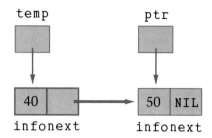

- `ptr := temp`

  `ptr` is made to point to the same place that `temp` points to:

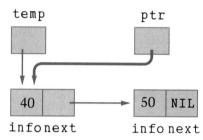

Now `ptr` points to the first of two cells in a linked list!

The rest of the program **traverses** the list and writes the `info` values as it goes:

- `Write (temp^.info:3)`

  The `info` field of the record pointed to by `temp` is written to the screen.

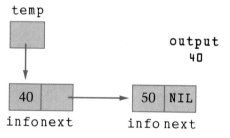

- `temp := temp^.next`

advancing a pointer

  We'll see lines like this over and over again in our programs. This statement does, for the pointer `temp`, what `i := i + 1` does for the `INTEGER` variable `i`. It **advances the pointer** by one cell. Here's why:

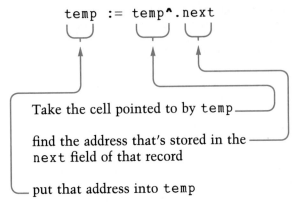

The overall effect is to make temp point to the same place that temp^.next used to point to:

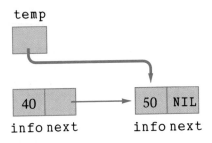

- Write (temp^.info:3)

  This statement writes the new value of temp^.info, which is 50.

14.2 Exercises

Key Words to Review

caret	NIL	advance a pointer
New	traverse	

Questions to Answer

QUE 14.2.1 Can you create the linked list that we created in Program BiggerList without having two pointer variables? Why, or why not?

QUE 14.2.2 With the definitions and declarations in Program PointDemo, explain the meaning of the expression

        ptr^.next

QUE 14.2.3 Explain why the declaration of a pointer variable creates just one storage location, and not an entire linked list.

QUE 14.2.4   Explain the effect of the statement

```
ptr := temp
```

in Program TwoPointers.

Experiments to Try

Experiments with Program PointDemo:

EXP 14.2.1   Change Write (ptr^.info:3) to Write (ptr:10).

EXP 14.2.2   Change Write (ptr^.info:3) to Write (ptr^.next:10).

EXP 14.2.3   Remove the statement ptr^.next := NIL.

EXP 14.2.4   Remove the statement ptr^.info := 50.

EXP 14.2.5   Remove the statement New (ptr).

EXP 14.2.6   Switch the lines that assign values to ptr^.info and ptr^.next.

EXP 14.2.7   Switch the lines that define info : INTEGER and next : ptrType.

EXP 14.2.8   Move the definition of ptrType so that it comes after the definition of cellType.

EXP 14.2.9   Add a new line ptr := ptr^.next just before the END. Then try to add an additional line after it that writes the value 50 from the list.

EXP 14.2.10   Add the following declarations:

```
TYPE
   intPtrType = ^INTEGER;
VAR
   intPtr : intPtrType;
```

to your program. Then put intPtr := ptr anywhere in the main body of the program.

EXP 14.2.11   Redo Exercise Exp.14.2.10. This time, see if it helps to add ptr := NIL right before intPtr := ptr.

Experiments with Program TwoPointers:

EXP 14.2.12   Change ptr := temp to temp := ptr.

EXP 14.2.13   Change temp^.next := ptr to temp^.next := temp and, just before the Write, add several ptr := ptr^.nexts.

EXP 14.2.14   After the Write, add two identical ptr := ptr^.next lines. (This will definitely give you an error diagnostic—the diagnostic that you see most often when you write programs involving pointers. Study this error carefully. If you can grasp what's going on you'll be able to debug 90 percent of your pointer programs.)

EXP 14.2.15   Redo Exercise Exp.14.2.14, but first remove the statement temp^.next := ptr.

Experiments with Program BiggerList:

EXP 14.2.16   Change the last line to Write (ptr^.info:3).

EXP 14.2.17   Change the last line to Write (ptr^.next^.info:3).

EXP 14.2.18   Have the last two statements in the program be executed twice.

EXP 14.2.19   After the second Write, add a new line ptr := ptr^.next. Then try to add an additional line after it that writes the value 40 from the list.

Changes to Make

CHA 14.2.1   Modify Program BiggerList so that it stores the numbers 50, 40, and 30 in a linked list that's three cells long.

CHA 14.2.2   In Program BiggerList change the call to New so that it says New (ptr). How do you change the rest of the program so that it achieves the same effect as the old version?

Scales to Practice

PRA 14.2.1   Write a program which creates a list with two cells that point to one another.

PRA 14.2.2   Write a program which creates a list in which the last cell points to itself.

14.3

Linked List Operations

In this chapter we'll treat linked lists as an abstract data type; that is, our main programs won't directly change or examine any lists. Instead, they'll *call subprograms* that do the changing and examining. We'll design a separate subprogram for each operation that can be performed on a linked list, and we'll reuse each subprogram. In other words, we'll carry our subprograms from one main program to another. We'll think of this collection of subprograms as our **tool set**. When we need to do anything with a linked list, we'll call one of the subprograms in our tool set.

a tool set

Now here's how our tool set turns linked lists into an abstract data type: *Once we're done writing a subprogram, we won't look again at the code inside its body.* In order to trace the action of a program, we'll simply remember what action each subprogram performs and make drawings based on our knowledge of those actions.

Let's begin by creating subprograms from the statements in Program BiggerList (Section 14.2). The first statement in the program's body is used to *initialize* the list.

```
ptr := NIL
```

initializing a linked list

(Just like counters and accumulators, linked lists have to be initialized.) So we create a procedure Initialize:

```
PROCEDURE Initialize (VAR ptr : ptrType);
{Initializes a linked list.}

BEGIN {Initialize}
  ptr := NIL
END;   {Initialize}
```

Many of our linked list programs will start with a call to this procedure. In Program BiggerList the code

```
New (temp);
temp^.info := some value;
temp^.next := ptr;
ptr        := temp
```

adding a cell to a linked list

appears twice. It adds two new cells to the list. We can turn this code into a subprogram:

```
PROCEDURE Push (VAR ptr : ptrType ;
                    i       : INTEGER);
{Pushes a new cell onto a linked list.}

  VAR
    temp : ptrType;

BEGIN {Push}
  New (temp);
  temp^.info := i;
  temp^.next := ptr;
  ptr        := temp
END;   {Push}
```

or perhaps into two subprograms:

```
PROCEDURE CreateCell (VAR temp : ptrType ;
                          i        : infoType;
                          ptr      : ptrType);
{Creates a new cell and places
'i' and 'ptr' into its fields.}

BEGIN {CreateCell}
  New (temp);
  temp^.info := i;
  temp^.next := ptr
END;   {CreateCell}

{----------}

PROCEDURE Push (VAR ptr : ptrType  ;
                    i       : infoType);
{Pushes a new cell onto a linked list.}

BEGIN {Push}
  CreateCell (ptr, i, ptr)
END;   {Push}
```

Taken together, these two procedures do exactly the same work as the original four lines in Program BiggerList. Procedure CreateCell makes a new cell and fills its info and next fields. Procedure Push calls

CreateCell in just the right way so that the new cell gets attached to the head of the list. In the bodies of our linked list programs we'll see repeated calls to Procedures CreateCell and Push.

Notice how we've substituted infoType for INTEGER in Procedures CreateCell and Push. This will help somewhat in making our procedures be *polymorphic*. (See Section 10.5.)

There's another useful procedure we can get from our BiggerList program. The last few lines in the program

```
Write (temp^.info:3);
temp := temp^.next;
Write (temp^.info:3)
```

writing the values in a list

are for traversing the list and writing the list's info values during the traversal. We can turn these lines into a procedure:

```
PROCEDURE WriteList (ptr : ptrType);
{Writes the info values stored in a linked list.}

  VAR
    temp : ptrType;
BEGIN {WriteList}
  temp := ptr;
  WHILE temp <> NIL DO
    BEGIN
      Write (temp^.info:4);
      temp := temp^.next
    END
END;   {WriteList}
```

Traces

• temp := ptr

This statement makes temp point to the same cell that ptr points to. It's the first cell whose info value gets written.

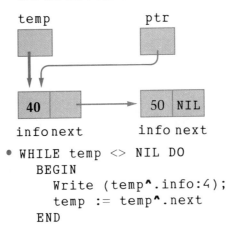

• WHILE temp <> NIL DO
    BEGIN
      Write (temp^.info:4);
      temp := temp^.next
    END

In a loop, we keep writing info values and then, with temp :=
temp^.next, advancing to the next cell. Here's a more detailed
description of the action:

First we write the value of temp^.info:

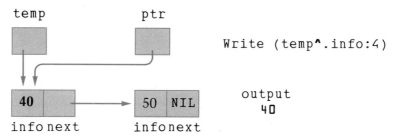

Write (temp^.info:4)

output
40

Then we advance the temp pointer to make it point to the next cell:

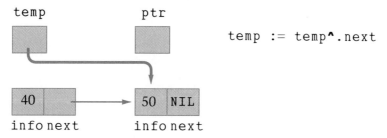

temp := temp^.next

Then we write the value of temp^.info again:

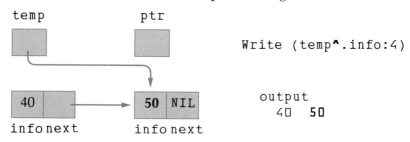

Write (temp^.info:4)

output
40   50

and so on, for each cell in the list. Of course, in this example our linked
list has only two cells, so the loop should end here. To see why it ends,
look at what happens when one more temp := temp^.next is
executed:

Before another temp := temp^.next is executed, temp^.next
has the value NIL.

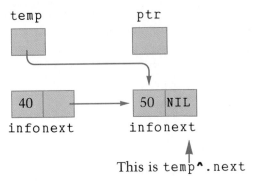

This is temp^.next

After temp := temp^.next is executed, temp has the value NIL.

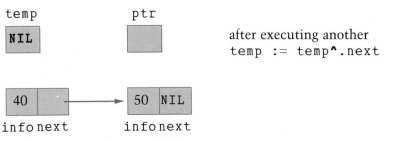

after executing another
temp := temp^.next

So now our WHILE temp <> NIL DO loop ends.

So now we have four procedures—Initialize, CreateCell, Push, and WriteList. These are the first in our catalog of linked list subprograms. In the next few sections we'll use the tools that we've created. Occasionally we'll change the names of the formal parameters to make the code more readable:

```
PROCEDURE Initialize (VAR ptr : ptrType);
{Initializes a linked list.}

BEGIN {Initialize}
  ptr := NIL
END;   {Initialize}

PROCEDURE Initialize (VAR stack : ptrType);
{Initializes a linked list.}

BEGIN {Initialize}
  stack := NIL
END;   {Initialize}
```

This won't make any difference in the way the subprograms behave.

It's almost time to solve some interesting problems using linked lists. But before you read on, make sure to learn what each of the procedures in our tool set does. Your understanding of the next several sections depends not so much on your dexterity with pointers, but rather on your familiarity with the procedures in our tool set.

Programming Style

a pointer as a result value

Take another look at Procedure `CreateCell`. It has only one `VAR` parameter, so it could be a function:

```
FUNCTION CreatedCell (i   : infoType;
                          ptr : ptrType  ) : ptrType;
{Creates a new cell and places
'i' and 'ptr' into its fields.}
  VAR
    newCell : ptrType;
BEGIN {CreatedCell}
  New (newCell);
  newCell^.info := i;
  newCell^.next := ptr;

  CreatedCell    := newCell
END;   {CreatedCell}
PROCEDURE Push (VAR ptr : ptrType  ;
                    i        : infoType);
{Pushes a new cell onto a linked list.}
BEGIN {Push}
  ptr := CreatedCell (i, ptr)
END;   {Push}
```

In Section 10.1 we said that the result types of functions could only be simple types. That wasn't quite true. Even though pointer types aren't considered to be simple types, a function can return a pointer as its result type.

14.3   Exercises

Key Words to Review

tool set

Questions to Answer

QUE 14.3.1   Explain the effect of the procedure call `CreateCell (ptr, i, ptr)`.

QUE 14.3.2   What happens when we make two identical calls to Procedure `CreateCell`, one right after another? And what about two identical calls to Procedure `Push`?

QUE 14.3.3   Explain the effect of the statement

```
temp := temp^.next
```

in Procedure `WriteList`.

Changes to Make

CHA 14.3.1   Turn Procedure `WriteList` into a new Procedure `LinearSearch` (see Section 10.5), which returns the *position* in the list (if any) where the `searchFor` value is stored.

CHA 14.3.2   Modify Procedure WriteList so that it uses recursion rather than iteration.

Scales to Practice

PRA 14.3.1   Write a function subprogram that accepts a pointer to a linked list and returns the number of cells in the list.

PRA 14.3.2   Read ten INTEGER values and store them in a linked list. Then examine the list to determine if, as you move from one cell to another, the values are non-decreasing.

PRA 14.3.3   Read ten INTEGER values and store them in a linked list pointed to by ptr1. Then read ten more INTEGER values and store them in a linked list pointed to by ptr2. Then examine the lists to find out if the values stored in them are identical.

PRA 14.3.4   Redo Exercise Pra.10.7.1, this time testing for similar linked lists.

PRA 14.3.5   Redo Exercise Wri.10.9.2, using linked lists instead of arrays.

PRA 14.3.6   Instead of making a linked list in this section, we could have stored our values in an array. One way to do this is to put a dummy value (−1, for instance) in the component that comes after the last value in the list:

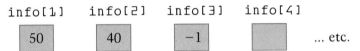

```
info[1]    info[2]    info[3]    info[4]
  50         40         −1                      ... etc.
```

Modify Procedures Initialize, CreateCell, Push, and WriteList so that they deal with an array rather than a linked list. Then write a test driver for these procedures.

PRA 14.3.7   Redo Exercise Pra.14.3.6, but this time start by declaring

```
TYPE
   listType = RECORD
                  info   : ARRAY [1..20] OF INTEGER;
                  unused : 1..21
              END;
VAR
   list : listType;
```

Instead of putting a dummy value after the last component of the list, we make list.unused be the index of the component where that dummy value would go.

PRA 14.3.8   Reread Exercise Pra.14.1.1. In that exercise, we presented a way to mimic linked lists without pointers, using only INTEGER values stored in an ordinary array. Rewrite Procedures Initialize, Push, CreateCell, and WriteList for lists of this kind.

14.4

Stacks

Specifications   Look once more at Program BiggerList. The number 40 is the last number that gets put into the list, but it's the first number that gets written.

last-in first-out   That's why the list that's created in Program BiggerList is called a last-in first-out (LIFO) list. Another name for a LIFO list is a **stack**. The word *stack* calls to mind a stack of plates on a spring-loaded cart in a cafeteria. The last plate to be **pushed** onto the stack, the plate that's on top, is always the first plate that gets popped off the stack.

In this section we test the procedures we created in Section 14.3 by making a stack that contains several cells.

Input: Several numbers.

Process: Store the numbers on a stack.

Output: The same numbers printed out in reverse order (that is, last-in first-out order).

This is the third program we've seen in which we reverse the order of input. The first was Program Reverse in Section 10.1, using an array. The second was Program RecReverse in Section 13.2, using recursion.

Program Example

```
PROGRAM StackDemo (input, output);
{Shows how a stack is created.}
   TYPE
      infoType = INTEGER;
      ptrType  = ^cellType;
      cellType = RECORD
                    info : infoType;
                    next : ptrType
                 END;
   VAR
      stack  : ptrType;
      number : infoType;

   {----------}
   {Put the linked list subprograms
    from Section 14.3 here.}
   {----------}
BEGIN {StackDemo}
   Initialize (stack);
   WriteLn    ('Enter several numbers, all on one line:');
   WHILE NOT Eoln DO
      BEGIN
         Read (number);
         Push (stack, number)
      END;
   WriteLn;
   WriteLn    ('The same numbers in reverse order are:');
   WriteList (stack)
END.  {StackDemo}
```

Sample Runs

```
Enter several numbers, all on one line:
50 40 30 20 10

The same numbers in reverse order are:
   10   20   30   40   50
```

Observations To recall what Procedure `Push` does, look at the diagrams in Section 14.2, and reread the code in the procedure's body. The first time we make the call

pushing cells onto a stack

```
Push (stack, number)
```

with `number` equal to 50 we get:

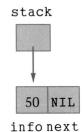

Then after another call to `Push`, with `number` equal to 40 we have

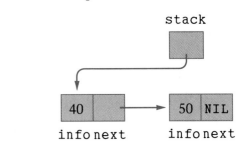

By the end of the fifth call to Procedure `Push`, the `stack` variable points to the first of five cells in a linked list:

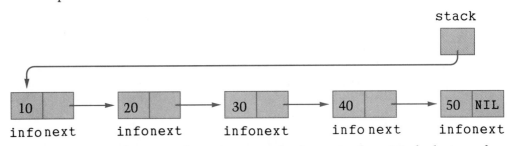

Notice how a stack's pointers work: they point from 10, the last number in, down to 50. By calling Procedure `WriteList` we print the list's values in last-in first-out order, just by following the pointers that we created.

We're actually using the word *stack* in two ways here. The whole list is a stack, but the pointer variable that points to the top of the list is also called `stack`. It turns out that this double usage makes the code easier to understand.

Further Discussion

referring to
cellType
before it's
defined

Let's take a closer look at the type definitions in Program `StackDemo`:

```
TYPE
  ptrType  = ^cellType;                    ←───── ptrType is defined by
                                                  referring to cellType

  cellType = RECORD                        ←───── cellType isn't define
              info : infoType;                    until the next line
              next : ptrType
             END;
```

Recall once again the rule from Section 3.5 that an identifier can't be used before it's been defined. In these type definitions we seem to have violated that rule because the identifier `cellType` is used on one line, and defined on the next line. But Pascal's scope rules contain loopholes that allow us to refer to

`^some-type`

before we've defined *some-type*. We take advantage of these loopholes whenever we define a linked list.

addresses and
abstraction

Pointers are interesting objects. They contain values that are a bit different from the values in our earlier programs. For example, we've emphasized that a pointer variable stores an address, and we've represented addresses with numbers like 2001, 2002, etc. So we may be tempted to try to `Write` the values of these addresses. But if we insert

`WriteLn (stack:10)`

into Program `StackDemo`, most compilers will give us an error diagnostic. That's because ANSI Standard Pascal doesn't treat addresses as `INTEGER`s (even though we use integers in our drawings to show how pointers work).

Here again we have the notion of *data abstraction*. Certain details about the data, namely the numeric values of addresses, are being hidden from us because these are details that we don't need to know. In fact, these are details that we're safer not knowing.

With the introduction of Procedure `New`, we're doing something that we've never done before. We're using executable statements, in the body of the program, to create memory locations where values can be stored. Instead of "creating" memory locations, we usually say that we're *allocating* memory locations. Until this point in the text we've never allocated memory with statements in the program's body. All memory was allocated in the program's `VAR` declarations with lines like

```
VAR
  a : ARRAY [1..10] OF INTEGER;
```

static and
dynamic
allocation

When we use `VAR` declarations, we're doing what's called **static allocation.** When we use statements in the body of the program, we're doing **dynamic allocation.** Dynamic allocation has some advantages over static allocation. Notice, for instance, that in Program `StackDemo`, we never declare how large the linked list will be. The list can grow indefinitely. On the other hand, when we declare an array, we're using static allocation, and when we give the range of indices, we're declaring exactly how large the array will be.

14.4   Exercises

Key Words to Review

stack	push	dynamic allocation
last-in first-out (LIFO)	static allocation	

Questions to Answer

QUE 14.4.1   Can we write Procedure `CreateCell` without using a local variable `temp`? Why, or why not?

QUE 14.4.2   Explain the difference between static and dynamic allocation.

QUE 14.4.3   The components of an array are stored in adjacent memory locations, but the contents of a linked list are not. In light of this difference, why can we never change the number of components of an array during the run of the program? Why can we change the number of cells in a linked list during the run of the program?

Experiments to Try

EXP 14.4.1   Remove the call to Procedure `Initialize` from Program `StackDemo`.

EXP 14.4.2   Change the body of Procedure `CreateCell` as follows:

```
BEGIN {CreateCell}
  New (ptr);
  ptr^.info := i;
  ptr^.next := ptr
END;   {CreateCell}
```

EXP 14.4.3   Change the type definition part of Program `StackDemo` to

```
TYPE
  infoType = INTEGER;
  ptrType  = ^RECORD
               info : infoType;
               next : ptrType
             END;
```

EXP 14.4.4   Change code in Program `StackDemo` as follows:

```
TYPE
  infoType = INTEGER;
  cellType = RECORD
               info : infoType;
               next : ^cellType
             END;
VAR
  stack   : ^cellType;
```

Changes to Make

CHA 14.4.1   Modify Program StackDemo so that, before it reads numbers from the keyboard, it pushes a cell with sentinel value −1 in its info field onto the stack. Then modify Procedure WriteList so that it stops when it sees this sentinel value.

Scales to Practice

PRA 14.4.1   Use the main body of Program StackDemo, exactly as it appears in this section, to test the procedures you wrote for Exercise Pra.14.3.8.

Programs and Subprograms to Write

Many of the exercises in this chapter can be done without explicitly using pointers. Instead of using pointers, do the exercises with calls to the subprograms in our tool set.

WRI 14.4.1   Write and test a subprogram that makes a copy of a stack. That is, stack1 and stack2 always point to different collections of cells, but after the call

        StackCopy (stack1, stack2)

the cells pointed to by stack2 have the same info values as the cells pointed to by stack1. *Hint:* Use the subprograms in our tool set along with a third stack tempStack.

WRI 14.4.2   Redo Exercise Wri.13.2.1, using a stack in place of recursion.

14.5

Stacks (Continued)

Specifications So far we've learned how to push numbers onto a stack and then write the numbers by traversing the stack. Now we'll do things a slightly different way. Instead of writing numbers by traversing the stack, we'll pop numbers **popping cells off** off the stack. When we pop a cell off a stack, we're actually *removing* that **of a stack** cell from the stack. The words *push* and *pop*, rather than *add* and *remove*, are used because they convey the last-in first-out spirit.

Designing a We'll start by creating the same stack that we created in Program
Program StackDemo:

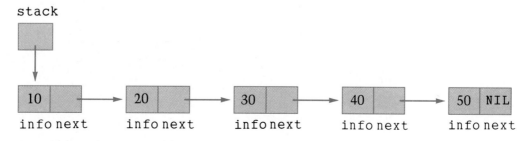

Then to remove a cell from the stack, we'll just advance the stack pointer:

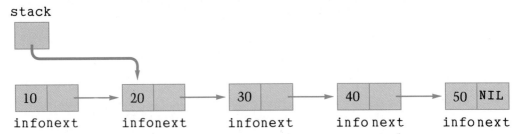

When we do this, we'll say that the cell with 10 in it has been "removed" from the stack, but in truth this cell isn't "gone"—it's just unreachable. There's nothing pointing to it, and it has no name of its own, so there's no longer any way to refer to this memory location in the code. For all practical purposes, this cell has been "removed" (popped) from the stack.

So the essence of Procedure Pop is just one statement that advances a pointer:

```
stack := stack^.next
```

Of course, before we remove a cell from the stack, we probably want to save the value in the cell's info field:

```
i := stack^.info
```

And we don't even want to try to remove a cell if the stack is already empty:

```
IF IsEmpty (stack) THEN
   WriteLn (Chr(7), 'Error: Empty stack')
```

Here's what we get when we put all this code together:

popping a stack

```
PROCEDURE Pop (VAR stack : ptrType   ;
                  VAR i     : infoType);
{Pops a cell off the stack.}

BEGIN {Pop}
  IF IsEmpty (stack) THEN
    WriteLn (Chr(7), 'Error: Empty stack')
  ELSE
    BEGIN
       i      := stack^.info;
       stack := stack^.next
    END
END;  {Pop}
```

Is the stack empty?

Now it's easy to tell if the stack IsEmpty:

```
FUNCTION IsEmpty (stack : ptrType) : BOOLEAN;
{Determines whether the stack is empty.}

BEGIN {IsEmpty}
  IsEmpty := (stack = NIL)
END;   {IsEmpty}
```

The stack variable will have NIL in it when the stack is initialized and again after we've Popped all the cells out of it. (Check this!)

The code for our new program follows.

**Program
Example**

```
PROGRAM StackDemo2 (input, output);
{Shows how a stack is created and destroyed.}

   TYPE
      infoType = INTEGER;
      ptrType  = ^cellType;
      cellType = RECORD
                      info : infoType;
                      next : ptrType
                   END;
   VAR
      stack  : ptrType;
      number : infoType;

   {----------}

   {Put the list subprograms
    (including Pop and IsEmpty) here.}

   {----------}

BEGIN {StackDemo2}
   Initialize (stack);
   WriteLn    ('Enter several numbers, all on one line:');

   WHILE NOT Eoln DO
      BEGIN
         Read (number);
         Push (stack, number)
      END;

   WriteLn;
   WriteLn    ('The same numbers in reverse order are:');
   WHILE NOT IsEmpty (stack) DO
      BEGIN
         Pop    (stack, number);
         Write (number:4)
      END
END.   {StackDemo2}
```

**Sample
Runs**

```
Enter several numbers, all on one line:
50 40 30 20 10

The same numbers in reverse order are:
   10   20   30   40   50
```

**Further
Discussion**

Notice that there's an IsEmpty subprogram, but there's no subprogram called IsFull. This is because we're using dynamic allocation. The size of a linked list can grow almost indefinitely.

*accidentally
losing a cell*

In the code for Procedure Push we lost a cell when we advanced the stack pointer, because, as we said, that cell had "no name of its own." This is true of all the cells in the lists we create—they have no names of their own. In the code we always declare variables to have type `ptrType`, never `cellType`. We never have a variable that holds a cell. The only way we refer to a cell is indirectly, by referring to something that points to the cell. Since cells don't have names of their own, they're said to be **anonymous**

Now notice that the effect of the statement

```
stack := stack^.next
```

is irreversible. Once we've advanced the `stack` pointer—say, from the 10-cell to the 20-cell—we can't go back and find the 10-cell again, because the 10-cell no longer has anything pointing to it. There's a moral here: *Be careful when you advance a pointer like* `stack`. *Do it only when you intend to lose a cell.*

In Programs `StackDemo` and `StackDemo2` the value of `stack` isn't changed directly by statements in the main body. Instead, changes to the value of `stack` are done in subprograms. The main program has to call a subprogram if it wants to change the value of `stack`. This is a nice safe programming practice: The values of "sensitive" variables are changed only within certain subprograms, where we know that the changes will be made correctly.

14.5   Exercises

Key Words to Review

pop   anonymous

Questions to Answer

QUE 14.5.1   What's the difference between traversing a stack and popping cells off the stack?

QUE 14.5.2   Under what circumstances is the effect of the following statement irreversible?

```
stack := stack^.next
```

Is there a context in which the effect of this statement can be undone?

QUE 14.5.3   It would be much harder to pop a cell off the top of a stack if the pointers pointed from the bottom of the stack toward the top. Why?

QUE 14.5.4   Would it be harder to push a cell onto the top of a stack if the pointers pointed from the bottom toward the top? Why, or why not?

Things to Check in a Manual

MAN 14.5.1   Does your implementation provide a way of creating a pointer to a cell that is not anonymous?

Experiments to Try

EXP 14.5.1   In Program StackDemo2 modify the WHILE condition so that ten values are popped off the stack, no matter how many were pushed onto it. Push only nine values onto the stack.

Changes to Make

CHA 14.5.1   Modify Program StackDemo2 so that, at any point during the program's execution, the user has the option of either pushing another number onto the stack or popping the top number (if there is one) off the stack.

CHA 14.5.2   Redo Exercise Cha.13.2.2, using a stack instead of recursion.

CHA 14.5.3   Redo Exercise Cha.13.2.3, using a stack instead of recursion.

CHA 14.5.4   The notion of *postponement* that we see in recursion can also be implemented nicely using a stack. Rewrite Procedure WriteBin from Section 13.3 so that the postponement is done using a stack rather than with recursion.

Scales to Practice

PRA 14.5.1   Implement Function IsEmpty and Procedure Pop using the alternate implementations of a list described in Exercises Pra.14.1.1, Pra.14.3.6, and Pra.14.3.7. Use the main body of Program StackDemo2, exactly as it appears in this section, to test your new subprograms.

Programs and Subprograms to Write

Reminder: Many of the exercises in this chapter can be done without explicitly using pointers. Instead of using pointers, use calls to the subprograms in our tool set.

WRI 14.5.1   Write and test a subprogram that reverses the values in a stack. After the call

```
StackReverse (stack)
```

the value that used to be on the top of the stack should be on the bottom, and vice versa.

WRI 14.5.2   Write a subprogram that *concatenates* two stacks; that is, it takes two smaller stacks and turns them into one large stack. All the values in one small stack are simply piled on top of the other small stack. (*Hint:* You don't need to move around lots of values. Just change a pointer or two.)

WRI 14.5.3   Rewrite Program Merge (Section 10.7) so that it merges two small stacks into one large stack. (*Hint:* You may want to finish this program with the subprogram you wrote for Exercise Wri.14.5.1.)

WRI 14.5.4   Redo Exercise Wri.13.4.2, using a stack instead of an array.

WRI 14.5.5   Rewrite the iterative Towers of Hanoi program (Exercise Wri.13.6.1) using three stacks to implement the three pegs.

14.6

Queues

Recent estimates indicate that the average American spends at least 50 hours a year waiting in lines.[2] Even when you're not standing in line behind another person, you're on waiting lists for courses or your program is waiting to snatch a slice of computer time from the programs that other people are running. Waiting lines are everywhere. They're fertile ground for problems in mathematics, computer science, and many other disciplines. In computer science, a waiting line is called by its British-English name; it's called a **queue.**

Designing a Program

first-in first-out

Let's begin by comparing queues and stacks. Recall that a stack is a last-in first-out list. What about a queue? If you're the first person to get into a waiting line, you should be the first person to get out (that is, the first person to receive service). This means a queue is a **first-in first-out (FIFO)** list.

When you enter a queue, you enter at the **rear,** but by the time you leave the queue, you leave from the **front.** This means it's convenient to have two pointers for each queue:

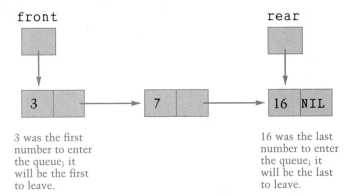

front

rear

| 3 | | → | 7 | | → | 16 | NIL |

3 was the first
number to enter
the queue; it
will be the first
to leave.

16 was the last
number to enter
the queue; it
will be the last
to leave.

So we'll need a `queue` variable that contains two pointers:

```
TYPE
   queueType = RECORD
                  front, rear : ptrType
               END;

VAR
   queue  : queueType;
```

In our queue subprograms we'll be referring to `queue.front` and `queue.rear`.

---

[2]From unpublished notes made by B. Burd during a visit to the State Office of Licensing and Motor Vehicles.

initializing a
queue

The queue subprograms are a little different from the stack subprograms, but not much. For instance, to `Initialize` a queue, we've got to set both its `front` and `rear` pointers to `NIL`:

```
PROCEDURE Initialize (VAR q : queueType);
{Initializes a queue.}

BEGIN {Initialize}
  WITH q DO
    BEGIN
      front := NIL;
      rear  := NIL
    END
END;   {Initialize}
```

Is the queue empty?

To see if the queue `IsEmpty` we can check either its `front` pointer or its `rear` pointer:

```
FUNCTION IsEmpty (q : queueType) : BOOLEAN;
{Determines whether the queue is empty.}

BEGIN {IsEmpty}
  IsEmpty := (q.front = NIL)
END;   {IsEmpty}
```

adding a cell to a queue

Now here's how we add a cell to the rear of the queue: First we create a new cell using the same subprogram we used in Section 14.3:

```
Create Cell (temp, i, NIL)
```

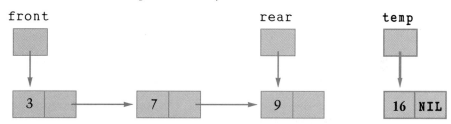

Then we make the last cell in the queue point to this new cell:

```
rear^.next := temp
```

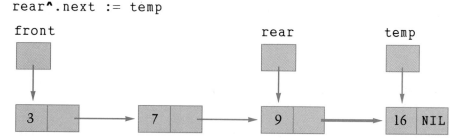

and then we make the `rear` variable point to this new cell:

```
rear := temp
```

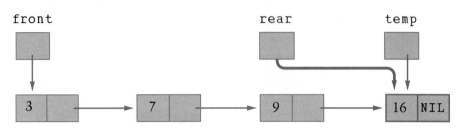

Putting it all together, we get

```
CreateCell (temp, i, NIL);
WITH q DO
  BEGIN
    rear^.next := temp;
    rear       := temp
  END
```

But what if the queue doesn't even have a "last" cell? If the queue IsEmpty, we simply create a new cell, and make the front and rear pointers point to it:

```
CreateCell (temp, i, NIL);
WITH q DO
  BEGIN
    front := temp;
    rear  := temp
  END
```

To get our AddCell procedure, we combine these two fragments of code:

```
PROCEDURE AddCell (VAR q : queueType;
                       i     : infoType);
{Adds a new cell to the rear of a queue.}
  VAR
    temp : ptrType;
BEGIN {AddCell}
  CreateCell (temp, i, NIL);
  WITH q DO
    BEGIN
      IF IsEmpty (q) THEN
        front := temp
      ELSE
        rear^.next := temp;
      rear := temp
    END
END;   {AddCell}
```

removing a cell from a queue   Now what about removing a cell from the queue? The essential step in removing a cell is to advance the front pointer:

```
front := front^.next
```

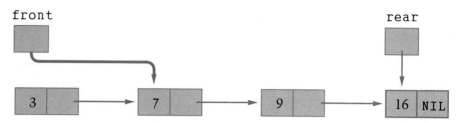

Of course, before we remove a cell, we probably want to save the value in the cell's `info` field:

```
i := front^.info
```

And we don't even want to try to remove a cell if the queue is already empty:

```
IF IsEmpty (q) THEN
   WriteLn (Chr(7), 'Error: Empty queue')
```

Putting this all together, we get

```
IF IsEmpty (q) THEN
   WriteLn (Chr(7), 'Error: Empty queue')
ELSE
   WITH q DO
     BEGIN
        i     := front^.info;
        front := front^.next
     END
```

Now look what this code does if it's removing the last remaining cell in a queue:

Before executing `front := front^.next`

This is `front^.next`
It has the value NIL

After executing front := front^.next

Since the queue becomes empty we should make both the front and the rear pointers be NIL. So let's add

```
IF front = NIL THEN
   rear := NIL
```

to the code for Procedure RemoveCell.

Now here's the procedure in its entirety:

```
PROCEDURE RemoveCell (VAR q : queueType;
                      VAR i : infoType);
{Removes a cell from the front of the queue.}

BEGIN {RemoveCell}
  IF IsEmpty (q) THEN
    WriteLn (Chr(7), 'Error: Empty queue')
  ELSE

    WITH q DO
      BEGIN
        i     := front^.info;
        front := front^.next;
        IF front = NIL THEN
          rear := NIL
      END
END;   {RemoveCell}
```

A program that tests our new queue subprograms follows.

**Program
Example**

```
PROGRAM QueueDemo (output);
{Adds and removes cells to (and from) a queue.}
  TYPE
    infoType  = INTEGER;
    ptrType   = ^cellType;
    cellType  = RECORD
                    info : infoType;
                    next : ptrType
                END;
    queueType = RECORD
                    front, rear : ptrType
                END;
```

```
        VAR
          queue  : queueType;
          number : infoType;

        {----------}

        {Put the queue subprograms here.}

        {----------}

      BEGIN {QueueDemo}
        Initialize (queue);
        AddCell    (queue, 3);
        AddCell    (queue, 7);
        AddCell    (queue, 16);

        RemoveCell (queue, number);
        WriteLn    ('Removed ', number:3);

        AddCell    (queue, 22);

        RemoveCell (queue, number);
        WriteLn    ('Removed ', number:3)
      END.  {QueueDemo}
```

Sample
Runs

```
Removed    3
Removed    7
```

Traces

Initialize (queue)

front   rear

NIL   NIL

AddCell (queue, 3)

front   rear

3 NIL

AddCell (queue, 7)

front   rear

3   →   7 NIL

AddCell (queue, 16)

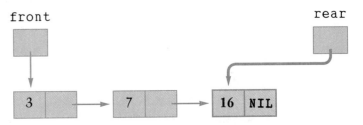

RemoveCell (queue, number)

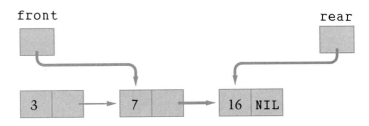

AddCell (queue, 22)

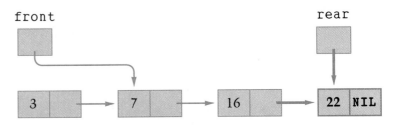

RemoveCell (queue, number)

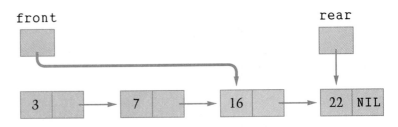

14.6   Exercises

Key Words to Review

queue   front
first-in first-out (FIFO)   rear

Questions to Answer

QUE 14.6.1   Explain how the statements in Program QueueDemo create a first-in first-out list.

QUE 14.6.2   It would be much harder to remove a cell from the front of a queue if the pointers pointed from the rear toward the front. Why?

QUE 14.6.3   Would it be harder to add a cell to the rear of a queue if the pointers pointed from the rear toward the front? Why, or why not?

Changes to Make

CHA 14.6.1   Modify Program QueueDemo so that, during the run of the program, the user determines when a value should be added to the queue, when a value should be removed from the queue, and when the program should stop running.

Scales to Practice

PRA 14.6.1   Implement each of the queue subprograms using the implementations of Exercises Pra.14.3.6 and Pra.14.3.7. Of course, you'll have to modify each implementation a bit in order to keep the queue from running off the edge of the array. Try using a circular array as in Exercise Pra.10.1.9. Use the main body of Program QueueDemo, exactly as it appears in this section, to test your new subprograms.

PRA 14.6.2   Implement each of the queue subprograms using the array implementation of a linked list, as described in Exercise Pra.14.1.1. Use the main body of Program QueueDemo, exactly as it appears in this section, to test your new subprograms.

Programs and Subprograms to Write

WRI 14.6.1   Repeat Exercise Wri.14.4.1 with queues instead of stacks.

WRI 14.6.2   Repeat Exercise Wri.14.5.1 with queues instead of stacks.

WRI 14.6.3   Repeat Exercise Wri.14.5.2 with queues instead of stacks.

WRI 14.6.4   Repeat Exercise Wri.14.5.3 with queues instead of stacks.

WRI 14.6.5   Redo Exercise Wri.7.5.2, using a *circularly linked list:*

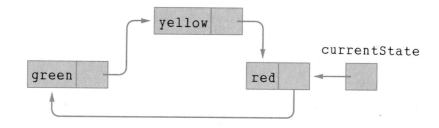

WRI 14.6.6   Write a program that creates a circularly linked list containing the numbers on a clock face. (See Exercise Wri.14.6.5.) Test your subprogram by having it write the hours in a whole day.

WRI 14.6.7   Modify Exercise Wri.14.6.6 so that it keeps track of 60 minutes rather than 12 hours.

WRI 14.6.8   Combine Exercises Wri.14.6.6 and Wri.14.6.7 so that, instead of being a single pointer, the `currentTime` is a record consisting of three pointers, `currentHours`, `currentMinutes`, and `currentSeconds`, plus a `BOOLEAN` value `amORpm`. Then write four procedures:

`Init`	initializes the `currentTime` to midnight
`Advance`	advances the value of `currentSeconds` by 1
`Change`	allows the user to change the `currentTime`
`Display`	displays the `currentTime`

This problem contains an excellent example of an abstract data type. The main program should make no reference to the clock as a linked structure. You should be able to change the clock into a simple collection of counters without changing the main program at all. The main program is unable to do anything except what's provided by the subprograms.

14.7

Using Queues

In this section we'll use a queue to solve a problem concerning a company's temporary employees. Keep in mind that this is only one of many problems that can be solved using queues.

A temporary-services employment agency maintains a list of available applicants. The names are entered into a queue on a first-come first-served basis. Along with each name, we store the applicant's number of years of experience. When a job becomes available, the applicant at the front of the queue (the person who's been waiting the longest) is removed from the queue. That applicant's name is sent to the new employer.

Specifications

Input: The letters A for *add* a new applicant or R for *remove* an applicant who's been waiting. Also, for each applicant being added, the applicant's name and number of years of experience.

Process: Store the applicants in a queue, so that they can be removed on a first-come first-served basis.

Output: When the user types an R, the next applicant's name and years of experience are written on the screen.

Designing a Program

Now that we have our queue subprograms written, all we have to do is write a main program to suit this particular problem. Here's the pseudocode:

```
Initialize the queue.
Repeat forever:
    Read an A or an R.
    If A then
        Read employee info.
        Add a Cell to the queue, with this info.
    If R then
        Remove a Cell from the queue.
        Write the cell's info to the screen.
```

Now here's something nice—we can use this chapter's queue subprograms (Initialize, AddCell, RemoveCell) without changing them at all! No modifications are needed. The trick that lets us do this is to define infoType as follows:

```
TYPE
    nameType  = PACKED ARRAY [1..20] OF CHAR;
    expType   = 0..30;
    infoType  = RECORD
                    name       : nameType;
                    experience : expType
                END;
```

Each of our queue subprograms works with this infoType just as well as with

```
TYPE
    infoType = INTEGER;
```

The code follows.

Program Example

```
PROGRAM Applicants (input, output);
{Processes applicants for temp services positions.}
    TYPE
        nameType  = PACKED ARRAY [1..20] OF CHAR;
        expType   = 0..30;
        infoType  = RECORD
                        name       : nameType;
                        experience : expType
                    END;
        ptrType   = ^cellType;
        cellType  = RECORD
                        info : infoType;
                        next : ptrType
                    END;
        queueType = RECORD
                        front, rear : ptrType
                    END;
    VAR
        queue   : queueType;
        tempInf : infoType;
        reply   : CHAR;
    {----------}
```

```
{Put the queue subprograms here,                    }
{but add a call to Dispose in RemoveCell:::          }
PROCEDURE RemoveCell (VAR q : queueType;
                      VAR i : infoType);
{Removes a cell from the front of the queue.}

  VAR                                         {Added line}
    temp : ptrType;                           {Added line}
BEGIN {RemoveCell}
  IF IsEmpty(q) THEN
    WriteLn (Chr(7), 'Error: Empty queue')
  ELSE

    WITH q DO
      BEGIN
        temp  := front;                       {Added line}
        i     := front^.info;
        front := front^.next;
        IF fror+ = NIL THEN
          rear .= NIL;
        Dispose (temp)                        {Added line}
      END
END; {RemoveCell}

{----------}

{Also, substitute the following for WriteList:::}

PROCEDURE WriteLnName (nam : nameType);
{Writes a name (assuming it's
 terminated with an asterisk).}

  VAR
    i : INTEGER;

BEGIN {WriteLnName}
  i := 1;
  WHILE nam[i] <> '*' DO
    BEGIN
      Write (nam[i]);
      i := i + 1
    END;
  WriteLn
END;   {WriteLnName}

{----------}

PROCEDURE ReadLnName (VAR nam : nameType);
{Reads a name; terminates it with an asterisk.}

  VAR
    i : INTEGER;
```

```
        BEGIN {ReadLnName}
          Write ('Name: ');
          i := 1;
          WHILE NOT Eoln (input) DO
            BEGIN
              Read (nam[i]);
              i := i + 1
            END;
          nam[i] := '*';
          ReadLn {don't forget this!}
        END;  {ReadLnName}

        {----------}

  BEGIN {Applicants}
    Initialize (queue);

    WHILE TRUE DO
      BEGIN
        WriteLn;
        Write  ('What next? A(dd), R(emove): ');
        ReadLn (reply);

        IF reply = 'A' THEN
          BEGIN
            ReadLnName (tempInf.name);
            Write      ('Years experience: ');
            ReadLn     (tempInf.experience);
            WriteLn;
            AddCell    (queue, tempInf)
          END

        ELSE IF reply = 'R' THEN
          BEGIN
            RemoveCell  (queue, tempInf);
            WriteLnName (tempInf.name);
            WriteLn     (tempInf.experience:2, ' years')
          END

        ELSE
          WriteLn (Chr(7), 'Invalid response; try again.')
      END
  END.  {Applicants}
```

Sample Runs

```
What next? A(dd), R(emove): A
Name: Barry Burd
Years experience: 21

What next? A(dd), R(emove): A
Name: Harriet Ritter
Years experience: 22

What next? A(dd), R(emove): A
Name: Sam Burd
Years experience: 4

What next? A(dd), R(emove): R
Barry Burd
21 years
```

```
What next? A(dd), R(emove): A
Name: Jennie Burd
Years experience: 1

What next? A(dd), R(emove): R
Harriet Ritter
22 years

What next? A(dd), R(emove): R
Sam Burd
 4 years

What next? A(dd), R(emove): r
<beep>Invalid response; try again.

What next? A(dd), R(emove): R
Jennie Burd
 1 years

What next? A(dd), R(emove): R
<beep>Error: Empty queue
Jennie Burd
 1 years

What next? A(dd), R(emove):
 <Interrupt>
```

Observations

an intentionally infinite loop

- WHILE TRUE DO

  The condition that's tested in this WHILE loop is always TRUE, so the execution of this loop will never end. This is an infinite loop. To get the program to stop running, the user has to perform some special action. On many computers, hitting control-C on the keyboard will do it. This causes the operating system to interrupt the run of the program. When this interrupt takes place, the program is aborted.

  Some problems lead naturally to programs that run forever. For instance, a program that monitors a hospital's fire-safety system should run all day, every day, all year round. We might envision Program Applicants running around the clock, in an office where services are available on an emergency basis, 24 hours a day.

- PROCEDURE RemoveCell (VAR q : queueType;
                                          VAR i : infoType);

    .

    .

  Dispose (temp)

Dispose

  Dispose is a pre-declared procedure. It's the opposite of New.

  When we call Procedure New we obtain a brand new cell for a pointer to point to. This brand new cell has to come from somewhere! It comes from a list of available cells, called the free list.

  The statement Dispose (temp) takes the cell pointed to by temp and returns it to the free list. We do this for two reasons:

  - We don't need that cell anymore. It represents an applicant that's already been sent to an employer.

- A computer's memory isn't indefinitely large, and neither is the free list. If we don't return this cell to the free list, it can never again be obtained by calling New. But then, since the program runs on and on indefinitely, the free list will eventually run out of cells.

- PROCEDURE RemoveCell (VAR q : queueType;
                       VAR i : infoType);

    .
    .
    .

i := front^.info

**record
assignment**

With our new definition of infoType, front^.info becomes a RECORD with two fields (name and experience). So this assignment statement, straight from our old Procedure RemoveCell, takes both fields of front^.info, and puts them into the infoType record variable i.

Values from

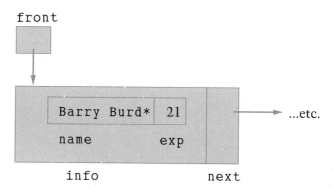

are assigned to

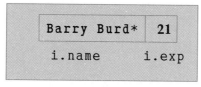

We're making use of a certain rule in Pascal:

A single assignment statement can be used to copy values from all the fields of one record to the fields of another record, as long as the same type name is used to declare both records.[3]

In this program, both i and front^.info are declared to be of type infoType.

---

[3]Like many other rules, this rule has its subtleties. See Exercises Exp.14.7.3 and Exp.14.7.4.

```
• i := 1;
  WHILE NOT Eoln (input) DO
    BEGIN
      Read (nam[i]);
      i := i + 1
    END;
  nam[i] := '*'
```

handling names of different lengths

Arrays of type `nameType` are 20 characters long, but we don't want to make the user type in a 10-character name and then 10 blanks. So we read characters until the user hits the return key. Then we make the next component be a non-letter character (such as an asterisk). When we design the `WriteLnName` procedure, we have it treat this asterisk as an "end-of-name" indicator. Of course, there are other ways we could be dealing with this same "end-of-name" problem. For an alternative approach, see Section 12.5.

Testing and Debugging

If you're not careful you can run into quite a bit of trouble using the pre-declared Procedure `Dispose`. Here's an example:

dangling reference

```
PROGRAM DanglingReference (output);
{Shows what happens when something
 points to a cell that's been Disposed.}

  TYPE
    infoType = INTEGER;
    ptrType  = ^cellType;
    cellType = RECORD
                    info : infoType;
                    next : ptrType
                 END;
    queueType = RECORD
                    front, rear : ptrType
                 END;
  VAR
    queue  : queueType;
    number : infoType;
    extra  : ptrType;

  {----------}

  {Put the queue subprograms here.}

  {----------}

BEGIN {DanglingReference}
  Initialize (queue);
  AddCell    (queue, 3);

  WITH queue DO
    BEGIN
      WriteLn (rear^.info:1);
      Dispose (front);
      New     (extra);
      extra^.info := 4;
      WriteLn (rear^.info:1)
    END
END.   {DanglingReference}
```

Let's trace this program and see what we get:

`Initialize (queue)`

`AddCell (queue, 3)`

`WriteLn (rear^.info:1)`

Output is 3.

`Dispose (front)`

The call to Procedure `Dispose` has no mention of `rear` in it, and generally an implementation isn't "smart" enough to know that anything other than `front` points to that no-longer-needed cell. So `rear` still points to something, but does it point to anything meaningful?

```
New (extra);
extra^.info := 4
```

`WriteLn (rear^.info:1)`

On many implementations, the output from this statement is the number 4! Why? Because the picture we expect to get, the one drawn above, isn't quite right. What really happens is this: when `New (extra)` is executed, the computer looks for a new cell in the free list, and finds the one that's just been Disposed.

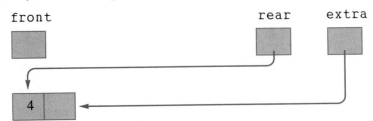

So after putting the number 4 into extra^.info, we have rear pointing to a cell with info field 4.

This nasty situation is called a **dangling reference**. It's like having a file cabinet that's shared by two roommates, Fred Front and Joe Rear. One roommate decides to clean out the file cabinet without telling the other!

At the heart of the dangling reference mess is an even deeper difficulty called **aliasing**. In Program DanglingReference the cell pointed to by front has two names: a "legal" name front^ and an "alias" rear^. The confusion we encountered happens because we can Dispose of the cell using its legal name and still have a way of referencing that cell with its alias. As you can see, aliasing has its dangers.

14.7 Exercises

Key Words to Review

interrupt	free list	aliasing
Dispose	dangling reference	

Questions to Answer

QUE 14.7.1 What changes had to be made to our queue subprograms in order to deal with the temporary services problem?

QUE 14.7.2 In Section 14.2 we said "When New is applied to the variable ptr it puts the address of a cellType into the variable ptr." Use the notion of a free list to show that our explanation in Section 14.2 was oversimplified a bit.

QUE 14.7.3 Why should you bother to Dispose of a cell that's being removed from a linked list?

QUE 14.7.4 What can happen when a pointer points to a cell that's already been Disposed?

Things to Check in a Manual

MAN 14.7.1 How can the user interrupt the run of a program on your implementation?

Experiments to Try

EXP 14.7.1 Run Program `DanglingReference` on your computer to see how your implementation deals with it.

EXP 14.7.2 In Program `DanglingReference` add `WriteLn (front^.info:1)` immediately after the call to `Dispose`.

EXP 14.7.3 Try to compile the following program. If it compiles, then run it.

```
PROGRAM Compatibility1 (output);
  TYPE
    rType = RECORD
                 i : INTEGER
            END;
    qType = rType;
  VAR
    r : rType;
    q : qType;
BEGIN {Compatibility1}
  r.i := 3;
  q   := r;
  WriteLn (q.i:1)
END.   {Compatibility1}
```

EXP 14.7.4 Try to compile the following program. If it compiles, then run it.

```
PROGRAM Compatibility2 (output);
  TYPE
    rType = RECORD
                 i : INTEGER
            END;
    qType = RECORD
                 i : INTEGER
            END;
  VAR
    r : rType;
    q : qType;
BEGIN {Compatibility2}
  r.i := 3;
  q   := r;
  WriteLn (q.i:1)
END.   {Compatibility2}
```

Changes to Make

CHA 14.7.1 Modify Procedure `ReadLnName` so that it does something sensible if the user enters a name containing twenty or more letters.

CHA 14.7.2 Modify Program `Applicants` so that it contains three queues—one for inexperienced applicants (one year or less), another for moderately experienced applicants (one to three years), and a third for very experienced applicants (more than three years). When an applicant is added, the applicant is automatically placed into the appropriate queue. When an applicant is needed, the user specifies the level of experience required and the program gets the applicant from the front of the correct queue.

Programs and Subprograms to Write

Each of the following exercises describes a real-life situation involving queues. Write programs to simulate each of these situations. Be sure to call Function Random of Section 9.5. A large result value from Function Random means "yes, an item arrives in the queue during this time interval." It can also mean "yes, an item can be removed from the queue during this time interval." A small result value means "no, an item doesn't arrive in the queue during this time interval." It can also mean "no, an item can't be removed from the queue during this time interval."

WRI 14.7.1   A bank has six tellers and only one waiting line. When any of the six tellers becomes available, the person at the front of the line goes to the teller for service.

WRI 14.7.2   A supermarket has ten cashiers with one waiting line for each cashier. Two of the ten cashiers have express lanes—for customers who require very little time to be checked out.

WRI 14.7.3   A computer's operating system has three queues—one for high-priority jobs (jobs with priority A), another for medium-priority jobs (B), and a third for low-priority jobs (C). Jobs take random amounts of time to run. The system spends half of every second running A priority jobs, a third of every second running B priority jobs, and a sixth of every second running C priority jobs. Once an A job begins running, it runs for half of every second until the job is completed. Similarly, a B job takes a third of every second until it's completed, and a C job takes a sixth of every second until it's completed.

WRI 14.7.4   Repeat Exercise Wri.14.7.3, but this time assume that after half of a second an A job not only gets replaced by a B job, but also gets thrown to the rear of the A queue. It doesn't get another half second until all the other jobs in the A queue get their turns. (Compare with Exercises Wri.14.6.5 and Wri.14.6.6.)

WRI 14.7.5   An intersection has a traffic light that changes (green to red to green, etc.) every thirty seconds.

WRI 14.7.6   A traffic intersection has a two-way stop sign. Cars coming from the north and from the south must always stop and yield to other traffic. Cars coming from the east or west can go straight through without stopping. Cars coming from any direction that need to turn left must yield to cars that are going straight through from the opposite direction.

WRI 14.7.7   Simulate the use of elevators described in Exercises Wri.12.8.4 and Wri.12.8.5.

14.8

Using Stacks

In Section 13.4 we showed that there's a natural connection between iteration and recursion. There's also a natural connection between stacks and recursion. Briefly stated, the connection is this: When a subprogram makes calls to itself, the various versions of the subprogram form a stack. The last version to be called will be the first version from which we return.

postfix
expressions

Instead of exploring this connection very deeply, we'll just take up where we left off in Section 13.6—we'll evaluate a postfix expression using a stack.

Specifications

Input: A postfix expression, containing natural numbers (integers without signs) and operators (+, −, *, and /). Each item in the expression (a number or a sign) is separated from its neighbors by at least one blank space.

Output: The value of the postfix expression.

Designing a Program

How do we interpret a postfix expression to get a numeric result? We simply read from left to right. Whenever we see an operator, we apply it to the two previous numbers. We just have to be careful when we say *the two previous numbers.* Let's look at the postfix expression 9 3 2 − +:

When we see the minus sign, the two previous numbers are 3 and 2:

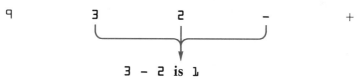

But then when we see the plus sign, the *two previous numbers* are 9 and 1. The 1 comes from having applied the minus sign:

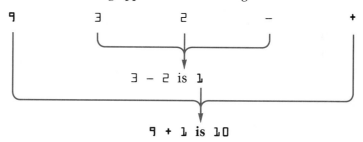

The same is true when we evaluate 9 3 − 2 +. When we apply the plus sign, the two previous numbers are 6 and 2. The 6 comes from having applied the minus sign:

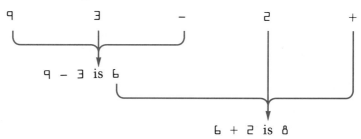

Now why do we need a stack to evaluate a postfix expression? When we evaluate 9 3 2 – +, the first number we encounter is 9, but 9 is the last number to be combined using +. Thus, evaluating a postfix expression means that the first number in is the last number to come out. This is exactly what a stack is designed to do.

Program Example

```
PROGRAM Postfix (input, output);
{Evaluates a postfix expression.}
  TYPE
    kindType  = (character, natral);
    natural   = 0..MAXINT;
    infoType  = INTEGER;
    ptrType   = ^cellType;
    cellType  = RECORD
                  info : infoType;
                  next : ptrType
                END;
    stackType = ptrType;

  VAR
    stack          : stackType;
    left, right,
    result, final  : INTEGER;
    c              : CHAR;
    n              : natural;
    kind           : kindType;

  {----------}

  {Put stack subprograms from
   Sections 14.3 and 14.5 here.}

  {----------}

  {Put Procedure ReadCharOrNat
   from Section 13.6 here.}

  {----------}
```

```
BEGIN  {Postfix}
  Initialize (stack);
  WriteLn    ('Enter a postfix expression: ');
  WHILE NOT Eoln DO
    BEGIN
      ReadCharOrNat (c, n, kind);
      IF kind = character THEN
        BEGIN
          Pop (stack, right);
          Pop (stack, left);
          CASE c OF
            '+': result := left + right;
            '-': result := left - right;
            '*': result := left * right;
            '/': result := left DIV right
          END;
          Push (stack, result)
        END
      ELSE
        Push (stack, n)
    END;
  Pop     (stack, final);
  WriteLn (final:5, ' is the value of this expression')
END.  {Postfix}
```

Sample Runs

```
Enter a postfix expression:
9 3 2 - +
   10 is the value of this expression
   _____


Enter a postfix expression:
9 3 - 2 +
    8 is the value of this expression
   _____


Enter a postfix expression:
4 -
<beep>Error: Empty stack
   -4 is the value of this expression
   _____


Enter a postfix expression:
100 101 -
   -1 is the value of this expression
   _____


Enter a postfix expression:
9<blank space><end-of-line indicator>
    9 is the value of this expression
```

In the last of our sample runs we highlight the need for an extra blank space. Program Postfix needs this blank space because, in this sample run, the input ends with a natural number. (See Exercise Que.14.8.6.)

Traces

Take the sample run with input 9 3 2 − +. After reading 9, 3, and 2, the stack looks like this:

visualizing a
stack

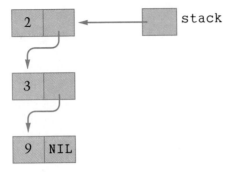

In this diagram we drew the cells one on top of another to emphasize the idea that a stack has a top and a bottom. Of course, if we're comfortable with the notion that a stack's pointers point from top to bottom, we can make abbreviated diagrams in which we show only the info portion of each cell.

```
2
3
9
```

The minus sign pops the 2 and 3 off the stack and pushes a 1 onto the stack:

```
2
3        becomes              which becomes         1
9                  9                                9
```

Then the plus sign pops the 1 and 9 off the stack, and pushes a 10 onto the stack:

```
1
9     becomes   empty   which becomes    10
                stack
```

Finally, the call Pop (stack, final) pops the last number 10 off the stack, and this 10 is written to the screen.

Programming Style

Look at the last few lines of Program Postfix. Instead of calling Procedure Pop:

Use your tool set!

```
Pop       (stack, final);
WriteLn (final:5, ' is the value of this expression')
```

we could have had a statement like

```
WriteLn (stack^.info:5, ' is the value of this expression')
```

in the main program. But this would have been cheating. The principle of data abstraction demands that we manipulate the stack *only* with subprograms and then only with subprograms whose sole purpose is to manipulate the stack. The main program should not directly put things on the stack, take things off the stack, or even examine the contents of the stack.

14.8   Exercises

Questions to Answer

QUE 14.8.1   Find the value of each of the following postfix expressions:
a. 3 9 – 15 2 + *   b. 8 62 31 9 2 – – – –

QUE 14.8.2   Turn each of the following postfix expressions into an equivalent infix expression:
a. 1 2 3 4 5 + – * /   b. 16 2 – 13 2 + 14 5 – * +

QUE 14.8.3   Turn each of the following infix expressions into an equivalent postfix expression:
a. (2 + 3) * (41 – 16)   b. (6 + ((3/4) – (5/6))) * 9   c. 8

QUE 14.8.4   Explain the output in each of this section's Sample Runs.

QUE 14.8.5   Compare the code of Program Postfix

```
Pop (stack, right);
Pop (stack, left)
```

with the corresponding code of Program Prefix (Section 13.6):

```
left  := Value (input);
right := Value (input)
```

Why do the variables left and right appear in one order when we pop a stack and in the opposite order when we use recursion?

QUE 14.8.6   Why do we need an extra blank space in the last of our Sample Runs? Why isn't this space needed in the other runs?

Changes to Make

CHA 14.8.1   The CASE statement in the main body of Program Postfix is vulnerable to bad input. If the user enters a character other than +, –, *, or /, the program will be aborted. Take measures to keep the program from being aborted when the user can simply be asked to supply better input.

CHA 14.8.2   Add code to Program Postfix to keep track of the number of values on the stack. Before popping the final value off the stack, the new program checks to make sure that there's only one value on the stack. If the stack contains more than one value, the program writes a warning message on the screen.

Scales to Practice

PRA 14.8.1   Modify the subprograms you wrote for Exercises Pra.14.3.6 and Pra.14.5.1 so that they store two stacks in just one array. The bottom of one stack is at the beginning of the array, and the bottom of the other stack is at the end of the array. As each stack grows, it grows toward the middle of the array.

Programs and Subprograms to Write

WRI 14.8.1   Look once again at Exercises Wri.10.4.7 and Wri.13.4.1. Then do the palindrome problem using a stack.

WRI 14.8.2   When profits are low, companies use a stack to decide who gets laid off first. The most recent people to be hired are the first to be laid off. Write a program, like Program Applicants of Section 14.7, that keeps track of employees who are hired and laid off.

WRI 14.8.3   Modify the program you wrote for Exercise Wri.14.8.2 so that it takes several of the company's departments into account. The sales and data processing departments are represented by two separate stacks. When the company wants to "trim the fat" in the sales department, it pops the top of that department's stack even though the most recent hire may have been in the data processing department.

WRI 14.8.4   Combine the program you wrote for Exercise Wri.14.8.3 with Program Applicants of Section 14.7. The new program tracks many aspects of hiring and firing for a company.

Things to Think About

THI 14.8.1   Look once again at Exercise Wri.14.8.2. Sometimes a company's layoffs are temporary; that is, the company intends to hire back the employees that were laid off as soon as positions become available. In what order should the employees be rehired? Does the company use a stack, a queue, or a combination of both structures? Explain.

14.9

Extracting Cells

In the examples we've seen so far, we've been removing cells from one of the ends of a list. Sometimes this isn't enough. What if someone in the middle of our waiting line decides to give up and go home? What if we have a list of employee information records, in alphabetical order by last name, and Jane Middler decides to quit?

arrays vs. linked lists

It's hard to remove a value from the middle of an array. In order to remove `Barry` from

Alan	Barry	Harriet	Jennie	Ruth	Sam

we need to do

Alan		Harriet	Jennie	Ruth	Sam

which becomes

| Alan | Harriet | | Jennie | Ruth | Sam | ⟵ Step 1
|------|---------|--|--------|------|-----|

and then

| Alan | Harriet | Jennie | | Ruth | Sam | ⟵ Step 2
|------|---------|--------|--|------|-----|

and

| Alan | Harriet | Jennie | Ruth | | Sam | ⟵ Step 3
|------|---------|--------|------|--|-----|

and finally

| Alan | Harriet | Jennie | Ruth | Sam | | ⟵ Step 4
|------|---------|--------|------|-----|--|

(By "hard" we mean that it takes $O(n)$ steps, where n is the number of values that come after the value we're removing.) But, as we'll see in this section, it's easy to remove a value from the middle of a linked list. (By "easy" we mean that it takes only three steps, no matter how many values come after the value that we're removing.)

Specifications

Input: Several numbers.

Process: Form a queue containing the numbers. Then **extract** a cell from the queue; that is, remove a cell from the middle of the queue.

Output: The `info` value that was in the extracted cell and the `info` values in the new queue after the cell has been extracted.

Designing a Program

We need a procedure that extracts a cell from a queue. Its heading looks like this:

```
PROCEDURE ExtractCell (middle : ptrType  ;
                       VAR i  : infoType);
```

how to extract a cell

`middle` should point to the cell that comes just before the one we'd like to extract, and `i` ends up containing the number that was in the extracted cell's `info` field.

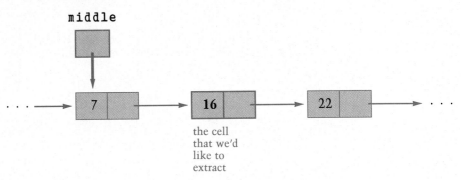

the cell
that we'd
like to
extract

Extracting a cell from the queue means changing only one pointer:

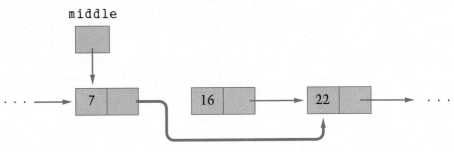

By changing just one pointer, we make the list bypass the 16-cell. Even though the 16-cell points to the 22-cell, the 16-cell is no longer pointed to by anything else in the list. For all practical purposes, the 16-cell has been removed from the list.

We'll implement this pointer change in two statements:

```
temp := middle^.next
```

> `temp` is made to point to the same cell that `middle^.next` points to

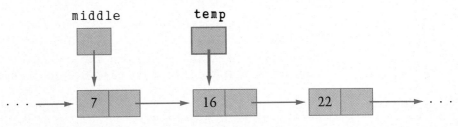

```
middle^.next := temp^.next
```

middle^.next is made to point to the same cell that
temp^.next points to

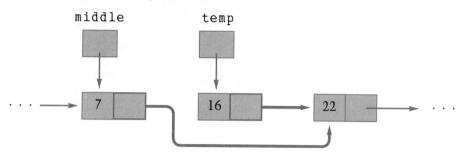

Now finding a value for i is easy:

```
i := temp^.info
```

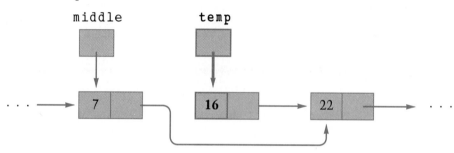

Here's the entire subprogram:

```
PROCEDURE ExtractCell (middle : ptrType  ;
                       VAR i  : infoType);
{Removes a cell from the middle of the queue.}
   VAR
     temp : ptrType;
BEGIN {ExtractCell}
   temp         := middle^.next;
   middle^.next := temp^.next;
   i            := temp^.info
END;   {ExtractCell}
```

A test driver for Procedure ExtractCell follows.

Program Example

```
PROGRAM ExtractTest (input, output);
{Test driver for Procedure ExtractCell.}

  TYPE
    infoType  = INTEGER;
    ptrType   = ^cellType;
    cellType  = RECORD
                     info : infoType;
                     next : ptrType
                  END;
    queueType = RECORD
                     front, rear : ptrType
                  END;

  VAR
    queue  : queueType;
    number : infoType;
    middle : ptrType;

  {----------}

  {Put the queue subprograms here, including
   Procedure ExtractCell.  Also include
   Procedure WriteList from Section 14.3.}

  {----------}

BEGIN {ExtractTest}
  Initialize (queue);
  WriteLn    ('Enter several numbers, all on one line:');

  WHILE NOT Eoln DO
    BEGIN
      Read    (number);
      AddCell (queue, number)
    END;

  middle := queue.front;
  middle := middle^.next;
  ExtractCell (middle, number);

  WriteLn;
  WriteLn    ('Extracted: ', number:4);
  Write      ('Now the queue contains: ');
  WriteList (queue.front)
END.  {ExtractTest}
```

Sample Runs

```
Enter several numbers, all on one line:
3 7 16 22 31

Extracted:   16
Now the queue contains:    3    7   22   31
```

Observations

- ```
  PROCEDURE ExtractCell (middle : ptrType  ;
                         VAR i  : infoType);
         .
         .
         .
  BEGIN
     .
     .
     .
    middle^.next := temp^.next
  ```
  ```

In the body of Procedure `ExtractCell` we make an assignment to the value of `middle^.next`, so wouldn't you think we have to make `middle` be a `VAR` parameter? Well we don't, because we're not changing the value of `middle`; that is, we're not making `middle` point to a different location. We're just changing the content of the location that `middle` already points to.

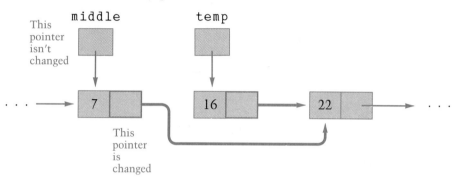

Since we're not changing the value of `middle`, we don't need to make `middle` be a `VAR` parameter.

Further Discussion

Extracting is easy.

If you're not already familiar with the way pointers work, Procedure `ExtractCell` may not seem as "easy" as we promised. But in terms of time consumption, the computer executes only three statements to `Extract a Cell`, no matter how many cells are in various parts of the list. This means that a cell can be removed from the middle of a linked list in a constant amount of time (= O(1) time). Compare this with the O(n) time that we calculated for removing a value from the middle of an array.

Now some students like to jump to conclusions at this point and say "Linked lists take O(1) time, and arrays take O(n) time, so linked lists must be better." This is an oversimplification. Linked lists are better for removing middle values, but they're not better for everything. If you have a problem where you very often need to remove middle values, then you should consider using linked lists. But arrays may be better for some other frequently used operations.

Programming Style

avoiding complicated pointer expressions

We could have written Procedure `ExtractCell` without a local `temp` variable:

```
PROCEDURE ExtractCell (middle : ptrType  ;
                          VAR i  : infoType);
{Removes a cell from the middle of the queue.}

BEGIN {ExtractCell}
   i             := middle^.next^.info;
   middle^.next := middle^.next^.next
END;   {ExtractCell}
```

If you take one of these expressions apart carefully, you'll find out what it means:

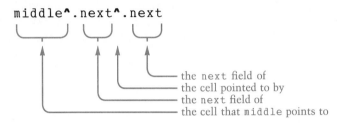

Of course it's easier to use `temp`, and it makes for a more readable program.

14.9   Exercises

Key Words to Review

extract

Questions to Answer

QUE 14.9.1   Explain why it takes O(n) time to remove a value from the middle of an array.

QUE 14.9.2   Assume that when we remove a value from the middle of an array we replace that value with a zero. With this assumption, rethink your answer to Exercise Que.14.9.1.

QUE 14.9.3   Explain why it takes O(1) time to remove a value from the middle of a linked list.

QUE 14.9.4   Assume that before we remove a value from the middle of a linked list we have to find that value in the list, starting from the front of the list and working our way toward the middle. With this assumption, rethink your answer to Exercise Que.14.9.3.

Experiments to Try

EXP 14.9.1   Try using Procedure `ExtractCell` to remove the cell that's at the front of a queue.

EXP 14.9.2   Call Procedure `ExtractCell` with `middle` pointing to the cell that's at the rear of the queue.

EXP 14.9.3   Call Procedure `ExtractCell` and give it `NIL` for the value of `middle`.

Changes to Make

CHA 14.9.1   Make Procedure `ExtractCell` robust enough to do something reasonable with the situation described in Exercise Exp.14.9.2.

CHA 14.9.2   Make Procedure `ExtractCell` robust enough to do something reasonable with the situation described in Exercise Exp.14.9.3.

CHA 14.9.3   Modify Procedure `ExtractCell` so that it extracts a cell from the middle of a stack.

14.10

Inserting Cells

We've just seen that we can extract a cell from a linked list very efficiently—in O(1) time. What about inserting a cell in the middle of a linked list?

Specifications

Input: Several numbers.

Process: Form a queue containing the numbers. Then *insert* a cell into the middle of the queue. Put the number 100 into its info field.

Output: The info values in the new queue, after the cell has been inserted.

Designing a Program

We need a procedure that inserts a cell into a queue. Its heading looks like this:

```
PROCEDURE InsertCell (middle : ptrType  ;
                      i      : infoType);
```

how to insert a cell

We'll insert a new cell just after the cell pointed to by middle, and we'll put the value of i in the new cell's info field.

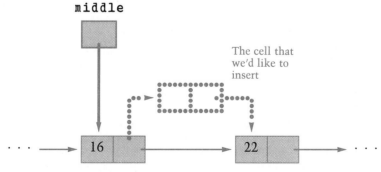

We implement the insertion in two steps. First we create a new cell, with info field i and next field the same as middle^.next:

```
CreateCell (temp, i, middle^.next)
```

The new cell's next field points to the same place that
middle^.next points to

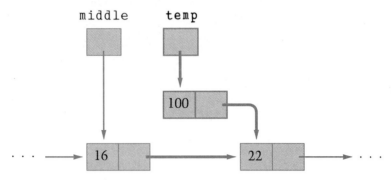

Then we change middle^.next so that it points to the new cell:

```
middle^.next := temp
```

middle^.next is made to point to the same place that
temp points to

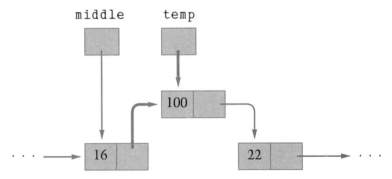

Here's the entire subprogram:

```
PROCEDURE InsertCell (middle : ptrType   ;
                      i      : infoType);
{Inserts a cell into the middle of a queue.}
   VAR
      temp : ptrType;
BEGIN {InsertCell}
   CreateCell (temp, i, middle^.next);
   middle^.next := temp
END;   {InsertCell}
```

A test driver for Procedure InsertCell follows.

**Program
Example**

```
PROGRAM InsertTest (input, output);
{Test driver for Procedure InsertCell.}
   TYPE
     infoType  = INTEGER;
     ptrType   = ^cellType;
     cellType  = RECORD
                       info : infoType;
                       next : ptrType
                   END;
     queueType = RECORD
                       front, rear : ptrType
                   END;

   VAR
     queue  : queueType;
     number : infoType;
     middle : ptrType;
     i      : 1..2;

   {----------}

   {Put the queue subprograms here,
    including Procedure InsertCell.}

   {----------}

BEGIN {InsertTest}
   Initialize (queue);
   WriteLn    ('Enter several numbers, all on one line:');

   WHILE NOT Eoln DO
     BEGIN
       Read (number);
       AddCell (queue, number)
     END;

   middle := queue.front;
   FOR i := 1 TO 2 DO
     middle := middle^.next;
   InsertCell (middle, 100);

   WriteLn;
   WriteLn    ('Inserted: ', 100);
   Write      ('Now the queue contains: ');
   WriteList (queue.front)
END.  {InsertTest}
```

**Sample
Runs**

```
Enter several numbers, all on one line:
3 7 16 22 31

Inserted:          100
Now the queue contains:    3    7   16 100   22   31
```

**Further
Discussion**

**arrays vs. linked
lists**

Once again we see how an operation on a linked list can be faster than the corresponding array operation. In this program we've managed to insert a value into the middle of a list in O(1) time. That is, we've inserted a new cell by manipulating a few pointers, and it didn't matter how many cells were already in the list.

Look at the corresponding array operation:

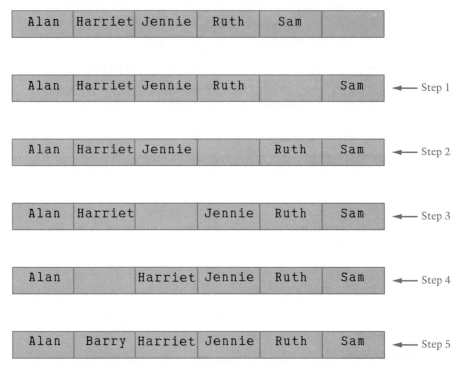

This takes O(n) time, where n is the number of values that come after the inserted value (the number of values that have to be moved in order to insert the new value).

14.10 Exercises

Key Words to Review

insert

Questions to Answer

QUE 14.10.1 Explain why it takes O(n) time to add a value in the middle of an array.

QUE 14.10.2 Assume that when we remove a value from the middle of an array we replace that value with a zero. This zero is just a dummy value. It doesn't have any particular significance in the problem we're trying to solve. It can be deleted without any ill effects. With this assumption, rethink your answer to Exercise Que.14.10.1.

QUE 14.10.3 Explain why it takes O(1) time to add a value in the middle of a linked list.

Experiments to Try

EXP 14.10.1   Try using Procedure `InsertCell` to add a cell at the front of a queue.

EXP 14.10.2   Call Procedure `InsertCell` with `middle` pointing to the cell that's at the rear of the queue.

EXP 14.10.3   Call Procedure `InsertCell` and give it `NIL` for the value of `middle`.

Changes to Make

CHA 14.10.1   Make Procedure `InsertCell` robust enough to do something reasonable with the situation described in Exercise Exp.14.10.3.

CHA 14.10.2   Modify Procedure `InsertCell` so that it inserts a cell into the middle of a stack.

CHA 14.10.3   Modify Program `Applicants` from Section 14.7 so that it includes an option to shove a person into the middle of the queue.

CHA 14.10.4   Do we need to make any changes to Procedure `InsertCell` if we want it to insert a cell into the circularly linked list of Exercise Wri.14.6.6? Explain.

CHA 14.10.5   Do we need to make any changes to Procedure `InsertCell` if we want it to insert a cell into the list described in Exercise Pra.14.2.2 (a list in which the last cell points to itself)? Explain.

14.11

Sorting with Linked Lists (Doubly Linked Lists)

Recall the binary search algorithm (Section 10.6). This algorithm involves "jumping" to the middle of an array. If you have a linked list instead of an array, then you don't want to use a binary search, because it's hard to find the middle of a linked list. By "hard" we mean that it takes O(n) time, where n is the number of cells in the list. You have to start at one end of the list and follow pointers until you get to the middle. This is like finding Jeffrey Smith in the phone book by starting with Aaacon Plumbing and turning the pages one by one. If you must use a linked list, it's better to do a linear search.

In the same way, some sorting algorithms work best with arrays, and others work best with linked lists. In this section we present a sorting

insertion sort   algorithm called the **insertion sort**. This sort works much better with linked lists than with arrays, because it's much easier to insert a new value into the middle of a linked list than into the middle of an array.

To write an insertion sort in the most straightforward way, we'll have to modify our ideas about linked lists a bit. At one point in the algorithm it'll be handy to refer to the `previous` cell in the linked list (as opposed to the `next` cell in the list). To do this most efficiently, each of our cells will have two pointers: one pointing to the `next` cell, and another pointing to the `previous` cell.

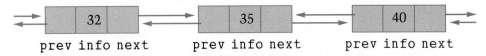

prev info next   prev info next   prev info next

doubly linked list

A list like this, in which each cell points to the cell before it and to the cell after it, is called a doubly linked list. Of course, a cell with two pointers takes up more space than a cell with only one pointer. But we'll be able to find the previous cell by just following the prev pointer, so having two pointers will save us some time. Here again, we see the time versus space trade-off.

Specifications

Input: A file with several INTEGER values in it.

Process: Do an insertion sort: Store the values in a linked list. Each time you read a new value from the input file, create a newCell for it in the linked list. To find out where the newCell should be inserted, start at the head of the list and keep moving forward until you've reached a cell containing a number that's larger than the new value.

Output: The INTEGER values, in non-decreasing order.

Designing a Program

First we need to declare a doubly linked list:

```
TYPE
   infoType = INTEGER;
   ptrType  = ^cellType;
   cellType = RECORD
                 prev : ptrType;
                 info : infoType;
                 next : ptrType
              END;
VAR
   head    : ptrType;
```

creating a cell

Then since we've got a new kind of list, we have to redesign our list subprograms. First we need a new Procedure CreateCell:

```
PROCEDURE CreateCell (VAR ptr : ptrType ;
                          pre     : ptrType ;
                          inf     : infoType;
                          nex     : ptrType);
{Creates a new cell and places 'pre'
 'inf' and 'nex' into its fields.}

BEGIN {CreateCell}
   New (ptr);
   WITH ptr^ DO
      BEGIN
         prev := pre;
         info := inf;
         next := nex
      END
END;   {CreateCell}
```

And here's what we might get when we call `CreateCell`:

head is made to point to a new cell with fields NIL, -MAXINT, and NIL.

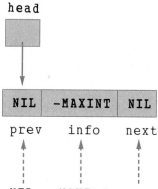

CreateCell (**head, NIL, -MAXINT, NIL**)

Let's see what happens if we follow this call with another call to `CreateCell`:

head^.next is made to point to a new cell. The prev field of the new cell points backwards to the cell that head points to; the cell's other fields contain MAXINT and NIL.

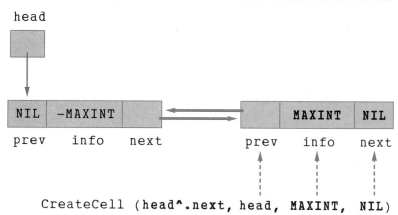

CreateCell (**head^.next, head, MAXINT, NIL**)

This is exactly how we want to initialize our doubly linked list for the insertion sort.

```
PROCEDURE Initialize (VAR head : ptrType);
{Initializes a doubly linked list.}

BEGIN {Initialize}
   CreateCell (head, NIL, -MAXINT, NIL);
   CreateCell (head^.next, head, MAXINT, NIL)
END;  {Initialize}
```

The `MAXINT` values serve a purpose similar to the extra `searchFor` value that we added to our array in Procedure `LinearSearch` (Section 10.5).

We'll also need a new Procedure InsertCell; but before we even do an insertion, we need to decide where we're going to insert a new cell. For instance, if we want to put the number 35 in the list, we have to find a cell that has a number larger than 35 in it. We can do this with a linear search. We start with a variable named larger pointing to the head of the list and then advance larger until it points to a number that's greater than 35:

```
PROCEDURE FindLargerInfo (head        : ptrType  ;
                          VAR larger : ptrType  ;
                          value       : infoType);
{Finds a cell whose info field is larger than 'value'.}

BEGIN {FindLargerInfo}
  larger := head;
  WHILE value > larger^.info DO
    larger := larger^.next
END;   {FindLargerInfo}
```

Now we can look at our new Procedure InsertCell:

```
PROCEDURE InsertCell (larger : ptrType  ;
                      value  : infoType);
{Inserts a cell into a doubly linked list.}

  VAR
    smaller, newCell : ptrType;
BEGIN {InsertCell}
  smaller        := larger^.prev;
  CreateCell (newCell, smaller, value, larger);
  smaller^.next := newCell;
  larger^.prev  := newCell
END;   {InsertCell}
```

Traces   Let's say we call InsertCell with value equal to 35 and larger pointing as pictured below:

Here's what happens as each statement in Procedure InsertCell is executed:

```
smaller := larger^.prev
```

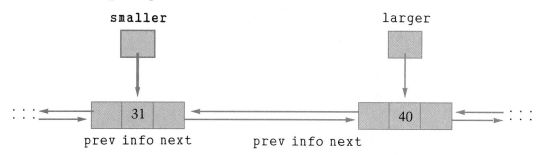

```
CreateCell (newCell, smaller, value, larger)
```

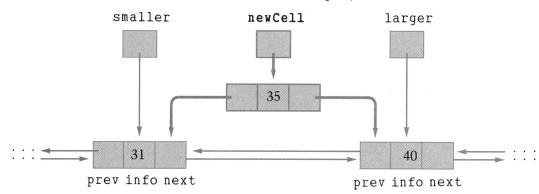

```
smaller^.next := newCell
```

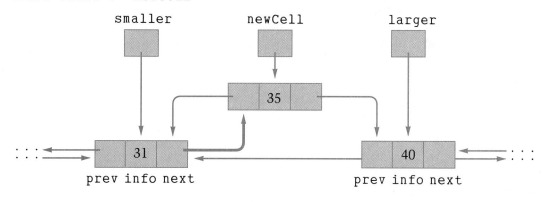

```
larger^.prev := newCell
```

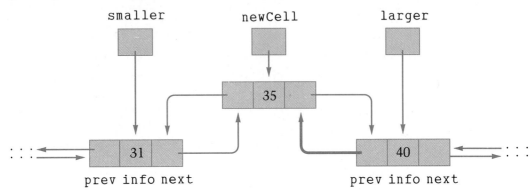

So a new cell with info value 35 is inserted right before the larger cell.

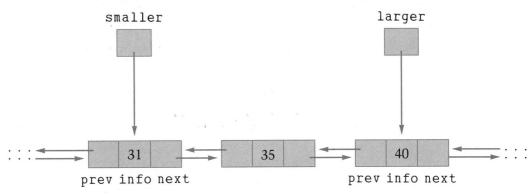

Now we've got the procedures we need to do an insertion sort:

Initialize the doubly linked list.
Loop:
    Read a number.
    Call FindLargerInfo to locate larger.
    Call InsertCell to put the number in a new cell that comes before the larger cell.

Program Example

```
PROGRAM InsertSortDriver (fInput, output);
{Test driver for Procedure InsertionSort.}
    TYPE
        infoType = INTEGER;
        ptrType  = ^cellType;
        cellType = RECORD
                        prev : ptrType;
                        info : infoType;
                        next : ptrType
                    END;
    VAR
        head    : ptrType;
        fInput  : TEXT;
```

```
{----------}

{Put the doubly linked list subprograms here,
 including Procedure FindLargerInfo.}

{----------}

PROCEDURE InsertionSort (VAR head : ptrType);
{Implements the insertion sort algorithm.}
   VAR
     value  : infoType;
     larger : ptrType;
BEGIN {InsertionSort}
   Reset       (fInput);
   Initialize (head);
   WHILE NOT Eof (fInput) DO
     BEGIN
       ReadLn          (fInput, value);
       FindLargerInfo (head, larger, value);
       InsertCell      (larger, value)
     END
END;   {InsertionSort}

{----------}

PROCEDURE WriteList (head : ptrType);
{Adapted from Procedure WriteList in Section
 14.3.  Modified for a doubly linked list
 with extra cells at both ends.}
   VAR
     temp : ptrType;
BEGIN {WriteList}
   temp := head^.next;
   WHILE temp^.next <> NIL DO
     BEGIN
       Write (temp^.info:4);
       temp := temp^.next
     END
END;   {WriteList}

{----------}

BEGIN {InsertSortDriver}
   InsertionSort (head);
   WriteLn        ('The values in non-decreasing order are: ');
   WriteList      (head)
END.   {InsertSortDriver}
```

Sample Runs

With this fInput file:

```
31
40
35
10
63
32
```

the output is

```
The values in non-decreasing order are:
  10  31  32  35  40  63
```

Observations

Why use a doubly linked list?

Program InsertSortDriver contains several references to the prev pointer. Some of them are needed only because we decided to create a doubly linked list. (That is, if our cells have prev pointers, then we need some statements that put values into these prev pointer fields.) But the essential use of prev pointers in the program is in the line

```
smaller := larger^.prev
```

Once we've found the larger cell, we have to know what cell comes before it, because we need to make that cell's next field point to the newCell. In order to find the cell that comes before the larger cell, we look at larger^.prev.

14.11   Exercises

Key Words to Review

insertion sort   doubly linked list

Questions to Answer

QUE 14.11.1   It's not practical to use the binary search algorithm (Section 10.6) on a linked list, because it's hard to jump to the middle of a linked list. What about the merge algorithm (Section 10.7)?

QUE 14.11.2   Is it practical to use the selection sort algorithm (Section 10.8) on a linked list? Why, or why not?

QUE 14.11.3   Describe the role of the two extra cells (containing −MAXINT and MAXINT) in Procedure InsertionSort.

Experiments to Try

EXP 14.11.1   Run Program InsertSortDriver with the numeric value of MAXINT somewhere in the fInput file.

EXP 14.11.2   Run Program InsertSortDriver with the numeric value of −MAXINT somewhere in the fInput file.

EXP 14.11.3   Start by putting MAXINT − 10 in the extra cell at the high end of the list (instead of MAXINT). Then run Program InsertSortDriver with the numeric value of MAXINT somewhere in the fInput file.

Changes to Make

CHA 14.11.1   Modify Procedure ExtractCell (Section 14.9) for a doubly linked list.

CHA 14.11.2   Rewrite Procedure `InsertionSort` so that it doesn't use extra cells with `-MAXINT` and `MAXINT` values.

CHA 14.11.3   Modify Program `InsertSortDriver` so that it stores values in a singly linked list (like the lists we've been using up until this section).

CHA 14.11.4   Use the insertion sort algorithm to sort values in an array rather than a linked list.

CHA 14.11.5   Modify Program `SelectionSortDriver` (Section 10.8) so that it sorts values stored in a linked list.

CHA 14.11.6   Create your own version of Function `IsAWin` in which the tic-tac-toe board is a linked structure containing nine cells. (See Section 11.3 for an "array" of `IsAWin` functions—`IsAWin1` through `IsAWin7`.)

Programs and Subprograms to Write

WRI 14.11.1   In the beginning of this section we used the word *hard* to describe the task of finding the middle cell in a linked list. By "hard" we meant that it takes $O(n)$ time—more time than it takes with an array. When we translate this "hardness" into program writing, it means that our subprogram will use an algorithm that appears to be awkward and unnecessarily cumbersome. See for yourself. Write a subprogram that accepts a pointer to the front of a list and returns a pointer to the cell in the middle of the list.

WRI 14.11.2   Redo Exercise Wri.10.8.5 so that the program sorts values stored in a linked list.

WRI 14.11.3   Redo Exercise Wri.11.4.1. In this version represent the imaginary world with a linked structure in which each cell contains a character string for its `info` and a pointer to each of its neighboring cells.

Things to Think About

THI 14.11.1   In Pascal every pointer variable points to a particular type of value. The type of value to which it points cannot be changed during the run of the program. But think about the way you use the `NIL` pointer in Pascal. Is there any sense in which the use of the `NIL` pointer is an exception to Pascal's rules?

THI 14.11.2   Can you categorize the kinds of problems that should be solved using arrays, and those that are better solved using linked lists? After describing some general categories, give examples of problems that fall into each category.

14.12

Trees

What is a tree?   In Sections 13.6 and 14.8 we wrote programs to find the values of prefix and postfix expressions. In this section we'll read a prefix expression and translate it into its familiar infix form. We'll do this by storing the expression in a linked structure called a **binary tree**.

A binary tree for the expression ((9 - 3) + (2 * 4)):

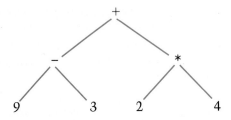

A binary tree for the expression (9 + (3 - 2)):

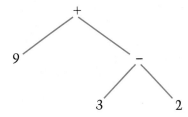

In our Pascal programs, we'll make binary trees with cells and pointers:

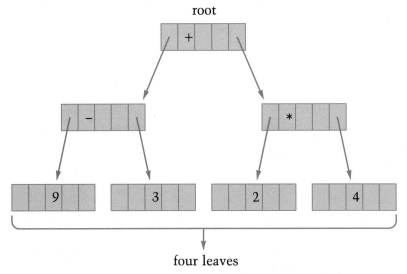

four leaves

As it's pictured, the tree grows downward. The topmost cell is called the **root** and the cells on the bottom are called leaves.

tree
terminology

To describe the tree in a little more detail, we switch metaphors from horticultural to genealogical. The root of the tree has two children—a left child and a right child. We say that the root is the parent of these two cells:

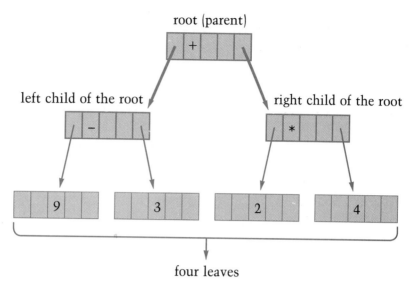

(Notice that each cell can have two children. That's why we call this a binary tree.)

Of course, one generation begets another generation. That happens with trees as well as with humans. So the root's children can have children of their own.

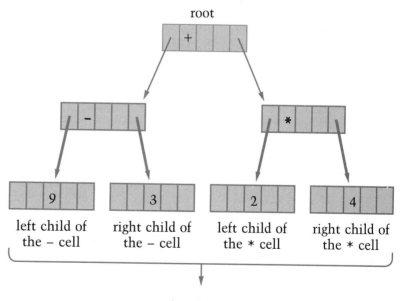

And now let's shift the terminology one more time. Let's use the variable name `root` for a pointer that points to the tree's top cell. Let's also use `left` child and `right` child to refer to the fields of a cell that point to the cell's children:

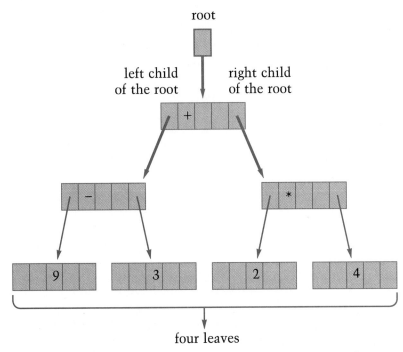

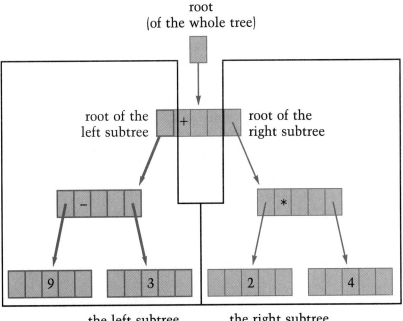

Now if you take a branch off a real-life tree, then what do you have? You have a little stick with branches and leaves of its own—a smaller version of the original tree. The same is true of trees in computer science. *If you take any part of a tree, from a particular pointer on downward, you get a tree.*

In particular, every binary tree has two **subtrees**—a **left subtree** and a **right subtree**. And each of these subtrees has its own root.

Now we can think of a binary tree as a combination of two subtrees: the left and right subtrees. This means we can

> *Deal with* a binary tree by
>   *dealing with* its left subtree, and then
>   *dealing with* its right subtree.

So, whatever we do with a binary tree, we usually do it using recursion. We'll emphasize this point over and over again as we design programs to deal with trees.

Specifications

Input: An expression in prefix form.

Process: Store the expression as a binary tree.

Output: The equivalent expression, in infix form.

Designing a Program

algorithms for binary trees

Look at any of this section's diagrams and you'll see that we store operator characters in some of our cells and natural numbers in others. If you read Section 12.6 you'll recognize that this problem is perfect for variant record types. To keep things simple, we'll use an ordinary record type for the cells in the tree; but if you want to improve on the work we do, try Exercise Cha.14.12.4.

Now our problem has two parts:

1. Make a tree for the given prefix expression.
2. Use the tree to make an infix expression.

In the next several paragraphs, we'll deal with each part separately.

Make a tree for the given prefix expression.   Recall from Section 13.6 how we handled a prefix expression:

> How to *get a value*:
> Read an item (a number or an operator).
> If the item is an operator character then
>   *get two more values*, and
>   apply the operator to those values.

We'll use a similar approach to create a tree from a prefix expression:

> How to *make a tree* for a prefix expression:
> Read an item (a number or an operator).
> Put the item on the tree.
> If the item is an operator character then read further to get two other prefix expressions. Use them to
>   *make the left subtree*, and
>   *make the right subtree*.

Notice the use of self-reference in this pseudocode. We make a tree by making its left subtree and then making its right subtree. Certainly when we implement this pseudocode in Pascal, we need to use recursion. So here's the code for Procedure MakeTree:

```
PROCEDURE MakeTree (VAR ptr : ptrType);
{Recursively makes a tree from the user's input.}
  VAR
    c    : CHAR;
    n    : natural;
    kind : kindType;
BEGIN {MakeTree}
  ReadCharOrNat (c, n, kind);
  CreateCell    (ptr, NIL, c, n, kind, NIL);

  IF kind = character THEN
    BEGIN
      MakeTree (ptr^.left);
      MakeTree (ptr^.right)
    END
END;  {MakeTree}
```

And here's how the code works with the prefix expression

+ - 9 3 * 2 4

• `ReadCharOrNat (c, n, kind);`
  `CreateCell    (ptr, NIL, c, n, kind, NIL)`

Reads the + sign and creates

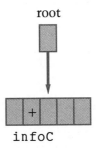

• `MakeTree (ptr^.left)`

Reads the prefix expression – 9 3 and creates

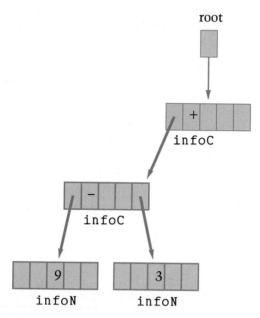

- MakeTree (ptr^.right)

Reads the prefix expression * 2 4 and creates

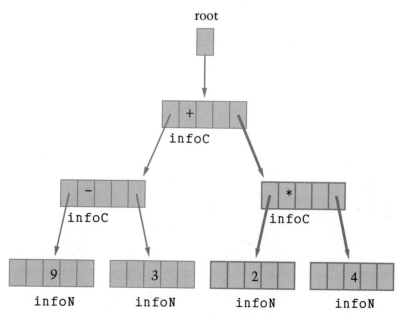

Use the tree to make an infix expression.   Let's look carefully at the tree for the expression ((9 − 3) + (2 * 4)). Notice that each of its subtrees is the tree for a smaller expression.

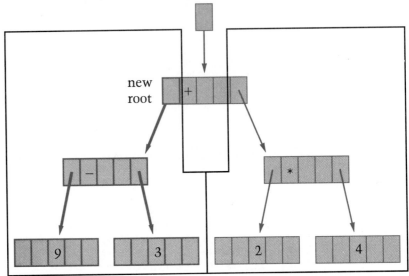

new
root

This tree represents the
infix expression (9 − 3)

So here's how we'll go about writing the infix version of the expression in this tree:

How to *write the infix version* of the whole tree:
write the infix version of the expression on the left subtree,
write the character on the root (+),
write the infix version of the expression on the right subtree.

And here's what we get when we do this:

How to *write* ((9 − 3) + (2 * 4)):
write (9 − 3)
write +
write (2 * 4)

Once again we're using self-reference: as part of our instructions to *write the infix version* of an expression, we're telling the computer twice to *write the infix version* of smaller parts of the expression. This means we're using recursion. In fact, we're using a recursive algorithm that's found in one tree

inorder traversal   program after another. It's an algorithm called **inorder traversal**:

How to *inorder traverse* a tree:
inorder traverse its left subtree,
do something with the cell that's in the middle,
inorder traverse its right subtree.

Here's the actual code that we'll use to write an infix expression:

```
PROCEDURE InOrder (ptr : ptrType);
{Implements the inorder traversal algorithm.}
BEGIN {InOrder}
  WITH ptr^ DO
    BEGIN

      IF left <> NIL THEN
        BEGIN
          Write   ('(');
          InOrder (left)
        END;

      WriteInfo (ptr);

      IF right <> NIL THEN
        BEGIN
          InOrder (right);
          Write   (')')
        END

    END
END;   {InOrder}
```

The complete program follows.

Program Example

```
PROGRAM MakeInfix (input, output);
{Reads a prefix expression; writes
 the equivalent infix expression.}
  TYPE
    kindType    = (character, natral);
    natural     = 0..MAXINT;
    ptrType     = ^cellType;
    cellType    = RECORD
                    left     : ptrType;
                    infoC    : CHAR;
                    infoN    : natural;
                    infoKind : kindType;
                    right    : ptrType
                  END;
  VAR
    root : ptrType;
  {----------}

  {Put Procedure ReadCharOrNat
   from Section 13.6 here.}
  {----------}

  PROCEDURE Initialize (VAR root : ptrType);
  {Initializes a tree.}
  BEGIN {Initialize}
    root := NIL
  END;   {Initialize}
  {----------}
```

```
            PROCEDURE CreateCell (VAR ptr : ptrType   ;
                                      lef     : ptrType   ;
                                      c       : CHAR      ;
                                      n       : natural   ;
                                      kind    : kindType ;
                                      rit     : ptrType );
   {Creates a new cell and places 'lef', 'c',
    'n', 'kind', and 'rit' into its fields.}
   BEGIN {CreateCell}
     New (ptr);
     WITH ptr^ DO
       BEGIN
         left     := lef;
         infoKind := kind;
         CASE infoKind OF
           character : infoC := c;
           natral    : infoN := n
         END;
         right    := rit
       END
   END;   {CreateCell}

   {----------}

   PROCEDURE MakeTree (VAR ptr : ptrType);
   {Recursively makes a tree from the user's input.}

     VAR
       c    : CHAR;
       n    : natural;
       kind : kindType;

   BEGIN {MakeTree}
     ReadCharOrNat (c, n, kind);
     CreateCell     (ptr, NIL, c, n, kind, NIL);

     IF kind = character THEN
       BEGIN
         MakeTree (ptr^.left);
         MakeTree (ptr^.right)
       END
   END;   {MakeTree}

   {----------}

   PROCEDURE InOrder (ptr : ptrType);
   {Implements the inorder traversal algorithm.}

     {----------}

     PROCEDURE WriteInfo (ptr : ptrType);
     {Writes either infoC or infoN.}

     BEGIN {WriteInfo}
       WITH ptr^ DO
         CASE infoKind OF
           character : Write (' ', infoC:1, ' ');
           natral    : Write (infoN:2)
         END
     END;   {WriteInfo}
```

```
              {----------}
          BEGIN {InOrder}
            WITH ptr^ DO
              BEGIN

                IF left <> NIL THEN
                  BEGIN
                    Write   ('(');
                    InOrder (left)
                  END;

                WriteInfo (ptr);

                IF right <> NIL THEN
                  BEGIN
                    InOrder (right);
                    Write   (')')
                  END

              END
          END;  {InOrder}

          {----------}

      BEGIN {MakeInfix}
        Initialize (root);

        WriteLn    ('Enter a prefix expression: ');
        MakeTree   (root);

        WriteLn;
        WriteLn    ('The equivalent infix expression is ');
        InOrder    (root)
      END.  {MakeInfix}
```

Sample Runs

```
Enter a prefix expression:
+ - 9 3 * 2 4

The equivalent infix expression is
(( 9 -  3) + ( 2 *  4))
```

```
Enter a prefix expression:
+ - 90 30 20

The equivalent infix expression is
((90 - 30) + 20)
```

```
Enter a prefix expression:
+ 90 - 30 20

The equivalent infix expression is
(90 + (30 - 20))
```

```
Enter a prefix expression:
42

The equivalent infix expression is
42
```

14.12   Exercises

Key Words to Review

binary tree	left child	left subtree
root	right child	right subtree
leaves	parent	inorder traversal
child	subtree	

Questions to Answer

QUE 14.12.1   Draw a binary tree for each of the following expressions:
  a. + * − 14 5 + 13 2 − 16 2   (prefix)
  b. 1 2 3 4 5 + − * /   (postfix)
  c. (6 + ((3/4) − (5/6))) * 9   (infix)
  d. 8

QUE 14.12.2   Trace the action of Program MakeInfix with each of the following prefix expressions:
  a. + − 90 30 20
  b. + 90 − 30 20
  c. + * − 14 5 + 13 2 − 16 2
  d. 42

QUE 14.12.3   Look at this section's Sample Runs and notice that in all but the last run the entire infix expression that's displayed by the program is in parentheses. Why does this happen for the first three runs, and why doesn't it happen for the last sample run?

Things to Check in a Manual

MAN 14.12.1   Does your implementation have special versions of New and Dispose for use with variant record types?

Experiments to Try

EXP 14.12.1   Change the body of Procedure InOrder as follows:

```
WITH ptr^ DO
  BEGIN
    Write ('(');
    IF left <> NIL THEN
      InOrder (left);
    WriteInfo (ptr);
    IF right <> NIL THEN
      InOrder (right);
    Write   (')')
  END
```

EXP 14.12.2   There's a variation on the inorder traversal algorithm called *postorder traversal*. Here's the pseudocode for postorder traversal:

> How to *postorder traverse* a tree:
> *postorder traverse* its left subtree,
> *postorder traverse* its right subtree,
> do something with the cell that's in the middle.

And here's the code:

```
IF left <> NIL THEN
   PostOrder (left);

IF right <> NIL THEN
   PostOrder (right);

WriteInfo (ptr)
```

Replace Procedure `InOrder` with Procedure `PostOrder` in Program `MakeInfix`. Run the new program a few times until you can describe exactly what it's doing.

EXP 14.12.3   There's a variation on the inorder traversal algorithm called *preorder traversal*. Here's the pseudocode for preorder traversal:

> How to *preorder traverse* a tree:
> do something with the cell that's in the middle,
> *preorder traverse* its left subtree,
> *preorder traverse* its right subtree.

And here's the code:

```
WriteInfo (ptr);

IF left <> NIL THEN
   PreOrder (left);

IF right <> NIL THEN
   PreOrder (right)
```

Replace Procedure `InOrder` with Procedure `PreOrder` in Program `MakeInfix`. Run the new program a few times until you can describe exactly what it's doing.

Changes to Make

CHA 14.12.1   Modify Program `MakeInfix` so that a record with three fields instead of three separate variables (c, n, and kind) gets passed back and forth between subprograms.

CHA 14.12.2   Modify Program `MakeInfix` so that, when writing an infix expression, it always omits the outermost parentheses.

CHA 14.12.3   Modify Program `MakeInfix` so that it writes the numeric *value* of the prefix expression.

CHA 14.12.4   Combine the work we did in Sections 12.6 and 13.6 on the procedure that reads either a character or a natural number. Use this in Program `MakeInfix` so that the cells of the tree belong to a variant record type. Each cell can store either an operator character or a natural number, but not both.

Programs and Subprograms to Write

WRI 14.12.1   Write and test a function subprogram that accepts a pointer to the root of a binary tree and returns the number of cells on the tree.

WRI 14.12.2   Write and test a function subprogram that accepts a pointer to the root of a binary tree and returns the number of leaves on the tree.

WRI 14.12.3   Write and test a function that accepts a binary tree and returns the height of a binary tree. The height of a binary tree is the largest number of cells on any path from the root to a leaf.

WRI 14.12.4   The information in a binary tree can actually be stored in an array. To create the array, we number the cells on the tree. We start at the top level and work our way downward, going from left to right along each level:

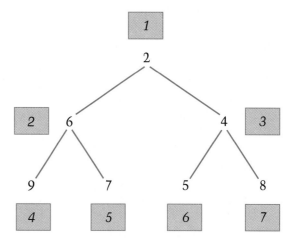

When all the cells have been numbered we can use the numbers as the cells' indices in the array.

a[1]	a[2]	a[3]	a[4]	a[5]	a[6]	a[7]
2	6	4	9	7	5	8

a. Write a function subprogram that accepts the index of a cell and returns the index of the cell's left child, if there is one. (*Hint:* Look at the way we've numbered the cells on the tree. Compare the number we assigned to a cell with the number we assigned to the cell's left child. Is there a pattern?)

b. Write a function subprogram that accepts the index of a cell and returns the index of the cell's right child, if there is one.

c. Write a function subprogram that accepts the index of a cell and checks to make sure that the number stored in the cell is smaller than the number stored in its children cells.

d. Write a function subprogram that checks to make sure that, for every cell on the tree, the number stored in the cell is smaller than the number stored in its children cells. A tree of this kind is called a *heap.*

Things to Think About

THI 14.12.1   In this section and other sections we eliminated the need for parentheses by switching from infix notation to prefix or postfix notation. Now look again at the expressions we used to represent *game trees* in Section 13.7.

((4 1) (2 3))

In these expressions we used parentheses to describe the shape of the tree. But maybe we can eliminate the need for parentheses in these game tree expressions. Describe a prefix representation for game trees. Then modify Program Minimax of Section 13.7 so that it accepts this new kind of expression.

14.13

Binary Tree Sort

In this section we present a sorting algorithm that's faster than the selection sort of Section 10.8. Instead of storing the values in an array, we'll store the values in a binary tree.

Specifications

Input: Same as selection sort.

Process: Do a **binary tree sort** Each time you read a new value, create a new cell for it on the binary tree. Do this in such a way that, when you do an inorder traversal of the tree, the values are visited in increasing order.

Output: Same as selection sort.

Designing a Program

Let's say you could build a tree that has the following nice properties:

algorithms for binary trees

1. The values stored on the left subtree are all smaller than the value stored at the root.

2. The values stored on the right subtree are all larger than the value stored at the root.

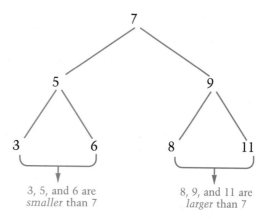

3, 5, and 6 are *smaller* than 7

8, 9, and 11 are *larger* than 7

Then let's say you traversed this tree with inorder traversal:

How to *inorder traverse* a tree:
  inorder traverse its left subtree,
  do something with the cell that's in the middle
  (write the number that's stored in its `info` field),
  inorder traverse its right subtree.

Then the values on the tree would be visited in the following way:

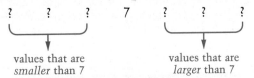

So the values would be written in something similar to increasing order.
    Now what if we could manage to build the tree in such a way that each of its subtrees obeyed properties 1 and 2 given above?

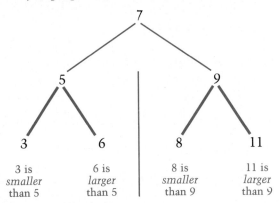

Then, because the inorder traversal algorithm is recursive, it would treat the subtrees the same way as it dealt with the original tree. Each subtree's values would be written in something similar to increasing order:

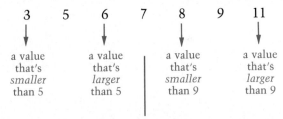

But now notice how the values in our example are being written exactly in increasing order. If we can manage to build a tree in which each subtree has properties 1 and 2, then inorder traversal will give us the tree's values in increasing order; that is, the values will have been sorted.

So how do we build a tree in which each subtree has properties 1 and 2? We'll do it with a recursive procedure called PlaceValue. As long as we're not at the end of the input file we'll keep doing

Read a value.
Place the value that we just read onto the tree.

As we did with so many other recursive subprograms, we'll derive the code for Procedure PlaceValue from the definitions. In this case, the "definitions" are properties 1 and 2.

How to *place the value we just read* onto the tree whose root is called ptr:

1. If the value we just read is less than ptr^.info then *place the value we just read* onto ptr^s left subtree
2. If the value we just read is greater than ptr^.info then *place the value we just read* onto ptr^s right subtree

This pseudocode uses self-reference, so of course it describes part of a recursive subprogram:

```
PROCEDURE PlaceValue (VAR ptr   : ptrType  ;
                          justRead : infoType);
   .
   .
WITH ptr^ DO
   IF justRead < info THEN
      PlaceValue (left, justRead)
   ELSE
      PlaceValue (right, justRead)
```

This is the essence of our tree-building algorithm. The only thing missing is the base case. When ptr is NIL, it means we've gone down as far as we can go on the tree:

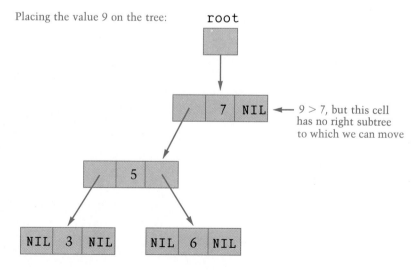

Placing the value 9 on the tree:

root

7 NIL ← 9 > 7, but this cell has no right subtree to which we can move

5

NIL 3 NIL   NIL 6 NIL

When `PlaceValue` has called itself so many times that `ptr` has become NIL, it's time to create a new cell to hold the value that we just read:

```
PROCEDURE PlaceValue (VAR ptr    : ptrType   ;
                           justRead : infoType);

BEGIN {PlaceValue}
  IF ptr = NIL THEN
    CreateCell (ptr, NIL, justRead, NIL)
  ELSE
    WITH ptr^ DO
      IF justRead < info THEN
        PlaceValue (left, justRead)
      ELSE
        PlaceValue (right, justRead)
END;   {PlaceValue}
```

Of course, definitions are nice, but does this code actually work? To see what happens when we run this code, read the Traces subsection that follows.

Program Example

```
PROGRAM BinaryTreeSort (input, output);
{Places values on a binary tree, then picks
 them off with an inorder traversal.}

  TYPE
    infoType = INTEGER;
    ptrType  = ^cellType;
    cellType = RECORD
                 left  : ptrType;
                 info  : infoType;
                 right : ptrType
               END;
  VAR
    root : ptrType;

  {----------}

  PROCEDURE Initialize (VAR root : ptrType);

  BEGIN {Initialize}
    root := NIL
  END;   {Initialize}

  {----------}

  PROCEDURE CreateCell (VAR ptr : ptrType ;
                            lef   : ptrType ;
                            inf   : infoType;
                            rit   : ptrType);
  {Creates a new cell and places 'lef'
   'inf' and 'rit' into its fields.}
```

```
BEGIN {CreateCell}
  New (ptr);
  WITH ptr^ DO
    BEGIN
      left := lef;
      info := inf;
      right:= rit
    END
END;  {CreateCell}

{----------}

PROCEDURE MakeTree (VAR root : ptrType);
{Makes a tree from the user's input.}

  VAR
    justRead : infoType;

  {----------}

  PROCEDURE PlaceValue (VAR ptr  : ptrType  ;
                            justRead : infoType);
  {Recursively moves downward to
   place a value on the tree.}

  BEGIN {PlaceValue}
    IF ptr = NIL THEN
      CreateCell (ptr, NIL, justRead, NIL)
    ELSE
      WITH ptr^ DO
        IF justRead < info THEN
          PlaceValue (left, justRead)
        ELSE
          PlaceValue (right, justRead)
  END;  {PlaceValue}

  {----------}

BEGIN {MakeTree}
  WHILE NOT Eof (input) DO
    BEGIN
      ReadLn      (justRead);
      PlaceValue (root, justRead)
    END
END;  {MakeTree}

{----------}

PROCEDURE InOrder (ptr : ptrType);
{Implements the inorder traversal algorithm.}

BEGIN  {InOrder}
  WITH ptr^ DO
    BEGIN
      IF left  <> NIL THEN
        InOrder (left);

      Write (info:3);

      IF right <> NIL THEN
        InOrder (right)
    END
END;  {InOrder}
```

```
                      {----------}
              BEGIN {BinaryTreeSort}
                WriteLn    ('Enter several integers, one on each line:');
                Initialize (root);
                MakeTree   (root);

                WriteLn    ('The values in non-decreasing order are:' );
                InOrder    (root)
              END.  {BinaryTreeSort}
```

Sample Runs

```
Enter several integers, one on each line:
7
5
6
3
9
<end-of-file indicator>
The values in non-decreasing order are:
   3  5  6  7  9
```

Traces

We'll illustrate the action of Program `BinaryTreeSort` using the data given in the Sample Run.

First, let's look at an iterative way to think about the behavior of Procedure `PlaceValue`: When we read a value from the input file, Procedure `PlaceValue` keeps "trickling down" the tree, sometimes moving to the left and sometimes moving to the right, until it finds where to create a new cell for the value that it just read. In more detail:

We start with an empty tree:

root

Then we read the value 7, and hang it on the root of the tree:

Putting 7 on the tree:

root

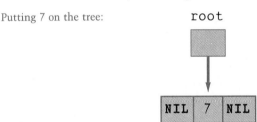

Then we read the value 5 and find that it's less than 7. So we hang it on the left subtree of the 7-cell:

Putting 5 on the tree:

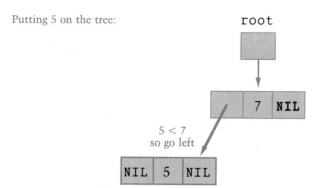

We do the same thing with the other values that we read, always starting at the root, and working our way down the tree, either to the left or to the right, until we reach a NIL. At that point we create a new cell to hold the value we just read:

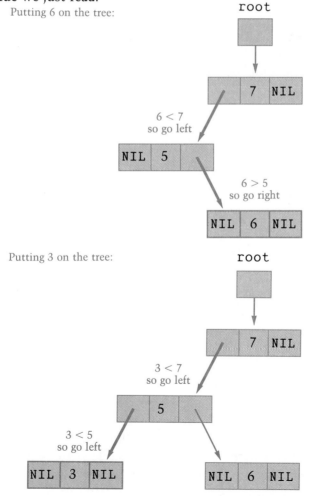

Putting 9 on the tree:

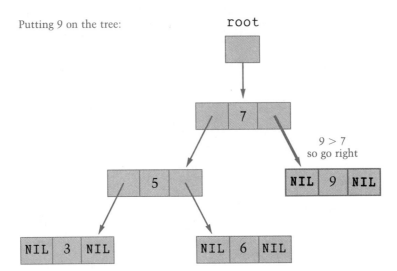

9 > 7
so go right

But now that we have a tree of values, our algorithm is only half finished. We still have to pick the values off of the tree with inorder traversal.

When we call a recursive subprogram, the subprogram calls itself, so we end up running many different versions of the same subprogram. In the case of Procedure InOrder we get one version for each cell on the tree. In each version, the formal parameter ptr has a different value—a value that points to one of the cells on the tree:

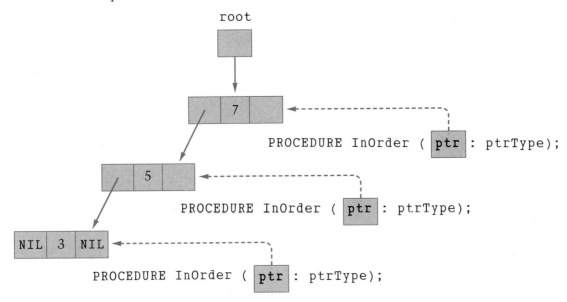

Each version of Procedure InOrder can call two more versions of the procedure—a version for ptr's left child and another version for ptr's right child:

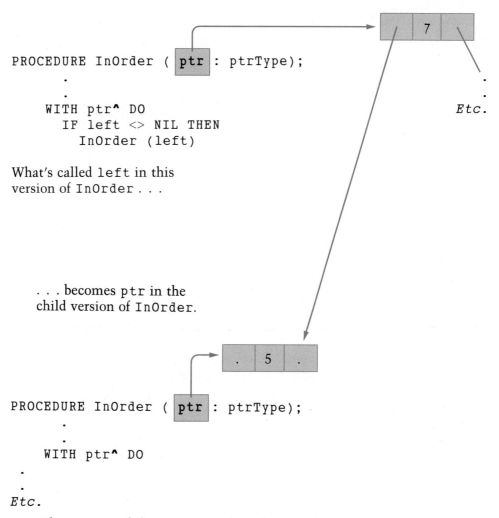

```
PROCEDURE InOrder ( ptr : ptrType);
        .
        .

    WITH ptr^ DO
       IF left <> NIL THEN
          InOrder (left)
```

What's called `left` in this
version of `InOrder` . . .

. . . becomes `ptr` in the
child version of `InOrder`.

```
PROCEDURE InOrder ( ptr : ptrType);
        .
        .

    WITH ptr^ DO
   .
   .
Etc.
```

Etc.

The essence of the `InOrder` algorithm is this:

A cell's *left* child is visited *before* the cell itself is visited;
A cell's *right* child is visited *after* the cell itself is visited.

So our various versions of Procedure `InOrder` are created and destroyed in
the following order:

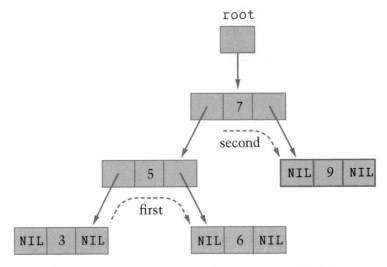

This is exactly what we want, because it manages to find the tree's values in the order 3, 5, 6, 7, 9; that is, in increasing order.

Structure

running time of binary tree sort

How long will it take to run a binary tree sort? The algorithm has two parts: `MakeTree` and `InOrder`. We'll do two separate (rough) calculations to find the running time of each part. Then we'll combine the results.

The running time of `MakeTree`: To make things simple, let's assume that `MakeTree` creates a **balanced tree**:

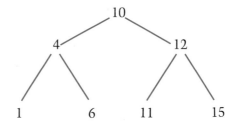

rather than an unbalanced tree:[4]

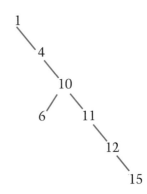

---

[4]We're stretching the truth a bit with this assumption. It's easy to see that Procedure `MakeTree` doesn't always create a balanced tree. See Exercise Que.14.13.4.

If we have a balanced tree with n values on it (give or take a few), the number of levels is the number of times we can divide n by 2. The reason for this is simple: Look at the balanced tree pictured. There are seven (nearly eight) values on the tree. The last level has four ($= 8/2$) values on it, the next-to-last level has two ($= 8/2/2$) values on it, and the top level has one ($= 8/2/2/2$) value on it. We did this kind of a calculation when we timed the binary search. The number of times n can be divided by 2 is called log n. So a balanced tree with nearly n values on it has log n levels.

Now the `MakeTree` algorithm goes roughly like this:

> For each value in the input file,
> > for each level on the tree, from top to bottom,
> > > carry the value downward, moving leftward or rightward.
> > When you've reached the bottom, create a new cell and put the new value in it.

If we replace each clause in this pseudocode with the corresponding number of steps, we get

> n times do:
> > *log* n times do:
> > > carry the value . . .

So the running of algorithm `MakeTree` takes n log n steps.

The running time of `InOrder`: Once we see clearly through `InOrder`'s elaborate recursion scheme, we see that

- There's one version of `InOrder` for each cell on the tree.
- Each version takes exactly three steps (call `InOrder (left)`, write the `info` value, call `InOrder (right)`).

So all these calls to Procedure `InOrder` take a total of $3n$ steps, which is $O(n)$ time.

Combining the running times for `MakeTree` and `InOrder`: First `MakeTree` runs, and then `InOrder` runs. The total number of steps is $(n$ log $n) + n$. If we make tables to see how the terms n log n and n grow as n becomes larger and larger, we'll see that n log n grows so fast that it dwarfs the n term:

n	vs.	$n \log n$
2		2
4		8
8		24
16		64
32		160
64		384
128		896
256		2048
512		4608
1024		10240

Thus, the running time of the whole binary tree sort is just $O(n \log n)$.

This is good! An $O(n \log n)$ algorithm is faster than an $O(n^2)$ algorithm. To show this, we'll assume we have six programs and that

Program `Constant`	takes	1 second to run
Program `Log`	takes	$\log n$ seconds to run
Program `Linear`	takes	n seconds to run
Program `NLogN`	takes	$n \log n$ seconds to run
Program `Quadratic`	takes	n^2 seconds to run
Program `Exponential`	takes	$2^n n$ seconds to run

Here's a chart showing running times of the six programs:

Running time (in seconds) of Programs

n	Constant	Log	Linear	NLogN	Quadratic	Exponential
1	1	1	1	1	1	2
2	1	1	2	2	4	8
3	1	2	3	5	9	24
4	1	2	4	8	16	64
5	1	3	5	12	25	160
6	1	3	6	16	36	384
7	1	3	7	20	49	896
8	1	3	8	24	64	2048
9	1	4	9	29	81	4608
10	1	4	10	34	100	10240

Since the binary tree sort is an $O(n \log n)$ algorithm, and selection sort is an $O(n^2)$ algorithm, a binary tree sort is faster than a selection sort. Once again, this assumes that the binary tree manages to stay balanced.

14.13   Exercises

Key Words to Review

binary tree sort   balanced tree

Questions to Answer

QUE 14.13.1   Trace Program `BinaryTreeSort` with input

```
7
10
9
12
10
```

QUE 14.13.2   We want to do a binary tree sort and someone "gives" us a tree with the following properties:

- The values stored on the left subtree are all smaller than the value stored at the root.

- The values stored on the right subtree are all larger than the value stored at the root.

Is this enough, or does the tree have to satisfy a stricter set of requirements? Explain your answer.

QUE 14.13.3   In tracing this section's Program Example, we described "an iterative way to think about the behavior of Procedure `PlaceValue`." And yet Procedure `PlaceValue` isn't iterative—it's recursive. Explain how executing Procedure `PlaceValue` has the same effect as the iterative behavior that we described in the trace.

QUE 14.13.4   If we give Program `BinaryTreeSort` the following sequence of numbers

```
1  4  10  11  12  15
```

does the program create a balanced tree? Verify your answer by making a diagram.

QUE 14.13.5   In Section 10.8 we used the formula

$$(n - 1) + (n - 2) + \ldots + 2 + 1 = \frac{n^2 - n}{2}$$

to show that the running time of the selection sort is $O(n^2)$. Use the same formula to show that it takes $O(n^2)$ time just to make the tree for the input of Exercise Que.14.13.4.

Experiments to Try

EXP 14.13.1   Add `WriteLns` to Procedure `PlaceValue` so that it displays the `info` values it encounters as it moves downward on the tree. It also displays the messages `Moving left` and `Moving right` as it goes.

Changes to Make

CHA 14.13.1   Procedure `InOrder` is quite useful, but each time you use it to solve a different problem, you might want to have `InOrder` do something slightly different as it "visits" each cell in the tree. Modify Procedure `InOrder` so that it has a procedural parameter called `Visit`. Test your new version of Procedure `InOrder` by putting it in Program `BinaryTreeSort` and passing it a procedure `WriteInfo`, which writes the value at the current cell.

CHA 14.13.2   Modify the program of Exercise Cha.14.13.1 so that it writes either the decimal or the binary representation of each cell's value, depending on which subprogram is passed to Procedure `InOrder`.

Programs and Subprograms to Write

WRI 14.13.1   The methods outlined in this section can be used to search as well as to sort. As we read the values in a file, we can create a binary tree with Procedure `MakeTree`. Then to find the value we're `searchingFor`, we can start at the root and repeatedly

> go left if `searchFor` is smaller than the value we're visiting, and
> go right if `searchFor` is larger than the value we're visiting.

Write a program that implements this binary tree search algorithm.

WRI 14.13.2   Write and test a subprogram that makes a copy of a binary tree. That is, `tree1` and `tree2` always point to different collections of cells, but after the call

    TreeCopy (tree1, tree2)

the cells pointed to by `tree2` have the same `info` values (and form the same tree shape) as the cells pointed to by `tree1`.

WRI 14.13.3   Write and test a subprogram that swaps all the left and right children in a binary tree. For example, if the tree starts out being

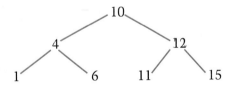

then the subprogram turns it into

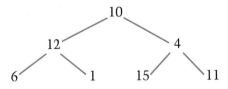

WRI 14.13.4   Write and test a subprogram that flips a binary tree around its vertical axis as if you're looking at it in a mirror.

WRI 14.13.5   Let's consider the problem of Section 12.8. In that section, we zeroed in on a particular item by asking questions and trimming down a set accordingly. There's another way to approach the same problem using trees: Have each non-leaf cell represent an *attribute*. Go left if the item you're looking for has that attribute, and go right if the item doesn't have the attribute.

   Write and test a program that creates this tree and then asks the user questions until it reaches a leaf of the tree.

WRI 14.13.6   Modify the program of Exercise Wri.14.13.5 so that, when it reaches a leaf, it asks the user if the item on that leaf is indeed the item the user was thinking about. If the user wasn't thinking about that item, the program

- asks the user for the name of the new item
- asks the user for an attribute (`animal?`, `big?`, `furry?`) that would differentiate this new item from the item that's already on the leaf
- enlarges the tree accordingly

14.14

Pointers without Linked Lists (Supplementary)

Until now we've been working with pointers as values that connect cells together. We've used pointers to create linked lists (stacks and queues) and other intricate linked structures (such as trees). But now it's time to create pointers that don't point from cell to cell. Instead they point to values that don't have pointer fields of their own. For instance, we can create a pointer that points to an `INTEGER`:

```
TYPE
  ptrType = ^INTEGER;
VAR
  intPtr : ptrType;
      .
      .
      .
New (intPtr)
```

intPtr

or a pointer that points to an array:

```
TYPE
  wordType  = PACKED ARRAY [1..5] OF CHAR;
  anyType   = ^wordType;
VAR
  arrPtr : anyType;
    .
    .
New (arrPtr)
```

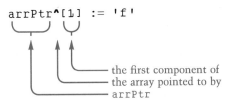

And remember what the caret symbol ^ means:

- When it's used in a type definition, it means *is a pointer to.* . . .
- When it's used in the body of a program or subprogram, it means *the thing pointed to by.* . . .

So in the type definitions just given, intPtr^ means *the* INTEGER *value pointed to by* intPtr, and arrPtr^ refers to *the array pointed to by* arrPtr. If we want to store the number 10 in the location pointed to by intPtr, we say

```
intPtr^ := 10
```

pointers to arrays

and if we want to store the letter f in an array's first component, we might say

```
arrPtr^[1] := 'f'
```

the first component of
the array pointed to by
arrPtr

Now what if we have two pointers, x and y—each pointing to an array that we've filled with characters?

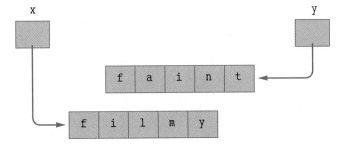

If we ever want to switch the words filmy and faint we can do it without moving lots of letters around. All we have to do is switch the addresses stored in x and y, so that x points to where y used to point, and y points to where x used to point:

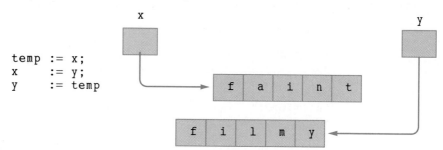

```
temp := x;
x    := y;
y    := temp
```

Certainly it's quicker to switch two addresses than to switch ten letters. As the words in the CHAR arrays become longer and longer, switching pointers becomes even more of a timesaver.

Specifications   The specs are the same as those for the selection sort of Section 10.8. But this time we'll sort five-letter words instead of INTEGERs. And when we switch two words, we'll do it by switching the values stored in two pointer variables.

Program Example

```
PROGRAM SelectionSortDriver (fInput, output);
{Test driver for Procedure SelectionSort.}
   CONST
      lo       = 1;
      hi       = 10;
      wordSize = 5;
   TYPE
      wordType  = PACKED ARRAY [1..wordSize] OF CHAR;
      anyType   = ^wordType;
      indexType = lo..hi;
      arrayType = ARRAY [indexType] OF anyType;
   VAR
      a       : arrayType;
      fInput  : TEXT;
   {----------}

PROCEDURE ReadArray (VAR fInput : TEXT; VAR a : arrayType);
{Reads unsorted values.}
   VAR
      i : indexType;
   {----------}
```

```
    PROCEDURE ReadLnWord (VAR fInput : TEXT    ;
                          VAR p        : anyType);
    {Reads a word.}
      VAR
        j : 1..wordSize;
    BEGIN {ReadLnWord}
      New (p);
      FOR j := 1 TO wordSize DO
        Read (fInput, p^[j]);
      ReadLn (fInput)
    END;   {ReadLnWord}
    {----------}
BEGIN {ReadArray}
  Reset (fInput);
  FOR i := lo TO hi DO
    ReadLnWord (fInput, a[i])
END;   {ReadArray}
{----------}
PROCEDURE SelectionSort (VAR a : arrayType);
{Implements the selection sort algorithm.}
  VAR
    start, minIndex : indexType;
  {----------}
  FUNCTION IndexOfSmallest (a            : arrayType;
                            start, finish : indexType) : indexType;
  {Returns the index of the smallest value in the array
   'a', between the 'start' and 'finish' components.}
    VAR
      minIndex, thisIndex : indexType;
  BEGIN {IndexOfSmallest}
    minIndex := start;
    FOR thisIndex := start+1 TO finish DO
      IF a[thisIndex]^ < a[minIndex]^ THEN
        minIndex := thisIndex;
    IndexOfSmallest := minIndex
  END;   {IndexOfSmallest}
  {----------}
  PROCEDURE Switch (VAR x, y : anyType);
  {Switches two values, x and y.}
    VAR
      temp : anyType;
  BEGIN {Switch}
    temp := x;
    x    := y;
    y    := temp
  END;   {Switch}
  {----------}
```

```
      BEGIN {SelectionSort}
        FOR start := 1 TO hi-1 DO
          BEGIN
            minIndex := IndexOfSmallest (a, start, hi);
            Switch (a[start], a[minIndex])
          END
      END;  {SelectionSort}

      {----------}

      PROCEDURE WriteArray (a : arrayType);
      {Writes sorted values.}

        VAR
          i : indexType;
      BEGIN {WriteArray}
        FOR i := lo TO hi DO
          Write (' ', a[i]^);
        WriteLn ('.')
      END;   {WriteArray}

      {----------}

    BEGIN {SelectionSortDriver}
      ReadArray      (fInput, a);
      SelectionSort (a);
      WriteArray     (a)
    END.   {SelectionSortDriver}
```

Sample Runs

With the following fInput file:

```
        every
        April
        filmy
        under
        lying
        ghost
        shyly
        calls
        faint
        woods
```

the output looks like this:

```
April calls every faint filmy ghost lying shyly under woods.
```

Observations

the syntax of
pointers to
arrays

Most of this code is taken directly from Program SelectionSortDriver in Section 10.8. What few changes we've made are due to the sorting of words rather than INTEGERs and the use of pointers. In the next few paragraphs we'll check to make sure that all the pointing is done correctly.

- TYPE
  ```
  wordType  = PACKED ARRAY [1..wordSize] OF CHAR;
  anyType   = ^wordType;
  indexType = lo..hi;
  arrayType = ARRAY [indexType] OF anyType;
  VAR
  a : arrayType;
  ```
  Here we have an array of pointers to wordType values.

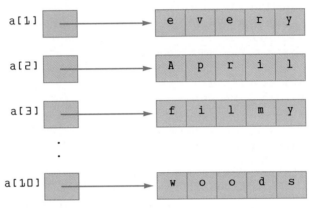

- IF a[thisIndex]^ < a[minIndex]^ THEN

  To see what this line does, we make a picture:

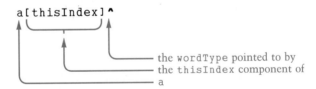

  the wordType pointed to by
  the thisIndex component of
  a

  Since a[thisIndex]^ is a word, it can be compared alphabetically with another word, a[minIndex]^. So it makes sense to do the comparison in the IF statement.

- PROCEDURE ReadLnWord (VAR fInput : TEXT   ;
                        VAR p   : anyType);

  .
  .

  ReadLnWord (fInput, a[i])

  Each component of a stores a pointer. So when ReadLnWord is called, a pointer is passed to the formal parameter p. This is just as it should be, since p's type (anyType) is a pointer type.

- New (p);

  .
  .

  Read (fInput, p^[j])

If you're not dealing with linked lists, it's easy to forget about calling New. But we still need to call it. After all, p is a pointer variable, so it needs to be made to point to something. In this instance, New makes p point to a wordType array.

Once p points to a wordType array, we can read CHAR values into the array's components. Once again, we check our syntax with a small diagram.

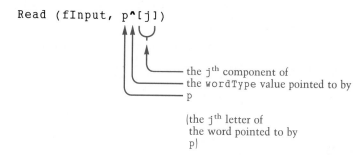

```
Read (fInput, p^[j])
```

the jth component of
the wordType value pointed to by
p

(the jth letter of
the word pointed to by
p)

According to the diagram, this Read gets a single letter, which is just right.

Some programming languages, like the C programming language, rely heavily on having pointers that point to non-linked values. Pascal places less emphasis on this technique, but still, there are Pascal programs in which it's very useful.

14.14   Exercises

Questions to Answer

QUE 14.14.1   With anyType defined as in Program SelectionSortDriver, explain why

```
VAR
   arrPtr : anyType;
      .
      .
   arrPtr^ := 'April'
```

would be legal.

QUE 14.14.2   With arrayType defined as in Program SelectionSortDriver, explain why

```
VAR
   a : arrayType;
      .
      .
   a[1]^[1] := 'f'
```

would be legal.

QUE 14.14.3   Is it possible to create a pointer that points to the first field of a cellType record rather than to the entire record? Explain your answer.

Experiments to Try

EXP 14.14.1 In Program SelectionSortDriver move the definition of anyType so that it comes before the definition of wordType.

EXP 14.14.2 Remove the name wordType from Program SelectionSortDriver. Instead define anyType with

```
TYPE
    anyType = ^PACKED ARRAY [1..wordSize] OF CHAR;
```

EXP 14.14.3 Run the following program. Then draw a picture to show how it works.

```
PROGRAM DoubleIndirect (output);

    TYPE
      ptrType    = ^INTEGER;
      ptrPtrType = ^ptrType;
    VAR
      p : ptrPtrType;
BEGIN {DoubleIndirect}
  New (p);
  New (p^);
  p^^ := 3;
  WriteLn (p^^)
END.   {DoubleIndirect}
```

EXP 14.14.4 Run a program containing:

```
PROCEDURE Switch (xPtr, yPtr : ptrType);
{Notice!!  xPtr and yPtr aren't VAR parameters!}

    VAR
      temp : INTEGER;

BEGIN {Switch}
  temp  := xPtr^;
  xPtr^ := yPtr^;
  yPtr^ := temp
END; {Switch}
    .
    .
ReadLn (xPtr^, yPtr^);
Switch (xPtr , yPtr );
WriteLn (xPtr^:3, yPtr^:3)
```

EXP 14.14.5 Can you create a pointer that points to a file?

EXP 14.14.6 Reread the explanation of a WITH statement's effect in Section 12.1. Then run the following program:

```
PROGRAM WITHTester (input, output);
    TYPE
      twoIntType = RECORD
                      x, y : INTEGER
                   END;
      ptrType    = ^twoIntType;

    VAR
      p1, p2: ptrType;
    {----------}
```

```
     PROCEDURE ReadLnRecord (VAR p : ptrType);
     BEGIN {ReadLnRecord}
       WITH p^ DO
         ReadLn (x, y)
     END;  {ReadLnRecord}

     {----------}
   BEGIN {WITHTester}
     New (p1);
     New (p2);

     WITH p1^ DO
       BEGIN
         Write           ('Enter two numbers for p1: ');
         ReadLnRecord (p1);
         Write           ('Enter two numbers for p2: ');
         ReadLnRecord (p2);

         p1 := p2;

         WriteLn;
         WriteLn;
         WriteLn ('No dots     : ',      x:3,      y:3);
         WriteLn ('Using p1^. : ', p1^.x:3, p1^.y:3);
         WriteLn ('Using p2^. : ', p2^.x:3, p2^.y:3)
       END
   END.   {WITHTester}
```

Changes to Make

CHA 14.14.1 Modify Program `SelectionSortDriver` so that it isn't restricted to five-letter words. See Section 12.5 for a good way to do it.

Programs and Subprograms to Write

WRI 14.14.1 Redo Exercise Wri.10.8.5 using the techniques of this section.

WRI 14.14.2 The inorder tree traversal algorithm (Sections 14.12 and 14.13) is one of several ways to traverse a tree in a depth-first fashion. The term *depth-first* refers to the fact that we go downward before we go across. For instance, we visit all the cells on a tree's leftmost path before we visit any of the cells on the right subtree. In contrast to a depth-first traversal, there's a breadth-first tree traversal. In a *breadth-first* traversal, we visit the root first, then we visit each of the root's children, then each of the root's grandchildren, etc.

The algorithm for performing a breadth-first traversal involves the use of a queue:

> Put the root on the queue.
> Repeat the following
>   remove a cell from the queue
>   do something with that cell
>   put that cell's children (if any) on the queue
> as long as there's still at least one cell on the queue.

But how can we "put a cell on the queue"? What we need is a queue whose `info` fields are pointers:

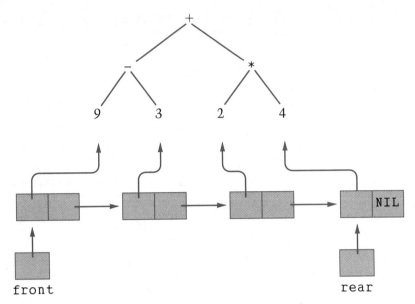

Write and test a procedure that does a breadth-first traversal of a tree that's created using Procedure MakeTree of Section 14.12.

Chapter Summary

A *pointer* is variable in which an address can be stored. The address refers to a memory location where a value is stored. This value can be an entire record, in which case one of the record's fields can be another pointer. When we create a chain of records with this technique, we call it a *linked list*. Each record in the list is called a *cell*.

The syntax of pointers is easier to understand if we remember the following rules:

- When a caret symbol ^ is used in a type definition, it means *is a pointer to. . . .*
- When a caret symbol ^ is used in the body of a program or subprogram, it means *the thing pointed to by. . . .*
- If we have two variables, say ptr and temp, in which pointers are stored, and we execute

   ptr := temp

   this makes ptr point to the same place that temp points to.

One way to make a pointer variable point to a cell is to call Pascal's pre-declared procedure New. Because this call is made during the run of the program, and not at compile time, we say that space for the cell is being allocated *dynamically*.

Two special kinds of linked lists, called *stacks* and *queues*, are useful in solving a wide variety of problems. A stack is a last-in first-out (LIFO) list. The last value to be *pushed* onto the list is always the first value to be *popped* off. To make a stack, we create a linked list with a pointer variable pointing to the top of the list. Each cell in the stack points to the cell directly below it. At the bottom of the stack we have a cell containing a NIL pointer.

A queue is a first-in first-out (FIFO) list. The first value to be added to the list is always the first value to be removed. To make a queue, we create a linked list with two special pointers—one pointing to the front of the list, and another pointing to the rear of the list. Each cell in the queue points toward the rear. The rearmost cell contains a NIL pointer.

Sometimes we need to extract a cell from the middle of a linked list or insert a cell into the middle of a linked list. These operations take $O(1)$ time, and the comparable array operations take $O(n)$ time. So if we frequently need to extract or insert values, we should consider representing the data with a linked list rather than an array.

Here's a table summarizing the differences between linked structures and arrays:

	Arrays	Linked Structures
allocation	static	dynamic
size	determined at compile time	determined at run time (and can change at run time)
size changes by	editing code	calling New, calling Dispose, moving pointers
shape	line (1-dimensional) rectangle (2-dimensional) cube (3-dimensional) etc.	can take on any shape (a line, a tree shape, etc.) depending on how the pointers are arranged

Performing Operations:

finding a value in the middle	"easy", $O(1)$ time	"hard", $O(n)$ time
inserting a value into the middle	"hard", $O(n)$ time	"easy", $O(1)$ time
removing a value from the middle	"hard", $O(n)$ time	"easy", $O(1)$ time

A doubly linked list is a list in which each cell points to the cell before it and the cell after it. A doubly linked list is useful when the problem demands that we can quickly find the previous cell as well as the next cell.

Another example of a linked structure is a *tree*. A *binary tree* is a tree in which each cell has at most two *children*. Each cell on a tree is the root of an entire subtree. Since trees contain subtrees, which themselves contain subtrees, we often use recursion to solve problems involving trees. One recursive algorithm, called *inorder* traversal, is used in many programs that deal with binary trees.

15

More on Files

15.1

File Windows: `Get` and `Put`

TEXT files

If you want to bake a cake, you can either use a mix or bake it from scratch. The same is true of input and output. Until now we've used Pascal's "premixed" procedures `Read`, `ReadLn`, `Write`, and `WriteLn`. In this section we'll use more primitive mechanisms to do input and output from scratch.[1]

First let's review what we mean by a TEXT file. Here's what a file of type TEXT looks like:

```
<character> <character> .. <character> <end-of-line indicator>
<character> <character> .. <character> <end-of-line indicator>
     .
     .
     .
<character> <character> .. <character> <end-of-line indicator>
<end-of-file indicator>
```

It's a sequence of *lines*, separated from one another by *end-of-line indicators.* The *characters* on these lines can be letters, digits, non-printing characters, etc.

Our first program example follows.

Program
Example

```
PROGRAM GetDemo (fInput, output);
{Demonstrates the pre-declared Get procedure.}
   VAR
      ch1, ch2, ch3, ch4 : CHAR;
      fInput             : TEXT;
```

---

[1]Note: The features discussed in this section are *not* available in Turbo Pascal. Consult your instructor or your Turbo Pascal manual for more details.

```
BEGIN {GetDemo}
  Reset (fInput);

  ch1 := fInput^;
  Get (fInput);

  ch2 := fInput^;
  Get (fInput);

  ch3 := fInput^;
  ch4 := fInput^;

  WriteLn (ch1, ch2, ch3, ch4)
END.  {GetDemo}
```

Sample Runs

With the following fInput file:

```
abcd
```

the output looks like this:

```
abcc
```

Observations

fInput is a TEXT file—a file containing CHARacters. By adding a caret to the file's name, we get fInput^—a CHAR-type variable. But fInput^ isn't just an ordinary CHAR variable. It's different from the variables we've been discussing up to this point in the book. fInput^ has a special relationship with the fInput file, which we're about to explore.

file windows and Get

First notice that we don't explicitly declare the variable fInput^ anywhere in the program. It's created automatically when we declare the file fInput:

```
VAR
  fInput : TEXT;
```

Then look carefully at the way values are placed into the variable fInput^. When Program GetDemo begins running, it calls

```
Reset (fInput)
```

and *this call places the first character of the* fInput *file into the* fInput^ *variable:*

The result of the call Reset (fInput):

fInput^   abcd

After this call to Procedure Reset has been made, we can use the statement

```
ch1 := fInput^
```

to place the letter a into the ordinary CHAR-type variable ch1.

Now once we've stored the letter a in the variable ch1, it would be nice if we could make fInput^ contain the next character in the fInput file. We can do this with Pascal's pre-declared procedure Get. The effect of calling

```
Get (fInput)
```

is to place the next character of the fInput file into the fInput^ variable:

The result of the call Get (fInput):

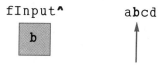

fInput^   abcd

Calling Procedure Get also has the effect of *advancing* our position in the file. In our diagram this means moving the arrow one character to the right, so that it points to the letter b—the next character in the file.

fInput^ is called the **file window** for the file fInput. The word *window* is meant to suggest that, at any given time, we can only catch a glimpse at one character of the many characters that are in the file. Be sure not to confuse the ^ in a file window with the ^ we use for pointers. They don't have much to do with one another.

Traces

Here's what happens during a run of Program GetDemo:

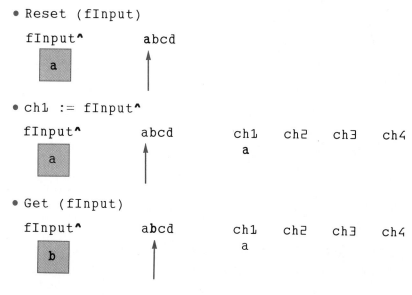

- Reset (fInput)

  fInput^   abcd

- ch1 := fInput^

  fInput^   abcd   ch1   ch2   ch3   ch4
                                 a

- Get (fInput)

  fInput^   abcd   ch1   ch2   ch3   ch4
                                 a

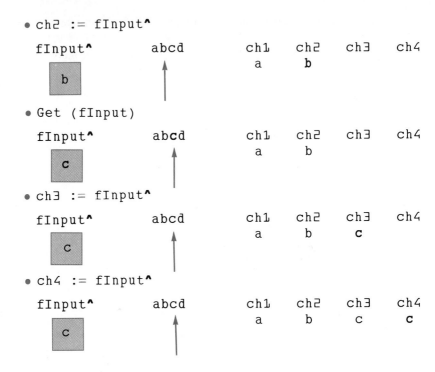

Notice that both ch3 and ch4 were assigned the value c. We didn't call Get between the two statements

        ch3 := fInput^

and

        ch4 := fInput^

so we didn't change the value stored in fInput^ and we didn't advance our position in the file fInput. After executing

        ch3 := fInput^

the file window still contained the same letter c.

Read vs. Get   Now if you think about an old familiar statement like

        Read (fInput, ch1)

you'll realize that it does the same thing that we've just done with

        ch1 := fInput^;
        Get (fInput)

When we Read a character variable, we're actually doing two things. We're *assigning* a value to the variable, and we're *changing* our position in the file, so that the next execution of Read sees a different character.

        To further emphasize this point, we'll rewrite Program GetDemo, using calls to Read:

<table>
</table>

Program Example

```
PROGRAM ReadReplacesGet (fInput, output);
{Does the same thing as Program GetDemo
 but uses Read instead of Get and fInput^.}
   VAR
     ch1, ch2, ch3, ch4 : CHAR;
     fInput             : TEXT;
BEGIN {ReadReplacesGet}
   Reset (fInput);

   Read (fInput, ch1);

   Read (fInput, ch2);

   Read (fInput, ch3);
   ch4 := ch3;

   WriteLn (ch1, ch2, ch3, ch4)
END.   {ReadReplacesGet}
```

Sample Runs

A run of ReadReplacesGet looks the same as a run of Program GetDemo.

changing the position within a file

The next program shows how Reset and Get can be used to move back and forth within a file.

Program Example

```
PROGRAM MoveAround (inFile, output);
{Uses Reset and Get to move around the inFile.}
   VAR
     ch1, ch2, ch3, ch4, ch5 : CHAR;
     inFile                  : TEXT;
BEGIN {MoveAround}
   Reset (inFile);

   ch1 := inFile^;
   Get (inFile);

   ch2 := inFile^;
   Reset (inFile);

   ch3 := inFile^;
   Get (inFile);

   ch4 := inFile^;
   Get (inFile);

   WriteLn (ch1, ch2, ch3, ch4);

   ch5 := inFile^;
   WriteLn ('**', ch5, '**');
   IF Eoln(inFile) THEN
      WriteLn ('At end of line.')
END.   {MoveAround}
```

Sample Runs

With the following inFile:

```
ab
```

the output looks like this:

```
abab
**  **
At end of line.
```

end-of-line indicators in a file

As you go through the program's trace, it will be important to remember that an inFile like this one contains more than just two letters:

```
ab<end-of-line indicator><end-of-file indicator>
```

On the most implementations you can create this inFile by starting up your editor, typing the two characters ab, and saving the file. You don't need to hit the return key to get the end-of-line indicator. The rules of ANSI Standard Pascal say that every line of a TEXT file, even the last line, ends with an end-of-line indicator. The last end-of-line indicator is placed in the file without your doing anything special to put it there.

Traces

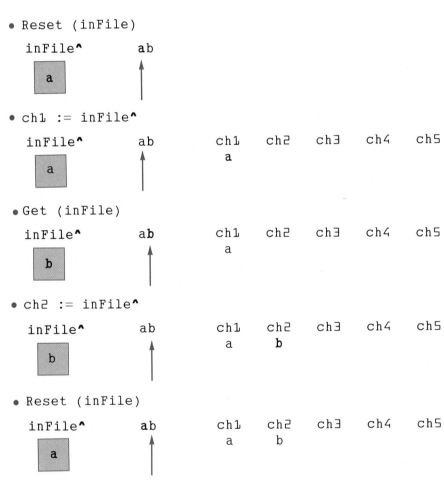

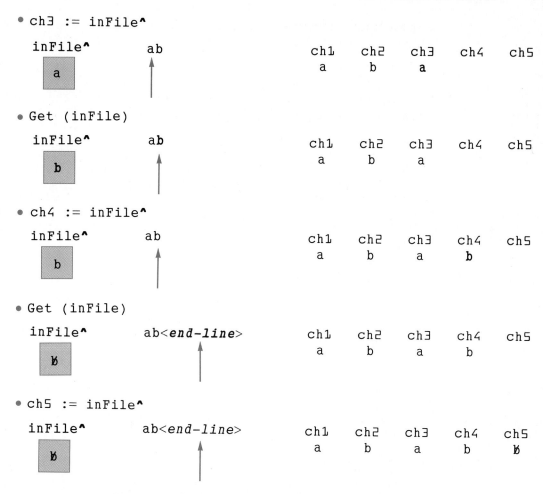

- ch3 := inFile^

  inFile^   ab

  a

ch1	ch2	ch3	ch4	ch5
a	b	a		

- Get (inFile)

  inFile^   ab

  b

ch1	ch2	ch3	ch4	ch5
a	b	a		

- ch4 := inFile^

  inFile^   ab

  b

ch1	ch2	ch3	ch4	ch5
a	b	a	b	

- Get (inFile)

  inFile^   ab<*end-line*>

  b̷

ch1	ch2	ch3	ch4	ch5
a	b	a	b	

- ch5 := inFile^

  inFile^   ab<*end-line*>

  b̷

ch1	ch2	ch3	ch4	ch5
a	b	a	b	b̷

examining an end-of-line indicator

ANSI Standard Pascal has an interesting rule concerning end-of-line indicators. When we Read an end-of-line indicator or examine an end-of-line indicator with a file window, we always see a blank space (pictured as a b̷ in our trace diagrams). This is different from what the pre-declared function Eoln does. Eoln returns TRUE if it's looking at the end-of-line indicator and FALSE if it's looking at anything else (a blank space, for instance).

- WriteLn ('**', ch5, '**')
  Writes ** **.

- IF Eoln(inFile) THEN
      WriteLn ('At end of line.')
  Writes At end of line.

Now here's a chart showing some of Pascal's pre-declared subprograms for doing input and output:

Input	Output
ReadLn	WriteLn
Read	Write
Reset	Rewrite
Get	Put

For each subprogram that does input there's a corresponding subprogram to do output. The subprogram that corresponds to Procedure Get is Procedure Put. Next we'll look at a small program that shows how Put works.

Program Example

```
PROGRAM GetAndPut (aFile, output);
{Demonstrates the pre-declared
 Get and Put procedures.}
  VAR
    ch1, ch2, ch3 : CHAR;
    aFile         : TEXT;
BEGIN {GetAndPut}
  Rewrite (aFile);

  aFile^ := 'x';
  Put (aFile);

  aFile^ := 'y';
  Put (aFile);

  aFile^ := 'z';
  Put (aFile);

  Reset (aFile);

  ch1 := aFile^;
  Get (aFile);

  ch2 := aFile^;
  Get (aFile);

  ch3 := aFile^;

  WriteLn (ch1, ch2, ch3)
END.  {GetAndPut}
```

Sample Runs

After we run Program GetAndPut, the aFile contains

    xyz

These characters also appear on the screen.

Observations

First you move a value into the file window with a statement like

Put

    aFile^ := 'x'

    aFile^

Then you call the pre-declared Procedure Put:

```
Put (aFile)
```

The call to Put does two things:[2] It copies whatever's in the file window into the file:

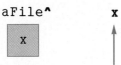

and it advances our position in the file in preparation for the next output operation:

Traces

- Rewrite (aFile)

Calling Procedure Rewrite positions us at the beginning of an empty aFile. If aFile had characters in it, they're gone after we call Procedure Rewrite.

- aFile^ := 'x';
  Put (aFile)

- aFile^ := 'y';
  Put (aFile)

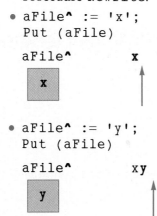

---

[2]According to the ANSI Standard, the value of aFile^ is undefined after a successful call to Procedure Put. Nevertheless, our diagrams will always show aFile^ to have its most recently acquired value.

```
aFile^ := 'z';
Put (aFile)
```

aFile^   xyz

```
┌─────┐
│  z  │          ↑
└─────┘          │
                 │
```

```
Reset (aFile)
```

aFile^   xyz

```
┌─────┐
│  x  │          ↑
└─────┘          │
                 │
```

Procedure Reset moves us back to the beginning of the file, in preparation for using the file as input (with Read or Get).

Don't forget to Put.   In Program GetAndPut, notice that very little happens until we call Put. Just doing aFile^ := 'x' doesn't move anything into aFile, and it doesn't advance our position in the file. This point is emphasized in the next example.

Program Example

```
PROGRAM PutDemo (aFile, output);
{Demonstrates the pre-declared Put procedure.}
   VAR
     ch1, ch2 : CHAR;
     aFile    : TEXT;
BEGIN {PutDemo}
   Rewrite (aFile);

   aFile^ := 'x';
   aFile^ := 'y';
   Put (aFile);
   aFile^ := 'z';
   Put (aFile);

   Reset (aFile);

   Read    (aFile, ch1, ch2);
   WriteLn (ch1, ch2)
END.   {PutDemo}
```

Sample Runs   After we run Program PutDemo, the aFile contains

       yz

These characters also appear on the screen.

Traces
```
aFile^ := 'x';
aFile^ := 'y';
Put (aFile)
```

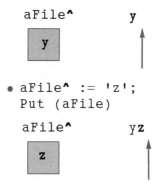

```
aFile^            y

    y
```

```
• aFile^ := 'z';
  Put (aFile)
```

```
aFile^           yz

    z
```

The first assignment, aFile^ := 'x', ends up having no noticeable effect, just as the first assignment in

```
x := 1;
x := 2;
Write (x:1)
```

would have no noticeable effect.

Write vs. Put   Now we'll redo Program GetAndPut, using calls to Write.

Program Example

```
PROGRAM WriteReplacesPut (aFile, output);
{Does the same thing as Program GetAndPut
 but uses Write instead of Get and fInput^.}
  VAR
    ch1, ch2, ch3 : CHAR;
    aFile         : TEXT;
BEGIN {WriteReplacesPut}
  Rewrite (aFile);
  Write (aFile, 'x');
  Write (aFile, 'y');
  Write (aFile, 'z');
  Reset (aFile);
  ch1 := aFile^;
  Get (aFile);
  ch2 := aFile^;
  Get (aFile);
  ch3 := aFile^;
  WriteLn (ch1, ch2, ch3)
END.  {WriteReplacesPut}
```

Sample Runs   A run of this program looks the same as a run of Program GetAndPut.

Observations

Reset and Rewrite

In this program, we use the familiar `Write` procedure along with our new `Get` procedure. `Read`s, `Get`s, `Write`s, and `Put`s can be mixed together in a program. Of course, if you mix these together, you must do it in a way that makes sense. Consider the following code fragments:

```
Reset (aFile);
Write (aFile, 'x')
```

or

```
Reset (aFile);
aFile^ := 'x';
Put     (aFile)
```

Either of these will give you an error diagnostic, because `Reset` prepares a file for input, not for output. Of course, it *is* legal to do the following:

```
Reset   (aFile);
Rewrite (aFile);
Write   (aFile, 'x')
```

because in this code, you prepare the file for output with `Rewrite` immediately before attempting the `Write`.

Rewrite erases a file.

Procedures `Reset` and `Rewrite` have one thing in common: Both procedures position us at the beginning of a file. But that's where the similarity ends. When you `Reset (aFile)`, you don't change the contents of aFile. But when you `Rewrite (aFile)` you erase anything that was already in aFile. This point is illustrated in the next example.

Program Example

```
PROGRAM MoveAroundAgain (aFile, output);
{Uses Rewrite, Put, and Reset to move around aFile.}
  VAR
    ch1, ch2, ch3 : CHAR;
    aFile         : TEXT;
BEGIN {MoveAroundAgain}
  Rewrite (aFile);

  Write (aFile, 'x');
  Write (aFile, 'y');
  Write (aFile, 'z');

  Rewrite (aFile);

  aFile^ := 'a';
  Put (aFile);
  aFile^ := 'b';
  Put (aFile);

  Rewrite (aFile);

  Write (aFile, 'pqr');

  Reset (aFile);

  Read    (aFile, ch1, ch2, ch3);
  WriteLn (ch1, ch2, ch3)
END.  {MoveAroundAgain}
```

Sample Runs

After we run Program MoveAroundAgain, the aFile contains

pqr

These characters also appear on the screen.

Traces

- Rewrite (aFile);
  Write (aFile, 'x');
  Write (aFile, 'y');
  Write (aFile, 'z')

  aFile^   **xyz**

- Rewrite (aFile)

  aFile^

- aFile^ := 'a';
  Put (aFile);
  aFile^ := 'b';
  Put (aFile)

  aFile^   **ab**

- Rewrite (aFile)

  aFile^

- Write (aFile, 'pqr')

  aFile^   **pqr**

• Reset (aFile)

aFile^   pqr

And so on.

15.1   Exercises

Key Words to Review

Get   Put   file window

Questions to Answer

QUE 15.1.1   Explain the relationship between Get and Read.

QUE 15.1.2   Did your answer in Exercise Que.15.1.1 depend on any assumptions about Reading a CHAR value rather than an INTEGER or a REAL number? Explain.

QUE 15.1.3   What can go wrong if we forget to call Get?

QUE 15.1.4   What can go wrong if we forget to call Put?

QUE 15.1.5   What can go wrong if we forget to call Reset or Rewrite?

QUE 15.1.6   What's the difference between Reset and Rewrite?

QUE 15.1.7   When we Read an end-of-line indicator or examine an end-of-line indicator with a file window, we always see a blank space. Explain this in terms of the notion of *abstraction*.

Things to Check in a Manual

MAN 15.1.1   Are Procedures Get and Put available on your implementation? If not, what features does your implementation offer to take the places of Get and Put?

MAN 15.1.2   Some implementations allow you to add data to the *end* of a file—a file that already contained data before your program began running. When you do this, we say that you are *appending* to an existing file. Does your implementation provide such a feature?

MAN 15.1.3   Does your implementation have a pre-declared procedure to Close a file? If so, what's the purpose of calling this procedure?

MAN 15.1.4   If you use Turbo Pascal, check the manual for more information on the way the end-of-line indicator is treated. It's different from what's done in the ANSI Standard.

Experiments to Try

EXP 15.1.1   Devise an experiment to find out if your implementation sees a blank space when it Reads or examines an end-of-line indicator.

EXP 15.1.2   In Program `MoveAroundAgain` add the statement

> `WriteLn (aFile^)`

immediately after the statement

> `Write (aFile, 'z')`

EXP 15.1.3   Run a program containing references to `input^` and `output^`.

EXP 15.1.4   Redo Exercise Exp.15.1.3, but add `Reset (input)` and `Rewrite (output)` at the top of the program.

EXP 15.1.5   Redo Exercise Exp.15.1.3, but add `Reset (output)` at the top of the program.

EXP 15.1.6   Redo Exercise Exp. 15.1.3, but add `Reset (input)`and `Rewrite (output)`in the middle of the program.

EXP 15.1.7   Does your implementation have a pre-declared procedure called `Page`? If so, what happens when a program executes `Page (output)`?

EXP 15.1.8   Does your implementation allow you to explicitly write an end-of-line indicator? Try it with the following statement:

> `Write (myFile, x, y, Chr(13), Chr(10), z)`

EXP 15.1.9   Can you write the bell sound to a file, read it, and then play it back to the user?

Changes to Make

CHA 15.1.1   Modify Program `OneBar` (Section 2.6) so that it uses `Put` instead of `Write`.

CHA 15.1.2   *(A continuation of Exercise Cha.15.1.1)* Further modify Program `OneBar` so that it uses `Get` instead of `Read`. Assume that `symbolsNeeded` is always a one-digit number.

CHA 15.1.3   Modify Program `Alphabet` (Section 7.4) so that it uses `Get` and `Put` instead of `Read` and `Write`.

15.2

Using File Windows

We've used file windows in several experimental programs but we haven't used them to do any useful work.[3] Why would we ever want to break

> `Read (fInput, ch1)`

into two statements

> `ch1 := fInput^;`
> `Get (fInput)`

---

[3]Note: The features discussed in this section are *not* available in Turbo Pascal. Consult your instructor or your Turbo Pascal manual for more details.

The answer is this: Occasionally Procedures Read and Write don't give us enough control. That is, in certain problems we need to do "half" of a Read without doing an "entire" Read.

Specifications   Recall Procedure ReadLnCharOrNat in Section 8.3. The procedure was designed to read either a CHARacter or a natural number. It had two VAR parameters, c (of type CHAR) and n (of type natural). Procedure ReadLnCharOrNat gave a meaningful value to either c or n depending on what the user entered on the keyboard.

Now let's get a little bit more ambitious. Let's have our procedure take just one item, a character or a natural, from a line that has several items on it.

An input line with seven items on it:

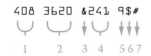

item count: 1   2   3 4   5 6 7

To take all the items from the preceding line, our new procedure ReadCharOrNat will need to be called seven times. Notice how numbers and characters are squeezed together on this line, without any intervening blank spaces. The human eye can tell where a number ends and a character begins, so a computer should be able to do it. Of course we won't squeeze together two numbers because if we do, even the human eye can't tell where one starts and the other begins:

item count: 1   2   3 4   5 6 7

Input: A line with several items in it. Each "item" is either a natural number or a character. Any two adjacent numbers are separated from one another by at least one blank space.

Process: Add 2 to each number and find the Successor of each character.

Output: The new list of items.

These are almost the same as the specs for Program CharNatTester in Section 8.3. The only difference is that the program of Section 8.3 accepted three items—characters or natural numbers—with each item on its own line. We can also compare this section's specs with the action of Procedure ReadCharOrNat in Section 13.6. The code in Section 13.6 accepted several items on a line, but all the items had to be separated from one another by blank spaces.

Designing a Program   Can we solve this problem without file windows, using just Procedure Read? Let's look at a slightly modified NS Chart for our old Procedure ReadLnCharOrNat:

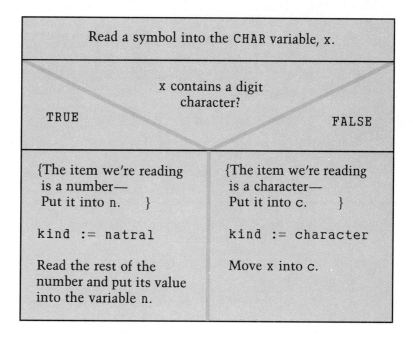

Why do we
need to use file
windows?

This looks OK, but if we apply it to our new specs we'll run into trouble. Think about what happens when we get to the ꟼ on the line

```
408 3620 &241 ꟼ$#
```
                    Read a ꟼ

First we "Read the ꟼ symbol into the CHAR variable x." After determining that ꟼ is a digit character we set kind equal to natral and then "Read the rest of the number." But there's no more number to read

```
408 3620 &241 ꟼ$#
```
                  Read a $

So instead of reading the rest of the number, we read a dollar sign. Now once we've read this non-digit character $, we can't read it again in the next call to ReadCharOrNat. This call to ReadCharOrNat used up the natural number ꟼ and the character $, even though we meant only for it to take a natural number.

What we need is to be able to "peek" at the characters in the file without actually reading them. Then we can

> peek at the ꟼ,
> determine that the ꟼ is part of a natural number,
> read the entire natural number (starting with the ꟼ)

As we saw in Section 15.1, we can easily "peek" at characters in a file using a file window.

Program Example

```
PROGRAM CharNatTester (input, output);
{A test driver for Procedure ReadCharOrNat.}
   TYPE
     kindType = (character, natral);
     natural  = 0..MAXINT;
   VAR
     c     : CHAR;
     n     : natural;
     kind  : kindType;

   {----------}

   PROCEDURE ReadCharOrNat (VAR inFile : TEXT     ;
                            VAR c      : CHAR      ;
                            VAR n      : natural   ;
                            VAR kind   : kindType);
   {Reads a value for c OR for n.
    Sets kind to
      character   if a value of c is read;
      natral      if a value of n is read.}

     {----------}

     PROCEDURE SkipBlanks (VAR inFile : TEXT);
     {Skips over blank spaces.}

       CONST
         blank = ' ';

     BEGIN {SkipBlanks}
       WHILE inFile^ = blank DO
         Get (inFile)
     END;  {SkipBlanks}

     {----------}

     FUNCTION IsDigit (x : CHAR) : BOOLEAN;
     {Answers the question "Is x one of the
      digit characters '0' to '9'?"}
     BEGIN {IsDigit}
       IsDigit := x IN ['0'..'9']
     END;  {IsDigit}

     {----------}

   BEGIN {ReadCharOrNat}
     SkipBlanks (inFile);
     IF IsDigit (inFile^) THEN
       BEGIN
         kind := natral;
         Read (inFile, n)
       END
     ELSE
       BEGIN
         kind := character;
         Read (inFile, c)
       END
   END;  {ReadCharOrNat}

   {----------}
```

```
BEGIN {CharNatTester}
  Write   ('Enter several lines containing ');
  WriteLn ('characters and natural numbers:');
  WriteLn;

  WHILE NOT Eof (input) DO
    BEGIN
      WriteLn ('.................');

      WHILE NOT Eoln (input) DO
        BEGIN
          ReadCharOrNat (input, c, n, kind);
          IF kind = character THEN
            Write (Succ(c) : 1, ' ')
          ELSE
            Write (n + 2   : 3, ' ')
        END;

      WriteLn;
      WriteLn;
      WriteLn;
      ReadLn (input)
    END
END.  {CharNatTester}
```

Sample Runs

```
Enter several lines containing characters and natural numbers:
5 x 321                        ←——— The user types this
.................
  7 y 323                      )——  The computer writes this
408 3620 &241 9$#              ←——— The user types this
.................
410 3622 ' 243  11 % $         )——  The computer writes this
<end-of-file indicator>
```

Observations Compare Procedure ReadLnCharOrNat in Section 8.3 with this section's ReadCharOrNat. File windows not only allow us to solve the revised problem, but they also make the code shorter and more readable.

Why are file windows useful?

Here's how we use the file window in Procedure ReadCharOrNat:

- IF IsDigit (inFile^) THEN

inFile   408 3620 &241 9$#

Peeking at this 9 we realize that we're about to read a natural number. So we go on and actually read the number 9 into the variable n.

• BEGIN
```
   kind := natral;
   Read (inFile, n)
END
```

Now notice what Read (inFile, n) does: Since the digit 9 hasn't already been read, the Read procedure can pick up the INTEGER value 9 *but it leaves the dollar sign unread*. The dollar sign that follows the digit 9 doesn't get "used up." It's available for reading by the next call to Procedure ReadCharOrNat. We're making use of an important feature of the pre-declared procedure Read in ANSI Standard Pascal: When the procedure reads a number, it keeps reading until it finds a character that doesn't belong to the number (like the dollar sign in this example) and it leaves that character for the next call to Read.[4]

• PROCEDURE ReadCharOrNat (**VAR inFile : TEXT; ...)**

        .
        .

```
ReadCharOrNat (input, c, n, kind)
```

input is a file.

Here's another example to show that the information typed in on the keyboard (the information that goes by the name input) is just another file. The heading of ReadCharOrNat tells us that the procedure expects a file, which it calls inFile. It's only in the call to ReadCharOrNat that we decide to have this procedure deal with input, the keyboard file.

Why are files passed by reference?

Now what about the words VAR inFile in the heading of Procedure ReadCharOrNat? In Section 4.2 we observed that when a file is a formal parameter in a subprogram, it needs to be a VAR parameter. But why? Does Procedure ReadCharOrNat actually change the file by reading it? The answer is yes. When we Read from a file, we change our position in the file. Remember that if ch1 is a CHAR variable then

```
Read (fInput, ch1)
```

does exactly the same work as

```
ch1 := fInput^;
Get (fInput)
```

When we change our position with Procedure Get we're actually changing something about the file. And if a procedure is going to change something about a formal parameter, that formal parameter needs to be a VAR parameter.

Actions can seem to be out of order.

Now look at the ordering of WriteLns, Reads, etc. in the main body of Program CharNatTester. Compare the code with the Sample Run. In the code, the instructions tell us to do things in a certain order:

---

[4]Turbo Pascal doesn't do it this way. Consult your instructor or your manuals.

```
WriteLn ('.................');          ◄──────── first
WHILE NOT Eoln (input) DO
  BEGIN
    ReadCharOrNat (input, c, n, kind); ◄──────── second
    IF kind = character THEN
      Write (Succ(c) : 1, ' ')
    ELSE                                 ⎫◄──────── third
      Write (n + 2   : 3, ' ')          ⎭
  END
END
```

But in the Sample Run, they seem to happen in a different order:

```
5 x 321              ◄──────────── three ReadCharOrNats
.................◄──────────── WriteLn ('.................')
   7 y 323           ◄──────────── three Writes
```

What's going on here?

To understand what's happening, we need to make some very fine distinctions. Four things happen as we use the keyboard for the program's input:

1. We type information on the keyboard.
2. This information is echoed on the screen.
3. The information is made available to the running program.
4. The information is used by the program. (It's read, examined with a file window, checked for end-of-line with Eoln, etc.)

Until now, we never had to distinguish among these four actions, but now we have to make it clear: *actions 3 and 4 don't happen until after we hit the return key.* So as we type

```
5 x 321
```

these characters are echoed on the screen *but the program receives nothing.* It's not until we finish off the line by hitting the return key

```
5 x 321<return key>
```

that the program receives a line's worth of information, examines the first character on the line, checks for end-of-line, etc. So the remarks we wrote beside our Sample Run were incorrect.

```
5 x 321              ◄───── three ReadCharOrNats  No, just echoing
.................    ◄───── WriteLn ('.................')
   7 y 323           ◄───── three Writes
```

So here's a much better description of what happens during a run of Program CharNatTester:

The program begins running. The program tries to check Eof (input) but can't do the check yet because it hasn't received any input.

The user hits several keys, which are echoed on the screen, and then . . .

`5 x 321<return>`

the user hits the return key.

Now at last the program has received a line of input. Having received this line of input, the code in the body of Program CharNatTester can now be executed as follows:

The program checks for Eof (input).
The program executes WriteLn ('..........').
The program checks for Eoln (input).

`7 y 323`

The program reads the 5 with Procedure ReadCharOrNat.
The program writes the value of 5 + 2.

The program reads the x with Procedure ReadCharOrNat.
The program writes the value of Succ('x').
Et cetera.

The crucial thing to notice is that the computer is executing statements in the order specified by the body of Program CharNatTester. It just appears as if statements are being executed out of order, because we're not used to making a distinction between Reading and echoing.

The most accurate way to describe what's happening is to talk in terms **buffers** of a **buffer**. A buffer is a collection of memory locations in which values are collected and stored up before they're made available to the program.

The computer's processor

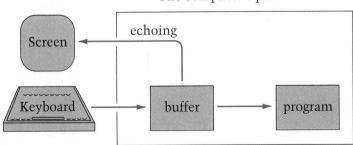

Whenever you type a character on the keyboard, the character is immediately placed in the buffer and echoed to your screen. But the character isn't sent from the buffer to the program until you hit your keyboard's return key. Hitting the return key tells the computer "I've typed a line of characters exactly the way I want it. Now send this line to the program!" If there weren't a buffer and every character was sent to the program as soon as it was typed, then it would be impossible to correct any mistakes with the backspace key.[5] If you typed in

```
Barry Bi<backspace>urd
```

then the program would receive the incorrect i before you had a chance to backspace over it.

15.2 Exercises

Key Words to Review

buffer

Questions to Answer

QUE 15.2.1 Explain why we need a file window to solve the `ReadCharOrNat` problem.

QUE 15.2.2 Let's assume, as we did in Section 13.6, that each item (each character or number) is separated from its neighbors by at least one blank space. Explain why we don't need file windows to solve this modified `ReadCharOrNat` problem.

QUE 15.2.3 Explain the differences between this section's Program `ReadCharOrNat` and the original Program `ReadLnCharOrNat` of Section 8.3. In particular, why did the original `ReadLnCharOrNat` need to read a number in one or more "pieces," whereas this section's `ReadCharOrNat` simply issues the call

```
Read (inFile, n)
```

QUE 15.2.4 In what sense is a file "changed" when we read a value from it?

QUE 15.2.5 Write a trace of the following program. Assume that the user types the letters abc when the program runs:

```
PROGRAM TraceMe2 (input, output);
   VAR
      x : CHAR;
   BEGIN {TraceMe2}
     WHILE NOT Eoln DO
       BEGIN
         Write   ('Enter a single character: ');
         Read    (x);
         WriteLn (x)
       END
   END.  {TraceMe2}
```

---

[5]On some systems, this is known as the "delete key."

Experiments to Try

EXP 15.2.1   Run a program containing

```
ReadLn  (anInt, aChar)
```

with the input

```
965*
```

EXP 15.2.2   What happens when you try to use `ReadLn` to input the numbers $-430+612$ (with no blank spaces between them) from the keyboard or from a disk file?

EXP 15.2.3   Try to modify Program `Minimum` (Section 5.4) so that it prompts the user for each integer value individually.

Changes to Make

CHA 15.2.1   Program `CharNatTester` behaves very badly if we give it a line of input that ends with blank spaces. Explain what happens, and modify the program so that it behaves reasonably with this kind of input.

CHA 15.2.2   In discussing the way `Read` handles numbers, we said that "When the procedure reads a number, it keeps reading until it finds a character that doesn't belong to the number and it leaves that character for the next call to `Read`." Now what if we have an implementation which insists that each number in its input is followed by at least one blank space (or by the end-of-line indicator)? Use a file window to modify this section's `ReadCharOrNat` so that it accounts for this possibility.

CHA 15.2.3   Modify Procedure `ReadCharOrNat` to get Procedure `ReadCharOrInt`, which accepts a number with or without a sign, as well as characters.

CHA 15.2.4   Redo Exercise Cha.12.5.2 using a file window.

CHA 15.2.5   Add the following new feature to the program you wrote for Exercises Cha.5.1.1, Cha.5.1.2, and Wri.8.3.1: Give the user the option of typing a number, followed by the letter f, followed by the return key. The input

```
--More--10f<return>
```

gets the program to *skip ten screenfuls* of the file and display the screenful that comes after these ten skipped screenfuls.

CHA 15.2.6   Here's one more variation on the theme of Exercise Cha.15.2.5: Give the user the option of typing a number, followed by the letter b, followed by the return key. The input

```
--More--10b<return>
```

gets the program to jump backward ten screenfuls in the file and then display a screenful.

Programs and Subprograms to Write

WRI 15.2.1   Write a program that reads a telephone number, given in the form

```
1(201)555-1932
```

and writes it in the form

```
201/555-1932
```

WRI 15.2.2   Write a program that removes the dashes from a social security number.

WRI 15.2.3   Redo Exercise Wri.8.4.4, this time insisting that there be no spaces in the time of day. If the program reads

```
8:19AM
```

then it writes

```
Eight nineteen in the morning.
```

WRI 15.2.4   One day a long time ago someone came into my office and said, "Here's an advertisement for a Pascal compiler that's only $19.95! For that price, we can't go wrong." When we got the disk it came with a note saying "This implementation of Pascal has INTEGERs but no REAL numbers. If you write subprograms to implement the REAL type, send them to us." Assume that in your implementation you can declare and store a REAL number, but you can't read a REAL number. Write a procedure ReadReal that reads a sign, several digits, a decimal point, and more digits, and converts this into a REAL value.

WRI 15.2.5   *(To do this problem, it helps to know some differential calculus.)* Write a program that performs a simple form of *symbolic computation*. It reads $5x^3$, meaning $5x^3$, and writes the derivative $15x^2$.

WRI 15.2.6   Modify the program of Exercise Wri.15.2.5 so that it handles formulas for *polynomial functions.* For instance, it reads

```
5x^3 + 4x^2 + 1x^1 + 6x^0
```

and writes

```
15x^2 + 8x + 1
```

15.3

Binary Files

What is a binary file?

Let's take a few numbers: 1, 9, and 10. How are these numbers stored inside the computer? The answer is a bit complicated. There are several ways to store each of these numbers. The way the numbers are stored depends on the purpose for which they're being used.

First let's assume that they're being stored in the INTEGER variables i, j, and k.

```
VAR
   i, j, k : INTEGER;
     .
     .
i := 1;
j := 9;
k := i + j
```

The best way to store INTEGER values is in binary form. (See Section 9.3.) Binary numbers can be added easily, because the rules for binary addition are simple:

$$\begin{array}{cccc}
0 & 1 & 0 & \\
+\,0 & +\,0 & +\,1 & \\
\hline
0 & 1 & 1 & \\
\end{array}$$

carry 1

$$\begin{array}{c}
1 \\
+\,1 \\
\hline
0 \\
\end{array}$$

For instance, here's how we add the binary representations of 1 and 9:

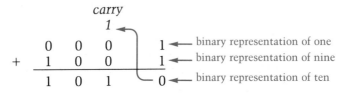

So *arithmetic* values (such as, values of type INTEGER) are stored, in one way or another, in *binary* form.

On the other hand, *character* values are stored in ASCII (or EBCDIC) form. Here's an example:

```
VAR
   a, b : CHAR;
   c    : PACKED ARRAY [1..2] OF CHAR;
     .
     .
a :=   '1';
b :=   '9';
c := '10'
```

The values actually stored in a, b, and c are:

a:	110001
b:	111001
c:	110001 110000

Here's why:

110001	are the binary	→	49	which are	→ 1
111001	representations	→	57	the ASCII	→ 9
110001 110000	of the numbers	→	49 48	codes for	→ 1 0

This way of representing values isn't very useful for doing arithmetic, but it makes it easy for us to store letters (starting with 65 for A) and other characters (such as, 32 for a blank space).

Neither a computer screen nor a computer printer is designed to do arithmetic. These devices are designed to reproduce characters. So these devices deal exclusively with ASCII codes. For instance, in order for the message

```
1 + 9 = 10
```

to appear on your screen, the screen has to receive the ASCII codes:

```
49 32 43 32 57 32 61 32 49 48
```

because

characters: 1 b + b 9 b = b 1 0
ASCII codes: 49 32 43 32 57 32 61 32 49 48

(Remember: A b symbol is our way of showing you where there's a blank space character.) So to execute the statement

```
Write (i:1, ' + ', j:1, ' = ', k:2)
```

text I/O

the computer has to convert INTEGER values into their corresponding ASCII codes. For instance, 10 has to be converted into the codes 49 and 48. The conversion process takes time. This form of input and output is called *text* input and output (or **text I/O**, for short). It's the kind of I/O you get when you create a TEXT file in Pascal. You can think of it as "displayable I/O" or "human-readable I/O."

But what if we're storing INTEGER values on a disk? Perhaps these values are written to the disk by one program and read from the disk by another program, with no human intervention in between. Why bother converting these binary INTEGER values into their ASCII character codes? Characters are meant to be read by people, and there aren't any people who can actually read the magnetic information stored on the surface of this disk. Why not just store the values in their binary form? This form of input and output is called **binary I/O**.

binary I/O

In this section, we'll see how to do binary I/O in Pascal.

Specifications The Barry Burd Marketing company sells various items (mostly books on computer science) through a mail-order catalog. Whenever an order or a check is received, a customer changes address, or some other customer business takes place, the company makes a note of this in a list called the list of customer *transactions*. Transactions are stored in order in the list by customer identification number. The customers with the lowest identification numbers are at the start of the list, etc.

The company gathers transactions into this list during each month. At the end of each month, the company uses the transaction list to update its *master* list. The master list contains the most up-to-date information on each of the company's customers. Just like the transaction list, the records in the master list are in order by customer identification number.

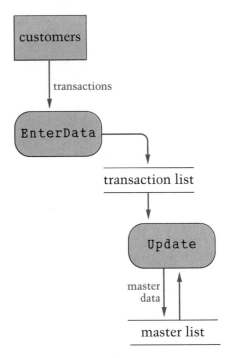

On the third day of each month, the company prepares a report that contains all the information in the master list in printed form. A copy of the report is given to each of the company's upper managers (see the diagram page 899).

analysis and data flow diagrams

We've just given a very brief **analysis** of the company's operations. We've described the company's existing procedures in words and sentences, but we've also used what's called a **data flow diagram** to help us visualize the system. This data flow diagram can serve as a guide as we move the company from a **manual** to an **automated system**. It helps us plan the software we'll need and the ways in which the software will be integrated with existing procedures.

So let's consider the system once again, this time thinking in terms of computers and programs.

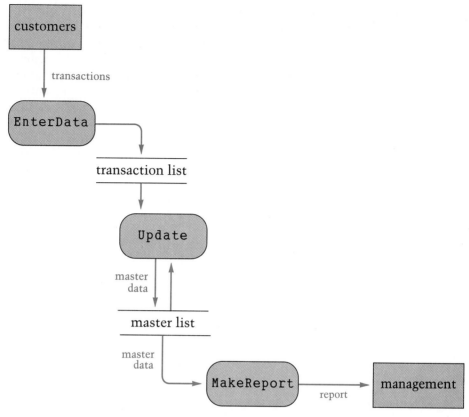

First we have a master file that potentially contains thousands of records. Each record is a collection of various data fields for one of the company's customers. In real life, such a record might contain the customer's name, address, phone number, purchase history, credit rating, etc. In our example, each customer record will contain only a few items of information.

The master file:

Harriet Ritter
ID # 101
Balance $52.63

Willy Katz
ID # 505
Balance $00.00

.

.

etc.

Why use a
binary file?

Most of the company's computer programs work with the data in its internal form; only a few of them read customer data from the keyboard or display it to the screen. In addition, the company has so many customers, and there's so much customer data, that it doesn't make sense to store the data as characters in a TEXT file. (Character storage takes up lots of space.) So the master file is a **binary file**—a file containing data in its binary form.

All month long, the company collects changes that need to be made to the master file. Such changes include adding a new customer, deleting an old customer, modifying a customer's address, etc. These changes are collected in another file, called the *transaction file*. The transaction file contains records, just like the master file. But the records in the transaction file reflect additions, deletions, and modifications that are to be made to records in the master file.

The transaction file:

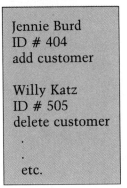

```
Jennie Burd
ID # 404
add customer

Willy Katz
ID # 505
delete customer
  .
  .
etc.
```

At the end of each month, the company runs its Update program. The transaction file is combined with the old master file, to create a new, up-to-date master file.

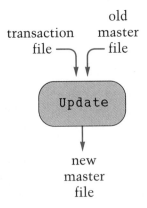

The combining algorithm is very much like the merging algorithm in Section 10.7, but care must be taken to differentiate among customers that should be added, deleted, or modified.

Here are some formal specs:

Input: The input to Program Update consists of two files: a transaction file (transF) and a master file (oldMasF). Each file consists of several customer records. Each customer record has four fields: name, customer identification number, current balance, and a special field called op (which stands for operation). The records in each file are stored so that their identification numbers are in *increasing* order.

Process: Depending on the value stored in the op field, each record in the transaction file represents either a new customer, to be added to the master file (when op has the value add); an old customer, to be deleted from the master file (when op has the value delete); or an old customer, whose name and/or balance need to be modified (when op has the value modify). Program Update reads records one at a time from the transaction file and the master file and creates a new master file that contains the necessary changes.

Output: The new master file (called newMasF) and an errorFile, containing records from the transaction file that have improper op codes, are out of order, etc.

Designing a Program

First we'll need to define a customer record type, called custRecType:

```
TYPE
   cardinal    = 0..MAXINT;
   nameType    = PACKED ARRAY [1..nameSize] OF CHAR;
   opType      = (add, delete, modify);
   custRecType =
     RECORD
       name    : nameType;
       id      : cardinal;
       balance : REAL;
       op      : opType
     END;
```

defining a binary file

Then we'll need to have a file of custRecTypes:

```
TYPE
   custFileType = FILE OF custRecType;
```

A file of type custFileType isn't a TEXT file—it's a binary file containing several custRecType values:

`<custRecType-value> <custRecType-value> .. <custRecType-value> <end-file>`

In this file, each custRecType-*value* is actually a combination of four things—a name, an id, a balance, and an op.

binary files vs. TEXT files

Notice that a file of type custFileType has no end-of-line indicators. A binary file is never written directly on the screen so it doesn't have to be divided into lines. Because of this, we won't be using ReadLn or WriteLn on a custFileType file. It doesn't make sense to use ReadLn or

WriteLn on anything but a TEXT file, because TEXT files are the only files with end-of-line indicators. Of course, we can still use Read and Write on binary files, and that's exactly what we'll do.

Now with these basic definitions under our belts, we can work on the strategy for Program Update. In Program Update we'll keep comparing records from the transFile and the oldMasFile, to decide what should go into the newMasFile. When we compare the customer identification numbers in two records, we'll either get

```
transRec.id > oldMasRec.id
transRec.id < oldMasRec.id
              or
transRec.id = oldMasRec.id
```

Let's deal with each of these possibilities in turn:

- transRec.id > oldMasRec.id

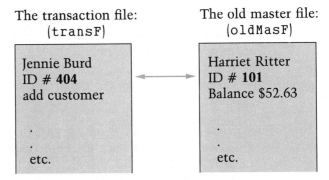

The transaction file:
(transF)

Jennie Burd
ID # 404
add customer

.
.
.
etc.

The old master file:
(oldMasF)

Harriet Ritter
ID # **101**
Balance $52.63

.
.
.
etc.

We're in the middle of a run of the Update program. We've processed all the records in the transaction file that come before this 404-record. We've also processed all the records in the old master file that come before the 101-record. From this we can conclude that the transFile contains no records concerning the customer with identification number 101. Why? Because the transFile's records are in increasing order by identification number. If identification number 101 appeared anywhere in the transFile, it would have come before identification number 404. Since there were no transactions this month concerning customer 101, we can copy the oldMasFile's 101 record to the newMasFile without any modifications.

- `transRec.id < oldMasRec.id`

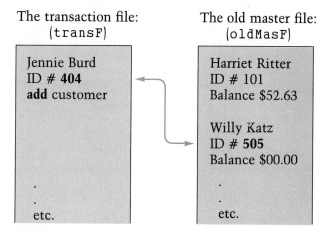

The transaction file:
(`transF`)

| Jennie Burd |
| ID # **404** |
| **add** customer |

The old master file:
(`oldMasF`)

| Harriet Ritter |
| ID # 101 |
| Balance $52.63 |
| |
| Willy Katz |
| ID # **505** |
| Balance $00.00 |

We're in the middle of a run of the `Update` program. We've processed all the records in the transaction file that come before this 404-record. We've also processed all the records in the old master file that come before the 505-record. From this we can conclude that the `oldMasFile` contains no records concerning the customer with identification number 404. Why? Because the `oldMasFile`'s records are in increasing order by identification number. If identification number 404 appeared anywhere in the `oldMasFile`, it would have come before identification number 505. What the `op` field says must be true: Customer 404 is a new customer who should be added from the `transFile`. We can copy the `transFile`'s record to the `newMasFile` without any modifications.

- `transRec.id = oldMasRec.id`

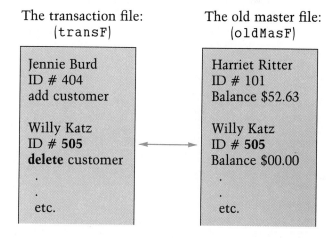

The transaction file:
(`transF`)

| Jennie Burd |
| ID # 404 |
| add customer |
| |
| Willy Katz |
| ID # **505** |
| **delete** customer |

The old master file:
(`oldMasF`)

| Harriet Ritter |
| ID # 101 |
| Balance $52.63 |
| |
| Willy Katz |
| ID # **505** |
| Balance $00.00 |

Both the `transFile` and the `oldMasFile` contain references to the customer with identification number 505. We have to look at the `op` field in the `transFile` to see if this customer should be deleted or this customer's information should be modified. The `op` field tells us that the customer should be deleted.

- `transRec.id = oldMasRec.id`   {another example:}

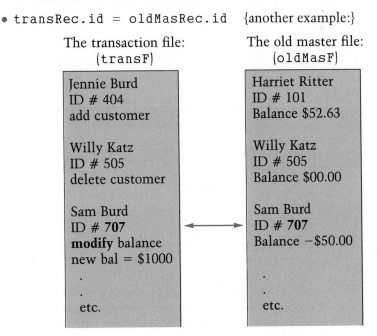

The transaction file:
(transF)

| Jennie Burd
ID # 404
add customer |
| Willy Katz
ID # 505
delete customer |
| Sam Burd
ID # **707**
modify balance
new bal = $1000 |
| .
.
.
etc. |

The old master file:
(oldMasF)

| Harriet Ritter
ID # 101
Balance $52.63 |
| Willy Katz
ID # 505
Balance $00.00 |
| Sam Burd
ID # **707**
Balance −$50.00 |
| .
.
.
etc. |

In this instance the `op` field tells us to modify some information about the customer. We'll copy the `oldMasFile`'s record to the `newMasFile`, but while we do it we'll change the customer's balance.

Now at last, here's the `Update` program.

Program Example

```
PROGRAM Update (transF, oldMasF, newMasF, errorF);
{Combines the transaction file and the old master
 file to obtain the updated new master file.  Any
 errors are placed in the error file.}
  {**                                              }
  {** The custRecType definitions:                 }
  {**                                              }
  CONST
    nameSize    = 20;
    dummyName   = '                    ';
    dummyBalance = 0.001;
```

```
TYPE
  cardinal   = 0..MAXINT;
  nameType   = PACKED ARRAY [1..nameSize] OF CHAR;
  opType     = (add, delete, modify);
  custRecType =
    RECORD
      name    : nameType;
      id      : cardinal;
      balance : REAL;
      op      : opType
    END;
  custFileType = FILE OF custRecType;
{**                                          }
{** End of the custRecType definitions.      }
{**                                          }
VAR
  transF, oldMasF, newMasF, errorF : custFileType;
  transRec, oldMasRec              : custRecType;
{**                                          }
{** The custRecType I/O routines:            }
{**                                          }
PROCEDURE ReadRecord (VAR aFile : custFileType;
                      VAR aRec  : custRecType);
{Reads a custRecType record from aFile.}

BEGIN {ReadRecord}
  IF Eof (aFile) THEN
    aRec.id := MAXINT
  ELSE
    Read (aFile, aRec)
END;  {ReadRecord}

{----------}

PROCEDURE WriteRecord (VAR aFile : custFileType;
                       aRec      : custRecType);
{Writes a custRecType record to aFile.}

BEGIN {WriteRecord}
  IF aRec.id <> MAXINT THEN
    Write (aFile, aRec)
END;  {WriteRecord}
{**                                          }
{** End of the custRecType I/O routines.     }
{**                                          }
PROCEDURE StartIO (VAR transF,  oldMasF,
                       newMasF, errorF  : custFileType;
                   VAR transR, oldMasR  : custRecType);
{Initializes the various files.}
```

```
BEGIN {StartIO}
  Reset      (transF);
  Reset      (oldMasF);
  Rewrite    (newMasF);
  Rewrite    (errorF);
  ReadRecord (transF,  transR);
  ReadRecord (oldMasF, oldMasR)
END;  {StartIO}
```

```
{**                                        }
{** The condition-testing functions:       }
{**                                        }
```

```
FUNCTION IsMoreInput (transR, oldMasR : custRecType) : BOOLEAN;
{Determines whether there are any more records
 in the transaction file or the old master file.}
```

```
BEGIN {IsMoreInput}
  IsMoreInput := (transR.id  <> MAXINT) OR
                 (oldMasR.id <> MAXINT)
END;  {IsMoreInput}
```

```
{----------}
```

```
FUNCTION ShouldAdd (transR, oldMasR : custRecType) : BOOLEAN;
{Determines whether a record in the transaction
 file should be added to the master file.}
```

```
BEGIN {ShouldAdd}
  ShouldAdd := (transR.id < oldMasR.id) AND
               (transR.op = add)
END;  {ShouldAdd}
```

```
{----------}
```

```
FUNCTION ShouldDelete (transR, oldMasR : custRecType) : BOOLEAN;
{Decides if a record should be deleted from the master file.}
```

```
BEGIN {ShouldDelete}
  ShouldDelete := (transR.id = oldMasR.id) AND
                  (transR.op = delete)
END;  {ShouldDelete}
```

```
{----------}
```

```
FUNCTION ShouldModify (transR, oldMasR : custRecType) : BOOLEAN;
{Decides if a record in the master file should be modified.}
```

```
BEGIN {ShouldModify}
  ShouldModify := (transR.id = oldMasR.id) AND
                  (transR.op = modify)
END;  {ShouldModify}
```

```
{----------}
```

```
FUNCTION ShouldCopyOld (transR, oldMasR : custRecType) : BOOLEAN;
{Determines whether a record should be copied
 from the old master file to the new master file.}
```

```
    BEGIN {ShouldCopyOld}
      ShouldCopyOld := transR.id > oldMasR.id
    END;  {ShouldCopyOld}

    {** End of                            }
    {** the condition-testing functions:  }
    {**                                    }

    PROCEDURE ModifyRecord (transR      : custRecType ;
                            VAR oldMasR : custRecType);
    {Modifies a record in preparation for its
     being written to the new master file.}
    BEGIN {ModifyRecord}
      IF transR.name    <> dummyName    THEN
        oldMasR.name    := transR.name;
      IF transR.balance <> dummyBalance THEN
        oldMasR.balance := transR.balance;
      oldMasR.op := transR.op
    END;  {ModifyRecord}

    {----------}

BEGIN {Update}
   StartIO (transF, oldMasF, newMasF, errorF, transRec, oldMasRec);

   WHILE IsMoreInput (transRec, oldMasRec) DO
       IF       ShouldAdd (transRec, oldMasRec) THEN
               BEGIN
                  WriteRecord (newMasF, transRec);
                  ReadRecord  (transF,  transRec)
               END
       ELSE IF ShouldDelete (transRec, oldMasRec) THEN
               BEGIN
                  ReadRecord (transF,  transRec);
                  ReadRecord (oldMasF, oldMasRec)
               END
       ELSE IF ShouldModify (transRec, oldMasRec) THEN
               BEGIN
                  ModifyRecord (transRec, oldMasRec);
                  ReadRecord    (transF,    transRec)
               END
       ELSE IF ShouldCopyOld (transRec, oldMasRec) THEN
               BEGIN
                  WriteRecord (newMasF, oldMasRec);
                  ReadRecord  (oldMasF, oldMasRec)
               END
       ELSE
               BEGIN
                  WriteRecord (errorF, transRec);
                  ReadRecord  (transF, transRec)
               END
END.  {Update}
```

Observations

writing an entire record

- `Write (aFile, aRec)`

When we introduced records in Chapter 12, we never even attempted to `Write` an entire recordful of values at once. Instead we wrote each field separately:

```
WriteLn (empRec.id, empRec.wage)
```

But when we write to a binary file, we can write a whole record at once. After all, a custFileType is defined to be a FILE OF custRecords.

```
<custRecType-value> <custRecType-value> .. <custRecType-value> <end-file>
```

So when we write to a custFileType file, we've got to place a custRecType-value in the file.

writing an enumerated-type value

And here's another notion from earlier chapters that needs rethinking. In Section 7.5 we announced that "input and output procedures for enumerated types are not part of ANSI Standard Pascal," so it might look strange that we can Write the value of aRec when aRec contains an enumerated-type op field. The truth is, our announcement in Section 7.5 was a simplification. In ANSI Standard Pascal we can use Read, Write, Get, Put, file windows, etc., to move enumerated type values to and from a binary file—but not a TEXT file.

Now what do these enumerated values "look like" when they're deposited onto a disk? Is the word modify represented with upper- or lowercase letters? Does add take up as many character spaces as modify? In a way, these questions don't make sense. A FILE OF custRecTypes isn't anything like a TEXT file. A binary file, like newMasFile, is meant to be stored on a disk, not written on a screen. Its contents aren't stored in the ASCII format. You'll see this if you try to examine the newMasFile with your editor. Some editors refuse to handle the file, with a message like

```
Cannot edit binary files.
```

Others just display funny-looking characters (dollar signs, bell sounds, returns, etc.) on the screen. The point is that binary files aren't meant to be displayed. They're meant only to be stored onto disk and retrieved from the disk.

"seeing" the contents of a binary file

Since the files used in Program Update are binary files, we can't use our editor to put information into these files or even to see what information is stored in them. How can we actually see what's in the newMasFile? We need a program that obtains data from the newMasFile and sends the data to the output file (that is, to the screen). Such a program follows.

Program Example

```
PROGRAM MakeReport (newMasF, output);
{Writes the information that's contained
 in the new master file onto the screen.}

  {Copy the custRecType definitions
   from Program Update here.}

  VAR
    newMasRec : custRecType;
    newMasF   : custFileType;
```

```
               {----------}
               {Copy the custRecType I/O routines
                from Program Update here.}
               {----------}
         BEGIN {MakeReport}
           Reset (newMasF);
           WITH newMasRec DO
             WHILE NOT Eof (newMasF) DO
               BEGIN
                 ReadRecord (newMasF, newMasRec);
                 WriteLn    ('Name    : ', name);
                 WriteLn    ('ID      : ', id);

                 IF balance <> dummyBalance THEN
                   WriteLn ('Balance : ', balance : 10:2);

                 Write ('Recently ');
                 CASE op OF
                   add    : WriteLn ('added');
                   delete : WriteLn ('deleted');
                   modify : WriteLn ('modified')
                 END;

                 WriteLn
               END
         END.   {MakeReport}
```

Observations

- `WriteLn ('ID        : ', id)`

  The transition from "un-displayable" to "displayable" customer identification numbers takes place during the execution of this `WriteLn`.
  Starting from the very first program in this book, an important purpose
  of `Write` and `WriteLn` has been to turn binary values into their ASCII
  equivalents. It would have been difficult to describe that aspect of
  `Write` and `WriteLn` in Chapter 2, so we saved it until this chapter.

- ```
  CASE op OF
    add    : WriteLn ('added');
    delete : WriteLn ('deleted');
    modify : WriteLn ('modified')
  END
  ```

  In ANSI Standard Pascal we can write enumerated values to a binary
  file, but not to a TEXT file (such as the `output` file). Pascal's
  pre-declared `Write` procedure can't turn the enumerated value `add`
  into the ASCII characters `'a'-'d'-'d'`, so we have to create our own
  `CASE` statement to display op values.

adding data to a
binary file

The `transFile` is a binary file, so we can't use our editor to put
information into it. We need a program that obtains data from the `input`
file (the keyboard) and sends the data to the `transFile`. The next program,
`EnterData`, does this. It's basically the reverse of `MakeReport`. It has a
  ```

few more lines of code than Program `MakeReport`, because it turns certain user responses into "dummy" values. For instance, when a user who doesn't want to enter a customer's name just hits the return key, Program `EnterData` puts twenty blanks in the name field.

Program Example

```
PROGRAM EnterData (input, transF, output);
{Copy the custRecType definitions
 from Program Update here.}

VAR
   transRec         : custRecType;
   transF           : custFileType;
   reply, opChar    : CHAR;
   i                : 1..21;   {nameSize + 1}

{----------}

{Copy the custRecType I/O routines
 from Program Update here.}

{----------}

PROCEDURE ReadLnName (VAR name : nameType);
{Reads a name field of up to twenty characters
 (or leaves the dummyName in the name field).}

   VAR
     i : 1..21;

BEGIN {ReadLnName}
   Write ('Name        (optional)  : ');
   name := dummyName;
   i := 1;
   WHILE NOT Eoln AND (i <= 20) DO
     BEGIN
       Read (name[i]);
       i := i + 1
     END;
   ReadLn
END;   {ReadLnName}

{----------}

PROCEDURE ReadLnId (VAR id : cardinal);
{Reads a customer identification number.}

BEGIN {ReadLnId}
   Write  ('Id          (required)  : ');
   ReadLn (id)
END;   {ReadLnId}

{----------}

PROCEDURE ReadLnBalance (VAR balance : REAL);
{Reads a customer's balance (or puts
 the dummyBalance in the balance field).}
```

```
BEGIN {ReadLnBalance}
  Write ('Balance    (optional)  : ');
  IF Eoln THEN
    balance := dummyBalance
  ELSE
    Read (balance);
  ReadLn
END;  {ReadLnBalance}
{----------}
PROCEDURE ReadLnOp (VAR op : opType);
{Reads an op field (add, delete or modify).}
BEGIN {ReadLnOp}
  REPEAT
    Write  ('Operation (a/d/m)     : ');
    ReadLn (opChar)
  UNTIL opChar IN ['A','a','D','d','M','m'];
  CASE opChar OF
    'A', 'a' : op := add;
    'D', 'd' : op := delete;
    'M', 'm' : op := modify
  END
END;  {ReadLnOp}
{----------}
BEGIN {EnterData}
  Rewrite (transF);
  WITH transRec DO
    REPEAT
      ReadLnName     (name);
      ReadLnId       (id);
      ReadLnBalance  (balance);
      ReadLnOp       (op);

      WriteRecord    (transF, transRec);
      WriteLn;

      Write          ('More? (Y/N) : ');
      ReadLn         (reply);
      WriteLn;
      WriteLn
    UNTIL (reply = 'N') OR (reply = 'n')
END.  {EnterData}
```

Sample Runs

We'll perform the following cycle two times:

Run EnterData.

Run Update.

Run MakeReport.

Here's a diagram that shows how the various files are used by these programs:

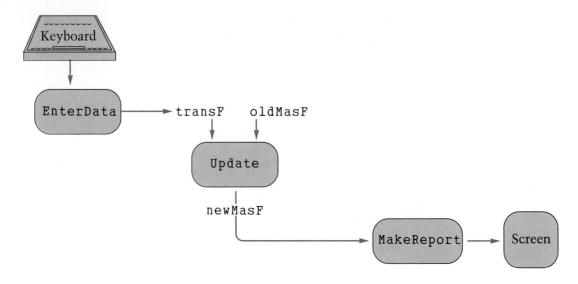

Between the runs we'll do a little "housekeeping" so that the computer can run each program against the appropriate files.

First we run Program `EnterData`. Here's what appears on the screen:

```
Name       (optional)  : Harriet Ritter
Id         (required)  : 101
Balance    (optional)  : 52.63
Operation (a/d/m)      : a
More? (Y/N) : y

Name       (optional)  :
Id         (required)  : 202
Balance    (optional)  :
Operation (a/d/m)      : a
More? (Y/N) : y

Name       (optional)  : Willy Katz
Id         (required)  : 505
Balance    (optional)  : 0.00
Operation (a/d/m)      : a
More? (Y/N) : y

Name       (optional)  : Sam Burd
Id         (required)  : 707
Balance    (optional)  : -50.00
Operation (a/d/m)      : a
More? (Y/N) : n
```

This creates a `transFile`.

Before running Program `Update`, we have to make sure that the `oldMasFile` exists. It doesn't need to have any customer records in it, but there has to be a file that the program can `Reset` when

```
Reset (oldMasF)
```

in Procedure `StartIO` is executed. On many implementations, we can create an empty `oldMasFile` by editing it, putting nothing in it, and saving it.

Once we've created `oldMasF`, we can run Program `Update`. This creates a `newMasF`. Nothing appears on the screen because Program `Update` has no statements that write to the screen.

To see the `newMasF`, we have to run Program `MakeReport`. Here's what appears on the screen when we run `MakeReport`:

```
Name    : Harriet Ritter
ID      :        101
Balance :         52.63
Recently added

Name    :
ID      :        202
Recently added

Name    : Willy Katz
ID      :        505
Balance :          0.00
Recently added

Name    : Sam Burd
ID      :        707
Balance :        -50.00
Recently added
```

Now we've done the `EnterData/Update/MakeReport` cycle one time. The second time through the cycle we'll make changes to the master file. We run Program `EnterData` again.

```
Name      (optional)  : Jennie Burd
Id        (required)  : 404
Balance   (optional)  : 0.01
Operation (a/d/m)     : a
More? (Y/N) : y

Name      (optional)  :
Id        (required)  : 505
Balance   (optional)  :
Operation (a/d/m)     : d
More? (Y/N) : y

Name      (optional)  :
Id        (required)  : 707
Balance   (optional)  : 1000.00
Operation (a/d/m)     : m
More? (Y/N) : n
```

This creates a new version of `transF`.

Before we run `Update` again, we have to make sure that `Update` can find the `oldMasF`. Remember that the last run of `Update` created a file called `newMasF`. This `newMasF` has to become the `oldMasF` before we can rerun `Update`. Here's a diagram:

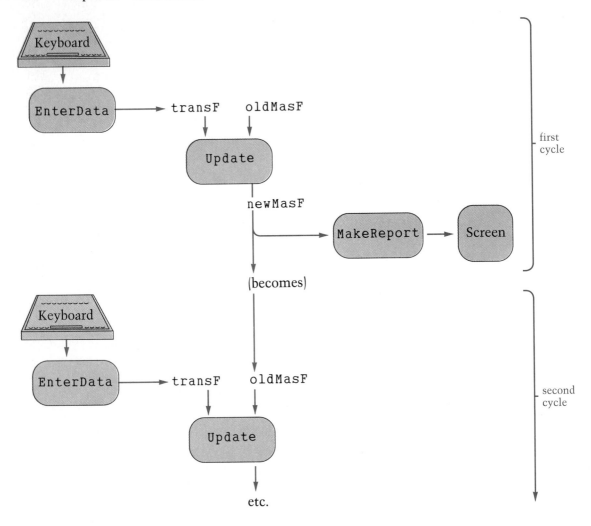

On some implementations the operating system has a rename command that you can use to change the name of the newMasF. Other implementations store several **generations** of a file. Instead of an oldMasF and a newMasF you get a whole family of files. The empty master file represents the first generation. Running Program Update creates the second generation. Running it again creates the third generation, etc. The operating system takes care of it for you. Each time Program Update is run, it's given the correct generation of the master file.

Having dealt one way or another with the oldMasF-vs.-newMasF problem, we can run Programs Update and MakeReport again. Here's what appears on the screen when we run MakeReport:

```
Name     : Harriet Ritter
ID       :          101
Balance  :        52.63
Recently added

Name     :
ID       :          202
Recently added

Name     : Jennie Burd
ID       :          404
Balance  :         0.01
Recently added

Name     : Sam Burd
ID       :          707
Balance  :      1000.00
Recently modified
```

Structure

many programs working together

Most problems in the real world are solved not by a single program, but by many programs working together. We've solved the file update problem with three programs called `Update`, `EnterData`, and `MakeReport`. All three of these programs made use of certain constant definitions, type definitions, and subprogram declarations. In ANSI Standard Pascal we'd need to repeat these definitions and declarations in each of the three programs. In this section we cheated a little bit—we just put comments in two of the programs, reminding us that the definitions and declarations needed to be copied. That's OK for now, but to get the programs to run we'd actually have to do the copying.

Of course, copying things from one program to another can be cumbersome, time consuming, and error-prone. If we want to change the definitions we have to change them in each program. If we forget to change one of the programs, we're in trouble. It would be much nicer if we didn't need to copy definitions and declarations from program to program. What we need at the very minimum is a language feature that allows us to **import** definitions and declarations into a program from some other unit.

```
PROGRAM MakeReport (newMasF, output);
{Writes the information that's contained
 in the new master file onto the screen.}

   USES custRecTypeDefs;    {Automatically places the
                             custRecType definitions here.}

   VAR
     newMasRec : custRecType;
     newMasF   : custFileType;
        .
        .
      etc.
```

Many versions of Pascal have features like this—especially the versions that support some form of *object-oriented programming*. And once we open the door to object-oriented programming a whole new way of thinking about software emerges. For more information on object-oriented programming, see Sections 3.9, 9.6, and 12.9.

15.3   Exercises

Key Words to Review

text I/O	data flow diagram	binary file
binary I/O	manual system	generations
analysis	automated system	import

Questions to Answer

QUE 15.3.1   Explain the reasoning behind each of the alternatives in the main body of Program Update.

QUE 15.3.2   If we can use Read and Write on a binary file, why can't we use ReadLn and WriteLn?

QUE 15.3.3   Why do we need Program EnterData? (That is, why can't we create this section's transFile using an editor?)

QUE 15.3.4   In this section we touched on data flow diagrams, but we didn't discuss any of the details about making them. Nevertheless, you probably know enough to make some preliminary data flow diagrams for several kinds of systems:
   a. Diagram the flow of information when a consumer makes a purchase and pays for it with a check. Include the roles of the consumer, the merchant, and the bank.
   b. Diagram the flow of information inside Program CryptoDriver (Section 10.4).
   c. Diagram the flow of information in a typical computer science course. Include elements such as the teacher, the students, the registrar, class notes, textbooks, assignments, exams, grades, etc.

Things to Check in a Manual

MAN 15.3.1   What's the best way to turn a newMasFile into an oldMasFile with your computer's operating system?

MAN 15.3.2   *(Direct access)* Some implementations allow you to choose a number—say 505—and immediately position a file window on the 505th entry of an existing file (the 505th customer record, for instance). Then you can Read the file from the 505th entry onward. You don't need a loop to Read the entries that come before the 505th entry. With a very large file this can save you quite a bit of time. Does your implementation provide such a feature?

MAN 15.3.3   *(Indexed access)* Here's a notion that's similar to the one we explored in Exercise Man.15.3.2. We'll explain it using this section's master file as an example. Some implementations allow you to choose a customer identification number—say, 505—and immediately position the file window on the entry whose id field contains the number 505. Then you can Read the entire record for customer 505. You don't need a loop to Read the entries that come before customer 505. This is a bit different from the feature we described in Exercise Man.15.3.2 because the record with id field 505 doesn't have to be the 505th record in the file. (There could be several unused identification numbers.) Does your implementation provide a feature of the kind we've just described?

MAN 15.3.4 Read the description of a TEXT file in your implementation's manual. How does it differ from a FILE OF CHAR?

MAN 15.3.5 In Section 5.1 we mentioned that "on many implementations the end-of-line indicator isn't a character at all. It's just a place that the computer keeps track of." Does your manual give any details about this?

MAN 15.3.6 Does your implementation provide a way of *importing* definitions and declarations into a program from some other unit? If so, can you use it to avoid having to copy definitions and subprograms from Program Update into Programs MakeReport and EnterData?

Experiments to Try

EXP 15.3.1 Run Program EnterData to create a binary transFile. Then try to examine the contents of the transFile with your editor.

EXP 15.3.2 In Procedure ReadRecord replace Read (aFile, aRec) with

```
aRec := aFile^;
Get (aFile)
```

In Procedure WriteRecord replace Write (aFile, aRec) with

```
aFile^ := aRec;
Put (aFile)
```

Notice that aFile is of type custFileType, which is a FILE OF custRecType. This has some important consequences: First, the file window aFile^ refers to an entire customer record (all four fields), so it makes sense to do aRec := aFile^ or aFile^ := aRec. Second, since aFile is composed of custRecType values, one call to Get or Put advances the file window aFile^ forward by an entire customer record (all four fields).

EXP 15.3.3 With the following definitions and declarations:

```
TYPE
   arrayType     = ARRAY[1..10] OF INTEGER;
   arrayFileType = FILE OF arrayType;
VAR
   anArray : arrayType;
   arrayF  : arrayFileType;
```

Can you read an entire array from the file with the statement

```
Read (arrayF, anArray)
```

EXP 15.3.4   Run the following program:

```
PROGRAM CompareFiles (tFile, bFile);
    VAR
      x     : INTEGER;
      tFile : TEXT;
      bFile : FILE OF INTEGER;
    BEGIN {CompareFiles}
      Rewrite (tFile);
      Rewrite (bFile);
      x := 7;
      Write (tFile, x, x+1);
      Write (bFile, x, x+1)
    END.  {CompareFiles}
```

After running the program, try to examine each of the files (tFile and bFile) with your editor.

EXP 15.3.5   Run the following program:

```
PROGRAM CompareFiles2 (tFile, bFile);
    VAR
      x     : CHAR;
      tFile : TEXT;
      bFile : FILE OF CHAR;
    BEGIN {CompareFiles2}
      Rewrite (tFile);
      Rewrite (bFile);
      x := 'x';
      Write (tFile, x, Succ(x));
      Write (bFile, x, Succ(x))
    END.  {CompareFiles2}
```

After running the program, try to examine each of the files (tFile and bFile) with your editor.

EXP 15.3.6   Some operating systems provide a way of "dumping" the contents of a file—that is, showing what's actually in the file without the intervention of an editor. (One of the editor's jobs is to display the file in an intelligible format.) If your operating system has such a feature, learn how to use it. Use it to dump the files created in Exercises Exp.15.3.4 and Exp.15.3.5.

EXP 15.3.7   Add the statement

```
Write (transF, id)
```

anywhere in Program EnterData.

EXP 15.3.8   Add the statement

```
Write (transF, 'added')
```

anywhere in Program EnterData.

EXP 15.3.9   Try to compile a program containing the following code:

```
TYPE
   fileType1 = FILE OF INTEGER;
   recType   = RECORD
                  field1 : CHAR;
                  field2 : fileType1
               END;
   fileType2 = FILE OF recType;
```

Changes to Make

CHA 15.3.1   Modify Program Applicants in Section 14.7 so that the program can "go to sleep." At the user's request, the program writes the information in its queue to a file and then ends its execution. Later, when the program is run again, the first thing it does is reload the queue from the file.

CHA 15.3.2   Redo Exercise Cha.11.4.4, this time reading values of the array from a binary file.

Programs and Subprograms to Write

WRI 15.3.1   A *mail merge program* deals with two files: an address file and a letter file. The address file contains several entries, such as

```
Dr. Barry Burd
21 Winding Way
Pittston, NJ 07940
Dear Dr. Burd

Ms. Grace A. Katz
Box A-11
Minneapolis, MN 55455
Dear Gracie
```

The letter file contains a form letter into which an address and salutation can be inserted. The mail merge program creates several copies of the form letter, one for each entry in the address file. Write a mail merge program.

WRI 15.3.2   Run the program you wrote for Exercise Wri.12.5.6 several times. Let the output of each run become the input for the next run. Run the program enough times to determine how many perfect shuffles it takes to restore a deck of cards to its original order. (*Hint:* It's not very many!)

WRI 15.3.3   (*Merge sort*) What do we do if we need to sort a collection of values so large that we can't store all the values in an array or a linked list? All the names in the Manhattan telephone directory might be just such a collection. In this situation we do an *external sort*. In each step in the execution of an external sort, most of the values we're sorting are stored on a disk file. To understand a particular kind of external sort called the *merge sort*, you should first review the algorithms implemented by Program Merge from Section 10.7 and Procedure SelectionSort from Section 10.8. When we combine the two algorithms we obtain the merge sort:

Do the following several times:
   Read several values from the disk file into the array.
   Sort the array with the selection sort.
   Write the sorted values to a new disk file.

(Now you have several disk files. The values in each of these files are sorted. So . . .)

Merge the first two files into one larger file. Note that this can be done *without* storing values in an array.

Merge the next pair of files into one larger file.

Etc.

(Now perhaps you've gone from eight small files to four larger files. So . . .)

Merge the first pair of larger files into one very large file.

Merge the next pair of larger files into one very large file.

Etc.

Keep merging pairs of files until you have only one enormous sorted file.

Write a program that implements this merge sort algorithm.

WRI 15.3.4   Write a program that helps you enter date records into a binary file. Each record contains a month, day, and year. A record also contains a fifty-character string with a reminder about something to do on that day. Write another program that searches for a date in the date-records file and writes all reminders pertaining to that date.

WRI 15.3.5   Add information about the year's calendar to the second program you wrote for Exercise Wri.15.3.4. The program uses this new information to decide if the date you've entered falls on a Saturday. If it does, the program writes not only that date's reminders, but Sunday's reminders as well.

WRI 15.3.6   Modify the program of Exercise Wri.14.13.6 so that the entire tree, along with the new items that have been added to it, is saved into a file before the program ends its execution. Later when the program is run again (possibly by a different user), the first thing the program does is reload the tree from the file.

15.4

A Pascal Program Is a File

During this course, you've used your editor to create both Pascal programs and TEXT input files. You can do this because programs are stored as TEXT files. A program is, after all, a sequence of characters separated, here and there, by end-of-line indicators. When you edit a program, you're actually creating, or making changes to, a TEXT file. When the program is compiled, that TEXT file is given as input to another program, called a *compiler*.

There's nothing mysterious about TEXT files or programs or the connection between them. You can easily create a program that reads another program as part of its input or writes another program as part of its output.

Specifications

preprocessor

The program in this section is an example of a **preprocessor**. A preprocessor makes changes to a program after the program is edited and before the program is given to the compiler.

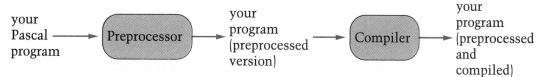

your
Pascal → Preprocessor → your program (preprocessed version) → Compiler → your program (preprocessed and compiled)
program

Input: A TEXT file, containing (1) on the first line, any characters at all, and (2) starting on the second line, a Pascal program.

Process: The first character on the first line is called oldCh. The rest of the characters on the first line form a string called newStr. Wherever oldCh appears in the Pascal program, it's replaced by newStr.

Output: The new Pascal program.

macro

Taken together, the oldCh and the newStr are called a **macro**. Our program will do what's called **macro substitution**. Wherever it finds the oldCh, it will substitute the newStr. The old program, with several occurrences of oldCh in it, is commonly called the **source**. The new program, with newStr substituted for oldCh, is usually called the **object**

Designing a Program

Our first job is to create a string type to hold the newStr. Fortunately, we already have one. We defined it in Section 12.5. In that section we created the vStringType:

```
vStringType = RECORD
                content : ARRAY [indexType] OF CHAR;
                length  : bigIndType
              END;
```

We designed this type in order to store strings of various lengths. Since we don't know in advance how long the newStr will be, this type from Section 12.5 is just what we need.

Now for the heart of the algorithm: Our preprocessor has to read the source program and turn it into an object program. To do this, it must examine characters from the source and write the appropriate characters to form the object. What constitutes an "appropriate character" depends on what you find in the source. There are three cases:

If you find the end-of-line indicator in the source
  go to a new line in the object (use WriteLn to do this)
If you find oldCh in the source
  write newStr in the object (that is, make the macro
    substitution)
If you find any other printable character in the source
  copy this character to the object

The code follows.

**Program
Example**

```
PROGRAM Preprocessor (source, object);
{Performs macro substitution.}
    CONST
      maxLength = 80;
    TYPE
      indexType   = 1..maxLength;
      bigIndType  = 0..maxLength;
      vStringType = RECORD
                         content : ARRAY [indexType] OF CHAR;
                         length  : bigIndType
                    END;
    VAR
      oldCh          : CHAR;
      newStr         : vStringType;
      source, object : TEXT;

    {----------}

    PROCEDURE ReadTilEoln (VAR source : TEXT        ;
                           VAR vStr   : vStringType);
    {Reads a vString from the source file.
     Keeps reading until it finds the end-of-line.}

      VAR
        index  : bigIndType;
        charIn : CHAR;

    BEGIN {ReadTilEoln}
      index := 0;

      WHILE NOT Eoln (source) DO
        BEGIN
          Read (source, charIn);
          index := index + 1;
          vStr.content[index] := charIn
        END;

      vStr.length := index;
      ReadLn (source)
    END;  {ReadTilEoln}

    {----------}

    PROCEDURE WriteVString (VAR object : TEXT        ;
                            vStr       : vStringType);
    {Writes a vString to the object file.}

      VAR
        i : indexType;

    BEGIN {WriteVString}
      WITH vStr DO
        FOR i := 1 TO length DO
          Write (object, content[i])
    END;  {WriteVString}

    {----------}
```

```
PROCEDURE ReadTheMacro (VAR source : TEXT         ;
                        VAR oldCh  : CHAR         ;
                        VAR newStr : vStringType);
{Reads a macro from the first line of the source file.}

BEGIN {ReadTheMacro}
  Read       (source, oldCh);
  ReadTilEoln (source, newStr)
END;  {ReadTheMacro}

{----------}

PROCEDURE MakeObject (VAR object : TEXT         ;
                      oldCh      : CHAR         ;
                      newStr     : vStringType);
{Creates the object file by substituting
 newStr for all occurrences of oldCh.}

  VAR
    c : CHAR;

BEGIN {MakeObject}
  WHILE NOT Eof (source) DO
    IF Eoln (source) THEN
      BEGIN
        WriteLn (object);
        ReadLn  (source)
      END
    ELSE
      BEGIN
        Read (source, c);
        IF c = oldCh THEN
          WriteVString (object, newStr)
        ELSE
          Write (object, c)
      END
END;  {MakeObject}

{----------}

BEGIN {Preprocessor}
  Reset        (source);
  ReadTheMacro (source, oldCh, newStr);

  Rewrite      (object);
  MakeObject   (object, oldCh, newStr)
END.  {Preprocessor}
```

Sample Runs

In Section 3.3 we examined a program to compute the interest on a loan. Program Interest was one of our first examples showing the difference between pass by reference and pass by value. At one point in Section 3.3 we removed the word VAR from the parameter list of Procedure AddInterest.

Now what if, in writing Program Interest, we leave off this word VAR by mistake? We might have a difficult time tracking down the error. Perhaps we'll want to add some extra WriteLns to the program to help us find out what's gone wrong. We can type each `WriteLn` separately, but maybe we can save ourselves some typing (and some typos) by using macro substitution.

So, let's add a macro to our incorrect version of Program `Interest`. The macro consists of a pound sign # followed by a `WriteLn`. We'd like to have the `WriteLn` inserted at several points in the program. Inside Program `Interest`, we put pound signs in the places where the `principal` variable might have new and interesting values:

```
#;WriteLn ('principal = ', principal:6:2);    {!!macro!!}
PROGRAM Interest (input, output);
{Tries to compute interest on
 a loan - why isn't it working?}

  VAR
    principal, intRate : REAL;

  {----------}

  PROCEDURE AddInterest (principal : REAL ;
                         intRate    : REAL);
  {Tries to add one year's
   interest - why isn't it working?}
  BEGIN {AddInterest}
    #
    principal := principal + (intRate/100.0 * principal)
    #
  END;   {AddInterest}

  {----------}

BEGIN {Interest}
    Write       ('Enter principal and interest rate: ');
    ReadLn      (principal, intRate);

    #
    AddInterest (principal, intRate);
    #

    WriteLn     ('New principal: ', principal:6:2)
END.    {Interest}
```

This is the input to Program `Preprocessor`. The output of Program `Preprocessor` is a new version of Program `Interest`, with the pound signs replaced by `WriteLn`s:

```
PROGRAM Interest (input, output);
{Tries to compute interest on
 a loan - why isn't it working?}

  VAR
    principal, intRate : REAL;

  {----------}
```

```
      PROCEDURE AddInterest (principal : REAL ;
                             intRate   : REAL);
      {Tries to add one year's
       interest - why isn't it working?}
      BEGIN {AddInterest}
        ;WriteLn ('principal = ', principal:6:2);   {!!macro!!}
        principal := principal + (intRate/100.0 * principal)
        ;WriteLn ('principal = ', principal:6:2);   {!!macro!!}
      END;   {AddInterest}

      {----------}

BEGIN {Interest}
   Write        ('Enter principal and interest rate: ');
   ReadLn       (principal, intRate);

   ;WriteLn ('principal = ', principal:6:2);   {!!macro!!}
   AddInterest (principal, intRate);
   ;WriteLn ('principal = ', principal:6:2);   {!!macro!!}

   WriteLn      ('New principal: ', principal:6:2)
END.   {Interest}
```

After running the preprocessor, we give the command to compile, link, and run the new Program Interest. Here's a sample run for our new Interest:

```
Enter principal and interest rate: 200.00 5.0
principal = 200.00
principal = 200.00
principal = 210.00
principal = 200.00
New principal: 200.00
```

When we examine the sample run, we notice that principal's value gets changed to 210.00 inside the subprogram, but it bounces back to 200.00 after we return from the subprogram. This reminds us that we've forgotten the word VAR in the subprogram's parameter list.

By the way, if you take one more look at the source and object programs you'll notice that we put semicolons before and after our new WriteLn. We did this because we wanted the WriteLn to surround a statement that had no semicolons.

Separates the WriteLn from
the assignment statement

↓

```
;WriteLn ('principal = ', principal:6:2);   {!!macro!!}
principal := principal + (intRate/100.0 * principal)
;WriteLn ('principal = ', principal:6:2);   {!!macro!!}
```

↑

Separates the assignment
statement from the WriteLn

Structure

A program is a file.

Here's a diagram that shows a run of our new program `Preprocessor`, along with a run of `Interest`:

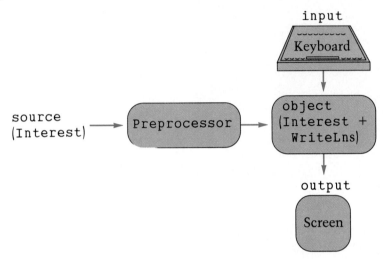

The preprocessed version of `Interest` figures into our diagram both as a program and a file. As the output of Program `Preprocessor`, it's a file. As the code that turns keyboard input (values for `principal` and `intRate`) into screen output (the new `principal`), it's a program.

Testing and Debugging

In debugging a program like Program `Interest`, it's often useful to put `WriteLns` in crucial places. But some editors are cumbersome to use. They make it difficult to add these extra statements to the program. Our preprocessor helps us. It allows us to add `WriteLns` by inserting only a few extra characters—some pound signs or other symbols.

automated
debuggers

The next step is to add `WriteLns` without even inserting pound signs. An **automated debugger** might run Program `Interest` and effectively insert `WriteLns` in places where the value of `principal` might change. Automated debuggers are very useful pieces of software.

Of course automated debuggers can be very sophisticated. Most of them have features that insert `WriteLns` for any and all of a program's variables. In addition, they allow the programmer to specify **breakpoints**. A breakpoint is a place in the program where execution should pause. When the run of a program reaches a breakpoint, the programmer is given several options. The programmer may instruct the computer to

- display the values of certain variables
- change the values of certain variables
- continue running the program

Some debuggers can make every statement in the program be a breakpoint. Each statement is displayed while it's being executed. The programmer gains insight into the nature of the program by watching the statements as they're executed—one statement, then the next, then the next.

When I think about the things software can do, I can't help but be amazed.

15.4   Exercises

Key Words to Review

preprocessor	source	automated debugger
macro	object	breakpoints
macro substitution		

Questions to Answer

QUE 15.4.1   In what way is a compiler very much like this section's Program `Preprocessor`?

QUE 15.4.2   Is an algorithm a file? Why, or why not?

QUE 15.4.3   Compare the `vString` subprograms in this section with those in Section 12.5. How are they different? Why are they different?

Experiments to Try

EXP 15.4.1   Add the following lines to Program `Interest`:

```
IF principal > 1000.00 THEN
  principal := principal + 10.00
      #
ELSE
  principal := principal + 20.00
```

Then run the preprocessor and try to compile and run the object file.

EXP 15.4.2   Try running the following program:

```
PROGRAM MakeProg (helloF);
  VAR
    helloF : TEXT;
BEGIN {MakeProg}
  Rewrite (helloF);
  WriteLn (helloF, 'PROGRAM SayHello (output);');
  WriteLn (helloF, 'BEGIN {SayHello}        ');
  WriteLn (helloF, '  WriteLn (''Hello'')    ');
  WriteLn (helloF, 'END.  {SayHello}         ')
END.  {MakeProg}
```

Then try compiling and running the program's output!

EXP 15.4.3   Run Program `Copy` of Section 5.1. For the `inFile` use Program `EolnDemo` (from the same section).

EXP 15.4.4   Run Program `Copy` of Section 5.1. For the `inFile` use Program `Copy` itself.

Changes to Make

CHA 15.4.1 Modify Program `Preprocessor` to handle a `newStr` that's more than one line long. To indicate that a `newStr` is continued on the next line, we put the backslash character \ at the end of the current line.

CHA 15.4.2 Modify Program `Preprocessor` to handle source text that contains several macros. The macros end when the preprocessor finds the word `PROGRAM` at the beginning of a line. Think carefully about the way macros can interact with one another. For instance, one macro can be

```
#WriteLn ('$');
```

and the next macro can be

```
$This is a message.
```

CHA 15.4.3 Look at the Testing and Debugging subsection of Section 6.1, and you'll find an incorrect version of Program `FindAverage`. Remove the extra `WriteLns` that we placed in this program and add a macro at the top to help debug the program.

Programs and Subprograms to Write

WRI 15.4.1 Write a program that reads an infix expression, consisting only of numbers, operators, and parentheses (no variables) and writes a file containing a short Pascal program to print the value of that expression. Test your work by running the short Pascal program.

WRI 15.4.2 Write a program called `Document` that extracts everything except the header lines and their neighboring prologue comments from another Pascal program. As the name suggests, Program `Document` strips a program of everything but its essential documentation.

WRI 15.4.3 Use the function you wrote in Exercise Wri.10.9.2 to solve the *global search and replace* problem: You're given a `smallString`, a `newString`, and a `largeString`. Wherever you find the `smallString` inside the `largeString`, replace it with the `newString`.

Things to Think About

THI 15.4.1 Is it possible to write a self-replicating program? A self-replicating program is one that creates a brand new file containing an exact copy of itself. It does this without having any input (so it can't read characters from its own file) and without calling on any of the operating system's `copy` commands.

THI 15.4.2 Is it possible to write a program that can read the text of another program, read the input to that other program, and tell whether or not that program will go into an infinite loop?

THI 15.4.3 What's the most important thing you've learned in studying Pascal? The most difficult? The most helpful? The most surprising?

Chapter Summary

A *file* is a collection of data. A file can be stored on a medium (such as a disk), but it can also be a "collection" of data in a less tangible sense. For instance the collection of all keys typed by the user during the run of a program is a file (called `input`). The collection of all characters displayed on the screen during the run of a program is also a file (called `output`).

For each file (except the keyboard file `input`) we must call the pre-declared procedure `Reset` before we can obtain data from the file. For each file (except the screen file `output`) we must call the pre-declared procedure `Rewrite` before we can place data into the file.

To move data to and from a file, we can call Pascal's pre-declared subprograms `Read`, `ReadLn`, `Write`, and `WriteLn`. But we have more control over input and output if we use file windows, along with the pre-declared subprograms `Get` and `Put`.

For each file (`aFile`, for instance) there's a corresponding *file window* `aFile^`. Using Pascal's pre-declared `Reset` and `Get` procedures we can fill the file window `aFile^` with a value from the `aFile`. Then we can copy that value into one of the program's "ordinary" variables with a statement like

```
aVar := aFile^
```

In addition to filling the file window, Procedures `Reset` and `Get` also position us at particular values in the file. Procedure `Reset` positions us at the beginning of the file in preparation for reading. Then, once we're already positioned at a particular value in a file, Procedure `Get` positions us at the next value in the file.

We can also position ourselves within a file using Pascal's pre-declared Procedures `Rewrite` and `Put`. Procedure `Rewrite` makes a file empty and positions us at the beginning of the file in preparation for writing. Procedure `Put` copies a value from the file window to the file and positions us at the next value in the file.

In between a program and a file we have a *buffer*. As we type keys on the keyboard, the characters we type are placed in the buffer and echoed on the screen. They're not made available to the program until we end the line by hitting the return key. When we hit the return key, the characters on that line leave the buffer and become available to the running program.

A `TEXT` file is a sequence of characters, separated into lines by end-of-line indicators. In contrast, a *binary* file is a sequence of values, all belonging to the same Pascal type. A `TEXT` file contains ASCII characters and its contents can be displayed and modified by an editor. In contrast, a binary file can contain information that's not part of the ASCII Character Set. Because of this, a binary file cannot be displayed in a useful way by an editor.

We can use `Write` and `Read` to move values to and from a binary file. Each such "value" belongs to a particular Pascal type. Even values that can't be written to `TEXT` files, such as records and enumerated type values, can be written to binary files. We cannot use `WriteLn` or `ReadLn` to move values to and from a binary file. We can't do it because binary files aren't composed of lines and don't have end-of-line indicators.

Finally, a Pascal program is a `TEXT` file. Because of this, we can create, display, and modify a Pascal program with an editor. We can also have one program be the input to another program. This happens whenever we compile a program. The Pascal program is the input to the compiler. The compiler's output is a new program containing machine language instructions that can be executed directly by the computer.

A Final Word

We repeat something from Section 2.4:

There's always a tendency, once you've found a solution to a problem, to push the problem aside and go on to something else. The thinking is something like "Whew! I solved that one—now I can forget about it. What's next?"

But in this book we stress over and over again that when you've found a solution to a problem, you should *step back and examine that solution.* When you look over your work, you can discover many things about it. Perhaps

you can improve upon it;

there's another way you could have done it;

it doesn't really work; or

it was really a stroke of genius.

APPENDIX A

Reserved Words in ANSI Standard Pascal

These words have the same meaning in every Pascal program and may not be used as identifiers:

AND	FUNCTION	PROGRAM
ARRAY	GOTO	RECORD
BEGIN	IF	REPEAT
CASE	IN	SET
CONST	LABEL	THEN
DIV	MOD	TO
DO	NIL	TYPE
DOWNTO	NOT	UNTIL
ELSE	OF	VAR
END	OR	WHILE
FILE	PACKED	WITH
FOR	PROCEDURE	

APPENDIX B

Pascal's Pre-defined and Pre-declared Identifiers

These identifiers are pre-defined (or pre-declared) for every Pascal program. Programmers are advised not to redefine (or re-declare) these names in CONST definitions, TYPE definitions, or VAR declarations.

Pre-defined constants:

MAXINT	FALSE	TRUE

Pre-defined types:

BOOLEAN	INTEGER	TEXT
CHAR	REAL	

Pre-defined variables:

input	output

Pre-declared procedures:

Dispose[1]	Page[2]	Reset
Get	Put	Rewrite
New[1]	Read	Unpack
Pack	ReadLn	Write
		WriteLn

Pre-declared functions:

Abs	Exp	Sin
Arctan	Ln	Sqr
Chr	Odd	Sqrt
Cos	Ord	Succ
Eof	Pred	Trunc
Eoln	Round	

---

[1]Dispose and New have additional forms (for use with pointers to variant records) that are not discussed in this text.

[2]The effect of Pascal's pre-declared Page procedure varies very much from one implementation to another. The general idea is to go to the top of the next page in preparation for the next Write or WriteLn.

APPENDIX C

Pascal Syntax Diagrams

This appendix describes the ISO Pascal standard. ANSI Standard Pascal is the same as the ISO standard except that the ANSI standard does not have conformant array parameters.

letter:

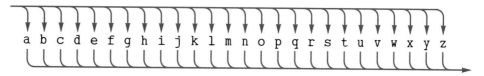

Each uppercase letter is equivalent in meaning to its lowercase counterpart, except within a character string.

digit:

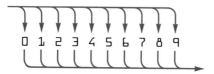

identifier:

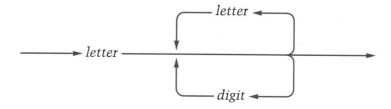

For added clarity we sometimes use the terms *constant identifier, variable identifier, field identifier, type identifier, procedure identifier, function identifier*. Each is synonymous with the word *identifier*.

directive:

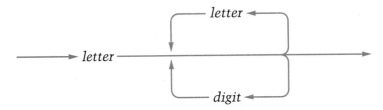

unsigned number:

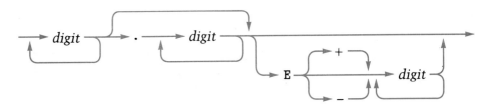

character string:

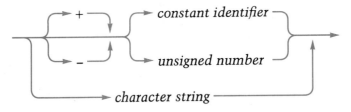

constant expression:

variable:

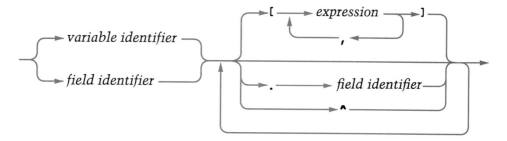

factor:

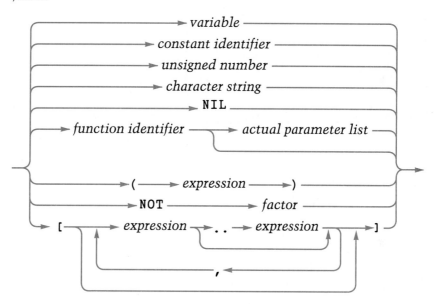

term:

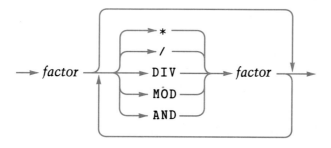

simple expression:

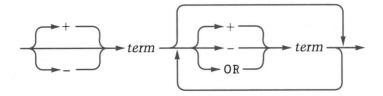

expression:

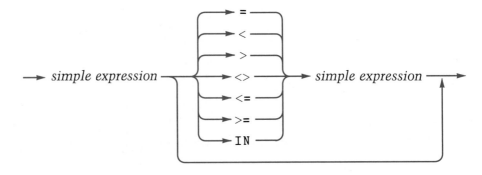

actual parameter list:

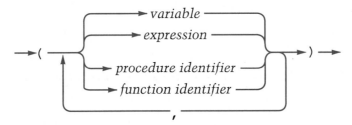

write parameter list:

→ (→ *expression* → : → *expression* → : → *expression* →) →

index type specification:

→ *identifier* → . . → *identifier* → : → *type identifier* →

conformant array schema:

formal parameter list:

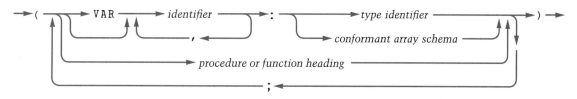

procedure or function heading:

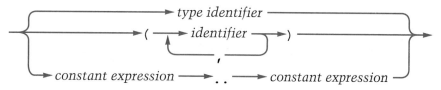

ordinal type:

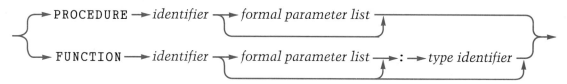

index list:

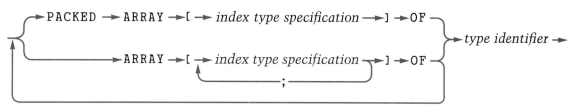

variant part:

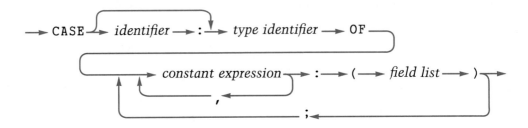

field list:

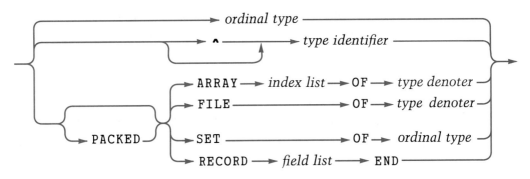

type denoter:

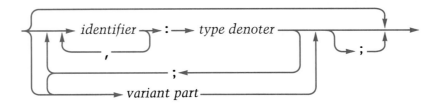

statement label:

→ *digit* → *digit* → *digit* → *digit* →

label declaration part:

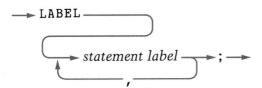

constant definition part:

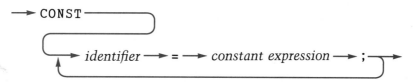

type definition part:

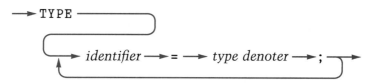

variable declaration part:

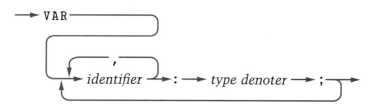

assignment statement:

procedure call:

while statement:

For clarity we occasionally use the word *condition* which is taken in these diagrams as a synonym for *expression*.

for statement:

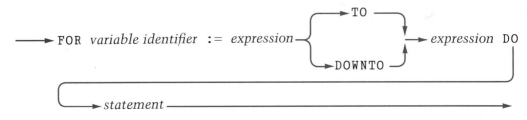

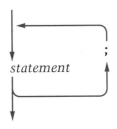

statement sequence:

repeat statement:

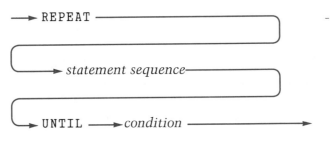

if statement:

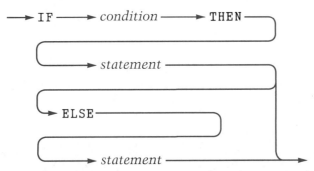

case statement:

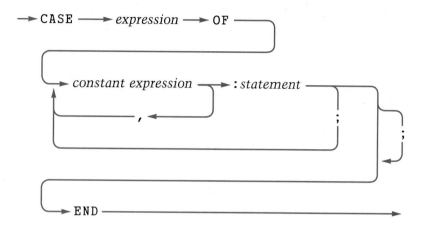

with statement:

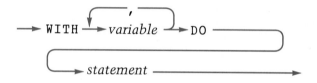

null statement:

⟶

goto statement:

⟶ GOTO ⟶ *statement label* ⟶

compound statement:

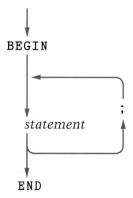

statement:

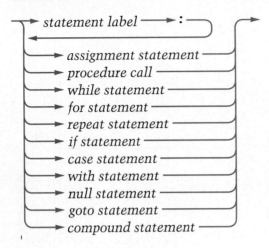

block:

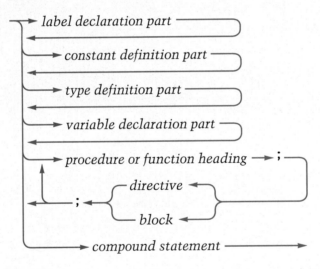

Pascal program:

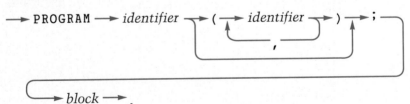

APPENDIX D

ASCII Character Set

The ASCII Character Set assigns meanings to the binary codes for the numbers 0 to 255. Normally the codes 32 to 126 represent printing characters and the other codes are non-printing. The following table gives the meanings of some of the non-printing codes. Many of the codes 0 through 31 are identified primarily with the communication of data from one device to another. Other non-printing codes used in general purpose programming are highlighted in bold in the table.

ASCII code	name	on a keyboard	use
0	NUL	ctrl-@	The null byte; used for padding or filling
1	SOH	ctrl-A	Start of heading with routing information
2	STX	ctrl-B	Start of text; ends heading, starts message
3	ETX	ctrl-C	End of text; ends one message, begins another
4	EOT	ctrl-D	End of transmission; ends the last message
5	ENQ	ctrl-E	Enquire; requests response
6	ACK	ctrl-F	Acknowledge; acknowledges receipt of info
7	BEL	ctrl-G	**Makes the bell sound**
8	BS	ctrl-H or Backspace	**Erases the character preceding the cursor**
9	HT	ctrl-I	**Horizontal tab; indents a few spaces**
10	LF	ctrl-J	**Line feed; goes to the next line**
11	VT	ctrl-K	**Vertical tab; goes down a few lines**
12	FF	ctrl-L	**Form feed; goes to the next page**
13	CR	ctrl-M or Return	**Carriage return; goes to start of the line**
14	SO	ctrl-N	Shift out — Encloses codes whose meaning
15	SI	ctrl-O	Shift in — is non-standard
16	DLE	ctrl-P	Data link escape; alters subsequent codes
17	DC1	ctrl-Q	**Device control 1; unfreezes the screen**
18	DC2	ctrl-R	Device control 2
19	DC3	ctrl-S	**Device control 3; freezes the screen**
20	DC4	ctrl-T	Device control 4
21	NAK	ctrl-U	Negative acknowledge; did not receive info
22	SYN	ctrl-V	Synchronize; gets sender/receiver in sync
23	ETB	ctrl-W	End transmission block (physical data block)
24	CAN	ctrl-X	Cancel last block or text because of error
25	EM	ctrl-Y	End of medium; Example: end of magnetic tape
26	SUB	ctrl-Z	Substitute this for an erroneous code
27	ESC	ctrl-[or Escape	**Changes meaning of subsequent codes or undoes an action**
28	FS	ctrl-\	File separator ⎤
29	GS	ctrl-]	Group separator ⎟ Separates the logical
30	RS	ctrl-^	Record separator ⎟ parts of a message
31	US	ctrl-_	Unit separator ⎦
127	DEL	Delete	**Erase the character at the cursor**

The next table describes the IBM® Extended ASCII Character Set. In this version of the ASCII Character Set, most of the codes from 0 to 255 represent printing characters. An implementation that uses the standard ASCII Character Set will agree with this table for the codes 32 (blank space) through 126 (the ~ character). To learn what your implementation does, consult your manuals.

How to read the table: The column of numbers on left side of the table gives the first digit or two of an ASCII code. The row of numbers at the top of the table gives the last digit of an ASCII code. So, for instance, the ASCII code for the letter A is 65, and the ASCII code for the letter z is 122.

Note: Some programming languages and manuals use hexadecimal or octal representations for the ASCII codes rather than the decimal values given in this table. For instance, the hexadecimal representation for decimal 122 (the ASCII code for z) is 7A. The octal representation for decimal 122 is 172. To find out how to convert among decimal, hexadecimal, and octal representations, see Exercises Cha.9.3.3 and Cha.9.3.4.

rightmost digit

leftmost digit(s)

	0	1	2	3	4	5	6	7	8	9
0		☺	☻	♥	♦	♣	♠	•	◘	○
1	◙	♂	♀	♪	♫	☼	►	◄	↕	‼
2	¶	§	▬	↨	↑	↓	→	←	∟	↔
3	▲	▼		!	"	#	$	%	&	'
4	(	)	*	+	,	-	.	/	0	1
5	2	3	4	5	6	7	8	9	:	;
6	<	=	>	?	@	A	B	C	D	E
7	F	G	H	I	J	K	L	M	N	O
8	P	Q	R	S	T	U	V	W	X	Y
9	Z	[	\	]	^	_	`	a	b	c
10	d	e	f	g	h	i	j	k	l	m
11	n	o	p	q	r	s	t	u	v	w
12	x	y	z	{	|	}	~		Ç	ü
13	é	â	ä	à	å	ç	ê	ë	è	ï
14	î	ì	Ä	Å	É	æ	Æ	ô	ö	ò
15	û	ù	ÿ	ö	Ü	¢	£	¥	₧	ƒ
16	á	í	ó	ú	ñ	Ñ	ª	º	¿	⌐
17	¬	½	¼	¡	«	»	░	▒	▓	│
18	┤	╡	╢	╖	╕	╣	║	╗	╝	╜
19	╛	┐	└	┴	┬	├	─	┼	╞	╟
20	╚	╔	╩	╦	╠	═	╬	╧	╨	╤
21	╥	╙	╘	╒	╓	╫	╪	┘	┌	█
22	▄	▌	▐	▀	α	ß	Γ	π	Σ	σ
23	µ	τ	Φ	Θ	Ω	δ	∞	φ	ε	∩
24	≡	±	≥	≤	⌠	⌡	÷	≈	°	•
25	·	√	ⁿ	²	■					

Notes: Codes 0, 127, and 255 do not represent printing characters in the IBM Extended ASCII Character Set. Code 32 represents the blank space character.

EBCDIC Character Set

The following table gives a portion of the EBCDIC Character Set. For hints on reading the table, see Appendix D.

leftmost digit(s) \ rightmost digit	0	1	2	3	4	5	6	7	8	9
0						HT		DEL		
1		VT	FF	CR						
2			BS							
3								LF		ESC
4								BEL		
5										
6										
7					¢	.	<	(	+	|
8	&									
9	!	$	*	)	;	¬	-	/		
10							^	'	%	—
11	>	?								
12			:	#	@	'	=	"		a
13	b	c	d	e	f	g	h	i		
14						j	k	l	m	n
15	o	p	q	r						
16			s	t	u	v	w	x	y	z
17								\	{	}
18	[	]								
19				A	B	C	D	E	F	G
20	H	I								J
21	K	L	M	N	O	P	Q	R		
22							S	T	U	V
23	W	X	Y	Z						
24	0	1	2	3	4	5	6	7	8	9
25										

Note: EBCDIC code 64 represents the blank space character.

APPENDIX F

Complete Programs in *Pascal by Example*

[S]Indicates a subprogram rather than a program. For many of these subprograms, test drivers are given in the text.

APPENDIX G

Index to Subsections

Subsections entitled	*appear in the following sections:*
Specifications	2.3, 2.4, 2.6, 3.1, 3.3, 3.4, 3.7, 3.8, 3.9, 4.1, 5.2, 5.4, 5.5, 6.1, 6.2, 6.3, 6.4, 6.5, 6.6, 7.2, 7.4, 7.5, 8.1, 8.2, 8.3, 8.5, 8.6, 9.1, 9.2, 9.3, 9.4, 9.5, 10.2, 10.4, 10.5, 10.6, 10.7, 10.8, 11.2, 11.3, 11.4, 11.5, 12.1, 12.2, 12.3, 12.4, 12.5, 12.6, 12.7, 12.8, 13.1, 13.2, 13.3, 13.4, 13.6, 13.7, 13.8, 14.4, 14.5, 14.7, 14.8, 14.9, 14.10, 14.11, 14.12, 14.13, 14.14, 15.2, 15.3, 15.4
Designing a program	2.3, 2.4, 2.6, 3.1, 3.4, 3.5, 3.7, 3.8, 3.9, 4.1, 5.1, 5.2, 5.3, 5.4, 5.5, 6.2, 6.3, 6.4, 6.5, 6.6, 7.4, 7.5, 8.1, 8.2, 8.3, 8.5, 8.6, 9.1, 9.2, 9.3, 9.4, 9.6, 10.2, 10.3, 10.4, 10.5, 10.7, 10.8, 11.2, 11.3, 11.4, 12.2, 12.3, 12.8, 13.1, 13.2, 13.3, 13.4, 13.6, 13.7, 14.5, 14.6, 14.7, 14.8, 14.9, 14.10, 14.11, 14.12, 14.13, 15.2, 15.3, 15.4
Traces	2.4, 2.5, 2.6, 3.1, 3.4, 3.5, 5.4, 6.4, 8.2, 10.5, 10.6, 10.7, 10.8, 13.1, 13.2, 13.3, 14.2, 14.3, 14.6, 14.8, 14.11, 14.13, 15.1
Programming style	2.2, 2.4, 2.6, 3.4, 3.8, 4.1, 5.5, 6.1, 6.2, 6.6, 7.1, 8.2, 8.3, 8.4, 9.1, 9.4, 10.4, 10.5, 11.2, 11.4, 12.3, 12.4, 14.3, 14.8, 14.9
Structure	2.3, 2.6, 3.1, 3.5, 3.8, 6.1, 6.2, 6.4, 6.6, 8.5, 9.3, 9.4, 10.5, 10.6, 10.8, 12.3, 13.1, 13.3, 14.13, 15.3, 15.4
Testing and debugging	3.4, 3.7, 4.2, 5.4, 6.1, 6.2, 7.2, 8.2, 8.5, 8.6, 9.1, 9.2, 9.5, 11.3, 14.7, 15.4

APPENDIX H

An Annotated Bibliography

The early development of the Pascal programming language can be found in:

1. "The Programming Language Pascal" by Niklaus Wirth, *Acta Informatica 1*, pp. 35–63, Springer-Verlag, 1971.

2. *Systematic Programming: An Introduction* by Niklaus Wirth, Prentice-Hall, 1973.

For the official description of ANSI Standard Pascal see:

1. *The American Pascal Standard with Annotations* prepared by Henry Ledgard, Springer-Verlag, 1984.

2. *ANSI/IEEE 770 X3.97–1983(R1990)*, released by the American National Standards Institute (ANSI) and the Institute of Electrical and Electronic Engineers (IEEE).

For descriptions of the ISO Standard Pascal (which includes conformant array parameters—not part of the ANSI standard) see:

1. *Pascal User Manual and Report* by Kathleen Jensen and Niklaus Wirth, Springer-Verlag, 1985.

2. *ISO 7185 Specification for Computer Programming Language Pascal*, released by the International Organization for Standardization (ISO).

An extended Pascal standard, with many more features than ANSI Standard Pascal, is described in a document numbered *ANSI/IEEE 770 X 3.160–1990*. A copy of this document is available from the American National Standards Institute (ANSI).

An extremely rigorous definition of the Pascal programming language is given in "An Axiomatic Definition of the Programming Language PASCAL" by C. A. R. Hoare and Niklaus Wirth. It appeared in *Acta Informatica 2*, pp. 335–355, Springer-Verlag, 1973.

For an opposing point of view you should read "Why Pascal Is Not My Favorite Programming Language" by Brian W. Kernighan, a 1981 Computing Science Technical Report (CSTR) from Bell Laboratories. For a copy, call Bell Laboratories in Murray Hill, New Jersey and ask for CSTR #100.

Since you've learned Pascal you might want to learn Modula-2, a Pascal-like language with more modern features for importing and exporting code from various files. The language is described in *Programming in Modula-2* by Niklaus Wirth, Springer-Verlag, 1985.

In this text we used Turbo Pascal to demonstrate principles of object-oriented programming. The exact syntax of Turbo Pascal, and its features related to object-oriented programming, are discussed authoritatively in the language manuals that accompany that software product. Contact Borland International in Scotts Valley, California for more details.

Programming style is discussed in detail in *The Elements of Programming Style* by Brian Kernighan and P. J. Plauger, McGraw-Hill, 1978.

To read more about testing and debugging, pick up a copy of *The Art of Software Testing* by Glenford J. Myers, John Wiley & Sons, Inc., 1979.

For a book on many aspects of the programming endeavor, read *The Psychology of Computer Programming* by Gerald Weinberg, Van Nostrand Reinhold, 1988.

Nassi-Shneiderman charts (NS charts) were first discussed in an article called "Flowchart techniques for structured programming" by I. Nassi and B. Shneiderman in the *SIGPLAN Notices* (the Special Interest Group on Programming Languages of the Association for Computing Machinery), Vol. 8, No. 8, August 1973.

Our definition of Artificial Intelligence comes from a book entitled *Artificial Intelligence* by Elaine Rich, McGraw-Hill, 1983.

The pseudorandom number generators in Chapter 9 come from an article entitled "Random Number Generators: Good ones are hard to find" by S. Park and K. Miller, in the *Communications of the ACM* (Association for Computing Machinery), Vol. 31, No. 10, October 1988.

No bibliography in computer science would be complete without referring to *The Art of Computer Programming*, a series of books by Donald Knuth, published by Addison-Wesley. The first three volumes' latest editions were published in 1974, 1981, and 1973 respectively. Four other volumes have been announced. The series is unparalleled in its breadth and depth of coverage on algorithms.

The landmark reference on information hiding is an article called "On the criteria used in decomposing systems into modules" by D. L. Parnas. It first appeared in the *Communications of the ACM* (Association for Computing Machinery), Vol. 15, 1972, pp. 1053–1058.

For a good source of real-life data get a copy of the *Statistical Abstract of the United States*, published yearly by the Department of Census of the U.S. Department of Commerce.

APPENDIX I

Selected Exercises—Solutions and Hints

Chapter 1
Que 1.1.2 a. user **b.** programmer **c.** neither **d.** user **e.** neither
Que 1.2.4 a and **c** are the same (see Sections 10.5 and 10.6).
Que 1.3.3 a. hardware **b.** software **c.** neither **d.** software
Que 1.3.4 a. medium **b.** device **c.** device **d.** medium **Que 1.3.10 a.** disk
b. tape **Que 1.4.3 a.** command **c.** statement

Chapter 2
Que 2.1.1 a. yes **b.** no **c.** no **d.** yes **e.** yes **Que 2.1.2 a.** (a+b)/2.0
b. 3.142*r*r **c.** x*x + 3*x + 5 **Que 2.1.4 a.** 5.0 **b.** 7.2 **c.** 0.064
Que 2.1.6 a, c, d, and g are legal program headings. **Que 2.1.7** This restricted
form of a REAL number consists of one or more digits, followed by a decimal
point, followed again by one or more digits.
Cha 2.1.2

```
VAR
   couponTotal, couponChange      : REAL;
couponTotal  := (salePrice - 1.00) + couponTax;
couponChange := amtTendered - couponTotal;
WriteLn ('total with coupon  ', couponTotal :6:2);
WriteLn ('change with coupon ', couponChange:6:2)
```

Wri 2.1.5

```
PROGRAM Wri215 (output);
{Computes total cost of buying and installing new tires.}
   VAR
      eachTire, excisePerTire, totalLabor, totalCost : REAL;
BEGIN {Wri215}
   eachTire     := 97.50;
   excisePerTire := 10.25;
   totalLabor    := 15.00;
   totalCost := 4.0 * (eachTire + excisePerTire) + totalLabor;
   Writeln ('Total cost for four tires: ', totalCost:6:2)
END.  {Wri215}
{Total cost for four tires: 446.00}
```

954

Que 2.2.6 a. 2   **b.** 2   **c.** 14   **d.** 16   **e.** 16   **f.** 0   **g.** 1

Wri 2.2.1

```
PROGRAM Cola (input, output);
{Computes the number of six-packs
 from the number of bottles.}
  VAR
    bottles, sixPacks, leftOver : INTEGER;
BEGIN {Cola}
  Write  ('How many bottles? ');
  ReadLn (bottles);
  sixPacks := bottles DIV 6;
  leftOver := bottles MOD 6;
  WriteLn (sixPacks:3, ' six packs with   ',
           leftOver:3, ' bottles left over')
END. {Cola}
```

Wri 2.3.1

```
IF totalSales < 10000.00 THEN
  commission := 0.05 * totalSales
ELSE
  commission := 0.07 * totalSales
```

Cha 2.4.1

```
IF score1 < score2 THEN
  BEGIN
    temp1  := score1;
    temp2  := score2;
    score1 := temp2;
    score2 := temp1
  END
```

Pra 2.4.1

```
temp := a;
a    := b;
b    := c;
c    := d;
d    := temp
```

Pra 2.5.1

```
PROCEDURE Obtain (VAR r1, r2: REAL; VAR code : INTEGER);
{Prompts for values and reads them from the keyboard.}
BEGIN {Obtain}
  Write  ('Enter two real numbers:                ');
  ReadLn (r1, r2);
  Write  ('Sum (0) or product (any other number)? ');
  ReadLn (code);
END;   {Obtain}
```

Que 2.6.1 c, d, and **e.** After switching, these names might be misleading. **f.** Great cartoon, but uninformative as variable names.

Wri 2.6.4

```
Write  ('Enter the current temperature: ');
ReadLn (temp);
WHILE  (low <= temp) AND (temp <= high) DO
  BEGIN
    Write  ('Enter the current temperature: ');
    ReadLn (temp);
  END
```

Chapter 3
Que 3.1.4 In Wri 2.5.2 the Fahrenheit temperature can be a value parameter. So can the ages of children in Wri 2.5.4. Anywhere else?
Que 3.1.5

```
PROCEDURE QuoAndRem (num1, num2                 : INTEGER ;
                     VAR quotient, remainder : INTEGER);
```

Wri 3.1.1

```
PROCEDURE WriteInColumn (num : REAL);
{Writes positive number in left column;
 writes negative number in right column.}
BEGIN {WriteInColumn}
  IF num >= 0.0 THEN
    WriteLn (num:8:2)
  ELSE
    WriteLn ('            ', num:8:2)
END;   {WriteInColumn}
```

Que 3.2.3 no   **Que 3.2.4** Yes, but we should use pass by value.
Cha 3.2.1

```
PROCEDURE Switch (score1, score2 : INTEGER; VAR a, z : INTEGER);
  ...
Switch (score1, score2, a, z);
```

Que 3.3.5 No. A procedure call cannot threaten to change the value of the number `100.00`.

Pra 3.3.1

```
PROCEDURE CountTimesCalled (VAR count : INTEGER);
{Writes a message every third time it's been called.}
BEGIN {CountTimesCalled}
   count := count + 1;
   IF count MOD 3 = 0 THEN
     WriteLn ('That makes three more!')
END;  {CountTimesCalled}
```

Wri 3.4.1

```
FUNCTION SixPacks (bottles : INTEGER) : INTEGER;
{Finds the number of six packs from the number of bottles.}
BEGIN {SixPacks}
  SixPacks := bottles DIV 6
END;  {SixPacks}
```

Que 3.5.2 yes **Que 3.5.3** no

Cha 3.6.1 `Trunc(Sqrt(number))`

Pra 3.7.1 `Round (number / 100.0) * 100`

Wri 3.7.3 `5.2 * Exp (0.36 * Ln (m))`

Cha 3.8.2

```
    PROCEDURE InsureOrder (VAR a, z : INTEGER);
    {Insures that a is greater than or equal to z.}
      {----------}
      PROCEDURE Switch (VAR a, z : INTEGER);
      {Switches the values of two numbers, a and z.}
        VAR
          temp : INTEGER;
      BEGIN {Switch}
        temp := a;
        a    := z;
        z    := temp
      END;  {Switch}
      {----------}
    BEGIN {InsureOrder}
      IF a < z THEN
        Switch (a, z)
    END;  {InsureOrder}
```

Chapter 4
Cha 4.1.2

```
Read  (inFile,  ch);
Write (outFile, ch);
Write (output,  ch);
WHILE ch <> '.' DO
  BEGIN
    Read  (inFile, ch);
    Write (outFile, ch);
    Write (output, ch)
  END
```

Chapter 5
Wri 5.1.4 Section 10.5 will help you do this one.

Que 5.4.1 false
Cha 5.4.1

```
IF (available < min) AND (available >= size) THEN
  min := available
```

Cha 5.4.6

```
IF ch <> ' ' THEN
  Write (outFile, ch);
Write (output,  ch)
```

Pra 5.4.4

```
ReadLn (inFile, lastNum);
lineNum := 1;
WHILE NOT Eof(inFile) DO
  BEGIN
    ReadLn (inFile, thisNum);
    lineNum := lineNum + 1;
    IF thisNum <> lastNum THEN
      WriteLn ('Number changes on line ', lineNum:3);
    lastNum := thisNum
  END
```

Que 5.5.2 NoNesting:8 paths but one can never be taken, AvoidNesting:4, UseMaxFunction:4

Cha 5.5.3

```
IF a > c THEN
  writeMe := a                {1}
    ...
IF NOT Odd (writeMe) THEN
  BEGIN
    Write  ('The largest is ');
    WriteLn (writeMe:5)
  END
```

Que 5.6.4 no

Chapter 6
Wri 6.1.1

```
wCount := 0;
mCount := 0;
WriteLn ('Enter w''s and m''s:');
WHILE NOT Eof (input) DO
  BEGIN
    ReadLn (charIn);
    IF charIn = 'w' THEN
      wCount := wCount + 1;
    IF charIn = 'm' THEN
      mCount := mCount + 1;
    IF (charIn <> 'w') AND (charIn <> 'm') THEN
      WriteLn ('Enter w or m')
  END;
total := wCount + mCount;
IF total <> 0 THEN
  BEGIN
    WriteLn ('Women: ', wCount*100/total:5:1, '%');
    WriteLn ('Men:   ', mCount*100/total:5:1, '%')
  END
```

Que 6.2.4 The details of initializing and incrementing the loop counter are hidden. (These details are "abstracted.")
Cha 6.2.1 See Program Iterative in Section 13.4.
Cha 6.3.2

```
pastPrev := 1;
WriteLn (pastPrev:12);
prev := 1;
WriteLn (prev:12);
FOR count := 3 TO termsNeeded DO
  ...
```

Pra 6.4.1

```
FOR a := 1 TO 4 DO
  FOR b := 1 TO 4 DO
    FOR c := 1 TO 4 DO
      FOR d := 1 TO 4 DO
        WriteLn (a:1, b:1, c:1, d:1)
```

Cha 6.5.1

```
FOR row := 1 TO n DO
  BEGIN
    FOR column := 1 TO row-1 DO
      Write ('    ');
    FOR column := row TO n DO
      Write (row * column:4);
    WriteLn
  END
```

Wri 6.6.3

```
REPEAT
  Read (inFile, ch)
UNTIL ch <> ' ';
WriteLn (ch)
```

Chapter 7

Que 7.1.4 c and e are not legal.   **Que 7.1.6** b isn't legal.   **Que 7.2.2 a.** m is an INTEGER, x is REAL, m*x is REAL, n is an INTEGER, m*x + n is REAL.
Cha 7.2.1

```
WriteLn ('The average of the grades is ', Round(average):3)
```

Wri 7.3.3

```
WHILE Abs(Sqr(guess) - number) > error DO
  guess := guess - ((Sqr(guess) - number)/(2*guess))
```

Pra 7.4.4

```
ch := 'a';
WHILE ch <= 'z' DO
  BEGIN
    Write (ch:2);
    ch := Succ(Succ(ch))
  END
```

Que 7.5.3

```
TYPE
  dayType = (Monday, Tuesday, Thursday, Friday);
```

Wri 7.5.2

```
IF stoplight = red THEN
  NextLight := green
ELSE
  NextLight := Succ (stoplight)
```

Chapter 8

Que 8.1.1 c is FALSE; the others are TRUE.   **Que 8.1.2 d.** (x MOD 3 = 0) AND
(y MOD 3 = 0) AND (z MOD 3 = 0)

Wri 8.1.3

```
sum    := (addend1 AND NOT addend2) OR
          (NOT addend1 AND addend2);
carry := addend1 AND addend2
```

Cha 8.2.3

```
VAR
  aBiggest, bBiggest, cBiggest : BOOLEAN;
  ...
aBiggest := (a >= b) AND (a >= c);
  ...
IF aBiggest THEN
  WriteLn (a:5:1);
  ...
```

Que 8.3.2 when the user enters a single digit character   **Cha 8.3.1** See Procedure
ReadCharOrNat in Section 13.6.   **Que 8.4.3** Neither c nor d can be used.

Wri 8.4.1

```
IF totalSales < 1000.00 THEN
  fraction := 0.05
ELSE IF totalSales < 5000.00 THEN
  fraction := 0.06
    ...
ELSE IF totalSales < 23000.00 THEN
  fraction := 0.08
ELSE
  fraction := 0.0825
```

Wri 8.6.1

```
Read (ch);
isIdentifier := isLetter (ch);
WHILE isIdentifier AND NOT Eoln (input) DO
  BEGIN
    Read (ch);
    isIdentifier := isLetter (ch) OR isDigit (ch)
  END
```

Que 8.7.4 The control variable in a FOR statement; the case-index in a CASE statement.

Chapter 9
Que 9.2.1 Each variable takes a value that's created during one iteration and stores that value for use during the next iteration.   **Que 9.3.1 a.** 101010   **b.** 0 **c.** 1000000   **Que 9.3.3** The binary representation gets an additional bit—a zero. It's the rightmost bit.

Pra 9.3.1

```
NextInt := (intIn MOD 10) + 1
```

Que 9.4.2 Perhaps the exponential-time program takes $2^n n$ seconds to run, whereas the linear time program takes n decades to run. Or perhaps the exponential-time program is running on a fast computer and the linear-time program is running on a slow computer.
Wri 9.4.2

```
Write ('{');
power := IntegerExp (2, nBits) DIV 2;
count := nBits - 1;
WHILE power > 0  DO
   BEGIN
      bit      := decimal DIV power;
      IF bit = 1 THEN
         Write (count:3, ',');
      count := count - 1;
      decimal := decimal MOD power;
      power   := power DIV 2
   END;
Write ('}')
```

Cha 9.5.1

```
10.0 * Random(seed)
Trunc (10.0 * Random(seed)) + 1
 {but what can you do when Random returns a number very close to 1.0?}
5.0 * Random(seed) + 5.0
```

Que 9.6.2 See the CONST definition in the HoursUnit of Section 3.9.

Chapter 10
Que 10.1.1 no   **Que 10.1.2** no

Pra 10.1.3

```
sum := 0;
i   := 0;
WHILE NOT Eof (input) DO
  BEGIN
    i := i + 1;
    ReadLn (num[i]);
    sum := sum + num[i]
  END;
av := sum / i;
FOR j := 1 to i DO
  IF num[j] > av THEN
    WriteLn (num[j]:6:2)
```

Pra 10.1.5

```
FOR i := 1 TO 10 DO
  IF x[i] = y[i] THEN
    WriteLn (i:2)
```

Wri 10.2.1

```
FOR i := 1 TO 10 DO
  Read (price[i]);
ReadLn;
FOR i := 1 TO 10 DO
  Read (quantity[i]);
ReadLn;
cost := 0.0;
FOR i := 1 TO 10 DO
  cost := cost + price[i] * quantity[i]
```

Que 10.3.1 yes   **Que 10.3.2** no
Cha 10.3.2

```
FOR grade := 0 TO 100 DO
  FOR recount := 1 TO howMany[grade] DO
    Write (grade:3)
```

Wri 10.4.1

```
i := 0;
WHILE NOT Eoln (input) AND (i < 79) DO
  BEGIN
    i := i + 1;
    Read (name[i])
  END;
name[i+1] := '*';
ReadLn;
i := 1;
WHILE (name[i] <> '*') AND (i < 80) DO
  BEGIN
    Write (name[i]:1);
    i := i + 1
  END;
WriteLn
```

Que 10.5.2

```
WHILE a[i] <> searchFor DO
  i := i + 1
```

Que 10.5.3 the average of all cases
Cha 10.5.3

```
IF searchFor <> 0 THEN
  a[hi-2] := 0
ELSE                 {a[hi-2] must not equal searchFor}
  a[hi-2] := -1;
a[hi-1] := searchFor;
a[hi]   := searchFor;
i := lo;
WHILE (a[i] <> searchFor) OR (a[i+1] <> searchFor) DO
  i := i + 1
```

Wri 10.7.2 *Hint:* Start by assuming that each student is in a single-student group. For each student in the x array, check to see if there's another student whose group is lower in the x array and higher in the y array. If so, combine the two students' groups.

Wri 10.8.5

```
FOR start := 1 TO hi-1 DO
  FOR other := start+1 TO hi DO
    IF a[start] > a[other] THEN
      Switch (a[start], a[other])
```

Que 10.9.1 b is legal.   **Wri 10.9.1** Watch out for the string with no blank spaces.

Chapter 11
Que 11.1.1 Not necessarily
Pra 11.1.2

```
FOR row := 1 TO 5 DO
  FOR col := 1 TO 5 DO
    a[row, col] := 1;
FOR row := 2 TO 4 DO
  FOR col := 2 TO 4 DO
    a[row, col] := 0
```

Cha 11.2.3

```
TYPE
  anyType = PACKED ARRAY [1..20] OF CHAR;
FOR i := lo TO hi DO
  BEGIN
    FOR j := 1 TO 20 DO
      Read (fInput, a[i][j]);
    ReadLn (fInput)
  END
FOR i := lo TO hi DO
  Write (a[i]:20)
```

Pra 11.2.4

```
existsRow := FALSE;
FOR row := 1 TO 4 DO
  BEGIN
    everyCol := TRUE;
    FOR col := 1 TO 4 DO
      BEGIN
        existsNum := FALSE;
        FOR r := 1 TO 4 DO
          IF a[r,col] < a[row,col] THEN
            existsNum := TRUE;
        IF NOT existsNum THEN
          everyCol := FALSE
      END;
    IF everyCol THEN
      existsRow := TRUE
  END
```

Que 11.3.1 The phrase *brute force* describes an algorithm which takes the most obvious approach, which is often not the most elegant or efficient approach.
Que 11.3.3 Functions have names which are nouns; procedures have names which are verbs.   **Que 11.5.4** There's no such thing as an array which is conformant. Only a formal parameter in a subprogram can be described as being "conformant."

Chapter 12
Wri 12.2.2

```
TYPE
  natural    = 0..MAXINT;
  intRecType = RECORD
                 principal, intRate : REAL;
                 nYears             : INTEGER;
               END;
VAR
  intRec : intRecType;
PROCEDURE AddInterest (VAR intRec : intRecType);
{Adds several years' interest.}
  VAR
    y : natural;
BEGIN {AddInterest}
  WITH intRec DO
    FOR y := 1 TO nYears DO
      principal := principal + (intRate/100.0 * principal)
END;  {AddInterest}
```

Wri 12.4.3

```
PROCEDURE AddIntToRat (i        : INTEGER  ;
                       r        : rational ;
                       VAR rSum : rational);
{Adds an integer to a rational.}
  VAR
    rTemp : rational;
BEGIN {AddIntToRat}
  rTemp.num   := i;
  rTemp.denom := 1;
  AddRats (r, rTemp, rSum)
END;   {AddIntToRat}
```

Wri 12.4.4 *Hint:* See the program that finds the greatest common divisor (Exercise Wri.9.5.6). **Que 12.5.3 a.** empArray[67].id **Cha 12.5.2** See Procedure ReadCharOrNat in Section 13.6. **Wri 12.5.2** vStr.length := 0 **Que 12.7.1** No element can occur more than once in a set. **Wri 12.7.1**

```
FOR i := 1 TO 10 DO
  intSetUnion[i] := intSet1[i] OR intSet2[i]
```

Pra 12.8.2 IF ch IN ['A'..'Z', 'a'..'z'] THEN

Chapter 13
Wri 13.1.1

```
IF a MOD b = 0 THEN
  Gcd := b
ELSE
  Gcd := Gcd (a MOD b, b)
```

Cha 13.3.3

```
IF exponent > 0 THEN
  IntegerExp := base * IntegerExp (base, exponent-1)
ELSE
  IntegerExp := 1
```

Cha 13.4.3

```
IF n = 1 THEN
  Factorial := 1
ELSE
  Factorial := n * Factorial (n-1)
```

Que 13.6.1 a. 29   **Que 13.6.2 a.** $(((1*2)/3)*4)/5$
Que 13.6.3 a. / * 2 3 - 4 5
Wri 13.6.2

```
IF NumberOfRings (ringSet) = 1 THEN
  BEGIN
    Write   ('Move ring ', TheRingIn(ringSet) : 3);
    WriteLn (' from ', fromPeg, ' to ', toPeg    )
  END
ELSE
  BEGIN
    largeRing := LargestRingIn (ringSet);
    otherPeg  := ThePegNotIn ([fromPeg, toPeg]);
    Move (ringSet-[largeRing], fromPeg,  otherPeg);
    Move ([largeRing]        , fromPeg,  toPeg  );
    Move (ringSet-[largeRing], otherPeg, toPeg  )
  END
```

Cha 13.7.3

```
FUNCTION Min (level, leafLevel : positive) : INTEGER;
  VAR
    a, b : INTEGER;
BEGIN {Min}
  IF level = leafLevel-1 THEN
    BEGIN
      Read (a);
      Read (b)
    END
  ELSE
    BEGIN
      a := Max (level + 1, leafLevel);
      b := Max (level + 1, leafLevel)
    END;
  IF a < b THEN
    Min := a
  ELSE
    Min := b
END;   {Min}
```

Chapter 14

Pra 14.2.2 Create a cell with ptr pointing to it. Then execute the statement ptr^.next := ptr. Then create the other cells in the list.

Cha 14.3.2

```
IF ptr <> NIL THEN
  BEGIN
    Write      (ptr^.info:4);
    WriteList (ptr^.next)
  END
```

Pra 14.3.1

```
count := 0;
temp  := ptr;
WHILE temp <> NIL DO
  BEGIN
    count := count + 1;
    temp := temp^.next
  END;
ListLength := count
```

Wri 14.5.1 *Hint:* When we move values, one by one, from one stack to another, the values in the new stack are the reverse of the values in the old stack. So in this problem we use two temporary stacks.

Que 14.8.2 b. (16-2) + ((13+2)*(14-5))   **Que 14.8.3 c.** 8

Wri 14.8.1

```
FOR i := 1 TO size DIV 2 DO
  BEGIN
    Read (ch);
    Push (stack, ch)
  END;
IF Odd (size) THEN
  Read (ch);
isPalin := TRUE;
WHILE NOT IsEmpty (stack) DO
  BEGIN
    Read (ch);
    Pop (stack, ch2);
    IF ch <> ch2 THEN
      isPalin := FALSE
  END
```

Que 14.9.2 This kind of removal takes $O(1)$ time.   **Que 14.9.4** This kind of removal takes $O(n)$ time.

Cha 14.11.1

```
tempLeft          := middle^.prev;
tempRight         := middle^.next;
tempLeft^.next    := tempRight;
tempRight^.prev   := tempLeft;
i                 := middle^.info
```

Wri 14.12.1

```
IF root = NIL THEN
  NumCells := 0
ELSE
  WITH root^ DO
    NumCells := 1 + NumCells (left) + NumCells (right)
```

Wri 14.12.4 a. If a cell has index n then the cell's left child has index $2n$ and the cell's right child has index $2n + 1$.   **Que 14.13.2** This is not enough.
Que 14.13.4 It is not a balanced tree.

Chapter 15
Que 15.1.2 In a TEXT file, Get always advances the file window by one CHARacter—never by one INTEGER.
Que 15.1.7 Details about ends of lines are hidden from the programmer.

Cha 15.1.1

```
WHILE symbolsWritten < symbolsNeeded DO
  BEGIN
    output^ := symbol;
    Put (output);
    symbolsWritten := symbolsWritten + 1
  END
```

Cha 15.2.4

```
WHILE input^ = ' ' DO
  Get (input)
```

Wri 15.4.1

```
i := 0;
WHILE NOT Eoln DO
  BEGIN
    i := i + 1;
    Read (expr[i])
  END;
FOR j := i+1 TO 50 DO
  expr[j] := ' ';
Rewrite   (evalF);
WriteLn   (evalF, 'PROGRAM Eval (output);  ');
WriteLn   (evalF, 'BEGIN {Eval}             ');
IF i > 0 THEN
  WriteLn (evalF, '  WriteLn (', expr, ')   ');
WriteLn   (evalF, 'END.  {Eval}             ')
```

Credits and Acknowledgments

The Syntax diagrams in this text are reproduced and adapted from IEEE standard 770X3.97-1983 (reaffirmed, 1990), IEEE Pascal Computer Programming Language, copyright © 1983 by the Institute of Electrical and Electronics Engineers, Inc., used with the permission of the IEEE.

Page ii (opposite title page): Quote from Weinberg: *The Psychology of Computer Programming*, p. 5, © 1971, Van Nostrand Reinhold: New York. Used with permission.

Pages 221 and 222: Poems from *One Hundred Haiku* by Daniel Buchanan. Japan Publications, Inc. © 1973.

Pages 452 and 453: From "Random Number Generators: Good Ones Are Hard to Find," by S. Park and K. Miller, *Communications of the Association for Computing Machinery*, Vol. 31, No. 10 October, 1988. Used with permission.

Page 944: IBM® is a registered trademark of International Business Machines Corporation.

Index

Note: Numbers in boldface represent a page number where a definition, or the principal description of a term, can be found. Terms from disciplines other than computer science are referenced under the *applications* heading.

B	
C	
D	4
E	5
F	6
G	7
H	8
I	9
J	0